Oxford Dictionary of
Humorous Quotations

OXFORD DICTIONARY OF

Humorous Quotations

FIFTH EDITION

EDITED BY
Gyles Brandreth

OXFORD
UNIVERSITY PRESS

OXFORD
UNIVERSITY PRESS

Great Clarendon Street, Oxford OX2 6DP,
United Kingdom

Oxford University Press is a department of the University of Oxford.
It furthers the University's objective of excellence in research, scholarship,
and education by publishing worldwide. Oxford is a registered trade mark of
Oxford University Press in the UK and in certain other countries

© Oxford University Press 2013
© Selection and arrangement Ned Sherrin, Oxford University Press 1995, 2001, 2005, 2008

The moral rights of the author have been asserted
Database right Oxford University Press (maker)

First edition published 1995
Second edition published 2001
Third edition published 2005
Fourth edition published 2008
Fifth edition published 2013

Impression: 2

British Library Cataloguing in Publication Data
Data available

Library of Congress Cataloging in Publication Data
Data available

ISBN 978-0-19-968136-5

Printed in Italy by L.E.G.O. S.p.A. - Lavis TN

Contents

Project Team

COMMISSIONING EDITOR	Joanna Harris
ASSOCIATE EDITOR	Susan Ratcliffe
READING PROGRAMME	Jean Harker
	Verity Mason
LIBRARY RESEARCH	Ralph Bates
DATA CAPTURE	Susanne Charlett
PROOFREADING	Kim Allen

Introduction

....

I am proud to be the editor of the fifth edition of the *Oxford Dictionary of Humorous Quotations*. To coin a phrase, I am the man for the job. For more than fifty years I have been messing about in quotes. I suppose I have always had a short attention span and an eye and an ear for the pithy, witty, and wise. At school I discovered the detective stories of Dorothy L. Sayers and her hero, the aristocratic sleuth Lord Peter Wimsey, became an early role model. In *Have His Carcase*, Sayers has Lord Peter confess: 'I always have a quotation for everything—it saves original thinking.' I could not put it better myself.

I have been collecting quotations actively since the age of eleven. In the early days, I copied them out, by the dozen, in small blue notebooks. The very first to feature in my childhood anthology was a favourite of my father's—a line from Saki's *Reginald*: 'The cook was a good cook, as cooks go; and as cooks go, she went.' As a small boy, I was tickled pink by the cleverness of Saki's wordplay. (I still am.)

As a writer, Saki (Hector Hugh Monro) acknowledged his debt to Lewis Carroll, Rudyard Kipling, and Oscar Wilde, and his own style as a story-teller, wit, and wordsmith went on to influence many others, including A. A. Milne, P. G. Wodehouse, and Noël Coward. All these men—who feature prominently in the pages that follow—were among my father's favourites. It was my father who explained to me that, technically, a quotation is simply an extract from something someone has written or said. What makes a quotation worth noting—and collecting—is its 'quotability'. According to my dad, a quotable quotation has to pass several tests. Is it memorable? Do you want to share it with others? Does it stand on its own? Is it interesting in itself? And, if it's intended to be a humorous quotation, is it funny?

When I first began collecting quotations it was just for the fun of them, but quite quickly I began to realize how useful they could be. I used them in school essays to give my plodding prose a bit of a lift. (Read on and you'll find that's a knack that's not deserted me.) I used them in conversation in the hope of raising a laugh. (If ever you have heard me on the radio playing *Just A Minute*, you will know that old habits die hard.) I used them in school debates to give my schoolboy utterances a rhetorical flourish. (And when I was an MP I did exactly the same thing.)

By the time I got to university, in the late 1960s, and was following, hopefully, in the footsteps of the likes of Gladstone and Asquith, John Buchan and Tony Benn as President of the Oxford Union, I don't think I had an original thought in my head. I was just a mass of other men's gems. And, as well as my notebooks crammed with random jottings from the great and the good, I now had several small boxes of cards featuring quips arranged alphabetically by subject and author and carefully cross-indexed.

It was at Oxford that I started to meet some of the people I was quoting. Robert Morley (actor), Frank Muir (with Denis Norden, creator of *Take It From Here*, a radio favourite of my childhood), and Clement Freud (grandson of Sigmund and matchless raconteur) were three of the professional humourists who kindly came to speak at the Union when I was President. Each lived up to his reputation—as did several of the politicians I first met then, notably Norman St John-Stevas (Conservative), Jeremy Thorpe (Liberal), and Michael Foot (Labour). You will find contributions from all of them here.

In fact, I realize as I write that, as well as collecting quotations over the past half-century, I have also been collecting the people I most like to quote.

There is almost no one who was born over the past one hundred years and who is quoted in the *Dictionary* whom I have not met. Kingsley Amis, Alan Ayckbourn, Alan Bennett, Maurice Bowra, Craig Brown, George Burns, Quentin Crisp, T. S. Eliot, Jackie Mason, John Mortimer, Joan Rivers, Stephen Sondheim, Tom Stoppard, Peter Ustinov, the Queen—I've known them all. Well, I have shaken their hands ... It's a start. (Joan Rivers is diminutive, by the way, and wonderfully wicked. I had lunch in New York with Quentin Crisp days before he died. He talked non-stop for about two hours, repeating his most famous lines with great charm, as if they were being new-minted just for me. Jackie Mason is the only one in that list with whom I did not feel comfortable. Off-stage, he struck me as a cold fish. I was interviewing him for the *Sunday Telegraph* and I think he felt he had already given enough interviews to last a lifetime. He thought his show would sell out without any help from me. He was right, no doubt.) Inevitably, some who feature in the pages that follow I have known better than others. I am the father of one of those quoted, but rest assured that the quotations from Benet Brandreth that appear here do so on merit alone. (It was my own father who gave me my contempt for nepotism.)

I was honoured to know the first editor of the *Oxford Dictionary of Humorous Quotations* quite well. Ned Sherrin was a writer, broadcaster, television producer, and theatre director. He was also an anecdotalist with few peers. I first came across him in the 1960s when he was riding the crest of the satire wave he helped to create as the producer of the BBC television series *That Was The Week That Was*. In 1971 I presented my own first BBC radio series, *A Rhyme in Time*. One of the resident panellists on the show was Caryl Brahms, a kind and witty woman whose chief claim to fame was (and will forever be) the comic novels she wrote with S. J. Simon in the 1930s and 1940s. After Simon's death, Caryl teamed up with Ned and they collaborated on a series of books and plays and musicals. In the 1980s Ned and I teamed up to write a television situation comedy together for ITV. It was called *The Old Boy* and was all about a prime minister living in reluctant retirement. It did not get very far because Peter Ustinov, who was due to play the lead, pulled out at the last minute. (Perhaps he had received a call from Jackie Mason?)

From the 1980s onward I met up regularly with Ned. He always made me laugh and he always amazed me by having ever at the ready an amusing and apposite story whatever the subject or person under discussion. Together we compiled an anthology of anecdotes and put-downs about the worlds of theatre and music (*Cutting Edge, or 'Back in the Knife Box, Miss Sharp'*), and at the last lunch at which he spoke in public, before throat cancer cruelly silenced him, we sat side by side—and he talked about this book.

Ned is largely responsible for all the classic quotations you will find here—from both sides of the Atlantic. He knew his Mark Twain and his Dorothy Parker as well as his Dr Johnson, his Charles Dickens, and his Sydney Smith. He is wholly responsible for all the song lyrics. No one knew the lyrics of W. S. Gilbert, Noël Coward, Ira Gershwin, E. Y. Harburg, Lorenz Hart, Cole Porter, and Stephen Sondheim as Ned did. In fact, I think he was almost too fond of them and, in editing this edition, boldly I have cut some of Ned's darlings to make way for a few of my own.

In the pages that follow I hope you will find all that you would expect to find, and plenty of surprises as well. There is a place here for all types and conditions of people—politicians, playwrights, philosophers, philanderers, performers, priests, and poets, from Diane Abbott MP to Benjamin Zephaniah—with one *proviso*. This is a dictionary of humorous quotations. To get in you have got to make the editor laugh. Or smile. Or at least raise an eyebrow in wry amusement.

In my lifetime, I have been lucky enough to know the professional funny men and women of several generations. When I was young, I was befriended by the comedian Cyril Fletcher and, through him and others, I got to know and admire a whole generation of entertainers—Wee George Wood, Arthur Askey, Tommy Trinder, Ted Ray, Max Wall—who began their careers in music-hall and variety. In the late 1960s, when I started to work in radio and television, I began to meet the stars who I had first found funny when I was a boy: Kenneth Williams, Frankie Howerd, Harry Worth, and Dick Emery among them. Soon I found myself working with comedians of every ilk, from the more sophisticated (Dave Allen, Bob Monkhouse) to the less so (Frank Carson, Charlie Williams) and now, in the teens of the twenty-first century, I find I am friends with a raft of younger comics—Jack Whitehall, David Mitchell, Russell Kane, Milton Jones, John Bishop—who weren't even alive when I first played a working men's club in Manchester, as the support act to Bernard Manning. (I shared a dressing room with the stripper, but that's another story.)

The funniest people I have seen on stage include Jim Davidson (yes), Victoria Wood, Ken Dodd, and Barry Humphries in his guise as Dame Edna Everage. The funniest people I have had dinner with include Alan Bennett, Kenneth Williams, Vincent Price, and the actor and casting director, Noel Davis. What surprised me when I had finished work on this edition of the *Dictionary* was how few of these very funny people had made my final cut. The reason is this: people who are funny in the flesh—on stage, on TV, across the dinner table—aren't necessarily so droll pinned down on the page and confined within quotation marks. Frankie Howerd in full flow was hilarious, but it was his stage *persona* and his manner of delivery that were funny rather than his material.

Comedians do feature in the pages that follow and some of them get more credit than is perhaps their due. We know Bob Hope said funny things, but how many of them did he think of himself? Does it matter? Because this is an Oxford Dictionary of Quotations and, rightly, we take these matters seriously, the *Dictionary*'s Associate Editor, Susan Ratcliffe, and her team at the Oxford University Press, have done their best to give every quotation a reliable attribution. It is not always easy. Very often, a comedian's scriptwriter (or, indeed, a politician's) is a shadowy figure whose name is destined never to be known. And, sometimes, it is simply impossible to discover 'who said it' and 'who said it first'. For example, which contemporary British comedian said this: 'My dad used to say "always fight fire with fire", which is probably why he got thrown out of the fire brigade'? Some believe it was Peter Kay who said it first. Others are adamant it was Harry Hill. Do you toss a coin to arrive at the truth?

Who first said, 'I have to go on working. I've discovered that money is the one thing keeping me in touch with my children'? It is a good line, isn't it? I am certain I thought of it. My first wife is equally certain I stole it—from whom she does not know. ('I call her my "first wife". I am still married to her. I only call her that to keep her on her toes ...' Now, *that* line I did steal, from the broadcaster and humorist Kenneth Robinson, in about 1982. But who *he* stole it from I cannot tell you.)

Some modern comedians are very sensitive about their material and pounce if they think you have purloined a line that they originated. Comics and wits of an earlier era were less precious. Oscar Wilde was famously relaxed about people who pinched his quips—and not at all ashamed of borrowing other men's flowers to rearrange in verbal bouquets of his own.

Oscar Wilde, I think, is the person most quoted in this book—not surprisingly. He made it his business to be witty and I have been collecting his choicest lines for as long as I can remember. In 1961, when I was thirteen, I was given his Complete Works and read them from cover to cover—all 1,118 pages. I cannot have understood much, but I relished the language and learnt by heart his 'Phrases and Philosophies for the Use of the Young'. My favourite is still this one: 'Wickedness is a myth invented by good people to account for the curious attractiveness of others.'

As a boy, I felt a special kinship with Oscar Wilde because I was a pupil at an English boarding school called Bedales, where Cyril, the older of Wilde's two sons, had been at school. The founder of Bedales, John Badley, was a friend of the Wilde family, and still alive and living in the school grounds when I was a boy. Mr Badley told me (in 1965, at around the time of his hundredth birthday) that he believed that much of Oscar's 'spontaneous wit' was, in fact, 'carefully studied'. He recalled staying at a house party in Cambridge with Oscar and travelling back with him to London by train. Assorted fellow guests came to the station to see them on their way. At the moment the train was due to pull out, Wilde delivered a valedictory quip, then the guard blew the whistle and waved his green flag, the admirers on the platform cheered, Wilde sank back into his seat and the train moved off. Unfortunately, it only moved a yard or two before juddering to a halt. The group on the platform gathered again outside the compartment occupied by Wilde and Badley. Oscar hid behind his newspaper and hissed at his companion, 'They've had my parting shot. I only prepared one.'

When I told this story to the actor Donald Sinden he volunteered that Wilde's friend, Lord Alfred Douglas, whom Sir Donald had got to know in the 1940s, had told him too that much of Wilde's spontaneous wit was carefully worked out in advance—and frequently repeated. Lord Alfred Douglas also claimed to be the originator of several of Wilde's most famous lines.

I hope you will find that all the attributions in this book are accurate. Susan Ratcliffe and her team have been dogged in their researches. For example,

I wanted to include this line in the collection: 'Under pressure, people admit to murder, setting fire to the village church, or robbing a bank, but never to being bores.' In other books and on the world-wide web, the quotation is attributed to Elsa Maxwell, American columnist and hostess. But did she actually say it? And, if so, when, where, and to whom? Nobody seems to know for sure. Just because something is repeated *ad nauseam* on the web does not mean that it is true. The line has made the final cut because I like it, but it appears with the *caveat* that it is 'attributed' to Mrs Maxwell. Hand on heart, we cannot promise that she actually ever said it.

We are not entirely sure that King George V ever said 'Bugger Bognor', either. According to legend, these were the King's last words. In January 1936, when the royal physician told the dying monarch he'd soon be on the mend and recuperating at his favourite seaside resort, His Majesty retorted 'Bugger Bognor'—and expired. That is too good to be the true story. I think *this* version is much more likely ... In 1929, several years before his death, the King is in Bognor convalescing from an earlier illness. He is recovering well and he is about to go home when a deputation from the town council comes to call on His Majesty, both to pay its dutiful respects and humbly to beg that the town might in future be given the signal honour of being known as Bognor Regis. The town council's request is duly conveyed to the sovereign by his private secretary. That's when the king says, 'Bugger Bognor!'—and the private secretary returns to the delegation. 'His Majesty is touched by your request,' he reports, 'and graciously pleased to accede to it.'

This is the *Oxford Dictionary of Humorous Quotations*. We have to get things right. When a quotation is of doubtful origin, we make that clear. When we absolutely don't know who said it first, but can't resist it, we give credit to a character called 'Anonymous'. When we have a good line that crops up in several forms, we pick the version we most trust and the one that best expresses the idea involved. For example, Shakespeare (like Wilde) often used exactly the same joke in different ways in different plays. This, I think, was the Bard's favourite joke:

Art thou his father?
Ay, sir, so his mother says, if I may believe her.

That's how Shakespeare gives us the gag in *The Taming of the Shrew*, act V, scene 1. The same joke crops up again in *Much Ado About Nothing*, act I, scene 1:

I think this is your daughter.
Her Mother hath many times told me so ...

And in *Love's Labour's Lost*, act II, scene 1:

Pray you sir, whose daughter?
Her mother's I have heard ...

And again in *The Merchant of Venice*, act II, scene 2:

I am Launcelot the Jew's Man, and I am sure Margery your wife is my mother ...

And half-a-dozen times more.

Many people have made this *Dictionary* possible. William Shakespeare and Oscar Wilde are two of them. My late father and Ned Sherrin, of course, are two more. (Both barristers, as it happens, and Exeter College, Oxford, men.) Others to thank for their contributions include Gerry Hanson, Merlin Holland, Matthew Horsford, Jeremy Nicholas, Ken Thomson, and Roger Lewis. (Roger Lewis, incidentally, is one of the funniest writers of our time—though he does not feature in the book. With some writers, the laughter comes by the page rather than the gobbet.) As well as Susan Ratcliffe and her team in Oxford, two people, in particular, have ensured that this edition of the *Dictionary* is not locked in antiquity and has a much broader and better representation of contemporary and female contributions than before. They are my wife Michele Brown (author, publisher, and sometime editor of *Hammer & Tongues, A Dictionary of Women's Wit and Humour*) and my daughter, Saethryd Brandreth, who has searched far and wide for quotations that reflect our time and yet look as though they might stand the test of time.

It has been a pleasure and an honour to edit this edition of the *Oxford Dictionary of Humorous Quotations*. Now you have it in your hands, let me sign off in contemporary fashion by simply saying, 'Enjoy'. I would have said, 'Have a nice day', but then I remembered that when someone said that to Peter Ustinov, he replied, 'Thank you, but I have other plans.' That's the joy of this line of work. I always have a quotation for everything—it saves original thinking.

Gyles Brandreth

How to Use the Dictionary

Finding a quotation...

...on a subject

The dictionary is arranged by subject, so quotations about **Food** or **Love** are grouped together. Some subjects cover related topics such as **Apology and Excuses**, and others cover opposites such as **Hope and Despair**. A list of all the subjects can be found on page xv. If the subject you want is not listed, try looking for the word and related terms in the Keyword Index.

...if you know the words

If you want to find out about a particular quotation, you can find it by looking in the Keyword Index, where the most significant words from each entry are indexed with a reference to help you find it (see **Using the indexes** below).

...by an author

If you are looking for quotations by a particular author, you can find them by looking in the Author Index, which guides you to all of the quotations from each author (see **Using the indexes** below).

About the order...

...of subjects

The subjects are arranged in alphabetical order from **Academic Life** to **Youth**. For joint subjects such as **Sleep and Dreams** the main entry is found at **Sleep**, and a cross-reference will direct you there from **Dreams**.

...of quotations

Within each theme, quotations are given in alphabetical order of author surname. After the text of the quotation the author is given, followed by a note of its source. Essential background information is given before the quotation text in an italicized note, while supplementary or explanatory information is given after it.

Quotations which are in general currency but which are not at present traceable to a specific source are described as 'attributed'; quotations which are popularly attributed to an author but whose authenticity is doubted include a note such as 'perhaps apocryphal'.

Looking elsewhere in the book...

...for related subjects

After each heading, cross references are given to any related subjects which may also be relevant: for example '**Business** see also **Management**'.

...for related quotations

Where one quotation is closely linked to another, a cross reference will direct you to the related quotation. Such references are to the name of the subject (sometimes in shortened form), followed by the number of the quotation within the subject: 'see CRIME 5' means look at the fifth quotation in the subject **Crime and Punishment**.

Using the indexes...

...keywords

The most significant words from each quotation appear in the Keyword Index. Each instance of a keyword, abbreviated to its initial letter, is given with a short section of the surrounding text to help identify it. Both the headwords and the sections of text are in alphabetical order. To simplify searching, words are indexed in their standard British English form, regardless of spelling in the original.

...authors

Each author who appears in the text is included in the Author Index, followed by a list of references to their quotations. Authors are listed in alphabetical order of surname.

...references

Index references are to the name of the subject (sometimes in shortened form), followed by the number of the item within the subject: FAMILY 7 means the seventh item in the subject **The Family**.

List of Themes

Academic Life

see also **EDUCATION**

....

Old professors never die, they merely lose their faculties.   **Stephen Fry**

1 You can always tell a Harvard man, but you can't tell him much.
- **James Barnes** 1866-1936 American writer: attributed

2 I was not unpopular [at school]…It is Oxford that has made me insufferable.
- **Max Beerbohm** 1872-1956 English critic, essayist, and caricaturist: *More* (1899) 'Going Back to School'

3 In my day, the principal concerns of university students were sex, smoking dope, rioting and learning. Learning was something you did only when the first three weren't available.
- **Bill Bryson** 1951- American travel writer: *The Lost Continent* (1989)

4 No academic person is ever voted into the chair until he has reached an age at which he has forgotten the meaning of the word 'irrelevant'.
- **Francis M. Cornford** 1874-1943 English academic: *Microcosmographia Academica* (1908)

5 Old professors never die, they merely lose their faculties.
- **Stephen Fry** 1957- English comedian, actor, and writer: *The Liar* (1991)

6 JOHNSON: I had no notion that I was wrong or irreverent to my tutor.
BOSWELL: That, Sir, was great fortitude of mind.
JOHNSON: No, Sir; stark insensibility.
- **Samuel Johnson** 1709-84 English poet, critic, and lexicographer: James Boswell *Life of Samuel Johnson* (1791) 31 October 1728

7 I find that the three major administrative problems on campus are sex for the students, athletics for the alumni, and parking for the faculty.
- **Clark Kerr** 1911-2003 American academic: speech at the University of Washington, in *Time* magazine 17 November 1958

8 That state of resentful coma that…dons dignify by the name of research.
- **Harold Laski** 1893-1950 British Labour politician: letter to Oliver Wendell Holmes, 10 October 1922

9 Most people tire of a lecture in ten minutes; clever people can do it in five. Sensible people never go to lectures at all.
- **Stephen Leacock** 1869-1944 Canadian humorist: *My Discovery of England* (1922)

10 In university they don't tell you that the greater part of the law is learning to tolerate fools.
- **Doris Lessing** 1919- English writer: *Martha Quest* (1952)

11 *of writer friends with degrees in English:*
University seems to have turned them into Conan the Grammarians, who fret over perfect sentence construction.
- **Kathy Lette** 1958- Australian writer: in *Daily Telegraph* 30 November 2002

12 The Socratic method is a game at which only one (the professor) can play.
- **Ralph Nader** 1934- American consumer protectionist: Joel Seligman *The High Citadel* (1978)

13 Liberals have invented whole college majors—psychology, sociology, women's studies— to prove that nothing is anybody's fault.
- **P. J. O'Rourke** 1947- American humorous writer: *Give War a Chance* (1992)

14 Very nice sort of place, Oxford, I should think, for people that like that sort of place. They teach you to be a gentleman there. In the Polytechnic they teach you to be an engineer or such like.
- **George Bernard Shaw** 1856-1950 Irish dramatist: *Man and Superman* (1903)

15 *replying to Woodrow Wilson's 'And what*

in your opinion is the trend of the modern English undergraduate?':
Steadily towards drink and women, Mr President.
- **F. E. Smith** 1872-1930 British Conservative politician and lawyer: attributed

16 I expect you'll be becoming a schoolmaster, sir. That's what most of the gentlemen does, sir, that gets sent down for indecent behaviour.
- **Evelyn Waugh** 1903-66 English novelist: *Decline and Fall* (1928)

Acting

see also **ACTORS, FILM STARS, THEATRE**

....

Shakespeare is so tiring. You never get a chance to sit down unless you're a king.
George S. Kaufman and **Howard Teichmann**

1 METHOD ACTOR: What is my motivation?
ABBOTT: Your job.
- **George Abbott** 1887-1995 American director, producer, and dramatist: in *New York Times* 2 February 1995

2 For an actress to be a success, she must have the face of a Venus, the brains of a Minerva, the grace of Terpsichore, the memory of a Macaulay, the figure of Juno, and the hide of a rhinoceros.
- **Ethel Barrymore** 1879-1959 American actress: George Jean Nathan *The Theatre in the Fifties* (1953)

3 Every actor has a natural animosity towards every other actor, present or absent, living or dead.
- **Louise Brooks** 1906-85 American actress: *Lulu in Hollywood* (1982)

4 Like acting with 210 pounds of condemned veal.
of a dull actor
- **Coral Browne** 1913-91 Australian actress: attributed

5 *auditioning a one-legged man for the role of Tarzan:*
The leg division, Mr Spiggot. You are deficient in it to the tune of one. Your right leg, I like…it's a lovely leg for the role…I've got nothing against your right leg. The trouble is—neither have you.
- **Peter Cook** 1937-95 English comedian and actor: *Not Only But Also* (BBC2 TV, 1964) 'One Leg Too Few'

6 Don't put your daughter on the stage, Mrs Worthington,
Don't put your daughter on the stage.
Though they said at the school of acting
She was lovely as Peer Gynt,
I'm afraid on the whole
An ingénue role
Would emphasize her squint.
- **Noël Coward** 1899-1973 English dramatist: 'Mrs Worthington' (1935)

7 CLAUDETTE COLBERT: I knew these lines backwards last night.
NOËL COWARD: And that's just the way you're saying them this morning.
- **Noël Coward** 1899-1973 English dramatist: Cole Lesley *The Life of Noel Coward* (1976)

8 *noted for his 'Method' acting:*
Just on the chance I might one day have to speak on an evening such as this I've actually stayed in character as myself for the last 55 years.
- **Daniel Day-Lewis** 1957- English actor: accepting a Best Actor award at the BAFTAs, 10 February 2013

9 She's the only sylph I ever saw, who could stand upon one leg, and play the tambourine on her other knee, like a sylph.
- **Charles Dickens** 1812-70 English novelist: *Nicholas Nickleby* (1839)

10 I found out that acting was hell. You spend all your time trying to do what

they put people in asylums for.
- **Jane Fonda** 1937- American actress: attributed; J. R. Colombo *Wit and Wisdom of the Moviemakers* (1979)

11 *when asked to say something terrifying during rehearsals for Peter Brook's* Oedipus *in 1968:*
We open in two weeks.
- **John Gielgud** 1904-2000 English actor: Peter Hay *Theatrical Anecdotes* (1987)

12 *when asked by Michael Hordern for advice before playing Lear for the first time:*
All I can tell you is, get a light Cordelia.
- **John Gielgud** 1904-2000 English actor: attributed, in *New York Times* 4 May 1995

13 An actor is a kind of a guy who if you ain't talking about him ain't listening.
- **George Glass** 1910-84 American film producer: Bob Thomas *Brando* (1973); said to be quoted frequently by Marlon Brando

14 I acted so tragic the house rose like magic,
The audience yelled 'You're sublime.'
They made me a present of Mornington Crescent
They threw it a brick at a time.
- **W. F. Hargreaves** 1846-1919 British songwriter: 'The Night I Appeared as Macbeth' (1922)

15 Acting is the most minor of gifts and not a very high-class way to earn a living. Shirley Temple could do it at the age of four.
- **Katharine Hepburn** 1907-2003 American actress: attributed; Nigel Rees *Cassell's Movie Quotations* (2000)

16 *on reticent British acting:*
I am well, except for a slight cold caught watching Sir Gerald du Maurier making love.
- **George S. Kaufman** 1889-1961 American dramatist: Ilka Chase *Past Imperfect* (1942)

17 Shakespeare is so tiring. You never get a chance to sit down unless you're a king.
- **George S. Kaufman** 1889-1961 and **Howard Teichmann** 1916-87 American dramatists: *The Solid Gold Cadillac* (1953); spoken by Josephine Hull

18 *on being refused membership of an exclusive golf-club:*
I'm *not* an actor, and I enclose my press cuttings to prove it.
- **Victor Mature** 1915-99 American actor: Ned Sherrin *Cutting Edge* (1984)

19 *on nudity:*
The part never calls for it. And I've never ever used that excuse. The box office calls for it.
- **Helen Mirren** 1945- English actress: in *Independent* 22 March 1994

20 When you do Shakespeare they think you must be intelligent because they *think* you understand what you're saying.
- **Helen Mirren** 1945- English actress: interviewed on *Ruby Wax Meets...*; in *Mail on Sunday* 16 February 1997

21 The only thing wrong with performing was that you couldn't phone it in.
- **Robert Mitchum** 1917-97 American actor: attributed; in *Sunday Times* (Magazine section) 11 May 1980

22 I used to work for a living, then I became an actor.
- **Roger Moore** 1927- English actor: in *Independent* 1 July 1989

23 *on the part of Lear:*
When you've the strength for it, you're too young; when you've the age you're too old. It's a bugger, isn't it?
- **Laurence Olivier** 1907-89 English actor: in *Sunday Telegraph* 4 May 1986

24 *on being congratulated on his performance as the Captain in Strindberg's bleak play about the misery of marriage,* The Dance of Death:
It wasn't difficult. There isn't a line that I haven't said to one of my three wives.
- **Laurence Olivier** 1907-89 English actor: Michael Meyer *Not Prince Hamlet* (1989)

25 The difference between being a director and being an actor is the difference between being the carpenter banging the nails into the wood, and being the piece of wood the nails are being banged into.
- **Sean Penn** 1960- American actor: in *Guardian* 28 November 1991

26 Acting is merely the art of keeping a large group of people from coughing.
- **Ralph Richardson** 1902-83 English actor: in *New York Herald Tribune* 19 May 1946

27 I don't care for Lady Macbeth in the streetwalking scene.
- **Edward Linley Sambourne** 1844-1910 English cartoonist: R. G. C. Price *A History of Punch* (1957)

28 The best actors in the world, either for tragedy, comedy, history, pastoral, pastoral-comical, historical-pastoral, tragical-historical, tragical-comical-historical-pastoral, scene individable, or poem unlimited.
- **William Shakespeare** 1564-1616 English dramatist: *Hamlet* (1601)

29 I wish sir, you would practise this without me. I can't stay dying here all night.
- **Richard Brinsley Sheridan** 1751-1816 Irish dramatist: *The Critic* (1779)

30 I told Mad Frankie Fraser 'I'm doing Hamlet'—he said, 'I'll do him for you.'
- **Arthur Smith** 1954- English comedian: *Arthur Smith's Hamlet*

31 *to an over-genteel actress in an Egyptian drama:*
Oh my God! Remember you're in Egypt.

The *skay* is only seen in Kensington.
- **Herbert Beerbohm Tree** 1852-1917 English actor-manager: M. Peters *Mrs Pat* (1984)

32 *to a motley collection of American females, assembled to play ladies-in-waiting to a queen:*
Ladies, just a little more virginity, if you don't mind.
- **Herbert Beerbohm Tree** 1852-1917 English actor-manager: Alexander Woollcott *Shouts and Murmurs* (1923)

33 *definition of acting:*
Shouting in the evenings.
- **Patrick Troughton** 1920-87 British actor: recalled as heard in a radio interview; Michael Simkins *What's My Motivation?* (2004)

34 Talk low, talk slow, and don't say much.
- **John Wayne** 1907-79 American actor: attributed

35 They say an actor is only as good as his parts. Well, my parts have done me pretty well, darling.
- **Barbara Windsor** 1937- English actress: in *Times* 13 February 1999

36 Acting is like sex. You should do it, not talk about it.
- **Joanne Woodward** 1930- American actress: attributed, 1987; in Nigel Rees *Cassell's Movie Quotations* (2000)

Actors

see also **ACTING, FILM STARS**

....

Dramatic art, in her opinion, is knowing how to fill a sweater. **Bette Davis**

1 *Alfred Hitchcock, who was directing her in* Torn Curtain, *complained that a spotlight was 'making a hell of a line over her head':*
That's my halo.
- **Julie Andrews** 1935- English actress and singer: Robert Windeler *Julie Andrews* (1970)

2 My only regret in the theatre is that I could never sit out front and watch me.
- **John Barrymore** 1882-1942 American actor: Eddie Cantor *The Way I See It* (1959)

3 Nobody thought Mel Gibson could play

a Scot but look at him now! Alcoholic and a racist!
- **Frankie Boyle** 1972- British comedian: at the Edinburgh Festival, 2006, in *Independent* 26 August 2006

4 This Thane of Cawdor would be unnerved by Banquo's valet, never mind Banquo's ghost.
of Michael Hordern in Macbeth *in 1959*
- **Alan Brien** 1925-2008 English journalist: Diana Rigg *No Turn Unstoned* (1982)

5 Tallulah Bankhead barged down the

Nile last night as Cleopatra—and sank.
- **John Mason Brown** 1900-69 American critic: in *New York Post* 11 November 1937

6 You were the first person I thought of to play a chimpanzee.
asking Helena Bonham Carter to star in Planet of the Apes
- **Tim Burton** 1958- American film director: in *Scotsman* 3 March 2010

7 Tallulah [Bankhead] is always skating on thin ice. Everyone wants to be there when it breaks.
- **Mrs Patrick Campbell** 1865-1940 English actress: in *Times* 13 December 1968

8 *of a rival:*
Such a clever actress. Pity she does her hair with Bovril.
- **Mrs Patrick Campbell** 1865-1940 English actress: in *Ned Sherrin in his Anecdotage* (1993); attributed

9 *the daughter of Sybil Thorndike and Lewis Casson explaining to a telephone enquiry why neither of her charitably inclined parents was at home:*
Daddy is reading Shakespeare Sonnets to the blind and Mummy's playing Shakespeare to the lepers.
- **Ann Casson** 1915-90 British actress: recounted by Emlyn Williams; James Harding *Emlyn Williams* (1987)

10 She [Edith Evans] took her curtain calls as though she had just been un-nailed from the cross.
- **Noël Coward** 1899-1973 English dramatist: diary, 25 October 1964

11 *seeing a poster for 'Michael Redgrave and Dirk Bogarde in* The Sea Shall Not Have Them*':*
I fail to see why not; everyone else has.
- **Noël Coward** 1899-1973 English dramatist: Sheridan Morley *The Quotable Noël Coward* (1999)

12 Anna Neagle playing Queen Victoria always made me think that Albert must have married beneath him.
- **Noël Coward** 1899-1973 English dramatist: Sheridan Morley *The Quotable Noël Coward* (1999)

13 Dramatic art, in her opinion, is knowing how to fill a sweater.
on Jayne Mansfield
- **Bette Davis** 1908-89 American actress: attributed

14 *of Creston Clarke as King Lear:*
He played the King as though under momentary apprehension that someone else was about to play the ace.
- **Eugene Field** 1850-95 American writer: review attributed to Field; in *Denver Tribune* c.1880

15 Dear Ingrid—speaks five languages and can't act in any of them.
of Ingrid Bergman
- **John Gielgud** 1904-2000 English actor: Ronald Harwood *The Ages of Gielgud* (1984); attributed

16 People like to hear me say 'shit' in my gorgeous voice.
of his popularity in America
- **John Gielgud** 1904-2000 English actor: in *New Yorker* 10 July 2000; attributed

17 My dear fellow, I never saw anything so funny in my life, and yet it was not in the least bit vulgar.
of Beerbohm Tree's Hamlet (1892)
- **W. S. Gilbert** 1836-1911 English writer: D. Bispham *A Quaker Singer's Recollections* (1920)

18 On the stage he was natural, simple, affecting;
'Twas only that when he was off he was acting.
of David Garrick
- **Oliver Goldsmith** 1730-74: *Retaliation* (1774)

19 Many actors want to play Hamlet and Macbeth, and ever since I became an actor from the very beginning, I just wanted to play a Shetland pony. I can't explain why.
- **Dustin Hoffman** 1937- American actor: in *Observer* 30 January 2005

20 She was good at playing abstract confusion in the same way that a midget is good at being short.
on Marilyn Monroe
- **Clive James** 1939 Australian critic and writer: *Visions Before Midnight* (1977)

21 Massey won't be satisfied until
he's assassinated.
on Raymond Massey's 'sincerity' in playing
Lincoln
- **George S. Kaufman** 1889-1961 American
dramatist: Howard Teichmann *George S.*
Kaufman (1973)

22 I've made so many movies playing a
hooker that they don't pay me in the
regular way any more. They leave it on
the dresser.
- **Shirley MacLaine** 1934– American actress:
in *New Woman* July 1989

23 There were three things that Chico was
always on—a phone, a horse or a broad.
- **Groucho Marx** 1890-1977 American film
comedian: Ned Sherrin *Cutting Edge* (1984)

24 I'd like to work with her again in
something appropriate. Perhaps
Macbeth.
after starring opposite Barbra Streisand in
Hello, Dolly!
- **Walter Matthau** 1920-2000 American
actor: Anne Edwards *Streisand: It Only*
Happens Once (1996)

25 *watching Spencer Tracy on the set of*
Dr Jekyll and Mr Hyde *(1941):*
Which is he playing now?
- **W. Somerset Maugham** 1874-1965 English
novelist: attributed; Leslie Halliwell *The*
Filmgoer's Book of Quotes (1978 edn)

26 Left eyebrow raised, right eyebrow
raised.
summary of his acting range
- **Roger Moore** 1927– English actor: David
Brown *Star Billing* (1985)

27 *of Katharine Hepburn at the first night of*
The Lake *(1933):*
She ran the whole gamut of the
emotions from A to B, and put some
distance between herself and a
more experienced colleague [Alison
Skipworth] lest she catch acting from
her.
- **Dorothy Parker** 1893-1967 American critic:
attributed

28 Any man who hates dogs and babies
can't be all bad.
of W. C. Fields, and often attributed to him
- **Leo Rosten** 1908-97 American writer and
social scientist: speech at Masquers' Club
dinner, 16 February 1939

29 Through it all, I have remained
consistently and nauseatingly adorable.
In fact, I have been known to cause
diabetes.
- **Meg Ryan** 1961– American actress: at
Women in Hollywood luncheon, 1999

30 It is greatly to Mrs Patrick Campbell's
credit that, bad as the play was, her
acting was worse.
review of Sardou Fedora *1 June 1895*
- **George Bernard Shaw** 1856-1950 Irish
dramatist: *Our Theatre in the Nineties* (1932)

31 As Virgilia in *Coriolanus* she yearns so
hungrily that I longed to throw her a
fish.
of Claire Bloom in 1955
- **Kenneth Tynan** 1927-80 English critic:
Curtains (1961)

32 Forty years ago he was Slightly in *Peter*
Pan, and you might say that he has been
wholly in *Peter Pan* ever since.
of Noël Coward
- **Kenneth Tynan** 1927-80 English theatre
critic: *Curtains* (1961)

33 ALISON SKIPWORTH: You forget I've been
an actress for forty years.
MAE WEST: Don't worry, dear. I'll keep
your secret.
- **Mae West** 1892-1980 American actress:
G. Eells and S. Musgrove *Mae West* (1989)

34 *on the Burton-Taylor* Private Lives *in 1964:*
He's miscast and she's Miss Taylor.
- **Emlyn Williams** 1905-87 Welsh dramatist:
James Harding *Emlyn Williams* (1987)

35 She was like a sinking ship firing on the
rescuers.
of Mrs Patrick Campbell in her later years
- **Alexander Woollcott** 1887-1943 American
writer: *While Rome Burns* (1944) 'The First
Mrs Tanqueray'

Advertising

The consumer isn't a moron; she is your wife.   **David Ogilvy**

1 While you were out your exterminator
called.
*heading of leaflet left in a New York
letter-box*
 ▪ **Anonymous**: Sylvia Townsend Warner
letter to David Garnett, 12 May 1967

2 Surely any society that permits the
substitution of 'kwik' for 'quick'
and 'e.z.' for 'easy' does not deserve
Shakespeare, Eliot or Michener.
on the language of advertising
 ▪ **Russell Baker** 1925- American journalist:
column in *New York Times*; Ned Sherrin
Cutting Edge (1984)

3 Doing business without advertising is
like winking at a girl in the dark. You
know what you are doing but nobody
else does.
 ▪ **Stewart Henderson Britt** 1907-79
American advertising consultant: in *New
York Herald Tribune* 30 October 1956

4 It is far easier to write ten passably
effective sonnets, good enough to take
in the not too enquiring critic, than one
effective advertisement that will take in
a few thousand of the uncritical buying
public.
 ▪ **Aldous Huxley** 1894-1963 English novelist:
On the Margin (1923) 'Advertisement'

5 Advertising may be described as
the science of arresting human
intelligence long enough to get

money from it.
 ▪ **Stephen Leacock** 1869-1944 Canadian
humorist: *Garden of Folly* (1924)

6 I think that I shall never see
A billboard lovely as a tree.
Perhaps, unless the billboards fall,
I'll never see a tree at all.
 ▪ **Ogden Nash** 1902-71 American humorist:
'Song of the Open Road' (1933)

7 The consumer isn't a moron; she is
your wife.
 ▪ **David Ogilvy** 1911-99 British-born
advertising executive: *Confessions of an
Advertising Man* (1963)

8 Advertising is the rattling of a stick
inside a swill-bucket.
 ▪ **George Orwell** 1903-50 English novelist:
Keep the Aspidistra Flying (1936)

9 If the client moans and sighs,
Make his logo twice the size.
 ▪ **John Trench** 1920-2003 English writer:
attributed, perhaps apocryphal; in *Times*
14 March 2003 (obituary)

10 *asked why he had made a commercial for
American Express:*
To pay for my American Express.
 ▪ **Peter Ustinov** 1921-2004 British actor: in
Ned Sherrin in his Anecdotage (1993)

11 Don't sell the steak, sell the sizzle.
 ▪ **Elmer Wheeler** American salesman: 1930s
advertising slogan, attributed

Advice

··

When in doubt buy shoes.   **Marcelle D'Argy Smith**

1 Never play cards with a man called
Doc. Never eat at a place called Mom's.
Never sleep with a woman whose
troubles are worse than your own.
- **Nelson Algren** 1909-81 American novelist:
in *Newsweek* 2 July 1956

2 It's not who you know, it's how you
use them.
- **Ed Arriens** 1977– British television
producer: attributed

3 Consult, *v.* To seek another's approval
of a course already decided on.
- **Ambrose Bierce** 1842-c.1914 American
writer: *The Cynic's Word Book* (1906)

4 Be yourself. That's the worst advice you
could give an impressionist.
- **Rory Bremner** 1961– British impressionist
and comedian: attributed

5 She generally gave herself very good
advice (though she very seldom
followed it).
- **Lewis Carroll** 1832-98 English writer: *Alice's
Adventures in Wonderland* (1865)

6 Start every day with a smile and get it
over with.
- **W. C. Fields** 1880-1946 American humorist:
attributed, perhaps apocryphal

7 *appearing as an agony aunt on an American
television show:*
QUESTION: My fiancé gave me a car, a
mink coat, and a stove. Is it proper for
me to accept these gifts?
GABOR: Of course not! Send back the
stove.
- **Zsa Zsa Gabor** 1917– Hungarian-born
actress: *TV Guide Roundup* (1960)

8 Always buy a good pair of shoes and a
good bed—if you're not in one you're
in the other.
advice from her mother
- **Gloria Hunniford** 1941– British broadcaster:
in *Mail on Sunday* 16 June 2002

9 Don't forgive and never forget; do
unto others before they do unto you;
and third and most importantly, keep
your eye on your friends, because your
enemies will take care of themselves.
- **David Jacobs** 1939– American
screenwriter: *Dallas* (CBS TV, 1987),
spoken by Larry Hagman as J.R. Ewing; see
lifestyle 3

10 It's useless to hold a person to anything
he says while he's in love, drunk or
running for office.
- **Shirley MacLaine** 1934– American actress:
attributed

11 Don't accept rides from strange men,
and remember that all men are strange
as hell.
- **Robin Morgan** 1941– American feminist:
Sisterhood is Powerful (1970)

12 Never trust a dog with orange
eyebrows,
Always get the young man's name and
address,
Never get between two mirrors,
And always wear completely clean
underwear every day because you
never knew when you were going
to be knocked down and killed by a
runaway horse and if people found
you had unsatisfactory underwear
on, you'd die of shame.
*advice given to Desiderata Hollow by her
grandmother*
- **Terry Pratchett** 1948– English fantasy
writer: *Witches Abroad* (1991)

13 When in doubt buy shoes.
- **Marcelle D'Argy Smith** British journalist:
attributed; in *Independent* 20 August 1997

14 Dr Ruth says we women should tell
our lovers how to make love to us. My
boyfriend goes nuts if I tell him how to
drive.
- **Pam Stone** 1959– American comedian:
attributed

15 Above all, gentlemen, not the slightest zeal.
   ▪ **Charles-Maurice de Talleyrand** 1754-1838 French statesman: P. Chasles *Voyages d'un critique à travers la vie et les livres* (1868)

16 Always be sincere, even if you don't mean it.
   ▪ **Harry S. Truman** 1884-1972 American Democratic statesman: attributed

Age and Ageing

see also **MIDDLE AGE, OLD AGE**

....

I can remember when the air was clean and sex was dirty. **George Burns**

1 Pushing forty? She's clinging on to it for dear life.
   one actress discussing another
   ▪ **Anonymous**: saying, sometimes wrongly attributed to Ivy Compton-Burnett

2 It's sad to grow old—but nice to ripen.
   ▪ **Brigitte Bardot** 1934- French actress: Tony Crawley *Bébé: the Films of Brigitte Bardot* (1975)

3 I can remember when the air was clean and sex was dirty.
   ▪ **George Burns** 1896-1996 American comedian: attributed, perhaps apocryphal

4 Grandchildren don't make a man feel old; it's the knowledge that he's married to a grandmother.
   ▪ **G. Norman Collie**: attributed, 1955

5 The years that a woman subtracts from her age are not lost. They are added to the ages of other women.
   ▪ **Diane de Poitiers** 1499-1566 French mistress of Henri II: attributed

6 When a man fell into his anecdotage it was a sign for him to retire from the world.
   ▪ **Benjamin Disraeli** 1804-81 British Tory statesman and novelist: *Lothair* (1870)

7 Life begins at 40—but so do fallen arches, rheumatism, faulty eyesight, and the tendency to tell the same story to the same person three or four times.
   ▪ **William Feather** 1889-1981 American writer: attributed

8 I'm over the hill, but nobody prepared me for what was going to be on the other side.
   on being 70
   ▪ **Jane Fonda** 1937- American actress: in *Mail on Sunday* 6 January 2008

9 QUESTIONER: Which of the Gabors is the oldest?
   ZSA ZSA: She vould never admit it, but it's Mama.
   ▪ **Zsa Zsa Gabor** 1917- Hungarian-born actress: Earl Wilson *Hot Times: True Tales of Hollywood and Broadway* (1984)

10 When I wake up in the morning, I don't feel anything until noon, and then it's time for my nap.
   ▪ **Bob Hope** 1903-2003 American comedian: accepting an award from Vietnam veterans, 23 May 1985

11 You know you're getting old when the candles cost more than the cake.
   ▪ **Bob Hope** 1903-2003 American comedian: attributed

12 *the new five ages of man:*
   Lager, Aga, Saga, Viagra, Gaga.
   ▪ **Virginia Ironside** 1945- English journalist: at an *Oldie* lunch, in *Guardian* 23 February 2013

13 I do not call myself really old yet. Not till a young woman offers me her seat in a railway compartment will that tragedy really be mine.
   ▪ **E. V. Lucas** 1868-1938 English writer: *London Lavender* (1912)

14 A woman telling her true age is like a buyer confiding his final price to an Armenian rug dealer.
   ▪ **Mignon McLaughlin** 1913-83 American writer: *Complete Neurotic's Notebook* (1981)

15 I will never forget it! It was on the occasion of Ernie's eightieth birthday. He rang me up and said, 'Soph, Soph! I just married me a twenty-year old girl. What do you think of that?' I said to him, 'Ernie, when I am eighty I shall marry me a twenty-year-old boy. And let me tell you something, Ernie: twenty goes into eighty a helluva lot more than eighty goes into twenty!'
  - **Bette Midler** 1945- American actress: *A View from a Broad* (1980)

16 When you've reached a certain age and think that a face-lift or a trendy way of dressing will make you feel twenty years younger, remember—nothing can fool a flight of stairs.
  - **Denis Norden** 1922- English humorist: attributed

17 George, you're too old to get married again. Not only can't you cut the mustard, honey, you're too old to open the jar.
  at a dinner to honour George Burns
  - **LaWanda Page** 1920-2002 American comedienne: George Burns *The Third time Round* (1980)

18 Age is a question of mind over matter.

If you don't mind, it doesn't matter.
  - **Leroy ('Satchel') Paige** 1906-82 American baseball player: Bert Sugar *Book of Sports Quotes* (1979)

19 I said to my husband, my boobs have gone, my stomach's gone, say something nice about my legs. He said, 'Blue goes with everything'.
  - **Joan Rivers** 1933- American comedienne: attributed; Michèle Brown and Ann O'Connor *Hammer and Tongues* (1986)

20 Just remember, once you're over the hill you begin to pick up speed.
  - **Charles Monroe Schulz** 1922-2000 American cartoonist: *Peanuts*

21 I feel like I'm twenty again—but with arthritis.
  on his latest Rambo film
  - **Sylvester Stallone** 1946- American actor and film director: in *Daily Star* 11 February 2008

22 One should never trust a woman who tells one her real age. A woman who would tell one that, would tell one anything.
  - **Oscar Wilde** 1854-1900 Irish dramatist and poet: *A Woman of No Importance* (1893)

Ambition

I always wanted to be somebody, but now I realise I should have been more specific.   **Lily Tomlin**

1 *seeing a commemorative stone engraved 'Laid by the Poet Laureate' (John Masefield):*
  Every nice girl's ambition.
  - **John Betjeman** 1906-84 English poet: Bevis Hillier *Betjeman: the Bonus of Laughter* (2004)

2 At the age of six I wanted to be a cook. At seven I wanted to be Napoleon. And my ambition has been growing steadily ever since.
  - **Salvador Dali** 1904-89 Spanish painter: *The Secret Life of Salvador Dali* (1948)

3 People assume you slept your way to the top. Frankly, I couldn't sleep my way to the middle.
  - **Joni Evans** American publisher: in *New York Times* 23 July 1986

4 My grandfather once told me that there two kinds of people: those who do the work and those who take the credit. He told me to try to be in the first group; there was much less competition there.
  - **Indira Gandhi** 1917-84 Indian stateswoman: attributed, 1960s

5 The average Hollywood film star's ambition is to be admired by an

American, courted by an Italian, married to an Englishman, and have a French boyfriend.
- **Katharine Hepburn** 1907-2003 American actress: in *New York Journal-American* 22 February 1954

6 Nothing makes a man so adventurous as an empty pocket.
- **Victor Hugo** 1802-85 French writer: *The Hunchback of Notre Dame* (1831)

7 For years politicians have promised the moon, I'm the first one to be able to deliver it.
- **Richard Milhous Nixon** 1913-94 American Republican statesman: on the first moon landing, 20 July 1969; attributed

8 Everybody wants to save the earth; nobody wants to help Mom do the dishes.
- **P. J. O'Rourke** 1947- American humorous writer: *All the Trouble in the World* (1994)

9 A self-made man is one who believes in luck and sends his son to Oxford.
- **Christina Stead** 1902-83 Australian novelist: *House of All Nations* (1938)

10 I always wanted to be somebody, but now I realise I should have been more specific.
- **Lily Tomlin** 1939- American comedienne and actress: attributed

11 *on being advised against joining the overcrowded legal profession:*
There is always room at the top.
- **Daniel Webster** 1782-1852 American politician: attributed

America

see also **TOWNS**

The thing that impresses me most about America is the way parents obey their children.   **Edward VIII**

1 California is a fine place to live—if you happen to be an orange.
- **Fred Allen** 1894-1956 American humorist: in *American Magazine* December 1945

2 They're the experts where personality is concerned, the Americans; they've got it down to a fine art.
- **Alan Bennett** 1934- English writer: *Talking Heads* (1988)

3 Our bombs are incredibly smart. In fact, our bombs are better educated than the average high school graduate. At least they can find Kuwait.
- **A. Whitney Brown** 1952- American comedian: *Saturday Night Live* (NBC TV) 9 February 1991

4 I had forgotten just how flat and empty it [middle America] is. Stand on two phone books almost anywhere in Iowa and you get a view.
- **Bill Bryson** 1951- American travel writer: *The Lost Continent* (1989)

5 When you're born, you get a ticket to the freak show. If you're born in America, you get a front row seat.
- **George Carlin** 1937-2008 American comedian: James Sullivan *Seven Dirty Words: The Life and Crimes of George Carlin* (2010)

6 When I was a boy I was told that anybody could become President. I'm beginning to believe it.
- **Clarence Darrow** 1857-1938 American lawyer: Irving Stone *Clarence Darrow for the Defence* (1941)

7 The thing that impresses me most about America is the way parents obey their children.
- **Edward VIII** 1894-1972 British king: in *Look* 5 March 1957

8 I'm as corny as Kansas in August I'm as normal as blueberry pie...
...High as a flag on the fourth of July.
- **Oscar Hammerstein II** 1895-1960 American songwriter: 'I'm in Love with a Wonderful Guy' (1949)

9 Once we had a Roosevelt
Praise the Lord!
Now we're stuck with Nixon, Agnew,
  Ford
Brother, can you spare a rope!
- **E. Y. Harburg** 1898-1981 American songwriter: parody of 'Brother Can You Spare a Dime?', written for the *New York Times* at the time of Watergate

10 I could come back to America...to die—
but never, never to live.
- **Henry James** 1843-1916 American novelist: letter to Mrs William James, 1 April 1913

11 Never criticize Americans. They have the best taste that money can buy.
- **Miles Kington** 1941-2008 English humorist: *Welcome to Kington* (1989)

12 *the universal philosophy of young America:*
I can do that.
- **Ed Kleban** 1939-87 American songwriter: song-title (1975)

13 So I really think that American gentlemen are the best after all, because kissing your hand may make you feel very very good but a diamond and safire bracelet lasts forever.
- **Anita Loos** 1893-1981 American writer: *Gentlemen Prefer Blondes* (1925)

14 The continental United States slopes gently from east to west, with the result that everything with a screw loose rolls into California.
- **John Naughton** 1946- Irish academic: in *Observer* 30 September 2012

15 Wherever there is suffering, injustice and oppression, the Americans will show up, six months late, and bomb the country next to where it's happening.
- **P. J. O'Rourke** 1947- American humorous writer: *Peace Kills* (2004)

16 I like to be in America!
O.K. by me in America!
Ev'rything free in America
For a small fee in America!
- **Stephen Sondheim** 1930- American songwriter: 'America' (1957)

17 In the United States there is more space where nobody is than where anybody is. That is what makes America what it is.
- **Gertrude Stein** 1874-1946 American writer: *The Geographical History of America* (1936)

18 In America any boy may become President and I suppose it's just one of the risks he takes!
- **Adlai Stevenson** 1900-65 American Democratic politician: speech in Detroit, 7 October 1952

19 'American girls *do* have regrets', Amy said, 'That is what distinguishes them from French girls.'
- **Amanda Vail** 1921-66 American writer: *Love Me Little* (1957)

20 In Europe, when a rich woman has an affair with a conductor, they have a baby. In America, she endows an orchestra for him.
- **Edgard Varèse** 1885-1965 French-born American composer: Herman G. Weinberg *Saint Cinema* (1970)

21 The land of the dull and the home of the literal.
- **Gore Vidal** 1925-2012 American writer: *Reflections upon a Sinking Ship* (1969)

22 MRS ALLONBY: They say, Lady Hunstanton, that when good Americans die they go to Paris.
LADY HUNSTANTON: Indeed? And when bad Americans die, where do they go to?
LORD ILLINGWORTH: Oh, they go to America.
- **Oscar Wilde** 1854-1900 Irish dramatist: *A Woman of No Importance* (1893)

23 The youth of America is their oldest tradition. It has been going on now for three hundred years.
- **Oscar Wilde** 1854-1900 Irish dramatist: *A Woman of No Importance* (1893)

Anger and Argument

Reason always means what someone else has got to say.   **Elizabeth Gaskell**

1 Sir Roger told them, with the air of a man who would not give his judgement rashly, that much might be said on both sides.
   - **Joseph Addison** 1672-1719 English writer: *The Spectator* 20 July 1711

2 Anger makes dull men witty, but it keeps them poor.
   - **Francis Bacon** 1561-1626 English courtier: *Works* (1859) 'Baconiana'

3 I expect to pass through this world but once and therefore if there is anybody that I want to kick in the crutch I had better kick them in the crutch *now*, for I do not expect to pass this way again.
   while lunching at the Reform Club with a bishop at the next table
   - **Maurice Bowra** 1898-1971 English critic: Arthur Marshall *Life's Rich Pageant* (1984)

4 Violence is the repartee of the illiterate.
   - **Alan Brien** 1925-2008 English journalist: in *Punch* 7 February 1973

5 The time for action is past. Now is the time for senseless bickering!
   - **Ashleigh Brilliant** 1933- American writer and cartoonist: attributed

6 I've never won an argument with her; and the only times I thought I had I found out the argument wasn't over yet.
   of his wife Rosalynn
   - **Jimmy Carter** 1924- American Democratic statesman: in *Reader's Digest* March 1979

7 'My idea of an agreeable person,' said Hugo Bohun, 'is a person who agrees with me.'
   - **Benjamin Disraeli** 1804-81 British Conservative statesman: *Lothair* (1870)

8 What counts is not necessarily the size of the dog in the fight—it's the size of the fight in the dog.
   - **Dwight D. Eisenhower** 1890-1969 American Republican statesman: remark, Republican National Committee Breakfast, 31 January 1958

9 I'll not listen to reason...Reason always means what someone else has got to say.
   - **Elizabeth Gaskell** 1810-65 English novelist: *Cranford* (1853)

10 Those who in quarrels interpose, Must often wipe a bloody nose.
   - **John Gay** 1685-1732 English poet and dramatist: *Fables* (1727) 'The Mastiffs'

11 There is no arguing with Johnson; for when his pistol misses fire, he knocks you down with the butt end of it.
   - **Oliver Goldsmith** 1730-74 Irish writer: James Boswell *Life of Samuel Johnson* (1934 ed.) 26 October 1769

12 Any stigma, as the old saying is, will serve to beat a dogma.
   - **Philip Guedalla** 1889-1944 British historian: *Masters and Men* (1923)

13 When you get angry, they tell you, count to five before you reply. Why should I count to five? It's what happens *before* you count to five which makes life interesting.
   - **David Hare** 1947- English dramatist: *The Secret Rapture* (1988)

14 You may easily play a joke on a man who likes to argue—agree with him.
   - **E. W. Howe** 1853-1937 American novelist and editor: *Country Town Sayings* (1911)

15 The only person who listens to both sides of a husband and wife argument is the woman in the next apartment.
   - **Sam Levenson** 1911-80 American humorist: *You Can Say That Again, Sam!* (1975)

16 It's my rule never to lose me temper till it would be dethrimental to keep it.
   - **Sean O'Casey** 1880-1964 Irish dramatist: *The Plough and the Stars* (1926)

17 I storm and I roar, and I fall in a rage, And missing my whore, I bugger my page.
   - **Charles Sackville** 1638-1706 English poet: 'Regime d'vivre' (often attributed to Lord Rochester, but probably not by him)

18 John Major's self-control in cabinet was rigid. The most angry thing he would ever do was to throw down his pencil.
   - **Gillian Shephard** 1940– English Conservative politician: in November 1999

19 *when two royal dukes walking on either side of him told him that they were trying to decide if he was a greater fool or rogue:*
   Why, i'faith, I believe I am between *both*.
   - **Richard Brinsley Sheridan** 1751–1816 Irish dramatist: Walter Jerrold *Bon-Mots* (1893)

20 *on seeing two Edinburgh women hurling insults at one another across an alleyway:*
   Those two women will never agree;
   they are arguing from different premises.
   - **Sydney Smith** 1771–1845 English essayist: Peter Virgin *Sydney Smith* (1994)

21 My uncle Toby would never offer to answer this by any other kind of argument, than that of whistling half a dozen bars of Lillabullero.
   - **Laurence Sterne** 1713–68 English novelist: *Tristram Shandy* (1759–67)

22 He never let the sun go down on his wrath, though there were some colourful sunsets while it lasted.
   of W. G. Grace
   - **A. A. Thomson** 1894–1968 English writer: Alan Gibson *The Cricket Captains of England* (1979)

Animals and Birds

see also CATS

....

The cow is of the bovine ilk; One end is moo, the other, milk. **Ogden Nash**

1 The lion and the calf shall lie down together but the calf won't get much sleep.
   - **Woody Allen** 1935– American film director, writer, and actor: in *New Republic* 31 August 1974

2 *on the qualities a good pig should have:*
   The shoulders of a parlour maid and the buttocks of a cook.
   - **Anonymous**: saying of unknown origin

3 *Puella Rigensis ridebat*
   Quam tigris in tergo vehebat;
   Externa profecta,
   Interna revecta,
   Risusque cum tigre manebat.
   There was a young lady of Riga
   Who went for a ride on a tiger;
   They returned from the ride
   With the lady inside,
   And a smile on the face of the tiger.
   - **Anonymous**: R. L. Green (ed.) *A Century of Humorous Verse* (1959)

4 *during his time in the Lords the eighth Earl of Arran was concerned with measures for homosexual reform and the protection of badgers, interests concisely summed up by a fellow peer:*
   Teaching people not to bugger badgers and not to badger buggers.
   - **Anonymous**: in *Ned Sherrin in his Anecdotage* (1993)

5 I think animal testing is a terrible idea; they get all nervous and give the wrong answers.
   - **Anonymous**: modern saying

6 The Tiger, on the other hand, is kittenish and mild,
   He makes a pretty play fellow for any little child;
   And mothers of large families (who claim to common sense)
   Will find a Tiger well repay the trouble and expense.
   - **Hilaire Belloc** 1870–1953 British writer and Liberal politician: 'The Tiger' (1896)

7 Ornithology used to be an arcane hobby for embittered schoolmasters, dotty spinsters and lonely little boys, but now it is as normal a weekend

occupation as rug-making or
wife-swapping.
- **Kyril Bonfiglioli** 1928-85 English writer:
  Don't Point that Thing at Me (1972)

8 To my mind, the only possible pet
is a cow. Cows love you...They will
listen to your problems and never ask
a thing in return. They will be your
friends for ever. And when you get tired
of them, you can kill and eat them.
Perfect.
- **Bill Bryson** 1951- American travel writer:
  Neither Here Nor There (1991)

9 A hen is only an egg's way of making
other eggs.
- **Samuel Butler** 1835-1902 English novelist:
  Life and Habit (1877)

10 I am fond of pigs. Dogs look up to us.
Cats look down on us. Pigs treat us as
equal.
- **Winston Churchill** 1874-1965 British
  Conservative statesman: M. Gilbert *Never
  Despair* (1988); attributed

11 Animals generally return the love
you lavish on them by a swift bite in
passing—not unlike friends and wives.
- **Gerald Durrell** 1925-95 English zoologist
  and writer: attributed

12 *after an operation to remove a fishbone stuck
in her throat:*
After all these years of fishing, the fish
are having their revenge.
- **Queen Elizabeth, the Queen Mother**
  1900-2002: in November 1982, attributed;
  Christopher Dobson (ed.) *Queen Elizabeth
  the Queen Mother: Chronicle of a Remarkable
  Life* (2000)

13 A horse is dangerous at both ends and
uncomfortable in the middle.
- **Ian Fleming** 1908-64 English writer:
  attributed

14 Honey bees are amazing creatures.
I mean, think about it, do earwigs
make chutney?
- **Eddie Izzard** 1962- British comedian:
  Unrepeatable (1994)

15 Arabs of means rode none but she-
camels, since they...were patient and
would endure to march long after
they were worn out, indeed until they
tottered with exhaustion and fell in their
tracks and died: whereas the coarser
males grew angry, flung themselves
down when tired, and from sheer rage
would die there unnecessarily.
- **T. E. Lawrence** 1888-1935 English soldier
  and writer: *Seven Pillars of Wisdom* (1926)

16 No animal should ever jump up on the
dining room furniture unless absolutely
certain that he can hold his own in the
conversation.
- **Fran Lebowitz** 1946- American writer:
  Social Studies (1982)

17 Where are you going
With your fetlocks blowing in the...
    wind
I want to shower you with sugar lumps
And ride you over...fences
I want to polish your hooves every
    single day
And bring you to the horse...dentist.
*'My Lovely Horse' as sung by Fathers Ted and
Dougal*
- **Graham Linehan** 1968- and **Arthur
  Mathews** 1959- Irish writers: 'A Song for
  Europe' (1996), episode from *Father Ted*
  (Channel 4 TV, 1995-8)

18 Oh, a wondrous bird is the pelican!
His beak holds more than his belican.
He takes in his beak
Food enough for a week.
But I'll be darned if I know how the
    helican.
- **Dixon Lanier Merritt** 1879-1972 American
  editor: in *Nashville Banner* 22 April 1913

19 One disadvantage of being a hog is that
at any moment some blundering fool
may try to make a silk purse out of
your wife's ear.
- **J. B. Morton** 1893-1975 British journalist:
  By the Way (1931)

20 My mother made me ride horses when
I was young. I didn't like it. They're too
difficult to steer.
- **Stirling Moss** 1929- British motor-racing
  driver: in *Observer* 1 July 2012

21 God in His wisdom made the fly
And then forgot to tell us why.
- **Ogden Nash** 1902-71 American humorist:
  'The Fly' (1942)

22 The turtle lives 'twixt plated decks
Which practically conceal its sex.
I think it clever of the turtle
In such a fix to be so fertile.
- **Ogden Nash** 1902-71 American humorist:
'Autres Bêtes, Autres Moeurs' (1931)

23 The cow is of the bovine ilk;
One end is moo, the other, milk.
- **Ogden Nash** 1902-71 American humorist:
'The Cow' (1931)

24 Four legs good, two legs bad.
- **George Orwell** 1903-50 English novelist:
Animal Farm (1945)

25 It costs me never a stab nor squirm
To tread by chance upon a worm.
'Aha, my little dear,' I say,
'Your clan will pay me back some day.'
- **Dorothy Parker** 1893-1967 American critic
and humorist: 'Thoughts for a Sunshiny
Morning' (1928)

26 I live in a city. I know sparrows from
starlings. After that everything's a duck
as far as I'm concerned.
- **Terry Pratchett** 1948- English fantasy
writer: *Monstrous Regiment* (2003)

27 There was one poor tiger that hadn't *got*
a Christian.
- **Punch** 1841-1992 English humorous weekly
periodical: vol. 68 (1875)

28 I know two things about the horse
And one of them is rather coarse.
- **Naomi Royde-Smith** c.1875-1964 English
novelist and dramatist: in *Weekend Book*
(1928)

29 So, naturalists observe, a flea
Hath smaller fleas that on him prey;
And these have smaller fleas to bite
'em,
And so proceed *ad infinitum*.
- **Jonathan Swift** 1667-1745 Irish poet and
satirist: 'On Poetry' (1733)

30 If I were a cassowary
On the plains of Timbuctoo,
I would eat a missionary,
Cassock, band, and hymn-book too.
- **Samuel Wilberforce** 1805-73
English prelate: impromptu verse,
attributed

Apology and Excuses

'Dogs must be carried on the escalators.' Took me forty minutes to find one.
Harry Worth

1 CUSTOMER'S VOICE: In six days, do you
hear me, in six days, God made the
world…And you are not bloody well
capable of making me a pair of trousers
in three months!
TAILOR'S VOICE: But my dear Sir, my
dear Sir, look—at the world—and
look—at my trousers.
- **Samuel Beckett** 1906-89 Irish writer:
Endgame (1957)

2 VERY SORRY CAN'T COME. LIE FOLLOWS
BY POST.
*message to the Prince of Wales, on being
summoned to dine at the eleventh hour*
- **Lord Charles Beresford** 1846-1919 British
politician: Ralph Nevill *The World of Fashion
1837-1922* (1923)

3 Several excuses are always less
convincing than one.
- **Aldous Huxley** 1894-1963 English novelist:
Point Counter Point (1928)

4 One of those telegrams of which
M. de Guermantes had wittily fixed the
formula: 'Cannot come, lie follows'.
- **Marcel Proust** 1871-1922 French novelist:
Le Temps retrouvé (Time Regained, 1926)

5 *on being asked to apologize for calling a fellow
MP a liar:*
Mr Speaker, I said the honourable
member was a liar it is true and I am sorry
for it. The honourable member may place
the punctuation where he pleases.
- **Richard Brinsley Sheridan** 1751-1816 Irish
dramatist and Whig politician: attributed

6 Excuses are like assholes, Taylor—
everybody's got one.
- **Oliver Stone** 1946- American film
director: *Platoon* (1986 film), spoken by
John McGinley as Sgt O'Neill

7 It is a good rule in life never to apologize.
The right sort of people do not want
apologies, and the wrong sort take a
mean advantage of them.
- **P. G. Wodehouse** 1881-1975 English-born
writer: *The Man Upstairs* (1914)

8 I nearly missed the show tonight.
I got to the Underground and saw
this sign: 'Dogs must be carried on the
escalators.' Took me forty minutes to
find one.
- **Harry Worth** 1917-89 English comedian:
Gyles Brandreth diary 3 August 1968

Appearance

see also **FACES, HAIR**

....

It costs a lot of money to look this cheap. **Dolly Parton**

1 I'll tell you what, he doesn't suit
daylight, does he?
*a fan of Michael Parkinson overheard by
the veteran presenter at a book signing in
Wolverhampton*
- **Anonymous**: in *Express* 2 October 2008

2 It often means vanity and sometimes
drink.
*explaining his mistrust of 'men with waxed
moustaches'*
- **Lord Baden-Powell** 1857-1941 English
soldier and founder of the Boy Scout
movement: *Scouting for Boys* (1908)

3 *to her former lover Lord Alington as he dined
with another woman in a restaurant:*
Don't you recognize me with my
clothes on?
- **Tallulah Bankhead** 1903-68 American
actress: Bryony Lavery *Tallulah Bankhead*
(1999)

4 I refuse to think of them as chin hairs.
I think of them as stray eyebrows.
- **Janette Barber** 1953- American comedian
and producer: attributed

5 She is not so much dressed as richly
upholstered.
- **J. M. Barrie** 1860-1937 Scottish writer and
dramatist: *The Will* (performed 1913)

6 I know I looked awful because my
mother phoned and said I looked
lovely.
after getting a makeover on television
- **Jo Brand** 1957- English comedian: in
Sunday Telegraph 28 December 2003

7 After forty a woman has to choose
between losing her figure or her face.
My advice is to keep your face, and stay
sitting down.
- **Barbara Cartland** 1901-2000 English writer:
Libby Purves 'Luncheon à la Cartland'; in
Times 6 October 1993

8 It was a blonde. A blonde to make a
bishop kick a hole in a stained glass
window.
- **Raymond Chandler** 1888-1959 American
writer: *Farewell, My Lovely* (1940)

9 Glamour is on a life-support machine
and not expected to live.
- **Joan Collins** 1933- British actress: in
Independent 24 April 1999

10 Edith Sitwell, in that great Risorgimento
cape of hers, looks as though she were
covering a teapot or a telephone.
- **Noël Coward** 1899-1973 English dramatist,
actor, and composer: William Marchant
The Pleasure of his Company (1975)

11 Sunburn is very becoming—but only when it is even—one must be careful not to look like a mixed grill.
- Noël Coward 1899-1973 English dramatist, actor, and composer: *This Year of Grace* (1939)

12 The most delightful advantage of being bald—one can *hear* snowflakes.
- R. G. Daniels 1916-93 British magistrate: in *Observer* 11 July 1976

13 A drag queen's like an oil painting: You gotta stand back from it to get the full effect.
- Harvey Fierstein 1954- American dramatist and actor: *Torch Song Trilogy* (1979)

14 When she's narrow, she's narrow as an arrow
And she's broad, where a broad, should be broad.
- Oscar Hammerstein II 1895-1960 American songwriter: 'Honey Bun' (1949)

15 I got into moisturiser when I played football. If you're out in all weathers you have to take care of your face.
- Vinnie Jones 1965- English footballer and actor: in *Independent* 28 December 2002

16 Sure, deck your lower limbs in pants;
Yours are the limbs, my sweeting.
You look divine as you advance—
Have you seen yourself retreating?
- Ogden Nash 1902-71 American humorist: 'What's the Use?' (1940)

17 In Los Angeles everyone has perfect teeth. It's crocodile land.
- Gwyneth Paltrow 1972- American actress: in *Sunday Times* 3 February 2002

18 It costs a lot of money to look this cheap.
- Dolly Parton 1946- American singer and songwriter: attributed, perhaps apocryphal

19 Prince Charles' ears are so big he could hang-glide over the Falklands.
- Joan Rivers 1933- American comedienne: from stand up routine, early 1980s

20 My body is a temple, and my temple needs redecorating.
explaining why she's having more plastic surgery at the age of 78
- Joan Rivers 1933- American comedienne: in *Daily Mail* 26 January 2012

21 The musician's flabby, redundant figure sat up in bewildered semi-consciousness, like an ice-cream that has been taught to beg.
- Saki 1870-1916 Scottish writer: *The Chronicles of Clovis* (1911)

22 EDINA: What you don't realize is that inside, inside of me there is a thin person screaming to get out.
MOTHER: Just the one, dear?
- Jennifer Saunders 1958- English actress and writer: *Absolutely Fabulous* (BBC1 TV, 1993) 'Fat'

23 MRS CANDOUR: I'll swear her colour is natural—I have seen it come and go—
LADY TEAZLE: I dare swear you have, ma'am; it goes of a night and comes again in the morning.
- Richard Brinsley Sheridan 1751-1816 Irish dramatist and Whig politician: *The School for Scandal* (1777)

24 Women never look so well as when one comes in wet and dirty from hunting.
- R. S. Surtees 1805-64 English novelist: *Mr. Sponge's Sporting Tour* (1853)

25 A man who can part the Red Sea but apparently not his own hairpiece.
of Charlton Heston
- Dick Vosburgh 1929-2007 and Denis King: *Beauty and the Beards* (2001)

26 It is only shallow people who do not judge by appearances.
- Oscar Wilde 1854-1900 Irish dramatist and poet: *The Picture of Dorian Gray* (1891)

27 The Right Hon. was a tubby little chap who looked as if he had been poured into his clothes and had forgotten to say 'When!'
- P. G. Wodehouse 1881-1975 English-born writer: *Very Good, Jeeves* (1930)

28 I was so ugly when I was born, the doctor slapped my mother.
- Henny Youngman 1906-98 American comedian: in *Times* 26 February 1998; obituary

Architecture

The physician can bury his mistakes, but the architect can only advise his client to plant vines.   **Frank Lloyd Wright**

1 In my experience, if you have to keep the lavatory door shut by extending your left leg, it's modern architecture.
   - **Nancy Banks-Smith** 1929- British journalist: in *Guardian* 20 February 1979

2 Sir Christopher Wren
   Said, 'I am going to dine with some men.
   If anybody calls
   Say I am designing St Paul's.'
   - **Edmund Clerihew Bentley** 1875-1956 English writer: 'Sir Christopher Wren' (1905)

3 Ghastly good taste, or a depressing story of the rise and fall of English architecture.
   - **John Betjeman** 1906-84 English poet: title of book (1933)

4 The Church's Restoration
   In eighteen-eighty-three
   Has left for contemplation
   Not what there used to be.
   - **John Betjeman** 1906-84 English poet: 'Hymn' (1931)

5 They said it was split-level and open-plan. But then again so is an NCP car park.
   - **Alan Carr** 1976- English comedian: attributed

6 Like a monstrous carbuncle on the face of a much-loved and elegant friend.
   - **Charles, Prince of Wales** 1948- heir apparent to the British throne: speech on the proposed extension to the National Gallery, London, 30 May 1984

7 My client—God—is in no hurry.
   of the church of the Sagrada Familia in Barcelona (begun 1884)
   - **Antonio Gaudí** 1853-1926 Spanish architect: attributed

8 Why is it only Tudor that we mock?
   - **Harry Hill** 1964- English comedian: attributed

9 A taste for the grandiose, like a taste for morphia, is, once it has been fully acquired, difficult to keep within limits.
   - **Osbert Lancaster** 1908-86 English writer and cartoonist: *Homes Sweet Homes* (1939)

10 A lot of nuns in a rugger scrum.
   on the exterior of the Sydney Opera House
   - **George Molnar** 1910-98 Hungarian-born Australian cartoonist: attributed

11 The green belt was a Labour idea and we are determined to build on it.
   - **John Prescott** 1938- British Labour politician: attributed by Paddy Ashdown, in *Independent* 22 September 1999; perhaps apocryphal

12 A singularly dreary street. What I would term Victorian Varicose.
   - **Peter Shaffer** 1926- English dramatist: *Lettice and Lovage* (rev. ed. 1989)

13 *on Brighton Pavilion:*
   As if St Paul's had come down and pupped.
   - **Sydney Smith** 1771-1845 English clergyman and essayist: Peter Virgin *Sydney Smith* (1994)

14 Whatever may be said in favour of the Victorians, it is pretty generally admitted that few of them were to be trusted within reach of a trowel and a pile of bricks.
   - **P. G. Wodehouse** 1881-1975 English-born writer: *Summer Moonshine* (1938)

15 The physician can bury his mistakes, but the architect can only advise his client to plant vines.
   - **Frank Lloyd Wright** 1867-1959 American architect: in *New York Times* 4 October 1953

Argument *see* ANGER AND ARGUMENT

The Aristocracy

see also **CLASS**

....

A duchess will be a duchess in a bath towel. It's all a matter of style.
Carol Lawrence

1 *the much-married Duke of Westminster had died the previous day:*
There was a bad fire next door; lots of smoke, but it turned out *not* to be the four bereaved Duchesses of Westminster committing suttee.
▪ **Chips Channon** 1897-1958 American-born British Conservative politician: diary, 21 July 1953

2 The Stately Homes of England,
How beautiful they stand,
To prove the upper classes
Have still the upper hand.
▪ **Noël Coward** 1899-1973 English dramatist, actor, and composer: 'The Stately Homes of England' (1938)

3 I can trace my ancestry back to a protoplasmal primordial atomic globule. Consequently, my family pride is something in-conceivable. I can't help it. I was born sneering.
▪ **W. S. Gilbert** 1836-1911 English writer: *The Mikado* (1885)

4 Hearts just as pure and fair
May beat in Belgrave Square
As in the lowly air
Of Seven Dials.
▪ **W. S. Gilbert** 1836-1911 English writer: *Iolanthe* (1882)

5 *replying to Harold Wilson's remark (on Home's leading the Conservatives to victory in the 1963 election) that 'the whole [democratic] process has ground to a halt with a fourteenth Earl':*
As far as the fourteenth earl is concerned, I suppose Mr Wilson, when you come to think of it, is the fourteenth Mr Wilson.
▪ **Lord Home** 1903-95 British Conservative statesman: in *Daily Telegraph* 22 October 1963

6 I am an ancestor.
reply when taunted on his lack of ancestry, having been made Duke of Abrantes, 1807
▪ **Marshal Junot** 1771-1813 French general: attributed

7 A duchess will be a duchess in a bath towel. It's all a matter of style.
▪ **Carol Lawrence** 1932- American actress: attributed, in *TV Guide* 1969

8 An aristocracy in a republic is like a chicken whose head has been cut off: it may run about in a lively way, but in fact it is dead.
▪ **Nancy Mitford** 1904-73 English writer: *Noblesse Oblige* (1956) 'The English Aristocracy'

9 I'll purge, and leave sack, and live cleanly, as a nobleman should do.
▪ **William Shakespeare** 1564-1616 English dramatist: *Henry IV, Part 1* (1597)

10 LORD ILLINGWORTH: A title is really rather a nuisance in these democratic days. As George Harford I had everything I wanted. Now I have merely everything that other people want.
▪ **Oscar Wilde** 1854-1900 Irish dramatist and poet: *A Woman of No Importance* (1893)

11 Those comfortably padded lunatic asylums which are known, euphemistically, as the stately homes of England.
▪ **Virginia Woolf** 1882-1941 English novelist: *The Common Reader* (1925)

The Armed Forces

see also **WAR**

....

Don't talk to me about naval tradition. It's nothing but rum, sodomy, and the lash.   **Winston Churchill**

1 Join the army, meet interesting people
   and kill them.
   - **Anonymous**: graffito, 1980s

2 My home at my uncle's brought me
   acquainted with a circle of admirals.
   Of *Rears* and *Vices*, I saw enough. No,
   do not be suspecting me of a pun,
   I entreat.
   Mary Crawford to a disapproving Edmund
   - **Jane Austen** 1775-1817 English novelist:
   Mansfield Park (1814)

3 We joined the Navy to see the world,
   And what did we see? We saw the sea.
   - **Irving Berlin** 1888-1989 American
   songwriter: 'We Saw the Sea' in *Follow the
   Fleet* (1936)

4 Don't talk to me about naval tradition.
   It's nothing but rum, sodomy, and the
   lash.
   - **Winston Churchill** 1874-1965 British
   Conservative statesman: Peter Gretton
   Former Naval Person (1968)

5 I can always guarantee that the Irish
   Citizen Army will fight, but I cannot
   guarantee that it will be on time.
   - **James Connolly** 1868-1916 Irish labour
   leader and nationalist: Diana Norman
   Terrible Beauty (1987)

6 Have you had any word
   Of that bloke in the 'Third',
   Was it Southerby, Sedgwick or Sim?
   They had him thrown out of the club in
   Bombay
   For, apart from his mess bills exceeding
   his pay,
   He took to pig-sticking in *quite* the
   wrong way.
   I wonder what happened to him!
   - **Noël Coward** 1899-1973 English dramatist,
   actor, and composer: 'I Wonder What
   Happened to Him' (1945)

7 For a soldier I listed, to grow great in
   fame,
   And be shot at for sixpence a-day.
   - **Charles Dibdin** 1745-1814 English
   songwriter and dramatist: 'Charity' (1791)

8 *to the Duke of Newcastle, who had
   complained that General Wolfe was a
   madman:*
   Mad, is he? Then I hope he will *bite*
   some of my other generals.
   - **George II** 1683-1760 British king: Henry
   Beckles Willson *Life and Letters of James
   Wolfe* (1909)

9 Stick close to your desks and never go
   to sea,
   And you all may be Rulers of the
   Queen's Navee!
   - **W. S. Gilbert** 1836-1911 English writer:
   HMS Pinafore (1878)

10 I'm very good at integral and
   differential calculus,
   I know the scientific names of beings
   animalculous;
   In short, in matters vegetable, animal,
   and mineral,
   I am the very model of a modern
   Major-General.
   - **W. S. Gilbert** 1836-1911 English writer:
   The Pirates of Penzance (1879)

11 Fortunately, the army has had much
   practice at ignoring impossible
   instructions.
   - **Michael Green** 1927- English writer:
   The Boy Who Shot Down an Airship (1988)

12 I had examined myself pretty
   thoroughly and discovered that I was
   unfit for military service.
   - **Joseph Heller** 1923-99 American novelist:
   Catch-22 (1961)

13 Ben Battle was a soldier bold,
   And used to war's alarms:

But a cannon-ball took off his legs,
So he laid down his arms!
- **Thomas Hood** 1799-1845 English poet and
  humorist: 'Faithless Nelly Gray' (1826)

14 For here I leave my second leg,
And the Forty-second Foot!
- **Thomas Hood** 1799-1845 English poet and
  humorist: 'Faithless Nelly Gray' (1826)

15 My parents were very pleased that I was
in the army. The fact that I hated it
somehow pleased them even more.
- **Barry Humphries** 1934- Australian actor
  and writer: *More Please* (1992)

16 No man will be a sailor who has
contrivance enough to get himself into
a jail; for being in a ship is being in a jail,
with the chance of being drowned...A
man in a jail has more room, better
food, and commonly better company.
- **Samuel Johnson** 1709-84 English poet,
  critic, and lexicographer: James Boswell
  Life of Samuel Johnson (1791) 16 March 1759

17 *as young army musician, having composed a
march for his regiment:*
GENERAL: Isn't it a little fast, Korngold?
The men can't march to that.
KORNGOLD: Ah yes, well, you see Sir,
this was composed for the retreat!
- **Erich Korngold** 1897-1957 Austrian-born
  American composer: Brendan G. Carroll
  The Last Prodigy (1997)

18 *of a general who sent his dispatches from
'Headquarters in the Saddle':*
The trouble with Hooker is that
he's got his headquarters where his
hindquarters ought to be.
- **Abraham Lincoln** 1809-65 American
  statesman: P. M. Zall *Abe Lincoln Laughing*
  (1982)

19 [Haig is] brilliant—to the top of his boots.
- **David Lloyd George** 1863-1945 British Liberal
  statesman: Paul Johnson (ed.) *The Oxford
  Book of Political Anecdotes* (1986); attributed

20 Join a Highland regiment, me boy.
The kilt is an unrivalled garment for
fornication and diarrhoea.
- **John Masters** 1914-83 British writer:
  Bugles and a Tiger (1956)

21 If these gentlemen had their way, they
would soon be asking me to defend the
moon against a possible attack from
Mars.
*of his senior military advisers, and their
tendency to see threats which did not exist*
- **Lord Salisbury** 1830-1903 British
  Conservative statesman: Robert Taylor *Lord
  Salisbury* (1975)

22 Napoleon's armies always used to
march on their stomachs shouting:
'Vive l'Intérieur!'
- **W. C. Sellar** 1898-1951 and **R. J. Yeatman**
  1898-1968: *1066 and All That* (1930)

23 Your friend the British soldier can stand
up to anything except the British War
Office.
- **George Bernard Shaw** 1856-1950 Irish
  dramatist: *The Devil's Disciple* (1901)

24 When the military man approaches, the
world locks up its spoons and packs off
its womankind.
- **George Bernard Shaw** 1856-1950 Irish
  dramatist: *Man and Superman* (1903)

25 As for being a General, well at the age
of four with paper hats and wooden
swords we're all Generals. Only some
of us never grow out of it.
- **Peter Ustinov** 1921-2004 British actor,
  director, and writer: *Romanoff and Juliet*
  (1956)

26 The General was essentially a man of
peace, except in his domestic life.
- **Oscar Wilde** 1854-1900 Irish dramatist
  and poet: *The Importance of Being Earnest*
  (1895)

Art

There are only two styles of portrait painting; the serious and the smirk.
Charles Dickens

1 A cow and calf are cut in half
And placed in separate cases
To call it art, however smart
Casts doubt on art's whole basis.
 • **Anonymous**: unattributed; in *Spectator* 5 July 2003

2 *an old lady on Epstein's controversial* Christ in Majesty:
I can never forgive Mr Epstein for his representation of Our Lord. So very un-English!
 • **Anonymous**: in *Ned Sherrin in his Anecdotage* (1993)

3 The floozie in the jacuzzi.
popular description of the statue of James Joyce's character Anna Livia Plurabelle in Croppy Acre Park, Dublin
 • **Anonymous**: comment, c.1988

4 Oh, I wish I could draw. I've always wanted to draw. I'd give my right arm to be able to draw. It must be very relaxing.
 • **Alan Ayckbourn** 1939- English dramatist: *Joking Apart* (1979)

5 Of course he [William Morris] was a wonderful all-round man, but the act of walking round him has always tired me.
 • **Max Beerbohm** 1872-1956 English critic, essayist, and caricaturist: letter to S. N. Behrman c.1953; *Conversations with Max* (1960)

6 The joy of conceptual art is that the description is everything. Oh yes, there is real artistry at work here. It just isn't on the walls but in the catalogue descriptions.
 • **Benet Brandreth** 1975- English lawyer: *The Brandreth Papers* (2011)

7 The artistic temperament is a disease that afflicts amateurs.
 • **G. K. Chesterton** 1874-1936 English essayist, novelist, and poet: *Heretics* (1905)

8 There is no more sombre enemy of good art than the pram in the hall.
 • **Cyril Connolly** 1903-74 English writer: *Enemies of Promise* (1938)

9 The thing what makes you know that Vernon Ward is a good painter is if you look at his ducks, you can see the eyes follow you around the room.
 • **Peter Cook** 1937-95 English comedian and actor: *Not Only But Also* (BBC2 TV, 1965) 'At the Art Gallery'

10 There are only two styles of portrait painting; the serious and the smirk.
 • **Charles Dickens** 1812-70 English novelist: *Nicholas Nickleby* (1839)

11 If I were alive in Rubens's time, I'd be celebrated as a model. Kate Moss would be used as a paint brush.
 • **Dawn French** 1957- British comedy actress: in *Sunday Times* 13 August 2006

12 *to a lawyer who had asked him why he laid such stress on 'the painter's eye':*
The painter's eye is to him what the lawyer's tongue is to you.
 • **Thomas Gainsborough** 1727-88 English painter: William Hazlitt *Conversations of James Northcote* (1830)

13 *on attempting to paint two actors, David Garrick and Samuel Foote:*
Rot them for a couple of rogues, they have everybody's faces but their own.
 • **Thomas Gainsborough** 1727-88 English painter: Allan Cunningham *The Lives of the Most Eminent Painters, Sculptors and Architects* (1829)

14 Then a sentimental passion of a vegetable fashion must excite your languid spleen,
An attachment à la Plato for a bashful young potato, or a not too French French bean!
Though the Philistines may jostle, you will rank as an apostle in the high aesthetic band,

If you walk down Piccadilly with a
poppy or a lily in your medieval
hand.
- **W. S. Gilbert** 1836-1911 English writer:
Patience (1881)

15 As my poor father used to say
In 1863,
Once people start on all this Art
Goodbye, moralitee!
- **A. P. Herbert** 1890-1971 English writer
and humorist: 'Lines for a Worthy Person'
(1930)

16 It's amazing what you can do with an E
in A-level art, twisted imagination and a
chainsaw
- **Damien Hirst** 1965- English artist: in
Observer 3 December 1995

17 I don't want justice, I want mercy.
on having his portrait painted
- **William Morris 'Billy' Hughes** 1862-1952
British-born Australian statesman: John
Thompson *On the Lips of Living Men* (1962)

18 There is, perhaps, no more dangerous
man in the world than the man with
the sensibilities of an artist but without
creative talent. With luck such men
make wonderful theatrical impresarios
and interior decorators, or else they
become mass murderers or critics.
- **Barry Humphries** 1934- Australian actor
and writer: *More Please* (1992)

19 Mr Landseer whose only merit as a
painter was the tireless accuracy with
which he recorded the more revoltingly
sentimental aspects of the woollier
mammals.
- **Osbert Lancaster** 1908-86 English writer
and cartoonist: *Homes Sweet Homes* (1939)

20 *when Carl André's* Equivalent VIII
*consisting of 120 bricks was exhibited at the
Tate Gallery in 1976:*
I think the fellow needs to have his hod
examined.
- **Osbert Lancaster** 1908-86: attributed

21 The adjective 'modern', when applied
to any branch of art, means 'designed
to evoke incomprehension, anger,
boredom or laughter'.
- **Philip Larkin** 1922-85 English poet: *All What
Jazz* (1985)

22 'What are you painting?' I said. 'Is it the
Heavenly Child?' 'No' he said, 'It is a
cow.'
- **Stephen Leacock** 1869-1944 Canadian
humorist: *Nonsense Novels* (1911)

23 Dali is the only painter of LSD without
LSD.
- **Timothy Leary** 1920-96 American
psychologist: Salvador Dali *Dali by Dali*
(1970)

24 If a scientist were to cut his ear off,
no one would take it as evidence of a
heightened sensibility.
- **Peter Medawar** 1915-87 English
immunologist and writer: 'J. B. S.' (1968)

25 Monet began by imitating Manet, and
Manet ended by imitating Monet.
- **George Moore** 1852-1933 Irish novelist:
Vale (1914)

26 To me, the *Mona Lisa* just looks like
she's chewing a toffee.
- **Justin Moorhouse** 1970- English
comedian: attributed, 2007

27 *on a South African statue of the Voortrekkers:*
Patriotism is the last refuge of the
sculptor.
- **William Plomer** 1903-73 South African
poet and novelist: Rupert Hart-Davis letter
to George Lyttelton, 13 October 1956

28 My art belongs to Dada.
- **Cole Porter** 1891-1964 American
songwriter: attributed

29 Epstein is a great sculptor. I wish he
would wash, but I believe Michelangelo
never did, so I suppose it is part of the
tradition.
- **Ezra Pound** 1885-1972 American poet:
Charles Norman *The Case of Ezra Pound*
(1948)

30 I don't think rock'n'roll songwriters
should worry about Art...As far as I'm
concerned, Art is just short for Arthur.
- **Keith Richards** 1943- English rock
musician: *Keith Richards: in His Own Words*
(1994)

31 *on the probable reaction to the painting of the
subjects of Turner's* Girls Surprised while
Bathing:
I should think devilish surprised to see

what Turner has made of them.
- **Dante Gabriel Rossetti** 1828-82 English poet and painter: O. Doughty *A Victorian Romantic* (1960)

32 Treat a work of art like you would a prince: let it speak to you first.
- **Arthur Schopenhauer** 1788-1860 German philosopher: attributed

33 I don't know what art is, but I do know what it isn't. And it isn't someone walking around with a salmon over his shoulder, or embroidering the name of everyone they have slept with on the inside of a tent.
- **Brian Sewell** 1931- British art critic: in *Independent* 26 April 1999

34 The photographer is like the cod which produces a million eggs in order that one may reach maturity.
- **George Bernard Shaw** 1856-1950 Irish dramatist: introduction to the catalogue for Alvin Langdon Coburn's exhibition at the Royal Photographic Society, 1906

35 What sight is sadder than the sight of a lady we admire admiring a nauseating picture.
- **Logan Pearsall Smith** 1865-1946 American-born man of letters: *Afterthoughts* (1931)

36 I always ask the sitter if they want truth or flattery. They always ask for truth, and I always give them flattery.
- **Ruskin Spear** 1911-90 British painter: attributed; in *Sunday Times* (Letters) 4 January 2004

37 Imagination without skill gives us modern art.
- **Tom Stoppard** 1937- British dramatist: *Artist Descending a Staircase* (1972)

38 I doubt that art needed Ruskin any more than a moving train needs one of its passengers to shove it.
- **Tom Stoppard** 1937- British dramatist: in *Times Literary Supplement* 3 June 1977

39 *the ingredients for a successful exhibition:*
You've got to have two out of death, sex and jewels.
- **Roy Strong** 1935- English art historian: in *Sunday Times* 23 January 1994

40 There is only one position for an artist anywhere: and that is, upright.
- **Dylan Thomas** 1914-53 Welsh poet: *Quite Early One Morning* (1954)

41 Painters are so bitchy. Magritte told Miró that Kandinsky had feet of Klee.
- **Dick Vosburgh** 1929-2007 American writer: told to Ned Sherrin

42 Mrs Ballinger is one of the ladies who pursue Culture in bands, as though it were dangerous to meet it alone.
- **Edith Wharton** 1862-1937 American novelist: *Xingu and Other Stories* (1916)

43 *advice on how to become an artist:*
All you need to know is which end of the brush to put in your mouth.
- **James McNeill Whistler** 1834-1903 American-born painter: quoted by Walter Sickert, lecture, Thanet School of Art, 23 November 1934

44 Yes—one does like to make one's mummy just as nice as possible!
on his portrait of his mother
- **James McNeill Whistler** 1834-1903 American-born painter: E. R. and J. Pennell *The Life of James McNeill Whistler* (1908)

45 *in his case against Ruskin, replying to the question: 'For two days' labour, you ask two hundred guineas?':*
No, I ask it for the knowledge of a lifetime.
- **James McNeill Whistler** 1834-1903 American-born painter: D. C. Seitz *Whistler Stories* (1913)

46 *on the 'Old Masters':*
They are all old but they are not all masters.
- **James McNeill Whistler** 1834-1903 American-born painter: quoted by Walter Sickert, lecture, Thanet School of Art, 23 November 1934

47 All that I desire to point out is the general principle that Life imitates Art far more than Art imitates Life.
- **Oscar Wilde** 1854-1900 Irish dramatist and poet: *Intentions* (1891) 'The Decay of Lying'

Audiences

The play was a great success, but the audience was a total failure. **Oscar Wilde**

1 The best audience is intelligent, well educated, and a little drunk.
- **Alben W. Barkley** 1877-1956 American politician: attributed; Jonathon Green *A Dictionary of Contemporary Quotations* (1982)

2 They eat their young.
on Glasgow music hall audiences
- **Harry Chapman**: attributed

3 They were really tough—they used to tie their tomatoes on the end of a yo-yo, so they could hit you twice.
- **Bob Hope** 1903-2003 American comedian: attributed

4 There was laughter in the back of the theatre, leading to the belief that someone was telling jokes back there.
- **George S. Kaufman** 1889-1961 American dramatist: Howard Teichmann *George S. Kaufman* (1973)

5 There still remains, to mortify a wit, The many-headed monster of the pit.
- **Alexander Pope** 1688-1744 English poet: *Imitations of Horace* (1737)

6 I know two kinds of audiences only— one coughing, and one not coughing.
- **Artur Schnabel** 1882-1951 Austrian-born pianist: *My Life and Music* (1961)

7 The play was a great success, but the audience was a total failure.
- **Oscar Wilde** 1854-1900 Irish dramatist and poet: after the first performance of *Lady Windermere's Fan*; Peter Hay *Theatrical Anecdotes* (1987)

Australia

By God what a site! By man what a mess! **Clough Williams-Ellis**

1 Australia is a huge rest home, where no unwelcome news is ever wafted on to the pages of the worst newspapers in the world.
- **Germaine Greer** 1939- Australian feminist: in *Observer* 1 August 1982

2 The only people keeping the spirit of irony alive in Australia are taxi drivers and homosexuals.
- **Barry Humphries** 1934- Australian entertainer and writer: in *Australian Woman's Weekly* February 1983

3 In a way Australia is like Catholicism. The company is sometimes questionable and the landscape is grotesque. But you always come back.
- **Thomas Keneally** 1935- Australian novelist: in *Woman's Day* 4 July 1983

4 When New Zealanders emigrate to Australia, it raises the average IQ of both countries.
- **Robert Muldoon** 1921-92 New Zealand statesman: attributed

5 In Australia,
Inter alia,
Mediocrities
Think they're Socrates.
- **Peter Porter** 1929- Australian poet: unpublished clerihew; Stephen Murray-Smith (ed.) *The Dictionary of Australian Quotations* (1984)

6 Cusins is a very nice fellow, certainly: nobody would ever guess that he was born in Australia.
- **George Bernard Shaw** 1856-1950 Irish dramatist: *Major Barbara* (1907)

7 By God what a site! By man what a mess!
of Sydney
- **Clough Williams-Ellis** 1883-1978 British architect: *Architect Errant* (1971)

Autobiography

see also **BIOGRAPHY**

....

To write one's memoirs is to speak ill of everybody except oneself.
Henri Philippe Pétain

1 Reformers are always finally neglected, while the memoirs of the frivolous will always eagerly be read.
- **Chips Channon** 1897-1958 American-born British Conservative politician: diary, 7 July 1936

2 An autobiography is an obituary in serial form with the last instalment missing.
- **Quentin Crisp** 1908-99 English writer: *The Naked Civil Servant* (1968)

3 *Giles Gordon's father had criticized the length of his son's entry in* Who's Who:
I've just measured it, with a ruler; it's exactly the same length as my male organ, which I've also just measured.
- **Giles Gordon** 1940- Scottish literary agent: *Aren't We Due a Royalty Statement?* (1993)

4 Autobiography is now as common as adultery and hardly less reprehensible.
- **John Grigg** 1924- British writer and journalist: in *Sunday Times* 28 February 1962

5 Autobiography—that unrivalled vehicle for telling the truth about other people.
- **Philip Guedalla** 1889-1944 British historian and biographer: C. David Stelling *Yea and Nay* (1923)

6 Next to the writer of real estate advertisements, the autobiographer is the most suspect of prose artists.
- **Donal Henahan** 1921-2012 American music critic: in *New York Times* 1977

7 Like all good memoirs it has not been emasculated by considerations of good taste.
- **Peter Medawar** 1915-87 English immunologist and writer: review of James D. Watson *The Double Helix* (1968)

8 Every autobiography...becomes an absorbing work of fiction, with something of the charm of a cryptogram.
- **H. L. Mencken** 1880-1956 American journalist and literary critic: *Minority Report* (1956)

9 To write one's memoirs is to speak ill of everybody except oneself.
- **Henri Philippe Pétain** 1856-1951 French soldier and statesman: in *Observer* 26 May 1946

10 Of all forms of fiction autobiography is the most gratuitous.
- **Tom Stoppard** 1937- British dramatist: *Lord Malquist and Mr Moon* (1966)

11 Only when one has lost all curiosity about the future has one reached the age to write an autobiography.
- **Evelyn Waugh** 1903-66 English novelist: *A Little Learning* (1964)

12 I shall not say why and how I became, at the age of fifteen, the mistress of the Earl of Craven.
- **Harriette Wilson** 1789-1846 English courtesan: opening words of *Memoirs* (1825)

Awards and Honours

Awards are like piles. Sooner or later, every bum gets one.   **Maureen Lipman**

1 You should always accept because of the pain it brings to your enemies.
- **Maurice Bowra** 1898-1971 English scholar and literary critic: quoted by Peter Hennessy in evidence to the House of Commons Select Committee on Public Administration, 11 March 2004

2 My career must be slipping. This is the first time I've been available to pick up an award.
- **Michael Caine** 1933- English film actor: at the Golden Globe awards, Beverly Hills, California, 24 January 1999

3 Oscar night at my house is called Passover.
- **Bob Hope** 1903-2003 American comedian: in *Daily Telegraph* 29 May 2003 (online edition)

4 I feel very humble. But I think I have the strength of character to fight it.
on receiving a Congressional Gold Medal from President Kennedy
- **Bob Hope** 1903-2003 American comedian: attributed; in *Times* 29 July 2003

5 Awards are like piles. Sooner or later, every bum gets one.
- **Maureen Lipman** 1946- British actress: in *Independent* 31 July 1999

6 I can't see the sense in it really. It makes me a Commander of the British Empire. They might as well make me a Commander of Milton Keynes—at least that exists.
on receiving an honorary CBE in 1992
- **Spike Milligan** 1918-2002 Irish comedian: attributed; in *Daily Telegraph* 28 February 2002

7 A very useful institution. It fosters a wholesome taste for bright colours, and gives old men who have good legs an excuse for showing them.
of the Order of the Garter, which had been awarded to both his father and grandfather

as well as the early Cecils
- **Lord Salisbury** 1830-1903 British Conservative statesman: in Houghton Papers; Andrew Roberts *Salisbury: Victorian Titan* (1999)

8 In the end I accepted the honour, because during dinner Venables told me, that, if I became Poet Laureate, I should always when I dined out be offered the liver-wing of a fowl.
on being made Poet Laureate in 1850
- **Alfred, Lord Tennyson** 1809-92 English poet: in *Alfred Lord Tennyson: A Memoir by his Son* (1897) vol. 1

9 *congratulated on being awarded a baronetcy:* Thanks—but more importantly than that, I have just been elected a member of Sunningdale Golf Club.
- **Denis Thatcher** 1915-2003 English businessman: attributed; in *Times* 27 June 2003

10 The cross of the Legion of Honour has been conferred upon me. However, few escape that distinction.
- **Mark Twain** 1835-1910 American writer: *A Tramp Abroad* (1880)

11 I had another convulsion of pleasure when Yale made me a Doctor of Literature, because I was not competent to doctor anybody's literature but my own.
- **Mark Twain** 1835-1910 American writer: *Autobiography* (1924)

12 Medals, they're like haemorrhoids. Sooner or later every asshole gets one.
- **Billy Wilder** 1906-2002 American screenwriter and director: Ed Sikov *On Sunset Boulevard: the life and times of Billy Wilder* (1998)

13 An OBE is what you get if you clean the toilets well at King's Cross Station.
explaining why he turned down an OBE in the Queen's 80th birthday honours' list
- **Michael Winner** 1935-2013 English film director and restaurant critic: in *Independent* 29 May 2006

Baseball

see also **SPORTS**

If people don't want to come out to the ball park, nobody's going to stop 'em.
Yogi Berra

1 One of the chief duties of the fan is to engage in arguments with the man behind him. This department of the game has been allowed to run down fearfully.
  - **Robert Benchley** 1889-1945 American humorist: Ralph S. Graben *The Baseball Reader* (1951)

2 Think! How the hell are you gonna think and hit at the same time?
  - **Yogi Berra** 1925- American baseball player: *Nice Guys Finish Seventh* (1976)

3 If people don't want to come out to the ball park, nobody's going to stop 'em.
  - **Yogi Berra** 1925- American baseball player: attributed

4 This game of baseball consists of tapping a ball with a piece of wood, then running like a lunatic.
  - **Henri Jean Dutiel**: *The Great American Parade* (1953)

5 Baseball is very big with my people. It figures. It's the only way we can get to shake a bat at a white man without starting a riot.
  - **Dick Gregory** 1932- American comedian and civil rights activist: D. H. Nathan (ed.) *Baseball Quotations* (1991)

6 *after leaving his sick-bed in October 1935 to attend the World Baseball Series in Detroit,* *and betting on the losers:*
I should of stood in bed.
  - **Joe Jacobs** 1896-1940 American boxing manager: John Lardner *Strong Cigars* (1951)

7 Take me out to the ball game,
Take me out with the crowd.
Buy me some peanuts and
  cracker-jack—
I don't care if I never get back.
  - **Jack Norworth** 1879-1959 American songwriter: 'Take Me Out to the Ball Game' (1908 song)

8 Don't look back. Something may be gaining on you.
a baseball pitcher's advice
  - **Leroy ('Satchel') Paige** 1906-82 American baseball player: in *Collier's* 13 June 1953

9 I don't think I can be expected to take seriously any game which takes less than three days to reach its conclusion.
a cricket enthusiast on baseball
  - **Tom Stoppard** 1937- British dramatist: in *Guardian* 24 December 1984

10 Baseball, it is said, is only a game. True. And the Grand Canyon is only a hole in Arizona. Not all holes, or games, are created equal.
  - **George F. Will** 1941- American columnist: *Men At Work: The Craft of Baseball* (1990)

Beauty

I always say beauty is only sin deep. **Saki**

1 It has been said that a pretty face is a passport. But it's not, it's a visa and it runs out fast.
  - **Julie Burchill** 1960 English journalist and writer: *Sex and Sensibility* (1992)

2 Every woman who is not absolutely ugly thinks herself handsome.
  - **Lord Chesterfield** 1694-1773 English writer and politician: *Letters to His Son* (1774)

3 I have a left shoulder-blade that is a miracle of loveliness. People come miles to see it. My right elbow has a fascination that few can resist.
▪ **W. S. Gilbert** 1836-1911 English writer: *The Mikado* (1885)

4 Manicures: Which are basically just holding hands with a stranger for forty-five minutes whilst listening to Enya.
▪ **Miranda Hart** 1972- English comedian: *Is It Just Me?* (2012)

5 I'm tired of all this nonsense about beauty being only skin-deep. That's deep enough. What do you want—an adorable pancreas?
▪ **Jean Kerr** 1923-2003 American writer: *The Snake has all the Lines* (1958)

6 A beautiful young lady is an act of nature. A beautiful old lady is a work of art.
introducing Sara Delano Roosevelt, mother of President Franklin D. Roosevelt
▪ **Louis Nizer** 1902-94 British- born American lawyer: remark, in *New York Times* 11 November 1994

7 I always say beauty is only sin deep.
▪ **Saki** 1870-1916 Scottish writer: *Reginald* (1904)

8 If beauty is truth, why don't women go to the library to have their hair done?
▪ **Lily Tomlin** 1939- American comedienne and actress: Sally Feldman (ed.) *Woman's Hour Book of Humour* (1993)

9 It is better to be beautiful than to be good. But…it is better to be good than to be ugly.
▪ **Oscar Wilde** 1854-1900 Irish dramatist and poet: *The Picture of Dorian Gray* (1891)

Betting and Gambling

Never give a sucker an even break.   **W. C. Fields**

1 It's one thing to ask your bank manager for an overdraft to buy 500 begonias for the borders in Haslemere, but quite another to seek financial succour to avail oneself of some of the 5–2 they're offering on Isle de Bourbon for the St Leger.
▪ **Jeffrey Bernard** 1932-97 English journalist: in *Guardian* 23 December 1978

2 People go to casinos for the same reason they go on blind dates: hoping to hit the jackpot. But mostly, you just wind up broke and alone in a bar.
▪ **Candace Bushnell** 1958- , **Darren Star** 1961- , and **Patrick King** 1954- American writers: *Sex and the City* (HBO TV, 2002), Sarah Jessica Parker as Carrie

3 Rowe's Rule: the odds are five to six that the light at the end of the tunnel is the headlight of an oncoming train.
▪ **Paul Dickson** 1939- American writer: in *Washingtonian* November 1978

4 Never give a sucker an even break.
▪ **W. C. Fields** 1880-1946 American humorist: title of a W. C. Fields film (1941); the catch-phrase (Fields's own) is said to have originated in the musical comedy *Poppy* (1923)

5 GAMBLER: Say, is this a game of chance? CUTHBERT J. TWILLIE: Not the way I play it.
▪ **W. C. Fields** 1880-1946 American humorist: *My Little Chickadee* (1940 film), spoken by W. C. Fields

6 Horse sense is a good judgement which keeps horses from betting on people.
▪ **W. C. Fields** 1880-1946 American humorist: attributed; Nigel Rees *Cassell Dictionary of Humorous Quotations* (1999)

7 Two-up is Australia's very own way of parting a fool and his money.
▪ **Germaine Greer** 1939- Australian feminist: in *Observer* 1 August 1982

8 *asked how his bridge-partner should have played a hand:*
Under an assumed name.
- **George S. Kaufman** 1889-1961 American dramatist: Scott Meredith *George S. Kaufman and the Algonquin Round Table* (1974)

9 I long ago come to the conclusion that all life is 6 to 5 against.
- **Damon Runyon** 1884-1946 American writer: in *Collier's* 8 September 1934, 'A Nice Price'

10 It may be that the race is not always to the swift, nor the battle to the strong— but that's the way to bet.
- **Damon Runyon** 1884-1946 American writer: attributed

11 There are two times in a man's life when he should not speculate: when he can't afford it and when he can.
- **Mark Twain** 1835-1910 American writer: *Following the Equator* (1897)

The Bible

A wonderful book, but there are some very queer things in it. **George V**

1 An apology for the Devil: It must be remembered that we have only heard one side of the case. God has written all the books.
- **Samuel Butler** 1835-1902 English novelist: *Notebooks* (1912)

2 The Bible...is a lesson in how not to write for the movies.
- **Raymond Chandler** 1888-1959 American writer: letter to Edgar Carter, 28 March 1947

3 A wonderful book, but there are some very queer things in it.
- **George V** 1865-1936 British king: K. Rose *King George V* (1983)

4 The number one book of the ages was written by a committee, and it was called the Bible.
- **Louis B. Mayer** 1885-1957 Russian-born American film executive: attributed

5 The Ten Commandments should be treated like an examination. Only six need to be attempted.
- **Bertrand Russell** 1872-1970 British philosopher and mathematician: attributed, perhaps apocryphal

6 LORD ILLINGWORTH: The Book of Life begins with a man and a woman in a garden.
MRS ALLONBY: It ends with Revelations.
- **Oscar Wilde** 1854-1900 Irish dramatist and poet: *A Woman of No Importance* (1893)

7 I read the book of Job last night. I don't think God comes well out of it.
- **Virginia Woolf** 1882-1941 English novelist: letter to Lady Robert Cecil, 12 November 1922

8 It's just called 'The Bible' now. We dropped the word 'Holy' to give it a more mass-market appeal.
a publisher's view
- **Judith Young**: attributed, 1989

Biography

see also **AUTOBIOGRAPHY**

Biography is the mesh through which our real life escapes.   **Tom Stoppard**

1 Biography should be written by an acute enemy.
   ■ **Arthur James Balfour** 1848-1930 British Conservative statesman: in *Observer* 30 January 1927

2 The Art of Biography
   Is different from Geography.
   Geography is about Maps,
   But Biography is about Chaps.
   ■ **Edmund Clerihew Bentley** 1875-1956 English writer: *Biography for Beginners* (1905) introduction

3 Biography, like big game hunting, is one of the recognized forms of sport, and it is as unfair as only sport can be.
   ■ **Philip Guedalla** 1889-1944 British historian and biographer: *Supers and Supermen* (1920)

4 I never read the life of any important person without discovering that he knew more and could do more than I could ever hope to know or to do in half a dozen lifetimes.
   ■ **J. B. Priestley** 1894-1984 English writer: *Apes and Angels* (1928)

5 I have done my best to die before this book is published. It now seems possible that I may not succeed...I shall try to keep my sense of humour and the perspective of eternity.
   letter to his biographer, Humphrey Carpenter, shortly before publication
   ■ **Robert Runcie** 1921-2000 English archbishop: H. Carpenter *Robert Runcie* (1996)

6 Biography is the mesh through which our real life escapes.
   ■ **Tom Stoppard** 1937- British dramatist: *The Invention of Love* (1997)

7 Discretion is not the better part of biography.
   ■ **Lytton Strachey** 1880-1932 English biographer: Michael Holroyd *Lytton Strachey* (1967)

8 Then there is my noble and biographical friend who has added a new terror to death.
   on Lord Campbell's Lives of the Lord Chancellors *being written without the consent of heirs or executors*
   ■ **Charles Wetherell** 1770-1846 English lawyer and politician: also attributed to Lord Lyndhurst (1772-1863)

9 Every great man nowadays has his disciples, and it is always Judas who writes the biography.
   ■ **Oscar Wilde** 1854-1900 Irish dramatist and poet: *Intentions* (1891) 'The Critic as Artist'

Birds *see* **ANIMALS AND BIRDS**

Birth and Pregnancy

···

I was caesarean born, but not so you'd notice. It's just that when I leave a house I go out through the window.   **Steven Wright**

1 I was very relieved when the child was born at the Chelsea and Westminster hospital. I had thought he would be born in a manger.
on the birth of Leo, son of Tony Blair
- **Leo Abse** 1917-2008 British Labour politician: in *Observer* 28 May 2000 'They said what...?'

2 If men had to have babies, they would only ever have one each.
while in late pregnancy
- **Diana, Princess of Wales** 1961-97 British princess: in *Observer* 29 July 1984

3 Having a baby is like getting a tattoo on your face. You really need to be certain it's what you want before you commit.
- **Elizabeth Gilbert** 1969- American writer: quoting her sister; *Eat, Pray, Love* (2006)

4 If men could get pregnant, abortion would be a sacrament.
- **Florynce Kennedy** 1916-2001 American lawyer: 'The Verbal Karate of Florynce R. Kennedy' (1973)

5 I didn't 'fall' pregnant! I was bloody well pushed.
- **Kathy Lette** 1958- Australian writer: *Foetal Attraction* (1993)

6 Having a baby is like trying to push a grand piano through a transom.
- **Alice Roosevelt Longworth** 1884-1980 American daughter of Theodore Roosevelt: Michael Teague *Mrs L* (1981)

7 When I was in labour the nurses would look at me and say, 'Do you still think blondes have more fun?'
- **Joan Rivers** 1933- American comedienne: attributed

8 I fear the seventh granddaughter and fourteenth grandchild becomes a very uninteresting thing—for it seems to me to go on like the rabbits in Windsor Park!
- **Victoria** 1819-1901 British queen: letter to the Crown Princess of Prussia, 10 July 1868

9 Impotence and sodomy are socially O.K. but birth control is flagrantly middle-class.
- **Evelyn Waugh** 1903-66 English novelist: 'An Open Letter' in Nancy Mitford (ed.) *Noblesse Oblige* (1956)

10 I was caesarean born, but not so you'd notice. It's just that when I leave a house I go out through the window.
- **Steven Wright** 1955- American comedian: attributed

The Body

see also **APPEARANCE, DESCRIPTION, FACES**

···

Imprisoned in every fat man a thin one is wildly signalling to be let out.
Cyril Connolly

1 The verandah over the toy shop.
Australian term for a beer belly.
- **Anonymous**: Richard Eyre *National Service: Diary of a Decade* (2003)

2 Be true to your teeth or they'll be false to you.
- **Anonymous**: American proverb

3 If I had the use of my body I would throw it out of the window.
- **Samuel Beckett** 1906-89 Irish writer: *Malone Dies* (1988)

4 All legs leave something to be desired, do they not? That is part of their function

and all of their charm.
- **Alan Bennett** 1934- English dramatist and actor: attributed

5 I'm the female equivalent of a counterfeit $20 bill. Half of what you see is a pretty good reproduction, the rest is a fraud.
- **Cher** 1946- American singer and actress: Doug McClelland *Star Speak: Hollywood on Everything* (1987)

6 Imprisoned in every fat man a thin one is wildly signalling to be let out.
- **Cyril Connolly** 1903-74 English writer: *The Unquiet Grave* (1944)

7 He's so small, he's the only man I know who has turn-ups on his underpants.
- **Jerry Dennis** American writer: attributed

8 He had but one eye, and the popular prejudice runs in favour of two.
- **Charles Dickens** 1812-70 English novelist: *Nicholas Nickleby* (1839)

9 If you could see my legs when I take my boots off, you'd form some idea of what unrequited affection is.
- **Charles Dickens** 1812-70 English novelist: *Dombey and Son* (1848)

10 What is man, when you come to think upon him, but a minutely set, ingenious machine for turning, with infinite artfulness, the red wine of Shiraz into urine?
- **Isak Dinesen** 1885-1962 Danish novelist and short-story writer: *Seven Gothic Tales* (1934) 'The Dreamers'

11 *to William Cecil, who suffered from gout:*
My lord, we make use of you, not for your bad legs, but for your good head.
- **Elizabeth I** 1533-1603 English queen: F. Chamberlin *Sayings of Queen Elizabeth* (1923)

12 Oh, how I regret not having worn a bikini for the entire year I was twenty-six.
- **Nora Ephron** 1941-2012 American screenwriter: *I Feel Bad About My Neck: And Other Thoughts On Being a Woman* (2008)

13 Being a woman is worse than being a farmer—There is so much harvesting and crop spraying to be done: legs to be waxed, underarms shaved, eyebrows plucked, feet pumiced, skin exfoliated and moisturized, spots cleansed, roots dyed, eyelashes tinted, nails filed, cellulite massaged, stomach muscles exercised...Is it any wonder girls have no confidence?
- **Helen Fielding** 1958- British writer: *Bridget Jones's Diary* (1996)

14 My body, on the move, resembles in sight and sound nothing so much as a bin-liner full of yoghurt.
- **Stephen Fry** 1957- English comedian, actor, and writer: *The Hippopotamus* (1995)

15 There is something between us.
- **Donald Hall** 1928- American poet: 'Breasts' (a one-line poem, 1971)

16 Mr Richards was a tall man with what must have been a magnificent build before his stomach went in for a career of its own.
- **Margaret Halsey** 1910-97 American writer: *Some of My Best Friends are Soldiers* (1944)

17 [Alfred Hitchcock] thought of himself as looking like Cary Grant. That's tough, to think of yourself one way and look another.
- **Tippi Hedren** 1930- American actress: interview in California, 1982; P. F. Boller and R. L. Davis *Hollywood Anecdotes* (1988)

18 What they call 'heart' lies much lower than the fourth waistcoat button.
- **Georg Christoph Lichtenberg** 1742-99 German scientist and drama critic: notebook (1776-79) in *Aphorisms* (1990)

19 *seaside postcard showing a very fat man whose stomach obscures the small boy at his feet:*
Can't see my little Willy.
- **Donald McGill** 1875-1962 English cartoonist: caption, *c.*1910; in 'Quote Unquote Newsletter', July 1994

20 *of Muhammad Ali:*
I'd like to borrow his body for just 48 hours. There are three guys I'd like to beat up and four women I'd like to make love to.
- **Jim Murray**: attributed

21 A bit of talcum
Is always walcum.
- **Ogden Nash** 1902-71 American humorist:
'The Baby' (1931)

22 If I see something sagging, dragging
or bagging, I'm going to have the stuff
tucked or plucked.
- **Dolly Parton** 1946- American singer and
songwriter: interview with Larry King,
12 July 2003

23 Cuddling up to a piece of gristle.
on Madonna
- **Guy Ritchie** 1968- English film director:
attributed, in *News of the World* 19 October
2008

24 My body is so bad, a Peeping Tom
looked in my window and pulled down
the shade.
- **Joan Rivers** 1933- American comedienne:
attributed

25 It's hard to be naked and not be
upstaged by your nipples.
- **Susan Sarandon** 1946- American actress:
in *Independent* 28 December 2002

26 Thou seest I have more flesh than
another man, and therefore more
frailty.
- **William Shakespeare** 1564-1616 English
dramatist: *Henry IV, Part 1* (1597)

27 The body of a young woman is God's
greatest achievement...Of course, He
could have built it to last longer but you
can't have everything.
- **Neil Simon** 1927- American dramatist: *The
Gingerbread Lady* (1970)

28 Bah! the thing is not a nose at all, but a
bit of primordial chaos clapped on to
my face.
- **H. G. Wells** 1866-1946 English novelist:
Select Conversations with an Uncle (1895)
'The Man with a Nose'

29 Let's forget the six feet and talk about
the seven inches.
- **Mae West** 1892-1980 American film actress:
G. Eells and S. Musgrove *Mae West* (1989)

30 Look how she moves! It's like Jell-O on
springs!
watching Marilyn Monroe
- **Billy Wilder** 1906-2002 and **I. A. L.
Diamond** 1915-88 American screenwriters:
Some Like It Hot (1959 film), spoken by Jack
Lemmon as Jerry

31 A lot of people are very critical of
modern reproductive processes without
understanding all the ins and outs.
- **Robert Winston** 1940- English physician
and broadcaster: attributed in *Private Eye*,
6 February 2004

32 The lunches of fifty-seven years had
caused his chest to slip down into the
mezzanine floor.
- **P. G. Wodehouse** 1881-1975 English-born
writer: *The Heart of a Goof* (1926)

33 You're a man, and that's a bonus
'Cause when you're swinging your
cojones
You'll show 'em what testosterone is.
- **David Yazbek** 1961- American writer and
musician: 'Man' in *The Full Monty* (musical,
2000)

Books

see also **DICTIONARIES, LIBRARIES, LITERATURE, READING, PUBLISHING**

Book—what they make a movie out of for television.   **Leonard Louis Levinson**

1 If you don't find it in the Index, look very
carefully through the entire catalogue.
- **Anonymous**: in *Consumer's Guide, Sears,
Roebuck and Co.* (1897); Donald E. Knuth
Sorting and Searching (1973)

2 Books and harlots have their quarrels in
public.
- **Walter Benjamin** 1892-1940 German
philosopher and critic: *One Way Street*
(1928)

3 My desire is…that mine adversary had
written a book.
  ▪ **Bible:** *Job*

4 The covers of this book are too far
apart.
  ▪ **Ambrose Bierce** 1842–c.1914 American
  writer: C. H. Grattan *Bitter Bierce* (1929)

5 *on Fanny Hill:*
The two most fascinating subjects in
the universe are sex and the eighteenth
century.
  ▪ **Brigid Brophy** 1929–95 Irish novelist: in *New
  Statesman* 15 November 1963

6 Whenever I am sent a new book on the
lively arts, the first thing I do is look for
myself in the index.
  ▪ **Julie Burchill** 1960– English journalist and
  writer: *The Spectator* 16 January 1992

7 *on hearing that a fellow guest was 'writing a
book':*
Neither am I.
  ▪ **Peter Cook** 1937–95 English satirist and
  actor: attributed (disclaimed as original
  by Cook); Nigel Rees *Cassell Dictionary of
  Humorous Quotations* (1999)

8 PETER BOGDANOVICH: I'm giving John
Wayne a book as a birthday present.
JOHN FORD: He's *got* a book.
  ▪ **John Ford** 1895–1973 American film director:
  Peter Bogdanovich *Who the Hell's in It?*
  (2004)

9 When the [Supreme] Court moved to
Washington in 1800, it was provided
with no books, which probably
accounts for the high quality of early
opinions.
  ▪ **Robert H. Jackson** 1892–1954 American
  lawyer: *The Supreme Court in the American
  System of Government* (1955)

10 One man is as good as another until he
has written a book.
  ▪ **Benjamin Jowett** 1817–93 English classicist:
  Evelyn Abbott and Lewis Campbell (eds.)
  Life and Letters of Benjamin Jowett (1897)

11 Synopsis of Previous Chapters: There
are no Previous Chapters.
  ▪ **Stephen Leacock** 1869–1944 Canadian
  humorist: *Nonsense Novels* (1911) 'Gertrude
  the Governess'

12 Book—what they make a movie out of
for television.
  ▪ **Leonard Louis Levinson** 1904–74: Laurence
  J. Peter (ed.) *Quotations for our Time* (1977)

13 I opened it at page 96—the secret page
on which I write my name to catch out
borrowers and book-sharks.
  ▪ **Flann O'Brien** 1911–66 Irish novelist and
  journalist: *Myles Away from Dublin* (1990)

14 This is not a novel to be tossed aside
lightly. It should be thrown with great
force.
  ▪ **Dorothy Parker** 1893–1967 American critic
  and humorist: R. E. Drennan *Wit's End*
  (1973)

15 'I thought you didn't like books,' said
Agnes. 'I don't,' said Granny, turning a
page. 'They can look you right in the
face and still lie.'
  ▪ **Terry Pratchett** 1948– English fantasy
  writer: *Maskerade* (1995)

16 *on proofs:*
They're a sort of trial run for the books
so's we can check that all the spelling
mistakes have been left in.
  ▪ **Terry Pratchett** 1948– English fantasy
  writer: *Maskerade* (1995)

17 I hate books; they only teach us to talk
about things we know nothing about.
  ▪ **Jean-Jacques Rousseau** 1712–78 French
  philosopher and novelist: *Émile* (1762)

18 *the Editors' acknowledgements:*
Their thanks are also due to their wife
for not preparing the index wrong.
There is no index.
  ▪ **W. C. Sellar** 1898–1951 and **R. J. Yeatman**
  1898–1968: *1066 and All That* (1930)

19 An index is a great leveller.
  ▪ **George Bernard Shaw** 1856–1950 Irish
  dramatist: G. N. Knight *Indexing* (1979);
  attributed, perhaps apocryphal

20 A best-seller is the gilded tomb of a
mediocre talent.
  ▪ **Logan Pearsall Smith** 1865–1946 American-
  born man of letters: *Afterthoughts* (1931) 'Art
  and Letters'

21 No furniture so charming as books.
  ▪ **Sydney Smith** 1771–1845 English clergyman
  and essayist: Lady Holland *Memoir* (1855)

22 Digressions, incontestably, are the sunshine;—they are the life, the soul of reading;—take them out of this book for instance,—you might as well take the book along with them.
 ▪ **Laurence Sterne** 1713-68 English novelist: *Tristram Shandy* (1759-67)

23 *title of her bestseller on punctuation taken from a badly punctuated wildlife manual:* Eats, shoots and leaves.
 ▪ **Lynne Truss** 1955- English writer: book title, 2003

24 A thick, old-fashioned heavy book with a clasp is the finest thing in the world to throw at a noisy cat.
 ▪ **Mark Twain** 1835-1910 American writer: Alex Ayres *The Wit and Wisdom of Mark Twain* (1987)

25 I haven't been so happy since the day Reader's Digest lost my address.
 ▪ **Dick Vosburgh** 1929-2007 American writer: *A Saint She Ain't* (1999)

26 Should not the Society of Indexers be known as Indexers, Society of, The?
 ▪ **Keith Waterhouse** 1929-2009 English writer: *Bookends* (1990)

27 In every first novel the hero is the author as Christ or Faust.
 ▪ **Oscar Wilde** 1854-1900 Irish dramatist and poet: attributed

28 There is no such thing as a moral or an immoral book. Books are well written, or badly written.
 ▪ **Oscar Wilde** 1854-1900 Irish dramatist and poet: *The Picture of Dorian Gray* (1891)

29 The good ended happily, and the bad unhappily. That is what fiction means.
 ▪ **Oscar Wilde** 1854-1900 Irish dramatist and poet: *The Importance of Being Earnest* (1895)

30 The scratching of pimples on the body of the bootboy at Claridges.
 of James Joyce's Ulysses
 ▪ **Virginia Woolf** 1882-1941 English novelist: letter to Lytton Strachey, 24 April 1922

Bores

Even the grave yawns for him.   **Herbert Beerbohm Tree**

1 A person who talks when you wish him to listen.
 ▪ **Ambrose Bierce** 1842-c.1914 American writer: definition of a bore; *Cynic's Word Book* (1906)

2 Everyone is a bore to someone. That is unimportant. The thing to avoid is being a bore to oneself.
 ▪ **Gerald Brenan** 1894-1987 British travel writer: *Thoughts in a Dry Season* (1978)

3 What's wrong with being a boring kind of guy?
 ▪ **George Bush** 1924- American Republican statesman: during the campaign for the Republican nomination; in *Daily Telegraph* 28 April 1988

4 Dullness is so much stronger than genius because there is so much more of it, and it is better organized and more naturally cohesive *inter se*. So the arctic volcano can do nothing against arctic ice.
 ▪ **Samuel Butler** 1835-1902 English novelist: *Notebooks* (1912)

5 VISITOR TO ETON: I hope that I am not boring you.
 PROVOST: Not yet.
 ▪ **Lord Hugh Cecil** 1869-1956 British Conservative politician and educationist: attributed; in *Dictionary of National Biography* (1917-)

6 He is not only dull in himself, but the cause of dullness in others.
 on a dull law lord
 ▪ **Samuel Foote** 1720-77 English actor and dramatist: James Boswell *Life of Samuel Johnson* (1934 ed.) 1783

7 A bore is a fellow who opens his mouth and puts his feats in it.
 ▪ **Henry Ford** 1863-1947 American car manufacturer: attributed

8 Most of my contemporaries at school entered the World of Business, the logical destiny of bores.
   - **Barry Humphries** 1934- Australian actor and writer: *More Please* (1992)

9 He was dull in a new way, and that made many people think him *great*.
   - **Samuel Johnson** 1709-84 English poet, critic, and lexicographer: of Thomas Gray; James Boswell *Life of Samuel Johnson* (1791) 28 March 1775

10 The boredom occasioned by too much restraint is always preferable to that produced by an uncontrolled enthusiasm for a pointless variety.
   - **Osbert Lancaster** 1908-86 English writer and cartoonist: *Pillar to Post* (1938)

11 Under pressure, people admit to murder, setting fire to the village church, or robbing a bank, but never to being bores.
   - **Elsa Maxwell** 1883-1963 American columnist and hostess: attributed

12 It is to be noted that when any part of this paper appears dull there is a design in it.
   - **Richard Steele** 1672-1729 Irish-born essayist and dramatist: *The Tatler* 7 July 1709

13 Life is too short, and the time we waste in yawning never can be regained.
   - **Stendhal** 1783-1842 French novelist: attributed

14 A bore is a man who, when you ask him how he is, tells you.
   - **Bert Leston Taylor** 1866-1901 American writer: *The So-Called Human Race* (1922)

15 Dylan talked copiously, then stopped. 'Somebody's boring me,' he said, 'I think it's me.'
   - **Dylan Thomas** 1914-53 Welsh poet: Rayner Heppenstall *Four Absentees* (1960)

16 He is an old bore. Even the grave yawns for him.
   of the actor Israel Zangwill
   - **Herbert Beerbohm Tree** 1852-1917 English actor-manager: Max Beerbohm *Herbert Beerbohm Tree* (1920)

17 In England people actually try to be brilliant at breakfast. That is so dreadful of them! Only dull people are brilliant at breakfast.
   - **Oscar Wilde** 1854-1900 Irish dramatist and poet: *An Ideal Husband* (1895)

Boxing

see also **SPORTS**

....

Boxing is show-business with blood.　**David Belasco**

1 I figure I'll be champ for about ten years and then I'll let my brother take over—like the Kennedys down in Washington.
   before becoming world heavyweight champion in 1964
   - **Muhammad Ali** 1942- American boxer: attributed, 1979

2 It's gonna be a thrilla, a chilla, and a killa,
   When I get the gorilla in Manila.
   - **Muhammad Ali** 1942- American boxer: in 1975; attributed

3 Boxing is show-business with blood.
   - **David Belasco** 1853-1931 American theatrical producer: in 1915; Michael Parkinson *Sporting Lives* (1993); later also used by Frank Bruno

4 Tall men come down to my height when I hit 'em in the body.
   - **Jack Dempsey** 1895-1983 American boxer: in 1920, attributed

5 I want to keep fighting because it is the only thing that keeps me out of the hamburger joints. If I don't fight, I'll eat this planet.
   - **George Foreman** 1948- American boxer: in *Times* 17 January 1990

6 We're all endowed with God-given talents. Mine happens to be hitting people in the head.
  ▪ **Sugar Ray Leonard** 1956– American boxer: Thomas Hauser *The Black Lights* (1986)

7 In boxing the right cross-counter is distinctly one of those things it is more blessed to give than to receive.
  ▪ **P. G. Wodehouse** 1881–1975 English-born writer: *The Pothunters* (1902)

The British

see also **ENGLAND, SCOTLAND, WALES**

Modest about our national pride—and inordinately proud of our national modesty. **Ian Hislop**

1 There's nothing the British like better than a bloke who comes from nowhere, makes it, and then gets clobbered.
  ▪ **Melvyn Bragg** 1939– English broadcaster and writer: in *Guardian* 23 September 1988; referring to Richard Burton

2 It is an interesting experience to become acquainted with a country through the eyes of the insane, and, if I may say, so a particularly useful grounding for life in Britain
  ▪ **Bill Bryson** 1951– American travel writer: *Notes from a Small Island* (1995)

3 *on British men:*
Grubby and distinctly grey around the underwear region.
  ▪ **Germaine Greer** 1939– Australian feminist: Graham Jones *I Don't Hate Men, But–; I Don't Hate Women, But–* (1986)

4 Listening to Britons dining out is like watching people play first-class tennis with imaginary balls.
  ▪ **Margaret Halsey** 1910–97 American writer: *With Malice towards Some* (1939)

5 Modest about our national pride—and inordinately proud of our national modesty.
  ▪ **Ian Hislop** 1960– English satirical journalist: *Stiff Upper Lip–An Emotional History of Britain* BBC2, 2 October 2012

6 British Beatitudes!…Beer, beef, business, bibles, bulldogs, battleships, buggery and bishops.
  ▪ **James Joyce** 1882–1941 Irish novelist: *Ulysses* (1922)

7 The Roman Conquest was, however, a *Good Thing*, since the Britons were only natives at the time.
  ▪ **W. C. Sellar** 1898–1951 and **R. J. Yeatman** 1898–1968: *1066 and All That* (1930)

8 What two ideas are more inseparable than Beer and Britannia?
  ▪ **Sydney Smith** 1771–1845 English clergyman and essayist: Hesketh Pearson *The Smith of Smiths* (1934)

9 *on the suggestion that, in his books, washing has some symbolic significance:*
I've noticed that the British are not given to it.
  ▪ **Gore Vidal** 1925–2012 American novelist and critic: attributed; in *Guardian* 27 February 1999

10 Other nations use 'force'; we Britons alone use 'Might'.
  ▪ **Evelyn Waugh** 1903–66 English novelist: *Scoop* (1938)

Bureaucracy and Form-Filling

see also **CIVIL SERVANTS, MANAGEMENT**

A camel is a horse designed by a committee.   **Alec Issigonis**

1 A memorandum is written not to inform the reader but to protect the writer.
- **Dean Acheson** 1893-1971 American politician: in *Wall Street Journal* 8 September 1977

2 Whenever I fill out an application, in the part that says 'If an emergency, notify:' I put 'DOCTOR'. What's my mother going to do?
- **Anonymous**: modern saying, often attributed to Steven Wright

3 This island is made mainly of coal and surrounded by fish. Only an organizing genius could produce a shortage of coal and fish at the same time.
- **Aneurin Bevan** 1897-1960 British Labour politician: speech at Blackpool 24 May 1945

4 Whatever was required to be done, the Circumlocution Office was beforehand with all the public departments in the art of perceiving— HOW NOT TO DO IT.
- **Charles Dickens** 1812-70 English novelist: *Little Dorrit* (1857)

5 The Pentagon, that immense monument to modern man's subservience to the desk.
- **Oliver Franks** 1905-92 English philosopher and administrator: in *Observer* 30 November 1952

6 *when his secretary suggested throwing away out-of-date files:*
A good idea, only be sure to make a copy of everything before getting rid of it.
- **Sam Goldwyn** 1882-1974 American film producer: Michael Freedland *The Goldwyn Touch* (1986)

7 *Gilbert Harding, applying for a US visa, was irritated by having to fill in a long form with many questions, including 'Is it your intention to overthrow the Government of the United States by force?':*
Sole purpose of visit.
- **Gilbert Harding** 1907-60 British journalist: W. Reyburn *Gilbert Harding* (1978)

8 Official dignity tends to increase in inverse ratio to the importance of the country in which the office is held.
- **Aldous Huxley** 1894-1963 English novelist: *Beyond the Mexique Bay* (1934)

9 *on his dislike of working in teams:*
A camel is a horse designed by a committee.
- **Alec Issigonis** 1906-88 British engineer: in *Guardian* 14 January 1991 'Notes and Queries' (attributed)

10 The truth in these matters may be stated as a scientific law: 'The persistence of public officials varies inversely with the importance of the matter on which they are persisting.'
- **Bernard Levin** 1928-2004 British journalist: *In These Times* (1986)

11 I think it will be a clash between the political will and the administrative won't.
- **Jonathan Lynn** 1943- and **Antony Jay** 1930- English writers: *Yes Prime Minister* vol. 2 (1987)

12 *filling in an embarkation form on a channel crossing:*
HAROLD NICOLSON: What age are you going to put, Osbert?
OSBERT SITWELL: What sex are you going to put, Harold?
- **Harold Nicolson** 1886-1968 English diplomat and writer: attributed, perhaps apocryphal

13 Perfection of planned layout is achieved only by institutions on the point of collapse.
- **C. Northcote Parkinson** 1909-93 English writer: *Parkinson's Law* (1958)

14 A committee should consist of three men, two of whom are absent.
- **Herbert Beerbohm Tree** 1852-1917 English actor-manager: Hesketh Pearson *Beerbohm Tree* (1956)

Business

see also **MANAGEMENT**

....

Commercialism is doing well that which should not be done at all.   **Gore Vidal**

1 Focus groups are people who are selected on the basis of their inexplicable free time and their common love of free sandwiches.
- **Scott Adams** 1957- American cartoonist: *The Dilbert Principle* (1996)

2 TO SUCCEED
Early to bed, early to rise,
Never get tight, and—advertise.
- **Anonymous**: marketing slogan, 1898; Wolfgang Mieder *Proverbs: A Handbook* (2004)

3 Our clients are coping with the stress of financial loss by soaking in a hot bath scented with my Rose Geranium bath crystals.
on the Wall Street crash
- **Elizabeth Arden** c.1880-1966 Canadian-born American beautician: attributed

4 Some are born great, some achieve greatness and some hire public relations officers.
- **Daniel Boorstin** 1914-2004 American historian: attributed

5 My first rule of consumerism is never to buy anything you can't make your children carry.
- **Bill Bryson** 1951- American travel writer: *The Lost Continent* (1989)

6 Price is what you pay. Value is what you get.
- **Warren Buffett** 1930- American businessman: letter to partners, 20 January 1966

7 Rule No 1: never lose money. Rule No 2: never forget rule No 1.
- **Warren Buffett** 1930- American businessman: in *Forbes 400* 27 October 1986

8 I always invest in companies an idiot could run, because one day one will.
- **Warren Buffett** 1930- American businessman: in *Mail on Sunday* 18 March 2007

9 Some accountants are comedians, but comedians are never accountants.
defending Ken Dodd on the charge of tax evasion
- **George Carman** 1929-2001 English lawyer: in *Times* 30 August 2000; attributed

10 I find it rather easy to portray a businessman. Being bland, rather cruel and incompetent comes naturally to me.
- **John Cleese** 1939- English comic actor and writer: in *Newsweek* 15 June 1987

11 A verbal contract isn't worth the paper it is written on.
- **Sam Goldwyn** 1882-1974 American film producer: Alva Johnston *The Great Goldwyn* (1937)

12 Accountants are the witch-doctors of the modern world and willing to turn their hands to any kind of magic.
- **Charles Harman** 1894-1970 English judge: speech, February 1964

13 The last stage of fitting the product to the market is fitting the market to the product.
- **Clive James** 1939- Australian critic and writer: in *Observer* 16 October 1989

14 A: I play it the company way
Where the company puts me, there
I'll stay.
B: But what is your point of view?
A: I have no point of view!
Supposing the company thinks…I think
so too!
- **Frank Loesser** 1910-69 American
songwriter: 'The Company Way' (1962)

15 The longer the title, the less important
the job.
- **George McGovern** 1922-2012 American
Democratic politician: attributed

16 Skill is fine and genius is splendid, but
the right contacts are more valuable
than either.
- **Archibald Hector McIndoe** 1900-60 New
Zealand plastic surgeon: Leonard Mosley
Faces from the Fire (1962)

17 *asked if there were signs of a depression in
London:*
If you mean that one could fire a gun
across the Savoy Grill without hitting
either a diner or an Italian waiter the
answer is 'No'
- **David Montague**: attributed, 1963

18 I think I was the first person at Motown
to ask where the money was going. And
that made me an enemy. Did I find out?
Honey, I found my way out the door.
- **Martha Reeves** 1941- American singer:
Gerri Hirshey *Nowhere to Run: the story of
soul music* (1985)

19 Running a company on market research
is like driving while looking in the rear
view mirror.
- **Anita Roddick** 1942-2007 English
businesswoman: in *Independent* 22 August
1997

20 Never invest your money in anything
that eats or needs repainting.
- **Billy Rose** 1899-1966 American producer
and songwriter: in *New York Post*
26 October 1957

21 *definition of insider trading:*
Stealing too fast.
- **Calvin Trillin** 1935- American journalist
and writer: 'The Inside on Insider Trading'
(1987)

22 It's a recession when your neighbour
loses his job; it's a depression when you
lose yours.
- **Harry S. Truman** 1884-1972 American
Democratic statesman: in *Observer* 13 April
1958

23 Put all your eggs in one basket—and
WATCH THAT BASKET.
- **Mark Twain** 1835-1910 American writer:
Pudd'nhead Wilson (1894)

24 The public be damned! I'm working for
my stockholders.
- **William H. Vanderbilt** 1821-85 American
railway magnate: comment to a news
reporter, 2 October 1882

25 [Commercialism is] doing well that
which should not be done at all.
- **Gore Vidal** 1925-2012 American novelist
and critic: in *Listener* 7 August 1975

26 Go to your business, I say, pleasure,
whilst I go to my pleasure, business.
- **William Wycherley** c.1640-1716 English
dramatist: *The Country Wife* (1675)

27 Nothing is illegal if one hundred well-
placed business men decide to do it.
- **Andrew Young** 1932- American politician:
Morris K. Udall *Too Funny to be President*
(1988)

Canada

Climb every Mountie.   **Dick Vosburgh** and **Denis King**

1 Canada is a country so square that even the female impersonators are women.
   ▪ **Richard Benner**: *Outrageous* (1977)

2 *definition of a Canadian:*
   Somebody who knows how to make love in a canoe.
   ▪ **Pierre Berton** 1920-2004 Canadian writer: in *Toronto Star* 22 December 1973

3 Americans are benevolently ignorant about Canada, while Canadians are malevolently well-informed about the United States.
   ▪ **John Bartlet Brebner** 1895-1957 Canadian historian: attributed

4 I don't even know what street Canada is on.
   ▪ **Al Capone** 1899-1947 American gangster: remark, 1931, Roy Greenaway *The News Game* (1966)

5 I see Canada as a country torn between a very northern, rather extraordinary, mystical spirit which it fears and its desire to present itself to the world as a Scotch banker.
   ▪ **Robertson Davies** 1913-95 Canadian novelist: *The Enthusiasms of Robertson Davies* (1990)

6 In any world menu, Canada must be considered the vichyssoise of nations—it's cold, half-French, and difficult to stir.
   ▪ **Stuart Keate** 1913-87 Canadian journalist: attributed

7 In Pierre Elliott Trudeau, Canada has at last produced a political leader worthy of assassination.
   ▪ **Irving Layton** 1912-2006 Canadian poet: *The Whole Bloody Bird* (1969)

8 *asked about Canadian sovereignty over the Arctic:*
   That's ours—lock, stock and iceberg.
   ▪ **Brian Mulroney** 1939- Canadian Conservative statesman: speaking to reporters, Ottawa, 5 April 1987

9 I'm world famous, Dr Parks said, all over Canada.
   ▪ **Mordecai Richler** 1931-2001 Canadian writer: *The Incomparable Atuk* (1963)

10 Climb every Mountie.
   ▪ **Dick Vosburgh** 1929-2007 and **Denis King**: *Beauty and the Beards* (2001)

Catchphrases *see* **COMEDY ROUTINES AND CATCHPHRASES**

Cats and Dogs

see also **ANIMALS**

A door is what a dog is perpetually on the wrong side of.   **Ogden Nash**

1 Rule of feline frustration: When your cat has fallen asleep on your lap and looks utterly content and adorable you will suddenly have to go the bathroom.
   ▪ **Anonymous**: Arthur Bloch *Murphy's Law and other reasons why things go wrong* (1977)

2 Cats, I always think, only jump into your lap to check if you are cold enough, yet, to eat.
   ▪ **Anne Enright** 1962- Irish novelist and short-story writer: *The Gathering* (2007)

3 To his dog, every man is Napoleon: hence the constant popularity of dogs.
- **Aldous Huxley** 1894-1963 English novelist: attributed; Evan Esar *The Treasury of Humorous Quotations* (1951)

4 Dogs who earn their living by appearing in television commercials in which they constantly and aggressively demand meat should remember that in at least one Far Eastern country they *are* meat.
- **Fran Lebowitz** 1946- American writer: *Social Studies* (1981)

5 I've never understood why women love cats. Cats are independent, they don't listen, they don't come in when you call, they like to stay out all night, and when they're home they like to be left alone and sleep. In other words, every quality that women hate in a man, they love in a cat.
- **Jay Leno** 1950- American comedian: attributed

6 Outside of a dog, a book is a man's best friend. Inside of a dog, it's too dark to read.
- **Groucho Marx** 1890-1977 American film comedian: Groucho Marx and Stefan Kanfer *The Essential Groucho* (2000)

7 A door is what a dog is perpetually on the wrong side of.
- **Ogden Nash** 1902-71 American humorist: 'A Dog's Best Friend is his Illiteracy' (1953)

8 If cats looked like frogs we'd realise what nasty cruel little bastards they are. Style. That's what people remember.
- **Terry Pratchett** 1948- English fantasy writer: *Lords and Ladies* (1992)

9 That indefatigable and unsavoury engine of pollution, the dog.
- **John Sparrow** 1906-92 English academic: letter to *Times* 30 September 1975

10 The more one gets to know of men, the more one values dogs.
- **A. Toussenel** 1803-85 French writer: *L'Esprit des bêtes* (1847); attributed to Mme Roland in the form 'The more I see of men, the more I like dogs'

11 If man could be crossed with a cat it would improve man, but it would deteriorate the cat.
- **Mark Twain** 1835-1910 American writer: notebook, 1894

12 The Aberdeen terrier gave me an unpleasant look and said something under its breath in Gaelic.
- **P. G. Wodehouse** 1881-1975 English-born writer: *The Code of the Woosters* (1938)

Censorship

....

I'm all in favour of free expression provided it's kept rigidly under control.
Alan Bennett

1 There are no alternatives to 'bastard' agreeable to me. Nevertheless I have offered them 'swine' in its place.
on changes to the text of Endgame *required by the Lord Chamberlain for the London production, summer 1958*
- **Samuel Beckett** 1906-89 Irish dramatist, novelist, and poet: James Knowlson *Damned to Fame* (1996)

2 I'm all in favour of free expression provided it's kept rigidly under control.
- **Alan Bennett** 1934- English dramatist and actor: *Forty Years On* (1969)

3 Everybody favours free speech in the slack moments when no axes are being ground.
- **Heywood Broun** 1888-1939 American journalist: in *New York World* 23 October 1926

4 I dislike censorship. Like an appendix it is useless when inert and dangerous when active.
- **Maurice Edelman** 1911-75 British Labour politician: Jonathon Green (ed.) *A Dictionary of Contemporary Quotations* (1982)

5 Will Hays is my shepherd, I shall not want, He maketh me to lie down in clean postures.
on the establishment of the 'Hays Office' in 1922 to monitor the Hollywood film industry
▪ **Gene Fowler** 1890-1960 American writer: Clive Marsh and Gaye Ortiz (eds.) *Explorations in Theology and Film* (1997)

6 It's red hot, mate. I hate to think of this sort of book getting into the wrong hands. As soon as I've finished this, I shall recommend they ban it.
▪ **Ray Galton** 1930- and **Alan Simpson** 1929- English writers: *The Missing Page* (BBC TV, 1960) words spoken by Tony Hancock

7 No less than twenty-two publishers and printers read the manuscript of *Dubliners* and when at last it was printed some very kind person bought out the entire edition and had it burnt in Dublin.
▪ **James Joyce** 1882-1941 Irish novelist: letter, 2 April 1932

8 Freedom of the press is guaranteed only to those who own one.
▪ **A. J. Liebling** 1904-63 American writer: 'The Wayward Press: Do you belong in Journalism?' (1960)

9 She sits among the cabbages and leeks.
substitution for 'she sits among the cabbages and peas', which was supposedly forbidden by a local watch committee
▪ **Marie Lloyd** 1870-1922 English music-hall artiste: attributed; Nigel Rees *Cassell Dictionary of Humorous Quotations* (1999)

10 Censorship, like charity, should begin at home, but, unlike charity, it should end there.
▪ **Clare Booth Luce** 1903-87 American diplomat, politician, and writer: attributed, 1982

11 We have long passed the Victorian Era when asterisks were followed after a certain interval by a baby.
▪ **W. Somerset Maugham** 1874-1965 English novelist: *The Constant Wife* (1926)

12 *on being appointed Irish film censor:*
I am between the devil and the Holy See.
▪ **James Montgomery** 1870-1943 Irish businessman and film censor: Ulick O'Connor *Oliver St John Gogarty* (1964)

13 I suppose that writers should, in a way, feel flattered by the censorship laws. They show a primitive fear and dread at the fearful magic of print.
▪ **John Mortimer** 1923-2009 English novelist, barrister, and dramatist: *Clinging to the Wreckage* (1982)

14 A censor is a man who knows more than he thinks you ought to.
▪ **Laurence J. Peter** 1919-90 Canadian writer: Jonathon Green (ed.) *A Dictionary of Contemporary Quotations* (1982)

15 Assassination is the extreme form of censorship.
▪ **George Bernard Shaw** 1856-1950 Irish dramatist: *The Showing-Up of Blanco Posnet* (1911) 'Limits to Toleration'

16 We are paid to have dirty minds.
▪ **John Trevelyan** 1903-86 British film censor: in *Observer* 15 November 1959

Certainty and Doubt

see also **RELIGION**

I'll give you a definite maybe. **Sam Goldwyn**

1 He used to be fairly indecisive, but now he's not so certain.
▪ **Peter Alliss** 1931- English golfer: Barry Fantoni (ed.) *Private Eye's Colemanballs 3* (1986)

2 I've never had a humble opinion. If you've got an opinion, why be humble about it?
▪ **Joan Baez** 1941- American singer and songwriter: in *Observer* 29 February 2004

3 The Flying Scotsman is no less splendid a sight when it travels north to Edinburgh than when it travels south to London. Mr Baldwin denouncing sanctions was as dignified as Mr Baldwin imposing them.
- **Lord Beaverbrook** 1879-1964 Canadian-born British newspaper proprietor and Conservative politician: in *Daily Express* 29 May 1937

4 Often undecided whether to desert a sinking ship for one that might not float, he would make up his mind to sit on the wharf for a day.
of Lord Curzon
- **Lord Beaverbrook** 1879-1964 Canadian-born British newspaper proprietor and Conservative politician: *Men and Power* (1956)

5 Oh! let us never, never doubt
What nobody is sure about!
- **Hilaire Belloc** 1870-1953 British writer and Liberal politician: 'The Microbe' (1897)

6 *when asked whether he really believed a horseshoe hanging over his door would bring him luck:*
Of course not, but I am told it works even if you don't believe in it.
- **Niels Bohr** 1885-1962 Danish physicist: A. Pais *Inward Bound* (1986)

7 The archbishop [Archbishop Runcie] is usually to be found nailing his colours to the fence.
- **Frank Field** 1942- British Labour politician: attributed in *Crockfords 1987/88* (1987); Geoffrey Madan records in his *Notebooks* that Harry Cust made a similar comment on A. J. Balfour, c.1904.

8 I'll give you a definite maybe.
- **Sam Goldwyn** 1882-1974 American film producer: attributed

9 Well, who you gonna believe, me or your own eyes?
- **Bert Kalmar** 1884-1947 and **others** screenwriters: *Duck Soup* (1933 film), spoken by Chico Marx as Chicolini

10 A young man who wishes to remain a sound atheist cannot be too careful of his reading.
- **C. S. Lewis** 1898-1963 English literary scholar: *Surprised by Joy* (1955)

11 Like all weak men he laid an exaggerated stress on not changing one's mind.
- **W. Somerset Maugham** 1874-1965 English novelist: *Of Human Bondage* (1915)

12 I wish I was as cocksure of anything as Tom Macaulay is of everything.
- **Lord Melbourne** 1779-1848 British Whig statesman: Lord Cowper *Preface to Lord Melbourne's Papers* (1889)

13 I am not denying anything I did not say.
- **Brian Mulroney** 1939- Canadian Conservative statesman: in *The Globe and Mail* 18 September 1986

14 Well, sir, you never can tell. That's a principle in life with me, sir, if you'll excuse my having such a thing, sir.
- **George Bernard Shaw** 1856-1950 Irish dramatist: *You Never Can Tell* (1898)

15 All right, have it your own way—you heard a seal bark!
- **James Thurber** 1894-1961 American humorist: cartoon caption; in *New Yorker* 30 January 1932

16 To try and find out the reason for everything is very dangerous and leads to nothing but disappointment and dissatisfaction, unsettling your mind and in the end making you miserable.
- **Victoria** 1819-1901 British Queen: letter to Princess Victoria of Hesse, 22 August 1883

17 A mind not so much open as permanently vulnerable to a succession of opposing certainties.
on Conservative politician David Howell
- **Hugo Young** 1938-2003 British journalist: *One of Us* (1991)

18 To convince Cézanne of anything is like teaching the towers of Notre Dame to dance.
- **Émile Zola** 1840-1902 French novelist: Lawrence Gowing 'The Great Transformation'

Challenges *see* **LIFE AND ITS CHALLENGES**

Champagne

Remember gentlemen, it's not just France we are fighting for, it's Champagne!
Winston Churchill

1 In victory, you deserve champagne, in defeat, you need it.
- **Anonymous**: modern saying, frequently associated with Napoleon I, but without evidence

2 *on champagne:*
I drink it when I am happy and when I am sad. Sometimes I drink it when I'm alone. When I have company I consider it obligatory. I trifle with it if I'm not hungry and drink it when I am. Otherwise I never touch it…unless I'm thirsty.
- **Lily Bollinger** 1899-1977 French businesswoman: attributed

3 Remember gentlemen, it's not just France we are fighting for, it's Champagne!
- **Winston Churchill** 1874-1965 British Conservative statesman: in 1918; attributed

4 Gentlemen, in the little moment that remains to us between the crisis and the catastrophe, we may as well take a glass of champagne.
during the Depression of the early 1930s
- **Paul Claudel** 1868-1955 French poet and diplomat: Claud Cockburn *In Time of Trouble* (1956)

5 There comes a time in every woman's life when the only thing that helps is a glass of champagne.
- **Bette Davis** 1908-89 American actress: Whitney Stine *Mother Goddam* (1985)

6 Three be the things I shall never attain: Envy, content, and sufficient champagne.
- **Dorothy Parker** 1893-1967 American critic and humorist: 'Inventory' (1937)

7 Champagne certainly gives one werry gentlemanly ideas, but for a continuance, I don't know but I should prefer mild hale.
- **R. S. Surtees** 1805-64 English novelist: *Jorrocks's Jaunts and Jollities* (1838)

Character

see also **SELF-KNOWLEDGE**

I've met a lot of hardboiled eggs in my time, but you're twenty minutes.
Billy Wilder

1 A gentleman is someone who can play the accordion, but doesn't.
- **Anonymous**: attributed

2 When people are on their best behaviour they aren't always at their best.
- **Alan Bennett** 1934- English dramatist and actor: *Dinner at Noon* (BBC television, 1988)

3 Show me a man who lives alone and has a perpetually clean kitchen, and 8 times out of 9 I'll show you a man with detestable spiritual qualities.
- **Charles Bukowski** 1920-94 German-born American writer: *Tales of Ordinary Madness* (1983)

4 The best measure of a man's honesty isn't his tax return. It's the zero adjust

on his bathroom scale.
- **Arthur C. Clarke** 1917-2008 English science fiction writer: attributed

5 I am so sorry. We have to stop there. I have just come to the end of my personality.
closing down an interview
- **Quentin Crisp** 1908-99 English writer: attributed, in *Times* 26 October 2002

6 We never knows wot's hidden in each other's hearts; and if we had glass winders there, we'd need keep the shutters up, some on us, I do assure you!
- **Charles Dickens** 1812-70 English novelist: *Martin Chuzzlewit* (1844)

7 Claudia's the sort of person who goes through life holding on to the sides.
- **Alice Thomas Ellis** 1932-2005 English novelist: *The Other Side of the Fire* (1983)

8 Those who stand for nothing fall for anything.
- **Alex Hamilton** 1936- British writer and broadcaster: 'Born Old' (radio broadcast), in *Listener* 9 November 1978

9 Shyness is egotism out of its depth.
- **Hugh Kingsmill** 1889-1949 English man of letters: Richard Ingrams *God's Apology* (1977)

10 He wanted to be the bride at every wedding and the corpse at every funeral.
on her father Theodore Roosevelt
- **Alice Roosevelt Longworth** 1884-1980 American socialite: attributed; early sources attribute the remark to 'one of his sons'

11 So cool, when he goes to bed, sheep count him.
- **David Mamet** 1947- American dramatist and director: *Heist* (2001 film), spoken by Ricky Jay as Pinky

12 He was a bit like a corkscrew. Twisted, cold and sharp.
- **Kate Cruise O'Brien** 1948-98 Irish writer: *A Gift Horse, and Other Stories* (1977)

13 He's so wet you could shoot snipe off him.
- **Anthony Powell** 1905-2000 English novelist: *A Question of Upbringing* (1951)

14 You can tell a lot about a fellow's character by his way of eating jellybeans.
- **Ronald Reagan** 1911-2004 American Republican statesman: in *New York Times* 15 January 1981

15 People will do things from a sense of duty which they would never attempt as a pleasure.
- **Saki** 1870-1916 Scottish writer: *The Chronicles of Clovis* (1911)

16 He was so crooked, you could have used his spine for a safety-pin.
- **Dorothy L. Sayers** 1893-1957 English writer: *The Nine Tailors* (1934)

17 A man does not have to be an angel in order to be a saint.
- **Albert Schweitzer** 1875-1965 Franco-German missionary: attributed; Lore Cowan *The Wit of Medicine* (1972)

18 He's too nervous to kill himself. He wears his seat belt in a drive-in movie.
- **Neil Simon** 1927- American dramatist: *The Odd Couple* (1966)

19 Few things are harder to put up with than the annoyance of a good example.
- **Mark Twain** 1835-1910 American writer: *Pudd'nhead Wilson* (1894)

20 CECIL GRAHAM: What is a cynic? LORD DARLINGTON: A man who knows the price of everything and the value of nothing.
- **Oscar Wilde** 1854-1900 Irish dramatist and poet: *Lady Windermere's Fan* (1892)

21 I am afraid that he has one of those terribly weak natures that are not susceptible to influence.
- **Oscar Wilde** 1854-1900 Irish dramatist and poet: *An Ideal Husband* (1895)

22 I've met a lot of hardboiled eggs in my time, but you're twenty minutes.
- **Billy Wilder** 1906-2002 American screenwriter and director: *Ace in the Hole* (1951 film, with Lesser Samuels and Walter Newman)

23 Slice him where you like, a hellhound is always a hellhound.
- **P. G. Wodehouse** 1881-1975 English-born writer: *The Code of the Woosters* (1938)

Children

see also **BIRTH, FAMILY, PARENTS, YOUTH**

Ask your child what he wants for dinner only if he's buying.   **Fran Lebowitz**

1 I don't work that way…The very idea that all children want to be cuddled by a complete stranger, I find completely amazing.
on her work for Save the Children
- **Anne, Princess Royal** 1950-   British princess: in *Daily Telegraph* 17 January 1998

2 Children: You spend the first two years of their life teaching them to walk and talk. Then you spend the next sixteen years telling them to sit down and shut up.
- **Anonymous**: saying

3 Being constantly with children was like wearing a pair of shoes that were expensive and too small. She couldn't bear to throw them out but they gave her blisters.
- **Beryl Bainbridge** 1934-2010 English novelist: *Injury Time* (1977)

4 A Trick that everyone abhors
In Little Girls is slamming Doors.
- **Hilaire Belloc** 1870-1953 British writer and Liberal politician: 'Rebecca' (1907)

5 And always keep a-hold of Nurse
For fear of finding something worse.
- **Hilaire Belloc** 1870-1953 British writer and Liberal politician: 'Jim' (1907)

6 The place is very well and quiet and the children only scream in a low voice.
- **Lord Byron** 1788-1824 English poet: letter 21 September 1813

7 I am fond of children (except boys).
- **Lewis Carroll** 1832-98 English writer and logician: letter to Kathleen Eschwege, 24 October 1879

8 *on being asked what sort of child he was:*
When paid constant attention, extremely lovable. When not, a pig.
- **Noël Coward** 1899-1973 English dramatist, actor, and composer: interview with David Frost in 1969

9 I'll thcream and thcream and thcream till I'm thick. And I *can*.
Violet Elizabeth Bott's habitual threat
- **Richmal Crompton** 1890-1969 English writer of books for children: *Still—William* (1925)

10 I want my children to have all the things I couldn't afford. Then I want to move in with them.
- **Phyllis Diller** 1917-2012 American actress: attributed

11 It is only rarely that one can see in a little boy the promise of a man, but one can almost always see in a little girl the threat of a woman.
- **Alexandre Dumas** 1824-95 French writer: attributed remark, 1895

12 There was never child so lovely but his mother was glad to get him asleep.
- **Ralph Waldo Emerson** 1803-82 American philosopher and poet: *Journal* 1836

13 O'er the rugged mountain's brow
Clara threw the twins she nursed,
And remarked, 'I wonder now
Which will reach the bottom first?'
- **Harry Graham** 1874-1936 British writer and journalist: 'Calculating Clara' (1899)

14 When Baby's cries grew hard to bear
I popped him in the Frigidaire.
I never would have done so if
I'd known that he'd be frozen stiff.
My wife said, 'George, I'm so
  unhappé!
Our darling's now completely *frappé*!
- **Harry Graham** 1874-1936 British writer and journalist: *Ruthless Rhymes for Heartless Homes* (1899) 'L'Enfant glacé'

15 Kids are the best, Apu. You can teach them to hate the things you hate. And they practically raise themselves,

what with the Internet and all.
Homer Simpson
- **Matt Groening** 1954- American humorist
  and satirist: *The Simpsons* 'Eight Misbehavin''
  (1999) written by Matt Selman

16 *at the first night of J. M. Barrie's* Peter Pan:
Oh, for an hour of Herod!
- **Anthony Hope** 1863-1933 English novelist:
  Denis Mackail *The Story of JMB* (1941)

17 The real menace in dealing with a
five-year-old is that in no time at all you
begin to sound like a five-year-old.
- **Jean Kerr** 1923-2003 American writer:
  Please Don't Eat the Daisies (1957)

18 *definition of a baby:*
A loud noise at one end and no sense of
responsibility at the other.
- **Ronald Knox** 1888-1957 English writer and
  Roman Catholic priest: attributed

19 The realization that it was not people
I disliked but children was for me
one of those celebrated moments of
revelation.
on growing up
- **Philip Larkin** 1922-85 English poet: *Required
  Writing* (1983) 'The Savage Seventh'

20 The parent who could see his boy as he
really is, would shake his head and say:
'Willie is no good; I'll sell him.'
- **Stephen Leacock** 1869-1944 Canadian
  humorist: *Essays and Literary Studies* (1916)

21 Ask your child what he wants for dinner
only if he's buying.
- **Fran Lebowitz** 1946- American writer:
  Social Studies (1981)

22 The knowingness of little girls
Is hidden underneath their curls.
- **Phyllis McGinley** 1905-78 American poet:
  'What Every Woman Knows' (1960)

23 *a nurse, excusing her illegitimate baby:*
If you please, ma'am, it was a very little
one.
- **Frederick Marryat** 1792-1848 English
  novelist: *Mr Midshipman Easy* (1836)

24 I love children, especially when they cry,
for then someone takes them away.
- **Nancy Mitford** 1904-73 English writer:
  attributed

25 All bachelors love dogs, and we would
love children just as much if they could
be taught to retrieve.
- **P. J. O'Rourke** 1947- American humorous
  writer: *The Bachelor Home Companion*
  (1987)

26 Every luxury was lavished on you—
atheism, breast-feeding, circumcision.
- **Joe Orton** 1933-67 English dramatist: *Loot*
  (1967)

27 Parents—especially step-parents—are
sometimes a bit of a disappointment
to their children. They don't fulfil the
promise of their early years.
- **Anthony Powell** 1905-2000 English
  novelist: *A Buyer's Market* (1952)

28 Go directly—see what she's doing, and
tell her she mustn't.
- **Punch** 1841-1992 English humorous weekly
  periodical: vol. 63 (1872)

29 I'm in that benign form of house arrest
that is looking after a baby.
- **J. K. Rowling** 1965- English novelist: in
  Sunday Times 12 June 2005

30 Childhood is Last Chance Gulch for
happiness. After that, you know too
much.
- **Tom Stoppard** 1937- British dramatist:
  Where Are They Now? (1973)

31 If you want your children to turn out
well, spend twice as much time with
them, and half as much money.
- **Abigail Van Buren** 1918-2013 American
  journalist: attributed, *c.* 1970

32 You will find as the children grow
up that as a rule children are a bitter
disappointment—their greatest object
being to do precisely what their parents
do not wish and have anxiously tried to
prevent.
- **Victoria** 1819-1901 British queen: letter to
  the Crown Princess of Prussia, 5 January
  1876

33 I love my children...I'm delighted to
see them come and delighted to see
them go.
- **Mary Wesley** 1912-2002 English novelist:
  attributed

34 The main purpose of children's parties is to remind you that there are children more awful than your own.
- **Katharine Whitehorn** 1928- English journalist: *How to Survive Children* (1975)

35 Children begin by loving their parents; after a time they judge them; rarely, if ever, do they forgive them.
- **Oscar Wilde** 1854-1900 Irish dramatist and poet: *A Woman of No Importance* (1893)

36 Like so many infants of tender years he presented to the eye the aspect of a mass murderer suffering from an ingrowing toenail.
- **P. G. Wodehouse** 1881-1975 English-born writer: *A Few Quick Ones* (1959)

Choice

. . . .

Anything except that damned Mouse. **George V**

1 More than any other time in history, mankind faces a crossroads. One path leads to despair and utter hopelessness. The other, to total extinction. Let us pray we have the wisdom to choose correctly.
- **Woody Allen** 1935- American film director, writer, and actor: *Side Effects* (1980)

2 That's a bit like asking a man crawling across the Sahara whether he would prefer Perrier or Malvern Water.
replying to a question by Ian McKellen on his sexual orientation
- **Alan Bennett** 1934- English dramatist and actor: attributed

3 I'll have what she's having.
woman to waiter, seeing Sally acting an orgasm
- **Nora Ephron** 1941-2012 American writer and journalist: *When Harry Met Sally* (1989 film)

4 *George V was asked which film he would like to see while convalescing:*
Anything except that damned Mouse.
- **George V** 1865-1936 British king: George Lyttelton letter to Rupert Hart-Davis, 12 November 1959

5 Economy is going without something you do want in case you should, some day, want something you probably won't want.
- **Anthony Hope** 1863-1933 English novelist: *The Dolly Dialogues* (1894)

6 A compromise in the sense that being bitten in half by a shark is a compromise with being swallowed whole.
- **P. J. O'Rourke** 1947- American humorous writer: *Parliament of Whores*

7 *in the post office, pointing at the centre of a sheet of stamps:*
I'll take that one.
- **Herbert Beerbohm Tree** 1852-1917 English actor-manager: Hesketh Pearson *Beerbohm Tree* (1956)

Christmas

....

I'm walking backwards for Christmas. **Spike Milligan**

1 There are six evacuated children in
our house. My wife and I hate them so
much that we have decided to *take away*
something from them for Christmas!
  - **Anonymous**: letter from a friend in the
    country; James Agate diary 22 December
    1939

2 *on her husband:*
  Fang is the cheapest man alive. On
  Christmas Eve, he puts the kids to bed,
  fires one shot, and tells them Santa has
  committed suicide.
  - **Phyllis Diller** 1917-2012 American actress:
    Like a Lampshade in a Whorehouse (2005,
    with Richard Buskin)

3 A Merry Christmas to all my friends
except two.
  - **W. C. Fields** 1880-1946 American humorist:
    attributed

4 *confessing she takes pretend baths to get away
from it all:*
  Sometimes I get in with no water and
  just lie there. I've been known to have
  five 'baths' on Christmas Day.
  - **Dawn French** 1957- British comedy
    actress: in *Sunday Times* 5 December 2004

5 I am a poor man, but I would gladly
give ten shillings to find out who
sent me the insulting Christmas card
I received this morning.
  - **George Grossmith** 1847-1912 and **Weedon
    Grossmith** 1854-1919 English writers: *The
    Diary of a Nobody* (1894)

6 DRIFTWOOD (GROUCHO MARX): It's all
right. That's—that's in every contract.
That's—that's what they call a sanity
clause.
FIORELLO (CHICO MARX): You can't fool
me. There ain't no Sanity Claus.
  - **George S. Kaufman** 1889-1961 and **Morrie
    Ryskind** 1895-1985 screenwriters: *A Night at
    the Opera* (1935 film)

7 A lovely thing about Christmas is that
it's compulsory, like a thunderstorm,
and we all go through it together.
  - **Garrison Keillor** 1942- American
    humorous writer and broadcaster: *Leaving
    Home* (1987) 'Exiles'

8 I'm walking backwards for Christmas
Across the Irish Sea.
  - **Spike Milligan** 1918-2002 Irish comedian:
    'I'm Walking Backwards for Christmas'
    (1956)

9 Christmas begins about the first of
December with an office party and
ends when you finally realize what you
spent, around April fifteenth of the
next year.
  - **P. J. O'Rourke** 1947- American humorous
    writer: *Modern Manners* (1984)

10 Christmas, that time of year when people
descend into the bunker of the family.
  - **Byron Rogers** 1942- Welsh writer: in *Daily
    Telegraph* 27 December 1993

11 Be nice to yu turkeys dis christmas,
Don't eat it, keep it alive,
It could be yu mate an not on yu plate
Say, Yo! Turkey I'm on your side.
  - **Benjamin Zephaniah** 1958- British poet:
    'Talking Turkeys!!' (1994)

The Cinema

see also **ACTING, FILM, FILM PRODUCERS, FILM STARS, HOLLYWOOD**

···

Our comedies are not to be laughed at. **Samuel Goldwyn**

1 This film wasn't released—it escaped.
on M.A.S.H.
- **Robert Altman** 1922-2006 American film director: attributed

2 There are no rules in filmmaking. Only sins. And the cardinal sin is dullness.
- **Frank Capra** 1897-1991 Italian-born American film director: in *People* 16 September 1991

3 Bring on the empty horses!
said while directing the 1936 film
The Charge of the Light Brigade
- **Michael Curtiz** 1888-1962 Hungarian-born American film director: David Niven *Bring on the Empty Horses* (1975)

4 GEORGES FRANJU: Movies should have a beginning, a middle and an end.
JEAN-LUC GODARD: Certainly. But not necessarily in that order.
- **Jean-Luc Godard** 1930- French film director: in *Time* 14 September 1981

5 *told that he could not film Radclyffe Hall's* The Well of Loneliness *as it dealt with lesbians:*
So, make them Latvians.
- **Sam Goldwyn** 1882-1974 American film producer: attributed; Topol *A Treasury of Jewish Wit, Wisdom and Humour* (1999)

6 Our comedies are not to be laughed at.
- **Sam Goldwyn** 1882-1974 American film producer: N. Zierold *Hollywood Tycoons* (1969)

7 Pictures are for entertainment, messages should be delivered by Western Union.
- **Sam Goldwyn** 1882-1974 American film producer: Arthur Marx *Goldwyn* (1976)

8 Let's have some new clichés.
- **Sam Goldwyn** 1882-1974 American film producer: attributed, perhaps apocryphal

9 'Do you have a leading lady for your film?'
'We're trying for the Queen, she sells.'
- **George Harrison** 1943-2001 English singer and songwriter: at a press conference in the 1960s; Ned Sherrin *Cutting Edge* (1984)

10 The length of a film should be directly related to the endurance of the human bladder.
- **Alfred Hitchcock** 1899-1980 British-born film director: attributed

11 The writer, in the eyes of many film producers, still seems to occupy a position of importance somewhere between the wardrobe lady and the tea boy, with this difference: it's often quite difficult to replace the wardrobe lady.
- **John Mortimer** 1923-2009 English novelist, barrister, and dramatist: *Clinging to the Wreckage* (1982)

12 *on the take-over of United Artists by Charles Chaplin, Mary Pickford, Douglas Fairbanks and D. W. Griffith:*
The lunatics have taken charge of the asylum.
- **Richard Rowland** c.1881-1947 American film producer: Terry Ramsaye *A Million and One Nights* (1926)

13 The trouble, Mr Goldwyn, is that you are only interested in art and I am only interested in money.
telegraphed version of the outcome of a conversation between Shaw and Sam Goldwyn
- **George Bernard Shaw** 1856-1950 Irish dramatist: Alva Johnson *The Great Goldwyn* (1937)

Cities *see* **TOWNS AND CITIES**

Civil Servants

Here lies a civil servant. He was civil To everyone, and servant to the devil.
C. H. Sisson

1 I confidently expect that we [civil servants] shall continue to be grouped with mothers-in-law and Wigan Pier as one of the recognized objects of ridicule.
  ▪ **Edward Bridges** 1892–1969 British civil servant: *Portrait of a Profession* (1950)

2 Give a civil servant a good case and he'll wreck it with clichés, bad punctuation, double negatives and convoluted apology.
  ▪ **Alan Clark** 1928–99 British Conservative politician: diary 22 July 1983

3 A civil servant doesn't make jokes.
  ▪ **Eugène Ionesco** 1912–94 French dramatist: *Tueur sans gages* (The Killer, 1958)

4 May I hasten to support Mrs McGurgle's contention that civil servants are human beings, and must be treated as such?
  ▪ **J. B. Morton** 1893–1975 British journalist: M. Frayn (ed.) *The Best of Beachcomber* (1963)

5 By the time the civil service has finished drafting a document to give effect to a principle, there may be little of the principle left.
  ▪ **Lord Reith** 1889–1971 British administrator and politician: *Into the Wind* (1949)

6 Here lies a civil servant. He was civil To everyone, and servant to the devil.
  ▪ **C. H. Sisson** 1914–2003 English poet: *The London Zoo* (1961)

Class

see also **ARISTOCRACY, SNOBBERY**

If the lower orders don't set us a good example, what on earth is the use of them?   **Oscar Wilde**

1 A gentleman never eats. He breakfasts, he lunches, he dines, but he *never* eats!
  ▪ **Anonymous**: Cole Porter's headmaster, c.1910; Caryl Brahms and Ned Sherrin *Song by Song* (1984)

2 His lordship may compel us to be equal upstairs, but there will never be equality in the servants' hall.
  ▪ **J. M. Barrie** 1860–1937 Scottish writer and dramatist: *The Admirable Crichton* (performed 1902)

3 You know you're working class when your TV is bigger than your bookcase.
  ▪ **Rob Beckett** English comedian: at the Edinburgh Festival fringe, August 2012

4 *when asked by interviewer Sandra Harris on the* Today *programme whether she thought British class barriers had come down:* Of course they have, or I wouldn't be sitting here talking to someone like you.
  ▪ **Barbara Cartland** 1901–2000 English writer: Jilly Cooper *Class* (1979)

5 I came upstairs into the world; for I was born in a cellar.
  ▪ **William Congreve** 1670–1729 English dramatist: *Love for Love* (1695)

6 Gentlemen do not take soup at luncheon.
  ▪ **Lord Curzon** 1859–1925 British Conservative politician; Viceroy of India 1898–1905: E. L. Woodward *Short Journey* (1942)

7 He [Lord Home] is used to dealing with estate workers. I cannot see how anyone can say he is out of touch.
comment on her father's becoming Prime Minister
- **Caroline Douglas-Home** 1937- : in *Daily Herald* 21 October 1963

8 We are all Adam's children but silk makes the difference.
- **Thomas Fuller** 1654-1734 English writer and physician: *Gnomologia* (1732)

9 The Earl, the Marquis, and the Dook,
The Groom, the Butler, and the
    Cook—...
The Aristocrat who banks with
    Coutts...
The Aristocrat who cleans our boots—
They all shall equal be.
- **W. S. Gilbert** 1836-1911 English writer of comic and satirical verse: *The Gondoliers* (1889)

10 Bow, bow, ye lower middle classes!
Bow, bow, ye tradesmen, bow, ye masses.
- **W. S. Gilbert** 1836-1911 English writer of comic and satirical verse: *Iolanthe* (1882)

11 When every one is somebodee,
Then no one's anybody.
- **W. S. Gilbert** 1836-1911 English writer of comic and satirical verse: *The Gondoliers* (1889)

12 Man he eat the barracuda,
Barracuda eat the bass
Bass he eat the little flounder,
'Cause the flounder lower class.
- **E. Y. Harburg** 1898-1981 American songwriter: 'For Every Fish' (1957)

13 *when William Douglas Home, son of the 13th Earl of Home, was sent to prison in 1944, his mother told him:*
Be sure to pack your evening clothes. The governor is bound to ask you to dine.
- **Lady Douglas Home** 1909-90: attributed

14 Will the people in the cheaper seats clap your hands? All the rest of you, if you'll just rattle your jewellery.
- **John Lennon** 1940-80 English pop singer and songwriter: at the Royal Variety Performance, 4 November 1963

15 Of all the hokum with which this country [America] is riddled the most odd is the common notion that it is free of class distinctions.
- **W. Somerset Maugham** 1874-1965 English novelist: *A Writer's Notebook* (1949) written in 1941

16 *definition of a gentleman:*
Someone who can make a grouse do for six.
- **Nigel Nicolson** 1917-2004 English writer: Adam Nicolson *Sea Room: an island life* (2002)

17 The upper middle classes like anything ecological: it assuages their guilt. Give your posh friends a bag of muddy parsnips. They'll love it.
- **Grayson Perry** 1960- English ceramic artist: in *Sunday Times* 2 December 2012

18 I no longer keep the coal in the bath. I keep it in the bidet.
- **John Prescott** 1938- British Labour politician: in *Independent* 3 July 1999

19 'She's leaving her present house and going to Lower Seymour Street.' 'I dare say she will, if she stays there long enough.'
- **Saki** 1870-1916 Scottish writer: *The Toys of Peace* (1919)

20 I don't want to talk grammar, I want to talk like a lady.
- **George Bernard Shaw** 1856-1950 Irish dramatist: *Pygmalion* (1916), spoken by Eliza Doolittle

21 The only infallible rule we know is, that the man who is always talking about being a gentleman never is one.
- **R. S. Surtees** 1805-64 English sporting journalist and novelist: *Ask Mamma* (1858)

22 Nothing is more bourgeois than to be afraid to look bourgeois.
- **Andy Warhol** 1927-87 American artist: Tom Wolfe *The Painted Word* (1975)

23 Really, if the lower orders don't set us a good example, what on earth is the use of them?
- **Oscar Wilde** 1854-1900 Irish dramatist and poet: *The Importance of Being Earnest* (1895)

24 I think factories would close down,
actually, if it wasn't for working-class
people.
▪ **Victoria Wood** 1953- British writer and
comedienne: *Victoria Wood—As Seen on TV*
BBC2 January 1985

The Clergy

see also **RELIGION**

....

There are three sexes—men, women, and clergymen. **Sydney Smith**

1 A priest is a man who is called Father by
everyone except his own children who
are obliged to call him Uncle.
▪ **Anonymous**: said to be an Italian saying
found in a French novel; Rupert Hart-Davis
letter to George Lyttelton, 15 July 1956

2 As for the British churchman, he goes
to church as he goes to the bathroom,
with the minimum of fuss and with no
explanation if he can help it.
▪ **Ronald Blythe** 1922- English writer:
The Age of Illusion (1963)

3 Don't like bishops…Blessed are the
meek my foot! They're all on the climb.
Ever heard of meekness stopping
a bishop from becoming a bishop?
Nor have I.
▪ **Maurice Bowra** 1898-1971 English scholar
and literary critic: in conversation while
lunching at the Reform Club with a bishop
at the next table; Arthur Marshall *Life's Rich
Pageant* (1984)

4 Poor Uncle Harry
Having become a missionary
Found the natives' morals rather crude.
He and Aunt Mary
Quickly imposed an arbitrary
Ban upon them shopping in the nude…
Uncle Harry's not a missionary now.
▪ **Noël Coward** 1899-1973 English dramatist,
actor, and composer: 'Uncle Harry' (1946)

5 The parson knows enough who knows
a duke.
▪ **William Cowper** 1731-1800 English poet:
'Tirocinium' (1785)

6 Mr Doctor, that loose gown becomes
you so well I wonder your notions
should be so narrow.
*to the Puritan Dr Humphreys, as he was
about to kiss her hand on her visit to Oxford
in 1566*
▪ **Elizabeth I** 1533-1603 English queen:
F. Chamberlin *Sayings of Queen Elizabeth*
(1923)

7 I remember the average curate at home
as something between a eunuch and a
snigger.
▪ **Ronald Firbank** 1886-1926 English novelist:
The Flower Beneath the Foot (1923)

8 This merriment of parsons is mighty
offensive.
▪ **Samuel Johnson** 1709-84 English poet,
critic, and lexicographer: James Boswell
Life of Samuel Johnson (1791) March 1781

9 Evangelical vicar, in want of a portable,
second-hand font, would dispose, for
the same, of a portrait, in frame, of the
Bishop, elect, of Vermont.
advertisement placed in a newspaper
▪ **Ronald Knox** 1888-1957 English writer and
Roman Catholic priest: W. S. Baring-Gould
The Lure of the Limerick (1968)

10 It's great being a priest, isn't it, Ted?
▪ **Graham Linehan** 1968- and **Arthur
Mathews** 1959- Irish writers: *Father Ted*
(Channel 4 TV, 1995) 'Good Luck,
Father Ted'

11 *to a clergyman who thanked him for the
enjoyment he'd given the world:*
And I want to thank you for all the

enjoyment you've taken out of it.
- **Groucho Marx** 1890-1977 American film comedian: Joe Adamson *Groucho, Harpo, Chico and sometimes Zeppo* (1973)

12 As the French say, there are three sexes—men, women, and clergymen.
- **Sydney Smith** 1771-1845 English clergyman and essayist: Lady Holland *Memoir* (1855)

13 A Curate—there is something which excites compassion in the very name of a Curate!!!
- **Sydney Smith** 1771-1845 English clergyman and essayist: *Edinburgh Review* (1822) 'Persecuting Bishops'

14 There is a species of person called a 'Modern Churchman' who draws the full salary of a beneficed clergyman and need not commit himself to any religious belief.
- **Evelyn Waugh** 1903-66 English novelist: *Decline and Fall* (1928)

15 *Merit*, indeed!…We are come to a pretty pass if they talk of *merit* for a bishopric.
- **Lord Westmorland** 1759-1841: Lady Salisbury, diary, 9 December 1835

16 The Bishop…was talking to the local Master of Hounds about the difficulty he had in keeping his vicars off the incense.
- **P. G. Wodehouse** 1881-1975 English-born writer: *Mr. Mulliner Speaking* (1929)

Colours

If I could find anything blacker than black, I'd use it.   **J. M. W. Turner**

1 I was shown round Tutankhamun's tomb in the 1920s. I saw all this wonderful pink on the walls and the artefacts. I was so impressed that I vowed to wear it for the rest of my life.
- **Barbara Cartland** 1901-2000 English writer: in *Irish Times* 28 March 1998

2 I cannot pretend to feel impartial about the colours. I rejoice with the brilliant ones, and am genuinely sorry for the poor browns.
- **Winston Churchill** 1874-1965 British Conservative statesman: *Thoughts and Adventures* (1932)

3 Gentlemen never wear brown in London.
- **Lord Curzon** 1859-1925 British Conservative politician: attributed; Nigel Rees *Cassell Dictionary of Humorous Quotations* (1999)

4 *on the choice of colour for the Model T Ford:*
Any colour—so long as it's black.
- **Henry Ford** 1863-1947 American car manufacturer and businessman: Allan Nevins *Ford* (1957)

5 It's just my colour: it's *beige*!
on her first view of the Parthenon
- **Elsie Mendl** 1865-1950 American socialite and interior decorator: Osbert Sitwell *Rat Week: An Essay on the Abdication* (1986)

6 If I could find anything blacker than black, I'd use it.
- **J. M. W. Turner** 1775-1851 English landscape painter: remark, 1844

7 Pink is the navy blue of India.
- **Diana Vreeland** 1903-89 American fashion editor: attributed, 1977

8 I think it pisses God off if you walk by the colour purple in a field somewhere and don't notice it.
- **Alice Walker** 1944- : *The Colour Purple* (1982)

Comebacks

....

'Which husband was the best lover?' 'Yours'   **Joan Collins**

1 NANCY ASTOR: If I were your wife
I would put poison in your coffee!
WINSTON CHURCHILL: And if I were
your husband I would drink it.
  ▪ Nancy Astor 1879-1964 American-born
  British Conservative politician: Consuelo
  Vanderbilt Balsan *Glitter and Gold* (1952)

2 *on finishing* Bill of Divorcement:
KATHARINE HEPBURN: Thank God,
I don't have to act with you any more.
BARRYMORE:I didn't know you ever had,
darling.
  ▪ John Barrymore 1882-1942 American actor:
  in *Time* 1942

3 PLAYER: I can see your tits from here.
BRADY: Well, when I sell you to Crewe,
you won't be able to see from there.
*as managing director of Birmingham City
Football Club*
  ▪ Karren Brady 1969- British
  businesswoman: *Strong Woman: Ambition,
  Grit and a Great Pair of Heels* (2012)

4 CHARLOTTE: Jack says that I have a fire
inside me.
CARRIE: You tell him they make a cream
for that.
  ▪ Candace Bushnell 1958- , **Darren Star**
  1961- , and **Patrick King** 1954- American
  writers: *Sex and the City* (HBO TV, 1998)
  Sarah Jessica Parker as Carrie and Kristin
  Davis as Charlotte

5 BESSIE BRADDOCK: Winston, you're
drunk.
CHURCHILL: Bessie, you're ugly. But
tomorrow I shall be sober.
  ▪ Winston Churchill 1874-1965 British
  Conservative statesman: an exchange with
  the Labour MP Bessie Braddock; J. L. Lane
  (ed.) *Sayings of Churchill* (1992)

6 *Joan Rivers interviewing Joan Collins about
her marriages:*
JOAN RIVERS: Which husband was the
best lover?

JOAN COLLINS: Yours.
  ▪ **Joan Collins** 1933- British actress:
  attributed, in *Ottawa Citizen* 11 October
  1997

7 KATHARINE HEPBURN: I fear I may be too
tall for you, Mr. Tracy.
SPENCER TRACY: Don't worry, I'll cut
you down to my size.
*apocryphal account of their first meeting in
1942; it was the film director Joe Mankiewicz
who said to Hepburn, 'He'll cut you down
to size'*
  ▪ **Katharine Hepburn** 1907-2003 American
  actress: Bill Davidson *Spencer Tracy* (1987)

8 I was mistaken for a prostitute once
in the last war. When a GI asked me
what I charged, I said, 'Well, dear, what
do your mother and sisters normally
ask for?'
  ▪ **Thora Hird** 1911-2003 English actress: in
  Independent 27 February 1999

9 *to Clare Boothe Luce, who had stood aside for
her saying, 'Age before Beauty':*
Pearls before swine.
  ▪ **Dorothy Parker** 1893-1967 American critic
  and humorist: R. E. Drennan *Wit's End* (1973)

10 FLO: I've never been so insulted in
my life.
HACKENBUSH: Well, it's early yet.
  ▪ **Robert Pirosh** 1910-89, **George Seaton**
  1911-79, and **George Oppenheimer**
  screenwriters: *A Day at the Races* (1937 film),
  spoken by Esther Muir and Groucho Marx

11 *responding to a savage review by Rudolph
Louis in* Münchener Neueste Nachrich
7 February 1906:
I am sitting in the smallest room of my
house. I have your review before me.
In a moment it will be behind me.
  ▪ **Max Reger** 1873-1916 German composer:
  Nicolas Slonimsky *Lexicon of Musical
  Invective* (1953)

12 Lots of grapefruit throughout the day
and plenty of virile young men...but

since her past escorts include Edward Kennedy, Frank Sinatra, Andy Williams and Julio Iglesias, I think the grapefruit deserves all the credit.

responding to Angie Dickinson; see **diets** 4
- **Anne Robinson** 1944- British television presenter: in *Daily Mirror* 2 October 1985

13 SMITH (TO THE COURT): At the time, my client was as drunk as a judge.
JUDGE (INTERJECTING): Mr Smith, I think you'll find the phrase is 'as drunk as a lord'.
SMITH: As your Lordship pleases.
- **F. E. Smith** 1872-1930 British Conservative politician and lawyer: attributed

14 *to Richard Adams, who had described Vidal's novel on Lincoln as 'meretricious'*
Really? Well, meretricious and a happy New Year to you too!
earlier uses of the response are attributed to Franklin P. Adams in the 1930s, and the NBC radio show starring the Marx Brothers, Flywheel, Shyster and Flywheel, in 1933
- **Gore Vidal** 1925-2012 American novelist and critic: on *Start the Week*, BBC radio, 1970s

15 EARL OF SANDWICH: 'Pon my soul, Wilkes, I don't know whether you'll die upon the gallows or of the pox.
WILKES: That depends, my Lord, whether I first embrace your Lordship's principles, or your Lordship's mistresses.
- **John Wilkes** 1727-97 English parliamentary reformer: Charles Petrie *The Four Georges* (1935); probably apocryphal

Comedy

see also **HUMOUR**

⋯⋯⋯

Comedy is the blues for people who can't sing. **Chris Rock**

1 I worked for a while as a stripper—that's when I realised I had a flair for comedy.
- **Jeanine Burnier** American comedienne: Michèle Brown and Ann O'Connor *Hammer and Tongues* (1986)

2 Comedy, like sodomy, is an unnatural act.
- **Marty Feldman** 1933-83 English comedian: in *Times* 9 June 1969

3 The funniest thing about comedy is that you never know why people laugh. I know *what* makes them laugh but trying to get your hands on the *why* of it is like trying to pick an eel out of a tub of water.
- **W. C. Fields** 1880-1946 American humorist: Richard J. Anobile *A Flask of Fields* (1972)

4 Some jokes are short and elegant, like a mathematical proof or a midget in a ball-gown.
- **Demetri Martin** 1973- American comedian: attributed

5 They laughed when I said I was going to be a comedian…They're not laughing now.
- **Bob Monkhouse** 1928-2003 English entertainer: attributed; *BBC News* 29 December 2003 (online edition)

6 Comedy is the blues for people who can't sing.
- **Chris Rock** 1965- American comedian: in *Spin* February 1993

7 Love, marriage and kids are fine, but I wouldn't give up an hour of comedy for them.
- **Frank Skinner** 1957- English comedian: in *Times* 11 August 2007

8 There are three basic rules for great comedy. Unfortunately no-one can remember what they are.
- **Arthur Smith** 1954- English comedian: attributed

Comedy Routines and Catchphrases

George—don't do that. **Joyce Grenfell**

1 CECIL: After you, Claude.
CLAUDE: No, after you, Cecil.
- **Ted Kavanagh** 1892-1958 New Zealand-born scriptwriter: catchphrase in *ITMA* (BBC radio programme, 1939-49)

2 Am I bovvered?
- **Catherine Tate** 1968- English actress and comedienne: teenager Lauren, in *The Catherine Tate Show* (BBC TV, 2004-6)

3 Art thou his father?
Ay, sir, so his mother says, if I may believe her.
- **William Shakespeare** 1564-1616 English dramatist: *The Taming of the Shrew* (1592)

4 Can I do you now, sir?
spoken by 'Mrs Mopp'
- **Ted Kavanagh** 1892-1958 New Zealand-born scriptwriter: catchphrase in *ITMA* (BBC radio programme, 1939-49)

5 Collapse of Stout Party.
supposed standard dénouement in Victorian humour
- **Anonymous**: R. Pearsall *Collapse of Stout Party* (1975) introduction

6 D'oh!
Homer J. Simpson's habitual expression of annoyance
- **Matt Groening** 1954- American humorist and satirist: *The Simpsons* (American TV series, 1990-)

7 Eat my shorts!
catchphrase associated with Bart Simpson
- **Matt Groening** 1954- American humorist and satirist: *The Simpsons* (American TV series, 1990-)

8 Ee, it was agony, Ivy.
- **Ted Ray** 1906-77 English comedian: catchphrase in *Ray's a Laugh* (BBC radio programme, 1949-61)

9 'Er indoors.
used by Arthur Daley (played by George Cole)
to refer to his wife
- **Leon Griffiths** 1928-92 English writer: ITV television series *Minder* (1979 onwards)

10 Fact.
David Brent's favourite assurance
- **Ricky Gervais** 1961- and **Stephen Merchant**: *The Office* (2001-3)

11 George—don't do that.
- **Joyce Grenfell** 1910-79 English comedy actress and writer: used as a recurring line in monologues about a nursery school, from the 1950s

12 GEORGE BURNS: Say goodnight, Gracie.
GRACIE ALLEN: Goodnight, Gracie.
- **George Burns** 1896-1996 American comedian: said to be customary conclusion to *The George Burns and Gracie Allen Show* (1950-58), although Burns in *Gracie: a Love Story* (1990) described this as a showbusiness myth

13 Hello, I'm Julian and this is my friend, Sandy.
- **Barry Took** 1928-2002 and **Marty Feldman** 1933-83: catchphrase in *Round the Horne* (BBC radio series, 1965-8), spoken by Hugh Paddick and referring to Kenneth Williams

14 Hello possums!
Dame Edna's habitual greeting to her fans
- **Barry Humphries** 1934- Australian actor and writer: *The Barry Humphries Show*: Dame Edna Everage

15 I 'ate you, Butler.
Inspector Blake (Stephen Lewis) to Stan Butler (Reg Varney)
- **Ronald Wolfe** and **Ronald Chesney**: *On the Buses* (1969-73).

16 I didn't get where I am today without —.
habitual boast of Reggie Perrin's boss CJ
- **David Nobbs** 1935- British comedy writer: BBC television series *The Fall and Rise of Reginald Perrin*, 1976-80

17 I don't mind if I do.
catchphrase spoken by 'Colonel Chinstrap'
- **Ted Kavanagh** 1892-1958 New Zealand-born scriptwriter: *ITMA* (BBC radio programme, 1939-49)

18 If you've got it, flaunt it!
- **Mel Brooks** 1926- American film director and actor: *The Producers* (1967 film)

19 I go—I come back.
catchphrase spoken by 'Ali Oop'
- **Ted Kavanagh** 1892-1958 New Zealand-born scriptwriter: *ITMA* (BBC radio programme, 1939-49)

20 I have a cunning plan.
Baldrick's habitual overoptimistic promise
- **Richard Curtis** 1956- and **Ben Elton** 1959- screenwriters: spoken by Tony Robinson, in the *Blackadder* television series (BBC TV 1987-2000)

21 I'm free!
cry of 'Mr Humphries' (played by John Inman) of Grace Brothers
- **David Croft** 1922- and **Jeremy Lloyd**: in *Are You Being Served?* (1973-83).

22 Is it cos I is black?
- **Sacha Baron Cohen** 1970- British comedian: as his character Ali G, originally in *The 11 O'Clock Show* (Channel 4 TV, 1998)

23 It's being so cheerful as keeps me going.
catchphrase spoken by 'Mona Lott'
- **Ted Kavanagh** 1892-1958 New Zealand-born scriptwriter: *ITMA* (BBC radio programme, 1939-49)

24 CORBETT: It's goodnight from me.
BARKER: And it's goodnight from him.
- **Ronnie Barker** 1929-2005 and **Ronnie Corbett** 1930- British comedians: in *The Two Ronnies*, 1971-87 BBC television series

25 It's *sooo* unfair!
habitual plaint of Kevin the Teenager
- **Harry Enfield** 1961- English comedian and writer: *Harry Enfield and Chums* (BBC TV, 1994)

26 I've arrived and to prove it I'm here!
- **Eric Sykes** 1923-2012 and **Max Bygraves** 1922-2012: *Educating Archie*, 1950-3 BBC radio comedy series

27 Nobody expects the Spanish Inquisition! Our chief weapon is surprise—surprise and fear...fear and surprise...our two weapons are fear and surprise—and ruthless efficiency...our *three* weapons are fear and surprise and ruthless efficiency and an almost fanatical devotion to the Pope...our *four*...no... *Amongst* our weapons—amongst our weaponry—are such elements as fear, surprise...I'll come in again.
- **Graham Chapman** 1941-89, **John Cleese** 1939- , and **others** British comedians: *Monty Python's Flying Circus* (BBC TV programme, 1970)

28 No sex, please—we're British.
- **Anthony Marriott** 1931- and **Alistair Foot**: title of play (1971)

29 Oh, calamity!
- **Robertson Hare** 1891-1979 English actor: catchphrase in *Yours Indubitably* (1956)

30 Ohhh, I don't *believe* it!
Victor Meldrew (Richard Wilson)
- **David Renwick** 1951- British television writer: *One Foot in the Grave* (BBC television series, 1989-)

31 Oh, titter ye not.
- **Frankie Howerd** 1922-92 British comedian: habitual adjuration to his audience, first introduced in *The Frankie Howerd Variety Show* 1978

32 Pass the sick bag, Alice.
referring to a canteen lady at the old Express building in Fleet Street, who conveyed plates of egg and chips to journalists at their desks
- **John Junor** 1919-97 British journalist and editor: in *Sunday Express* 28 December 1980

33 A play wot I wrote.
- **Eddie Braben** 1930-2013 English comedy writer: spoken by Ernie Wise, in *The Morecambe and Wise Show* (BBC Television, 1967-78; Thames Television, 1978-83)

34 Respect!
Ali G acknowledges quality
- **Sacha Baron Cohen** 1971- English comedian: *Da Ali G Show* (Channel 4 TV, 2000-1)

35 Shome mishtake, shurely?
- **Anonymous**: catchphrase in *Private Eye* magazine, 1980s

36 Shoulders back, lovely boy!
Sergeant-Major Williams (Windsor Davies) to
his concert party
- **Jimmy Perry** 1923- and **David Croft** 1922-
  screenwriters: *It Ain't Half Hot, Mum* (BBC
  TV, 1974-81)

37 So Harry says, 'You don't like me any
more. Why not?' And he says, 'Because
you've got so terribly pretentious.' And
Harry says, 'Pretentious? *Moi?*'
- **John Cleese** 1939- and **Connie Booth**
  1944- English and American-born comic
  actors: *Fawlty Towers* (BBC TV, 1979)

38 Stop messing about!
protest of Snide (Kenneth Williams)
- **Ray Galton** 1930- and **Alan Simpson**
  1929- English writers: *Hancock's Half Hour*
  (1954-9)

39 Take my wife—please!
- **Henny Youngman** 1906-98 American
  comedian: in *Times* 26 February 1998;
  obituary

40 ABBOTT: Now, on the St Louis team we
have Who's on first, What's on second,
I Don't Know is on third.
COSTELLO: That's what I want to
find out.
- **Bud Abbott** 1895-1974 and **Lou Costello**
  1906-59 American comedians: *Naughty*
  Nineties (1945 film)

41 They don't like it up 'em!
Lance-Corporal Jones (Clive Dunn)
- **Jimmy Perry** 1923- and **David Croft**
  1922- screenwriters: *Dad's Army* (BBC TV,
  1968-77)

42 Very interesting…but stupid.
- **Dan Rowan** 1922-87 and **Dick Martin** 1923-
  2008 American comedians: catchphrase
  in *Rowan and Martin's Laugh-In* (American
  television series, 1967-73)

43 What do you think of the show so far?
Rubbish!
- **Eric Morecambe** 1926-84 English
  comedian: on *The Morecambe and Wise*
  Show (BBC Television, 1968-78; Thames
  Television, 1978-83)

44 Yeah but no but yeah but no.
Vicky Pollard's habitual protest
- **Matt Lucas** 1974- and **David Walliams**
  1971- British comedians: spoken by Matt
  Lucas, in *Little Britain* (BBC TV, 2003-6)

45 SEAGOON: Ying tong iddle I po.
- **Spike Milligan** 1918-2002 Irish comedian:
  The Dreaded Batter Pudding Hurler in *The*
  Goon Show (BBC radio series) 12 October
  1954; catchphrase also used in *The Ying*
  Tong Song (1956)

46 You dirty old man!
Harold Steptoe (Harry H. Corbett) to his
father Albert
- **Ray Galton** 1930- and **Alan Simpson**
  1929- English writers: *Steptoe and Son*
  (BBC TV, 1962-5 and 1970-4).

47 You might very well think that.
I couldn't possibly comment.
the Chief Whip's habitual response to
questioning
- **Michael Dobbs** 1948- British novelist and
  broadcaster: *House of Cards* (BBC TV, 1990)

48 You plonker!
Del Boy Trotter (David Jason) to his brother
Rodney (Nicholas Lyndhurst)
- **John Sullivan** 1946-2011 English
  screenwriter: *Only Fools and Horses*
  (BBC TV, 1981-2003)

49 You stupid boy!
Captain Mainwaring (Arthur Lowe) to
Private Pike (Ian Lavender)
- **Jimmy Perry** 1923- and **David Croft**
  1922- screenwriters: *Dad's Army* (BBC TV,
  1968-77)

Computers and the Internet

see also **SCIENCE, TECHNOLOGY**

....

The email of the species is deadlier than the mail.   **Stephen Fry**

1 Now we have the World Wide Web (the only thing I know of whose shortened form—www—takes three times longer to say than what it's short for).
- **Douglas Adams** 1952-2001 English science fiction writer: *The Salmon of Doubt* (2002)

2 To err is human but to really foul things up requires a computer.
- **Anonymous**: in *Farmers' Almanac for 1978*

3 *Charles Babbage, inventor of the first mechanical computer, had sacrificed some very precious time to a lady, on the supposition that she understood as much as she thought she did:*
Now, Mr Babbage, there is only one thing that I want to know. If you put the question in wrong, will the answer come out right?
- **Anonymous**: Harriet Martineau *Autobiography* (1877)

4 A modern computer hovers between the obsolescent and the nonexistent.
- **Sydney Brenner** 1927-   British scientist: in *Science* 5 January 1990; attributed

5 Programming today is a race between software engineers striving to build bigger and better idiot-proof programs and the Universe trying to produce bigger and better idiots. So far, the Universe is winning.
- **Rick Cook** 1944-   American fantasy writer: *The Wizardry Compiled* (1989)

6 I am afraid it is a non-starter. I cannot even use a bicycle pump.
when asked whether she uses e-mail
- **Judi Dench** 1934-   English actress: in *Times* 13 February 1999

7 You can't retrieve your life (unless you're on Wikipedia, in which case you can retrieve an inaccurate version of it).
- **Nora Ephron** 1941-2012 American screenwriter and director: *I Remember Nothing and Other Reflections* (2012)

8 The email of the species is deadlier than the mail.
- **Stephen Fry** 1957-   English comedian, actor, and writer: in *Sunday Telegraph* 23 December 2001

9 Computer says No.
David Walliams as 'Carol'
- **Matt Lucas** 1974-   and **David Walliams** 1971-   British comedians: *Little Britain* (BBC TV, series 2, episode 1) 19 October 2004

10 Whenever I'm on my computer, I don't type 'lol'. I type 'lqtm': 'laugh quietly to myself'. It's more honest.
- **Demetri Martin** 1973-   American comedian: attributed

11 *of computers:*
But they are useless. They can only give you answers.
- **Pablo Picasso** 1881-1973 Spanish painter: in *Paris Review* 1964

12 A computer lets you make more mistakes faster than any invention in human history, with the possible exception of handguns and tequila.
- **Mitch Ratcliffe**: in *Technology Review* April 1992

13 Computers make it easier to do a lot of things, but most of the things they make it easier to do don't need to be done.
- **Andy Rooney** 1919-2011 American broadcaster: *Word for Word* (1986)

14 I think there is a world market for maybe five computers.
- **Thomas Watson Snr.** 1874-1956 American businessman; Chairman of IBM: commonly attributed, but not traced; stated by IBM to derive from a misunderstanding of an occasion on 28 April 1953 when Thomas Watson Jnr. informed a meeting of IBM stockholders that 'we expected to get orders for five machines, we came home with orders for 18'

15 Conjunctivitus.com—now there's a site for sore eyes.
- **Tim Vine** 1967- English comedian: attributed, 2012

16 We've all heard that a million monkeys banging on a million typewriters will eventually reproduce the entire works of Shakespeare. Now, thanks to the Internet, we know this is not true.
- **Robert Wilensky** 1951- American academic: in *Mail on Sunday* 16 February 1997

Conversation

see also **SPEECHES**

Faith, that's as well said, as if I had said it myself.   **Jonathan Swift**

1 When I left the dining room after sitting next to Mr Gladstone I thought he was the cleverest man in England, but after sitting next to Mr Disraeli I thought I was the cleverest woman in England.
view of a young lady taken into dinner by both on successive nights, sometimes attributed to Queen Victoria
- **Anonymous**: Princess Marie Louise *My Memories of Six Reigns* (1979)

2 From politics, it was an easy step to silence.
- **Jane Austen** 1775-1817 English novelist: *Northanger Abbey* (1818)

3 It was such a voice as icebergs might be supposed to use to speak to each other as they passed by night in the Arctic Sea.
- **E. F. Benson** 1867-1940 English novelist: *Miss Mapp* (1922)

4 Although there exist many thousand subjects for elegant conversation, there are persons who cannot meet a cripple without talking about feet.
- **Ernest Bramah** 1868-1942 English writer: *The Wallet of Kai Lung* (1900)

5 When you were quite a little boy somebody ought to have said 'hush' just once!
- **Mrs Patrick Campbell** 1865-1940 English actress: letter to George Bernard Shaw, 1 November 1912

6 'Then you should say what you mean,' the March Hare went on. 'I do,' Alice hastily replied; 'at least—at least I mean what I say—that's the same thing, you know.' 'Not the same thing a bit!' said the Hatter. 'Why, you might just as well say that "I see what I eat" is the same thing as "I eat what I see!" '
- **Lewis Carroll** 1832-98 English writer and logician: *Alice's Adventures in Wonderland* (1865)

7 Too much agreement kills a chat.
- **Eldridge Cleaver** 1935- American civil rights activist: *Soul on Ice* (1968)

8 Is it possible to cultivate the art of conversation when living in the country all the year round?
- **E. M. Delafield** 1890-1943 English writer: *The Diary of a Provincial Lady* (1930)

9 The fun of talk is to find what a man really thinks, and then contrast it with the enormous lies he has been telling all dinner, and, perhaps, all his life.
- **Benjamin Disraeli** 1804-81 British Tory statesman and novelist: *Lothair* (1870)

10 Blessed is the man who, having nothing to say, abstains from giving us wordy evidence of the fact.
- **George Eliot** 1819-80 English novelist: *Impressions of Theoprastus Such* (1879)

11 How time flies when you's doin' all the talking.
- **Harvey Fierstein** 1954- American dramatist and actor: *Torch Song Trilogy* (1979)

12 No man would listen to you talk if he didn't know it was his turn next.
- **E. W. Howe** 1853-1937 American novelist and editor: *Country Town Sayings* (1911)

13 If you are ever at a loss to support a flagging conversation, introduce the subject of eating.
- **Leigh Hunt** 1784-1859 English poet and essayist: J. A. Gere and John Sparrow (eds.) *Geoffrey Madan's Notebooks* (1981); attributed

14 A good housewife, she knew how to hash up the conversational remains of last night's dinner to furnish out this morning's lunch.
- **Aldous Huxley** 1894-1963 English novelist: *Point Counter Point* (1929)

15 I've just spent an hour talking to Tallulah [Bankhead] for a few minutes.
- **Fred Keating** 1897-1961 American actor: Denis Brian *Tallulah, Darling* (1980)

16 There are two things in ordinary conversation which ordinary people dislike—information and wit.
- **Stephen Leacock** 1869-1944 Canadian humorist: *The Boy I Left Behind Me* (1947)

17 The opposite of talking isn't listening. The opposite of talking is waiting.
- **Fran Lebowitz** 1946- American writer: *Social Studies* (1981)

18 No-one really listens to anyone else, and if you try it for a while you'll see why.
- **Mignon McLaughlin** 1913-83 American writer: *Complete Neurotic's Notebook* (1981)

19 Considering how foolishly people act and how pleasantly they prattle, perhaps it would be better for the world if they talked more and did less.
- **W. Somerset Maugham** 1874-1965 English novelist: *A Writer's Notebook* (1949) written in 1892

20 She plunged into a sea of platitudes, and with the powerful breast stroke of a channel swimmer made her confident way towards the white cliffs of the obvious.
- **W. Somerset Maugham** 1874-1965 English novelist: *A Writer's Notebook* (1949) written in 1919

21 He never knew what to say. If life was a party, he wasn't even in the kitchen.
- **Terry Pratchett** 1948- English fantasy writer: *Thief of Time* (2001)

22 *commenting that George Bernard Shaw's wife was a good listener:*
God knows she had plenty of practice.
- **J. B. Priestley** 1894-1984 English novelist, dramatist, and critic: *Margin Released* (1962)

23 You talkin' to me?
- **Paul Schrader** 1946- American screenwriter: *Taxi Driver* (1976 film); spoken by Robert de Niro as Travis Bickle

24 [Macaulay] has occasional flashes of silence, that make his conversation perfectly delightful.
- **Sydney Smith** 1771-1845 English clergyman and essayist: Lady Holland *Memoir* (1855)

25 —d! said my mother, 'what is all this story about?'— 'A Cock and a Bull,' said Yorick.
- **Laurence Sterne** 1713-68 English novelist: *Tristram Shandy* (1759-67)

26 *You* talked animatedly for some time about language being the aniseed trail that draws the hounds of heaven when the metaphysical fox has gone to earth; he must have thought you were barmy.
- **Tom Stoppard** 1937- British dramatist: *Jumpers* (rev. ed. 1986)

27 Faith, that's as well said, as if I had said it myself.
- **Jonathan Swift** 1667-1745 Irish poet and satirist: *Polite Conversation* (1738)

28 She never lets ideas interrupt the easy flow of her conversation.
- **Jean Webster** 1876-1916 American novelist: *Daddy-Long-Legs* (1912)

29 If one plays good music, people don't listen and if one plays bad music people don't talk.
- **Oscar Wilde** 1854-1900 Irish dramatist and poet: *The Importance of Being Earnest* (1895)

30 If one could only teach the English how to talk, and the Irish how to listen, society here would be quite civilized.
- **Oscar Wilde** 1854-1900 Irish dramatist and poet: *An Ideal Husband* (1895)

Cookery

see also **DIETS, FOOD**

For 30 years she served nothing but leftovers. The original meal was never found.   **Tracey Ullman**

1 English cooking: put things in hot water and take them out again after a while.
a French chef's view
 ▪ **Anonymous**: attributed

2 Anyone who tells a lie has not a pure heart, and cannot make a good soup.
 ▪ **Ludwig van Beethoven** 1770-1827 German composer: Ludwig Nohl *Beethoven Depicted by his Contemporaries* (1880)

3 Be content to remember that those who can make omelettes properly can do nothing else.
 ▪ **Hilaire Belloc** 1870-1953 British writer and Liberal politician: *A Conversation with a Cat* (1931)

4 Some women, it is said, like to cook. This book is not for them.
This book is for those of us who hate to, who have learned, through hard experience, that some activities become no less painful through repetition: childbearing, paying taxes, cooking. This book is for those of us who want to fold our big dishwater hands around a dry Martini instead of a wet flounder, come the end of a long day.
 ▪ **Peg Bracken** 1918-2007 American writer: *The 'I Hate to Cook' Book* (1960)

5 [My] standard position in regard to cooking is on the sofa with my feet up
 ▪ **Peg Bracken** 1918-2007 American writer: attributed, in *Guardian* 10 December 2007

6 The discovery of a new dish does more for the happiness of mankind than the discovery of a new star.
 ▪ **Anthelme Brillat-Savarin** 1755-1826 French jurist and gourmet: *Physiologie du Goût* (1826)

7 He said, 'I look for butterflies
That sleep among the wheat:

I make them into mutton-pies,
And sell them in the street.'
 ▪ **Lewis Carroll** 1832-98 English writer and logician: *Through the Looking-Glass* (1872)

8 I always give my bird a generous butter massage before I put it in the oven. Why? Because I think the chicken likes it—and, more importantly, I like it.
 ▪ **Julia Child** 1912-2004 American cook: attributed, but probably apocryphal

9 You cannot trust people who have such bad cuisine. It is the country with the worst food after Finland.
on the British
 ▪ **Jacques Chirac** 1932– French statesman: in *Times* 5 July 2005

10 I have made a *consommé* devoutly to be wished.
 ▪ **Noël Coward** 1899-1973 English dramatist, actor, and composer: Cole Lesley *Remembered Laughter* (1976); the phrase in fact appears as early as the nineteenth century

11 We approached our new microwave oven with the trepidation of two people returning to a reactor station after a leak.
 ▪ **Fanny Cradock** 1909-94 English cook: in *Daily Telegraph* 1979

12 An unwatched pot boils *immediately*.
 ▪ **H. F. Ellis** 1907-2000 English writer: in *Punch* February 1946

13 Old Italian chefs never die—they're just put out to pasta.
 ▪ **Shelby Friedman**: attributed

14 Heaven sends us good meat, but the Devil sends cooks.
 ▪ **David Garrick** 1717-79 English actor-manager: 'On Doctor Goldsmith's Characteristical Cookery' (1777)

15 She did not so much cook as
assassinate food.
- **Storm Jameson** 1891-1986 English novelist:
attributed

16 A cucumber should be well sliced, and
dressed with pepper and vinegar, and
then thrown out, as good for nothing.
- **Samuel Johnson** 1709-84 English poet,
critic, and lexicographer: James Boswell
Journal of a Tour to the Hebrides (1785)
5 October 1773

17 Sorry, I don't do offal.
*invited to help improve the food in the
Westminster kitchens*
- **Jamie Oliver** 1975- English chef and
broadcaster: in *Mail on Sunday* 15 June 2003

18 A woman always has half an onion left
over, no matter what the size of the
onion, the dish or the woman.
- **Terry Pratchett** 1948- English fantasy
writer: *Monstrous Regiment* (2003)

19 Her cooking is the missionary position
of cooking. That is how everybody starts.
defending Delia Smith
- **Egon Ronay** 1915-2010 Hungarian-born food
critic: in *Independent on Sunday* 1 November
1998

20 I read recipes the same way I read
science fiction. I get to the end and

I think, 'Well, that's not going to
happen'.
- **Rita Rudner** 1953- American comedienne
and writer: attributed

21 The cook was a good cook, as cooks go;
and as cooks go, she went.
- **Saki** 1870-1916 Scottish writer: *Reginald*
(1904)

22 'But why should you want to shield
him?' cried Egbert; 'the man is a
common murderer.' 'A common
murderer, possibly, but a very
uncommon cook.'
- **Saki** 1870-1916 Scottish writer: *Beasts and
Super-Beasts* (1914)

23 The most remarkable thing about my
mother is that for 30 years she served
nothing but leftovers. The original meal
was never found.
- **Tracey Ullman** 1959- English-born actress:
in *Observer* 23 May 1999

24 And now with some pleasure I find
that it's seven; and must cook dinner.
Haddock and sausage meat. I think it
is true that one gains a certain hold on
sausage and haddock by writing them
down.
- **Virginia Woolf** 1882-1941 English novelist:
diary, 8 March 1941

Countries and Peoples

see also **AMERICA, AUSTRALIA, BRITISH, CANADA, FRANCE, IRELAND**

Abroad is unutterably bloody and foreigners are fiends.   **Nancy Mitford**

1 I design coastlines. I got an award for
Norway.
- **Douglas Adams** 1952-2001 English science
fiction writer: *The Hitchhiker's Guide to the
Galaxy* (BBC radio, 1978)

2 It's where they commit suicide and the
king rides a bicycle, Sweden.
- **Alan Bennett** 1934- English dramatist and
actor: *Enjoy* (1980)

3 The sort of place to send your mother-
in-law for a month, all expenses paid.
of Pakistan, in a BBC Radio interview,

*17 March 1984; in April 1984 he was fined
£1000 for making the remark by the Test and
County Cricket Board*
- **Ian Botham** 1955- English cricketer: in
Times 20 March 1984

4 I'm a Red Sea pedestrian, and proud
of it!
Graham Chapman as 'Brian'
- **Graham Chapman** 1941-89, **John
Cleese** 1939- , and **others** British
comedians: *Monty Python's Life of Brian*
(1979 film)

5 They're Germans. Don't mention
the war.
- **John Cleese** 1939- and **Connie Booth**
1944- English and American-born comic
actors: *Fawlty Towers* (BBC TV programme,
1975)

6 *the French jazz critic Hugues Panassie had
given Condon a generally favourable notice:*
I don't see why we need a Frenchman
to come over here and tell us how to
play American music. I wouldn't think
of going to France and telling him how
to jump on a grape.
- **Eddie Condon** 1905-73 American jazz
musician: Bill Crow *Jazz Anecdotes* (1990)

7 To speak with your mouth full
And swallow with greed
Are national traits
Of the travelling Swede.
- **Duff Cooper** 1890-1954 British
Conservative politician, diplomat, and
writer: Philip Ziegler *Diana Cooper* (1981)

8 Don't let's be beastly to the Germans
When our Victory is ultimately won.
It was just those nasty Nazis who
persuaded them to fight
And their Beethoven and Bach are really
far worse than their bite,
- **Noël Coward** 1899-1973 English dramatist,
actor, and composer: 'Don't Let's Be
Beastly to the Germans' (1943)

9 Switzerland is a place where they don't
like to fight, so they get people to do
their fighting for them while they ski
and eat chocolate.
- **Larry David** 1947- American writer,
producer, and comedian: Curb Your
Enthusiasm (HBO TV, 2001) 'The Doll'

10 Get yourself a Geisha. The flower of Asia,
She's one with whom to take up.
At night your bed she'll make up,
And she'll be there when you wake up.
- **Howard Dietz** 1896-1983 American
songwriter: 'Get Yourself a Geisha' (1935)

11 When it comes to clichés, the Germans
are extremely diligent, efficient and
disciplined about living up to them.
- **Rainer Erlinger** 1965- German physician
and lawyer: in *Guardian* 27 January 2012

12 I'm not Jewish. I only look intelligent.
to Nazis in his cabaret audience, 1931
- **Werner Finck** 1902-78 German comedian:
Humphrey Carpenter *That Was Satire That
Was* (2000)

13 *on the reunification of Germany:*
It's like the Beatles coming together
again—let's hope they don't go on a
world tour.
- **Matt Frei** 1963- British journalist: in
Listener 21 June 1990

14 *on being asked his opinion of New Zealand:*
I find it hard to say, because when I was
there it seemed to be shut.
- **Clement Freud** 1924-2009 English
politician, broadcaster, and writer: *Quote...
Unquote* (BBC radio, 1978)

15 What cleanliness everywhere! You dare
not throw your cigarette into the lake.
No graffiti in the urinals. Switzerland
is proud of this; but I believe this is just
what she lacks: manure.
- **André Gide** 1869-1951 French novelist and
critic: diary, Lucerne, 10 August 1917

16 For he might have been a Roosian,
A French, or Turk, or Proosian,
Or perhaps Ital-ian!
But in spite of all temptations
To belong to other nations,
He remains an Englishman!
- **W. S. Gilbert** 1836-1911 English writer:
HMS Pinafore (1878)

17 Miles of cornfields, and ballet in the
evening.
of Russia
- **Alan Hackney** 1924-2009 English novelist:
Private Life (1958) (later filmed as *I'm All
Right Jack*, 1959)

18 Holland...lies so low they're only saved
by being dammed.
- **Thomas Hood** 1799-1845 English poet and
humorist: *Up the Rhine* (1840) 'Letter from
Martha Penny to Rebecca Page'

19 And we will all go together when
we go—
Every Hottentot and every Eskimo.
- **Tom Lehrer** 1928- American humorist:
'We Will All Go Together When We Go'
(1953)

20 In fact, I'm not really a *Jew*. Just Jew-*ish*.
Not the whole hog, you know.
- **Jonathan Miller** 1934- English writer and
director: *Beyond the Fringe* (1960 review)
'Real Class'

21 Frogs…are slightly better than Huns or
Wops, but abroad is unutterably bloody
and foreigners are fiends.
- **Nancy Mitford** 1904-73 English writer:
The Pursuit of Love (1945)

22 There's only two things I hate in this
world. People who are intolerant of
other people's cultures and the Dutch.
- **Mike Myers** 1963- Canadian actor:
Goldmember (2002 film, with Michael
McCullers), spoken by Michael Caine as
Nigel Powers

23 The people of Crete unfortunately
make more history than they can
consume locally.
- **Saki** 1870-1916 Scottish writer: *Chronicles of
Clovis* (1911)

24 I think he bought his doublet in Italy,
his round hose in France, his bonnet in
Germany, and his behaviour everywhere.
- **William Shakespeare** 1564-1616 English
dramatist: *The Merchant of Venice* (1596-8)

25 England and America are two countries
divided by a common language.
- **George Bernard Shaw** 1856-1950 Irish
dramatist: attributed in this and other forms,
but not found in Shaw's published writings

26 I look upon Switzerland as an inferior
sort of Scotland.
- **Sydney Smith** 1771-1845 English clergyman
and essayist: letter to Lord Holland, 1815

27 *a travelling companion on the Alps:*
They say if the Swiss had designed
these mountains, um, they'd be rather
flatter.
- **Paul Theroux** 1941- American novelist
and travel writer: 'Misery on the Orient
Express' in *Atlantic Monthly* July 1975

28 Lump the whole thing! say that the
Creator made Italy from designs by
Michael Angelo!
- **Mark Twain** 1835-1910 American writer:
The Innocents Abroad (1869)

29 I don't like Norwegians at all. The sun
never sets, the bar never opens, and the
whole country smells of kippers.
- **Evelyn Waugh** 1903-66 English novelist:
letter to Lady Diana Cooper, 13 July 1934

30 In Italy for thirty years under the
Borgias they had warfare, terror,
murder, bloodshed—they produced
Michelangelo, Leonardo da Vinci and
the Renaissance. In Switzerland they
had brotherly love, five hundred years
of democracy and peace and what did
that produce…? The cuckoo clock.
- **Orson Welles** 1915-85 American actor
and film director: *The Third Man* (1949
film); words added by Welles to Graham
Greene's script

31 I don't like Switzerland: it has
produced nothing but theologians
and waiters.
- **Oscar Wilde** 1854-1900 Irish dramatist and
poet: letter from Switzerland, 20 March
1899

The Country *see* **NATURE AND THE COUNTRY**

Cricket

see also **SPORTS**

....

Never read print, it spoils one's eye for the ball.　**W. G. Grace**

1 *when playing in a Lancashire league game, Dennis Lillee's ball hit the batsman on the leg. Although given out, the batsman remained at the crease, and Lillee insisted forcefully that he must go:*
I'd love to go Dennis but I daren't move. I think you've broken my bloody leg.
▪ **Anonymous**: Michael Parkinson *Sporting Lives* (1993)

2 *in Australian cricket, traditional line of wicket-keeper to new batsman:*
How's the wife and my kids?
▪ **Anonymous**: Simon Hughes *Yakking Around the World* (2000)

3 *the umpire to the bowler, after 'not out' was called when W. G. Grace was unexpectedly bowled first ball:*
They have paid to see Dr Grace bat, not to see you bowl.
▪ **Anonymous**: Harry Furniss *A Century of Grace* (1985); perhaps apocryphal

4 *after South Africa's 'Tufty' Mann had baffled George Mann of Middlesex with three successive deliveries in 1947:*
It is a clear case of Mann's inhumanity to Mann.
▪ **John Arlott** 1914-91 English journalist and broadcaster: *Another Word from Arlott* (1985)

5 *on being seen looking at a newspaper while fielding in the deep:*
I just wanted to find out who we were playing.
▪ **Warwick Armstrong** 1879-1947 Australian cricketer: during the 1921 Test match; G. F. Lamb *Apt and Amusing Quotations* (1988)

6 *on being approached for a contribution to W. G. Grace's testimonial:*
It's not in support of cricket but as an earnest protest against golf.
▪ **Max Beerbohm** 1872-1956 English critic, essayist, and caricaturist: attributed

7 The last positive thing England did for cricket was to invent it.
▪ **Ian Chappell** 1943- Australian cricketer: in *Mail on Sunday* 6 January 2002

8 Never read print, it spoils one's eye for the ball.
habitual advice to his players
▪ **W. G. Grace** 1848-1915 English cricketer: Harry Furniss *A Century of Grace* (1985)

9 Cricket—a game which the English, not being a spiritual people, have invented in order to give themselves some conception of eternity.
▪ **Lord Mancroft** 1914-87 British Conservative politician: *Bees in Some Bonnets* (1979)

10 *having watched a match at Lord's for several hours:*
MICHAEL DAVIE: Are you enjoying it?
GROUCHO MARX: It's great. When does it start?
▪ **Groucho Marx** 1890-1977 American film comedian: in *Daily Telegraph* 13 December 2005

11 It's a funny kind of month, October. For the really keen cricket fan it's when you discover your wife left you in May.
▪ **Denis Norden** 1922- English humorist: in *She* October 1977

12 Personally, I have always looked upon cricket as organized loafing.
view of a future archbishop of Canterbury in 1925
▪ **William Temple** 1881-1944 English theologian and archbishop: Michael Parkinson *Sporting Lives* (1993)

13 I need nine wickets from this match, and you buggers had better start drawing straws to see who I don't get.
to an opposing team
▪ **Freddie Trueman** 1931-2006 English cricketer: in *Ned Sherrin in his Anecdotage* (1993)

14 *asked if he thought anyone would surpass his*
achievement in taking 300 Test wickets:
If anyone beats it, they'll be bloody tired.
- **Freddie Trueman** 1931-2006 English
  cricketer: in 1964; quoted in obituary, *BBC
  Sport* (online edition) 1 July 2006

15 Fred, t'definitive volume on t'best fast
bowler that ever drew breath.
*suggested title for his biography; often quoted
as 't'finest bloody fast bowler…'*
- **Freddie Trueman** 1931-2006 English cricketer:
  Michael Parkinson *Sporting Profiles* (1995)

16 To the spectator, cricket is more a
therapy than a sport. It is like watching

fish dart about a pool.
- **Michael Wale** English journalist: Len
  Deighton and Adrian Bailey *London Dossier*
  (1967)

17 It's a well-known fact that, when I'm on
99, I'm the best judge of a run in all the
bloody world.
to Cyril Washbrook
- **Alan Wharton** 1923-93 English cricketer:
  Freddie Trueman *You Nearly Had Me That
  Time* (1978)

18 Cricket is basically baseball on valium.
- **Robin Williams** 1952- American actor:
  attributed

Crime and Punishment

see also **LAW, JUDGES**

One restaurant, you're in business, four restaurants it's the Mafia.   **Neil Simon**

1 It's a fairly unique position to have been
in: to have, at one stage, been in charge
of prison funding and then to have
been an inmate. I wish I'd been more
generous.
*former Chief Secretary to the Treasury
imprisoned for perjury in 1999*
- **Jonathan Aitken** 1942- British Conservative
  politician: in *Belfast Telegraph* 29 May 2000

2 I have kleptomania. But when it gets
bad, I take something for it.
- **Anonymous**: saying, associated with both
  Ken Dodd and Robert Benchley

3 Sammy, you've already lost one eye.
D'you wanna go for two?
gangster threatening Sammy Davis Jr
- **Anonymous**: Donald Zec *Put the Knife in
  Gently* (2003)

4 *Mafia hitman, on trial in Sicily for a double
murder:*
It was not me who killed those two
men because that night I was shooting
two other men.
- **Anonymous**: in *Mail on Sunday* 4 January
  2004 'Quotes of the Year'

5 When their lordships asked Bacon

How many bribes he had taken
He had at least the grace
To get very red in the face.
- **Edmund Clerihew Bentley** 1875-1956
  English writer: 'Bacon' (1939)

6 *to the prison chaplain who asked if he were
sewing (mailbags), when imprisoned for fraud:*
No, reaping.
- **Horatio Bottomley** 1860-1933 British
  newspaper proprietor and financier:
  S. T. Felstead *Horatio Bottomley* (1936)

7 What is robbing a bank compared with
founding a bank?
- **Bertolt Brecht** 1898-1956 German
  dramatist: *Die Dreigroschenoper* (1928)

8 Thieves respect property. They merely
wish the property to become their
property that they may more perfectly
respect it.
- **G. K. Chesterton** 1874-1936 English
  essayist, novelist, and poet: *The Man who
  was Thursday* (1908)

9 Thou shalt not steal; an empty feat,
When it's so lucrative to cheat.
- **Arthur Hugh Clough** 1819-61 English poet:
  'The Latest Decalogue' (1862)

10 Three juvenile delinquents,
Juvenile delinquents,
Happy as can be—we
Waste no time
On the wherefores and whys of it;
We like crime
And that's about the size of it.
- **Noël Coward** 1899-1973 English dramatist, actor, and composer: 'Three Juvenile Delinquents' (1949)

11 *of a burglar:*
He found it inconvenient to be poor.
- **William Cowper** 1731-1800 English poet: 'Charity' (1782)

12 *a prisoner before Mr Justice Darling objected to being called 'a professional crook':*
PRISONER: I've only done two jobs, and each time I've been nabbed.
LORD DARLING: It has never been suggested that you are successful in your profession.
- **Lord Darling** 1849-1936 English judge: Edward Maltby *Secrets of a Solicitor* (1929)

13 It's over, and can't be helped, and that's one consolation, as they always says in Turkey, ven they cuts the wrong man's head off.
- **Charles Dickens** 1812-70 English novelist: *Pickwick Papers* (1837)

14 It is quite a three-pipe problem, and I beg that you won't speak to me for fifty minutes.
- **Arthur Conan Doyle** 1859-1930 Scottish-born writer: *The Adventures of Sherlock Holmes* (1892) 'The Red-Headed League'

15 'Excellent,' I cried. 'Elementary,' said he.
- **Arthur Conan Doyle** 1859-1930 Scottish-born writer: *The Memoirs of Sherlock Holmes* (1894). 'Elementary, my dear Watson' is not found in any book by Conan Doyle, and first appears in P. G. Wodehouse *Psmith Journalist* (1915)

16 Major Strasser has been shot. Round up the usual suspects.
- **Julius J. Epstein** 1909-2001 and **others** American screenwriters: *Casablanca* (1942 film)

17 Hanging is too good for him. He must be posted to the infantry.
on being asked to endorse the execution of a cavalryman who sodomized his horse
- **Frederick the Great** 1712-86 Prussian monarch: Giles MacDonogh *Frederick the Great: a Life in Deed and Letters* (1999)

18 Awaiting the sensation of a short, sharp shock,
From a cheap and chippy chopper on a big black block.
- **W. S. Gilbert** 1836-1911 English writer: *The Mikado* (1885)

19 As some day it may happen that a victim must be found,
I've got a little list—I've got a little list
Of society offenders who might well be under ground
And who never would be missed—who never would be missed!
- **W. S. Gilbert** 1836-1911 English writer: *The Mikado* (1885)

20 It was beautiful and simple as all truly great swindles are.
- **O. Henry** 1862-1910 American short-story writer: *Gentle Grafter* (1908) 'Octopus Marooned'

21 Though he might be more humble, there is no police like Holmes.
- **Ernest Hornung** 1866-1921 English novelist: Arthur Conan Doyle *Memories and Adventures* (1924)

22 Let it appear in a criminal trial that the accused is a Sunday-school superintendent, and the jury says guilty almost automatically.
- **H. L. Mencken** 1880-1956 American journalist and literary critic: *Minority Report* (1956)

23 *on the campaign trail for Mayor of London:*
Death to anyone who drops chewing gum.
- **Steven Norris** 1945- British Conservative politician: in *Sunday Times* 13 June 2004

24 If I ever hear you accuse the police of using violence on a prisoner in custody again, I'll take you down to the station and beat the eyes out of your head.
- **Joe Orton** 1933-67 English dramatist: *Loot* (1966), spoken by Inspector Truscott

25 The most peaceable way for you, if you do take a thief, is, to let him show himself what he is and steal out of your company.
- **William Shakespeare** 1564-1616 English dramatist: *Much Ado About Nothing* (1598-9)

26 She starts to tell me how she's…married to an Italian with four restaurants on Long Island and right away I dig he's in with the mob. I mean one restaurant, you're in business, four restaurants it's the Mafia.
- **Neil Simon** 1927- American dramatist: *The Gingerbread Lady* (1970)

Critics and Criticism

A man who knows the way but can't drive the car. **Kenneth Tynan**

1 A bad review may spoil your breakfast but you shouldn't allow it to spoil your lunch.
- **Kingsley Amis** 1922-95 English novelist and poet: Giles Gordon *Aren't We Due a Royalty Statement?* (1993); attributed

2 Full many a gallant man lies slain
On Waterloo's ensanguined plain,
But none by bullet or by shot
Fell half so flat as Walter Scott.
comment on Scott's poem 'The Field of Waterloo' (1815), sometimes attributed to Thomas Erskine
- **Anonymous**: Una Pope-Hennessy *The Laird of Abbotsford* (1932)

3 It is a pity that the composer did not leave directions as to how flat he really did want it sung.
- **Anonymous**: review in *West Wilts Herald* 1893; Ned Sherrin *Cutting Edge* (1984)

4 Beware geeks bearing scripts.
headline to Nick Lowe's review of Troy
- **Anonymous**: in *Times Literary Supplement* 4 June 2004

5 There is less in this than meets the eye.
- **Tallulah Bankhead** 1903-68 American actress: of a revival of Maeterlinck's play 'Aglavaine and Selysette'; Alexander Woollcott *Shouts and Murmurs* (1922)

6 I have always thought it was a sound impulse by which he [Kipling] was driven to put his 'Recessional' into the waste-paper basket, and a great pity that Mrs Kipling fished it out and made

him send it to *The Times*.
- **Max Beerbohm** 1872-1956 English critic, essayist, and caricaturist: letter 30 October 1913

7 *apparent reassurance to a leading lady after a particularly bad first night:*
My dear, good is not the word.
- **Max Beerbohm** 1872-1956 English critic, essayist, and caricaturist: attributed; Nigel Rees *Cassell Dictionary of Humorous Quotations* (1999)

8 Critics are like eunuchs in a harem; they know how it's done, they've seen it done every day, but they're unable to do it themselves.
- **Brendan Behan** 1923-64 Irish dramatist: Jonathon Green (ed.) *A Dictionary of Contemporary Quotations* (1982)

9 Hebrews 13.8. [Jesus Christ, the same yesterday, and today, and forever.]
summing up the long-running 1920s Broadway hit Abie's Irish Rose
- **Robert Benchley** 1889-1945 American humorist: Peter Hay *Theatrical Anecdotes* (1987)

10 Listen, dear, you couldn't write 'fuck' in the dust on a Venetian blind.
to a Hollywood writer who had criticized Alan Bennett's 'An Englishman Abroad'
- **Coral Browne** 1913-91: attributed

11 COBBETT'S ENGLISH GRAMMAR This work has been published to the amount of fifty-five thousand copies, without ever having been mentioned

by the old shuffling bribed sots, called reviewers.
- **William Cobbett** 1762–1835 English reformer and journalist: *Cobbett's Political Register* (1825) 'A List of Mr Cobbett's Publications'

12 *on book reviewing:*
The thankless task of drowning other people's kittens.
- **Cyril Connolly** 1903–74 English writer: attributed; Stefan Collini *Common Reading* (2008)

13 *on the 1959 remake of* Ben Hur:
Loved Ben, hated Hur.
- **William Connor ('Cassandra')** 1909–67 English journalist: Robert Connor *Cassandra: Reflections in a Mirror* (1969)

14 It's about as long as *Parsifal*, and not as funny.
on Camelot
- **Noël Coward** 1899–1973 English dramatist, actor, and composer: Dick Richards *The Wit of Noël Coward* (1968)

15 *of Lionel Bart's musical* Blitz:
Just as long as the real thing and twice as noisy.
- **Noël Coward** 1899–1973 English dramatist, actor, and composer: Sheridan Morley *The Quotable Noël Coward* (1999)

16 *on leaving halfway through an especially cloying screening:*
My family has a history of diabetes.
- **Judith Crist** 1922–2012 American film critic: attributed, in *Esquire* 1976

17 You know who the critics are? The men who have failed in literature and art.
- **Benjamin Disraeli** 1804–81 British Tory statesman and novelist: *Lothair* (1870)

18 One of the most characteristic sounds of the English Sunday is the sound of Harold Hobson barking up the wrong tree.
on the notable theatre critic
- **Penelope Gilliatt** 1933–93 British writer: in *Encore* November–December 1959

19 I have knocked everything but the knees of the chorus girls, and nature has anticipated me there.
- **Percy Hammond** 1873–1936 American critic: Ned Sherrin *Cutting Edge* (1984)

20 Asking a working writer what he thinks about critics is like asking a lamp-post how it feels about dogs.
- **Christopher Hampton** 1946– English dramatist: in *Sunday Times Magazine* 16 October 1977

21 When I read something saying I've not done anything as good as *Catch-22* I'm tempted to reply, 'Who has?'
- **Joseph Heller** 1923–99 American novelist: in *Times* 9 June 1993

22 There is a sort of savage nobility about his firm reliance on his own bad taste.
of Richard Bentley's edition of Paradise Lost
- **A. E. Housman** 1859–1936 English poet: 'Introductory Lecture' (1892)

23 I want something that will keep me awake thinking it was the food I ate and not the show I saw.
after a disastrous preview
- **George S. Kaufman** 1889–1961 American dramatist: Howard Teichmann *George S. Kaufman* (1973)

24 The quickest way to start a punch-up between two British literary critics is to ask them what they think of the poems of Sir John Betjeman
- **Philip Larkin** 1922–85 English poet: introduction to *Collected Poems* (1971)

25 Mine was the kind of piece in which nobody knew what was going on, including the composer, the conductor, and the critics. Consequently I got pretty good notices.
- **Oscar Levant** 1906–72 American pianist: *A Smattering of Ignorance* (1940)

26 He took the praise as a greedy boy takes apple pie, and the criticism as a good dutiful boy takes senna-tea.
of Bulwer Lytton, whose novels he had criticized
- **Lord Macaulay** 1800–59 English politician and historian: letter, 5 August 1831

27 He takes the long review of things;
He asks and gives no quarter.
And you can sail with him on wings
Or read the book. It's shorter.
- **David McCord** 1897–1997 American poet: 'To A Certain Most Certainly Certain Critic' (1945)

28 I didn't like the play, but then I saw it under adverse conditions—the curtain was up.
- **Groucho Marx** 1890-1977 American film comedian: ad-lib, attributed in an interview by Marx to George S. Kaufman; Peter Hay *Broadway Anecdotes* (1989)

29 Reviewing here [in Baltimore] is a hazardous occupation. Once I spoke harshly of an eminent American novelist, and he retaliated by telling a very charming woman that I was non compos penis. In time she came to laugh at him as a liar.
- **H. L. Mencken** 1880-1956 American journalist and literary critic: letter to Hugh Walpole, 1922

30 And it is that word 'hummy', my darlings, that marks the first place in 'The House at Pooh Corner' at which Tonstant Weader fwowed up.
- **Dorothy Parker** 1893-1967 American critic and humorist: review in *New Yorker* 20 October 1928

31 In fact, now that you've got me right down to it, the only thing I didn't like about *The Barretts of Wimpole Street* was the play.
- **Dorothy Parker** 1893-1967 American critic and humorist: review in *New Yorker* 21 February 1931

32 *House Beautiful* is play lousy.
- **Dorothy Parker** 1893-1967 American critic and humorist: review in *New Yorker* 1933

33 Let my people go!
at a viewing of Exodus
- **Mort Sahl** 1926- Canadian-born American comedian: attributed, 1961; Nigel Rees *Cassell Dictionary of Humorous Quotations* (1999)

34 Last year I gave several lectures on 'Intelligence and the Appreciation of Music Among Animals'. Today I am going to speak to you about 'Intelligence and the Appreciation of Music Among Critics'. The subject is very similar.
- **Erik Satie** 1866-1925 French composer: Nat Shapiro (ed.) *An Encyclopedia of Quotations about Music* (1978)

35 Never pay any attention to what critics say...A statue has never been set up in honour of a critic!
- **Jean Sibelius** 1865-1957 Finnish composer: Bengt de Törne *Sibelius: A Close-Up* (1937)

36 I never read a book before reviewing it; it prejudices a man so.
- **Sydney Smith** 1771-1845 English clergyman and essayist: H. Pearson *The Smith of Smiths* (1934)

37 Of all the cants which are canted in this canting world,—though the cant of hypocrites may be the worst,—the cant of criticism is the most tormenting!
- **Laurence Sterne** 1713-68 English novelist: *Tristram Shandy* (1759-67)

38 As learned commentators view
In Homer more than Homer knew.
- **Jonathan Swift** 1667-1745 Irish poet and satirist: 'On Poetry' (1733)

39 *John Churton Collins, a rival of poet Edmund Gosse, launched a bitter critical attack on him. When Gosse took tea with Tennyson he found an ally who defined Collins as:*
A louse in the locks of literature.
- **Alfred, Lord Tennyson** 1809-92 English poet: Evan Charteris *Life and Letters of Sir Edmund Gosse* (1931)

40 My dear Sir: I have read your play. Oh, my dear Sir!
Yours faithfully.
rejecting a play
- **Herbert Beerbohm Tree** 1852-1917 English actor-manager: Peter Hay *Theatrical Anecdotes* (1987)

41 I believe that the trade of critic, in literature, music, and the drama, is the most degraded of all trades, and that it has no real value...However, let it go. It is the will of God that we must have critics, and missionaries, and Congressmen, and humorists, and we must bear the burden.
- **Mark Twain** 1835-1910 American writer: *Autobiography* (1924)

42 A critic is a man who knows the way but can't drive the car.
- **Kenneth Tynan** 1927-80 English theatre critic: in *New York Times Magazine* 9 January 1966

43 The original Greek is of great use in
elucidating Browning's translation of
the *Agamemnon*.
  ▪ **Robert Yelverton Tyrrell** 1844-1914 Irish
    classicist: habitual remark to students; Ulick
    O'Connor *Oliver St John Gogarty* (1964)

44 Critics search for ages for the wrong
word which, to give them credit, they
eventually find.
  ▪ **Peter Ustinov** 1921-2004 British actor,
    director, and writer: Ned Sherrin *Cutting
    Edge* (1984)

45 *Norman Mailer, annoyed at Vidal's literary
style of criticism, hit him over the head with a
glass tumbler:*
Ah, Mailer is, as usual, lost for words.
  ▪ **Gore Vidal** 1925-2012 American novelist
    and critic: attributed

46 Said a critic initialled E. N.
'Why does my wife like young men?'
A friend said: 'You fool,
Don't you know that the tool
Is mightier far than the pen?'
*in course of a feud with the music critic
Ernest Newman*
  ▪ **Peter Warlock** 1894-1930 English
    composer: attributed

47 WILDE: I shall always regard you as the
best critic of my plays.
TREE: But I have never criticized your
plays.
WILDE: That's why.
  ▪ **Oscar Wilde** 1854-1900 Irish dramatist and
    poet: conversation with Beerbohm Tree
    after the first-night success of *A Woman of
    No Importance*; Hesketh Pearson *Beerbohm
    Tree* (1956)

48 One must have a heart of stone to
read the death of Little Nell without
laughing.
  ▪ **Oscar Wilde** 1854-1900 Irish dramatist and
    poet: Ada Leverson *Letters to the Sphinx*
    (1930)

49 I HAVE BEEN LOOKING AROUND FOR AN
APPROPRIATE WOODEN GIFT AND AM
PLEASED HEREBY TO PRESENT YOU WITH
ELSIE FERGUSON'S PERFORMANCE IN HER
NEW PLAY.
*congratulatory telegram for George S.
Kaufman's fifth wedding anniversary*
  ▪ **Alexander Woollcott** 1887-1943 American
    writer: Howard Teichmann *George S.
    Kaufman* (1973)

50 This fictional account of the day-by-day
life of an English gamekeeper is still
of considerable interest to outdoor-
minded readers, as it contains many
passages on pheasant raising, the
apprehending of poachers, ways to
control vermin, and other chores and
duties of the professional gamekeeper.
Unfortunately one is obliged to wade
through many pages of extraneous
material in order to discover and savour
these sidelights on the management of
a Midlands shooting estate, and in this
reviewer's opinion this book cannot
take the place of J. R. Miller's *Practical
Gamekeeping*.
review of reissue of D. H. Lawrence Lady
Chatterley's Lover
  ▪ **Ed Zern** 1910-94 American humorous
    writer: in *Field and Stream* November 1959

Dance

···

I wish I could shimmy like my sister Kate, She shivers like the jelly on a plate.
Armand J. Piron

1 Dancing? Y-yes…dancing…I love…
dancing…(It makes me look like a coma
victim being stood up and zapped with
a cattle prod).
  ▪ **Jesse Armstrong** and **Sam Bain** 1971-
  British screenwriters: *Peep Show* (Channel 4
  TV, 2004), spoken by David Mitchell as
  Mark

2 I made the little buggers hop.
on conducting the Diaghilev Ballet
  ▪ **Thomas Beecham** 1879-1961 English
  conductor: attributed

3 *on dancing with another woman:*
Stately as a galleon, I sail across the
  floor,
Doing the Military Two-step, as in the
  days of yore…
So gay the band,
So giddy the sight,
Full evening dress is a must,
But the zest goes out of a beautiful
  waltz
When you dance it bust to bust.
  ▪ **Joyce Grenfell** 1910-79: 'Stately as a
  Galleon' (1978)

4 *on being asked whether the fashion for nudity*
would extend to dance:
No. You see there are portions of the
human anatomy which would keep
swinging after the music had finished.
  ▪ **Robert Helpmann** 1909-86 Australian
  dancer: Elizabeth Salter *Helpmann* (1978)

5 GROUCHO MARX: I could dance with you
till the cows come home. On second
thoughts, I'd rather dance with the
cows till you came home.
  ▪ **Bert Kalmar** 1884-1947 and **others**
  screenwriters: *Duck Soup* (1933 film)

6 Cheek to Cheek
Toes to Toes
Here's a dance you can do on a dime
Knees to Knees
Nose to Nose
Slowly move, and you're doin' 'The
  Slime'.
  ▪ **Jerry Leiber** 1933-2011 American songwriter:
  'The Slime' (1942)

7 Dancing is wonderful training for girls,
it's the first way you learn to guess what
a man is going to do before he does it.
  ▪ **Christopher Morley** 1890-1957 American
  writer: *Kitty Foyle* (1939)

8 He waltzes like a Protestant curate.
  ▪ **Kate O'Brien** 1897-1974 Irish novelist: *The
  Last of Summer* (1943)

9 I wish I could shimmy like my sister Kate,
She shivers like the jelly on a plate.
  ▪ **Armand J. Piron** 1888-1943 American jazz
  musician: 'Shimmy like Kate' (1919)

10 If the Louvre custodian can,
If the Guard Republican can,
If Van Gogh and Matisse and Cézanne
  can,
Baby, you can can-can too.
  ▪ **Cole Porter** 1891-1964 American
  songwriter: 'Can-Can' (1953)

11 [Dancing is] a perpendicular expression
of a horizontal desire.
  ▪ **George Bernard Shaw** 1856-1950 Irish
  dramatist: in *New Statesman* 23 March 1962

12 'Can you dance?' said the girl. Lancelot
gave a short, amused laugh. He was a
man who never let his left hip know
what his right hip was doing.
  ▪ **P. G. Wodehouse** 1881-1975 English-born
  writer: *Meet Mr Mulliner* (1927)

Dating

see also **MARRIAGE, RELATIONSHIPS, ROMANCE**

....

I would worship the ground you walk on, Audrey, if you only lived in a better neighbourhood.　**Billy Wilder**

1　*'Mrs Merton' to Debbie McGee:*
But what first, Debbie, attracted you to millionaire Paul Daniels?
- **Caroline Aherne** 1963–　English comedian: *The Mrs Merton Show* (BBC TV)

2　*Niles notices Roz checking out a man:*
NILES: Are you quite finished undressing him with your eyes?
ROZ: Oh, please. I'm already looking for my stockings and trying to remember where I parked my car.
- **David Angell** 1946-2001, **Peter Casey**, and **David Lee** American television producers: *Frasier* (NBC TV, 1996) 'A Crane's Critique', written by Dan Cohen and F. J. Pratt; spoken by David Hyde Pierce and Peri Gilpin

3　*of Woodrow Wilson:*
When the President proposed to the second Mrs Wilson, she was so surprised that she fell out of bed.
- **Anonymous**: anecdote, probably apocryphal; recalled by Anthony Howard in *Times* 1 April 2003

4　Tell me about yourself—your struggles, your dreams, your telephone number.
- **Peter Arno** 1904-68 American cartoonist: attributed

5　Courtship to marriage, as a very witty prologue to a very dull play.
- **William Congreve** 1670-1729 English dramatist: *The Old Bachelor* (1693)

6　I will not...sulk about having no boyfriend, but develop inner poise and authority and sense of self as woman of substance, complete *without* boyfriend, as best way to obtain boyfriend.
- **Helen Fielding** 1958–　British writer: *Bridget Jones's Diary* (1996)

7　A fine romance with no kisses.
A fine romance, my friend, this is.
We should be like a couple of hot tomatoes,
But you're as cold as yesterday's mashed potatoes.
- **Dorothy Fields** 1905-74 American songwriter: 'A Fine Romance' (1936 song)

8　On a plane...you can pick up more and better people than on any other public conveyance since the stagecoach.
- **Anita Loos** 1893-1981 American writer: in *New York Times Biographical Service* 1973

9　In European countries, there are more princes than dentists.
on finding a suitable man
- **Tara Palmer-Tomkinson** 1971–　English socialite: in *Sunday Times* 22 July 2012

10　When a girl marries she exchanges the attentions of many men for the inattention of one.
- **Helen Rowland** 1875-1950 American writer: Evan Esar *The Dictionary of Humorous Quotations* (1949)

11　Whenever I date a guy, I think: Is this the man I want my children to spend their weekends with?
- **Rita Rudner** 1953–　American comedienne and writer: attributed

12　Won't you come into the garden?
I would like my roses to see you.
- **Richard Brinsley Sheridan** 1751-1816 Irish dramatist and Whig politician: to a young lady; attributed

13　How can a bishop marry? How can he flirt? The most he can say is, 'I will see you in the vestry after service.'
- **Sydney Smith** 1771-1845 English clergyman and essayist: Lady Holland *Memoir* (1855)

14　An engagement should come on a young girl as a surprise, pleasant or unpleasant, as the case may be.
- **Oscar Wilde** 1854-1900 Irish dramatist and poet: *The Importance of Being Earnest* (1895)

15 *when courting his future wife (whom he married in 1949):*
I would worship the ground you walk on, Audrey, if you only lived in a better neighbourhood.
- **Billy Wilder** 1906-2002 American screenwriter and director: M. Zolotow *Billy Wilder in Hollywood* (1977)

16 All my friends started getting boyfriends. But I didn't want a boyfriend, I wanted a thirteen colour biro.
- **Victoria Wood** 1953- British writer and comedienne: attributed

Death

see also **EPITAPHS, FUNERALS, LAST WORDS, MURDER**

....

Either he's dead, or my watch has stopped.   **Groucho Marx**

1 It's not that I'm afraid to die. I just don't want to be there when it happens.
- **Woody Allen** 1935- American film director, writer, and actor: *Death* (1975)

2 I don't want to achieve immortality through my work...I want to achieve it through not dying.
- **Woody Allen** 1935- American film director, writer, and actor: Eric Lax *Woody Allen and his Comedy* (1975)

3 Death has got something to be said for it:
There's no need to get out of bed for it;
Wherever you may be,
They bring it to you, free.
- **Kingsley Amis** 1922-95 English novelist and poet: 'Delivery Guaranteed' (1979)

4 Regret to inform you Hand that rocked the cradle kicked the bucket.
- **Anonymous**: reported telegram; in *Ned Sherrin in his Anecdotage* (1993)

5 [Death is] nature's way of telling you to slow down.
- **Anonymous**: American life insurance proverb, in *Newsweek* 25 April 1960

6 I want to die in my sleep like my grandfather...not screaming and yelling like the passengers in his car.
- **Anonymous**: modern saying

7 Am I dying, or is this my birthday?
on seeing all her children assembled in her last illness
- **Nancy Astor** 1879-1964 American-born British Conservative politician: attributed

8 We met...Dr Hall in such very deep mourning that either his mother, his wife, or himself must be dead.
- **Jane Austen** 1775-1817 English novelist: letter to Cassandra Austen, 17 May 1799

9 Even death is unreliable: instead of zero it may be some ghastly hallucination, such as the square root of minus one.
- **Samuel Beckett** 1906-89 Irish dramatist, novelist, and poet: attributed

10 When I came back to Dublin, I was courtmartialled in my absence and sentenced to death in my absence, so I said they could shoot me in my absence.
- **Brendan Behan** 1923-64 Irish dramatist: *Hostage* (1958)

11 When I am dead, I hope it may be said:
'His sins were scarlet, but his books were read.'
- **Hilaire Belloc** 1870-1953 British writer and Liberal politician: 'On His Books' (1923)

12 What I like about Clive
Is that he is no longer alive.
There is a great deal to be said
For being dead.
- **Edmund Clerihew Bentley** 1875-1956 English writer: 'Clive' (1905)

13 I believe in reincarnation, so I've left all my money to myself.
- **Tony Blackburn** 1943- English disc jockey: in *The Oldie* May 2003

14 I saw that show 'Fifty Things To Do Before You Die'. I would have thought the obvious one was 'Shout For Help'.
- **Jimmy Carr** 1972- Irish comedian: attributed

15 This parrot is no more! It has ceased to be! It's expired and gone to meet its maker! This is a late parrot! It's a stiff! Bereft of life it rests in peace — if you hadn't nailed it to the perch it would be pushing up the daisies! It's rung down the curtain and joined the choir invisible! THIS IS AN EX-PARROT!
- **Graham Chapman** 1941-89, **John Cleese** 1939- , and **others** British comedians: *Monty Python's Flying Circus* (BBC TV programme, 1969)

16 Thou shalt not kill; but need'st not strive Officiously to keep alive.
- **Arthur Hugh Clough** 1819-61 English poet: 'The Latest Decalogue' (1862)

17 I'm amazed he was such a good shot.
on being told that his accountant had blown his brains out
- **Noël Coward** 1899-1973 English dramatist, actor, and composer: in *Ned Sherrin's Theatrical Anecdotes* (1991)

18 I read the *Times* and if my name is not in the obits I proceed to enjoy the day.
- **Noël Coward** 1899-1973 English dramatist, actor, and composer: attributed

19 He'd make a lovely corpse.
- **Charles Dickens** 1812-70 English novelist: *Martin Chuzzlewit* (1844)

20 Can I unmoved see thee dying
On a log,
Expiring frog!
- **Charles Dickens** 1812-70 English novelist: *Pickwick Papers* (1837)

21 Take away that emblem of mortality.
on being offered an air cushion to sit on, 1881
- **Benjamin Disraeli** 1804-81 British Tory statesman and novelist: Robert Blake *Disraeli* (1966)

22 When I die I want to decompose in a barrel of porter and have it served in all the pubs in Dublin. I wonder would they know it was me?
- **J. P. Donleavy** 1926- Irish-American novelist: *Ginger Man* (1955)

23 Some of you may die, but that is a sacrifice I am willing to make.
- **Ted Elliott** and **others** screenwriters: *Shrek* (2001 film), spoken by John Lithgow as Lord Farquaad

24 In this world nothing can be said to be certain, except death and taxes.
- **Benjamin Franklin** 1706-90 American politician, inventor, and scientist: letter to Jean Baptiste Le Roy, 13 November 1789

25 He makes a very handsome corpse and becomes his coffin prodigiously.
- **Oliver Goldsmith** 1730-74 Irish writer: *The Good-Natured Man* (1768)

26 Billy, in one of his nice new sashes,
Fell in the fire and was burnt to ashes;
Now, although the room grows chilly,
I haven't the heart to poke poor Billy.
- **Harry Graham** 1874-1936 British writer and journalist: 'Tender-Heartedness' (1899)

27 Once you're dead, you're made for life.
- **Jimi Hendrix** 1942-70 American rock musician: c.1968, attributed; Nigel Rees *Cassell Dictionary of Humorous Quotations* (1999)

28 *during his last illness:*
If Mr Selwyn calls again, show him up: if I am alive I shall be delighted to see him; and if I am dead he would like to see me.
- **Lord Holland** 1705-74 English Whig politician: J. H. Jesse *George Selwyn and his Contemporaries* (1844)

29 I had an interest in death from an early age. It fascinated me. When I heard 'Humpty Dumpty sat on a wall,' I thought, 'Did he fall or was he pushed?'
- **P. D. James** 1920- English writer: in *Paris Review* 1995

30 But there, everything has its drawbacks, as the man said when his mother-in-law died, and they came down upon him for the funeral expenses.
- **Jerome K. Jerome** 1859-1927 English writer: *Three Men in a Boat* (1889)

31 Depend upon it, Sir, when a man knows he is to be hanged in a fortnight,

it concentrates his mind wonderfully.
- **Samuel Johnson** 1709-84 English poet, critic, and lexicographer: James Boswell *Life of Samuel Johnson* (1791) 19 September 1777

32 *ex-President Eisenhower's death prevented her photograph appearing on the cover of* Newsweek*:*
Fourteen heart attacks and he had to die in my week. In MY week.
- **Janis Joplin** 1943-70 American singer: in *New Musical Express* 12 April 1969

33 *on how he would kill himself:*
With kindness.
- **George S. Kaufman** 1889-1961 American dramatist: Howard Teichmann *George S. Kaufman* (1973)

34 I detest life-insurance agents; they always argue that I shall some day die, which is not so.
- **Stephen Leacock** 1869-1944 Canadian humorist: *Literary Lapses* (1910)

35 Death is the most convenient time to tax rich people.
- **David Lloyd George** 1863-1945 British Liberal statesman: in *Lord Riddell's Intimate Diary of the Peace Conference and After,* 1918-23 (1933)

36 Either he's dead, or my watch has stopped.
- **Groucho Marx** 1890-1977 American film comedian: in *A Day at the Races* (1937 film; script by Robert Pirosh, George Seaton, and George Oppenheimer)

37 Death and taxes and childbirth! There's never any convenient time for any of them.
- **Margaret Mitchell** 1900-49 American novelist: *Gone with the Wind* (1936)

38 Jimmy Hoffa's most valuable contribution to the American labour movement came at the moment he stopped breathing—on July 30th, 1975.
- **Dan E. Moldea** American writer: *The Hoffa Wars* (1978)

39 One dies only once, and it's for such a long time!
- **Molière** 1622-73 French comic dramatist: *Le Dépit amoureux* (performed 1656, published 1662)

40 *on his deathbed, asked by an acquaintance how he was:*
Hovering between wife and death.
- **James Montgomery** 1870-1943 Irish businessman and film censor: Ulick O'Connor *Oliver St John Gogarty* (1964)

41 *during the Boxer rising it was erroneously reported that those besieged in the Legation quarter of Peking, including the* Times *correspondent Dr Morrison, had been massacred. Morrison cabled the paper:*
Have just read obituary in the Times. Kindly adjust pay to suit.
- **George Ernest Morrison** 1862-1920 Australian journalist: Claud Cockburn *In Time of Trouble* (1956); attributed

42 Drink and dance and laugh and lie
Love, the reeling midnight through
For tomorrow we shall die!
(But, alas, we never do.)
- **Dorothy Parker** 1893-1967 American critic and humorist: 'The Flaw in Paganism' (1937)

43 *on being told by Robert Benchley that Calvin Coolidge had died:*
How can they tell?
- **Dorothy Parker** 1893-1967 American critic and humorist: Ned Sherrin in *The Listener* 8 January 1987

44 Guns aren't lawful;
Nooses give;
Gas smells awful;
You might as well live.
- **Dorothy Parker** 1893-1967 American critic and humorist: 'Résumé' (1937)

45 Not louder shrieks to pitying heav'n are cast,
When husbands or when lapdogs breathe their last.
- **Alexander Pope** 1688-1744 English poet: *The Rape of the Lock* (1714)

46 'Don't think of it as dying,' said Death. 'Just think of it as leaving early to avoid the rush.'
- **Terry Pratchett** 1948- and **Neil Gaiman** 1960- English fantasy writers: *Good Omens* (1990)

47 Luca Brasi sleeps with the fishes.
- **Mario Puzo** 1920-99 American novelist: *The Godfather* (1972 film); spoken by Richard S. Castellano as Peter Clemenza

48 Next week, or next month, or next year I'll kill myself. But I might as well last out my month's rent, which has been paid up, and my credit for breakfast in the morning.
- **Jean Rhys** c.1890-1979 British novelist and short-story writer: *Good Morning, Midnight* (1967)

49 When I die sprinkle my ashes over the 80s.
- **Dave Lee Roth** 1955- American rock singer: attributed

50 Waldo is one of those people who would be enormously improved by death.
- **Saki** 1870-1916 Scottish writer: *Beasts and Super-Beasts* (1914)

51 Ain't it grand to be blooming well dead?
- **Leslie Sarony** 1897-1985 British songwriter: title of song (1932)

52 I read the obituaries every day just for the satisfaction of not seeing my name there.
- **Neil Simon** 1927- American dramatist: *Last of the Red Hot Lovers* (1970)

53 Death is always a great pity of course but it's not as though the alternative were immortality.
- **Tom Stoppard** 1937- British dramatist: *Jumpers* (rev. ed. 1986)

54 Early to rise and early to bed makes a male healthy and wealthy and dead.
- **James Thurber** 1894-1961 American humorist: 'The Shrike and the Chipmunks'; in *New Yorker* 18 February 1939

55 He was just teaching me my death duties.
on her deathbed, having been visited by her solicitor to put her affairs in order
- **Lady Tree** 1863-1937 English actress: in *Ned Sherrin in his Anecdotage* (1993)

56 *after his obituary appeared prematurely:*
The report of my death was an exaggeration.
usually quoted as, 'Reports of my death have been greatly exaggerated'
- **Mark Twain** 1835-1910 American writer: in *New York Journal* 2 June 1897

57 I refused to attend his funeral, but I wrote a very nice letter explaining that I approved of it.
on hearing of the death of a corrupt politician
- **Mark Twain** 1835-1910 American writer: James Munson (ed.) *The Sayings of Mark Twain* (1992)

58 Death is very sophisticated. It's like a Noel Coward comedy. You light a cigarette and wait for it in the library.
- **Theadora Van Runkle** 1928-2011 American costume designer: attributed, in *Viva* April 1974

59 *of Truman Capote's death:*
Good career move.
- **Gore Vidal** 1925-2012 American novelist and critic: attributed

60 Just think who we'd have been seen dead with!
on discovery that her name, with Noël Coward's, had been on the Nazi blacklist for arrest and probable execution
- **Rebecca West** 1892-1983 English novelist and journalist: postcard to Noël Coward, 1945

61 *at the mention of a huge fee for a surgical operation:*
Ah, well, then, I suppose that I shall have to die beyond my means.
- **Oscar Wilde** 1854-1900 Irish dramatist and poet: R. H. Sherard *Life of Oscar Wilde* (1906)

62 *of the wallpaper in the room where he was dying:*
One of us must go.
- **Oscar Wilde** 1854-1900 Irish dramatist and poet: attributed, probably apocryphal

Debt

see also **MONEY, POVERTY**

....

If I hadn't my debts I shouldn't have anything to think about.   **Oscar Wilde**

1 *on Allied war debts:*
They hired the money, didn't they?
- **Calvin Coolidge** 1872-1933 American
Republican statesman: John H. McKee
Coolidge: Wit and Wisdom (1933)

2 Any further letters and I shall remove
my overdraft.
*telegram, c.1959, to his bankers, who
had become alarmed at his expensive
undergraduate lifestyle*
- **Bobby Corbett** 1940-99: in his obituary,
Daily Telegraph 13 March 1999

3 Annual income twenty pounds, annual
expenditure nineteen nineteen six,
result happiness. Annual income
twenty pounds, annual expenditure
twenty pounds ought and six, result
misery.
- **Charles Dickens** 1812-70 English novelist:
David Copperfield (1850)

4 Good news rarely comes in a brown
envelope.
- **Henry D'Avigdor Goldsmid** 1909-76
British businessman and Conservative
politician: John Betjeman, letter to
Tom Driberg, 21 July 1976

5 [My father] taught me two things about
bills; always query them and never pay

till you have no alternative.
- **Miles Kington** 1941-2008 English humorist:
Welcome to Kington (1989)

6 In the midst of life we are in debt.
- **Ethel Watts Mumford** 1878-1940 American
humorist: *Altogether New Cynic's Calendar*
(1907, with Addison Mizner and Oliver
Herford)

7 If the spoken word is repeated often
enough, it is eventually written and thus
made permanent...Many a decent man
who has written a bad cheque knows
the truth of that.
- **Flann O'Brien** 1911-66 Irish novelist and
journalist: *Myles Away from Dublin* (1990)

8 I feel these days like a very large
flamingo. No matter what way I turn,
there is always a very large bill.
- **Joseph O'Connor** 1963- Irish novelist:
The Secret World of the Irish Male (1994)

9 The National Debt is a very Good
Thing and it would be dangerous to pay
it off, for fear of Political Economy.
- **W. C. Sellar** 1898-1951 and **R. J. Yeatman**
1898-1968: *1066 and All That* (1930)

10 If I hadn't my debts I shouldn't have
anything to think about.
- **Oscar Wilde** 1854-1900 Irish dramatist and
poet: *A Woman of No Importance* (1893)

Definitions

··

Knowledge is knowing a tomato is a fruit; Wisdom is not putting it in a fruit salad.   **Miles Kington**

1 *definition of an acquaintance:*
A person whom we know well enough to borrow from, but not well enough to lend to.
- **Ambrose Bierce** 1842–c.1914 American writer: *The Cynic's Word Book* (1906)

2 A pianoforte is a harp in a box.
- **Leigh Hunt** 1784–1859 English poet and essayist: *The Seer* (1840)

3 What is originality? Undetected plagiarism.
- **William Ralph Inge** 1860–1954 English writer: *Labels and Libels* (1929)

4 Discretion is the polite word for hypocrisy.
view from the centre of the 1963 Profumo Scandal
- **Christine Keeler** 1942–   English model and showgirl: attributed

5 Doorman: a genius who can open the door of your car with one hand, help you in with the other and still have one left for the tip.
- **Dorothy Kilgallen** 1913–65 American journalist: attributed, 1950

6 Knowledge is knowing a tomato is a fruit; Wisdom is not putting it in a fruit salad.
- **Miles Kington** 1941–2008 English humorist: in *Independent* 28 March 2003

7 A gossip is one who talks to you about others; a bore is one who talks to you about himself; and a brilliant conversationalist is one who talks to you about yourself.
- **Lisa Kirk** 1925–90 American actress and singer: in *New York Journal-American* 9 March 1954

8 Do you know the difference between involvement and commitment? Think of ham and eggs. The chicken is involved. The pig is committed.
- **Martina Navratilova** 1956–   Czech-born American tennis player: in *Newsweek* 6 September 1982

9 Being powerful is like being a lady—if you have to tell people you are, you aren't.
- **Margaret Thatcher** 1925–2013 British Conservative stateswoman: attributed; originally said by American trade unionist Jesse Carr, in *Newsweek* 27 September 1976, but now more commonly associated with Thatcher

Democracy

see also **GOVERNMENT, POLITICS**

··

Hell, I never vote for anybody. I always vote against.   **W. C. Fields**

1 Democracy means government by discussion, but it is only effective if you can stop people talking.
- **Clement Attlee** 1883–1967 British Labour statesman: speech at Oxford, 14 June 1957

2 Democracy must be something more than two wolves and a sheep voting on what to have for dinner.
- **James Bovard** 1956–   American writer: *Lost Rights* (1994)

3 A majority is always the best repartee.
  - **Benjamin Disraeli** 1804-81 British Tory statesman and novelist: *Tancred* (1847)

4 Hell, I never vote *for* anybody. I always vote *against*.
  - **W. C. Fields** 1880-1946 American humorist: Robert Lewis Taylor *W. C. Fields* (1950)

5 Democracy is the name we give the people whenever we need them.
  - **Robert, Marquis de Flers** 1872-1927 and **Armand de Caillavet** 1869-1915 French dramatists: *L'habit vert* (1913)

6 I always voted at my party's call,
  And I never thought of thinking for myself at all.
  - **W. S. Gilbert** 1836-1911 English writer: *HMS Pinafore* (1878)

7 *on John F. Kennedy's electoral victory in Wisconsin:*
  A triumph for democracy. It proves that a millionaire has just as good a chance as anybody else.
  - **Bob Hope** 1903-2003 American comedian: TV programme (1960); William Robert Faith *Bob Hope* (1983)

8 Democracy is the theory that the common people know what they want, and deserve to get it good and hard.
  - **H. L. Mencken** 1880-1956 American journalist and literary critic: *A Little Book in C major* (1916)

9 Under democracy one party always devotes its energies to trying to prove that the other party is unfit to rule—and both commonly succeed and are right.
  - **H. L. Mencken** 1880-1956 American journalist and literary critic: *Minority Report* (1956)

10 Every government is a parliament of whores. The trouble is, in a democracy the whores are us.
  - **P. J. O'Rourke** 1947- American humorous writer: *Parliament of Whores* (1991)

11 All animals are equal but some animals are more equal than others.
  - **George Orwell** 1903-50 English novelist: *Animal Farm* (1945)

12 *on the death of a supporter of Proportional Representation:*
  He has joined what even he would admit to be the majority.
  - **John Sparrow** 1906-92 English academic: J. A. Gere and John Sparrow (eds.) *Geoffrey Madan's Notebooks* (1981)

13 It's not the voting that's democracy, it's the counting.
  - **Tom Stoppard** 1937- British dramatist: *Jumpers* (1972)

14 Democracy is the recurrent suspicion that more than half of the people are right more than half of the time.
  - **E. B. White** 1899-1985 American humorist: in *New Yorker* 3 July 1944

15 Democracy means simply the bludgeoning of the people by the people for the people.
  - **Oscar Wilde** 1854-1900 Irish dramatist and poet: *Sebastian Melmoth* (1891)

16 *a voter canvassed by Wilkes had declared that he would sooner vote for the devil:*
  And if your friend is not standing?
  - **John Wilkes** 1727-97 English parliamentary reformer: Raymond Postgate 'That Devil Wilkes' (1956 rev. ed.)

Depression

Noble deeds and hot baths are the best cures for depression. **Dodie Smith**

1 Dr Sillitoes's got him on tablets for depression...A lot of better-class people get it apparently.
  - **Alan Bennett** 1934- English dramatist and actor: *Enjoy* (1980)

2 He's really turned his life around. He used to be depressed and miserable. Now he's miserable and depressed.
  - **David Frost** 1939- English broadcaster and writer: on TV-AM, 1984

3 Noble deeds and hot baths are the best cures for depression.
- **Dodie Smith** 1896-1990 English novelist and dramatist: *I Capture the Castle* (1949)

4 Depression is melancholy minus its charms.
- **Susan Sontag** 1933-2004 American writer: *Illness as Metaphor* (1978)

5 Depression is merely anger without enthusiasm.
- **Steven Wright** 1955- American comedian: attributed

Description

His smile bathed us like warm custard. **Basil Boothroyd**

1 Though I yield to no one in my admiration for Mr Coolidge, I do wish he did not look as if he had been weaned on a pickle.
- **Anonymous**: remark recorded in Alice Roosevelt Longworth *Crowded Hours* (1933)

2 *after a party given by Dorothy Parker:*
The less I behave like Whistler's Mother the night before, the more I look like her the morning after.
- **Tallulah Bankhead** 1903-68 American actress: R. E. Drennan *Wit's End* (1973)

3 About as cuddly as a cornered ferret.
of Anne Robinson
- **Lynn Barber** 1944- English journalist: in *Times* 27 October 2001

4 His smile bathed us like warm custard.
- **Basil Boothroyd** 1910-88 English writer: *Let's Move House* (1977)

5 A high altar on the move.
of Edith Sitwell
- **Elizabeth Bowen** 1899-1973 Anglo-Irish writer: V. Glendinning *Edith Sitwell* (1981)

6 Damn description, it is always disgusting.
- **Lord Byron** 1788-1824 English poet: letter 6 August 1809

7 What can you do with a man who looks like a female llama surprised when bathing?
of Charles de Gaulle
- **Winston Churchill** 1874-1965 British Conservative statesman: in conversation, c.1944; David Fraser *Alanbrooke* (1982)

8 Like the silver plate on a coffin.
describing Robert Peel's smile
- **John Philpot Curran** 1750-1817 Irish judge: quoted by Daniel O'Connell, House of Commons 26 February 1835

9 A day away from Tallulah is like a month in the country.
- **Howard Dietz** 1896-1983 American songwriter: *Dancing in the Dark* (1974)

10 *of Arnold Schwarzenegger:*
I once described him as looking like a brown condom full of walnuts.
- **Clive James** 1939- Australian critic and writer: in *Daily Mail* 20 August 2003

11 A man who so much resembled a Baked Alaska—sweet, warm and gungy on the outside, hard and cold within.
of C. P. Snow
- **Francis King** 1923- British writer: *Yesterday Came Suddenly* (1993)

12 His appearance with his large features and rich mane of hair suggested the attempt of some archaic sculptor only acquainted with sheep to achieve a lion by hearsay.
- **Osbert Lancaster** 1908-86 English writer and cartoonist: *All Done From Memory* (1953)

13 [He looks like] an explosion in a pubic hair factory.
of Paul Johnson
- **Jonathan Miller** 1934- English writer and director: Alan Watkins *Brief Lives* (1982)

14 Her face showed the kind of ferocious disbelief with which Goneril must have taken the news that her difficult old father King Lear had decided to retire and move in with her.
- **Frank Muir** 1920-98 English writer and broadcaster: *The Walpole Orange* (1993)

15 Rudyard Kipling's eyebrows are very odd indeed! They curl up black and furious like the moustache of a Neapolitan tenor.
- **Harold Nicolson** 1886-1968 English diplomat, politician, and writer: diary 8 January 1930

16 A rose-red sissy half as old as time.
- **William Plomer** 1903-73 South African poet and novelist: 'Playboy of the Demi-World: 1938' (1945)

17 She fitted into my biggest armchair as if it had been built round her by someone who knew they were wearing armchairs tight about the hips that season.
- **P. G. Wodehouse** 1881-1975 English writer: *My Man Jeeves* (1919)

18 Roderick Spode? Big chap with a small moustache and the sort of eye that can open an oyster at sixty paces?
- **P. G. Wodehouse** 1881-1975 English writer: *The Code of the Woosters* (1938)

Despair *see* HOPE AND DESPAIR

Diaries

I always say, keep a diary and some day it'll keep you. **Mae West**

1 A page of my Journal is like a cake of portable soup. A little may be diffused into a considerable portion.
- **James Boswell** 1740-95 Scottish lawyer: *Journal of a Tour to the Hebrides* (1785)

2 What is more dull than a discreet diary? One might just as well have a discreet soul.
- **Chips Channon** 1897-1958 American-born British Conservative politician: diary, 26 July 1935

3 To write a diary every day is like returning to one's own vomit.
- **Enoch Powell** 1912-98 British Conservative politician: interview in *Sunday Times* 6 November 1977

4 I have decided to keep a full journal, in the hope that my life will perhaps seem more interesting when it is written down.
- **Sue Townsend** 1946- English writer: *Adrian Mole: The Wilderness Years* (1993)

5 I always say, keep a diary and some day it'll keep you.
- **Mae West** 1892-1980 American film actress: *Every Day's a Holiday* (1937 film)

6 I never travel without my diary. One should always have something sensational to read in the train.
- **Oscar Wilde** 1854-1900 Irish dramatist and poet: *The Importance of Being Earnest* (1895)

Dictionaries

Defining what is unknown in terms of something equally unknown.   **Flann O'Brien**

1 Big dictionaries are nothing but
storerooms with infrequently visited
and dusty corners.
- **Richard W. Bailey** 1939-2011 American
lexicographer: *Images of English* (1991)

2 Like Webster's Dictionary, we're
Morocco bound.
- **Johnny Burke** 1908-64 American
songwriter: *The Road to Morocco* (1942 film),
title song

3 The greatest masterpiece in literature is
only a dictionary out of order.
- **Jean Cocteau** 1889-1963 French dramatist
and film director: attributed

4 Short dictionaries should be improved
because they are intended for people
who actually need help.
- **William Empson** 1906-84 English poet and
literary critic: attributed

5 *Lexicographer*. A writer of dictionaries,
a harmless drudge.
- **Samuel Johnson** 1709-84 English poet,
critic, and lexicographer: *A Dictionary of the
English Language* (1755)

6 *of his coinage of the phrase 'life's rich pageant':*
The compilers of *The Oxford Dictionary
of Quotations*...have finally decided that
the phrase, such as it is, was my own
invention and it is to be credited to
me. Let me assure you that this small
feather in my cap has not gone, so to
speak, to my head.
- **Arthur Marshall** 1910-89 British journalist:
Life's Rich Pageant (1984)

7 A bad business, opening dictionaries;
a thing I very rarely do. I try to make
it a rule never to open my mouth,
dictionaries, or hucksters' shops.
- **Flann O'Brien** 1911-66 Irish novelist and
journalist: *The Best of Myles* (1968)

8 *on dictionaries:*
Defining what is unknown in terms of
something equally unknown.
- **Flann O'Brien** 1911-66 Irish novelist and
journalist: *Myles Away from Dublin* (1990)

9 I've been in *Who's Who*, and I know
what's what, but it'll be the first time
I ever made the dictionary.
*on having an inflatable life jacket named
after her*
- **Mae West** 1892-1980 American actress:
letter to the RAF, early 1940s

Diets

You die of a heart attack but so what? You die thin.   **Bob Geldof**

1 The only time to eat diet food is while
you're waiting for the steak to cook.
- **Julia Child** 1912-2004 American cook:
attributed

2 Give me a dozen heart-breaks like that
if you think it would help me lose one
pound.
- **Colette** 1873-1954 French novelist: *Cheri* (1920)

3 I'm on a whisky diet. I've lost three days
already.
- **Tommy Cooper** 1921-84 British comedian:
attributed

4 So far I've always kept my diet secret
but now I might as well tell everyone
what it is...Lots of grapefruit
throughout the day and plenty of

virile young men.
- **Angie Dickinson** 1931– American actress: in *Daily Mirror* 1 October 1985; see **comebacks** 12

5 You die of a heart attack but so what? You die thin.
on the Atkins diet
- **Bob Geldof** 1954– Irish rock musician: in *Independent* 23 August 2003

6 I'm of the pie-eaters' liberation front. I'm fat and proud to be fat.
- **Boris Johnson** 1964– British Conservative politician: at the Conservative party conference; in *Independent* 5 October 2006

7 A great many people in Los Angeles are on strict diets that restrict their intake of synthetic foods. The reason for this seems to be the widely held belief that organically grown fruits and vegetables make the cocaine work faster.
- **Fran Lebowitz** 1946– American writer: *Social Studies* (1982)

8 Life, if you're fat, is a minefield—you have to pick your way, otherwise you blow up.
- **Miriam Margolyes** 1941– British-born actress: in *Observer* 9 June 1991

9 Is Elizabeth Taylor fat? Her favourite food is seconds.
- **Joan Rivers** 1933– American comedienne: attributed

10 EDINA: You are what you eat remember, darling.
SAFFY: Which would make you a large vegetarian tart.
- **Jennifer Saunders** 1958– English actress and writer: *Absolutely Fabulous* (BBC1 TV, 1993) 'Birthday'

11 Little snax,
Bigger slax.
- **Ruth S. Schenley** American writer: attributed; Michèle Brown and Ann O'Connor *Hammer and Tongues* (1986)

12 Free your mind, and your bottom will follow.
- **Sarah, Duchess of York** 1959– : slimming advice, 2001

Diplomacy

see also **POLITICS**

Forever poised between a cliché and an indiscretion. **Harold Macmillan**

1 *on the Council of Europe:*
If you open that Pandora's Box, you never know what Trojan 'orses will jump out.
- **Ernest Bevin** 1881-1951 British Labour politician and trade unionist: Roderick Barclay *Ernest Bevin and the Foreign Office* (1975)

2 We exchanged many frank words in our respective languages.
- **Peter Cook** 1937-95 English satirist and actor: *Beyond the Fringe* (1961 revue)

3 American *diplomacy*. It's like watching somebody trying to do joinery with a chainsaw.
- **James Hamilton-Paterson** 1941– English writer: *Griefwork* (1993)

4 Kissinger brought peace to Vietnam the same way Napoleon brought peace to Europe: by losing.
- **Joseph Heller** 1923-99 American novelist: *Good as Gold* (1979)

5 Diplomacy—lying in state.
- **Oliver Herford** 1863-1935 English-born American humorist: Laurence J. Peter (ed.) *Quotations for Our Time* (1977)

6 There cannot be a crisis next week. My schedule is already full.
- **Henry Kissinger** 1923– American politician: in *New York Times Magazine* 1 June 1969

7 The great nations have always acted like gangsters, and the small nations

like prostitutes.
- **Stanley Kubrick** 1928-99 American film
director: in *Guardian* 5 June 1963

8 *on the life of a Foreign Secretary:*
Forever poised between a cliché and an
indiscretion.
- **Harold Macmillan** 1894-1986 British
Conservative statesman: in *Newsweek*
30 April 1956

9 I liken the French/British relationship
to a very old married couple who often
think of killing each other but would
never dream of divorce.
*on the revelation that in 1956 the French
Prime Minister Guy Mollet suggested to
Anthony Eden a union between the United
Kingdom and France*
- **Denis MacShane** 1948- British Labour
politician: in *Times* (online edition)
15 January 2007

10 The French are masters of 'the dog ate
my homework' school of diplomatic
relations.
- **P. J. O'Rourke** 1947- American humorous
writer: *Holidays in Hell* (1988)

11 Lord Palmerston, with characteristic
levity had once said that only three
men in Europe had ever understood
[the Schleswig-Holstein question],
and of these the Prince Consort was
dead, a Danish statesman (unnamed)
was in an asylum, and he himself had
forgotten it.
- **Lord Palmerston** 1784-1865 British
statesman: R. W. Seton-Watson *Britain in
Europe 1789-1914* (1937)

12 The chief distinction of a diplomat is
that he can say no in such a way that

it sounds like yes.
- **Lester Bowles Pearson** 1897-1972 Canadian
statesman: Geoffrey Pearson *Seize the Day*
(1993)

13 In return for a handsomely bound
facsimile of Palestrina's music, the
Vicar of God was rewarded with a
signed photograph of the Grocer
and a gramophone record of himself
conducting an orchestra.
*of a meeting between the Pope and Edward
Heath*
- **Nicholas Shakespeare** 1957- British
writer: in *The Spectator* 19/26 December
1992

14 There is a story that when Mrs
Thatcher first met Gorbachev he gave
her a ball-point and she offered him
Labour-voting Scotland.
- **Nicholas Shakespeare** 1957- British
writer: in *The Spectator* 19/26 December
1992

15 A diplomat...is a person who can tell
you to go to hell in such a way that you
actually look forward to the trip.
- **Caskie Stinnett** 1911-98 American writer:
Out of the Red (1960) ch. 4

16 A diplomat these days is nothing but a
head-waiter who's allowed to sit down
occasionally.
- **Peter Ustinov** 1921-2004 British actor,
director, and writer: *Romanoff and Juliet*
(1956)

17 An ambassador is an honest man sent to
lie abroad for the good of his country.
- **Henry Wotton** 1568-1639 English poet
and diplomat: written in the album of
Christopher Fleckmore in 1604

Discontent *see* SATISFACTION AND DISCONTENT

Divorce

see also **MARRIAGE**

....

Love the quest; marriage the conquest; divorce the inquest.   **Helen Rowland**

1 It was partially my fault that we got divorced…I tended to place my wife under a pedestal.
  - **Woody Allen** 1935- American film director, writer, and actor: 'I Had a Rough Marriage' (monologue, 1964)

2 Your experience will be a lesson to all us men to be careful not to marry ladies in very high positions.
  to Lord Snowdon on the break-up of his marriage to Princess Margaret
  - **Idi Amin** 1925-2003 Ugandan president: attributed; Nigel Rees *Cassell Dictionary of Humorous Quotations* (1999)

3 The husband was a teetotaller, there was no other woman, and the conduct complained of was that he had drifted into the habit of winding up every meal by taking out his false teeth and hurling them at his wife.
  - **Arthur Conan Doyle** 1859-1930 Scottish-born writer: *The Adventures of Sherlock Holmes* (1892) 'A Case of Identity'

4 He taught me housekeeping; when I divorce I keep the house.
  - **Zsa Zsa Gabor** 1917- Hungarian-born film actress: of her fifth husband; Ned Sherrin *Cutting Edge* (1984)

5 I don't think I'll get married again. I'll just find a woman I don't like and give her a house.
  - **Lewis Grizzard** 1946-94 American humorous writer: attributed

6 A TV host asked my wife, 'Have you ever considered divorce?' She replied: 'Divorce never, murder often.'
  - **Charlton Heston** 1924-2008 American actor: in *Independent* 21 July 1999

7 *on how he and his wife managed to stay married for 33 years:*
  Well, we never wanted to get divorced at the same time.
  - **Bruce Paltrow** 1943-2002 American film producer: in *Daily Mail* 2 May 2013

8 Love the quest; marriage the conquest; divorce the inquest.
  - **Helen Rowland** 1875-1950 American writer: *Reflections of a Bachelor Girl* (1909)

9 Don't get mad, get everything.
  advice to wronged wives
  - **Ivana Trump** 1949- Czech former wife of Donald Trump: spoken in *The First Wives Club* (film, 1996)

Dogs *see* **CATS AND DOGS**

Doubt *see* **CERTAINTY AND DOUBT**

Dreams *see* **SLEEP AND DREAMS**

Dress

··

She wears her clothes, as if they were thrown on her with a pitchfork.
Jonathan Swift

1 If my jeans could talk they'd plead for
mercy.
  ▪ **Phyllis Diller** 1917-2012 American actress:
    The Joys of Ageing—And How to Avoid Them
    (1981)

2 *to Sir Frederick Ponsonby, who had proposed
  accompanying him in a tail-coat:*
  I thought everyone must know that a
  short jacket is always worn with a silk
  hat at a private view in the morning.
  ▪ **Edward VII** 1841-1910 British king: Philip
    Magnus *Edward VII* (1964)

3 *when Lord Harris appeared at Ascot in a
  brown bowler:*
  Goin' rattin', 'Arris?
  ▪ **Edward VII** 1841-1910 British king: Michael
    Hill *Right Royal Remarks* (2003)

4 When he buys his ties he has to ask if
  gin will make them run.
  ▪ **F. Scott Fitzgerald** 1896-1940 American
    novelist: *Notebooks* (1978)

5 *Dame Edna to Judy Steel:*
  Tell me the history of that frock, Judy.
  It's obviously an old favourite. You were
  wise to remove the curtain rings.
  ▪ **Barry Humphries** 1934- Australian actor
    and writer: *Another Audience with Dame
    Edna* (TV, 1984); Nigel Rees (ed.) *Cassell
    Dictionary of Humorous Quotations* (1999)

6 You should never have your best
  trousers on when you go out to fight for
  freedom and truth.
  ▪ **Henrik Ibsen** 1828-1906 Norwegian
    dramatist: *An Enemy of the People* (1882)

7 A silk dress in four sections, and shoes
  with high heels that would have broken
  the heart of John Calvin.
  ▪ **Stephen Leacock** 1869-1944 Canadian
    humorist: *Arcadian Adventures with the Idle
    Rich* (1914)

8 My little rebellion was to have my tie
  loose, with the top button of my shirt
  undone, but Paul'd always come up

to me and put it straight.
  ▪ **John Lennon** 1940-80 English pop singer
    and songwriter: *John Lennon: in His Own
    Words* (1980)

9 *when a waiter at Buckingham Palace spilled
  soup on her dress:*
  Never darken my Dior again!
  ▪ **Beatrice Lillie** 1894-1989 Canadian-born
    comedienne: *Every Other Inch a Lady* (1973)

10 A woman's dress should be like a
   barbed wire fence: serving its purpose
   without obstructing the view.
   ▪ **Sophia Loren** 1934- Italian actress: in *Mail
     on Sunday* 30 March 2003

11 There is something silly about a man
   who wears a white suit all the time,
   especially in New York.
   of Tom Wolfe
   ▪ **Norman Mailer** 1923-2007 American
     novelist and essayist: in *Smart* August 1989

12 *of 'Fred Fernackerpan, a Mystery Goblin',
   who walked about the town with his trousers
   deployed à la Grand Old Duke of York:*
   And when they were up they were up
   And when they were down they were
     down
   And when they were only half way up
   He was arrested.
   ▪ **Spike Milligan** 1918-2002 Irish comedian:
     Alexander Games *The Essential Spike
     Milligan* (2002)

13 *on being asked what she wore in bed:*
   Chanel No. 5.
   ▪ **Marilyn Monroe** 1926-62 American actress:
     Pete Martin *Marilyn Monroe* (1956)

14 The officers of this branch of the Force
   [the Obscene Publications Squad at
   Scotland Yard] have a discouraging club
   tie, on which a book is depicted being
   cut in half by a larger pair of scissors.
   ▪ **John Mortimer** 1923-2009 English novelist,
     barrister, and dramatist: *Clinging to the
     Wreckage* (1982)

15 There was a young belle of old Natchez
Whose garments were always in patchez.
When comment arose
On the state of her clothes,
She drawled, When Ah itchez,
    Ah scratchez.
  ▪ **Ogden Nash** 1902-71 American humorist:
  'Requiem' (1938)

16 The only really firm rule of taste
about cross dressing is that neither
sex should ever wear anything they
haven't yet figured out how to go to
the bathroom in.
  ▪ **P. J. O'Rourke** 1947- American humorous
  writer: *Modern Manners* (1984)

17 Fur is a subject that makes sensitive toes
curl in their leather shoes.
introducing a discussion on fur coats
  ▪ **Jeremy Paxman** 1950- British journalist
  and broadcaster: in *Mail on Sunday*
  13 February 2000 'Quotes of the Week'

18 My wife liked the costume. She asked
me to bring it home.
on his costume as Achilles in the film Troy
  ▪ **Brad Pitt** 1963- American actor: in CBS
  News (online ed.) 14 May 2004

19 A dress has no meaning unless it makes
a man want to take it off.
  ▪ **Françoise Sagan** 1935-2004 French novelist:
  in *Observer* 14 December 1969

20 We know Jesus can't have been English.
He is always wearing sandals, but never
with socks.
  ▪ **Linda Smith** 1958-2006 British comedian:
  in *Independent* 25 August 1994

21 She wears her clothes, as if they were
thrown on her with a pitchfork.
  ▪ **Jonathan Swift** 1667-1745 Irish poet and
  satirist: *Polite Conversation* (1738)

22 She wore far too much rouge last night,
and not quite enough clothes. That is
always a sign of despair in a woman.
  ▪ **Oscar Wilde** 1854-1900 Irish dramatist and
  poet: *An Ideal Husband* (1895)

Drink

see also **CHAMPAGNE, DRUNKENNESS, WINE**

Some weasel took the cork out of my lunch.   **W. C. Fields**

1 Let's get out of these wet clothes and
into a dry Martini.
  ▪ **Anonymous**: line coined in the 1920s by
  Robert Benchley's press agent and adopted
  by Mae West in *Every Day's a Holiday* (1937
  film)

2 Alcohol doesn't solve any problems…
but then again, neither does milk.
  ▪ **Anonymous**: modern saying

3 Only Irish coffee provides in a single
glass all essential food groups—alcohol,
caffeine, sugar and fat.
  ▪ **Anonymous**: modern saying

4 One reason why I don't drink is because
I wish to know when I am having a
good time.
  ▪ **Nancy Astor** 1879-1964 American-born
  British Conservative politician: in *Christian
  Herald* June 1960

5 At Dirty Dick's and Sloppy Joe's
We drank our liquor straight,
Some went upstairs with Margery,
And some, alas, with Kate.
  ▪ **W. H. Auden** 1907-73 English poet: 'The
  Sea and the Mirror' (1944)

6 I saw a notice which said 'Drink Canada
Dry' and I've just started.
  ▪ **Brendan Behan** 1923-64 Irish dramatist:
  attributed (probably not original); Nigel
  Rees *Cassell Dictionary of Humorous
  Quotations* (1999)

7 *on being told that the particular drink he was
consuming was slow poison:*
So who's in a hurry?
  ▪ **Robert Benchley** 1889-1945 American
  humorist: Nathaniel Benchley *Robert
  Benchley* (1955)

8 Often Daddy sat up very late working on a case of Scotch.
  ▪ **Robert Benchley** 1889-1945 American humorist: *Pluck and Luck* (1925)

9 I have taken more out of alcohol than alcohol has taken out of me.
  ▪ **Winston Churchill** 1874-1965 British Conservative statesman: Quentin Reynolds *By Quentin Reynolds* (1964)

10 *on being invited by a friend to dine at a Middle Eastern restaurant:*
  The aftertaste of foreign food spoils the clean, pure flavour of gin for hours.
  ▪ **Eddie Condon** 1905-73 American jazz musician: Bill Crow *Jazz Anecdotes* (1990)

11 *when seriously ill and given a blood transfusion:*
  This must be Fats Waller's blood. I'm getting high.
  ▪ **Eddie Condon** 1905-73 American jazz musician: Bill Crow *Jazz Anecdotes* (1990)

12 Sure I eat what I advertise. Sure I eat Wheaties for breakfast. A good bowl of Wheaties with Bourbon can't be beat.
  ▪ **Dizzy Dean** 1910-74 American baseball player: in *Guardian* 23 December 1978

13 I understand that absinthe makes the tart grow fonder.
  ▪ **Ernest Dowson** 1867-1900 English poet: letter to Arthur Moore, February 1889

14 There is wan thing, an' on'y wan thing, to be said in favour iv dhrink, an' that is that it has caused manny a lady to be loved that otherwise might've died single.
  ▪ **Finley Peter Dunne** 1867-1936 American humorous writer: *Mr. Dooley Says* (1910)

15 A man shouldn't fool with booze until he's fifty; then he's a damn fool if he doesn't.
  ▪ **William Faulkner** 1897-1962 American novelist: James M. Webb and A. Wigfall Green *William Faulkner of Oxford* (1965)

16 Some weasel took the cork out of my lunch.
  ▪ **W. C. Fields** 1880-1946 American humorist: *You Can't Cheat an Honest Man* (1939 film)

17 I always keep a supply of stimulant handy in case I see a snake—which I also keep handy.
  ▪ **W. C. Fields** 1880-1946 American humorist: Corey Ford *Time of Laughter* (1970); attributed

18 A woman drove me to drink and I never even had the courtesy to thank her.
  ▪ **W. C. Fields** 1880-1946 American humorist: attributed

19 Best while you have it use your breath, There is no drinking after death.
  ▪ **John Fletcher** 1579-1625 English dramatist: *The Bloody Brother*, or *Rollo Duke of Normandy* (with Ben Jonson and others, performed c.1616)

20 Maybe alcohol picks you up a little bit, but it sure lets you down in a hurry.
  ▪ **Betty Ford** 1918-2011 American First Lady: attributed; Frank S. Pepper *20th Century Quotations* (1984)

21 There is no such thing as a small whisky.
  ▪ **Oliver St John Gogarty** 1878-1957 Irish writer and surgeon: attributed

22 To alcohol! The cause of...and solution to...all of life's problems.
  Homer Simpson
  ▪ **Matt Groening** 1954- American humorist and satirist: *The Simpsons* 'Homer vs. the Eighteenth Amendment' (1997) written by John Swartzwelder

23 The House of Lords is sitting in its judicial capacity this afternoon, and while I may be drunk as a lord I must be sober as a judge.
  refusing another drink from the political journalist Robin Oakley
  ▪ **Lord Hailsham** 1907-2001 British Conservative politician: anecdote; in *Spectator* 5 April 2003

24 I went out with a guy who once told me I didn't need to drink to make myself more fun to be around. I told him, I'm drinking so that you're more fun to be around.
  ▪ **Chelsea Handler** 1975- American comedienne and writer: attributed

25 We drink one another's healths, and spoil our own.
  ▪ **Jerome K. Jerome** 1859-1927 English writer: *Idle Thoughts of an Idle Fellow* (1886)

26 Claret is the liquor for boys; port, for men; but he who aspires to be a hero (smiling) must drink brandy.
- **Samuel Johnson** 1709-84 English poet, critic, and lexicographer: James Boswell *Life of Samuel Johnson* (1791) 7 April 1779

27 When I makes tea I makes tea, as old mother Grogan said. And when I makes water I makes water...*Begob, ma'am,* says Mrs Cahill, *God send you don't make them in the one pot.*
- **James Joyce** 1882-1941 Irish novelist: *Ulysses* (1922)

28 The Lord above made liquor for temptation
To see if man could turn away from sin.
The Lord above made liquor for temptation—but
With a little bit of luck,
With a little bit of luck,
When temptation comes you'll give right in!
- **Alan Jay Lerner** 1918-86 American songwriter: 'With a Little Bit of Luck' (1956)

29 I don't drink liquor. I don't like it. It makes me feel good.
- **Oscar Levant** 1906-72 American pianist: in *Time* 5 May 1958

30 I distrust camels, and anyone else who can go a week without a drink.
- **Joe E. Lewis** 1902-71 American comedian: attributed

31 Heineken refreshes the parts other beers cannot reach.
- **Terry Lovelock**: slogan for Heineken lager, 1975 onwards

32 Love makes the world go round? Not at all. Whisky makes it go round twice as fast.
- **Compton Mackenzie** 1883-1972 English novelist: *Whisky Galore* (1947)

33 Prohibition makes you want to cry into your beer and denies you the beer to cry into.
- **Don Marquis** 1878-1937 American poet and journalist: *Sun Dial Time* (1936)

34 I'd hate to be a teetotaller. Imagine getting up in the morning and knowing that's as good as you're going to feel all day.
- **Dean Martin** 1917-95 American singer and actor: attributed; also attributed to Jimmy Durante and Frank Sinatra

35 I'm ombibulous. I drink every known alcoholic drink, and enjoy them all.
- **H. L. Mencken** 1880-1956 American journalist and literary critic: attributed

36 Candy
Is dandy
But liquor
Is quicker.
- **Ogden Nash** 1902-71 American humorist: 'Reflections on Ice-breaking' (1931)

37 I'll take a lemonade!...In a dirty glass!
- **Norman Panama** 1914-2003 and **Melvin Frank** 1913-88 screenwriters: in *Road to Utopia* (1946 film; words spoken by Bob Hope)

38 So make it another old-fashioned, please.
Leave out the cherry,
Leave out the orange,
Leave out the bitters,
Just make it a straight rye!
- **Cole Porter** 1891-1964 American songwriter: 'Make it Another Old-Fashioned, Please' (1940)

39 Look here, Steward, if this is coffee, I want tea; but if this is tea, then I wish for coffee.
- **Punch** 1841-1992 English humorous weekly periodical: vol. 123 (1902)

40 And the sooner the tea's out of the way, the sooner we can get out the gin, eh?
- **Henry Reed** 1914-86 English poet and dramatist: *Private Life of Hilda Tablet* (1954 radio play)

41 PORTER: Drink, sir, is a great provoker of three things.
MACDUFF: What three things does drink especially provoke?
PORTER: Marry, sir, nose-painting, sleep, and urine. Lechery, sir, it provokes, and unprovokes; it provokes the desire, but it takes away the performance.
- **William Shakespeare** 1564-1616 English dramatist: *Macbeth* (1606)

42 I'm only a beer teetotaller, not a
champagne teetotaller.
- **George Bernard Shaw** 1856-1950 Irish
dramatist: *Candida* (1898)

43 Alcohol…enables Parliament to do
things at eleven at night that no sane
person would do at eleven in the
morning.
- **George Bernard Shaw** 1856-1950 Irish
dramatist: *Major Barbara* (1907)

44 Gin was mother's milk to her.
- **George Bernard Shaw** 1856-1950 Irish
dramatist: *Pygmalion* (1916)

45 A bumper of good liquor
Will end a contest quicker
Than justice, judge, or vicar.
- **Richard Brinsley Sheridan** 1751-1816 Irish
dramatist and Whig politician: *The Duenna*
(1775)

46 *when told that drinking would ruin the coat
of his stomach:*
Then my stomach must digest its
waistcoat.
- **Richard Brinsley Sheridan** 1751-1816
Irish dramatist and Whig politician: in
Sheridaniana (1826)

47 First the man takes a drink,
Then the drink takes a drink,
Then the drink takes the man!
- **Edward Rowland Sill** 1841-87 American
educator and writer: 'An Adage from the
Orient' (1883)

48 Is that bottle just going to sit up there
or are you going to turn it into a lamp?
- **Neil Simon** 1927- American dramatist:
Last of the Red Hot Lovers (1970)

49 There are two things that will be
believed of any man whatsoever, and
one of them is that he has taken to drink.
- **Booth Tarkington** 1869-1946 American
novelist: *Penrod* (1914)

50 *of Edvard Grieg:*
Checking into the Betty Fjord Clinic.
- **Dick Vosburgh** 1929-2007 and **Denis King**:
Beauty and the Beards (2001)

51 I have a rare intolerance to herbs which
means I can only drink fermented
liquids, such as gin.
- **Julie Walters** 1950- British actress: in
Observer 14 March 1999

52 During one of my treks through
Afghanistan, we lost our corkscrew.
Compelled to live on food and water…
for several days.
- **Mae West** 1892-1980 and **W. C. Fields**
1880-1946: *My Little Chickadee* (1940 film),
spoken by W. C. Fields as Cuthbert J. Twillie

Driving

Speed has never killed anyone, suddenly becoming stationary…that's what
gets you. **Jeremy Clarkson**

1 *of Annie's parking:*
That's OK, we can walk to the kerb
from here.
- **Woody Allen** 1935- American film
director, writer, and actor: *Annie Hall*
(1977 film)

2 You're not stuck in traffic. You are
traffic.
- **Anonymous**: German transport campaign
slogan, in *Guardian* 4 September 2010

3 Have you ever noticed that anybody
driving slower than you is an idiot,
and anyone going faster than you is a
maniac?
- **George Carlin** 1937-2008 American
comedian: attributed

4 Speed has never killed anyone.
Suddenly becoming stationary, that's
what gets you.
- **Jeremy Clarkson** 1960- English
broadcaster: attributed, in *Sunday Times*
28 January 2007

5 I don't understand bus lanes. Why
do poor people have to get to places

quicker than I do?
- **Jeremy Clarkson** 1960– English broadcaster: attributed, in *Sydney Morning Herald* 1 February 2008

6 Somebody actually complimented me on my driving today. They left a little note on the windscreen. It said: 'Parking fine'.
- **Tommy Cooper** 1921-84 British comedian: attributed

7 [There are] only two classes of pedestrians in these days of reckless motor traffic—the quick, and the dead.
- **Lord Dewar** 1864-1930 British industrialist: George Robey *Looking Back on Life* (1933)

8 A woman driver is one who drives like a man and gets blamed for it.
- **Patricia Ledger**: in *Toledo Blade* 15 April 1958

9 In Milan, traffic lights are instructions. In Rome, they are suggestions. In Naples, they are Christmas decorations.
- **Antonio Martino** 1942– Italian politician: in *Sunday Times* 24 February 2002

Drugs

Reality is a crutch for people who can't cope with drugs.   **Lily Tomlin**

1 I'll tell you what, that crack is really moreish.
- **Jesse Armstrong** and **Sam Bain** 1971– British screenwriters: *Peep Show* (Channel 4 TV, 2004), spoken by Matt King as Super Hans

2 LSD? Nothing much happened, but I did get the distinct impression that some birds were trying to communicate with me.
- **W. H. Auden** 1907-73 English poet: George Plimpton (ed.) *The Writer's Chapbook* (1989)

3 Cocaine habit-forming? Of course not. I ought to know. I've been using it for years.
- **Tallulah Bankhead** 1903-68 American actress: *Tallulah* (1952)

4 *the number one thing he has learned after fifty years in the business:*
You start out playing rock 'n' roll so you can have sex and do drugs. But you end up doing drugs so you can still play rock 'n' roll and have sex.
- **Mick Jagger** 1943– English rock musician: on *The Late Show* (CBS TV) 11 December 2012

5 *warning his young son John to avoid opium on account of its 'terrible binding effect'*
Have you ever seen the pictures of the wretched poet Coleridge? He smoked opium. Take a look at Coleridge, he was green about the gills and a stranger to the lavatory.
- **Clifford Mortimer** British lawyer: John Mortimer *Clinging to the Wreckage* (1982)

6 Sure thing, man. I used to be a laboratory myself once.
on being asked to autograph a fan's school chemistry book
- **Keith Richards** 1943– English rock musician: in *Independent on Sunday* 7 August 1994

7 Reality is a crutch for people who can't cope with drugs.
- **Lily Tomlin** 1939– American comedienne and actress: attributed; Phil Hammond and Michael Mosley *Trust Me (I'm a Doctor)* 1999

8 Cocaine is God's way of saying you're making too much money.
- **Robin Williams** 1952– American actor: in *New York Magazine* 31 August 1981

Drunkenness and Hangovers

see also **DRINK**

But I'm not so think as you drunk I am. **J. C. Squire**

1 R-E-M-O-R-S-E!
Those dry Martinis did the work for
me;
Last night at twelve I felt immense,
Today I feel like thirty cents.
My eyes are bleared, my coppers hot,
I'll try to eat, but I cannot.
It is no time for mirth and laughter,
The cold, grey dawn of the morning
after.
  ▪ **George Ade** 1866-1944 American humorist
  and dramatist: *The Sultan of Sulu* (1903)

2 *asked to devise an advertising slogan for
Guinness:*
Guinness makes you drunk.
  ▪ **Brendan Behan** 1923-64 Irish dramatist:
  attributed, perhaps apocryphal

3 One evening in October, when I was
one-third sober,
An' taking home a 'load' with manly
pride;
My poor feet began to stutter, so I lay
down in the gutter,
And a pig came up an' lay down by my
side;
Then we sang 'It's all fair weather when
good fellows get together,'
Till a lady passing by was heard to say:
'You can tell a man who "boozes" by
the company he chooses'
And the pig got up and slowly walked
away.
  ▪ **Benjamin Hapgood Burt** 1880-1950
  American songwriter: 'The Pig Got Up and
  Slowly Walked Away' (1933)

4 Take the juice of two quarts of whisky.
recommended hangover cure
  ▪ **Eddie Condon** 1905-73 American jazz
  musician: in *New York Sunday News* 10 June
  1951

5 I often sit back and think 'I wish I'd
done that' and find out later that

I already have.
  ▪ **Richard Harris** 1930-2002 Irish actor: in *Sun*
  19 May 1988

6 I don't get hangovers. You have to stop
drinking to get a hangover.
  ▪ **Lemmy** 1945- English rock musician: in
  Observer 10 November 2002

7 You're not drunk if you can lie on the
floor without holding on.
  ▪ **Dean Martin** 1917-95 American singer and
  actor: Paul Dickson *Official Rules* (1978)

8 You can always tell that the crash is
coming when I start getting tender
about Our Dumb Friends. Three
highballs and I think I'm St Francis of
Assisi.
  ▪ **Dorothy Parker** 1893-1967 American critic
  and humorist: *Here Lies* (1939)

9 One more drink and I'd have been
under the host.
  ▪ **Dorothy Parker** 1893-1967 American
  critic and humorist: Howard Teichmann
  George S. Kaufman (1973)

10 But I'm not so think as you drunk I am.
  ▪ **J. C. Squire** 1884-1958 English man of letters:
  'Ballade of Soporific Absorption' (1931)

11 *a drunken reveller, deciding to look out to see
what sort of night it is, inadvertently stumbles
into a larder; he reports back:*
Hellish dark, and smells of cheese!
  ▪ **R. S. Surtees** 1805-64 English sporting
  journalist and novelist: *Handley Cross* (1843)

12 [An alcoholic:] A man you don't like
who drinks as much as you do.
  ▪ **Dylan Thomas** 1914-53 Welsh poet:
  Constantine Fitzgibbon *Life of Dylan
  Thomas* (1965)

13 *on being given aspirin from a small tin box by
Jeeves:*
Thank you, Jeeves. Don't slam the lid.
  ▪ **P. G. Wodehouse** 1881-1975 English-born
  writer: *Ring for Jeeves* (1953)

14 At the present moment, the whole
Fleet's lit up. When I say 'lit up',
I mean lit up by fairy lamps.
*engaged to make a live outside broadcast
of the Spithead Review, Woodrooffe
was so overcome by his reunion with
many old Naval colleagues that the
celebrations sabotaged his ability to*
commentate
- **Thomas Woodrooffe** 1899-1978 British
naval officer: reporting on the Spithead
Review, 20 May 1937

15 My dad was the town drunk. Usually
that's not so bad, but New York City?
- **Henny Youngman** 1906-98 American
comedian: attributed

Eating

see also **FOOD**

....

Never eat more than you can lift.   **Jim Henson**

1 The French, they say, live to eat. The
English, on the other hand, eat to die.
- **Martin Amis** 1949- English novelist:
Money (1984)

2 I believe that if ever I had to practise
cannibalism, I might manage if there
were enough tarragon around.
- **James Beard** 1903-85 American chef: in
New York Times 24 January 1985

3 Good to eat, and wholesome to digest,
as a worm to a toad, a toad to a snake,
a snake to a pig, a pig to a man, and a
man to a worm.
on the cycle of digestion
- **Ambrose Bierce** 1842-c.1914 American
writer: *The Enlarged Devil's Dictionary*
(1967)

4 In general they [my children] refused to
eat anything that hadn't danced on TV.
- **Erma Bombeck** 1927-96 American
humorist: *Motherhood: The Second Oldest
Profession* (1984)

5 The healthy stomach is nothing if not
conservative. Few radicals have good
digestions.
- **Samuel Butler** 1835-1902 English novelist:
Notebooks (1912)

6 'There's nothing like eating hay when
you're faint'…'I didn't say there was
nothing *better*,' the King replied, 'I said
there was nothing *like* it.'
- **Lewis Carroll** 1832-98 English writer and
logician: *Through the Looking-Glass* (1872)

7 'It's very easy to talk,' said Mrs Mantalini.
'Not so easy when one is eating a
demnition egg,' replied Mr Mantalini; 'for
the yolk runs down the waistcoat, and
yolk of egg does not match any waistcoat
but a yellow waistcoat, demmit.'
- **Charles Dickens** 1812-70 English novelist:
Nicholas Nickleby (1839)

8 Never eat more than you can lift.
Miss Piggy's advice
- **Jim Henson** 1936-90 American puppeteer:
attributed

9 The trouble with eating Italian food is that
five or six days later you're hungry again.
- **George Miller**: attributed

10 Chopsticks are one of the reasons the
Chinese never invented custard.
- **Spike Milligan** 1918-2002 Irish comedian:
attributed

11 We each day dig our graves with our
teeth.
- **Samuel Smiles** 1812-1904 English writer:
Duty (1880)

12 Serenely full, the epicure would say,
Fate cannot harm me, I have dined to-day.
- **Sydney Smith** 1771-1845 English clergyman
and essayist: Lady Holland *Memoir* (1855)
'Receipt for a Salad'

13 He found that a fork in his inexperienced
hand was an instrument of chase rather
than capture.
- **H. G. Wells** 1866-1946 English novelist:
Kipps (1905)

Economics

see also **MONEY**

....

The safest way to double your money is to fold it over and put it in your pocket.
Frank McKinney Hubbard

1 No real English gentleman, in his secret soul, was ever sorry for the death of a political economist.
 ▪ **Walter Bagehot** 1826–77 English economist and essayist: *Estimates of some Englishmen and Scotchmen* (1858) 'The First Edinburgh Reviewers'

2 A man explained inflation to his wife thus: 'When we married you measured 36-24-36. Now you're 42-42-42. There's more of you, but you're not worth as much.'
 ▪ **Joel Barnett** 1923– British Labour politician: attributed; in *Mail on Sunday* 5 October 2003

3 John Stuart Mill,
 By a mighty effort of will,
 Overcame his natural *bonhomie*
 And wrote 'Principles of Political Economy'.
 ▪ **Edmund Clerihew Bentley** 1875–1956 English writer: 'John Stuart Mill' (1905)

4 It's the economy, stupid.
 slogan on a sign put up at the Clinton presidential campaign headquarters
 ▪ **James Carville** 1944– American political consultant: campaign slogan, 1992

5 I never could make out what those damned dots meant.
 as Chancellor, on decimal points
 ▪ **Lord Randolph Churchill** 1849–94 British Conservative politician: W. S. Churchill *Lord Randolph Churchill* (1906)

6 Not all Germans believe in God, but they all believe in the Bundesbank.
 ▪ **Jacques Delors** 1925– French socialist politician: attributed, in *Guardian* 11 December 1992

7 Trickle-down theory—the less than elegant metaphor that if one feeds the horse enough oats, some will pass through to the road for the sparrows.
 ▪ **J. K. Galbraith** 1908–2006 Canadian-born American economist: *The Culture of Contentment* (1992)

8 I could seek to ease his pain, but only by giving him an aspirin.
 the Governor of the Bank of England on economic problems of the small businessman
 ▪ **Eddie George** 1938–2009 English banker: interview on *The Money Programme* BBC2 TV, 28 February 1999

9 Balancing the budget is like going to heaven. Everybody wants to do it, but nobody wants to do what you have to do to get there.
 ▪ **Phil Gramm** 1942– American Republican politician: in a television interview, 16 September 1990

10 In '29 when the banks went bust, Our coins still read 'In God We Trust'.
 ▪ **E. Y. Harburg** 1898–1981 American songwriter: 'Federal Reserve' (1965)

11 The safest way to double your money is to fold it over and put it in your pocket.
 ▪ **Frank McKinney Hubbard** 1868–1930 American humorist: attributed

12 *claiming to have been the first person to explain monetarism to Margaret Thatcher:*
 It makes one feel like the geography teacher who showed a map of the world to Genghis Khan.
 ▪ **Peter Jay** 1937– British economist: in *Tory !Tory! Tory!* (BBC Four television documentary) 8 March 2006

13 If economists could manage to get themselves thought of as humble, competent people, on a level with

dentists, that would be splendid!
- **John Maynard Keynes** 1883-1946 English economist: 'Economic Possibilities for our Grandchildren'; David Howell *Blind Victory* (1986)

14 Expenditure rises to meet income.
- **C. Northcote Parkinson** 1909-93 English writer: *The Law and the Profits* (1960)

15 An economist is an expert who will know tomorrow why the things he predicted yesterday didn't happen today
- **Laurence J. Peter** 1919-90 Canadian writer: attributed

16 The only function of economic forecasting is to make astrology look respectable.
- **Ezra Solomon** 1920-2002 Burmese-born American economist: in *Reader's Digest* 1985; often wrongly attributed to J. K. Galbraith following a humorous piece in *U.S. News & World Report* 7 March 1988

Education

see also **ACADEMIC, EXAMINATIONS**

I won't say ours was a tough school, but we had our own coroner.   **Lenny Bruce**

1 *an unnamed Professor of English at Ohio University:*
I am returning this otherwise good typing paper to you because someone has printed gibberish all over it and put your name at the top.
- **Anonymous**: quoted in *New Scientist*, 1996

2 I read Shakespeare and the Bible and I can shoot dice. That's what I call a liberal education.
- **Tallulah Bankhead** 1903-68 American actress: attributed

3 Education with socialists, it's like sex, all right so long as you don't have to pay for it.
- **Alan Bennett** 1934- English dramatist and actor: *Getting On* (1972)

4 I won't say ours was a tough school, but we had our own coroner. We used to write essays like: What I'm going to be if I grow up.
- **Lenny Bruce** 1925-66 American comedian: attributed

5 C-l-e-a-n, clean, verb active, to make bright, to scour. W-i-n, win, d-e-r, der, winder, a casement. When the boy knows this out of the book, he goes and does it.
- **Charles Dickens** 1812-70 English novelist: *Nicholas Nickleby* (1839)

6 Life isn't like coursework, baby. It's one damn essay crisis after another.
- **Boris Johnson** 1964- British Conservative politician: in *Observer* 15 May 2005

7 Take up car maintenance and find the class is full of other thirty-something women like me, looking for a fella.
- **Marian Keyes** 1963- Irish writer: 'Late Opening at the Last Chance Saloon' (1997)

8 Stand firm in your refusal to remain conscious during algebra. In real life, I assure you, there is no such thing as algebra.
- **Fran Lebowitz** 1946- American writer: *Social Studies* (1981)

9 At school I never minded the lessons. I just resented having to work terribly hard at playing.
- **John Mortimer** 1923-2009 English novelist, barrister, and dramatist: *A Voyage Round My Father* (1971)

10 Seriousness is stupidity sent to college.
- **P. J. O'Rourke** 1947- American humorous writer: *Give War a Chance* (1992)

11 The schoolteacher is certainly underpaid as a childminder, but ludicrously overpaid as an educator.
- **John Osborne** 1929-94 English dramatist: in *Observer* 21 July 1985 'Sayings of the Week'

12 GROUCHO MARX: With a little study you'll
go a long way, and I wish you'd start now.
- **S. J. Perelman** 1904-79 American humorist:
Monkey Business (1931 film)

13 There's al-gebra. That's like sums with
letters…for people whose brains aren't
clever enough for numbers, see?
- **Terry Pratchett** 1948- English fantasy
writer: *Jingo* (1997)

14 You can't expect a boy to be vicious till
he's been to a good school.
- **Saki** 1870-1916 Scottish writer: *Reginald in
Russia* (1910)

15 For every person who wants to teach
there are approximately thirty who
don't want to learn—much.
- **W. C. Sellar** 1898-1951 and **R. J. Yeatman**
1898-1968: *And Now All This* (1932)
introduction

16 Me havin' no education, I had to use my
brains.
- **Bill Shankly** 1913-81 Scottish footballer
and football manager: Hugh McIlvanney
McIlvanney on Football (1994)

17 He who can, does. He who cannot,
teaches.
- **George Bernard Shaw** 1856-1950 Irish
dramatist: *Man and Superman* (1903)
'Maxims: Education'

18 *Educ*: during the holidays from Eton.
- **Osbert Sitwell** 1892-1969 English writer:
entry in *Who's Who* (1929)

19 Soap and education are not as sudden as
a massacre, but they are more deadly in
the long run.
- **Mark Twain** 1835-1910 American writer:
A Curious Dream (1872) 'Facts concerning
the Recent Resignation'

20 'We class schools, you see, into four
grades: Leading School, First-rate
School, Good School, and School.
Frankly,' said Mr Levy, 'School is
pretty bad.'
- **Evelyn Waugh** 1903-66 English novelist:
Decline and Fall (1928)

21 Any one who has been to an English
public school will always feel
comparatively at home in prison.
It is the people brought up in the gay
intimacy of the slums, Paul learned,
who find prison so soul-destroying.
- **Evelyn Waugh** 1903-66 English novelist:
Decline and Fall (1928)

22 Assistant masters came and went…
Some liked little boys too little and
some too much.
- **Evelyn Waugh** 1903-66 English novelist:
A Little Learning (1964)

23 In England, at any rate, education
produces no effect whatsoever. If it
did, it would prove a serious danger
to the upper classes, and probably
lead to acts of violence in Grosvenor
Square.
- **Oscar Wilde** 1854-1900 Irish dramatist
and poet: *The Importance of Being Earnest*
(1895)

24 'Didn't Frankenstein get married?'
'Did he?' said Eggy. 'I don't know.
I never met him. Harrow man,
I expect.'
- **P. G. Wodehouse** 1881-1975 English-born
writer: *Laughing Gas* (1936)

Enemies

I detest him more than cold boiled veal. **Lord Macaulay**

1 I wouldn't piss in his ear if his brain was on fire.
indicating your level of dislike for someone
 ▪ **Anonymous**: quoted as a traditional expression of the Southern US; Bill Clinton *My Life* (2004)

2 Friends come and go, but enemies accumulate.
 ▪ **Anonymous**: saying in American government circles, from at least the 1970s

3 I do not love thee, Dr Fell.
The reason why I cannot tell;
But this I know, and know full well,
I do not love thee, Dr Fell.
 ▪ **Thomas Brown** 1663-1704 English satirist: written while an undergraduate at Christ Church, Oxford, of which Dr Fell was Dean

4 The Bible tells us to love our neighbours and also to love our enemies; probably because they are generally the same people.
 ▪ **G. K. Chesterton** 1874-1936 English essayist, novelist, and poet: in *Illustrated London News* 16 July 1910

5 I detest him more than cold boiled veal.
of the Tory essayist and politician John Wilson Croker
 ▪ **Lord Macaulay** 1800-59 English politician and historian: letter 5 August 1831

6 People wish their enemies dead—but I do not; I say give them the gout, give them the stone!
 ▪ **Lady Mary Wortley Montagu** 1689-1762 English writer: W. S. Lewis et al. (eds.) *Horace Walpole's Correspondence* (1973)

7 *asked on his deathbed if he forgave his enemies:* I have none. I had them all shot.
 ▪ **Ramón María Narváez** 1800-68 Spanish general: Antony Beevor *The Battle For Spain* (2006)

8 Any kiddie in school can love like a fool, But hating, my boy, is an art.
 ▪ **Ogden Nash** 1902-71 American humorist: 'Plea for Less Malice Toward None' (1933)

9 I find that forgiving one's enemies is a most curious morbid pleasure; perhaps I should check it.
 ▪ **Oscar Wilde** 1854-1900 Irish dramatist and poet: letter ?20 April 1894

10 A man cannot be too careful in the choice of his enemies.
 ▪ **Oscar Wilde** 1854-1900 Irish dramatist and poet: *The Picture of Dorian Gray* (1891)

England

see also **BRITISH, TOWNS**

If an Englishman gets run down by a truck he apologizes to the truck.
Jackie Mason

1 The English instinctively admire any man who has no talent and is modest about it
 ▪ **James Agate** 1877-1947 British drama critic and novelist: diary 15 March 1946

2 Boasting about modesty is typical of the English.
 ▪ **Anonymous**: unattributed; in *Mail on Sunday* 21 February 1999 'Quotes of the Week'

3 An Englishman considers himself a self-made man, and thereby relieves the Almighty of a dreadful responsibility.
- **Anonymous**: unattributed; in *Times* 23 February 1999

4 The North, where England tucks its shirt in its underpants.
- **Simon Armitage** 1963- English poet: *All Points North* (1998)

5 I'm English and as such crave disappointment.
- **Bill Bailey** 1964- English comedian: attributed

6 I only said the English weren't famous for sex, that's all. Like the Boat Race, in out, in out, in out, then everyone collapsed over their oars.
- **Julian Barnes** 1946- English novelist: *England, England* (1998)

7 The English may not like music, but they absolutely love the noise it makes.
- **Thomas Beecham** 1879-1961 English conductor: in *New York Herald Tribune* 9 March 1961

8 He was born an Englishman and remained one for years.
- **Brendan Behan** 1923-64 Irish dramatist: *Hostage* (1958)

9 The English like eccentrics. They just don't like them living next door.
- **Julian Clary** 1959- English comedian: in *Daily Telegraph* 2 September 1992

10 The country has grown too small for its boots.
of England
- **Claud Cockburn** 1904-81 British writer and journalist: *View from the West* (1961)

11 Mad dogs and Englishmen
Go out in the midday sun.
- **Noël Coward** 1899-1973 English dramatist, actor, and composer: 'Mad Dogs and Englishmen' (1931)

12 Very flat, Norfolk.
- **Noël Coward** 1899-1973 English dramatist, actor, and composer: *Private Lives* (1930)

13 The English can be explained by their Anglo-Saxon heritage and the influence of the Methodists. But I prefer to explain them in terms of tea, roast beef and rain. A people is first what it eats, drinks and gets pelted with.
- **Pierre Daninos** 1913-2005 French writer: *Major Thompson and I* (1957)

14 Kent, sir—everybody knows Kent—apples, cherries, hops, and women.
- **Charles Dickens** 1812-70 English novelist: *Pickwick Papers* (1837)

15 Because I am an Englishman
I spent most of my life in a state of embarrassment.
- **Colin Firth** 1960- British actor: interview, The-Talks.com, 2 May 2012

16 He is an Englishman!
For he himself has said it,
And it's greatly to his credit,
That he is an Englishman!
- **W. S. Gilbert** 1836-1911 English writer: *HMS Pinafore* (1878)

17 Contrary to popular belief, English women do not wear tweed nightgowns.
- **Hermione Gingold** 1897-1987 English actress: in *Saturday Review* 16 April 1955

18 The truth is that every Englishman's house is his hospital, particularly the bathroom.
- **Oliver St John Gogarty** 1878-1957 Irish writer and surgeon: *As I Was Going Down Sackville Street* (1937)

19 Even crushed against his brother in the Tube, the average Englishman pretends desperately that he is alone.
- **Germaine Greer** 1939- Australian feminist: *The Female Eunuch* (1970)

20 The English never smash in a face. They merely refrain from asking it to dinner.
- **Margaret Halsey** 1910-97 American writer: *With Malice Toward Some* (1938)

21 My parents were English. We were too poor to be British.
on his British origins
- **Bob Hope** 1903-2003 American comedian: in *Times* 29 July 2003

22 Not to be English was for my family so terrible a handicap as almost to place the sufferer in the permanent invalid class.
- **Osbert Lancaster** 1908-86 English writer and cartoonist: *All Done From Memory* (1953)

23 The old English belief that if a thing is unpleasant it is automatically good for you.
- **Osbert Lancaster** 1908-86 English writer and cartoonist: *Homes Sweet Homes* (1939)

24 I speak as your native guide to the mysterious tribe called the English. Dress code is everything. You can be a card-carrying Nazi, you can pay gigolos to eat gnocchi out of your navel and you won't be pilloried—as long as you never, ever wear linen with tweed.
- **Kathy Lette** 1958- Australian writer: *Foetal Attraction* (1993)

25 In England it is very dangerous to have a sense of humour.
- **E. V. Lucas** 1868-1938 English journalist, essayist, and critic: *365 Days and One More* (1926)

26 If an Englishman gets run down by a truck he apologizes to the truck.
- **Jackie Mason** 1931- American comedian: in *Independent* 20 September 1990

27 An Englishman, even if he is alone, forms an orderly queue of one.
- **George Mikes** 1912-87 Hungarian-born writer: *How to be an Alien* (1946)

28 The English are busy; they don't have time to be polite.
- **Montesquieu** 1689-1755 French political philosopher: *Pensées et fragments inédits...* (1901)

29 Man does not strive after happiness; only the Englishman does that.
- **Friedrich Nietzsche** 1844-1900 German philosopher: *Twilight of the Idols* (1889)

30 I think the English are bipolar. 'We're the greatest, no we're terrible'—that's a constant English struggle. Crime is down, there's little poverty—yet it's always the worst time to have lived here.
- **Dara O Briain** 1972- Irish comedian: attributed

31 It is hard to tell where the MCC ends and the Church of England begins.
- **J. B. Priestley** 1894-1984 English novelist, dramatist, and critic: in *New Statesman* 20 July 1962

32 We really *like* dowdiness in England.

It's absolutely incurable in us, I believe.
- **Peter Shaffer** 1926- English dramatist: *Whom Do I Have the Honour of Addressing?* (1990)

33 An Englishman thinks he is moral when he is only uncomfortable.
- **George Bernard Shaw** 1856-1950 Irish dramatist: *Man and Superman* (1903)

34 Englishmen never will be slaves: they are free to do whatever the Government and public opinion allow them to do.
- **George Bernard Shaw** 1856-1950 Irish dramatist: *Man and Superman* (1903)

35 Wensleydale lies between Tuesleydale and Thursleydale.
- **Arthur Smith** 1954- English comedian: attributed

36 This Englishwoman is so refined
She has no bosom and no behind.
- **Stevie Smith** 1902-71 English poet and novelist: 'This Englishwoman' (1937)

37 What a pity it is that we have no amusements in England but vice and religion!
- **Sydney Smith** 1771-1845 English clergyman and essayist: Hesketh Pearson *The Smith of Smiths* (1934)

38 As an Englishman does not travel to see Englishmen, I retired to my room.
- **Laurence Sterne** 1713-68 English novelist: *A Sentimental Journey* (1768)

39 He is a typical Englishman, always dull and usually violent.
- **Oscar Wilde** 1854-1900 Irish dramatist and poet: *An Ideal Husband* (1895)

40 You should study the Peerage, Gerald... It is the best thing in fiction the English have ever done.
- **Oscar Wilde** 1854-1900 Irish dramatist and poet: *A Woman of No Importance* (1893)

41 The inherited stupidity of the race— sound English common sense.
- **Oscar Wilde** 1854-1900 Irish dramatist and poet: *The Picture of Dorian Gray* (1891)

42 I did a picture in England one winter and it was so cold I almost got married.
- **Shelley Winters** 1922-2006 American actress: attributed; John Walker (ed.) *Halliwell's Who's Who in the Movies* 13th ed. (1999)

43 I like a man to be a clean, strong,
upstanding Englishman who can look
his gnu in the face and put an ounce of
lead in it.
- **P. G. Wodehouse** 1881-1975 English-born
writer: *Mr. Mulliner Speaking* (1929)

Epitaphs

see also **DEATH**

Keep off the grass.   **Peter Ustinov**

1 *invited to write his own epitaph:*
He finally met his deadline.
- **Douglas Adams** 1952-2001 English science
fiction writer: on BBC Radio 4 *Quote
Unquote*

2 In bloom of life
She's snatched from hence
She had not room
To make defence;
For Tiger fierce
Took life away,
And here she lies
In a bed of clay
Until the Resurrection Day.
*of Hannah Twynnoy, who had been attacked by
an escaped tiger from a travelling circus in 1703*
- **Anonymous**: gravestone in Malmesbury
churchyard

3 Here lies a poor woman who always
was tired,
For she lived in a place where help
wasn't hired.
Her last words on earth were, Dear
friends I am going
Where washing ain't done nor sweeping
nor sewing,
And everything there is exact to my
wishes,
For there they don't eat and there's no
washing of dishes…
Don't mourn for me now, don't mourn
for me never,
For I'm going to do nothing for ever
and ever.
- **Anonymous**: epitaph in Bushey
churchyard, before 1860; destroyed by 1916

4 Here lies Fred,
Who was alive and is dead:
Had it been his father,
I had much rather;
Had it been his brother,
Still better than another;
Had it been his sister,
No one would have missed her;
Had it been the whole generation,
Still better for the nation:
But since 'tis only Fred,
Who was alive and is dead,—
There's no more to be said.
*epitaph for Frederick, Prince of Wales, killed
by a cricket ball in 1751*
- **Anonymous**: Horace Walpole *Memoirs of
George II* (1847)

5 *suggested epitaph for an unnamed movie
queen whose love-life had been notorious:*
She sleeps alone at last.
- **Robert Benchley** 1889-1945 American
humorist: attributed

6 John Adams lies here, of the parish of
Southwell,
A carrier who carried his can to his
mouth well;
He carried so much, and he carried so fast,
He could carry no more—so was
carried at last;
For the liquor he drank, being too much
for one,
He could not carry off—so he's now
carri-on.
- **Lord Byron** 1788-1824 English poet: 'Epitaph
on John Adams of Southwell, a Carrier who
Died of Drunkenness' (1807)

7 Alan died suddenly at Saltwood on
Sunday 5th September. He said he
would like it to be stated that he
regarded himself as having gone to join
Tom and the other dogs.
  ▪ **Alan Clark** 1928-99 British Conservative
  politician: death announcement in *Times*
  8 September 1999

8 *on the death of US President Warren G.
Harding:*
The only man, woman or child who
wrote a simple declarative sentence
with seven grammatical errors is dead.
  ▪ **e. e. cummings** 1894-1962 American poet:
  attributed

9 Believing that his hate for queers
Proclaimed his love for God,
He now (of all queer things, my dears)
Lies under his first sod.
on John Gordon (1890–1974), editor of the
Sunday Express
  ▪ **Paul Dehn** 1912-76 English screenwriter:
  Nigel Rees *Cassell Dictionary of Humorous
  Quotations* (1999)

10 Under this stone, Reader, survey
Dead Sir John Vanbrugh's house of clay.
Lie heavy on him, Earth! for he
Laid many heavy loads on thee!
  ▪ **Abel Evans** 1679-1737 English poet and
  divine: 'Epitaph on Sir John Vanbrugh,
  Architect of Blenheim Palace'

11 Here lies W. C. Fields. I would rather be
living in Philadelphia.
  ▪ **W. C. Fields** 1880-1946 American humorist:
  suggested epitaph for himself; in *Vanity Fair*
  June 1925

12 Here Skugg
Lies snug
As a bug
In a rug.
  ▪ **Benjamin Franklin** 1706-90 American
  politician, inventor, and scientist: letter
  to Georgiana Shipley on the death of her
  squirrel, 26 September 1772

13 John Le Mesurier wishes it to be known
that he conked out on November 15th.
He sadly misses family and friends.
  ▪ **John Le Mesurier** 1912-83 English actor:
  death announcement in *Times* 16 November
  1983

14 Malcolm Lowry
Late of the Bowery
His prose was flowery
And often glowery
He lived, nightly, and drank, daily,
And died playing the ukelele.
*epitaph he had prepared, which his wife
refused to use on his tombstone*
  ▪ **Malcolm Lowry** 1909-57 English novelist:
  Javier Marias *Written Lives* (2000)

15 Poor G.K.C., his day is past—
Now God will know the truth at last.
  ▪ **E. V. Lucas** 1868-1938 English journalist,
  essayist, and critic: mock epitaph for G. K.
  Chesterton; Dudley Barker *G. K. Chesterton*
  (1973)

16 Here lie I, Martin Elginbrodde:
Hae mercy o' my soul, Lord God;
As I wad do, were I Lord God,
And ye were Martin Elginbrodde.
  ▪ **George MacDonald** 1824-1905 Scottish
  writer and poet: *David Elginbrod* (1863)

17 *epitaph for a waiter:*
By and by
God caught his eye.
  ▪ **David McCord** 1897-1997 American poet:
  'Remainders' (1935)

18 Here lies Spike Milligan. I told you
I was ill.
his chosen epitaph
  ▪ **Spike Milligan** 1918-2002 Irish comedian: in
  Daily Telegraph 28 February 2002

19 Beneath this slab
John Brown is stowed.
He watched the ads,
And not the road.
  ▪ **Ogden Nash** 1902-71 American humorist:
  'Lather as You Go' (1942)

20 Excuse My Dust.
  ▪ **Dorothy Parker** 1893-1967 American
  critic and humorist: suggested epitaph for
  herself; Alexander Woollcott *While Rome
  Burns* (1934) 'Our Mrs Parker'

21 *epitaph for Maurice Bowra:*
Without you, Heaven would be too dull
    to bear,
And Hell would not be Hell if you are
    there.
  ▪ **John Sparrow** 1906-92 English academic: in
  Times Literary Supplement 30 May 1975

22 *when asked what he would like to see on his tombstone:*
Keep off the grass.
- **Peter Ustinov** 1921-2004 British actor, director, and writer: attributed; in *Mail on Sunday* 4 April 2004

23 I always thought I'd like my tombstone to be blank. No epitaph, and no name. Well, actually I'd like it to say 'figment'.
- **Andy Warhol** 1927-87 American artist: *America* (1985)

Examinations

....

I evidently knew more about economics than my examiners.   **John Maynard Keynes**

1 I was thrown out of N.Y.U. my freshman year for cheating on my metaphysics final, you know. I looked within the soul of the boy sitting next to me.
- **Woody Allen** 1935- American film director, writer, and actor: *Annie Hall* (1977 film, with Marshall Brickman), as Alvy Singer

2 Truth is no more at issue in an examination than thirst at a wine-tasting or fashion at a striptease.
- **Alan Bennett** 1934- English dramatist and actor: *The History Boys* (2004)

3 I wrote my name at the top of the page. I wrote down the number of the question '1'. After much reflection I put a bracket round it thus '(1)'. But thereafter I could not think of anything connected with it that was either relevant or true....It was from these slender indications of scholarship that Mr Welldon drew the conclusion that I was worthy to pass into Harrow. It is very much to his credit.
- **Winston Churchill** 1874-1965 British Conservative statesman: *My Early Life* (1930)

4 He had ambitions, at one time, to become a sex maniac, but he failed his practical.
- **Les Dawson** 1934-93 English comedian: attributed; Fred Metcalf (ed.) *Penguin Dictionary of Modern Humorous Quotations* (1987)

5 *explaining why he performed badly in the Civil Service examinations:*
I evidently knew more about economics than my examiners.
- **John Maynard Keynes** 1883-1946 English economist: Roy Harrod *Life of John Maynard Keynes* (1951)

6 In examinations those who do not wish to know ask questions of those who cannot tell.
- **Walter Raleigh** 1861-1922 English lecturer and critic: *Laughter from a Cloud* (1923) 'Some Thoughts on Examinations'

7 Do not on any account attempt to write on both sides of the paper at once.
- **W. C. Sellar** 1898-1951 and **R. J. Yeatman** 1898-1968: *1066 and All That* (1930) 'Test Paper 5'

8 *Whistler had been found 'deficient in chemistry' in a West Point examination:*
Had silicon been a gas, I would have been a major-general by now.
- **James McNeill Whistler** 1834-1903 American-born painter: E. R. and J. Pennell *The Life of James McNeill Whistler* (1908)

9 *in his viva at Oxford Wilde was required to translate a passage from the Greek version of the New Testament. Having acquitted himself well, he was stopped:*
Oh, do let me go on, I want to see how it ends.
- **Oscar Wilde** 1854-1900 Irish dramatist and poet: James Sutherland (ed.) *The Oxford Book of Literary Anecdotes* (1975)

Excuses *see* **APOLOGY**

Exercise

....

Exercise is the yuppie version of bulimia.   **Barbara Ehrenreich**

1 I'd love to go to the gym, but I just can't get my head around the footwear.
  - **Victoria Beckham** 1974– British pop singer: interview, GMTV, in *Daily Mail* 15 May 2008

2 The only reason I would take up jogging is so that I could hear heavy breathing again.
  - **Erma Bombeck** 1927–96 American humorist: attributed

3 The two best exercises in the world are making love and dancing but a simple one is to stand on tiptoe.
  - **Barbara Cartland** 1901–2000 English writer: in 1972, attributed; in *Guardian* 22 May 2000

4 *on exercise:*
  I'm at an age when my back goes out more than I do.
  - **Phyllis Diller** 1917–2012 American actress: *The Joys of Ageing—And How to Avoid Them* (1981)

5 Exercise is the yuppie version of bulimia.
  - **Barbara Ehrenreich** 1941– American sociologist and writer: *The Worst Years of Our Lives* (1991) 'Food Worship'

6 For exercise, I wind my watch.
  - **Robert Maxwell** 1923–91 Czech-born British publisher: attributed

7 A bear, however hard he tries, Grows tubby without exercise.
  - **A. A. Milne** 1882–1956 English writer: 'Teddy Bear' (1924)

8 The only exercise I take is walking behind the coffins of friends who took exercise.
  - **Peter O'Toole** 1932– British actor: in *Mail on Sunday* 27 December 1998 'Quotes of the Year'

9 Avoid running at all times.
  - **Leroy ('Satchel') Paige** 1906–82 American baseball player: *How To Stay Young* (1953)

10 If God had wanted us to bend over, He would have put diamonds on the floor.
  - **Joan Rivers** 1933– American comedienne: attributed

11 I used to jog but the ice cubes kept falling out of my glass.
  - **Dave Lee Roth** 1955– American rock singer: attributed

12 I try to keep fit. I've got these parallel bars at home. I run at them and try to buy a drink from both of them.
  - **Arthur Smith** 1954– English comedian: attributed

13 I don't take enough exercise, but what is the longest-lived animal in the world? The giant tortoise is 120 years old and it hardly moves.
  - **Terry Wogan** 1938– Irish broadcaster: in *Times* 23 June 2007

Exploration *see* TRAVEL AND EXPLORATION

Faces

see also **APPEARANCE**

....

I tried to shave off my eyebrows once and my trousers fell down. **Denis Healey**

1 Frazier is so ugly that he should
donate his face to the US Bureau
of Wild Life.
  - **Muhammad Ali** 1942– American boxer:
  in *Guardian* 23 December 1972 'Sports
  Quotes of the Year'

2 My job is
Keeping faces clean
And nobody knows
De stubble
I've seen
Burma-Shave.
  - **Anonymous**: Burma-Shave advertisement,
  1950

3 If she'd played Lady Godiva, the horse
would have stolen the show.
on an actress not known for her looks
  - **Anonymous**: twentieth-century saying

4 My face looks like a wedding cake left
out in the rain.
  - **W. H. Auden** 1907–73 English poet:
  Humphrey Carpenter *W. H. Auden* (1981)

5 In appearance Dior is like a bland
country curate made out of pink
marzipan.
of Christian Dior
  - **Cecil Beaton** 1904–80 English
  photographer: *The Glass of Fashion* (1954)

6 He had the sort of face that makes
you realise God does have a sense
of humour.
  - **Bill Bryson** 1951– American travel writer:
  Neither Here Nor There (1991)

7 *of W. H. Auden's heavily wrinkled face:*
Were a fly to attempt to cross it, it
would break its leg.
  - **Lord David Cecil** 1902–86 British
  biographer and critic: A. L. Rowse diary,
  30 May 1960

8 Time marches on and eventually you
realize it is marching across your face.
  - **Robert Harling** 1951– American writer:
  Steel Magnolias (1989 film), spoken by
  Dolly Parton as Truvy

9 I tried to shave off my eyebrows once
and my trousers fell down.
  - **Denis Healey** 1917– British Labour
  politician: in *Observer* 21 August 2005

10 I kept thinking, if his face was that
wrinkled, what did his balls look like?
after drawing W. H. Auden
  - **David Hockney** 1937– British artist:
  attributed

11 Her face was her chaperone.
  - **Rupert Hughes** 1872–1956 American writer:
  attributed

12 A face made of broken commandments.
  - **John Masefield** 1878–1967 English poet:
  Sard Harker (1924)

Failure

Kids, you tried your best, and you failed miserably. The lesson is, never try.
Matt Groening

1 *during a rehearsal at the Royal Court, Beckett encouraged an actor who had lamented, 'I'm failing':*
Go on failing. Go on. Only next time, try to fail better.
- **Samuel Beckett** 1906-89 Irish dramatist, novelist, and poet: Tony Richardson *Long Distance Runner* (1993)

2 Failure is the condiment that gives success its flavour.
- **Truman Capote** 1924-84 American writer: *The Dogs Bark* (1977)

3 If at first you don't succeed, failure may be your style.
- **Quentin Crisp** 1908-99 English writer: in *Sunday Telegraph* 28 September 1999

4 I have not failed. I've just found 10,000 ways that won't work.
- **Thomas Alva Edison** 1847-1931 American inventor: the commonly-quoted version of an incident recounted in F. L. Dyer and T. C. Martin *Edison: His Life and Inventions* (1910)

5 If at first you don't succeed, try, try again. Then quit. No use being a damn fool about it.
- **W. C. Fields** 1880-1946 American humorist: attributed

6 Kids, you tried your best, and you failed miserably. The lesson is, never try.
Homer Simpson
- **Matt Groening** 1954- American humorist and satirist: *The Simpsons* 'Burns' Heir' (1994) written by Jace Richdale

7 Come forth, Lazarus! And he came fifth and lost the job.
- **James Joyce** 1882-1941 Irish novelist: *Ulysses* (1922)

8 Whoever said 'It's not whether you win or lose that counts' probably lost.
- **Martina Navratilova** 1956- Czech-born American tennis player: attributed

9 Anybody seen in a bus over the age of 30 has been a failure in life.
- **Loelia, Duchess of Westminster** 1902-93: in *Times* 4 November 1993; habitual remark

Fame

Stardom isn't a profession; it's an accident.   **Lauren Bacall**

1 A celebrity is a person who works hard all his life to become well known, and then wears dark glasses to avoid being recognized.
- **Fred Allen** 1894-1956 American humorist: Laurence J. Peter (ed.) *Quotations for our Time* (1977)

2 Someone once asked me if my dream was to live on in the hearts of people, and I said I would prefer to live on in my apartment.
- **Woody Allen** 1935- American film director, writer, and actor: in *Rolling Stone* 9 April 1987

3 To live in *Who's Who*
And to die in *The Times*,
To be one of the few
To live in *Who's Who*,
What would I not do?—
I'd commit frightful crimes
To live in *Who's Who*

And to die in *The Times*.
- **Anonymous**: unattributed; in *Times* 3 January 2004

4 Stardom isn't a profession; it's an accident.
- **Lauren Bacall** 1924- American actress: in *Observer* 19 March 1995 'Sayings of the Week'

5 *asked at a press conference what it was like to act with a 'screen legend' like Nicole Kidman:* She's not a legend, she's a beginner. You can't be a legend at whatever age she is.
- **Lauren Bacall** 1924- American actress: in *Sunday Telegraph* 12 September 2004

6 Oh, the self-importance of fading stars. Never mind, they will be black holes one day.
- **Jeffrey Bernard** 1932-97 English journalist: in *The Spectator* 18 July 1992

7 Oblivion...fame's eternal dumping ground.
- **Ambrose Bierce** 1842-c.1914 American writer: *The Enlarged Devil's Dictionary* (1967)

8 They were so far down the bill I thought they were the printers.
on Morecambe and Wise in early posters and playbills
- **Eddie Braben** 1930-2013 English comedy writer: William Cook (ed.) *Eric Morecambe Unseen* (2005)

9 A legend in his own lunchtime.
of Dennis Main Wilson
- **David Climie** 1920-95 English screenwriter: Ned Sherrin *Theatrical Anecdotes* (1991); also attributed to Christopher Wordsworth of Clifford Makins

10 They usually ask you, 'Are you you?'... In fact, I've even been thinking of printing up some cards that just say, 'Yes, I am,' so I can get one out before they even say anything.
on signing autographs
- **Jarvis Cocker** 1963- English musician: interview in *Q Magazine* November 1995

11 Becoming famous has taken the place of going to heaven.
- **Jarvis Cocker** 1963- English musician: in *Guardian* 17 October 2011

12 One dreams of the goddess Fame and winds up with the bitch Publicity.
- **Peter De Vries** 1910-93 American novelist: *The Mackerel Plaza* (1958)

13 Fancy being remembered around the world for the invention of a mouse!
- **Walt Disney** 1901-66 American animator and film producer: during his last illness; Leonard Mosley *Disney's World* (1985)

14 If all else fails, immortality can always be assured by adequate error.
often quoted as 'by a spectacular error'
- **J. K. Galbraith** 1908-2006 Canadian-born American economist: *Money, Whence It Came, Where It Went* (1995)

15 ARTHUR: I think I'll take a bath.
HOBSON: I'll alert the media.
- **Steve Gordon** 1938-82 American film director: *Arthur* (1981 film); Dudley Moore as Arthur Bach, and John Gielgud as his valet Hobson

16 I'm afraid of losing my obscurity. Genuineness only thrives in the dark. Like celery.
- **Aldous Huxley** 1894-1963 English novelist: *Those Barren Leaves* (1925)

17 The main advantage of being famous is that when you bore people at dinner parties they think it is their fault.
- **Henry Kissinger** 1923- American politician: James Naughtie in *Spectator* 1 April 1995; attributed

18 The best fame is a writer's fame: it's enough to get a table at a good restaurant, but not enough that you get interrupted when you eat.
- **Fran Lebowitz** 1946- American writer: in *Observer* 30 May 1993 'Sayings of the Week'

19 *on being asked what it was like to be famous:* It's like having a string of pearls given you. It's nice, but after a while, if you think of it at all, it's only to wonder if they're real or cultured.
- **W. Somerset Maugham** 1874-1965 English novelist: *A Writer's Notebook* (1949) written in 1941

20 *Wayne and Garth meet Alice Cooper:* We're not worthy! We're not worthy!
- **Mike Myers** 1963- Canadian actor: *Wayne's World* (1992 film)

21 You can't shame or humiliate modern celebrities. What used to be called shame and humiliation is now called publicity.
- **P. J. O'Rourke** 1947- American humorous writer: *Give War a Chance* (1992)

22 *to Labour MP Chris Bryant, whose photograph in his Y-fronts had appeared on a gay website:*
Ah, Bryant, there you are. Nearly didn't recognise you with your clothes on.
- **Nicholas Soames** 1948- British Conservative politician: attributed; in *Mail on Sunday* 4 January 2004

23 *on being approached by a fan a few years after her retirement in 1930:*
Get away dear, I don't need you anymore.
- **Norma Talmadge** 1893-1957 American film actress: Jeanine Basinger *Silent Stars* (2000)

24 *on rumours she would be posing for* Playboy:
Oh sure—and next month I'm dressing up as a sea bass for the front cover of *Field and Stream*!
- **Elizabeth Taylor** 1932-2011 English-born American actress: attributed

25 Modern fame is nothing. I'd rather have an acre of land.
- **Alfred, Lord Tennyson** 1809-92 English poet: Hallam Tennyson *Alfred Lord Tennyson; A Memoir by his Son* (1897)

26 When I pass my name in such large letters I blush, but at the same time instinctively raise my hat.
- **Herbert Beerbohm Tree** 1852-1917 English actor-manager: Hesketh Pearson *Beerbohm Tree* (1956)

27 One day you are a signature, next day you're an autograph.
- **Billy Wilder** 1906-2002 American screenwriter and director: Charlotte Chandler *Nobody's Perfect* (2002)

The Family

see also **CHILDREN, PARENTS**

....

It is a wise father that knows his own child.   **William Shakespeare**

1 What is wrong with a little incest? It is both handy and cheap.
- **James Agate** 1877-1947 British drama critic and novelist: on *The Barretts of Wimpole Street*; attributed, perhaps apocryphal

2 And my parents finally realize that I'm kidnapped and they snap into action immediately: They rent out my room.
- **Woody Allen** 1935- American film director, writer, and actor: Eric Lax *Woody Allen and his Comedy* (1975)

3 Like getting a telegram from the mortuary.
on becoming a grandfather
- **Martin Amis** 1949- English novelist: at Hay on Wye Literary Festival, 6 June 2010, in *Daily Mail* 7 June 2010

4 My mother-in-law broke up my marriage. My wife came home from work one day and found us in bed together.
- **Lenny Bruce** 1925-66 American comedian: attributed; Fred Metcalf (ed.) *The Penguin Dictionary of Modern Humorous Quotations*

5 I should, many a good day, have blown my brains out, but for the recollection that it would have given pleasure to my mother-in-law; and, even *then*, if I could have been certain to haunt her...
- **Lord Byron** 1788-1824 English poet: letter, 28 January 1817

6 The first half of our lives is ruined by our parents, the second half by our children.
- **Clarence Darrow** 1857-1938 American lawyer: attributed

7 My grandmother started walking five miles a day when she was sixty. She's ninety-seven now, and we don't know

where the hell she is.
- **Ellen DeGeneres** 1958– American comedian and actress: attributed

8 If you must go flopping yourself down, flop in favour of your husband and child, and not in opposition to 'em.
- **Charles Dickens** 1812–70 English novelist: *A Tale of Two Cities* (1859)

9 Accidents will occur in the best-regulated families.
- **Charles Dickens** 1812–70 English novelist: *David Copperfield* (1850)

10 We do everything alike
We look alike, we dress alike,
We walk alike, we talk alike,
and what is more we hate each other
    very much.
- **Howard Dietz** 1896–1983 American songwriter: 'Triplets' (1937)

11 John Donne, Anne Donne, Un-done.
in a letter to his wife, on being dismissed from the service of his father-in-law, Sir George More
- **John Donne** 1572–1631 English poet and divine: Izaak Walton *The Life of Dr Donne* (first printed in *LXXX Sermons*, 1640)

12 You know what they say, if at first you don't succeed, you're not the eldest son.
- **Stephen Fry** 1957– English comedian, actor, and writer: *Paperweight* (1992)

13 As a child my family's menu consisted of two choices: take it or leave it.
- **Buddy Hackett** 1924–2003 American comedian: attributed

14 MIRANDA: Good morning Mum how are you?
PENNY: Don't get emotional, we're not Spanish.
- **Miranda Hart** 1972– English comedian: *Miranda* (BBC TV, 2012)

15 I'm also told that the latest popular game in America is called Incest—all the family can join in!
- **Rupert Hart-Davis** 1907–99 British writer and publisher: letter to George Lyttelton, 14 November 1959

16 If Gloria hadn't divorced me she might never have become her own daughter-in-law.
of his ex-wife, Gloria Grahame, who had married her former stepson
- **Cy Howard** 1915–93 American screenwriter: in *Ned Sherrin in his Anecdotage* (1993)

17 A dysfunctional family is any family with more than one person in it.
- **Mary Karr** 1955– American poet: *The Liars Club* (1995)

18 *of his appointment of his brother Robert:*
I see nothing wrong with giving Robert some legal experience as Attorney General before he goes out to practice law.
- **John F. Kennedy** 1917–63 American Democratic statesman: Bill Adler *The Complete Kennedy Wit* (1967)

19 I've been out where the Blues begin,
Stopping at home with my kith and kin,
Where the handclasp's firm, and the
    smile is humorous,
And Family Friends are a bit too
    numerous.
- **Phyllis McGinley** 1905–78 American poet: 'Ordeal by Family' (1960)

20 The English take breeding of horses and dogs more seriously than children. God forbid the wrong drop of blood should get into their Labrador. But their children marry everywhere.
- **Princess Michael of Kent** 1945– in *Observer* 20 February 2005

21 We kept Mommy on a pedestal—it was the only way we could keep Daddy off her.
of family life as one of twelve children
- **Dolly Parton** 1946– American singer and songwriter: review of her show at the Hammersmith Apollo, London; in *Observer* 24 November 2002

22 I want to spend more time with my family, but I'm not sure they want to spend more time with me.
- **Esther Rantzen** 1940– English broadcaster: in *Independent* 29 April 2000

23 I find it difficult to take much interest in a man whose father was a dragon.
apologizing for his inability to appreciate William Morris's epic poem Sigurd the Volsung *(1876)*
- **Dante Gabriel Rossetti** 1828–82 English poet and painter: Osbert Sitwell *Noble Essences* (1950)

24 *Chutzpa* is that quality enshrined in a
man who, having killed his mother and
father, throws himself on the mercy of
the court as an orphan.
- **Leo Rosten** 1908-97 American writer and
social scientist: *The Joys of Yiddish* (1968)

25 *questionnaire for would-be Kings in the Wars
of the Roses:*
What have you done with your mother?
(If *Nun*, write *None*.)
- **W. C. Sellar** 1898-1951 and **R. J. Yeatman**
1898-1968: *1066 and All That* (1930)

26 It is a wise father that knows his own child.
- **William Shakespeare** 1564-1616 English
dramatist: *The Merchant of Venice* (1596-8)

27 My father is a bastard
My Ma's an S.O.B.
My Grandpa's always plastered
My Grandma pushes tea
My sister wears a moustache
My brother wears a dress
Goodness gracious, that's why I'm a mess.
- **Stephen Sondheim** 1930- American
songwriter: 'Gee, Officer Krupke' (1957)

28 The young ladies entered the drawing-
room in the full fervour of sisterly
animosity.
- **R. S. Surtees** 1805-64 English sporting
journalist and novelist: *Mr Sponge's Sporting
Tour* (1853)

29 If a man's character is to be abused,
say what you will, there's nobody like a
relation to do the business.
- **William Makepeace Thackeray** 1811-63
English novelist: *Vanity Fair* (1847-8)

30 I'm off to see if X Mansions is really razed
to the ground, as I have an uncle who lives
there and I know I'm in his will!
- **Ernest Thesiger** 1879-1961 English actor:
during the war; in *Ned Sherrin in his
Anecdotage* (1993)

31 I'm Charley's aunt from Brazil—where
the nuts come from.
- **Brandon Thomas** 1856-1914 English
dramatist: *Charley's Aunt* (1892)

32 I suppose that the high-water mark of
my youth in Columbus, Ohio, was the
night the bed fell on my father.
- **James Thurber** 1894-1961 American
humorist: *My Life and Hard Times* (1933)

33 All happy families resemble one
another, but each unhappy family is
unhappy in its own way.
- **Leo Tolstoy** 1828-1910 Russian novelist:
Anna Karenina (1875-7)

34 Familiarity breeds contempt—and
children.
- **Mark Twain** 1835-1910 American writer:
Notebooks (1935)

35 Wherever my dad is now, he's looking
down on me...not because he's dead
but because he is very condescending.
- **Jack Whitehall** 1988- British comedian:
comedy routine, August 2010

36 To lose one parent, Mr Worthing, may
be regarded as a misfortune; to lose
both looks like carelessness.
- **Oscar Wilde** 1854-1900 Irish dramatist and
poet: *The Importance of Being Earnest* (1895)

37 To be born, or at any rate bred, in a
hand-bag, whether it had handles or
not, seems to me to display a contempt
for the ordinary decencies of family life
that reminds one of the worst excesses
of the French Revolution.
- **Oscar Wilde** 1854-1900 Irish dramatist and
poet: *The Importance of Being Earnest* (1895)

38 It is no use telling me that there are bad
aunts and good aunts. At the core, they
are all alike. Sooner or later, out pops
the cloven hoof.
- **P. G. Wodehouse** 1881-1975 English-born
writer: *The Code of the Woosters* (1938)

39 As a rule, you see, I'm not lugged into
Family Rows. On the occasions when
Aunt is calling to Aunt like mastodons
bellowing across primeval swamps
and Uncle James's letter about Cousin
Mabel's peculiar behaviour is being shot
round the family circle...the clan has a
tendency to ignore me.
- **P. G. Wodehouse** 1881-1975 English-born
writer: *The Inimitable Jeeves* (1923)

40 It was that strange, almost unearthly
light which comes into the eyes of
wronged uncles when they see a chance
of getting a bit of their own back from
erring nephews.
- **P. G. Wodehouse** 1881-1975 English-born
writer: *Uncle Dynamite* (1948)

Family Life

There's no such thing as fun for the whole family.   **Jerry Seinfeld**

1 Teenagers are God's punishment for having sex.
  ▪ **Anonymous**: modern saying

2 Being constantly with children was like wearing a pair of shoes that were expensive and too small. She couldn't bear to throw them out but they gave her blisters.
  ▪ **Beryl Bainbridge** 1934-2010 English novelist: *Injury Time* (1977)

3 The truth is that parents are not really interested in justice. They just want quiet.
  ▪ **Bill Cosby** 1937- American comedian and actor: *Fatherhood* (1986)

4 The awe and dread with which the untutored savage contemplates his mother-in-law are amongst the most familiar facts of anthropology.
  ▪ **James George Frazer** 1854-1941 Scottish anthropologist: *The Golden Bough* (2nd ed., 1900)

5 A man…is *so* in the way in the house!
  ▪ **Elizabeth Gaskell** 1810-65 English novelist: *Cranford* (1853)

6 I was decorating, so I got out my step-ladder. I don't get on with my real ladder.
  ▪ **Harry Hill** 1964- English comedian: attributed

7 Living with a teenage daughter is like living under the Taliban. Mothers are not allowed to dance, sing, flirt, laugh loudly or wear short skirts.
  ▪ **Kathy Lette** 1958- Australian writer: *To Love, Honour and Betray* (2011)

8 The reason grandparents and grandchildren get along so well is that they have a common enemy.
  ▪ **Sam Levenson** 1911-80 American humorist: attributed

9 One would be in less danger
From the wiles of the stranger
If one's own kin and kith
Were more fun to be with.
  ▪ **Ogden Nash** 1902-71 American humorist: 'Family Court' (1931)

10 My Mom said she learned how to swim when someone took her out in the lake and threw her off the boat. I said 'Mom, they weren't trying to teach you how to swim'.
  ▪ **Paula Poundstone** 1959- American comedian: attributed

11 I knew I was an unwanted baby when I saw that my bath toys were a toaster and a radio.
  ▪ **Joan Rivers** 1933- American comedienne: Joey Adams *Roast of the Town* (1986)

12 There's no such thing as fun for the whole family.
  ▪ **Jerry Seinfeld** 1954- American comedian: attributed

13 Children and zip fasteners do not respond to force…Except occasionally.
  ▪ **Katharine Whitehorn** 1928- English journalist: *Observations* (1970)

14 After a good dinner one can forgive anybody, even one's own relations.
  ▪ **Oscar Wilde** 1854-1900 Irish dramatist and poet: *A Woman of No Importance* (1893)

Fashion

see also **DRESS**

His socks compelled one's attention without losing one's respect.   **Saki**

1 It is totally impossible to be well dressed in cheap shoes.
   ▪ **Hardy Amies** 1909-2003 English couturier: *The Englishman's Suit* (1994)

2 FIRST WOMAN: Whenever I'm down in the dumps, I get myself another hat.
   SECOND WOMAN: I always wondered where you found them.
   ▪ **Anonymous**: much used in pantomime scripts from the 1930s onwards

3 *of Asquith's first wife:*
   She lived in Hampstead and had no clothes.
   ▪ **Margot Asquith** 1864-1945 British political hostess: Chips Channon diary, 31 October 1937

4 It would be mortifying to the feelings of many ladies, could they be made to understand how little the heart of man is affected by what is costly or new in their attire.
   ▪ **Jane Austen** 1775-1817 English novelist: *Northanger Abbey* (1818)

5 I never cared for fashion much. Amusing little seams and witty little pleats. It was the girls I liked.
   ▪ **David Bailey** 1938- English photographer: in *Independent* 5 November 1990

6 *of Dior's New Look:*
   Clothes by a man who doesn't know women, never had one, and dreams of being one!
   ▪ **Coco Chanel** 1883-1971 French couturière: in *Vanity Fair* June 1994

7 Saint Laurent has excellent taste. The more he copies me, the better taste he displays.
   ▪ **Coco Chanel** 1883-1971 French couturière: attributed, 1971

8 There are easier things in this life than being a drag queen. But, I ain't got no choice. Try as I may, I just can't walk in flats.
   ▪ **Harvey Fierstein** 1954- American dramatist and actor: *Torch Song Trilogy* (1979)

9 Wearing underwear is as formal as I ever hope to get.
   ▪ **Ernest Hemingway** 1899-1961 American novelist: A. E. Hotchner *Papa Hemingway* (1983)

10 My only complaint about having a father in fashion is that every time I'm about to go to bed with a guy I have to look at my dad's name all over his underwear.
   ▪ **Marci Klein** 1967- American television producer: in *Newsweek* 17 October 1994

11 When anything becomes the fashion, that's the time to put a bomb under it.
   ▪ **Joan Littlewood** 1914-2002 English theatre director: attributed, 1961

12 How can you expect to convert England if you use a cope like that?
   ▪ **Augustus Welby Pugin** 1812-52 English architect and designer: to an unidentified Catholic priest; Bernard Ward *The Sequel to Catholic Emancipation* (1915)

13 I base my fashion sense on what doesn't itch.
   ▪ **Gilda Radner** 1946-89 American comedian and actress: attributed

14 Don't wear perfume in the garden— unless you want to be pollinated by bees.
   ▪ **Anne Raver** American journalist: in *New York Times* 21 June 1992

15 PIRATE: I'm gonna teach you the meaning of pain.
   ELIZABETH: You like pain? Try wearing a corset.
   ▪ **Terry Rossio** and **Ted Elliott** screenwriters: *Pirates of the Caribbean* (2003 film)

16 I wish I had invented blue jeans.
on his only regret
- **Yves Saint Laurent** 1936-2008 French couturier: in *Ritz* no. 85 (1984)

17 His socks compelled one's attention without losing one's respect.
- **Saki** 1870-1916 Scottish writer: *Chronicles of Clovis* (1911)

18 Her frocks are built in Paris, but she wears them with a strong English accent.
- **Saki** 1870-1916 Scottish writer: *Reginald* (1904)

19 Women dress alike all over the world: they dress to be annoying to other women.
- **Elsa Schiaparelli** 1896-1973 Italian-born French fashion designer: attributed, c.1950

20 I blame the women's movement for 10 years in a boiler suit.
- **Jill Tweedie** 1936-93 British journalist: attributed

21 If Botticelli were alive today he'd be working for *Vogue*.
- **Peter Ustinov** 1921-2004 British actor, director, and writer: in *Observer* 21 October 1962 'Sayings of the Week'

22 I like to dress egos. If you haven't got an ego today, you can forget it.
- **Gianni Versace** 1949-97 Italian fashion designer: in *Guardian* 16 July 1997; obituary

23 It is charming to totter into vogue.
- **Horace Walpole** 1717-97 English writer and connoisseur: letter to George Selwyn, 2 December 1765

24 *to Ada Leverson, who with her husband visited Wilde on the morning he left Pentonville:*
How marvellous of you to know exactly the right hat to wear at seven o'clock in the morning to meet a friend who has been away.
- **Oscar Wilde** 1854-1900 Irish dramatist and poet: Rupert Hart-Davis (ed.) *Selected Letters of Oscar Wilde* (1979)

Feminism

see also **WOMEN**

....

Militant feminists, I take my hat off to them. They don't like that.   **Milton Jones**

1 Women who seek to be equal to men lack ambition.
- **Anonymous**: feminist slogan, c. 1980, sometimes wrongly attributed to Marilyn Monroe

2 The suffragettes were triumphant. Woman's place was in the gaol.
- **Caryl Brahms** 1901-82 and **S. J. Simon** 1904-48: *No Nightingales* (1944)

3 A good part—and definitely the most fun part—of being a feminist is about frightening men.
- **Julie Burchill** 1960- English journalist and writer: in *Time Out* 16 November 1989

4 The feminist movement seems to have beaten the manners out of men, but I didn't see them put up a lot of resistance.
- **Clarissa Dickson Wright** 1947- English chef and broadcaster: in *Mail on Sunday* 24 September 2000 'Quotes of the Week'

5 Make policy, not coffee.
- **Betty Friedan** 1921-2006 American feminist: slogan for the National Organisation for Women's Political Caucus, 1971

6 Women go to so much trouble yet accept a man's pot belly, warts, bad breath, wind, stubble, baldness and ugliness.
- **Germaine Greer** 1939- Australian feminist: Graham Jones *I Don't Hate Men, But—; I Don't Hate Women, But—* (1986)

7 Militant feminists, I take my hat off to
them. They don't like that.
 • **Milton Jones** 1964- English comedian:
 attributed

8 BETTY FRIEDAN: Don't you hate women
being treated as a sexual plaything?
JESSICA MITFORD: But Betty, you're not a
plaything, you're a war toy!
 • **Jessica Mitford** 1917-96 British writer:
 attributed; in *Guardian* 7 February 2006

9 Batman doesn't want a baby in order
to feel he's 'done everything'. He's just
saved Gotham again! If this means
that Batman must be a feminist role
model…then so be it.
 • **Caitlin Moran** 1975- English journalist:
 How to Be a Woman (2012)

10 Feminism is the result of a few ignorant
and literal-minded women letting the
cat out of the bag about which is the
superior sex.
 • **P. J. O'Rourke** 1947- American humorous
 writer: *Modern Manners* (1984)

11 God made man and then said I can do
better than *that* and made woman.
 • **Adela Rogers St Johns** 1894-1988 American
 journalist: *Some Are Born Great* (1974)

12 We can't reduce women to equality.
Equality is a step down for most women.
 • **Phyllis Schafly** 1924- American lawyer:
 attributed, early 1970s

13 Like every good little feminist-in-
training in the sixties, I burned my
bra—and now it's the nineties and
I realize Playtex had supported me
better than any man I have ever known.
 • **Susan Sweetzer**: Amanda Newman *Women
 are from Venus, Men are from Hell* (1999)

14 The Queen is most anxious to enlist
every one who can speak or write
to join in checking this mad, wicked
folly of 'Woman's Rights', with all its
attendant horrors, on which her poor
feeble sex is bent, forgetting every sense
of womanly feeling and propriety.
 • **Victoria** 1819-1901 British queen: letter to
 Theodore Martin, 29 May 1870

15 I myself have never been able to find out
precisely what feminism is: I only know
that people call me a feminist whenever
I express sentiments that differentiate
me from a doormat or a prostitute.
 • **Rebecca West** 1892-1983 English novelist and
 journalist: in 1913; *The Young Rebecca* (1982)

Film

see also **CINEMA, FILM PRODUCERS, FILM STARS**

It's more than magnificent, it's mediocre. **Sam Goldwyn**

1 Several tons of dynamite are set off in
this picture [*Tycoon*]; none of it under
the right people.
 • **James Agee** 1909-55 American writer: in
 The Nation 14 February 1948

2 We didn't need dialogue. We had faces.
on silent films
 • **Charles Brackett** 1892-1969 and **Billy Wilder**
 1906-2002 screenwriters: *Sunset Boulevard*
 (1950 film, with D. M. Marshman Jr), spoken
 by Gloria Swanson as Norma Desmond

3 *Adolph Zukor had protested at the escalating
costs of* The Ten Commandments:
What do you want me to do? Stop
shooting now and release it as *The Five
Commandments*?
 • **Cecil B. De Mille** 1881-1959 American film
 producer: M. LeRoy *Take One* (1974)

4 Let's bring it up to date with some
snappy 19th-century dialogue.
 • **Sam Goldwyn** 1882-1974 American film
 producer: King Vidor *A Tree is a Tree* (1953)

5 *of one of his own films:*
It's more than magnificent, it's mediocre.
 • **Sam Goldwyn** 1882-1974 American film
 producer: attributed, perhaps apocryphal

6 GOLDWYN: I hope you didn't think it was
too blood and thirsty.

THURBER: Not only did I think so but I was horror and struck.
of The Secret Life of Walter Mitty, *Goldwyn's 1947 film of Thurber's story*
- **Sam Goldwyn** 1882-1974 American film producer: Michael Freedland *The Goldwyn Touch* (1986)

7 It would have been cheaper to lower the Atlantic!
of the disaster movie Raise the Titanic
- **Lew Grade** 1906-98 British television producer and executive: *Still Dancing: My Story* (1987)

8 I'm not [biting my fingernails]. I'm biting my knuckles. I finished the fingernails months ago.
- **Joseph L. Mankiewicz** 1909-93 American screenwriter, producer, and director: while directing Elizabeth Taylor in *Cleopatra* (1963); Dick Sheppard *Elizabeth* (1975)

9 Anything but Beethoven. Nobody wants to see a movie about a blind composer.
- **Jack Warner** 1892-1978 Canadian-born American film producer: J. Lawrence *Actor* (1975)

10 I didn't have to act in 'Tarzan, the Ape Man'—just said, 'Me Tarzan, you Jane.'
- **Johnny Weissmuller** 1904-84 American film actor: in *Photoplay Magazine* June 1932 (the words 'Me Tarzan, you Jane' do not occur in the 1932 film)

11 *asking Graham Greene to give a final polish to a rewrite of the last part of the screenplay for* Ben Hur:
You see, we find a kind of anticlimax after the Crucifixion.
- **Sam Zimbalist** 1904-58 American film producer: Graham Greene *Ways of Escape* (1980)

Film Producers and Directors

see also **CINEMA, FILM**

....

If I made Cinderella, the audience would immediately be looking for a body in the coach.   **Alfred Hitchcock**

1 Cecil B. de Mille
Rather against his will,
Was persuaded to leave Moses
Out of 'The Wars of the Roses'.
- **Nicholas Bentley** 1907-78 English writer and illustrator: 'Cecil B. de Mille' (1938)

2 Ah don't believe Ah know which pictures are yours. Do you make the Mickey Mouse brand?
to Irving Thalberg
- **William Faulkner** 1897-1962 American novelist: Max Wilk *The Wit and Wisdom of Hollywood* (1972)

3 *resigning from the Motion Picture Producers and Distributors of America in 1933:*
Gentlemen, include me out.
- **Sam Goldwyn** 1882-1974 American film producer: Michael Freedland *The Goldwyn Touch* (1986)

4 PRODUCTION ASSISTANT: But Mr Goldwyn, you said you wanted a spectacle.
GOLDWYN: Yes, but goddam it, I wanted an intimate spectacle!
- **Sam Goldwyn** 1882-1974 American film producer: attributed, perhaps apocryphal

5 That's the way with these directors, they're always biting the hand that lays the golden egg.
- **Sam Goldwyn** 1882-1974 American film producer: Alva Johnston *The Great Goldwyn* (1937)

6 Hitchcock was more careful about how the birds were treated than he was about me. I was just there to be pecked.
on the filming of The Birds
- **Tippi Hedren** 1930- American actress: Charlotte Chandler *It's Only A Movie: Alfred Hitchcock* (2005)

7 A pig in a silk suit who sends flowers.
of Sam Spiegel
- **Katharine Hepburn** 1907-2003 American
  actress: Natasha Fraser-Cavassoni *Sam
  Spiegel* (2003)

8 If I made Cinderella, the audience
would immediately be looking for a
body in the coach.
- **Alfred Hitchcock** 1899-1980 British-born
  film director: in *Newsweek* 11 June 1956

9 I can't tell you [the perfect ending to
a script]…I thought of the answer
after 5.30.
*to Jack Warner, who imposed a strict nine-to-
five-thirty schedule on his scriptwriters*
- **Norman Krasna** 1909-84 American
  screenwriter: M. Freedland *Warner Brothers*
  (1983)

10 Jack Warner has oilcloth pockets so he
can steal soup.
- **Wilson Mizner** 1876-1933 American
  dramatist: Max Wilk *The Wit and Wisdom
  of Hollywood* (1972)

11 He decided to make it [*Daisy Miller*]
exactly as it stood; he crammed James's
words into Cybill's mouth like fish into
a letterbox.
on Peter Bogdanovich
- **Frederic Raphael** 1931– British novelist
  and screenwriter: *Cuts and Bruises: Personal
  Terms* 3 (2006)

12 Tsar of all the rushes.
of Louis B. Mayer
- **B. P. Schulberg** 1892-1957 American film
  producer: Norman Zierold *The Hollywood
  Tycoons* (1969)

13 Once a month the sky falls on my head,
I come to, and I see another movie
I want to make.
- **Steven Spielberg** 1947– American film
  director and producer: in *Time* 8 June 1998

14 *on Roman Polanski:*
The four foot Pole you wouldn't want
to touch with a ten foot pole.
- **Kenneth Tynan** 1927-80 English theatre critic:
  Halliwell's Who's Who in the Movies (2001)

15 To Raoul Walsh a tender love scene is
burning down a whorehouse.
- **Jack Warner** 1892-1978 Canadian-born
  American film producer: P. F. Boller and
  R. L. Davis *Hollywood Anecdotes* (1988)

16 I like the old masters, by which I mean
John Ford, John Ford, and John Ford.
- **Orson Welles** 1915-85 American actor and
  film director: P. F. Boller and R. L. Davis
  Hollywood Anecdotes (1988)

17 Johnny, it's the usual slashed-wrist
shot…Keep it out of focus. I want to
win the foreign picture award.
- **Billy Wilder** 1906-2002 American
  screenwriter and director: to his lighting
  cameraman, John Seitz, when filming
  Sunset Boulevard (1950); P. F. Boller and
  R. L. Davis *Hollywood Anecdotes* (1988)

18 A modern-day Robin Hood, who
steals from the rich and steals from
the poor.
of Sam Spiegel
- **Billy Wilder** 1906-2002 American
  screenwriter and director: Natasha Fraser-
  Cavassoni *Sam Spiegel* (2003)

19 ANONYMOUS: What is an associate
producer?
BILLY WILDER: Anybody who's prepared
to associate with a producer.
- **Billy Wilder** 1906-2002 American
  screenwriter and director: attributed

20 The first nine commandments for a
director are 'Thou shalt not bore.'
The tenth is 'Thou shalt have the right
of final cut.'
- **Billy Wilder** 1906-2002 American
  screenwriter and director: attributed,
  perhaps apocryphal

21 An actor entering through the door,
you've got nothing. But if he enters
through the window, you've got a
situation.
- **Billy Wilder** 1906-2002 American
  screenwriter and director: attributed

Film Stars

see also CINEMA, FILM

....

It's not what I do, but the way I do it. It's not what I say, but the way I say it.
Mae West

1 Can't act. Slightly bald. Also dances.
studio official's comment on Fred Astaire
- **Anonymous**: Bob Thomas *Astaire* (1985)

2 They used to shoot her through gauze.
You should shoot me through linoleum.
on Shirley Temple
- **Tallulah Bankhead** 1903-68 American actress: attributed

3 JOE GILLIS: You used to be in pictures.
You used to be big.
NORMA DESMOND: I am big. It's the pictures that got small.
- **Charles Brackett** 1892-1969 and **Billy Wilder** 1906-2002 screenwriters: *Sunset Boulevard* (1950 film)

4 *of Greta Garbo:*
A rather boring old Swede, but luckily she loves doing the washing-up.
- **Gladys Cooper** 1888-1971 English actress: Sheridan Morley *Asking for Trouble* (2002)

5 Like watching an affair between a mad rocking-horse and a rawhide suitcase.
of Jeanette MacDonald and Nelson Eddy in the film of his Bitter Sweet
- **Noël Coward** 1899-1973 English dramatist, actor, and composer: diary 1 July 1946

6 *asked what it was like to kiss Marilyn Monroe:*
It's like kissing Hitler.
- **Tony Curtis** 1925-2010 American actor: A. Hunter *Tony Curtis* (1985)

7 Nowadays Mitchum doesn't so much act as point his suit at people.
- **Russell Davies** 1946- British journalist: in *Sunday Times* 18 September 1983

8 *during the making of* Lifeboat *in 1944, Mary Anderson asked Hitchcock what he thought her 'best side' for photography was:*
My dear, you're sitting on it.
- **Alfred Hitchcock** 1899-1980 British-born film director: D. Spoto *Life of Alfred Hitchcock* (1983)

9 That man's ears make him look like a taxi-cab with both doors open.
of Clark Gable
- **Howard Hughes Jr.** 1905-76 American businessman and film producer: Charles Higham and Joel Greenberg *Celluloid Muse* (1969)

10 She is a phenomenon of nature, like Niagara Falls or the Grand Canyon. You can't talk to it. It can't talk to you. All you can do is stand back and be awed by it.
of Marilyn Monroe
- **Nunnally Johnson** 1897-1977 American film producer: Peter Harry Brown and Patte B. Barham *Marilyn, the Last Take* (1990)

11 *approaching an unwelcoming Greta Garbo and peering up under the brim of her floppy hat:*
Pardon me, Ma'am...I thought you were a guy I knew in Pittsburgh.
- **Groucho Marx** 1890-1977 American film comedian: David Niven *Bring on the Empty Horses* (1975)

12 *asked if she really had nothing on in a calendar photograph:*
I had the radio on.
- **Marilyn Monroe** 1926-62 American actress: in *Time* 11 August 1952

13 Elizabeth [Taylor] is a wonderful movie actress: she has a deal with the film lab— she gets better in the bath overnight.
- **Mike Nichols** 1931- American film director: in *Vanity Fair* June 1994

14 Wet, she was a star—dry she ain't.
of the swimmer Esther Williams and her 1940s film career
- **Joe Pasternak** 1901-91 American film producer: attributed

15 *on hearing that Ronald Reagan was seeking nomination as Governor of California:*
No, no. Jimmy Stewart for governor—

Reagan for his best friend.
- **Jack Warner** 1892-1978 Canadian-born American film producer: Max Wilk *The Wit and Wisdom of Hollywood* (1972)

16 It's not what I do, but the way I do it. It's not what I say, but the way I say it.
- **Mae West** 1892-1980 American film actress: G. Eells and S. Musgrove *Mae West* (1989)

17 *on Marilyn Monroe's unpunctuality:*
My Aunt Minnie would always be punctual and never hold up production, but who would pay to see my Aunt Minnie?
- **Billy Wilder** 1906-2002 American screenwriter and director: P. F. Boller and R. L. Davis *Hollywood Anecdotes* (1988)

Fishing

I love fishing. It's like transcendental meditation with a punch-line. **Billy Connolly**

1 If fishing is a religion, fly fishing is high church.
- **Tom Brokaw** 1940- American journalist: in *International Herald Tribune* 10 September 1991

2 I love fishing. It's like transcendental meditation with a punch-line.
- **Billy Connolly** 1942- Scottish comedian: *Gullible's Travels* (1982)

3 Fishing is unquestionably a form of madness but, happily, for the once-bitten there is no cure.
- **Lord Home** 1903-95 British Conservative statesman: *The Way the Wind Blows* (1976)

4 Fly fishing may be a very pleasant amusement; but angling or float fishing I can only compare to a stick and a string, with a worm at one end and a fool at the other.
- **Samuel Johnson** 1709-84 English poet, critic, and lexicographer: attributed; Hawker *Instructions to Young Sportsmen* (1859); also attributed to Jonathan Swift

5 It is to be observed that 'angling' is the name given to fishing by people who can't fish.
- **Stephen Leacock** 1869-1944 Canadian humorist: attributed

6 It has always been my private conviction that any man who pits his intelligence against a fish and loses has it coming.
- **John Steinbeck** 1902-68 American novelist: in *Punch* 25 August 1954

Flattery *see* PRAISE AND FLATTERY

Flying

There's nothing like an airport for bringing you down to earth. **Richard Gordon**

1 Airline travel is hours of boredom interrupted by moments of stark terror.
- **Al Boliska** Canadian broadcaster: Laurence J. Peter *Quotations for our Time* (1977)

2 There's nothing like an airport for bringing you down to earth.
- **Richard Gordon** 1921- English surgeon: *Doctor in the Swim* (1962)

3 My inclination to go by the Air Express is confirmed by the crash they had yesterday, which will make them more careful in the immediate future.
- **A. E. Housman** 1859-1936 English poet: letter, 17 August 1920

4 I feel about airplanes the way I feel about diets. It seems to me that they are

wonderful things for other people to go on.

- **Jean Kerr** 1923-2003 American writer: *The Snake Has All the Lines* (1958)

5 I'm always amazed to hear of air crash victims so badly mutilated that they have to be identified by their dental records. What I can't understand is, if they don't know who you are, how do they know who your dentist is?

- **Paul Merton** 1957- English comedian: attributed

6 You know the oxygen masks on airplanes? I don't think there's really any oxygen. They're just to muffle the screams.

- **Rita Rudner** 1953- American comedienne and writer: attributed

7 *on airline food:*
The shiny stuff is tomatoes.
The salad lies in a group.
The curly stuff is potatoes,
The stuff that moves is soup.
Anything that is white is sweet,
Anything that is brown is meat.
Anything that is grey—don't eat.

- **Stephen Sondheim** 1930- American songwriter: 'Do I Hear a Waltz?' (1965)

Food

see also **COOKERY, DIETS**

....

Cauliflower is nothing but cabbage with a college education.   **Mark Twain**

1 I will not eat oysters. I want my food dead—not sick, not wounded—dead.

- **Woody Allen** 1935- American film director, writer, and actor: attributed

2 *Daphne offers to cook for Niles and Maris:*
NILES: Just bear in mind: she can't have shellfish, poultry, red meat, saturated fats, nitrates, wheat, starch, sulphites, MSG or dairy…Did I say nuts?
FRASIER: Oh, I think that's implied!

- **David Angell** 1946-2001, **Peter Casey**, and **David Lee** American television producers: *Frasier* (NBC TV, 1994) 'A Mid-Winter Night's Dream', written by Chuck Ranberg and Anne Flett-Giordano; spoken by David Hyde Pierce and Kelsey Grammer

3 *dining with her Cabinet:*
MRS THATCHER: Steak.
WAITER: And the vegetables?
MRS THATCHER: Oh, they'll have steak too.

- **Anonymous**: *Spitting Image* ITV

4 Shake and shake
The catsup bottle,
None will come,
And then a lot'll.

- **Richard Armour** 1906-89 American writer: Laurence J. Peter (ed.) *Quotations for our Time* (1977)

5 You realise tinned food is just for crackheads and wars?

- **Jesse Armstrong** and **Sam Bain** 1971- British screenwriters: *Peep Show* (Channel 4 TV, 2003), spoken by Robert Webb as Jez

6 Frosties are just cornflakes for people who can't deal with reality.

- **Jesse Armstrong** and **Sam Bain** 1971- British screenwriters: *Peep Show* (Channel 4 TV, 2005), spoken by David Mitchell as Mark

7 *making toast for breakfast:*
Brown for first course, white for pudding. Brown's the savoury and white's the treat.

- **Jesse Armstrong** and **Sam Bain** 1971- British screenwriters: *Peep Show* (Channel 4 TV, 2003), spoken by David Mitchell as Mark

8 There's no such thing as a little garlic.

- **Arthur Baer** 1886-1969 American journalist: Frank Muir *The Frank Muir Book* (1976)

9 *Snails*. I find this a somewhat disturbing dish, but the sauce is divine. What I do is order escargots, and tell them to 'hold' the snails.
Miss Piggy's view
▪ **Henry Beard** 1945- American humorist: *Miss Piggy's Guide to Life* (1981)

10 A gourmet who thinks of calories is like a tart who looks at her watch.
▪ **James Beard** 1903-85 American chef: attributed

11 A gourmet can tell from the flavour whether a woodcock's leg is the one on which the bird is accustomed to roost.
▪ **Lucius Beebe** 1902-66 American writer: Laurence J. Peter (ed.) *Quotations for our Time* (1977)

12 *of a woman on Cape Cod:*
She ate so many clams that her stomach rose and fell with the tide.
▪ **Helen Choate Bell** American socialite: Louis Kronenberger *The Cutting Edge* (1970)

13 One of the sauces which serve the French in place of a state religion.
on mayonnaise
▪ **Ambrose Bierce** 1842-*c*.1914 American writer: *The Enlarged Devil's Dictionary* (1967)

14 I've always thought Alfred showed a marked lack of ingenuity over cakes— why didn't he cut off the burnt bits, and ice the rest?
▪ **Madeline Bingham** English writer: *Something's Burning: The Bad Cook's Guide* (1968)

15 *from the recipe for Skid Road Stroganoff:*
Add the flour, salt, paprika, and mushrooms, stir, and let it cook five minutes while you light a cigarette and stare sullenly at the sink.
▪ **Peg Bracken** 1918-2007 American writer: *The 'I Hate to Cook' Book* (1960)

16 *of pepper:*
Always be sure it's coarse-ground, because a lot of people feel that anything that's peppered should look as though it had been fished out of a gravel pit.
▪ **Peg Bracken** 1918-2007 American writer: *The 'I Hate to Cook' Book* (1960)

17 *asked if he liked vegetables:*
I don't know. I have never eaten them... No, that is not quite true. I once ate a pea.
▪ **Beau Brummell** 1778-1840 English dandy: Lewis Melville *Beau Brummell* (1924)

18 I'm President of the United States, and I'm not going to eat any more broccoli!
▪ **George Bush** 1924- American Republican statesman: in *New York Times* 23 March 1990

19 If you are afraid of butter, use cream.
▪ **Julia Child** 1912-2004 American cook: attributed but almost certainly apocryphal, deriving from a description of Child's cookery in Julie Powell's obituary notice in *New York Times* 18 August 2004

20 I never see an egg brought on my table but I feel penetrated with the wonderful change it would have undergone but for my gluttony; it might have been a gentle useful hen, leading her chickens with a care and vigilance which speaks shame to many women.
▪ **St John de Crévècoeur** 1735-1813 French-born American writer: *Letters from an American Farmer* (1782)

21 Peanuts! What's happened to peanuts! Now every bugger's allergic to peanuts. It's true, you open a packet of peanuts now and a bunch of five year olds in a five mile radius slam to the floor jabbing themselves with fucking adrenaline.
▪ **Lee Evans** 1964- English comedian: attributed

22 [Cheese is] milk's leap toward immortality.
▪ **Clifton Fadiman** 1904-99 American critic: *Any Number Can Play* (1957)

23 Roast Beef, Medium, is not only a food. It is a philosophy.
▪ **Edna Ferber** 1887-1968 American writer: foreword to *Roast Beef, Medium* (1911)

24 Of soup and love, the first is the best.
▪ **Thomas Fuller** 1654-1734 English writer and physician: *Gnomologia* (1732)

25 It takes some skill to spoil a breakfast— even the English can't do it.
▪ **J. K. Galbraith** 1908-2006 Canadian-born American economist: *Ambassador's Journal* (1969)

26 Donuts. Is there anything they *can't* do?
Homer Simpson
- **Matt Groening** 1954– American humorist and satirist: *The Simpsons* 'Marge vs the Monorail' (2002), written by Conan O'Brien

27 'For what we are about to receive,
Oh Lord, 'tis Thee we thank,'
Said the cannibal as he cut a slice
Of the missionary's shank.
- **E. Y. Harburg** 1898–1981 American songwriter: 'The Realist' (1965)

28 I ate his liver with some fava beans and a nice chianti.
- **Thomas Harris** 1940– and **Ted Tally** 1952– screenwriters: *The Silence of the Lambs* (1991 film)

29 Oh, I was down by Manly Pier
Drinking tubes of ice-cold beer
With a bucket full of prawns upon me knee.
But when I'd swallowed the last prawn
I had a technicolour yawn
And I chundered in the old Pacific sea.
- **Barry Humphries** 1934– Australian actor and writer: 'Chunder Down Under' (1964)

30 Vegetarianism is harmless enough, though it is apt to fill a man with wind and self-righteousness.
- **Robert Hutchinson** 1871–1960 Scottish physician: address to the British Medical Association, Winnipeg, 1930

31 What proper man would plump for bints
Ahead of After-Eight thin mints?
True pleasure for a man of parts
Is tarts in him, not him in tarts.
- **Clive James** 1939– Australian critic and writer: Ned Sherrin *Cutting Edge* (1984)

32 Garlic bread—it's the future, I've tasted it.
Brian Potter envisages a reborn Phoenix Club
- **Peter Kay** 1973– British comedian: *Phoenix Nights* 'Brian Gets Everyone Back Together' (Series 2, 2002)

33 It has nothing to do with frogs' legs. No amphibian is harmed in the making of this dish.
explaining toad-in-the-hole to an American audience
- **Nigella Lawson** 1960– British journalist and cookery writer: in *Sunday Times* 6 October 2002

34 Large, naked, raw carrots are acceptable as food only to those who live in hutches eagerly awaiting Easter.
- **Fran Lebowitz** 1946– American writer: *Metropolitan Life* (1978)

35 *her anti-aging secrets:*
A love of life, spaghetti and the odd bath in virgin olive oil. Everything I have I owe to spaghetti.
- **Sophia Loren** 1934– Italian actress: in *Sunday Times* 28 August 2005

36 The piece of cod passeth all understanding.
- **Edwin Lutyens** 1869–1944 English architect: Robert Lutyens *Sir Edwin Lutyens* (1942)

37 You are offered a piece of bread and butter that feels like a damp handkerchief and sometimes, when cucumber is added to it, like a wet one.
- **Compton Mackenzie** 1883–1972 English novelist: *Vestal Fire* (1927)

38 It's all right, the white wine came up with the fish.
at a formal dinner at the home of the producer Arthur Hornblow Jr., having left the dinner table to be sick
- **Herman J. Mankiewicz** 1897–1953 American screenwriter: Max Wilk *The Wit and Wisdom of Hollywood* (1972); also claimed by Howard Dietz

39 For those who want to eat efficiently, God made the banana, complete with its own colour-co-ordinated carrying case.
- **Judith Martin** 1938– American journalist: *Miss Manners' Guide to Excruciatingly Correct Behaviour, Freshly Updated* (2005)

40 People often feed the hungry so that nothing may disturb their own enjoyment of a good meal.
- **W. Somerset Maugham** 1874–1965 English novelist: *A Writer's Notebook* (1949) written in 1896

41 *to a friend who had said that he hated English food:*
All you have to do is eat breakfast three times a day.
- **W. Somerset Maugham** 1874–1965 English novelist: Ted Morgan *Somerset Maugham* (1980)

42 *on having matzo balls for the third time at Arthur Miller's parents:*
Isn't there any other part of the matzo you can eat?
- **Marilyn Monroe** 1926-62 American actress: attributed

43 No man is lonely eating spaghetti; it requires so much attention.
- **Christopher Morley** 1890-1957 American writer: attributed

44 Parsley
Is gharsley.
- **Ogden Nash** 1902-71 American humorist: 'Further Reflections on Parsley' (1942)

45 I understand the big food companies are developing a tearless onion. I think they can do it—after all, they've already given us tasteless bread.
- **Robert Orben** 1927- American comedy writer: attributed

46 Never serve oysters in a month that has no paycheck in it.
- **P. J. O'Rourke** 1947- American humorous writer: *The Bachelor Home Companion* (1987)

47 A fruit is a vegetable with looks and money. Plus, if you let fruit rot, it turns into wine, something Brussels sprouts never do.
- **P. J. O'Rourke** 1947- American humorous writer: *The Bachelor's Home Companion* (1987)

48 I like the *philosophy* of the sandwich, as it were. It typifies my attitude to life, really. It's all there, it's fun, it looks good, and you don't have to wash up afterwards.
- **Molly Parkin** 1932- Welsh writer: attributed

49 The mountain sheep are sweeter,
But the valley sheep are fatter;
We therefore deemed it meeter
To carry off the latter.
- **Thomas Love Peacock** 1785-1866 English novelist and poet: 'The War-Song of Dinas Vawr' (1823)

50 Cheese. Shropshire Blue—it's so high in calorific content you need only rub against it, and that's enough.
on why he is so large
- **Eric Pickles** 1952- British Conservative politician: in *Daily Mail* 4 February 2013

51 I've had a taste of society
And society has had a taste of me.
the oyster ending up back in the sea after a day of social climbing
- **Cole Porter** 1891-1964 American songwriter: 'The Tale of the Oyster' (1929)

52 Dinner at the Huntercombes' possessed 'only two dramatic features—the wine was a farce and the food a tragedy'.
- **Anthony Powell** 1905-2000 English novelist: *The Acceptance World* (1955)

53 Any domestic food store, raided furtively in the middle of the night, always contains, no matter what its daytime inventory, half a jar of elderly mayonnaise, a piece of very old cheese, and a tomato with white mould growing on it.
- **Terry Pratchett** 1948- English fantasy writer: *Mort* (1987)

54 Botticelli isn't a wine, you Juggins! Botticelli's a *cheese*!
- **Punch** 1841-1992 English humorous weekly periodical: vol. 106 (1894)

55 BISHOP: I'm afraid you've got a bad egg, Mr Jones.
CURATE: Oh no, my Lord, I assure you! Parts of it are excellent!
- **Punch** 1841-1992 English humorous weekly periodical: vol. 109 (1895)

56 Cheese it is a peevish elf
It digests all things but itself.
- **John Ray** 1627-1705 English naturalist: *English Proverbs* (1670)

57 Does your chewing-gum lose its flavour on the bedpost overnight?
- **Billy Rose** 1899-1966 and **Marty Bloom** American songwriters: 'Does the spearmint lose its flavour on the bedpost overnight?' (1924 song) as revived by British musician Lonnie Donegan (1931-2002) in 1959

58 OSCAR: I got brown sandwiches and green sandwiches...Well, what do you say?
MURRAY: What's the green?
OSCAR: It's either very new cheese or very old meat.
- **Neil Simon** 1927- American dramatist: *The Odd Couple* (1966)

59 If there is a pure and elevated pleasure in this world it is a roast pheasant with bread sauce. Barn door fowls for dissenters but for the real Churchman, the thirty-nine times articled clerk—the pheasant, the pheasant.
- **Sydney Smith** 1771–1845 English clergyman and essayist: letter to R. H. Barham, 15 November 1841

60 Madam, I have been looking for a person who disliked gravy all my life; let us swear eternal friendship.
- **Sydney Smith** 1771–1845 English clergyman and essayist: Lady Holland *Memoir* (1855)

61 Shepherd's pie peppered with actual shepherd on top.
one of Mrs Lovett's variations on Sweeney Todd's human meat pies
- **Stephen Sondheim** 1930– American songwriter: 'A Little Priest' (1979)

62 Cauliflower is nothing but cabbage with a college education.
- **Mark Twain** 1835–1910 American writer: *Pudd'nhead Wilson* (1894)

63 Beulah, peel me a grape.
- **Mae West** 1892–1980 American film actress: in *I'm No Angel* (1933 film)

64 MOTHER: It's broccoli, dear.
CHILD: I say it's spinach, and I say the hell with it.
- **E. B. White** 1899–1985 American humorist: cartoon caption in *New Yorker* 8 December 1928

65 An egg is always an adventure.
- **Oscar Wilde** 1854–1900 Irish dramatist and poet: Laurence Housman *Echo de Paris: A Study from Life* (1923)

66 When I ask for a watercress sandwich, I do not mean a loaf with a field in the middle of it.
- **Oscar Wilde** 1854–1900 Irish dramatist and poet: Max Beerbohm letter to Reggie Turner, 15 April 1893

67 I was so darned sorry for poor old Corky that I hadn't the heart to touch my breakfast. I told Jeeves to drink it himself.
- **P. G. Wodehouse** 1881–1975 English writer: *My Man Jeeves* (1919)

68 One doughnut doesn't do a thing. You've got to eat 20 a day for five weeks before you get results.
on plumping up to play Bridget Jones
- **Renee Zellweger** 1969– American actress: in *Mail on Sunday* 15 June 2003

Foolishness

see also **IGNORANCE**

....

A man may be a fool and not know it, but not if he is married.   **H. L. Mencken**

1 *New Year Resolutions*
 1. To refrain from saying witty, unkind things, unless they are really witty and irreparably damaging.
 2. To tolerate fools more gladly, provided this does not encourage them to take up more of my time.
- **James Agate** 1877–1947 British drama critic and novelist: diary 2 January 1942

2 I sometimes wonder if the manufacturers of foolproof items keep a fool or two on their payroll to test things.
- **Alan Coren** 1938–2007 English humorist: *Seems Like Old Times* (1989)

3 How much a dunce that has been sent to roam
Excels a dunce that has been kept at home?
- **William Cowper** 1731–1800 English poet: 'The Progress of Error' (1782)

4 Two things are infinite, the universe and human stupidity, and I am not yet completely sure about the universe.
- **Albert Einstein** 1879–1955 German-born theoretical physicist: attributed; Frederick S. Perls *In and Out the Garbage Pail* (1969)

5 The idiot who praises, with enthusiastic tone,

All centuries but this, and every country but his own.
- **W. S. Gilbert** 1836-1911 English writer: *The Mikado* (1885)

6 Every man is a damn fool for at least five minutes every day. Wisdom consists in not exceeding that limit.
- **Elbert Hubbard** 1859-1915 American writer: Dale Carnegie *How to Stop Worrying and Start Living* (1948); Hubbard's own words in *The Fra* (1909) were 'even the best men are locoed logically half an hour every day...'

7 Chicolini here may talk like an idiot, and look like an idiot, but don't let that fool you: he really is an idiot.
- **Bert Kalmar** 1884-1947 and **others** screenwriters: *Duck Soup* (1933 film), spoken by Groucho Marx as Rufus T. Firefly

8 I could name eight people—half of those eight are barmy. How many apples short of a picnic?
on his Tory critics
- **John Major** 1943- British Conservative statesman: comment, 19 September 1993

9 A man may be a fool and not know it, but not if he is married.
- **H. L. Mencken** 1880-1956 American journalist and literary critic: Laurence J. Peter (ed.) *Quotations for our Time* (1977)

10 After you'd known Christine for any length of time, you found yourself fighting a desire to look into her ear to see if you could spot daylight coming the other way.
- **Terry Pratchett** 1948- English fantasy writer: *Maskerade* (1995)

11 *Sheridan's son Tom announced that when he became an MP he would proclaim his independence of party by writing 'To Let' on his forehead:*
And, under that, Tom, write 'unfurnished'.
- **Richard Brinsley Sheridan** 1751-1816 Irish dramatist and Whig politician: Walter Jerrold *Bon-Mots* (1893)

12 'A soldier,' cried my Uncle Toby, interrupting the corporal, 'is no more exempt from saying a foolish thing, Trim, than a man of letters.'—'But not so often, an' please your honour,' replied the corporal.
- **Laurence Sterne** 1713-68 English novelist: *Tristram Shandy* (1759-67)

13 How haughtily he lifts his nose, To tell what every schoolboy knows.
- **Jonathan Swift** 1667-1745 Irish poet and satirist: 'The Journal' (1727)

14 Hain't we got all the fools in town on our side? and ain't that a big enough majority in any town?
- **Mark Twain** 1835-1910 American writer: *The Adventures of Huckleberry Finn* (1884)

Football

see also **SPORTS**

....

Football is a simple game; 22 men chase a ball for 90 minutes and at the end, the Germans win. **Gary Lineker**

1 Why is there only one ball for 22 players? If you gave a ball to each of them, they'd stop fighting for it.
comment of a football widow, posted on an anti-World Cup website
- **Anonymous:** in *Daily Telegraph* 28 December 1998 'Sporting Quotes of the Year'

2 *George Best was often told by Matt Busby not to bother to turn up for Busby's team talks to Manchester United:*
It wasn't worth his coming. It was a very simple team talk. All I used to say was: 'Whenever possible, give the ball to George.'
- **Matt Busby** 1909-94 Scottish football manager: Michael Parkinson *Sporting Lives* (1993)

3 *on meetings with players:*
We talk about it for 20 minutes and
then we decide I was right.
- **Brian Clough** 1935-2004 English football
  manager: attributed; in *Channel 4 News*
  20 September 2004 (online edition)

4 Football's football; if that weren't the
case, it wouldn't be the game it is.
- **Garth Crooks** 1958- English football
  player: Barry Fantoni (ed.) *Private Eye's
  Colemanballs 2* (1984)

5 United will no longer be a football
club, it will be a giant Old Trafford fruit
machine.
- **Tommy Docherty** 1928- Scottish football
  manager: in *Mail on Sunday* 13 September
  1998 'Quotes of the Week'

6 *of Stan Bowles:*
If only he could pass a betting shop like
he does a football.
- **Reg Drury** 1928-2003 English journalist: in
  Times 28 June 2003 (obituary)

7 Football, wherein is nothing but beastly
fury, and extreme violence, whereof
proceedeth hurt, and consequently
rancour and malice do remain with
them that be wounded.
- **Thomas Elyot** 1499-1546 English diplomatist
  and writer: *Book of the Governor* (1531)

8 *when asked by Sir Stanley Rous whether
she thought anyone had played well in a
particularly dull football Cup Final:*
Yes, the band.
- **Elizabeth II** 1926- British queen:
  attributed; Michèle Brown and Ann
  O'Connor *Hammer and Tongues* (1986)

9 The only thing that Norwich didn't get
was the goal that they finally got.
- **Jimmy Greaves** 1940- English
  footballer: Barry Fantoni (ed.) *Private Eye's
  Colemanballs 2* (1984)

10 The natural state of the football fan is
bitter disappointment, no matter what
the score.
- **Nick Hornby** 1957- British novelist and
  journalist: *Fever Pitch* (1992)

11 I don't think some of the people who
come to Old Trafford can spell football,
never mind understand it.
- **Roy Keane** 1971- Irish football player and
  manager: in *Belfast Telegraph* 9 November
  2000

12 The nice aspect about football is that, if
things go wrong, it's the manager who
gets the blame.
before his first match as captain of England
- **Gary Lineker** 1960- English footballer: in
  Independent 12 September 1990

13 Football is a simple game; 22 men chase
a ball for 90 minutes and at the end, the
Germans win.
- **Gary Lineker** 1960- English footballer:
  attributed

14 Oh, he's football crazy, he's football mad
And the football it has robbed him o'
    the wee bit sense he had.
And it would take a dozen skivvies, his
    clothes to wash and scrub,
Since our Jock became a member of
    that terrible football club.
- **Jimmy McGregor** 1930- Scottish singer:
  'Football Crazy' (1960)

15 What's a geriatric? A German footballer
scoring three goals.
- **Bob Monkhouse** 1928-2003 English
  entertainer: attributed; in *BBC News* (UK
  edition, online) 29 December 2003

16 I think football would become an even
better game if someone could invent a
ball that kicks back.
- **Eric Morecambe** 1926-84 English
  comedian: attributed

17 Nobody cares if Le Saux is gay or not.
It is the fact that he openly admits to
reading *The Guardian* that makes him
the most reviled man in football.
- **Piers Morgan** 1965- English journalist:
  letter to *Guardian*, 5 March 1999

18 To say that these men paid their shillings
to watch twenty-two hirelings kick a
ball is merely to say that a violin is wood
and catgut, that *Hamlet* is so much paper
and ink. For a shilling the Bruddersford
United AFC offered you Conflict and Art.
- **J. B. Priestley** 1894-1984 English novelist,
  dramatist, and critic: *Good Companions*
  (1929)

19 We didn't underestimate them. They were a lot better than we thought.
on Cameroon's football team
- **Bobby Robson** 1933-2009 English footballer and manager: in *Guardian* 24 December 1990 'Sports Quotes of the Year'

20 The first ninety minutes are the most important.
- **Bobby Robson** 1933-2009 English footballer and manager: attributed

21 Some people think football is a matter of life and death…I can assure them it is much more serious than that.
- **Bill Shankly** 1913-81 Scottish footballer and football manager: in *Guardian* 24 December 1973 'Sports Quotes of the Year'

22 [Gary Lineker is] the Queen Mother of football.
- **Arthur Smith** 1954- and **Chris England**: *An Evening with Gary Lineker* (1990)

23 The English football team—brilliant on paper, shit on grass.
- **Arthur Smith** 1954- and **Chris England**: *An Evening with Gary Lineker* (1990)

24 Football and cookery are the two most important subjects in the country.
having been appointed a director of Norwich City football club
- **Delia Smith** 1941- English cookery expert: in *Observer* 23 February 1997 'Said and Done'

25 REPORTER: So, Gordon, in what areas do you think Middlesbrough were better than you today?
GORDON STRACHAN: What areas? Mainly that big green one out there…
- **Gordon Strachan** 1957- Scottish football manager: attributed

26 I tell you what son, playing football is a lot easier than directing a funeral.
comparing his two careers
- **Ray Wilson** 1934- English footballer: Simon Hattenstone *The Best of Times: What became of the heroes of '66?* (2006)

Form-Filling *see* BUREAUCRACY

France

How can you govern a country which has 246 varieties of cheese?
Charles de Gaulle

1 France is the only place where you can make love in the afternoon without people hammering on your door.
- **Barbara Cartland** 1901-2000 English writer: in *Guardian* 24 December 1984

2 Every wise and thoroughly worldly wench
Knows there's always something fishy about the French!
- **Noël Coward** 1899-1973 English dramatist, actor, and composer: 'There's Always Something Fishy about the French' (1933)

3 Dinners, soirées, poets, erratic millionaires, painters, translations, lobsters, absinthe, music, promenade, oysters, sherry, aspirin, pictures, Sapphic heiresses, editors, books, sailors. And How!
- **Hart Crane** 1899-1932 American poet: postcard from Paris, 1929

4 How can you govern a country which has 246 varieties of cheese?
- **Charles de Gaulle** 1890-1970 French soldier and statesman: Ernest Mignon *Les Mots du Général* (1962)

5 Unlike the cosy little A-roads in England, their French counterparts tended to be both straight and lined with trees, in order, it was said, that the German army might more easily find their way to Paris, and march in the shade while they did so.
- **Guy Fraser-Sampson** English writer: *Lucia on Holiday* (2012)

6 Bonjourr, you cheese-eating surrender monkeys.
Groundskeeper Willie as French teacher
- **Matt Groening** 1954- American humorist and satirist: *The Simpsons* (1995) 'Round Springfield'

7 *on being told, when estimating it would take him three years to complete his dictionary of the English language, that it had taken forty members of the Academie Française forty years to compile the French dictionary:*
Sir, thus it is. This is the proportion. Let me see; forty times forty is sixteen hundred. As three to sixteen hundred, so is the proportion of an Englishman to a Frenchman.
- **Samuel Johnson** 1709-84 English poet, critic, and lexicographer: James Boswell *Life of Johnson* (1791) 1747

8 The French are always too wordy and need cutting by half before they start.
- **Miles Kington** 1941-2008 English humorist: in *Spectator* 16 December 2006

9 No matter how politely or distinctly you ask a Parisian a question he will persist in answering you in French.
- **Fran Lebowitz** 1946- American writer: *Metropolitan Life* (1978)

10 Boy, those French, they have a different word for everything!
- **Steve Martin** 1945- American comedian: attributed

11 The Riviera isn't only a sunny place for shady people.
- **W. Somerset Maugham** 1874-1965 English novelist: *Strictly Personal* (1941)

12 Yet, who can help loving the land that has taught us
Six hundred and eighty-five ways to dress eggs?
- **Thomas Moore** 1779-1852 Irish musician and songwriter: *The Fudge Family in Paris* (1818)

13 It just proves that fifty million Frenchmen can't be wrong. They eat horses instead of ride them.
having been crippled in a riding accident in 1937
- **Cole Porter** 1891-1964 American songwriter: G. Eells *The Life that Late He Led* (1967)

14 Cannes is where you lie on the beach and stare at the stars—or vice versa.
- **Rex Reed** 1938- American critic: attributed

15 Everything is easier in France. We pay more taxes, but the hospitals don't kill you.
- **Kristin Scott Thomas** 1960- English actress: in *Daily Telegraph* 17 January 2005

16 France is a country where the money falls apart in your hands and you can't tear the toilet paper.
- **Billy Wilder** 1906-2002 American screenwriter and director: Leslie Halliwell *The Filmgoer's Book of Quotes* (1973)

Friends

see also **ENEMIES**

He hasn't an enemy in the world, and none of his friends like him.   **Oscar Wilde**

1 When you are in jail a good friend will be bailing you out. A best friend will be in the cell next to you saying 'Damn that was fun'.
- **Anonymous**: traditional saying, recently frequently attributed to Groucho Marx

2 I may be wrong, but I have never found deserting friends conciliates enemies.
- **Margot Asquith** 1864-1945 British political hostess: *Lay Sermons* (1927)

3 Champagne for my real friends, and real pain for my sham friends.
his favourite toast
- **Francis Bacon** 1909-92 Irish painter: Michael Peppiatt *Francis Bacon* (1996)

4 *definition of an acquaintance:*
A degree of friendship called slight
when its object is poor or obscure, and
intimate when he is rich or famous.
  - **Ambrose Bierce** 1842–c.1914 American
    writer: *The Cynic's Word Book* (1906)

5 *during an audience with the Pope:*
I expect you know my friend Evelyn
Waugh, who, like your holiness, is a
Roman Catholic.
  - **Randolph Churchill** 1911–68 British
    Conservative politician: attributed; in
    Penguin Dictionary of Modern Quotations
    (1971)

6 Rough diamonds are a girl's best friend.
  - **Jilly Cooper** 1937– English writer: *Angels
    Rush In* (1990)

7 To find a friend one must close one eye.
To keep him—two.
  - **Norman Douglas** 1868–1952 Scottish-born
    novelist and essayist: *South Wind* (1917)

8 Most of my friends seem either to be
dead, extremely deaf, or living in the
wrong part of Kent.
  - **John Gielgud** 1904–2000 English actor: in
    Sunday Times 14 February 1988

9 [Friends are] God's apology for relations.
  - **Hugh Kingsmill** 1889–1949 English man of
    letters: Michael Holroyd *The Best of Hugh
    Kingsmill* (1970)

10 The capacity for friendship is God's way
of apologizing for our families.
  - **Jay McInerney** 1955– American writer:
    The Last of the Savages (1996)

11 Money couldn't buy friends but you got
a better class of enemy.
  - **Spike Milligan** 1918–2002 Irish comedian:
    Puckoon (1963)

12 Scratch a lover, and find a foe.
  - **Dorothy Parker** 1893–1967 American
    critic and humorist: 'Ballade of a Great
    Weariness' (1937)

13 If it is abuse,—why one is always
sure to hear of it from one damned
goodnatured friend or another!
  - **Richard Brinsley Sheridan** 1751–1816 Irish
    dramatist and Whig politician: *The Critic*
    (1779)

14 You had only two friends in the world,
and having killed one you can't afford to
irritate the other.
  - **Tom Stoppard** 1937– British dramatist:
    Artist Descending a Staircase (1973)

15 *on Harold Macmillan's sacking seven of his
Cabinet on 13 July 1962:*
Greater love hath no man than this, that
he lay down his friends for his life.
  - **Jeremy Thorpe** 1929– British Liberal
    politician: D. E. Butler and Anthony King
    The General Election of 1964 (1965)

16 It takes your enemy and your friend,
working together, to hurt you to the
heart: the one to slander you and the
other to get the news to you.
  - **Mark Twain** 1835–1910 American writer:
    Following the Equator (1897)

17 Unfortunately we have little in common
except a mutual knowledge of a story
by Charlotte Yonge in which the hero is
an albino curate with eyes like rubies.
This is cordial, but not enough.
  - **Sylvia Townsend Warner** 1893–1978
    English writer: letter, 31 October 1967

18 We cherish our friends not for their
ability to amuse us, but for ours to
amuse them.
  - **Evelyn Waugh** 1903–66 English novelist:
    diary, 10 June 1963

19 He [Bernard Shaw] hasn't an enemy in
the world, and none of his friends like
him.
  - **Oscar Wilde** 1854–1900 Irish dramatist and
    poet: George Bernard Shaw *Sixteen Self
    Sketches* (1949)

Funerals

....

I hope you go before me because I don't want you singing at my funeral.
Spike Milligan

1 Curious but authenticated fact that a funeral is the only gathering to which the majority of men ever go willingly.
  ▪ **E. M. Delafield** 1890-1943 English writer: *The Diary of a Provincial Lady* (1930)

2 *said at the funeral of the escapologist Harry Houdini, while carrying his coffin:*
  I bet you a hundred bucks he ain't in here.
  ▪ **Charles Bancroft Dillingham** 1868-1934 American theatrical manager: in 1926, attributed

3 You can't get buried quickly at Bexhill on Sea—it's like getting a table at the Caprice.
  ▪ **David Hare** 1947- English dramatist: Richard Eyre *National Service: Diary of a Decade* (2003)

4 At his funeral in Omaha he filled the church to capacity. He was a draw right to the finish.
  after the death of the boxer Vince Foster in 1949
  ▪ **Jack Hurley:** Jonathon Green and Don Atyeo (eds.) *The Book of Sports Quotes* (1979)

5 There is nothing like a morning funeral for sharpening the appetite for lunch.
  ▪ **Arthur Marshall** 1910-89 British journalist: *Life's Rich Pageant* (1984)

6 *fax sent to Harry Secombe:*
  I hope you go before me because I don't want you singing at my funeral.
  ▪ **Spike Milligan** 1918-2002 Irish comedian: attributed; in *Daily Telegraph* 28 February 2002

7 I have nothing against undertakers personally. It's just that I wouldn't want one to bury my sister.
  ▪ **Jessica Mitford** 1917-96 British writer: in *Saturday Review* 1 February 1964

8 *on Teddy Kennedy arriving for Aristotle Onassis's funeral:*
  Looking like a priestly hustler peddling indulgences.
  ▪ **Christina Onassis** 1950-88 American-born Greek businesswoman: Peter Evans *Nemesis: the True Story of Aristotle* (2004)

9 [Memorial services are the] cocktail parties of the geriatric set.
  ▪ **Ralph Richardson** 1902-83 English actor: Ruth Dudley Edwards *Harold Macmillan* (1983)

10 Well, it only proves what they always say—give the public something they want to see, and they'll come out for it.
  on the crowds attending the funeral of the movie tycoon Harry Cohn, 2 March 1958
  ▪ **Red Skelton** 1913-97 American comedian: attributed

The Future *see* PAST, PRESENT, AND FUTURE

Gambling *see* BETTING AND GAMBLING

Games *see* SPORTS AND GAMES

Gardens

....

Eleven months' hard work and one month's acute disappointment.
John Heathcoat Amory

1 Everyone with a garden, however small, should have a few acres of woodland.
   - **Anonymous**: saying, sometimes attributed to Lord Rothschild or to an unidentified Director of the Royal Horticultural Society

2 A delectable sward, shaved as close as a bridegroom and looking just as green.
   - **Basil Boothroyd** 1910-88 English humorist: *Let's Move House* (1977)

3 I will keep returning to the virtues of sharp and swift drainage, whether a plant prefers to be wet or dry…I would have called this book Better Drains, but you would never have bought it or borrowed it for bedtime.
   - **Robin Lane Fox** 1946- English historian: *Better Gardening* (1982)

4 Eleven months' hard work and one month's acute disappointment.
   on gardening
   - **John Heathcoat Amory**: attributed; in *Guardian* 3 February 2006

5 'I distinguish the picturesque and the beautiful, and I add to them, in the laying out of the grounds, a third and distinct character, which I call *unexpectedness*.'

'Pray, Sir,' said Mr Milestone, 'by what name do you distinguish this character, when a person walks round the grounds for the second time?'
   - **Thomas Love Peacock** 1785-1866 English novelist and poet: *Headlong Hall* (1816)

6 Mort…had about the same talent for horticulture that you would find in a dead starfish.
   - **Terry Pratchett** 1948- English fantasy writer: *Mort* (1987)

7 'All really grim gardeners possess a keen sense of humus.' Capt. W. D. Pontoon.
   - **W. C. Sellar** 1898-1951 and **R. J. Yeatman** 1898-1968: *Garden Rubbish* (1930); chapter heading

8 What a man needs in gardening is a cast iron back, with a hinge in it.
   - **Charles Dudley Warner** 1829-1900 American writer: *My Summer in a Garden* (1870)

9 Perennials are the ones that grow like weeds, biennials are the ones that die this year instead of next and hardy annuals are the ones that never come up at all.
   - **Katharine Whitehorn** 1928- English journalist: *Observations* (1970)

The Generation Gap

see also **CHILDREN, PARENTS**

....

It is the one war in which everyone changes sides.   **Cyril Connolly**

1 *on the similarities between teenagers and their grandparents:*
   They're both on drugs, they both detest you, and neither of them has a job.
   - **Jasper Carrott** 1945- English comedian: in *Observer* 11 January 2004

2 What's the point in growing old if you can't hound and persecute the young?
   - **Kenneth Clarke** 1940- British Conservative politician: in *Observer* 27 May 2007 'Quotes of the Week'

3 It is the one war in which everyone changes sides.
- **Cyril Connolly** 1903-74 English writer: Tom Driberg, speech in House of Commons, 30 October 1959

4 Grown-ups never understand anything for themselves, and it is tiresome for children to be always and forever explaining things to them.
- **Antoine de Saint-Exupéry** 1900-44 French novelist: *Le Petit Prince* (1943)

5 When I was young, the old regarded me as an outrageous young fellow, and now that I'm old the young regard me as an outrageous old fellow.
- **Fred Hoyle** 1915-2001 English astrophysicist: in *Scientific American* March 1995

6 The young have aspirations that never come to pass, the old have reminiscences of what never happened.
- **Saki** 1870-1916 Scottish writer: *Reginald* (1904)

7 The denunciation of the young is a necessary part of the hygiene of older people, and greatly assists the circulation of their blood.
- **Logan Pearsall Smith** 1865-1946 American-born man of letters: *Afterthoughts* (1931) 'Age and Death'

8 There is more felicity on the far side of baldness than young men can possibly imagine.
- **Logan Pearsall Smith** 1865-1946 American-born man of letters: *Afterthoughts* (1931) 'Age and Death'

9 When I was a boy of 14, my father was so ignorant I could hardly stand to have the old man around. But when I got to be 21, I was astonished at how much the old man had learned in seven years.
- **Mark Twain** 1835-1910 American writer: attributed in *Reader's Digest* September 1939, but not traced in his works

10 Two things my parents did for me as a child stand head and shoulders above what parents usually do for their children. They had me in Egypt and they set me a vivid example of everything I didn't want to be when I grew up.
- **Jill Tweedie** 1936-93 British journalist: *Eating Children* (1993)

11 When I was your age...I had been an inconsolable widower for three months, and was already paying my addresses to your admirable mother.
- **Oscar Wilde** 1854-1900 Irish dramatist and poet: *An Ideal Husband* (1895)

Gifts

What do you give to the man who's had everyone?   **Alana Stewart**

1 How do you tell the difference between men's real gifts and their guilt gifts? Guilt gifts are nicer.
- **Anonymous**: saying

2 To a woman, having flowers sent to her is thoughtful. To a man, sending flowers is a way of being thoughtful without putting any thought in to it. It's like foreign aid.
- **Roy Blount Jr** 1941- American writer: *What Men Don't Tell Women* (1984)

3 I kinda like it when you forget to give me presents. It makes me feel like we're married.
- **Abe Burrows** 1910-85 American librettist: *Guys and Dolls* (1950)

4 Mrs Thatcher tells us she has given the French president a piece of her mind...not a gift I would receive with alacrity.
- **Denis Healey** 1917- British Labour politician: in *Today* 5 September 1989

5 *offering peanuts to Helen Hayes:*
I wish they were emeralds.
the line worked. And twenty years later,

he gave her emeralds. 'I wish they were peanuts,' he said
- **Charles MacArthur** 1895-1956 American dramatist: attributed, *c.* 1925

6 Ever since Eve gave Adam the apple, there has been a misunderstanding between the sexes about gifts.
- **Nan Robertson** 1926-2009 American journalist: in *New York Times* 28 November 1957

7 From my experience of life I believe my personal motto should be 'Beware of men bearing flowers.'
- **Muriel Spark** 1918-2006 British novelist: *Curriculum Vitae* (1992)

8 *on ex-husband Rod Stewart:*
What do you give to the man who's had everyone?
- **Alana Stewart** 1945- American actress: attributed

God

see also **RELIGION**

....

I'm sorry, we don't do God.   **Alastair Campbell**

1 If it turns out that there is a God, I don't think that he's evil. But the worst that you can say about him is that basically he's an underachiever.
- **Woody Allen** 1935- American film director, writer, and actor: *Love and Death* (1975 film)

2 Not only is there no God, but try getting a plumber on weekends.
- **Woody Allen** 1935- American film director, writer, and actor: in *New Yorker* 27 December 1969 'My Philosophy'

3 If only God would give me some clear sign! Like making a large deposit in my name at a Swiss bank.
- **Woody Allen** 1935- American film director, writer, and actor: 'Selections from the Allen Notebooks' in *New Yorker* 5 November 1973

4 God is silent, now if only we can get Man to shut up.
- **Woody Allen** 1935- American film director, writer, and actor: 'Remembering Needleman' (1976)

5 God is not dead but alive and working on a much less ambitious project.
- **Anonymous**: graffito quoted in *Guardian* 26 November 1975

6 Dear Sir,
Your astonishment's odd:
I am always about in the Quad.

And that's why the tree
Will continue to be,
Since observed by
Yours faithfully,
God.
- **Anonymous**: reply to verse by Ronald Knox (see **god** 30); Langford Reed *Complete Limerick Book* (1924)

7 Not odd
Of God:
Goyim
Annoy 'im.
- **Anonymous**: in *Leo Rosten's Book of Laughter* (1986); see **god** 12, **god** 22

8 If absolute power corrupts absolutely, where does that leave God?
- **Anonymous**: overheard at the Garrick Club, 26 May 1991; Milton Shulman *Voltaire, Goldberg and Others* (2000)

9 CLAIRE: How do you know you're...God?
EARL OF GURNEY: Simple. When I pray to Him I find I'm talking to myself.
- **Peter Barnes** 1931-2004 English dramatist: *The Ruling Class* (1969)

10 If I were Her what would really piss me off the worst is that they cannot even get My gender right for Christsakes.
- **Roseanne Barr** 1953- : *Roseanne* (1990)

11 *Birrell once saw a man treat George Eliot rudely:*
I sat down in a corner and prayed to God

to blast him. God did nothing, and ever since I have been an agnostic.
- **Augustine Birrell** 1850-1933 British essayist: Harold Laski, letter to Oliver Wendell Holmes, 21 January 1928

12 But not so odd
As those who choose
A Jewish God,
But spurn the Jews.
- **Cecil Browne** 1932- American businessman: reply to verse by William Norman Ewer; see **god** 7, **god** 22

13 God will not always be a Tory.
- **Lord Byron** 1788-1824 English poet: letter, 2 February 1821

14 I'm sorry, we don't do God.
Tony Blair's Director of Communications, when Blair was asked about his Christian faith in an interview for Vanity Fair *magazine*
- **Alastair Campbell** 1957- British journalist: in *Daily Telegraph* 5 May 2003

15 He's not the Messiah! He's a very naughty boy!
Brian's mother to his would-be followers
- **Graham Chapman** 1941-89, **John Cleese** 1939- , and **others** British comedians: *Monty Python's Life of Brian* (1979 film)

16 I am prepared to meet my Maker. Whether my Maker is prepared for the great ordeal of meeting me is another matter.
- **Winston Churchill** 1874-1965 British Conservative statesman: at a news conference in Washington in 1954

17 Thou shalt have one God only; who Would be at the expense of two?
- **Arthur Hugh Clough** 1819-61 English poet: 'The Latest Decalogue' (1862)

18 I've absolutely no idea if God exists. It seems unlikely to me, but then—does a trout know that I exist?
- **Billy Connolly** 1942- Scottish comedian: in *Independent on Sunday* 16 December 2012

19 Do I believe in God? Let's say we have a working relationship.
- **Noël Coward** 1899-1973 English dramatist, actor, and composer: Sheridan Morley *The Quotable Noël Coward* (1999)

20 I don't believe in God because I don't believe in Mother Goose.
- **Clarence Darrow** 1857-1938 American lawyer: speech in Toronto in 1930

21 Our only hope rests on the off-chance that God does exist.
- **Alice Thomas Ellis** 1932-2005 English novelist: *Unexplained Laughter* (1985)

22 How odd
Of God
To choose
The Jews.
- **William Norman Ewer** 1885-1976 British writer: *Week-End Book* (1924); see **god** 7, **god** 12

23 The world is disgracefully managed, one hardly knows to whom to complain.
- **Ronald Firbank** 1886-1926 English novelist: *Vainglory* (1915)

24 If sexual experiences were theoretically minimal, social expectations were on the contrary great. Once there was a Drag Hunt Ball just outside Oxford, to which I had unaccountably failed to be asked. I asked God to so something about it, and God recklessly killed poor King George VI, as a result of which the Hunt Ball was cancelled.
- **Antonia Fraser** 1932- British writer: Ann Thwaite (ed.) *My Oxford* (1977)

25 Forgive, O Lord, my little jokes on Thee
And I'll forgive Thy great big one on me.
- **Robert Frost** 1874-1963 American poet: 'Cluster of Faith' (1962)

26 Did God who gave us flowers and trees, Also provide the allergies?
- **E. Y. Harburg** 1898-1981 American songwriter: 'A Nose is a Nose is a Nose' (1965)

27 God will pardon me, it is His trade.
- **Heinrich Heine** 1797-1856 German poet: on his deathbed, in Alfred Meissner *Heinrich Heine. Erinnerungen* (1856); see **royalty** 7

28 The great act of faith is when a man decides he is not God.
- **Oliver Wendell Holmes Jr.** 1841-1935 American lawyer: letter to William James, 24 March 1907

29 *to an undergraduate trying to excuse himself from attendance at early morning chapel on the plea of loss of faith:*
You will find God by tomorrow morning, or leave this college.
- **Benjamin Jowett** 1817-93 English classicist: Kenneth Rose *Superior Person* (1969)

30 There once was a man who said, 'God Must think it exceedingly odd
If he finds that this tree
Continues to be
When there's no one about in the Quad.'
- **Ronald Knox** 1888-1957 English writer and Roman Catholic priest: Langford Reed *Complete Limerick Book* (1924); see **god** 6

31 God is love, but get it in writing.
- **Gypsy Rose Lee** 1914-70 American striptease artiste: attributed

32 I don't know why it is that the religious never ascribe common sense to God.
- **W. Somerset Maugham** 1874-1965 English novelist: *A Writer's Notebook* (1949) written in 1941

33 The chief contribution of Protestantism to human thought is its massive proof that God is a bore.
- **H. L. Mencken** 1880-1956 American journalist and literary critic: *Minority Report* (1956)

34 It is impossible to imagine the universe run by a wise, just and omnipotent God, but it is quite easy to imagine it run by a board of gods. If such a board actually exists it operates precisely like the board of a corporation that is losing money.
- **H. L. Mencken** 1880-1956 American journalist and literary critic: *Minority Report* (1956)

35 Satan probably wouldn't have talked so big if God had been his wife.
- **P. J. O'Rourke** 1947- American humorous writer: *Modern Manners* (1984)

36 God can stand being told by Professor Ayer and Marghanita Laski that He doesn't exist.
- **J. B. Priestley** 1894-1984 English novelist, dramatist, and critic: in *Listener* 1 July 1965

37 *what he plans to say to God when they meet:*
I've made a lot of mistakes, but, boy, you've made a lot more.
- **Burt Reynolds** 1936- American actor: in *Sunday Times* 17 February 2002

38 Those who set out to serve both God and Mammon soon discover that there is no God.
- **Logan Pearsall Smith** 1865-1946 American-born man of letters: *Afterthoughts* (1931) 'Other People'

39 Her conception of God was certainly not orthodox. She felt towards Him as she might have felt towards a glorified sanitary engineer; and in some of her speculations she seems hardly to distinguish between the Deity and the Drains.
of Florence Nightingale
- **Lytton Strachey** 1880-1932 English biographer: *Eminent Victorians* (1918)

40 If you talk to God, you are praying; if God talks to you, you have schizophrenia. If the dead talk to you, you are a spiritualist; if God talks to you, you are a schizophrenic.
- **Thomas Szasz** 1920-2012 Hungarian-born psychiatrist: *The Second Sin* (1973) 'Schizophrenia'

41 Only one thing, is impossible for God: to find any sense in any copyright law on the planet.
- **Mark Twain** 1835-1910 American writer: Notebook 23 May 1903

42 God was left out of the Constitution but was furnished a front seat on the coins of the country.
- **Mark Twain** 1835-1910 American writer: *Mark Twain in Eruption* (1940)

Golf

see also **SPORTS**

....

Golf is a good walk spoiled.   **Mark Twain**

1 *on the golf course, on being asked by Nancy Cunard, 'What is your handicap?'*
Drink and debauchery.
- **Lord Castlerosse** 1891-1943: Philip Ziegler *Diana Cooper* (1981)

2 QUESTION: What is your handicap?
ANSWER: I'm a colored, one-eyed Jew—do I need anything else?
- **Sammy Davis Jnr.** 1925-90 American entertainer: *Yes I Can* (1965)

3 One who has to shout 'Fore' when he putts.
definition of a Coarse Golfer
- **Michael Green** 1927- English writer: *The Art of Coarse Golf* (1967)

4 Men who would face torture without a word become blasphemous at the short fourteenth. It is clear that the game of golf may well be included in that category of intolerable provocations which may legally excuse or mitigate behaviour not otherwise excusable.
- **A. P. Herbert** 1890-1971 English writer and humorist: *Misleading Cases* (1935)

5 If you watch a game, it's fun. If you play it, it's recreation. If you work at it, it's golf.
- **Bob Hope** 1903-2003 American comedian: in *Reader's Digest* October 1958

6 I consider it unsportsmanlike to hit a sitting ball.
on why he disliked golf
- **Ernest Hornung** 1866-1921 English novelist: attributed; Julian Barnes *Arthur and George* (2005)

7 I'm playing like Tarzan and scoring like Jane.
- **Chi Chi Rodriguez** 1935- Puerto Rican golfer: attributed, 1982

8 Golf is a good walk spoiled.
- **Mark Twain** 1835-1910 American writer: Alex Ayres *Greatly Exaggerated: the Wit and Wisdom of Mark Twain* (1988); attributed

9 The uglier a man's legs are, the better he plays golf—it's almost a law.
- **H. G. Wells** 1866-1946 English novelist: *Bealby* (1915)

10 The least thing upset him on the links. He missed short putts because of the uproar of the butterflies in the adjoining meadows.
- **P. G. Wodehouse** 1881-1975 English writer: *The Clicking of Cuthbert* (1922)

11 Golf...is the infallible test. The man who can go into a patch of rough alone, with the knowledge that only God is watching him, and play his ball where it lies, is the man who will serve you faithfully and well.
- **P. G. Wodehouse** 1881-1975 English writer: *The Clicking of Cuthbert* (1922)

Gossip

I hate to spread rumours, but what else can one do with them?   **Amanda Lear**

1 I know that's a secret, for it's whispered every where.
   - **William Congreve** 1670-1729 English dramatist: *Love for Love* (1695)

2 They come together like the Coroner's Inquest, to sit upon the murdered reputations of the week.
   - **William Congreve** 1670-1729 English dramatist: *The Way of the World* (1700)

3 A secret in the Oxford sense: you may tell it to only one person at a time.
   - **Oliver Franks** 1905-92 English philosopher and administrator: in *Sunday Telegraph* 30 January 1977

4 It's the gossip columnist's business to write about what is none of his business.
   - **Louis Kronenberger** 1904-80 American critic: *The Cart and the Horse* (1964)

5 I hate to spread rumours, but what else can one do with them?
   - **Amanda Lear** French singer: in an interview in 1978; Jonathon Green (ed.) *A Dictionary of Contemporary Quotations* (1978)

6 If you haven't got anything good to say about anyone come and sit by me.
   - **Alice Roosevelt Longworth** 1884-1980 American socialite: maxim embroidered on a cushion; Michael Teague *Mrs L: Conversations with Alice Roosevelt Longworth* (1981)

7 She proceeds to dip her little fountain-pen filler into pots of oily venom and to squirt this mixture at all her friends.
   of the society hostess Mrs Ronnie Greville
   - **Harold Nicolson** 1886-1968 English diplomat, politician, and writer: diary, 20 July 1937

8 I hope there's a tinge of disgrace about me. Hopefully, there's one good scandal left in me yet.
   - **Diana Rigg** 1938- British actress: in *Times* 3 May 1999

9 No one gossips about other people's secret virtues.
   - **Bertrand Russell** 1872-1970 British philosopher and mathematician: *On Education Especially in Early Childhood* (1926)

10 I'm called away by particular business— but I leave my character behind me.
   - **Richard Brinsley Sheridan** 1751-1816 Irish dramatist and Whig politician: *The School for Scandal* (1777)

11 Here is the whole set! a character dead at every word.
   - **Richard Brinsley Sheridan** 1751-1816 Irish dramatist and Whig politician: *The School for Scandal* (1777)

12 Gossip is just news running ahead of itself in a red satin dress.
   - **Liz Smith** 1923- American journalist: in *Working Woman* 1982

13 It is perfectly monstrous the way people go about, nowadays, saying things against one behind one's back that are absolutely and entirely true.
   - **Oscar Wilde** 1854-1900 Irish dramatist and poet: *A Woman of No Importance* (1893)

14 There is only one thing in the world worse than being talked about, and that is not being talked about.
   - **Oscar Wilde** 1854-1900 Irish dramatist and poet: *The Picture of Dorian Gray* (1891)

Government

see also **DEMOCRACY, POLITICS**

We all know that Prime Ministers are wedded to the truth, but like other married couples they sometimes live apart.   **Saki**

1 The first requirement of a statesman is that he be dull.
   ▪ **Dean Acheson** 1893–1971 American politician: in *Observer* 21 June 1970

2 There is, in fact, no law or government at all [in Italy]; and it is wonderful how well things go on without them.
   ▪ **Lord Byron** 1788–1824 English poet: letter, 2 January 1821

3 Democracy means government by the uneducated, while aristocracy means government by the badly educated.
   ▪ **G. K. Chesterton** 1874–1936 English essayist, novelist, and poet: in *New York Times* 1 February 1931

4 Like most Chief Whips he [Michael Jopling] knew who the shits were.
   ▪ **Alan Clark** 1928–99 British Conservative politician: diary, 17 June 1987

5 A wartime Minister of Information is compelled, in the national interest, to such continuous acts of duplicity that even his natural hair must grow to resemble a wig.
   of Brendan Bracken
   ▪ **Claud Cockburn** 1904–81 British writer and journalist: *Crossing the Line* (1958)

6 Distrust of authority should be the first civic duty.
   ▪ **Norman Douglas** 1868–1952 Scottish-born novelist and essayist: *An Almanac* October (1941)

7 But the privilege and pleasure
   That we treasure beyond measure
   Is to run on little errands for the
      Ministers of State.
   ▪ **W. S. Gilbert** 1836–1911 English writer: *The Gondoliers* (1889)

8 'Do you pray for the senators, Dr Hale?'
   'No, I look at the senators and I pray for the country.'
   ▪ **Edward Everett Hale** 1822–1909 American Unitarian clergyman: Van Wyck Brooks *New England Indian Summer* (1940)

9 This we learn from Watergate
   That almost any creep'll
   Be glad to help the Government
   Overthrow the people.
   ▪ **E. Y. Harburg** 1898–1981 American songwriter: 'History Lesson' (1976)

10 This high official, all allow,
   Is grossly overpaid;
   There wasn't any Board, and now
   There isn't any Trade.
   ▪ **A. P. Herbert** 1890–1971 English writer and humorist: 'The President of the Board of Trade' (1922)

11 People must not do things for fun. We are not here for fun. There is no reference to fun in any Act of Parliament.
   ▪ **A. P. Herbert** 1890–1971 English writer and humorist: *Uncommon Law* (1935) 'Is it a Free Country?'

12 Office hours are from 12 to 1 with an hour off for lunch.
   of the US Senate
   ▪ **George S. Kaufman** 1889–1961 American dramatist: Howard Teichmann *George S. Kaufman* (1973)

13 We are a government of laws. Any laws some government hack can find to louse up a man who's down.
   ▪ **Murray Kempton** 1917–97 American journalist: in *New York Post* 21 December 1955

14 I work for a Government I despise for ends I think criminal.
   ▪ **John Maynard Keynes** 1883–1946 English economist: letter to Duncan Grant, 15 December 1917

15 How is the world ruled and how
do wars start? Diplomats tell lies to
journalists and then believe what they
read.
- **Karl Kraus** 1874-1936 Austrian satirist:
  Aphorisms and More Aphorisms (1909)

16 *on suggestions that the US should draft a*
Constitution for Iraq:
We might as well give them ours.
We aren't using it.
- **Jay Leno** 1950- American comedian:
  attributed; in *Mail on Sunday* 7 September
  2003

17 One of these days the people of
Louisiana are going to get good
government—and they aren't going
to like it.
- **Huey Long** 1893-1935 American
  Democratic politician: attributed

18 *describing the traditional method of running*
the economy:
[Like] looking up trains in last year's
Bradshaw.
- **Harold Macmillan** 1894-1986 British
  Conservative statesman: as Chancellor
  of the Exchequer, 1956; in Alistair Horne
  Macmillan (1988)

19 There are two reasons for making an
appointment. Either there was nobody
else; or there *was* somebody else.
- **Lord Normanbrook** 1902-67 British civil
  servant: Anthony Sampson *The Changing*
  Anatomy of Britain (1982)

20 I don't want to abolish government.
I simply want to reduce it to the size
where I can drag it into the bathroom
and drown it in the bathtub.
- **Grover Norquist** 1956- American lobbyist:
  interview on National Public Radio,
  Morning Edition, 25 May 2001

21 The nine most terrifying words in the
English language are, 'I'm from the
government and I'm here to help.'
on assistance to farmers
- **Ronald Reagan** 1911-2004 American
  Republican statesman: at a press
  conference in Chicago, 2 August 1986

22 When you stop being a minister,
you get in the back of the car and

it doesn't go anywhere.
- **Malcolm Rifkind** 1946- British Conservative
  politician: in *Times* 7 May 2010

23 Are you labouring under the impression
that I read these memoranda of yours?
I can't even lift them.
to Leon Henderson
- **Franklin D. Roosevelt** 1882-1945 American
  Democratic statesman: J. K. Galbraith
  Ambassador's Journal (1969)

24 We all know that Prime Ministers are
wedded to the truth, but like other
married couples they sometimes live
apart.
- **Saki** 1870-1916 Scottish writer: *The*
  Unbearable Bassington (1912)

25 Members [of civil service orders] rise
from CMG (known sometimes in
Whitehall as 'Call Me God') to the
KCMG ('Kindly Call Me God') to—for
a select few governors and super-
ambassadors—the GCMG ('God Calls
Me God').
- **Anthony Sampson** 1926-2004 British
  writer: *Anatomy of Britain* (1962)

26 A government which robs Peter to pay
Paul can always depend on the support
of Paul.
- **George Bernard Shaw** 1856-1950 Irish
  dramatist: *Everybody's Political What's*
  What? (1944)

27 It's a very sobering feeling to be up in
space and realize that one's safety factor
was determined by the lowest bidder on
a government contract.
- **Alan Shepard** 1923-98 American astronaut:
  in 1961, attributed in various forms

28 I don't mind how much my Ministers
talk, so long as they do what I say.
- **Margaret Thatcher** 1925-2013 British
  Conservative stateswoman: in *Observer*
  27 January 1980

29 *of his first Cabinet meeting as Prime Minister:*
An extraordinary affair. I gave them
their orders and they wanted to stay
and discuss them.
- **Duke of Wellington** 1769-1852 British
  soldier and statesman: Peter Hennessy
  Whitehall (1990)

30 Now that the House of Commons is
trying to become useful, it does a great
deal of harm.
- **Oscar Wilde** 1854-1900 Irish dramatist and
poet: *An Ideal Husband* (1895)

31 *the White House in the time of President
Eisenhower:*
The Tomb of the Well-Known Soldier.
- **Emlyn Williams** 1905-87 Welsh dramatist:
James Harding *Emlyn Williams* (1987)

Hair

Ronald Reagan doesn't dye his hair, he's just prematurely orange.　**Gerald Ford**

1 *when asked by his barber how he would like
his hair cut:*
In silence.
- **Archelaus** d. 399 BC Macedonian king:
Plutarch *Moralia*

2 Libby…was what we used to call a
'suicide blonde' (dyed by her own
hand).
- **Saul Bellow** 1915-2005 American novelist:
*Him With His Foot in His Mouth and Other
Stories* (1984)

3 I have learned—and this may be the
most important thing I say to you
today—hair matters. Pay attention to
your hair, because everyone else will.
- **Hillary Rodham Clinton** 1947- American
lawyer and politician: speech to students at
Yale, 20 May 2001

4 Not having to worry about your hair

any more is the secret upside of death.
- **Nora Ephron** 1941-2012 American
screenwriter and director: *I Feel Bad About
My Neck* (2008)

5 Ronald Reagan doesn't dye his hair, he's
just prematurely orange.
- **Gerald Ford** 1909-2006 American
Republican statesman: in 1974, attributed

6 A hair in the head is worth two in the
brush.
- **Oliver Herford** 1863-1935 English-born
American humorist: attributed

7 He has turned almost alarmingly
blond—he's gone past platinum,
he must be plutonium, his hair is
coordinated with his teeth.
on Robert Redford in The Sting
- **Pauline Kael** 1919-2001 American film critic:
in *The New Yorker* 31 December 1973

Handwriting

The dawn of legibility in his handwriting has revealed his utter inability to spell.
Ian Hay

1 That exquisite handwriting like a fly
which has been trained at the Russian
ballet.
of George Bernard Shaw's handwriting
- **James Agate** 1877-1947 British drama critic
and novelist: diary, 22 September 1944

2 I never saw Monty James's writing but
doubt whether he can have been more
illegible than Lady Colefax: the only
hope of deciphering *her* invitations,

someone said, was to pin them up on
the wall and *run* past them!
- **Rupert Hart-Davis** 1907-99 English
publisher: letter to George Lyttelton,
13 November 1955

3 The dawn of legibility in his handwriting
has revealed his utter inability to spell.
- **Ian Hay** 1876-1952 Scottish novelist and
dramatist: attributed; perhaps used in a
dramatization of *The Housemaster* (1938)

4 *of Foreign Office handwriting:*
Iron railings leaning out of the
perpendicular.
- **Lord Palmerston** 1784-1865 British
statesman: J. A. Gere and John Sparrow
(eds.) *Geoffrey Madan's Notebooks*
(1981)

5 No individual word was decipherable,
but, with a bold reader, groups could
be made to conform to a scheme

based on probabilities.
- **Edith Œ. Somerville** 1858-1949 and **Martin
Ross** 1862-1915 Irish writers: *In Mr Knox's
Country* (1915)

6 I know that handwriting...I remember
it perfectly. The ten commandments in
every stroke of the pen, and the moral
law all over the page.
- **Oscar Wilde** 1854-1900 Irish dramatist and
poet: *An Ideal Husband* (1895)

Hangovers *see* DRUNKENNESS AND HANGOVERS

Happiness

see also HOPE, SATISFACTION

Life would be very pleasant if it were not for its enjoyments.   **R. S. Surtees**

1 Happy as a bastard on Father's Day.
Australian expression
- **Anonymous**: Richard Eyre *National Service:
Diary of a Decade* (2003)

2 The great pleasure in life is doing what
people say you cannot do.
- **Walter Bagehot** 1826-77 English economist
and essayist: in *Prospective Review* 1853

3 Happiness is good health—and a bad
memory.
- **Ingrid Bergman** 1915-82 Swedish actress:
J. R. Colombo *Colombo's Hollywood: Wit
and Wisdom of the Moviemakers* (1979)

4 Happiness is having a large, loving,
caring, close-knit family in another city.
- **George Burns** 1896-1996 American
comedian: attributed

5 Let us have wine and women, mirth
and laughter,
Sermons and soda-water the day after.
- **Lord Byron** 1788-1824 English poet:
Don Juan (1819-24)

6 Happiness is...finding two olives in your
martini when you're hungry.
- **Johnny Carson** 1925-2005 American
broadcaster and comedian: *Happiness is—a
Dry Martini* (1966)

7 There's no greater bliss in life than
when the plumber eventually comes to
unblock your drains. No writer can give
that sort of pleasure.
- **Victoria Glendinning** 1937-   English
biographer and novelist: in *Observer*
3 January 1993

8 12.35 p.m.—The phone rings. I am not
amused. This is not my favourite way
to wake up. My favourite way to wake
up is to have a certain French movie
star whisper softly to me at two-thirty
in the afternoon that if I want to get to
Sweden in time to pick up my Nobel
Prize for Literature I had better ring for
breakfast. This occurs rather less often
than one might wish.
- **Fran Lebowitz** 1946-   American writer:
Metropolitan Life (1978)

9 There's no pleasure on earth that's
worth sacrificing for the sake of an
extra five years in the geriatric ward
of the Sunset Old People's Home,
Weston-Super-Mare.
- **John Mortimer** 1923-2009 English writer
and barrister: *Rumpole's Last Case* (1987)

10 Men who are unhappy, like men who

sleep badly, are always proud of the fact.
- **Bertrand Russell** 1872-1970 British philosopher and mathematician: *The Conquest of Happiness* (1930)

11 He's simply got the instinct for being unhappy highly developed.
- **Saki** 1870-1916 Scottish writer: *Chronicles of Clovis* (1911)

12 But a lifetime of happiness! No man alive could bear it: it would be hell on earth.
- **George Bernard Shaw** 1856-1950 Irish dramatist: *Man and Superman* (1903)

13 There are two tragedies in life. One is not to get your heart's desire. The other is to get it.
- **George Bernard Shaw** 1856-1950 Irish dramatist: *Man and Superman* (1903)

14 Life would be very pleasant if it were not for its enjoyments.
- **R. S. Surtees** 1805-64 English sporting journalist and novelist: *Mr Facey Romford's Hounds* (1865)

15 Let us all be happy, and live within our means, even if we have to borrer the money to do it with.
- **Artemus Ward** 1834-67 American humorist: *Artemus Ward in London* (1867)

16 A cigarette is the perfect type of a perfect pleasure. It is exquisite, and it leaves one unsatisfied. What more can one want?
- **Oscar Wilde** 1854-1900 Irish dramatist and poet: *The Picture of Dorian Gray* (1891)

17 All the things I really like to do are either illegal, immoral, or fattening.
- **Alexander Woollcott** 1887-1943 American writer: R. E. Drennan *Wit's End* (1973)

Headlines

Sticks nix hick pix.   **Anonymous**

1 Headless Body in Topless Bar.
- **Anonymous**: headline in *New York Post* 15 April 1983

2 Dr Fuchs off to south ice.
headline on the departure of a Polar expedition
- **Anonymous**: in *Liverpool Daily Post, c.* 1960s; Fritz Spiegl *Keep Taking the Tabloids* (1983)

3 Queen to skip Chuck nups.
announcing that the Queen would not attend the wedding of Charles, Prince of Wales, and Camilla Parker Bowles
- **Anonymous**: headline in *New York Post* 23 February 2005

4 Sticks nix hick pix.
on the lack of enthusiasm for farm dramas among rural populations
- **Anonymous**: headline in *Variety* 17 July 1935

5 It's The Sun Wot Won It.
following the 1992 general election
- **Anonymous**: headline in *Sun* 11 April 1992

6 NUT SCREWS WASHERS AND BOLTS.
reported headline in a Chinese newspaper above the story of an escapee from an asylum who broke into a laundry and raped several laundresses before escaping
- **Anonymous**: Claud Cockburn *I, Claud* (1967)

7 If Kinnock wins today will the last person to leave Britain please turn out the lights.
on election day, showing Neil Kinnock's head inside a light bulb
- **Anonymous**: headline in *Sun* 9 April 1992

8 If I rescued a child from drowning, the Press would no doubt headline the story 'Benn grabs child.'
- **Tony Benn** 1925- British Labour politician: in *Observer* 2 March 1975

9 *with which Cockburn claimed to have won a competition at* The Times *for the dullest headline:*
Small earthquake in Chile. Not many dead.
- **Claud Cockburn** 1904-81 British writer and journalist: *In Time of Trouble* (1956)

10 SIXTY HORSES WEDGED IN CHIMNEY
  The story to fit this sensational headline
  has not turned up yet.
  ▪ **J. B. Morton** 1893-1975 British journalist:
  Michael Frayn (ed.) *The Best of Beachcomber*
  (1963)

11 Marquis's Son Unused to Wine.
  ▪ **Evelyn Waugh** 1903-66 English novelist:
  headline in *Brideshead Revisited* (1945)

Health *see* SICKNESS AND HEALTH

Heaven and Hell

I have friends in both places.   **Mark Twain**

1 *of Lord Curzon, who at the age of thirty-nine
  had been created Viceroy of India:*
  For all the rest of his life Curzon was
  influenced by his sudden journey to
  heaven at the age of thirty-nine, and
  then by his return seven years later to
  earth, for the remainder of his mortal
  existence.
  ▪ **Lord Beaverbrook** 1879-1964 Canadian-
  born British newspaper proprietor and
  Conservative politician: *Men and Power*
  (1956)

2 I always say, as you know, that if my
  fellow citizens want to go to Hell I will
  help them. It's my job.
  ▪ **Oliver Wendell Holmes Jr.** 1841-1935
  American lawyer: letter to Harold Laski,
  4 March 1920

3 Whose love is given over-well
  Shall look on Helen's face in hell
  Whilst they whose love is thin and wise
  Shall see John Knox in Paradise.
  ▪ **Dorothy Parker** 1893-1967 American critic
  and humorist: 'Partial Comfort' (1937)

4 The Devil himself had probably
  re-designed Hell in the light of
  information he had gained from
  observing airport layouts.
  ▪ **Anthony Price** 1928- English writer and
  editor: *The Memory Trap* (1989)

5 My idea of heaven is, eating *pâté de foie
  gras* to the sound of trumpets.
  ▪ **Sydney Smith** 1771-1845 English clergyman
  and essayist: view ascribed by Smith to his
  friend Henry Luttrell; Peter Virgin *Sydney
  Smith* (1994)

6 I have friends in both places.
  ▪ **Mark Twain** 1835-1910 American writer:
  Archibald Henderson *Mark Twain* (1911)

7 If Max [Beaverbrook] gets to Heaven he
  won't last long. He will be chucked out
  for trying to pull off a merger between
  Heaven and Hell…after having secured
  a controlling interest in key subsidiary
  companies in both places, of course.
  ▪ **H. G. Wells** 1866-1946 English novelist:
  A. J. P. Taylor *Beaverbrook* (1972)

Heroes

....

We can't all be heroes because somebody has to sit on the curb and clap as they go by.   **Will Rogers**

1 Show me a hero and I will write you a tragedy.
  - **F. Scott Fitzgerald** 1896-1940 American novelist: Edmund Wilson (ed.) *The Crack-Up* (1945) 'Note-Books E'

2 The important thing when you are going to do something brave is to have someone on hand to witness it.
  - **Michael Howard** 1922–   English historian: in *Observer* 18 May 1980

3 I'm a hero wid coward's legs, I'm a hero from the waist up.
  - **Spike Milligan** 1918-2002 Irish comedian: *Puckoon* (1963)

4 Genghis Khan was not exactly lovable but I suppose he is my favourite historical character because he was damned efficient.
  - **Kerry Packer** 1937-2005 Australian media tycoon: in 1979, attributed; Jonathon Green *A Dictionary of Contemporary Quotations* (1982)

5 We can't all be heroes because someone has to sit on the curb and clap as they go by.
  - **Will Rogers** 1879-1935 American actor and humorist: attributed, Laurence J. Peter *Quotations for Our Time* (1977)

6 But be not afraid of greatness: some men are born great, some achieve greatness, and some have greatness thrust upon them.
  - **William Shakespeare** 1564-1616 English dramatist: *Twelfth Night* (1601)

History

....

History repeats itself; historians repeat one other.   **Rupert Brooke**

1 I often think it odd that it should be so dull, for a great deal of it must be invention.
  on history
  - **Jane Austen** 1775-1817 English novelist: *Northanger Abbey* (1818)

2 History is a commentary on the various and continuing incapabilities of men. What is history? History is women following behind with the buckets.
  - **Alan Bennett** 1934–   English dramatist and actor: *The History Boys* (2004)

3 I was still a medieval historian, not a profession, I imagine, with a high sexual strike rate.
  - **Alan Bennett** 1934–   English dramatist and actor: *Untold Stories* (2005)

4 An account, mostly false, of events, mostly unimportant, which are brought about by rulers, mostly knaves, and soldiers, mostly fools.
  definition of history
  - **Ambrose Bierce** 1842-c.1914 American writer: *The Cynic's Word Book* (1906)

5 History repeats itself; historians repeat one other.
  - **Rupert Brooke** 1887-1915 English poet: letter to Geoffrey Keynes, 4 June 1906

6 People who make history know nothing about history. You can see that in the sort of history they make.
  - **G. K. Chesterton** 1874-1936 English essayist, novelist, and poet: J. A. Gere and John Sparrow (eds.) *Geoffrey Madan's Notebooks* (1981)

7 One of the lessons of history is Nothing is often a good thing to do and always a clever thing to say.
 ▪ **Will Durant** 1855-1981 American historian: in *Reader's Digest* November 1972

8 History teaches us that men and nations behave wisely once they have exhausted all other alternatives.
 ▪ **Abba Eban** 1915-2002 Israeli diplomat: speech in London 16 December 1970

9 History is more or less bunk.
 ▪ **Henry Ford** 1863-1947 American car manufacturer and businessman: in *Chicago Tribune* 25 May 1916

10 Does Magna Carta mean nothing to you? Did she die in vain?
 ▪ **Ray Galton** 1930- and **Alan Simpson** 1929- English scriptwriters: *Hancock's Half Hour* (BBC radio, 1959) 'Twelve Angry Men', spoken by Tony Hancock

11 History unravels gently, like an old sweater. It has been patched and darned many times, reknitted to suit different people, shoved in a box under the sink of censorship to be cut up for the dusters of propaganda, yet it always— eventually—manages to spring into its old familiar shape. History has a habit of changing the people who think they are changing it. History always has a few tricks up its frayed sleeve. It's been around a long time.
 ▪ **Terry Pratchett** 1948- English fantasy writer: *Mort* (1987)

12 People don't alter history any more than birds alter the sky, they just make brief patterns in it.
 ▪ **Terry Pratchett** 1948- English fantasy writer: *Mort* (1987)

13 History is not what you thought. *It is what you can remember.*
 ▪ **W. C. Sellar** 1898-1951 and **R. J. Yeatman** 1898-1968: *1066 and All That* (1930) 'Compulsory Preface'

14 The Cavaliers (Wrong but Wromantic) and the Roundheads (Right but Repulsive).
 ▪ **W. C. Sellar** 1898-1951 and **R. J. Yeatman** 1898-1968: *1066 and All That* (1930)

15 AMERICA was thus clearly top nation, and History came to a .
 ▪ **W. C. Sellar** 1898-1951 and **R. J. Yeatman** 1898-1968: *1066 and All That* (1930)

16 SWINDON: What will history say?
 BURGOYNE: History, sir, will tell lies as usual.
 ▪ **George Bernard Shaw** 1856-1950 Irish dramatist: *The Devil's Disciple* (1901)

17 History is about arrogance, vanity and vapidity—who better than me to present it?
 ▪ **David Starkey** 1945- English historian: in *Mail on Sunday* 10 October 2004

18 Like most of those who study history, he [Napoleon III] learned from the mistakes of the past how to make new ones.
 ▪ **A. J. P. Taylor** 1906-90 British historian: in *Listener* 6 June 1963

19 History gets thicker as it approaches recent times.
 ▪ **A. J. P. Taylor** 1906-90 British historian: *English History 1914-45* (1965), bibliography

20 *on being asked what would have happened in 1963, had Khrushchev and not Kennedy been assassinated:*
 With history one can never be certain, but I think I can safely say that Aristotle Onassis would not have married Mrs Khrushchev.
 ▪ **Gore Vidal** 1925-2012 American novelist and critic: in *Sunday Times* 4 June 1989

21 Human history becomes more and more a race between education and catastrophe.
 ▪ **H. G. Wells** 1866-1946 English novelist: *Outline of History* (1920)

22 The one duty we owe to history is to rewrite it.
 ▪ **Oscar Wilde** 1854-1900 Irish dramatist and poet: *Intentions* (1891) 'The Critic as Artist' pt. 1

23 History started badly and hav been geting steadily worse.
 ▪ **Geoffrey Willans** 1911-58 and **Ronald Searle** 1920-2012: *Down with Skool!* (1953)

Holidays and Leisure

see also **WORK**

....

There is a French widow in every bedroom.   **Gerard Hoffnung**

1 Continental breakfasts are very sparse, usually just a pot of tea or coffee and a teensy roll that looks like a suitcase handle. My advice is to go right to lunch without pausing.
  ▪ **Henry Beard** 1945- American humorist: *Miss Piggy's Guide to Life* (1981)

2 BASIL: May I ask what you were hoping to see out of a Torquay bedroom window? Sydney Opera House, perhaps? The Hanging Gardens of Babylon? Herds of wildebeeste sweeping majestically...
  ▪ **John Cleese** 1939- and **Connie Booth** 1944- English and American-born comic actors: *Fawlty Towers* (1979) 'Communication Problems'

3 There's sand in the porridge and sand in the bed,
  And if this is pleasure we'd rather be dead.
  ▪ **Noël Coward** 1899-1973 English dramatist, actor, and composer: 'The English Lido' (1928)

4 I don't think we can do better than 'Good old Broadstairs'.
  ▪ **George Grossmith** 1847-1912 and **Weedon Grossmith** 1854-1919: *The Diary of a Nobody* (1894)

5 *supposedly quoting a letter from a Tyrolean landlord:*
  Standing among savage scenery, the hotel offers stupendous revelations. There is a French widow in every bedroom, affording delightful prospects.
  ▪ **Gerard Hoffnung** 1925-59 German-born artist and musician: speech at the Oxford Union, 4 December 1958

6 Some time before the end of August, I will grab a week's leave, like a half-starved sealion snatching an airborne mackerel; and whatever happens that leave will not be taken in some boarding-house in Eastbourne. It will not take place in Cornwall or Scotland or the Norfolk Broads. I say stuff Skegness. I say bugger Bognor. I am going to take a holiday abroad.
  refusing to be pressured into a hypocritical 'staycation' for the sake of political appearances
  ▪ **Boris Johnson** 1964- British Conservative politician: in *Daily Telegraph* 22 July 2008

7 Twenty-four hour room service generally refers to the length of time that it takes for the club sandwich to arrive.
  ▪ **Fran Lebowitz** 1946- American writer: *Social Studies* (1982)

8 I suppose we all have our recollections of our earlier holidays, all bristling with horror.
  ▪ **Flann O'Brien** 1911-66 Irish novelist and journalist: *Myles Away from Dublin* (1990)

9 I want to register a complaint...You know who sneaked into my stateroom at three o'clock this morning?... Nobody, and that's my complaint.
  ▪ **S. J. Perelman** 1904-79 and **others** screenwriters: *Monkey Business* (1931 film), spoken by Groucho Marx

10 The great advantage of a hotel is that it's a refuge from home life.
  ▪ **George Bernard Shaw** 1856-1950 Irish dramatist: *You Never Can Tell* (1898)

11 I like to have exciting evenings on holiday, because after you've spent 8 hours reading on the beach you don't feel like turning in early with a good book.
  ▪ **Arthur Smith** 1954- English comedian: *The Live Bed Show* (1995)

12 Life is too short for second-rate hotels.
  ▪ **Herbert Beerbohm Tree** 1852-1917 English actor-manager: Madeleine Bingham *The Great Lover* (1978)

Hollywood

see also **CINEMA, FILM**

A place where they'll pay you a thousand dollars for a kiss and fifty cents for your soul.   **Marilyn Monroe**

1 Hollywood is a place where people from Iowa mistake each other for stars.
■ **Fred Allen** 1894-1956 American humorist: Maurice Zolotow *No People like Show People* (1951)

2 Hollywood is the only place in the world where an amicable divorce means each one gets 50 per cent of the publicity.
■ **Lauren Bacall** 1924- American actress: in *People* February 1988; J. Vitullo-Martin and J. R. Moskin *The Executive's Book of Quotations* (1994)

3 I'm not very keen on Hollywood. I'd rather have a nice cup of cocoa really.
■ **Noël Coward** 1899-1973 English dramatist, actor, and composer: letter to his mother, 1937; Cole Lesley *The Life of Noel Coward* (1976)

4 Remember all the time…that Hollywood is an Oriental city. As long as you do that you might survive.
■ **Olivia De Havilland** 1916- American actress: Dirk Bogarde *Snakes and Ladders* (1978)

5 Hollywood is bounded on the north, south, east, and west by agents.
■ **William Fadiman** 1909-99 American film producer: *Hollywood Now* (1972)

6 Hollywood is the only place on earth where you can get stabbed in the back while you're climbing a ladder.
■ **William Faulkner** 1897-1962 American novelist: Joseph Blotner *Faulkner* (1984)

7 Working in Hollywood does give one a certain expertise in the field of prostitution.
■ **Jane Fonda** 1937- American actress: J. R. Colombo *Wit and Wisdom of the Moviemakers* (1979)

8 The only place you can wake up in the morning and hear the birds coughing in the trees.
■ **Joe Frisco** 1889-1958 American vaudeville artiste: attributed

9 Hollywood is strange when you're in trouble. Everyone is afraid it's contagious.
■ **Judy Garland** 1922-69 American actress: Simon Rose *Classic Film Guide* (1995)

10 Every country gets the circus it deserves. Spain gets bullfights. Italy gets the Catholic Church. America Hollywood.
■ **Erica Jong** 1942- American novelist: *How to Save Your Own Life* (1977)

11 Lunch Hollywood-style—a hot dog and vintage wine.
■ **Harry Kurnitz** 1907-68 American dramatist: Max Wilk *The Wit and Wisdom of Hollywood* (1971)

12 Behind the phoney tinsel of Hollywood lies the real tinsel.
■ **Oscar Levant** 1906-72 American pianist: Laurence J. Peter (ed.) *Quotations for our Time* (1977)

13 Being a writer in Hollywood is like going into Hitler's Eagle's Nest with a great idea for a bar-mitzvah.
■ **David Mamet** 1947- American dramatist and director: in *Sunday Times* 1 August 2004

14 A trip through a sewer in a glass-bottomed boat.
■ **Wilson Mizner** 1876-1933 American dramatist: Alva Johnston *The Legendary Mizners* (1953), reworked by Mayor Jimmy Walker into 'A reformer is a guy who rides through a sewer in a glass-bottomed boat'

15 Working for Warner Bros is like fucking a porcupine: it's a hundred

pricks against one.
- **Wilson Mizner** 1876-1933 American dramatist: David Niven *Bring On the Empty Horses* (1975)

16 Hollywood is a place where they'll pay you a thousand dollars for a kiss and fifty cents for your soul.
- **Marilyn Monroe** 1926-62 American actress: J. R. Colombo *Wit and Wisdom of the Moviemakers* (1979)

17 *Gandhi* was everything the voting members of the Academy would like to be: moral, tanned and thin.
- **Joe Morgenstern** 1932- American film critic: in *Los Angeles Herald-Examiner* April 1983

18 Hollywood, the Versailles of Los Angeles.
- **Jan Morris** 1926- Welsh writer: *Destinations* (1980)

19 Hollywood money isn't money. It's congealed snow, melts in your hand, and there you are.
- **Dorothy Parker** 1893-1967 American critic and humorist: Malcolm Cowley (ed.) *Writers at Work* 1st Series (1958)

20 There was the actor who put in his will that he wanted to be cremated and ten per cent of his ashes thrown in his agent's face.
- **Harry Richman** 1895-1972 American entertainer: attributed, 1940s

21 Hollywood: They know only one word of more than one syllable here, and that is fillum.
- **Louis Sherwin**: Laurence J. Peter (ed.) *Quotations for our Time* (1977)

22 This is the biggest electric train any boy ever had!
- **Orson Welles** 1915-85 American actor and film director: Leo Rosten *Hollywood* (1941)

The Home and Housework

Hatred of domestic work is a natural and admirable result of civilization.
Rebecca West

1 WIFE: Cooking! Cleaning! Why should women do it?
HUSBAND: You're quite right—let's get an au pair girl.
- **Mel Calman** 1931-94 English cartoonist: *Couples* (1972)

2 They tell me there is no more toilet paper in the house. How can I be expected to act a romantic part and remember to order TOILET PAPER!
- **Mrs Patrick Campbell** 1865-1940 English actress: Margot Peters *Mrs Pat* (1984)

3 Conran's Law of Housework—it expands to fill the time available plus half an hour.
- **Shirley Conran** 1932- English writer: *Superwoman 2* (1977)

4 Tho' the pipes that supply the bathroom burst
And the lavatory makes you fear the worst,

It was used by Charles the First
Quite informally,
And later by George the Fourth
On a journey North.
- **Noël Coward** 1899-1973 English dramatist, actor, and composer: 'The Stately Homes of England' (1938)

5 There was no need to do any housework at all. After the first four years the dirt doesn't get any worse.
- **Quentin Crisp** 1908-99 English writer: *The Naked Civil Servant* (1968)

6 The graveyards are full of women whose houses were so spotless you could eat off the floor. Remember the second wife always has a maid.
- **Heloise Cruse** 1919-77 American writer: in *Saturday Evening Post* 2 March 1963

7 Mrs Crupp had indignantly assured him that there wasn't room to swing a cat there; but, as Mr Dick justly observed

to me, sitting down on the foot of
the bed, nursing his leg, 'You know,
Trotwood, I don't want to swing a cat.
I never do swing a cat. Therefore, what
does that signify to *me*!'
- **Charles Dickens** 1812-70 English novelist:
David Copperfield (1850)

8 Housework can't kill you, but why take
a chance?
- **Phyllis Diller** 1917-2012 American actress:
Phyllis Diller and Richard Buskin *Like A
Lampshade in a Whorehouse: my life in
comedy* (2005)

9 Cleaning your house while your kids
are still growing is like shovelling the
walk before it stops snowing.
- **Phyllis Diller** 1917-2012 American actress:
Phyllis Diller's Housekeeping Hints (1966)

10 Home is the place where, when you
    have to go there,
They have to take you in.
- **Robert Frost** 1874-1963 American poet:
'The Death of the Hired Man' (1914)

11 *congratulating Margaret Thatcher on
10 Downing Street:*
I never seem to meet a good estate
agent.
- **John Gielgud** 1904-2000 English actor:
Sheridan Morley *Asking for Trouble* (2002)

12 What's the good of a home if you are
never in it?
- **George Grossmith** 1847-1912 and **Weedon
Grossmith** 1854-1919: *The Diary of a Nobody*
(1894)

13 The worst thing about work in the
house or home is that whatever you
do it is destroyed, laid waste or eaten
within twenty-four hours.
- **Alexandra Hasluck** 1908-93 Australian
writer: attributed

14 I want a house that has got over all its
troubles; I don't want to spend the rest
of my life bringing up a young and
inexperienced house.
- **Jerome K. Jerome** 1859-1927 English writer:
They and I (1909)

15 All I need is room enough to lay a hat
and a few friends.
- **Dorothy Parker** 1893-1967 American critic
and humorist: R. E. Drennan *Wit's End* (1973)

16 I hate housework! You make the beds,
you do the dishes—and six months later
you have to start all over again.
- **Joan Rivers** 1933- American comedienne:
attributed, 1984

17 The only advantage of not being too
good a housekeeper is that your guests
are so pleased to feel how very much
better they are.
- **Eleanor Roosevelt** 1884-1962 American
humanitarian and diplomat: *Eleanor
Roosevelt's My Day: Her Acclaimed Columns
1936-1945* (1989)

18 Addresses are given to us to conceal our
whereabouts.
- **Saki** 1870-1916 Scottish writer: *Reginald in
Russia* (1910)

19 Home life as we understand it is no
more natural to us than a cage is natural
to a cockatoo.
- **George Bernard Shaw** 1856-1950 Irish
dramatist: *Getting Married* (1911) preface
'Hearth and Home'

20 *on being encountered drinking a glass of
wine in the street, while watching his theatre,
the Drury Lane, burn down, on 24 February
1809:*
A man may surely be allowed to take a
glass of wine by his own fireside.
- **Richard Brinsley Sheridan** 1751-1816 Irish
dramatist and Whig politician: T. Moore
Life of Sheridan (1825)

21 It looks different when you're sober.
I thought I had twice as much furniture.
- **Neil Simon** 1927- American dramatist:
The Gingerbread Lady (1970)

22 *asked who wore the trousers at home:*
I do. I wear the trousers. And I wash
and iron them, too.
- **Denis Thatcher** 1915-2003 English
businessman: attributed; in *Times*
27 June 2003

23 The national sport of England is
obstacle racing. People fill their
rooms with useless and cumbersome
furniture, and spend the rest of their
lives in trying to dodge it.
- **Herbert Beerbohm Tree** 1852-1917 English
actor manager: Hesketh Pearson *Beerbohm
Tree* (1956)

24 Hatred of domestic work is a natural and admirable result of civilization.
   ▪ **Rebecca West** 1892-1983 English novelist and journalist: in *The Freewoman* 6 June 1912

25 When it comes to housework the one thing no book of household management can ever tell you is how to begin. Or maybe I mean *why*.
   ▪ **Katharine Whitehorn** 1928- English journalist: *Roundabout* (1962)

26 Everything's getting on top of me. I can't switch off. I've got a self-cleaning oven—I have to get up in the night to see if it's doing it.
   ▪ **Victoria Wood** 1953- British writer and comedienne: *Mens Sana in Thingummy Doodah* (1990)

Honours *see* AWARDS AND HONOURS

Hope and Despair

see also **HAPPINESS, OPTIMISM, SATISFACTION**

Blessed is the man who expects nothing, for he shall never be disappointed.
Alexander Pope

1 A minor form of despair, disguised as a virtue.
   definition of patience
   ▪ **Ambrose Bierce** 1842-c.1914 American writer: *The Devil's Dictionary* (1911)

2 There are bad times just around the corner,
   There are dark clouds travelling through the sky
   And it's no good whining
   About a silver lining
   For we know from experience that they won't roll by,
   With a scowl and a frown
   We'll keep our peckers down
   And prepare for depression and doom and dread,
   We're going to unpack our troubles from our old kitbag
   And wait until we drop down dead.
   ▪ **Noël Coward** 1899-1973 English dramatist, actor, and composer: 'There are Bad Times Just Around the Corner' (1953)

3 I have known him come home to supper with a flood of tears, and a declaration that nothing was now left but a jail; and go to bed making a calculation of the expense of putting bow-windows to the house, 'in case anything turned up,' which was his favourite expression.
   ▪ **Charles Dickens** 1812-70 English novelist: *David Copperfield* (1850)

4 Hope is the feeling you have that the feeling you have isn't permanent.
   ▪ **Jean Kerr** 1923-2003 American writer: *Finishing Touches* (1973)

5 but wotthehell
   archy wotthehell
   it s cheerio
   my deario that
   pulls a lady through.
   ▪ **Don Marquis** 1878-1937 American poet and journalist: *archy and mehitabel* (1927) 'cheerio my deario'

6 but wotthehell archy wotthehell
   jamais triste archy jamais triste
   that is my motto.
   ▪ **Don Marquis** 1878-1937 American poet and journalist: *archy and mehitabel* (1927) 'mehitabel sees paris'

7 When I am sad and weary
   When I think all hope has gone
   When I walk along High Holborn

I think of you with nothing on.
- **Adrian Mitchell** 1932-2008 English poet, novelist, and dramatist: 'Celia, Celia'

8 'Blessed is the man who expects nothing, for he shall never be disappointed' was the ninth beatitude.
- **Alexander Pope** 1688-1744 English poet: letter to Fortescue, 23 September 1725

9 Despair is a black leather jacket that everyone looks good in. Hope is a frilly, pink dress that exposes the knees.
- **Rebecca Solnit** 1961- American writer: attributed

10 *the wife of a late 19th-century master at Eton College:*
In all disagreeable circumstances remember the three things which I always say to myself:
I am an Englishwoman.
I was born in wedlock.
I am on dry land.
- **Blanche Warre-Cornish**: *Bensoniana & Cornishiana* (1935)

11 If you think nobody cares if you're alive, try missing a couple of car payments.
- **Earl Wilson** 1907-87 American journalist: attributed

Hospitality *see* PARTIES AND HOSPITALITY

House of Lords

The House of Lords is a perfect eventide home.   **Baroness Stocks**

1 The difference between the House of Commons and the House of Lords is the difference between a newly poured glass of champagne and one that has stood for five days.
- **Clement Attlee** 1883-1967 British Labour statesman: James Nelson *Wisdom for Our Time!* (1961)

2 The British House of Lords is the British Outer Mongolia for retired politicians.
- **Tony Benn** 1925- British Labour politician: in *Observer* 4 February 1962

3 MRS THATCHER: I do not create peers to have them vote against me in the House of Lords.
LORD DENHAM: Prime Minister, even you should know better than to expect me to find you a majority during Gold Cup week.
exchange between the Prime Minister and the Leader of the House of Lords
- **Lord Denham** 1927- British Conservative politician: Peter Hennessy *The Prime Minister* (2000)

4 The House of Peers, throughout the war, Did nothing in particular,

And did it very well.
- **W. S. Gilbert** 1836-1911 English writer: *Iolanthe* (1882)

5 While the Commons must bray like an ass every day
To appease their electoral hordes,
We don't say a thing till we've something to say—
There's a lot to be said for the Lords.
- **A. P. Herbert** 1890-1971 English writer and humorist: *Big Ben* (1946)

6 I will be sad if I either look up or down after my death and don't see my son fast asleep on the same benches on which I have slept.
- **Lord Onslow** 1938-2011 British Conservative politician: in *Times* 31 October 1998 'Quotes of the Week'

7 *on the quality of debate in the House of Lords:*
It is, I think, good evidence of life after death.
- **Donald Soper** 1903-98 British Methodist minister: in *Listener* 17 August 1978

8 The House of Lords is a perfect eventide home.
- **Baroness Stocks** 1891-1975 British writer: *My Commonplace Book* (1970)

9 The House of Lords, an illusion
to which I have never been able to
subscribe—responsibility without
power, the prerogative of the eunuch
throughout the ages.
- **Tom Stoppard** 1937- British dramatist:
Lord Malquist and Mr Moon (1966)

Housework *see* HOME AND HOUSEWORK

The Human Race

Man is the Only Animal that Blushes. Or needs to. **Mark Twain**

1 Well, of course, people are only
human…But it really does not seem
much for them to be.
- **Ivy Compton-Burnett** 1884-1969 English
novelist: *A Family and a Fortune* (1939)

2 *of other people:*
They are usually a mistake.
- **Quentin Crisp** 1908-99 English writer: in
Spectator 20 November 1999

3 I got disappointed in human nature as
well and gave it up because I found it
too much like my own.
- **J. P. Donleavy** 1926- Irish-American
novelist: *A Fairy Tale of New York* (1973)

4 Human beings can get used to virtually
anything, given plenty of time and no
choice in the matter whatsoever.
- **Tom Holt** 1961- English novelist: *Open
Sesame* (1997)

5 All God's children are not beautiful.
Most of God's children are, in fact,
barely presentable.
- **Fran Lebowitz** 1946- American writer:
Metropolitan Life (1978)

6 Men have an extraordinarily erroneous
opinion of their position in nature; and
the error is ineradicable.
- **W. Somerset Maugham** 1874-1965 English
novelist: *A Writer's Notebook* (1949) written
in 1896

7 Man is one of the toughest of animated
creatures. Only the anthrax bacillus can
stand so unfavourable an environment

for so long a time.
- **H. L. Mencken** 1880-1956 American
journalist and literary critic: *Minority Report*
(1956)

8 I wish I loved the Human Race;
I wish I loved its silly face;
I wish I liked the way it walks;
I wish I liked the way it talks;
And when I'm introduced to one
I wish I thought *What Jolly Fun!*
- **Walter Raleigh** 1861-1922 English lecturer
and critic: 'Wishes of an Elderly Man' (1923)

9 People differ. Some object to the fan
dancer, and others to the fan.
- **Elizabeth W. Spalding**: attributed; Dorothy
Sarnoff *Speech Can Change Your Life* (1971)

10 I'm dealing in rock'n'roll. I'm, like,
I'm not a bona fide human being.
- **Phil Spector** 1940- American record
producer and songwriter: attributed

11 The only man who wasn't spoilt by
being lionized was Daniel.
- **Herbert Beerbohm Tree** 1852-1917 English
actor-manager: Hesketh Pearson *Beerbohm
Tree* (1956)

12 Man is the Only Animal that Blushes.
Or needs to.
- **Mark Twain** 1835-1910 American writer:
Following the Equator (1897)

13 Reality is something the human race
doesn't handle very well.
- **Gore Vidal** 1925-2012 American novelist
and critic: in *Radio Times* 3 January 1990

14 This world is a comedy to those that
think, a tragedy to those that feel.
- **Horace Walpole** 1717-97 English writer and
connoisseur: letter to Anne, Countess of
Upper Ossory, 16 August 1776

15 The real problem of humanity is
the following: we have Paleolithic
emotions, medieval institutions, and
god-like technology.
- **Edward O. Wilson** 1929- American
sociobiologist: debate at the Harvard
Museum of Natural History, Cambridge,
Mass., 9 September 2009

16 'Have you ever seen Spode eat
asparagus?'
'No.'
'Revolting. It alters one's whole
conception of Man as Nature's last
word.'
- **P. G. Wodehouse** 1881-1975 English-born
writer: *The Code of the Woosters* (1938)

Humour

see also **COMEDY**, **WIT**

....

What do you mean, funny? Funny-peculiar or funny ha-ha?   **Ian Hay**

1 The marvellous thing about a joke with
a double meaning is that it can only
mean one thing.
- **Ronnie Barker** 1929-2005 English
comedian: *Sauce* (1977)

2 Mark my words, when a society has to
resort to the lavatory for its humour,
the writing is on the wall.
- **Alan Bennett** 1934- English dramatist and
actor: *Forty Years On* (1969)

3 When you tell an Iowan a joke, you can
see a kind of race going on between his
brain and his expression.
- **Bill Bryson** 1951- American travel writer:
The Lost Continent (1989)

4 Without humour you cannot run a
sweetie-shop, let alone a nation.
- **John Buchan** 1875-1940 Scottish novelist:
Castle Gay (1930)

5 Good jests ought to bite like lambs, not
dogs: they should cut, not wound.
- **Charles II** 1630-85 British monarch:
attributed; Stephen Leacock 'A
Rehabilitation of Charles II' in *Essays and
Literary Studies* (1916)

6 A joke's a very serious thing.
- **Charles Churchill** 1731-64 English poet:
The Ghost (1763)

7 Freud's theory was that when a joke
opens a window and all those bats and
bogeymen fly out, you get a marvellous
feeling of relief and elation. The trouble
with Freud is that he never had to play the
old Glasgow Empire on a Saturday night
after Rangers and Celtic had both lost.
- **Ken Dodd** 1927- British comedian: in
Guardian 30 April 1991 (quoted in many,
usually much contracted, forms since the
mid-1960s)

8 A difference of taste in jokes is a great
strain on the affections.
- **George Eliot** 1819-80 English novelist:
Daniel Deronda (1876)

9 'Tis ever thus with simple folk—an
accepted wit has but to say 'Pass the
mustard', and they roar their ribs out!
- **W. S. Gilbert** 1836-1911 English writer: *The
Yeoman of the Guard* (1888)

10 What do you mean, funny? Funny-
peculiar or funny ha-ha?
- **Ian Hay** 1876-1952 Scottish novelist and
dramatist: *The Housemaster* (1938)

11 A sober God-fearing man whose idea of
a good joke was to lie about his age.
- **Joseph Heller** 1923-99 American novelist:
Catch-22 (1961)

12 The only way to amuse some people is to slip and fall on an icy pavement.
- **E. W. Howe** 1853-1937 American novelist and editor: *Country Town Sayings* (1911)

13 It's an odd job, making decent people laugh.
- **Molière** 1622-73 French comic dramatist: *La Critique de l'école des femmes* (1663)

14 Good taste and humour…are a contradiction in terms, like a chaste whore.
- **Malcolm Muggeridge** 1903-90 British journalist: in *Time* 14 September 1953

15 Satire is a lesson, parody is a game.
- **Vladimir Nabokov** 1899-1977 Russian novelist: *Strong Opinions* (1974)

16 That's the Irish people all over—they treat a joke as a serious thing and a serious thing as a joke.
- **Sean O'Casey** 1880-1964 Irish dramatist: *The Shadow of a Gunman* (1923)

17 Laughter is pleasant, but the exertion is too much for me.
- **Thomas Love Peacock** 1785-1866 English novelist and poet: *Nightmare Abbey* (1818)

18 Everything is funny as long as it is happening to Somebody Else.
- **Will Rogers** 1879-1935 American actor and humorist: *The Illiterate Digest* (1924) 'Warning to Jokers: lay off the prince'

19 There's no trick to being a humorist when you have the whole government working for you.
- **Will Rogers** 1879-1935 American actor and humorist: in Laurence J. Peter *Quotations for Our Time* (1977)

20 For every ten jokes, thou hast got an hundred enemies.
- **Laurence Sterne** 1713-68 English novelist: *Tristram Shandy* (1769)

21 It would be a sad reflection on any satirical programme if no one ended up taking offence at some point.
- **Meera Syal** 1963- British actress and writer: in *Independent* 30 November 2002

22 Humour is emotional chaos remembered in tranquillity.
- **James Thurber** 1894-1961 American humorist: in *New York Post* 29 February 1960

23 That joke was lost on the foreigner—guides cannot master the subtleties of the American joke.
- **Mark Twain** 1835-1910 American writer: *The Innocents Abroad* (1869)

24 Laughter would be bereaved if snobbery died.
- **Peter Ustinov** 1921-2004 British actor, director, and writer: in *Observer* 13 March 1955

25 It's hard to be funny when you have to be clean.
- **Mae West** 1892-1980 American film actress: Joseph Weintraub *The Wit and Wisdom of Mae West* (1967)

26 She had a penetrating sort of laugh. Rather like a train going into a tunnel.
- **P. G. Wodehouse** 1881-1975 English writer: *The Inimitable Jeeves* (1923)

Husbands

see also **MARRIAGE**

....

Husbands are like fires. They go out when unattended.   **Zsa Zsa Gabor**

1 The most popular labour-saving device today is still a husband with money.
- **Joey Adams** 1911-99 American comedian: *Cindy and I* (1959)

2 *showing Lord Esher the corpse of her notoriously unfaithful husband, King Edward VII:*
Now at least I know where he is!
- **Queen Alexandra** 1844-1925: Piers Brandon *Our Own Dear Queen* (1986)

3 My husband will never chase another
woman. He's too fine, too decent,
too old.
on her husband, George Burns
- **Gracie Allen** 1895-1964 American
comedienne: attributed

4 Bigamy is having one husband too
many. Monogamy is the same.
- **Anonymous**: Erica Jong *Fear of Flying* (1973)

5 If a woman laughs at her husband's
joke, it means he has told a new joke or
he has a new wife.
- **Anonymous**: saying

6 I married beneath me, all women do.
- **Nancy Astor** 1879-1964 American-born
British Conservative politician: in *Dictionary
of National Biography 1961-1970* (1981)

7 My husband said he needed more space,
so I locked him outside.
- **Roseanne Barr** 1953- American comedienne
and actress: from her stand-up routine

8 I knew her when she didn't know where
her next husband was coming from.
- **Anne Baxter** 1923-85 American actress:
attributed, but probably apocryphal; Ned
Sherrin *Cutting Edge* (1984)

9 Being a husband is a whole-time job.
That is why so many husbands fail. They
cannot give their entire attention to it.
- **Arnold Bennett** 1867-1931 English novelist:
The Title (1918)

10 Never marry a man who hates his
mother, because he'll end up hating you.
- **Jill Bennett** 1931-90 English actress: in
Observer 12 September 1982 'Sayings of the
Week'

11 I am about to be married—and am of
course in all the misery of a man in
pursuit of happiness.
- **Lord Byron** 1788-1824 English poet: letter,
15 October 1814

12 Yblessed be god that I have wedded fyve!
Welcome the sixte, whan that evere he
shal.
- **Geoffrey Chaucer** c.1343-1400 English poet:
The Canterbury Tales 'The Wife of Bath's
Prologue'

13 A girl can wait for the right man, but
in the meantime that doesn't mean she

can't have a wonderful time with the
wrong ones.
- **Cher** 1946- American singer and actress:
in *Birmingham Post* 30 December 2003

14 Every woman should marry an
archaeologist because she grows
increasingly attractive to him as she
grows increasingly to resemble a ruin.
- **Agatha Christie** 1890-1976 English writer
of detective fiction: Russell H. Fitzgibbon
The Agatha Christie Companion (1980);
attributed, perhaps apocryphal

15 I've never yet met a man who could
look after me. I don't need a husband.
What I need is a wife.
- **Joan Collins** 1933- British actress: in
Sunday Times 27 December 1987

16 To catch a husband is an art, to keep
him a job.
- **Simone de Beauvoir** 1908-86 French
novelist and feminist: attributed

17 The desire to get married is a basic and
primal instinct in women. It's followed
by another basic and primal instinct: the
desire to be single again.
- **Nora Ephron** 1941-2012 American
screenwriter and director: attributed; in
Globe and Mail 28 June 2012

18 Husbands are like fires. They go out
when unattended.
- **Zsa Zsa Gabor** 1917- Hungarian-born
actress: in *Newsweek* 28 March 1960

19 *when asked how many husbands she had had:*
You mean apart from my own?
- **Zsa Zsa Gabor** 1917- Hungarian-born
actress: K. Edwards *I Wish I'd Said That* (1976)

20 The best thing about being married
is having someone who puts out the
rubbish.
- **Ulrika Jonsson** 1967- Swedish television
presenter: in *Mail on Sunday* 30 October
2005

21 The husband who wants a happy
marriage should learn to keep his
mouth shut and his cheque book open.
- **Groucho Marx** 1890-1977 American film
comedian: attributed

22 I'm Henery the Eighth, I am!
Henery the Eighth, I am, I am!

I got married to the widow next door,
She's been married seven times before.
Every one was a Henery,
She wouldn't have a Willie or a Sam.
I'm her eighth old man named Henery
I'm Henery the Eighth, I am!
- **Fred Murray:** 'I'm Henery the Eighth, I Am!' (1911)

23 He tells you when you've got on too
    much lipstick,
And helps you with your girdle when
    your hips stick.
- **Ogden Nash** 1902-71 American humorist: 'The Perfect Husband' (1949)

24 To keep your marriage brimming
With love in the loving cup,
Whenever you're wrong, admit it,
Whenever you're right, shut up.
- **Ogden Nash** 1902-71 American humorist: 'A Word to Husbands' (1957)

25 WIFE OF TWO YEARS' STANDING: Oh yes!
I'm sure he's not so fond of me as at
first. He's away so much, neglects me
dreadfully, and he's so cross when he
comes home. What *shall* I do?
WIDOW: Feed the brute!
- **Punch** 1841-1992 English humorous weekly periodical: vol. 89 (1885)

26 Trust your husband, adore your
husband, and get as much as you can in
your own name.
- **Joan Rivers** 1933- American comedienne: attributed

27 A husband is what is left of a lover, after
the nerve has been extracted.
- **Helen Rowland** 1875-1950 American writer: *A Guide to Men* (1922)

28 When you see what some girls marry,
you realise how they must hate to work
for a living.
- **Helen Rowland** 1875-1950 American writer: *Reflections of a Bachelor Girl* (1909)

29 She will keep no fool, sir, till she be
married, and fools are as like husbands
as pilchards are to herrings—the
husband's the bigger.
- **William Shakespeare** 1564-1616 English dramatist: *Twelfth Night* (1601)

30 A husband should not insult his wife
publicly, at parties. He should insult her
in the privacy of the home.
- **James Thurber** 1894-1961 American humorist: *Thurber Country* (1953)

31 He would grab me in his arms, hold me
close—and tell me how wonderful he was.
of her ex-husband Vittorio Gassman
- **Shelley Winters** 1922-2006 American actress: attributed, 1955

32 Chumps always make the best
husbands. When you marry, Sally, grab
a chump. Tap his forehead first, and
if it rings solid, don't hesitate. All the
unhappy marriages come from the
husbands having brains.
- **P. G. Wodehouse** 1881-1975 English-born writer: *The Adventures of Sally* (1920)

Hypocrisy

Most people sell their souls, and live with a good conscience on the proceeds.
Logan Pearsall Smith

1 There are moments when we
in the British press can show
extraordinary sensitivity; these
moments usually coincide with
the death of a proprietor, or a
proprietor's wife.
- **Craig Brown** 1957- British satirist: *Craig Brown's Greatest Hits* (1993)

2 In England the only homage which they
pay to Virtue—is hypocrisy.
- **Lord Byron** 1788-1824 English poet: letter, 11 May 1821

3 We are so very 'umble.
Uriah Heep
- **Charles Dickens** 1812-70 English novelist: *David Copperfield* (1850)

4 He combines the manners of a Marquis with the morals of a Methodist.
- **W. S. Gilbert** 1836-1911 English writer: *Ruddigore* (1887)

5 'Ye'es, ye'es,' he finally observed with a certain dry relish, 'ye'es, I think I see some adulterers down there.'
in the Press Gallery of the House of Commons during the Profumo scandal
- **Maurice Green** 1906-87: recorded by Colin Welch; Ned Sherrin *Cutting Edge* (1984)

6 If I were two-faced would I be wearing this one?
- **Abraham Lincoln** 1809-65 American statesman: attributed

7 In 1969 I published a small book on Humility. It was a pioneering work which has not, to my knowledge, been superseded.
- **Lord Longford** 1905-2001 British Labour politician and philanthropist: in *The Tablet* 22 January 1994

8 An orgy looks particularly alluring seen through the mists of righteous indignation.
- **Malcolm Muggeridge** 1903-90 British journalist: *The Most of Malcolm Muggeridge* (1966) 'Dolce Vita in a Cold Climate'

9 King David and King Solomon
Led merry, merry lives,
With many, many lady friends,
And many, many wives;
But when old age crept over them—
With many, many qualms!—
King Solomon wrote the Proverbs
And King David wrote the Psalms.
- **James Ball Naylor** 1860-1945 American writer and physician: 'King David and King Solomon' (1935)

10 Most people sell their souls, and live with a good conscience on the proceeds.
- **Logan Pearsall Smith** 1865-1946 American-born man of letters: *Afterthoughts* (1931) 'Other People'

11 I hope you have not been leading a double life, pretending to be wicked and being really good all the time. That would be hypocrisy.
- **Oscar Wilde** 1854-1900 Irish dramatist and poet: *The Importance of Being Earnest* (1895)

Ideas

I had a monumental idea this morning, but I didn't like it.   **Sam Goldwyn**

1 I ran into Isosceles. He has a great idea for a new triangle!
- **Woody Allen** 1935- American film director, writer, and actor: *If the Impressionists had been Dentists* (1978)

2 The only reason some people get lost in thought is because it's unfamiliar territory.
- **Paul Fix** 1901-83 American actor: attributed

3 An original idea. That can't be too hard. The library must be full of them.
- **Stephen Fry** 1957- English comedian, actor, and writer: *The Liar* (1991)

4 I had a monumental idea this morning, but I didn't like it.
- **Sam Goldwyn** 1882-1974 American film producer: N. Zierold *Hollywood Tycoons* (1969)

5 The chief end of man is to frame general ideas—and…no general idea is worth a damn.
- **Oliver Wendell Holmes Jr.** 1841-1935 American lawyer: letter to Morris R. Cohen, 12 April 1915

6 It is better to entertain an idea than to take it home to live with you for the rest of your life.
- **Randall Jarrell** 1914-65 American poet: *Pictures from an Institution* (1954)

7 There are some ideas so wrong that only a very intelligent person could believe in them.
- **George Orwell** 1903-50 English novelist: attributed

8 The English approach to ideas is not to kill them, but to let them die of neglect.
- **Jeremy Paxman** 1950- British journalist and broadcaster: *The English: a portrait of a people* (1998)

9 My sole inspiration is a telephone call from a producer.
- **Cole Porter** 1891-1964 American songwriter: *The Cole Porter Story* (with Richard G. Hubler, 1965)

Idleness

I'm burning the midday oil!   **Ronald Reagan**

1 If I am doing nothing, I like to be doing nothing to some purpose. That is what leisure means.
- **Alan Bennett** 1934- English dramatist and actor: *A Question of Attribution* (1989)

2 I do nothing, granted. But I see the hours pass—which is better than trying to fill them.
- **E. M. Cioran** 1911-95 Romanian-born French philosopher: in *Guardian* 11 May 1993

3 It is impossible to enjoy idling thoroughly unless one has plenty of work to do.
- **Jerome K. Jerome** 1859-1927 English writer: *Idle Thoughts of an Idle Fellow* (1886) 'On Being Idle'

4 My son's taken up meditation—at least it's better than sitting doing nothing.
- **Max Kauffman** American artist: attributed

5 *on being accused of idleness:*
I'm burning the midday oil!
- **Ronald Reagan** 1911-2004 American Republican statesman: attributed, William Doyle *Inside the Oval Office* (1999)

6 We start at three o'clock in the afternoon, we go through to dinner time, we have one break...nose to the grindstone.
on rehearsals for the Rolling Stones 50th anniversary tour
- **Ronnie Wood** 1947- English rock musician: in *New Musical Express* 23 October 2012

Ignorance

You know everybody is ignorant, only on different subjects.   **Will Rogers**

1 Mr Kremlin himself was distinguished for ignorance, for he had only one idea,—and that was wrong.
- **Benjamin Disraeli** 1804-81 British Tory statesman and novelist: *Sybil* (1845)

2 *on being asked why he had defined* pastern *in his dictionary as the 'knee' of a horse:*
Ignorance, madam, pure ignorance.
- **Samuel Johnson** 1709-84 English poet, critic, and lexicographer: James Boswell *Life of Samuel Johnson* (1791) 1755

3 *in response to the comment on another lawyer,* 'It may be doubted whether any man of our generation has plunged more deeply into the

sacred fount of learning':
Or come up drier.
- **Abraham Lincoln** 1809-65 American statesman: Leon Harris *The Fine Art of Political Wit* (1965)

4 You know everybody is ignorant, only on different subjects.
- **Will Rogers** 1879-1935 American actor and humorist: in *New York Times* 31 August 1924

5 Reports that say that something hasn't happened are always interesting to me, because as we know, there are known knowns; there are things we know we know. We also know there are known

unknowns; that is to say we know there are some things we do not know. But there are also unknown unknowns—the ones we don't know we don't know.
- **Donald Rumsfeld** 1932- American Republican politician and businessman: news briefing, February 2002; the statement won the Plain English Campaign's Foot in Mouth award

6 Ignorance is like a delicate exotic fruit; touch it and the bloom is gone.
- **Oscar Wilde** 1854-1900 Irish dramatist and poet: *The Importance of Being Earnest* (1895)

Insults and Invective

see also COMEBACKS

....

Simply a shiver looking for a spine to run up.   **Paul Keating**

1 Helen Hayes was suffering from fallen archness.
on her appearance in The Wren
- **Franklin P. Adams** 1881-1960 American journalist and humorist: Helen Hayes and Sandford Dody On Reflection (1969)

2 The reason Michael Jackson entitled his album *Bad* was because he couldn't spell *Indescribable*.
- **Anonymous**: in 1987; Nigel Rees (ed.) *Cassell Dictionary of Humorous Quotations* (1999)

3 Lord Birkenhead is very clever but sometimes his brains go to his head.
- **Margot Asquith** 1864-1945 British political hostess: in *Listener* 11 June 1953 'Margot Oxford' by Lady Violet Bonham Carter

4 The *t* is silent, as in *Harlow*.
to Jean Harlow, who had been mispronouncing her first name
- **Margot Asquith** 1864-1945 British political hostess: T. S. Matthews *Great Tom* (1973)

5 *Mr Bennet dissuading his daughter Mary from continuing to sing:*
You have delighted us long enough.
- **Jane Austen** 1775-1817 English novelist: *Pride and Prejudice* (1813)

6 I didn't know he'd been knighted. I knew he'd been doctored.
on rival conductor Malcolm Sargent's knighthood
- **Thomas Beecham** 1879-1961 English conductor: attributed

7 If there is anybody here that I have forgotten to insult, I apologize.
leaving a gathering
- **Johannes Brahms** 1833-97 German composer: attributed; Oscar Levant *A Smattering of Ignorance* (1940)

8 *shouting at his whist partner:*
Ye stupid auld bitch—I beg yer pardon, mem. I mistook ye for my wife.
- **Lord Braxfield** 1722-99: attributed; quoted in *Literary Review* November 2003

9 The 'g' is silent—the only thing about her that is.
of Camille Paglia
- **Julie Burchill** 1960- English journalist and writer: in *The Spectator* 16 January 1992

10 Lillian Gish may be a charming person, but she is not Ophelia. She comes on stage as if she had been sent for to sew rings on the new curtains.
- **Mrs Patrick Campbell** 1865-1940 English actress: Margot Peters *Mrs Pat* (1984)

11 *to an elderly scientist who had bored her by talking interminably about the social organization of ants, which have 'their own police force and their own army':*
No navy, I suppose?'
- **Mrs Patrick Campbell** 1865-1940 English actress: James Agate diary, 11 February 1944

12 When he said we were trying to make a fool of him I could only murmur that

the Creator had beat us to it.

- **Ilka Chase** 1905-78 American actress and writer: *Past Imperfect* (1945)

13 I have derived continued benefit from criticism at all periods of my life and I do not remember any time when I was ever short of it.

- **Winston Churchill** 1874-1965 British Conservative statesman: in House of Commons 27 November 1914

14 She's been kissed oftener than a police-court Bible and by much the same class of people.

- **Robertson Davies** 1913-95 Canadian novelist: *Fifth Business* (1970)

15 Why am I so good at playing bitches? I think it's because I'm not a bitch. Maybe that why Miss Crawford always plays ladies.

- **Bette Davis** 1908-89 American actress: *This 'n That* (1987, with Michael Herskowitz)

16 He is just about the nastiest little man I've ever known. He struts sitting down.

on American politician Thomas E. Dewey

- **Lillian Dykstra** American journalist: to Franz Dykstra, 8 July 1952, James T. Patterson *Mr Republican* (1972)

17 *on hearing that Nancy Mitford was borrowing a friend's villa 'to finish her book':*

Oh really? What exactly is she reading?

- **Edith Evans** 1888-1976 English actress: attributed

18 [Ernest Hemingway's *The Sun Also Rises* is about] bullfighting, bullslinging, and bull—.

- **Zelda Fitzgerald** 1900-47: Marion Meade *What Fresh Hell Is This?* (1988)

19 I won't say she was silly, but I think one of us was silly, and it wasn't me.

- **Elizabeth Gaskell** 1810-65 English novelist: *Wives and Daughters* (1866)

20 No one can have a higher opinion of him than I have—and I think he is a dirty little beast.

- **W. S. Gilbert** 1836-1911 English writer: attributed

21 There never was a Churchill from John of Marlborough down that had either morals or principles.

- **W. E. Gladstone** 1809-98 British Liberal statesman: in conversation in 1882, recorded by Captain R. V. Briscoe; R. F. Foster *Lord Randolph Churchill* (1981)

22 A very weak-minded fellow I am afraid, and, like the feather pillow, bears the marks of the last person who has sat on him!

of Lord Derby

- **Earl Haig** 1861-1928 British general: letter to Lady Haig, 14 January 1918

23 *on being criticized by Geoffrey Howe:*

Like being savaged by a dead sheep.

- **Denis Healey** 1917- British Labour politician: speech, House of Commons 14 June 1978

24 Some men are born mediocre, some men achieve mediocrity, and some men have mediocrity thrust upon them. With Major Major it had been all three.

- **Joseph Heller** 1923-99 American novelist: *Catch-22* (1961)

25 When you cannot answer your opponent's logic, do not be discouraged—You can still call him vile names.

- **Elbert Hubbard** 1859-1915 American writer: 'Colonel William D'Alton Mann' in *Hundred-Point-Men* (1998)

26 *to a subordinate:*

You couldn't pour piss out of a boot if the instructions were printed on the heel.

- **Lyndon Baines Johnson** 1908-73 American Democratic statesman: Robert Caro *The Years of Lyndon Johnson: Master of the Senate*

27 As an actress, her only flair is in her nostrils.

of Candice Bergen

- **Pauline Kael** 1919-2001 American film critic: in *Life* 8 April 1966

28 This little flower, this delicate little beauty, this cream puff, is supposed to be beyond personal criticism...He is simply a shiver looking for a spine to run up.

of John Hewson, the Australian Liberal leader

- **Paul Keating** 1944- Australian Labor statesman: in *Ned Sherrin in his Anecdotage* (1993)

29 There's nothing wrong with you that reincarnation won't cure.
- **Jack E. Leonard** 1910-73 American comedian: attributed

30 *on Stephen A. Douglas's doctrine of 'popular sovereignty':*
Has it not got down as thin as the homeopathic soup that was made by boiling the shadow of a pigeon that had starved to death?
- **Abraham Lincoln** 1809-65 American statesman: speech at Quincy, Illinois, 12 October 1858

31 The truckman, the trashman and the policeman on the block may call me Alice but you may not.
to Senator Joseph McCarthy
- **Alice Roosevelt Longworth** 1884-1980 American socialite: Michael Teague *Mrs. L* (1981)

32 *on hearing that a Hollywood agent had swum safely in shark-infested waters:*
I think that's what they call professional courtesy.
- **Herman J. Mankiewicz** 1897-1953 American screenwriter: attributed; Nigel Rees *Cassell Dictionary of Humorous Quotations* (1999)

33 I never forget a face, but in your case I'll be glad to make an exception.
- **Groucho Marx** 1890-1977 American film comedian: Leo Rosten *People I have Loved, Known or Admired* (1970) 'Groucho'

34 I've had a perfectly wonderful evening, but this wasn't it.
- **Groucho Marx** 1890-1977 American film comedian: attributed, but denied by Marx in *Salt Lake Tribune* 11 March 1962

35 The only thing Madonna will ever do like a virgin is give birth in a stable.
- **Bette Midler** 1945- American actress: attributed

36 If you say a modern celebrity is an adulterer, a pervert and a drug addict, all it means is that you've read his autobiography.
- **P. J. O'Rourke** 1947- American humorous writer: *Give War a Chance* (1992)

37 The affair between Margot Asquith and Margot Asquith will live as one of the prettiest love stories in all literature.
- **Dorothy Parker** 1893-1967 American critic and humorist: review of Margot Asquith's *Lay Sermons*; in *New Yorker* 22 October 1927

38 *on hearing that a well-known English actress, famous for her love affairs with members of the legal profession, had broken her leg:*
She must have done it sliding down a barrister.
- **Dorothy Parker** 1893-1967 American critic and humorist: John Keats *You Might As Well Live* (1970)

39 *on Marion Davies, mistress of Randolph Hearst and aspiring movie actress:*
Miss Davies has two expressions—joy and indigestion.
- **Dorothy Parker** 1893-1967 American critic and humorist: attributed; early sources cite an anonymous reviewer

40 I'm not offended at all, because I know I'm not a dumb blonde. I also know I'm not blonde.
- **Dolly Parton** 1946- American singer and songwriter: M. Palmer *Small Talk, Big Names: 40 Years of Rock Quotes* (1993)

41 A cherub's face, a reptile all the rest.
- **Alexander Pope** 1688-1744 English poet: of Lord Hervey; 'An Epistle to Dr Arbuthnot' (1735)

42 A wit with dunces, and a dunce with wits.
- **Alexander Pope** 1688-1744 English poet: *The Dunciad* (1742)

43 Don't look at me, Sir, with—ah—in that tone of voice.
- **Punch** 1841-1992 English humorous weekly periodical: vol. 87 (1884)

44 Elizabeth Taylor is wearing Orson Welles designer jeans.
- **Joan Rivers** 1933- American comedienne: attributed; Ned Sherrin *Cutting Edge* (1984)

45 Diana Rigg is built like a brick mausoleum with insufficient flying buttresses.
review of Abelard and Heloise in 1970
- **John Simon** 1925- American critic: Diana Rigg *No Turn Unstoned* (1982)

46 *on being approached by the secretary of the Athenaeum, which he had been in the habit of*

using as a convenience on the way to his office:
Good God, do you mean to say this place is a club?

- **F. E. Smith** 1872–1930 British Conservative politician and lawyer: attributed

47 JUDGE: You are extremely offensive, young man.
SMITH: As a matter of fact, we both are, and the only difference between us is that I am trying to be, and you can't help it.

- **F. E. Smith** 1872–1930 British Conservative politician and lawyer: Lord Birkenhead *Earl of Birkenhead* (1933)

48 *on a proposal to surround St Paul's with a wooden pavement:*
Let the Dean and Canons lay their heads together and the thing will be done.

- **Sydney Smith** 1771–1845 English clergyman and essayist: H. Pearson *The Smith of Smiths* (1934)

49 [Richard Nixon is] the kind of politician who would cut down a redwood tree, and then mount the stump and make a speech on conservation.

- **Adlai Stevenson** 1900–65 American Democratic politician: Fawn M. Brodie *Richard Nixon* (1983)

50 I regard you with an indifference closely bordering on aversion.

- **Robert Louis Stevenson** 1850–94 Scottish novelist: *New Arabian Nights* (1882)

51 Hey girls, seen much of Cinderella since the wedding?
upon meeting two ugly sisters

- **John Sullivan** 1946–2011 English screenwriter: *Only Fools and Horses* (BBC TV, 1981–2003), spoken by David Jason as Del Boy

52 He never chooses an opinion, he just wears whatever happens to be in style.

- **Leo Tolstoy** 1828–1910 Russian novelist: attributed

53 *when pressed by a gramophone company for a written testimonial:*
Sirs, I have tested your machine. It adds a new terror to life and makes death a long-felt want.

- **Herbert Beerbohm Tree** 1852–1917 English actor-manager: Hesketh Pearson *Beerbohm Tree* (1956)

54 There, standing at the piano, was the original good time who had been had by all.

- **Kenneth Tynan** 1927–80 English theatre critic: at an Oxford Union Debate, while an undergraduate; attributed (also attributed to Bette Davis of a passing starlet)

55 Looking and sounding not unlike Hitler, but without the charm.
on William F. Buckley Jr.

- **Gore Vidal** 1925–2012 American novelist and critic: in *Time* 1969

56 Every other inch a gentleman.

- **Rebecca West** 1892–1983 English novelist and journalist: of Michael Arlen; Victoria Glendinning *Rebecca West* (1987)

57 CECILY: When I see a spade I call it a spade.
GWENDOLEN: I am glad to say that I have never seen a spade.

- **Oscar Wilde** 1854–1900 Irish dramatist and poet: *The Importance of Being Earnest* (1895)

58 Yes, dear Frank [Harris], we believe you: you have dined in every house in London, *once*.

- **Oscar Wilde** 1854–1900 Irish dramatist and poet: William Rothenstein *Men and Memories* (1931)

59 She's been on more laps than a napkin.

- **Walter Winchell** 1897–1972 American journalist: attributed, in *Reader's Digest* (1937)

Intelligence and Intellectuals

see also **MIND**

....

Genius is one per cent inspiration, ninety-nine per cent perspiration.
Thomas Alva Edison

1 On the planet Earth Man had always assumed that he was more intelligent than dolphins because he had achieved so much...the wheel, New York, wars, and so on, whilst all the dolphins had ever done was muck about in the water having a good time. But conversely the dolphins believed themselves to be more intelligent than man for precisely the same reasons.
- **Douglas Adams** 1952-2001 English science fiction writer: *The Hitchhiker's Guide to the Galaxy* (BBC radio, 1978)

2 *definition of an intellectual:*
Someone who can listen to the William Tell Overture without thinking of the Lone Ranger.
- **Anonymous**: attributed to many people from the mid-twentieth-century

3 To the man-in-the-street, who,
    I'm sorry to say,
Is a keen observer of life,
The word 'Intellectual' suggests straight away
A man who's untrue to his wife.
- **W. H. Auden** 1907-73 English poet: *New Year Letter* (1941)

4 *to H.G. Wells:*
It is all very well to be able to write books, but can you wag your ears?
- **J. M. Barrie** 1860-1937 Scottish writer and dramatist: J. A. Hammerton *Barrie: The Story of a Genius* (1929)

5 I am sure some people think I have not got the brains to be that clever, but I do have the brains.
on how he intentionally picked up a yellow card in England's World Cup match against Wales
- **David Beckham** 1975- English footballer: in *Mail on Sunday* 17 October 2004

6 Men of genius are so few that they ought to atone for their fewness by being at any rate ubiquitous.
- **Max Beerbohm** 1872-1956 English critic, essayist, and caricaturist: letter to W. B. Yeats, 11 July 1911

7 But—Oh! ye lords of ladies intellectual,
Inform us truly, have they not hen-
    pecked you all?
- **Lord Byron** 1788-1824 English poet: *Don Juan* (1819-24)

8 Genius is one per cent inspiration, ninety-nine per cent perspiration.
- **Thomas Alva Edison** 1847-1931 American inventor: said c.1903; in *Harper's Monthly Magazine* September 1932

9 With the thoughts I'd be thinkin'
I could be another Lincoln,
If I only had a brain.
- **E. Y. Harburg** 1898-1981 American songwriter: 'If I Only Had a Brain' (1939)

10 Whenever I hear the word culture...I release the safety-catch of my Browning!
often attributed to Hermann Goering, and quoted as 'Whenever I hear the word culture, I reach for my pistol!'
- **Hanns Johst** 1890-1978 German dramatist: *Schlageter* (1933)

11 Probably the greatest concentration of talent and genius in this house except for perhaps those times when Thomas Jefferson ate alone.
of a dinner for Nobel Prizewinners at the White House
- **John F. Kennedy** 1917-63 American Democratic statesman: in *New York Times* 30 April 1962

12 *I think, therefore I am* is the statement of an intellectual who underrates toothaches.
- **Milan Kundera** 1929- Czech novelist: *Immortality* (1991)

13 No one in this world, so far as I know—
and I have searched the records for years,
and employed agents to help me—has
ever lost money by underestimating the
intelligence of the great masses of the
plain people.
- **H. L. Mencken** 1880-1956 American
journalist and literary critic: in *Chicago
Tribune* 19 September 1926

14 She does not understand the concept
of Roman numerals. She thinks we just
fought World War Eleven.
- **Joan Rivers** 1933- American comedienne:
attributed

15 My wish was that my husband should
be distinguished for intellect, and my
children too. I have had my wish,—and
I now wish that there were a little less
intellect in the family so as to allow for
a little more common sense.
- **Frances Rossetti** 1800-86: William Rossetti
(ed.) *Dante Gabriel Rossetti: His Family
Letters with a Memoir* (1895)

16 What is a highbrow? He is a man who

has found something more interesting
than women.
- **Edgar Wallace** 1875-1932 English thriller
writer: in *New York Times* 24 January 1932

17 I have nothing to declare except my
genius.
- **Oscar Wilde** 1854-1900 Irish dramatist
and poet: at the New York Custom House;
Frank Harris *Oscar Wilde* (1918)

18 'Jeeves is a wonder.'
'A marvel.'
'What a brain.'
'Size nine-and-a-quarter, I should say.'
'He eats a lot of fish.'
- **P. G. Wodehouse** 1881-1975 English-born
writer: *Thank You, Jeeves* (1934)

19 I know I've got a degree. Why does
that mean I have to spend my life
with intellectuals? I've got a life-
saving certificate but I don't spend my
evenings diving for a rubber brick with
my pyjamas on.
- **Victoria Wood** 1953- British writer and
comedienne: *Mens Sana in Thingummy
Doodah* (1990)

The Internet *see* COMPUTERS AND THE INTERNET

Invective *see* INSULTS AND INVECTIVE

Ireland and the Irish

see also COUNTRIES

I'm Irish. We think sideways. **Spike Milligan**

1 PAT: He was an Anglo-Irishman.
MEG: In the blessed name of God what's
that?
PAT: A Protestant with a horse.
- **Brendan Behan** 1923-64 Irish dramatist:
Hostage (1958)

2 We've never been cool, we're hot. Irish
people are Italians who can't dress,

Jamaicans who can't dance.
- **Bono** 1960- Irish rock star: interview,
25 February 2001; in *Independent* 26 February
2001

3 Where would the Irish be without
someone to be Irish at?
- **Elizabeth Bowen** 1899-1973 British novelist
and short-story writer, born in Ireland: *The
House in Paris* (1935)

4 In some parts of Ireland the sleep which knows no waking is always followed by a wake which knows no sleeping.
 - **Mary Wilson Little**: *Reveries of a Paragrapher* (1897)

5 I'm Irish. We think sideways.
 - **Spike Milligan** 1918-2002 Irish comedian: in *Independent on Sunday* 20 June 1999

6 He'd...settled into a life of Guinness, sarcasm and late late nights, the kind of life that American academics think real Dubliners lead.
 - **Joseph O'Connor** 1963- Irish novelist: *Cowboys and Indians* (1991)

7 Gladstone...spent his declining years trying to guess the answer to the Irish Question; unfortunately whenever he was getting warm, the Irish secretly changed the Question.
 - **W. C. Sellar** 1898-1951 and **R. J. Yeatman** 1898-1968: *1066 and All That* (1930)

8 An Irishman's heart is nothing but his imagination.
 - **George Bernard Shaw** 1856-1950 Irish dramatist: *John Bull's Other Island* (1907)

9 *denying that he was Irish:*
Because a man is born in a stable, that does not make him a horse.
 - **Duke of Wellington** 1769-1852 British soldier and statesman: Paul Johnson (ed.) *The Oxford Book of Political Anecdotes* (1986)

Jewellery

A diamond is the only kind of ice that keeps a girl warm.   **Elizabeth Taylor**

1 Every engagement ring should have at least one diamond or there is something very wrong—with the ring and the relationship.
 - **Francis Boulle** 1988- British businessman: *Boulle's Jewels, The Business of Life* (2012)

2 Don't ever wear artistic jewellery; it *wrecks* a woman's reputation.
 - **Colette** 1873-1954 French novelist: *Gigi* (1944)

3 You've got so much ice on your hands I could skate on them.
to Liberace
 - **John Curry** 1949-94 British skater: Ned Sherrin *Cutting Edge* (1984)

4 I never hated a man enough to give him diamonds back.
 - **Zsa Zsa Gabor** 1917- Hungarian-born actress: in *Observer* 25 August 1957

5 Men grow cold as girls grow old
And we all lose our charms in the end.
But square cut or pear shape,
These rocks won't lose their shape,
Diamonds are a girl's best friend.
 - **Leo Robin** 1900-84 American songwriter: 'Diamonds are a Girl's Best Friend' (1949)

6 A diamond is the only kind of ice that keeps a girl warm.
 - **Elizabeth Taylor** 1932- English-born American actress: attributed

Journalism *see* **NEWSPAPERS AND JOURNALISM**

Judges

see also CRIME, LAW

....

I don't want to know what the law is, I want to know who the judge is.
Roy M. Cohn

1 Reform! Reform! Aren't things bad enough already?
   - **Mr Justice Astbury** 1860-1939 British judge: attributed

2 *affecting not to recognize Lord Campbell, the newly appointed Lord Chancellor, whom he encountered enveloped in a huge fur coat:*
   I beg your pardon, My Lord. I mistook you for the Great Seal.
   - **Richard Bethell** 1800-73 British lawyer: J. B. Atlay *Victorian Chancellors* (1908)

3 CONVICTED CRIMINAL: As God is my judge—I am innocent.
   LORD BIRKETT: He isn't; I am, and you're not!
   - **Lord Birkett** 1883-1962 English barrister and judge: attributed; Matthew Parris *Scorn* (1994)

4 I always approach Judge [Lemuel] Shaw as a savage approaches his fetish, knowing that he is ugly but feeling that he is great.
   - **Rufus Choate** 1799-1859 American lawyer and politician: Van Wyck Brooks *The Flowering of New England* (1936)

5 I don't want to know what the law is, I want to know who the judge is.
   - **Roy M. Cohn** 1927-86 American lawyer: in *New York Times Book Review* 3 April 1988

6 Did you mail that cheque to the Judge?
   - **Roy M. Cohn** 1927-86 American lawyer: spoken to an aide, at breakfast with Ned Sherrin, 1978

7 Yes, I could have been a judge but I never had the Latin, never had the Latin for the judging…—and so I became a miner instead.
   - **Peter Cook** 1937-95 English satirist and actor: *Beyond the Fringe* (1961 revue)

8 *the judge Sir James Mansfield had suggested that the Court might sit on Good Friday:*
   If your Lordship pleases. But your Lordship will be the first judge who has done so since Pontius Pilate.
   the Court did not *sit*
   - **William Davy** d. 1780: Edward Parry *The Seven Lamps of Advocacy* (1923)

9 *of Judges Learned and Augustus Hand:*
   Quote Learned, and follow 'Gus'.
   - **Robert H. Jackson** 1892-1954 American lawyer and judge: Hershel Shanks *The Art and Craft of Judging* (1968)

10 I always feel that there should be some comfort derived from any question from the bench. It is clear proof that the inquiring Justice is not asleep.
   - **Robert H. Jackson** 1892-1954 American lawyer and judge: 'Advocacy before the Supreme Court: Suggestions for Effective Presentation' (1951)

11 Poor fellow, I suppose he fancied he was on the bench.
   on hearing that a judge had slept through his play Pizarro
   - **Richard Brinsley Sheridan** 1751-1816 Irish dramatist and Whig politician: Walter Jerrold *Bon-Mots* (1893)

12 JUDGE: I have read your case, Mr Smith, and I am no wiser now than I was when I started.
   SMITH: Possibly not, My Lord, but far better informed.
   - **F. E. Smith** 1872-1930 British Conservative politician and lawyer: Lord Birkenhead *F. E.* (1959)

13 JUDGE WILLIS: Mr Smith, have you ever heard of a saying by Bacon—the great Bacon—that youth and discretion are ill-wed companions?

SMITH: Indeed I have, your Honour; and has your Honour ever heard of a saying by Bacon—the great Bacon—that a much talking Judge is like an ill-tuned cymbal?

- **F. E. Smith** 1872-1930 British Conservative politician and lawyer: Lord Birkenhead *F. E.* (1959)

14 JUDGE: What do you suppose I am on the Bench for, Mr Smith?
SMITH: It is not for me, Your Honour, to attempt to fathom the inscrutable workings of Providence.

- **F. E. Smith** 1872-1930 British Conservative politician and lawyer: Lord Birkenhead *F. E.* (1959 ed.)

Kissing

....

Kissing don't last: cookery do!　**George Meredith**

1 What do you get when you kiss a guy?
You get enough germs to catch
  pneumonia.
After you do, he'll never phone you.
- **Hal David** 1921-2012 American songwriter: 'I'll Never Fall In Love Again' (1968 song)

2 A fine romance with no kisses.
A fine romance, my friend, this is.
We should be like a couple of hot
  tomatoes,
But you're as cold as yesterday's mashed
  potatoes.
- **Dorothy Fields** 1905-74 American songwriter: 'A Fine Romance' (1936 song)

3 Oh, innocent victims of Cupid,
Remember this terse little verse;
To let a fool kiss you is stupid,
To let a kiss fool you is worse.
- **E. Y. Harburg** 1898-1981 American songwriter: 'Inscriptions on a Lipstick' (1965)

4 Being kissed by a man who *didn't* wax
his moustache was—like eating an egg
without salt.
- **Rudyard Kipling** 1865-1936 English writer and poet: *The Story of the Gadsbys* (1889) 'Poor Dear Mamma'

5 *on being discovered by his wife with a chorus girl:*
I wasn't kissing her, I was just
whispering in her mouth.
- **Chico Marx** 1891-1961 American film comedian: Groucho Marx and Richard J. Anobile *Marx Brothers Scrapbook* (1973)

6 When women kiss it always reminds
one of prize-fighters shaking hands.
- **H. L. Mencken** 1880-1956 American journalist and literary critic: *Chrestomathy* (1949)

7 Kissing don't last: cookery do!
- **George Meredith** 1828-1909 English novelist and poet: *The Ordeal of Richard Feverel* (1859)

8 A kiss can be a comma, a question mark
or an exclamation point. That's basic
spelling that every woman ought to
know.
- **Mistinguett** 1875-1956 French actress: in *Theatre Arts* December 1955

9 I smoked my first cigarette and kissed
my first woman on the same day. I have
never had time for tobacco since.
- **Arturo Toscanini** 1867-1957 Italian conductor: in *Observer* 30 June 1946

Language

see also **LANGUAGES**, **WORDS**

This is the sort of English up with which I will not put.   **Winston Churchill**

1 Sentence structure is innate but whining is acquired.
- **Woody Allen** 1935- American film director, writer, and actor: 'Remembering Needleman' (1976)

2 Don't swear, boy. It shows a lack of vocabulary.
- **Alan Bennett** 1934- English dramatist and actor: *Forty Years On* (1969)

3 If *Miss* means respectably unmarried, and *Mrs* respectably married, then *Ms* means nudge, nudge, wink, wink.
- **Angela Carter** 1940-92 English novelist: 'The Language of Sisterhood' in C. Ricks (ed.) *The State of the Language* (1980)

4 Would you convey my compliments to the purist who reads your proofs and tell him or her that I write in a sort of broken-down patois which is something like the way a Swiss waiter talks, and that when I split an infinitive, God damn it, I split it so it will stay split.
- **Raymond Chandler** 1888-1959 American writer of detective fiction: letter to Edward Weeks, 18 January 1947

5 This is the sort of English up with which I will not put.
- **Winston Churchill** 1874-1965 British Conservative statesman: Ernest Gowers *Plain Words* (1948) 'Troubles with Prepositions'

6 Where in this small-talking world can I find
A longitude with no platitude?
- **Christopher Fry** 1907-2005 English dramatist: *The Lady's not for Burning* (1949)

7 Backward ran sentences until reeled the mind.
satirizing the style of Time *magazine*
- **Wolcott Gibbs** 1902-58 American critic: in *New Yorker* 28 November 1936 'Time... Fortune...Life...Luce'

8 When you're lying awake with a dismal headache, and repose is taboo'd by anxiety,
I conceive you may use any language you choose to indulge in, without impropriety.
- **W. S. Gilbert** 1836-1911 English writer: *Iolanthe* (1882)

9 Though 'Bother it' I may Occasionally say,
I never use a big, big D—
- **W. S. Gilbert** 1836-1911 English writer: *HMS Pinafore* (1878)

10 There was so little English in that answer that President Chirac would have been happy with it.
- **William Hague** 1961- British Conservative politician: confronting John Prescott at Prime Minister's questions in the House of Commons, 29 March 2006

11 The minute a phrase becomes current it becomes an apology for not thinking accurately to the end of the sentence.
- **Oliver Wendell Holmes Jr.** 1841-1935 American lawyer: letter to Harold Laski, 2 July 1917

12 *on the first-person plural pronoun:*
The only person entitled to use the imperial 'we' in speaking of himself is a king, an editor, and a man with a tapeworm.
- **Robert G. Ingersoll** 1833-99 American agnostic: in *Los Angeles Times* 6 October 1914

13 The Achilles heel which has bitten us in the backside all year has stood out like a sore thumb.
- **Andy King** 1956- English footballer: in *Observer* 18 December 2005

14 The subjunctive mood is in its death throes, and the best thing to do is

to put it out of its misery as soon as possible.

- **W. Somerset Maugham** 1874-1965 English novelist: *A Writer's Notebook* (1949) written in 1941

15 My spelling is Wobbly. It's good spelling but it Wobbles, and the letters get in the wrong places.

- **A. A. Milne** 1882-1956 English writer: *Winnie-the-Pooh* (1926)

16 All those exclamation marks, you notice? Five? A sure sign of someone who wears his underpants on his head.

- **Terry Pratchett** 1948- English fantasy writer: Maskerade (1995)

17 A dog cannot relate his autobiography; however eloquently he may bark, he cannot tell you that his parents were honest though poor.

- **Bertrand Russell** 1872-1970 British philosopher and mathematician: *Human Knowledge: It's Scope and Limits* (1948)

18 Save the gerund and screw the whale.

- **Tom Stoppard** 1937- British dramatist: *The Real Thing* (1988 rev. ed.)

19 The four most beautiful words in our common language: I told you so.

- **Gore Vidal** 1925-2012 American novelist and critic: in *Independent* 1 November 2000

20 *title for a language-monitoring organization:* Association for the Annihilation of the Aberrant Apostrophe.

- **Keith Waterhouse** 1929-2009 English writer: in *Daily Mail* 22 February 1988

21 'Feather-footed through the plashy fen passes the questing vole'…'Yes,' said the Managing Editor. 'That must be good style.'

- **Evelyn Waugh** 1903-66 English novelist: *Scoop* (1938)

22 Good intentions are invariably ungrammatical.

- **Oscar Wilde** 1854-1900 Irish dramatist and poet: attributed

Languages

see also **LANGUAGE, WORDS**

....

You know the trouble with the French, they don't even have a word for entrepreneur.　**George W. Bush**

1 The Norwegian language has been described as German spoken underwater.

- **Anonymous**: Nigel Rees *Cassell Dictionary of Humorous Quotations* (1999)

2 If you understand English, press 1. If you do not understand English, press 2.
recorded message on Australian tax helpline

- **Anonymous**: in *Mail on Sunday* 30 July 2000 'Quotes of the Week'

3 The letter is written in the tongue of the Think Tanks, a language more difficult to master than Basque or Navaho and spoken only where strategic thinkers clump together in Institutes.

- **Russell Baker** 1925- American journalist and columnist: in *New York Times* 8 April 1981

4 Is there no Latin word for Tea? Upon my soul, if I had known that I would have let the vulgar stuff alone.

- **Hilaire Belloc** 1870-1953 British writer and Liberal politician: 'On Tea' (1908)

5 You know the trouble with the French, they don't even have a word for entrepreneur.

- **George W. Bush** 1946- American Republican statesman: attributed, probably apocryphal

6 Speak in French when you can't think of the English for a thing.
- **Lewis Carroll** 1832–98 English writer and logician: *Through the Looking-Glass* (1872)

7 If the King's English was good enough for Jesus Christ, it's good enough for Texas.
view of the first woman Governor of Texas, 1924
- **Miriam A. 'Ma' Ferguson** 1875–1961 American Democratic politician: Christopher Meyer *D.C. Confidential* (2005)

8 I hear it's the Hebrew in Heaven, sir. Spanish is seldom spoken.
- **Ronald Firbank** 1886–1926 English novelist: *Concerning the Eccentricities of Cardinal Pirelli* (1926)

9 Weep not for little Léonie
Abducted by a French Marquis!
Though loss of honour was a wrench
Just think how it's improved her
    French.
- **Harry Graham** 1874–1936 British writer and journalist: 'Compensation' (1930)

10 All pro athletes are bilingual. They speak English and profanity.
- **Gordie Howe** 1928– Canadian ice-hockey player: in *Toronto Star* 27 May 1975

11 There even are places where English completely disappears.
In America, they haven't used it for years!
- **Alan Jay Lerner** 1918–86 American songwriter: 'Why Can't the English?' (1956)

12 *when Khrushchev began banging his shoe on the desk:*
Perhaps we could have a translation, I could not quite follow.
- **Harold Macmillan** 1894–1986 British Conservative statesman: during his speech to the United Nations, 29 September 1960

13 Listen, someone's screaming in agony— fortunately I speak it fluently.
- **Spike Milligan** 1918–2002 Irish comedian: *The Goon Show* 'The Scarlet Capsule' (BBC Radio, 1959)

14 I can speak Esperanto like a native.
- **Spike Milligan** 1918–2002 Irish comedian: attributed; in *Daily Telegraph* 28 February 2002

15 Waiting for the German verb is surely the ultimate thrill.
- **Flann O'Brien** 1911–66 Irish novelist and journalist: *The Hair of the Dogma* (1977)

16 *on being told the English have no word equivalent to* sensibilité:
Yes we have. Humbug.
- **Lord Palmerston** 1784–1865 British statesman: attributed

17 Don't you guys know you're in Hollywood? Speak German.
when a number of people began speaking in Hungarian at a Hollywood party
- **Otto Preminger** 1906–86 Austrian-born American film director: Anthony Heilbut *Exiled in Paradise* (1983)

18 KENNETH: If you're so hot, you'd better tell me how to say she has ideas above her station.
BRIAN: Oh, yes, I forgot. It's fairly easy, old boy. *Elle a des idées au-dessus de sa gare.*
- **Terence Rattigan** 1911–77 English dramatist: *French without Tears* (1937)

19 Remember that you are a human being with a soul and the divine gift of articulate speech: that your native language is the language of Shakespeare and Milton and The Bible; and don't sit there crooning like a bilious pigeon.
- **George Bernard Shaw** 1856–1950 Irish dramatist: *Pygmalion* (1916)

20 Egad I think the interpreter is the hardest to be understood of the two!
- **Richard Brinsley Sheridan** 1751–1816 Irish dramatist and Whig politician: *The Critic* (1779)

21 They spell it Vinci and pronounce it Vinchy; foreigners always spell better than they pronounce.
- **Mark Twain** 1835–1910 American writer: *The Innocents Abroad* (1869)

22 I once heard a Californian student in Heidelberg say, in one of his calmest moods, that he would rather decline two drinks than one German adjective.
- **Mark Twain** 1835–1910 American writer: *A Tramp Abroad* (1880)

23 An unalterable and unquestioned law of the musical world required that the German text of French operas sung by Swedish artists should be translated into

Italian for the clearer understanding of English-speaking audiences.

- **Edith Wharton** 1862-1937 American novelist: *The Age of Innocence* (1920)

24 There had crept a look of furtive shame, the shifty, hangdog look which announces that an Englishman is about to talk French.

- **P. G. Wodehouse** 1881-1975 English writer: *The Luck of the Bodkins* (1935)

25 'What asses these Frenchmen are. Why can't they talk English?'
'They are possibly more to be pitied than censured, m'lord. Early upbringing no doubt has a lot to do with it.'

- **P. G. Wodehouse** 1881-1975 English writer: *Ring for Jeeves* (1953)

Last Words

see also **DEATH**

....

Die, my dear Doctor, that's the last thing I shall do!   **Lord Palmerston**

1 He had been, he said, an unconscionable time dying; but he hoped that they would excuse it.

- **Charles II** 1630-85 British king: Lord Macaulay *History of England* (1849)

2 Do you know the famous last words of the Fatted Calf? 'I hear the young master has returned.'

- **Monja Danischewsky** 1911-94 Russian-born British screenwriter and producer: told to the editor

3 I will not go down to posterity talking bad grammar.

- **Benjamin Disraeli** 1804-81 British Tory statesman and novelist: while correcting proofs of his last Parliamentary speech, 31 March 1881; Robert Blake *Disraeli* (1966)

4 No it is better not. She would only ask me to take a message to Albert.
near death, declining a proposed visit from Queen Victoria

- **Benjamin Disraeli** 1804-81 British Tory statesman and novelist: Robert Blake *Disraeli* (1966)

5 *when Queen Caroline, on her deathbed, urged him to marry again:*
No, I shall have mistresses.

- **George II** 1683-1760 British king: John Hervey *Memoirs of the Reign of George II* (1848)

6 *on his deathbed in 1936, when someone remarked 'Cheer up, your Majesty, you will soon be at Bognor again':*
Bugger Bognor.
alternatively, the comment may have been made in 1929, when it was proposed that the town be renamed Bognor Regis following the king's convalescence there

- **George V** 1865-1936 British king: Kenneth Rose *King George V* (1983); attributed

7 Leave the shower curtain on the inside of the tub.

- **Conrad Hilton** 1887-1979 American hotelier: last words; attributed, perhaps apocryphal

8 Dying is easy. Comedy is hard.

- **Edmund Kean** c.1787-1833 English actor: last words, probably apocryphal; similar last words are attributed to the actor Edmund Gwenn (1875-1959), who is said to have responded to the remark 'I guess dying can be very hard' with 'Yes, but not as hard as playing comedy'

9 *Lady Eldon had suggested that she should read to him from his own New Testament:*
No...Awfully jolly of you to suggest it, though.

- **Ronald Knox** 1888-1957 English writer and Roman Catholic priest: Evelyn Waugh *Life of Ronald Knox*

10 I'm always angry when I'm dying.
John Mortimer's father's last words

- **Clifford Mortimer** British lawyer: John Mortimer *A Voyage Round My Father* (1971)

11 Die, my dear Doctor, that's the last thing I shall do!
- **Lord Palmerston** 1784-1865 British statesman: E. Latham *Famous Sayings and their Authors* (1904)

12 *last words, as the priest was leaving her room:* One moment, Monsieur Le Curé, and we will depart together.
- **Madame de Pompadour** 1721-64 French favourite of Louis XV: attributed

13 Bring down the curtain, the farce is played out.
- **François Rabelais** c.1494-c.1553 French humanist: last words, attributed, but probably apocryphal; Jean Fleury *Rabelais et ses oeuvres* (1877)

14 Put that bloody cigarette out!
before being shot by a sniper in World War One
- **Saki** 1870-1916 Scottish writer: attributed, perhaps apocryphal

15 They couldn't hit an elephant at this distance...
immediately prior to being killed by enemy fire

at the battle of Spotsylvania in the American Civil War, May 1864
- **John Sedgwick** 1813-64 American Union general: Robert E. Denney *The Civil War Years* (1992)

16 If this is dying, then I don't think much of it.
- **Lytton Strachey** 1880-1932 English biographer: Michael Holroyd *Lytton Strachey* (1967)

17 I find, then, I am but a bad anatomist.
cutting his throat in prison, he severed his windpipe instead of his jugular, and lingered for several days
- **Wolfe Tone** 1763-98 Irish nationalist: Oliver Knox *Rebels and Informers* (1998)

18 This is no time for making new enemies.
on being asked to renounce the Devil, on his deathbed
- **Voltaire** 1694-1778 French writer and philosopher: attributed

The Law

see also **CRIME, JUDGES**

....

If this is justice, I am a banana. **Ian Hislop**

1 *dismissing a prisoner in the 19th century:* You have been acquitted by a Limerick jury, and you may now leave the dock without any other stain upon your character.
- **Richard Adams** Irish judge: Maurice Healy *The Old Munster Circuit* (1939)

2 Laws are like sausages. It's better not to see them being made.
- **Otto von Bismarck** 1815-98 German statesman: attributed, but not traced and probably apocryphal

3 Equity does not demand that its suitors shall have led blameless lives.
- **Louis Brandeis** 1856-1941 American lawyer: in *Loughran v. Loughran* 1934

4 The one great principle of the English law is, to make business for itself.
- **Charles Dickens** 1812-70 English novelist: *Bleak House* (1853)

5 This contract is so one-sided that I am surprised to find it written on both sides of the paper.
- **Lord Evershed** 1899-1966 British judge: Lord Denning *Closing Chapter* (1983)

6 A jury consists of twelve persons chosen to decide who has the better lawyer.
- **Robert Frost** 1874-1963 American poet: attributed; Evan Esar *The Dictionary of Humorous Quotations* (1949)

7 I was sued by a woman who claimed that she became pregnant because she watched me on the television and I bent

her contraceptive coil.
- **Uri Geller** 1946- : in *Sunday Times*
17 December 2000

8 The Law is the true embodiment
Of everything that's excellent.
It has no kind of fault or flaw,
And I, my Lords, embody the Law.
- **W. S. Gilbert** 1836-1911 English writer:
Iolanthe (1882)

9 When constabulary duty's to be done,
A policeman's lot is not a happy one.
- **W. S. Gilbert** 1836-1911 English writer:
The Pirates of Penzance (1879)

10 Let's find out what everyone is doing,
And then stop everyone from doing it.
- **A. P. Herbert** 1890-1971 English writer
and humorist: 'Let's Stop Somebody from
Doing Something' (1930)

11 *an attempt is made to write a cheque on a cow:*
'Was the cow crossed?'
'No, your worship, it was an open cow.'
- **A. P. Herbert** 1890-1971 English writer
and humorist: *Uncommon Law* (1935) 'The
Negotiable Cow'

12 *on the award of £600,000 libel damages to
Sonia Sutcliffe against Private Eye:*
If this is justice, I am a banana.
- **Ian Hislop** 1960- English satirical
journalist: in *Guardian* 25 May 1989

13 Legal writing is one of those rare
creatures, like the rat and the cockroach,
that would attract little sympathy even
as an endangered species.
- **Richard Hyland** 1949- American lawyer:
'A Defense of Legal Writing' (1986)

14 No-one obeys the speed limit except a
motorised rickshaw.
- **Boris Johnson** 1964- British Conservative
politician: in *Daily Telegraph* 12 July 2001

15 *when Knox was Attorney General Theodore
Roosevelt requested a legal justification for his
acquisition of the Panama Canal:*
Oh, Mr President, do not let so great
an achievement suffer from any taint of
legality.
- **Philander C. Knox** 1853-1921 American
lawyer and Republican politician: Tyler
Dennett *John Hay: From Poetry to Politics*

16 If you want to get ahead in this world

get a lawyer—not a book.
on self-help books
- **Fran Lebowitz** 1946- American writer:
Social Studies (1981)

17 In England, justice is open to all—like
the Ritz Hotel.
- **James Mathew** 1830-1908 Irish judge:
R. E. Megarry *Miscellany-at-Law* (1955)

18 However harmless a thing is, if the law
forbids it most people will think it wrong.
- **W. Somerset Maugham** 1874-1965 English
novelist: *A Writer's Notebook* (1949) written
in 1896

19 Injustice is relatively easy to bear; what
stings is justice.
- **H. L. Mencken** 1880-1956 American
journalist and literary critic: *Prejudices, Third
Series* (1922)

20 Here [in Paris] they hang a man first,
and try him afterwards.
- **Molière** 1622-73 French comic dramatist:
Monsieur de Pourceaugnac (1670)

21 Going to court is just an expensive habit.
- **Keith Richards** 1943- English rock musician:
Barbara Charone *Keith Richards* (1979)

22 The first thing we do, let's kill all the
lawyers.
- **William Shakespeare** 1564-1616 English
dramatist: *Henry VI, Part 2* (1592)

23 MASTER OF THE ROLLS: Really, Mr Smith,
do give this court credit for some little
intelligence.
SMITH: That is the mistake I made in the
court below, my lord
- **F. E. Smith** 1872-1930 British Conservative
politician and lawyer: Gyles Brandreth
The Law is an Ass (1984)

24 Some circumstantial evidence is very
strong, as when you find a trout in the
milk.
- **Henry David Thoreau** 1817-62 American
writer: diary, 11 November 1850

25 By the argument of counsel it was shown
that at half-past ten in the morning on
the day of the murder…[the defendant]
became insane, and remained so for
eleven and a half hours exactly.
- **Mark Twain** 1835-1910 American writer:
'A New Crime' (1875)

26 Whenever a copyright law is to be made or altered, then the idiots assemble.
- **Mark Twain** 1835-1910 American writer: *Notebook* 23 May 1903

27 JUDGE: Are you trying to show contempt for this court?
WEST: No, I'm doing my best to hide it.
- **Mae West** 1892-1980 American film actress: *My Little Chickadee* (1940 film, with W. C. Fields)

28 Naturally a detective doesn't want to look like a detective, and give the whole thing away right at the start.
- **P. G. Wodehouse** 1881-1975 English writer: *The Man with Two Left Feet* (1917)

29 *on juries:*
Asking the ignorant to use the incomprehensible to decide the unknowable.
- **Hiller B. Zobel** 1932- American judge: 'The Jury on Trial' in *American Heritage* July-August 1995; see **sports** 35

Lawyers

....

If law school is so hard to get through, how come there are so many lawyers?
Calvin Trillin

1 I have knowingly defended a number of guilty men. But the guilty never escape unscathed. My fees are sufficient punishment for anyone.
- **F. Lee Bailey** 1933- American lawyer: in *Los Angeles Times* 9 January 1972

2 Johnson observed, that 'he did not care to speak ill of any man behind his back, but he believed the gentleman was an *attorney*.'
- **Samuel Johnson** 1709-84 English poet, critic, and lexicographer: James Boswell *Life of Samuel Johnson* (1791) 1770

3 Whatever fees we [Judge Logan and I] earn at a distance, if not paid *before*, we notice we never hear of after the work is done. We therefore, are growing a little sensitive on the point.
- **Abraham Lincoln** 1809-65 American statesman: letter 2 November 1842

4 I don't know as I want a lawyer to tell me what I cannot do. I hire him to tell me how to do what I want to do.
- **J. P. Morgan** 1837-1913 American financier and philanthropist: Ida M. Tarbell *The Life of Elbert H. Gary* (1925)

5 No brilliance is needed in the law. Nothing but common sense, and relatively clean finger nails.
- **John Mortimer** 1923-2009 English novelist, barrister, and dramatist: *A Voyage Round My Father* (1971)

6 Professional men, they have no cares; Whatever happens, they get theirs.
- **Ogden Nash** 1902-71 American humorist: 'I Yield to My Learned Brother' (1935)

7 I'm trusting in the Lord and a good lawyer.
on the Iran-Contra affair
- **Oliver North** 1943- American Marine Corps officer: in Observer 7 December 1986

8 Went down and spoke at some lawyers' meeting last night. They didn't think much of my little squib yesterday about driving the shysters out of their profession. They seemed to kinder doubt just who would have to leave.
- **Will Rogers** 1879-1935 American actor and humorist: 'Mr. Rogers is Hob Nobbing With Leaders of the Bar'

9 If law school is so hard to get through, how come there are so many lawyers?
- **Calvin Trillin** 1935- American journalist and writer: attributed

10 What chance has the ignorant, uncultivated liar against the educated expert? What chance have I...against a lawyer?
- **Mark Twain** 1835-1910 American writer: 'On the Decay of the Art of Lying' (1882)

Leisure *see* **HOLIDAYS AND LEISURE**

Letters

Dear 338171 (May I call you 338?).   **Noël Coward**

1 I would have answered your letter
sooner, but you didn't send one.
- **Goodman Ace** 1899-1982 American
humorist: letter to Groucho Marx, 1950

2 *formula with which to return unsolicited
manuscripts:*
Mr James Agate regrets that he has no
time to bother about the enclosed in
which he has been greatly interested.
- **James Agate** 1877-1947 British drama critic
and novelist: diary, 3 January 1936

3 One of the pleasures of reading old
letters is the knowledge that they need
no answer.
- **Lord Byron** 1788-1824 English poet:
attributed, but probably apocryphal

4 *using Lawrence's military number:*
Dear 338171 (May I call you 338?).
- **Noël Coward** 1899-1973 English dramatist,
actor, and composer: letter to T. E.
Lawrence, 25 August 1930

5 *in reply to a letter from executives of CBS
headed 'From the desk of':*
Dear Desk,...
- **Noël Coward** 1899-1973 English dramatist,
actor, and composer: c. 1955-6; Sheridan
Morley *A Talent to Amuse* (1985)

6 Sir, My pa requests me to write to you,
the doctors considering it doubtful
whether he will ever recuvver the use
of his legs which prevents his holding
a pen.
- **Charles Dickens** 1812-70 English novelist:
Nicholas Nickleby (1839)

7 It is wonderful how much news there is
when people write every other day; if
they wait for a month, there is nothing
that seems worth telling.
- **O. Douglas** 1877-1948 Scottish writer: *Penny
Plain* (1920)

8 [Charles Lamb's] sayings are generally

like women's letters; all the pith is in the
postscript.
- **William Hazlitt** 1778-1830 English essayist:
Conversations of James Northcote (1826-7)

9 A man seldom puts his authentic self
into a letter. He writes it to amuse
a friend or to get rid of a social or
business obligation, which is to say, a
nuisance.
- **H. L. Mencken** 1880-1956 American
journalist and literary critic: *Minority Report*
(1956)

10 I have made this [letter] longer than
usual, only because I have not had the
time to make it shorter.
- **Blaise Pascal** 1623-62 French
mathematician, physicist, and moralist:
Lettres Provinciales (1657)

11 *circular sent out to forestall unwanted
visitors:*
Mr J. Ruskin is about to begin a work
of great importance and therefore
begs that in reference to calls and
correspondence you will consider him
dead for the next two months.
- **John Ruskin** 1819-1900 English art and
social critic: attributed

12 *Wilde had sent a letter on 'Fashion in Dress'
to the* Daily Telegraph, *but explained in a
covering letter to the proprietor:*
I don't wish to sign my name, though
I am afraid everybody will know
who the writer is: one's style is one's
signature always.
- **Oscar Wilde** 1854-1900 Irish dramatist and
poet: letter, 2 February 1891

13 I have known men come to London
full of bright prospects and seen them
complete wrecks in a few months
through a habit of answering letters.
- **Oscar Wilde** 1854-1900 Irish dramatist and
poet: W. B. Yeats *Four Years* (1921)

14 I have no need of your God-damned
sympathy. I only wish to be entertained
by some of your grosser reminiscences.
- **Alexander Woollcott** 1887-1943 American
writer: letter to Rex O'Malley, 1942

Libraries

see also **BOOKS**

....

*Mr Cobb took me into his library and showed me his books, of which he had a
complete set.*   **Ring Lardner**

1 RUTH: They'll sack you.
NORMAN: They daren't. I reorganized
the Main Index. When I die, the secret
dies with me.
- **Alan Ayckbourn** 1939- English dramatist:
Round and Round the Garden (1975)

2 If you file your waste-paper basket for
50 years, you have a public library.
- **Tony Benn** 1925- British Labour politician:
in *Daily Telegraph* 5 March 1994

3 There is nowhere in the world where
sleep is so deep as in the libraries of the
House of Commons.
- **Chips Channon** 1897-1958 American-born
British Conservative politician: diary,
16 December 1937

4 Th' first thing to have in a libry is a
shelf. Fr'm time to time this can be
decorated with lithrachure. But th'
shelf is th' main thing.
- **Finley Peter Dunne** 1867-1936 American
humorous writer: *Mr Dooley Says* (1910)

5 I've been drunk for about a week now,
and I thought it might sober me up to
sit in a library.
- **F. Scott Fitzgerald** 1896-1940 American
novelist: *The Great Gatsby* (1925)

6 Mr Cobb took me into his library and
showed me his books, of which he had
a complete set.
- **Ring Lardner** 1885-1933 American writer:
R. E. Drennan *Wit's End* (1973)

7 The Librarian was, of course, very
much in favour of reading in general,
but readers in particular got on his
nerves...He liked people who loved
and respected books, and the best
way to do that, in the Librarian's
opinion, was to leave them on the
shelves where Nature intended them
to be.
- **Terry Pratchett** 1948- English fantasy
writer: *Men at Arms* (1993)

Lies

see also **TRUTH**

A little inaccuracy sometimes saves tons of explanation. **Saki**

1 It reminds me of the small boy who jumbled his biblical quotations and said: 'A lie is an abomination unto the Lord, and a very present help in trouble.'
- **Anonymous**: recalled by Adlai Stevenson; Bill Adler *The Stevenson Wit* (1966)

2 She [Lady Desborough] tells enough white lies to ice a wedding cake.
- **Margot Asquith** 1864-1945 British political hostess: Lady Violet Bonham Carter 'Margot Oxford' in *Listener* 11 June 1953

3 Matilda told such Dreadful Lies,
It made one Gasp and Stretch one's Eyes;
Her Aunt, who, from her Earliest Youth,
Had kept a Strict Regard for Truth,
Attempted to Believe Matilda:
The effort very nearly killed her.
- **Hilaire Belloc** 1870-1953 British writer and Liberal politician: 'Matilda' (1907)

4 *of propaganda:*
That branch of the art of lying which consists in very nearly deceiving your friends without quite deceiving your enemies.
- **Francis M. Cornford** 1874-1943 English academic: *Microcosmographia Academica* (1922 ed.)

5 What you take for lying in an Irishman is only his attempt to put an herbaceous border on stark reality.
- **Oliver St John Gogarty** 1878-1957 Irish writer and surgeon: *Going Native* (1940)

6 Telling lies is a bit like tiling bathrooms—if you don't know how to do it properly, it's best not to try.
- **Tom Holt** 1961- English novelist: *Falling Sideways* (2002)

7 By the time you say you're his,
Shivering and sighing
And he vows his passion is
Infinite, undying—
Lady, make a note of this:
One of you is lying.
- **Dorothy Parker** 1893-1967 American critic and humorist: 'Unfortunate Coincidence' (1937)

8 *on being told that Lord Astor claimed that her allegations, concerning himself and his house parties at Cliveden, were untrue:*
He would, wouldn't he?
- **Mandy Rice-Davies** 1944- English model and showgirl: in *Guardian* 1 July 1963

9 A little inaccuracy sometimes saves tons of explanation.
- **Saki** 1870-1916 Scottish writer: *The Square Egg* (1924)

10 In exceptional circumstances it is necessary to say something that is untrue in the House of Commons.
- **William Waldegrave** 1946- British Conservative politician: in *Guardian* 9 March 1994

11 Untruthful! My nephew Algernon? Impossible! He is an Oxonian.
- **Oscar Wilde** 1854-1900 Irish dramatist and poet: *The Importance of Being Earnest* (1895)

Life and its Challenges

see also **LIFESTYLE**

....

Life is something to do when you can't get to sleep.   **Fran Lebowitz**

1 Life! Don't talk to me about life.
   - **Douglas Adams** 1952-2001 English science fiction writer: *The Hitchhiker's Guide to the Galaxy* (BBC radio, 1978), Marvin the Paranoid Android

2 If you can't be a good example, then you'll just have to be a horrible warning.
   - **Catherine Aird** 1930- English writer: in *St Louis Post-Dispatch* 1 November 1989

3 I feel that life is—is divided up into the horrible and the miserable.
   - **Woody Allen** 1935- American film director, writer, and actor: *Annie Hall* (1977 film, with Marshall Brickman)

4 Life doesn't imitate art. It imitates bad television.
   - **Woody Allen** 1935- American film director, writer, and actor: *Husbands and Wives* (1992 film)

5 Life is a sexually transmitted disease.
   - **Anonymous**: graffito found on the London Underground

6 Nothing matters very much and very few things matter at all.
   - **Arthur James Balfour** 1848-1930 British Conservative statesman: Clodagh Anson *Book: discreet memoirs* (1931)

7 Life, you know, is rather like opening a tin of sardines. We are all of us looking for the key.
   - **Alan Bennett** 1934- English dramatist and actor: *Beyond the Fringe* (1961 revue) 'Take a Pew'

8 Brought up in the provinces in the forties and fifties one learned early the valuable lesson that life is generally something that happens elsewhere.
   - **Alan Bennett** 1934- English dramatist and actor: introduction to *Talking Heads* (1988)

9 There are things you just can't do in life. You can't beat the phone company, you can't make a waiter see you until he's ready to see you, and you can't go home again.
   - **Bill Bryson** 1951- American travel writer: *The Last Continent* (1989)

10 There's always somebody about to ruin your day, if not your life.
   - **Charles Bukowski** 1920-94 German-born American writer: *Pulp* (1994)

11 It's a funny old world—a man's lucky if he gets out of it alive.
   - **Walter de Leon** and **Paul M. Jones** screenwriters: *You're Telling Me* (1934 film); spoken by W. C. Fields

12 *Auntie Mame's view:*
   Life is a banquet, and some poor suckers are starving to death.
   - **Patrick Dennis** 1921-76 American writer: *Auntie Mame* (1956)

13 I find I always have to write something on a steamed mirror.
   - **Elaine Dundy** 1921-2008 American writer: attributed; Laurence J. Peter *Quotations for Our Time* (1977)

14 Life is like riding a bicycle. To keep your balance you must keep moving.
   - **Albert Einstein** 1879-1955 German-born theoretical physicist: letter to his son Eduard, 5 February 1930

15 All men are equal—all men, that is to say, who possess umbrellas.
   - **E. M. Forster** 1879-1970 English novelist: *Howard's End* (1910)

16 Just when you've squared up to the solemn realization that life is a bitch, it turns round and does something nice, just to confuse you.
   - **Tom Holt** 1961- English novelist: *The Better Mousetrap* (2008)

17 Life is just one damned thing after another.
- **Elbert Hubbard** 1859-1915 American writer: in *Philistine* December 1909 (often attributed to Frank Ward O'Malley)

18 Most of one's life…is one prolonged effort to prevent oneself thinking.
- **Aldous Huxley** 1894-1963 English novelist: *Mortal Coils* 1922

19 Do you know how helpless you feel if you have a full cup of coffee in your hand and you start to sneeze?
- **Jean Kerr** 1923-2003 American writer: *Mary, Mary* (performed 1961)

20 Life doesn't wait to be asked: it comes grinning in, sits down uninvited and helps itself to bread and cheese, and comments uninhibitedly on the decorations.
- **Philip Larkin** 1922-85 English poet: letter, 25 May 1958

21 Life is something to do when you can't get to sleep.
- **Fran Lebowitz** 1946- American writer: *Metropolitan Life* (1978)

22 For the happiest life, days should be rigorously planned, nights left open to chance.
- **Mignon McLaughlin** 1913-83 American writer: *Complete Neurotic's Notebook* (1981)

23 The living are the dead on holiday.
- **Maurice Maeterlinck** 1862-1949 Belgian poet, dramatist, and essayist: *Before the Great Silence* (1935)

24 There's one thing to be said for inviting trouble: it generally accepts.
- **Mae Maloo**: attributed, in *Reader's Digest* September 1976

25 Laugh it off, laugh it off; it's all part of life's rich pageant.
- **Arthur Marshall** 1910-89 British journalist and former schoolmaster: *The Games Mistress* (recorded monologue, 1937)

26 Whenever I investigate a smell, I find that the answer is always bad. It's never: 'What is that? [sniff] muffins'!
- **Demetri Martin** 1973- American comedian: attributed

27 It's not true that life is one damn thing after another—it's one damn thing over and over.
- **Edna St Vincent Millay** 1892-1950 American poet: letter to Arthur Davison Ficke, 24 October 1930

28 There are three ingredients in the good life: learning, earning, and yearning.
- **Christopher Morley** 1890-1957 American writer: *Parnassus on Wheels* (1917)

29 Today's tears are tomorrow's yawn.
- **Matthew Parris** 1949- British journalist: in *Times* 7 February 2013

30 There are few things in this world more reassuring than an unhappy lottery winner.
- **Tony Parsons** 1953- English writer: in *Mirror* 2 November 1998

31 You're born naked and the rest is drag.
- **RuPaul** 1960- American drag queen: attributed, 1990s

32 I *love* living. I have some problems with my *life*, but living is the best thing they've come up with so far.
- **Neil Simon** 1927- American dramatist: *Last of the Red Hot Lovers* (1970)

33 Life itself is a universally fatal sexually transmitted disease.
- **Petr Skrabanek** 1940-94 and **James McCormick**: *Follies and Fallacies in Medicine* (1990)

34 Life is a gamble at terrible odds—if it was a bet, you wouldn't take it.
- **Tom Stoppard** 1937- British dramatist: *Rosencrantz and Guildenstern are Dead* (1967)

35 Oh, isn't life a terrible thing, thank God?
- **Dylan Thomas** 1914-53 Welsh poet: *Under Milk Wood* (1954)

36 We're all in this together—by ourselves.
- **Lily Tomlin** 1939- American comedienne and actress: attributed

37 What a queer thing Life is! So unlike anything else, don't you know, if you see what I mean.
- **P. G. Wodehouse** 1881-1975 English-born writer: *My Man Jeeves* (1919)

Lifestyle

Never try to keep up with the Joneses. Drag them down to your level.
Quentin Crisp

1 Have fun. And go home when you're tired.
   - **George Abbott** 1887-1995 American director, producer, and dramatist: in obituary, *New York Times* 2 February 1995

2 What is the secret of my long life? I really don't know—cigarettes, whisky and wild, wild women!
   the oldest British survivor of the First World War
   - **Henry Allingham** 1896-2009 English airman: in *Daily Telegraph* 10 November 2005 (online edition)

3 Do unto others before they do unto you.
   - **Anonymous**: traditional saying; see **advice** 9

4 The only thing I regret about my life is the length of it. If I had to live my life again I'd make all the same mistakes— only sooner.
   - **Tallulah Bankhead** 1903-68 American actress: Laurence J. Peter (ed.) *Quotations for our Time* (1977)

5 I had always thought that once you grew up you could do anything you wanted—stay up all night or eat ice-cream straight out of the container.
   - **Bill Bryson** 1951- American travel writer: *The Lost Continent* (1989)

6 Never try to keep up with the Joneses. Drag them down to your level.
   - **Quentin Crisp** 1908-99 English writer: in *Times* 22 November 1999

7 If *A* is a success in life, then *A* equals *x* plus *y* plus *z*. Work is *x*; *y* is play; and *z* is keeping your mouth shut.
   - **Albert Einstein** 1879-1955 German-born theoretical physicist: in *Observer* 15 January 1950

8 Most people die without ever having lived. Luckily for them, they don't realize it.
   - **Henrik Ibsen** 1828-1906 Norwegian dramatist: attributed, Michael Meyer *Henrik Ibsen* vol. 3 (1971)

9 Puberty is a phase...Fifteen years of rejection is a lifestyle.
   - **Susan Kolinsky**: *Sex and the City* 'The Turtle and the Hare' (1998), spoken by Stanford (Willie Garson)

10 You only live once, and the way I live, once is enough.
   - **Frank Sinatra** 1915-98 American singer and actor: attributed, in *Times* 16 May 1998

11 As life goes on, don't you find that all you need is about two real friends, a regular supply of books, and a Peke?
   - **P. G. Wodehouse** 1881-1975 English writer: letter 28 October 1930

Literature

see also **BOOKS, POETRY, WRITING**

....

When I want to read a novel, I write one. **Benjamin Disraeli**

1 We men have got love well weighed up;
our stuff
Can get by without it.
Women don't seem to think that's good
enough;
They write about it.
  ▪ **Kingsley Amis** 1922-95 English novelist and
  poet: 'A Bookshop Idyll' (1956)

2 Literature's always a good card to play
for Honours. It makes people think that
Cabinet ministers are educated.
  ▪ **Arnold Bennett** 1867-1931 English novelist:
  The Title (1918)

3 Dr Weiss, at forty, knew that her life had
been ruined by literature.
  ▪ **Anita Brookner** 1928- British novelist and
  art historian: A Start in Life (1981)

4 A well-written Life is almost as rare as a
well-spent one.
  ▪ **Thomas Carlyle** 1795-1881 Scottish
  historian and political philosopher: Critical
  and Miscellaneous Essays (1838)

5 'What is the use of a book',
thought Alice, 'without pictures or
conversations?'
  ▪ **Lewis Carroll** 1832-98 English writer and
  logician: Alice's Adventures in Wonderland
  (1865)

6 If my books had been any worse,
I should not have been invited to
Hollywood, and if they had been any
better, I should not have come.
  ▪ **Raymond Chandler** 1888-1959 American
  writer: letter to Charles W. Morton,
  12 December 1945

7 When I want to read a novel, I write
one.
  ▪ **Benjamin Disraeli** 1804-81 British Tory
  statesman and novelist: W. Monypenny
  and G. Buckle Life of Benjamin Disraeli
  (1920)

8 listening to readings from Tolkien's Lord
of the Rings:
Oh fuck, not another elf!
  ▪ **Hugo Dyson** 1896-1975 English academic:
  A. N. Wilson C. S. Lewis (1990)

9 How rare, how precious is frivolity!
How few writers can prostitute all their
powers! They are always implying, 'I am
capable of higher things.'
  ▪ **E. M. Forster** 1879-1970 English novelist:
  Abinger Harvest (1936)

10 What greater service could I have
performed for German literature than
that I didn't bother with it?
  ▪ **Frederick the Great** 1712-86 Prussian king:
  K. Biedermann Friedrich der Grosse (1859)

11 He knew everything about literature
except how to enjoy it.
  ▪ **Joseph Heller** 1923-99 American novelist:
  Catch-22 (1961)

12 It's with bad sentiments that one makes
good novels.
  ▪ **Aldous Huxley** 1894-1963 English novelist:
  letter, 10 July 1962

13 It takes a great deal of history to
produce a little literature.
  ▪ **Henry James** 1843-1916 American novelist:
  Hawthorne (1879)

14 The notice which you have been
pleased to take of my labours, had it
been early, had been kind; but it has
been delayed till I am indifferent, and
cannot enjoy it; till I am solitary, and
cannot impart it; till I am known,
and do not want it.
  ▪ **Samuel Johnson** 1709-84 English poet,
  critic, and lexicographer: letter to Lord
  Chesterfield, 7 February 1755; James Boswell
  Life of Samuel Johnson (1791)

15 A beginning, a muddle, and an end.
on the 'classic formula' for a novel
  ▪ **Philip Larkin** 1922-85 English poet: in New
  Fiction January 1978

16 Literature is mostly about having sex
and not much about having children.
Life is the other way round.
- **David Lodge** 1935- English novelist:
The British Museum is Falling Down (1965)

17 From the moment I picked up your
book until I laid it down, I was
convulsed with laughter. Some day
I intend reading it.
- **Groucho Marx** 1890-1977 American
film comedian: a blurb written for S. J.
Perelman's 1928 book *Dawn Ginsberg's
Revenge*

18 In literature as in love, we are
astonished at what is chosen by others.
- **André Maurois** 1885-1967 French writer:
attributed

19 *explaining to Queen Victoria why he did not
wish to read* Oliver Twist:
It's all among workhouses and Coffin
Makers and Pickpockets...I wish to
avoid them.
- **Lord Melbourne** 1779-1848 British Whig
statesman: A. N. Wilson *The Victorians*
(2002)

20 I have only ever read one book in
my life, and that is *White Fang*. It's so
frightfully good I've never bothered to
read another.
Uncle Matthew's view of literature
- **Nancy Mitford** 1904-73 English writer:
Love in a Cold Climate (1949)

21 And I'll stay off Verlaine too; he was
always chasing Rimbauds.
- **Dorothy Parker** 1893-1967 American critic
and humorist: 'The Little Hours' (1939)

22 If, with the literate, I am
Impelled to try an epigram,
I never seek to take the credit;

We all assume that Oscar said it.
- **Dorothy Parker** 1893-1967 American
critic and humorist: 'A Pig's-Eye View of
Literature' (1937)

23 Nearly all our best men are dead!
Carlyle, Tennyson, Browning, George
Eliot!—I'm not feeling very well myself.
- **Punch** 1841-1992 English humorous weekly
periodical: vol. 104 (1893)

24 I have known her pass the whole
evening without mentioning a single
book, or *in fact anything unpleasant,*
at all.
- **Henry Reed** 1914-86 English poet and
dramatist: *A Very Great Man Indeed* (1953)

25 Is Moby Dick the whale or the man?
- **Harold Ross** 1892-1951 American journalist
and editor: James Thurber *The Years with
Ross* (1959)

26 In view of her penchant
For something romantic,
De Sade is too trenchant
And Dickens too frantic,
And Stendhal would ruin
The plan of attack
As there isn't much blue in
The Red and the Black.
- **Stephen Sondheim** 1930- American
songwriter: 'Now' (1972)

27 You're familiar with the tragedies of
antiquity, are you? The great homicidal
classics?
- **Tom Stoppard** 1937- British dramatist:
Rosencrantz and Guildenstern are Dead
(1967)

28 Like playing Beethoven on the kazoo.
*on his translation of Shakespeare into text
messages*
- **John Sutherland** 1938- English writer: in
Mail on Sunday 20 November 2005

Love

see also **DATING, MARRIAGE, ROMANCE, SEX**

....

Love is the delusion that one woman differs from another.   **H. L. Mencken**

1 MARK: Oh right, so, now she's finished with you, suddenly you're in love with her again?
JEZ: Exactly. Duh! That's how love works Mark.
- **Jesse Armstrong** and **Sam Bain** 1971-British screenwriters: *Peep Show* (Channel 4 TV, 2007), spoken by David Mitchell and Robert Webb

2 Even logical positivists are capable of love.
- **A. J. Ayer** 1910-89 English philosopher: Kenneth Tynan *Profiles* (1989)

3 The test for true love is whether you can endure the thought of cutting your sweetheart's toe-nails.
- **W. N. P. Barbellion** 1889-1919 English diarist: *Journal of a Disappointed Man* (1919)

4 Make love to every woman you meet. If you get five percent on your outlays it's a good investment.
- **Arnold Bennett** 1867-1931 English novelist: Laurence J. Peter (ed.) *Quotations for our Time* (1977)

5 It is a curious thought, but it is only when you see people looking ridiculous, that you realize just how much you love them.
- **Agatha Christie** 1890-1976 English writer: *Agatha Christie: An Autobiography* (1977)

6 Love and a cottage! Eh, Fanny! Ah, give me indifference and a coach and six!
- **George Colman, the Elder** 1732-94 and **David Garrick** 1717-79: *The Clandestine Marriage* (1766)

7 Would I were free from this restraint, Or else had hopes to win her; Would she could make of me a saint, Or I of her a sinner.
- **William Congreve** 1670-1729 English dramatist: 'Pious Selinda Goes to Prayers' (song)

8 They made love as though they were an endangered species.
- **Peter De Vries** 1910-93 American novelist: Laurence J. Peter (ed.) *Quotations for our Time* (1977)

9 Barkis is willin'.
- **Charles Dickens** 1812-70 English novelist: *David Copperfield* (1850)

10 Oh, Mrs Corney, what a prospect this opens! What a opportunity for a jining of hearts and house-keepings!
- **Charles Dickens** 1812-70 English novelist: *Oliver Twist* (1838)

11 Love is a piano dropped out a four story window
And you were in the wrong place at the wrong time.
- **Ani DiFranco** 1970- American singer and songwriter: 'Two Little Girls'

12 The magic of first love is our ignorance that it can ever end.
- **Benjamin Disraeli** 1804-81 British Tory statesman and novelist: *Henrietta Temple* (1837)

13 What is commonly called love, namely the desire of satisfying a voracious appetite with a certain quantity of delicate white human flesh.
- **Henry Fielding** 1707-54 English novelist and dramatist: *Tom Jones* (1749)

14 How happy could I be with either, Were t'other dear charmer away!
- **John Gay** 1685-1732 English poet and dramatist: *The Beggar's Opera* (1728)

15 Holding hands at midnight
'Neath a starry sky...
Nice work if you can get it,
And you can get it if you try.
- **Ira Gershwin** 1896-1983 American songwriter: 'Nice Work If You Can Get It' (1937 song)

16 So I fell in love with a rich attorney's
Elderly ugly daughter.
- **W. S. Gilbert** 1836-1911 English writer: *Trial
by Jury* (1875)

17 Love is a perky elf dancing a merry
little jig and then suddenly he turns on
you with a miniature machine gun.
- **Matt Groening** 1954- American humorist
and satirist: attributed

18 In the spring a young man's fancy
lightly turns to
thoughts of love;
And in summer,
and in autumn,
and in winter—
See above.
- **E. Y. Harburg** 1898-1981 American
songwriter: 'Tennyson Anyone?' (1965)

19 When I'm not near the girl I love,
I love the girl I'm near.
…When I can't fondle the hand I'm
fond of
I fondle the hand at hand.
- **E. Y. Harburg** 1898-1981 American
songwriter: 'When I'm Not Near the Girl
I Love' (1947 song)

20 The broken dates,
The endless waits,
The lovely loving and the hateful hates,
The conversation and the flying
plates—
I wish I were in love again.
- **Lorenz Hart** 1895-1943 American
songwriter: 'I Wish I Were in Love Again'
(1937 song)

21 Love's like the measles—all the worse
when it comes late in life.
- **Douglas Jerrold** 1803-57 English dramatist
and journalist: *The Wit and Opinions of
Douglas Jerrold* (1859) 'Love'

22 You ain't nothin' but a hound dog,
Quit snoopin' round my door
You can wag your tail but I ain't gonna
feed you no more.
- **Jerry Leiber** 1933-2011 and **Mike Stoller**
1933- : 'Hound Dog' (1956 song)

23 Tell me, George, if you had to do it
all over would you fall in love with
yourself again.
to George Gershwin
- **Oscar Levant** 1906-72 American pianist:
David Ewen *The Story of George Gershwin*
(1943)

24 Love's a disease. But curable.
- **Rose Macaulay** 1881-1958 English novelist:
Crewe Train (1926)

25 Love is the delusion that one woman
differs from another.
- **H. L. Mencken** 1880-1956 American journalist
and literary critic: *Chrestomathy* (1949)

26 Oh, life is a glorious cycle of song,
A medley of extemporanea;
And love is a thing that can never go
wrong;
And I am Marie of Roumania.
- **Dorothy Parker** 1893-1967 American critic
and humorist: 'Comment' (1937)

27 Four be the things I'd been better
without:
Love, curiosity, freckles, and doubt.
- **Dorothy Parker** 1893-1967 American critic
and humorist: 'Inventory' (1937)

28 Love is the fart
Of every heart:
It pains a man when 'tis kept close,
And others doth offend, when 'tis let
loose.
- **John Suckling** 1609-42 English poet and
dramatist: 'Love's Offence' (1646)

29 If love is the answer, could you rephrase
the question?
- **Lily Tomlin** 1939- American comedienne
and actress: attributed; David Housham
and John Frank-Keyes *Funny Business* (1992)

30 Love conquers all things—except
poverty and toothache.
- **Mae West** 1892-1980 American film actress:
attributed

31 To love oneself is the beginning of a
lifelong romance.
- **Oscar Wilde** 1854-1900 Irish dramatist and
poet: *An Ideal Husband* (1895)

Management

see also **BUREAUCRACY**

Only the paranoid survive.   **Andrew Grove**

1 Assistant heads must roll!
traditional solution to management problems in broadcasting
- **Anonymous**: in *Guardian* 30 June 2004

2 I was to learn later in life that we tend to meet any new situation by reorganizing; and a wonderful method it can be for creating the illusion of progress while producing confusion, inefficiency, and demoralization.
- **Anonymous**: modern saying, frequently (and wrongly) attributed to Petronius Arbiter

3 Meetings are a great trap…However, they are indispensable when you don't want to do anything.
- **J. K. Galbraith** 1908-2006 Canadian-born American economist: diary, 22 April 1961

4 When people say. 'Oh, would you rather be thought of as a funny man or a great boss?' My answer's always the same: to me they're not mutually exclusive.
David Brent as manager
- **Ricky Gervais** 1961- and **Stephen Merchant**: *The Office* (Series 1, Episode 2; 2001)

5 Only the paranoid survive.
dictum on which he has long run his company, the Intel Corporation
- **Andrew Grove** 1936- Hungarian-born American businessman: in *New York Times* 18 December 1994

6 The man who is denied the opportunity of taking decisions of importance begins to regard as important the decisions he is allowed to take.
- **C. Northcote Parkinson** 1909-93 English writer: *Parkinson's Law* (1958)

7 It is difficult to get a man to understand something when his salary depends on his not understanding it.
- **Upton Sinclair** 1878-1968 American novelist and social reformer: *I, Candidate for Governor* (1935)

8 Lunch is for wimps.
- **Stanley Weiser** and **Oliver Stone** 1946- screenwriters: *Wall Street* (1987 film), spoken by Michael Douglas

9 Any committee that is the slightest use is composed of people who are too busy to sit on it for a second longer than they have to.
- **Katharine Whitehorn** 1928- English journalist: *Observations* (1970)

10 Don't say yes until I finish talking!
characteristic instruction
- **Darryl F. Zanuck** 1902-79 American film producer: Mel Gussow *Don't Say Yes Until I Finish Talking* (1971)

Manners

Manners are especially the need of the plain.   **Evelyn Waugh**

1 Etiquette is the noise you don't make when you are eating soup.
  - **Anonymous**: traditional saying

2 My grandmother took a bath every year, whether she was dirty or not.
  - **Brendan Behan** 1923-64 Irish dramatist: *Brendan Behan's Island* (1962)

3 It looked bad when the Duke of Fife Left off using a knife; But people began to talk When he left off using a fork.
  - **Edmund Clerihew Bentley** 1875-1956 English writer: 'The Duke of Fife' (1905)

4 A man telephoned a friend at two o'clock in the morning. 'I do hope I haven't disturbed you,' he said cheerily. 'Oh no,' the friend replied, 'that's quite all right. I had to get up to answer the telephone anyway.'
  - **Carl Brandt**: attributed, in *Reader's Digest* 1942

5 INTERVIEWER: You've been accused of vulgarity.
  MEL BROOKS: Bullshit!
  - **Mel Brooks** 1926- American film director and comic actor: interview in *Playboy*, Maurice Yacowar *The Comic Art of Mel Brooks* (1981)

6 You know what charm is: a way of getting the answer yes without having asked any clear question.
  - **Albert Camus** 1913-60 French novelist, dramatist, and essayist: *La Chute* (1956)

7 Curtsey while you're thinking what to say. It saves time.
  - **Lewis Carroll** 1832-98 English writer and logician: *Through the Looking-Glass* (1872)

8 Don't let us be familiar or fond, nor kiss before folks, like my Lady Fadler and Sir Francis…Let us be very strange and well-bred: Let us be as strange as if we had been married a great while, and as well-bred as if we were not married at all.
  - **William Congreve** 1670-1729 English dramatist: *The Way of the World* (1700)

9 Vulgarity is the garlic in the salad of charm.
  - **Cyril Connolly** 1903-74 English writer: *Enemies of Promise* (1960)

10 The English never speak to anyone unless they have been properly introduced (except in case of shipwreck).
  - **Pierre Daninos** 1913-2005 French writer: *Major Thompson and I* (1957)

11 Suspect all extraordinary and groundless civilities.
  - **Thomas Fuller** 1654-1734 English writer and physician: *Gnomologia* (1734)

12 NOTE FROM FELLOW DINNER GUEST: Talk to the woman on your left.
  HEATH (PASSING THE NOTE BACK): I have.
  - **Edward Heath** 1916-2005 British Conservative statesman: attributed

13 To Americans, English manners are far more frightening than none at all.
  - **Randall Jarrell** 1914-65 American poet: *Pictures from an Institution* (1954)

14 'What are you doing for dinner tonight?'
  'Digesting it.'
  to a dinner invitation arriving at 8.30 pm
  - **George S. Kaufman** 1889-1961 American dramatist: Howard Teichmann *George S. Kaufman* (1973)

15 I've always had good manners. I always take the cigarette out of my mouth before kissing someone.
  - **Ian Kilminster** 1945- English pop singer: in *Times* 27 October 2012

16 Eccentricity, to be socially acceptable, had still to have at least four or five

generations of inbreeding behind it.
- **Osbert Lancaster** 1908-86 English writer and cartoonist: *All Done From Memory* (1953)

17 *as the pantomime dame Mother Goose:*
The bus was so crowded—even the men were standing.
- **Dan Leno** 1860-1904 English entertainer: attributed, 1904

18 I have noticed that the people who are late are often so much jollier than the people who have to wait for them.
- **E. V. Lucas** 1868-1938 English journalist, essayist, and critic: *365 Days and One More* (1926)

19 *aged four, having had hot coffee spilt over his legs:*
Thank you, madam, the agony is abated.
- **Lord Macaulay** 1800-59 English politician and historian: G. O. Trevelyan *Life and Letters of Lord Macaulay* (1876)

20 Good manners are a combination of intelligence, education, taste, and style mixed together so that you don't need any of those things.
- **P. J. O'Rourke** 1947- American humorous writer: *Modern Manners* (1984)

21 Do you suppose I could buy back my introduction to you?
- **S. J. Perelman** 1904-79 and **others** screenwriters: *Monkey Business* (1931 film), spoken by Groucho Marx

22 I am a woman of the world, Hector; and I can assure you that if you will only take the trouble always to do the perfectly correct thing, and to say the perfectly correct thing, you can do just what you like.
- **George Bernard Shaw** 1856-1950 Irish dramatist: *Heartbreak House* (1919)

23 Everyone knows that the real business of a ball is either to look out for a wife, to look after a wife, or to look after somebody else's wife.
- **R. S. Surtees** 1805-64 English sporting journalist and novelist: *Mr Facey Romford's Hounds* (1865)

24 *Somerset Maugham excused his leaving early when dining with Lady Tree by saying, 'I must look after my youth':*
Next time do bring him. We adore those sort of people.
- **Lady Tree** 1863-1937 English actress: in *Ned Sherrin in his Anecdotage* (1993); a similar story is told of Maugham and Lady Cunard

25 This is a free country, madam. We have a right to share your privacy in a public place.
- **Peter Ustinov** 1921-2004 British actor, director, and writer: *Romanoff and Juliet* (1956)

26 Orthodoxy is my doxy; heterodoxy is another man's doxy.
- **William Warburton** 1698-1779 English theologian and bishop: to Lord Sandwich; Joseph Priestley *Memoirs* (1807)

27 Manners are especially the need of the plain. The pretty can get away with anything.
- **Evelyn Waugh** 1903-66 English novelist: in *Observer* 15 April 1962

28 I am very sorry to hear that Duff [Cooper] was surprised and grieved to hear that I had detested him for 23 years. I must have nicer manners than people normally credit me with.
- **Evelyn Waugh** 1903-66 English novelist: letter to Lady Diana Cooper, 29 August 1953

29 Duty is what one expects from others, it is not what one does oneself.
- **Oscar Wilde** 1854-1900 Irish dramatist and poet: *A Woman of No Importance* (1893)

Marriage

see also **DIVORCE, HUSBANDS, LOVE, SEX, WEDDINGS**

....

Advice to persons about to marry.—'Don't.' **Punch**

1 I think people should mate for life. Like pigeons, or Catholics.
- **Woody Allen** 1935- : *Manhattan* (1979 film, with Marshall Brickman), spoken by Woody Allen

2 After a while, marriage is a sibling relationship—marked by occasional, and rather regrettable, episodes of incest.
- **Martin Amis** 1949- English novelist: *Yellow Dog* (2003)

3 [Marriage is] the only war where one sleeps with the enemy.
- **Anonymous**: Mexican saying; Ned Sherrin *Cutting Edge* (1984)

4 All marriages are happy. It's the living together afterwards that causes all the trouble.
- **Anonymous**: traditional saying

5 The marriage suffered a setback in 1965 when the husband was killed by the wife.
- **Anonymous**: in *The New Law Journal* 1968 vol. 117

6 They start with all that sucking and blowing and in the end you lose your house.
comparing marriage to the Florida hurricanes
- **Anonymous**: in *New Statesman* 20 November 2000

7 A man cannot marry before he has studied anatomy and has dissected at the least one woman.
- **Honoré de Balzac** 1799–1850 French novelist: *Physiology of Marriage* (1904)

8 I'm not going to make the same mistake once.
on marriage
- **Warren Beatty** 1937- American actor, film director, and screenwriter: attributed; Bob Chieger *Was It Good For You Too?* (1983)

9 Love matches are formed by people who pay for a month of honey with a life of vinegar.
- **Countess of Blessington** 1789–1849 Irish novelist: *Desultory Thoughts and Reflections* (1839)

10 It was very good of God to let Carlyle and Mrs Carlyle marry one another and so make only two people miserable instead of four.
- **Samuel Butler** 1835–1902 English novelist: letter, 21 November 1884

11 I have great hopes that we shall love each other all our lives as much as if we had never married at all.
- **Lord Byron** 1788–1824 English poet: letter to Annabella Milbanke, 5 December 1814

12 Love and marriage, love and marriage, Go together like a horse and carriage.
- **Sammy Cahn** 1913-93 American songwriter: 'Love and Marriage' (1955 song)

13 The deep, deep peace of the double-bed after the hurly-burly of the chaise-longue.
- **Mrs Patrick Campbell** 1865-1940 English actress: Alexander Woollcott *While Rome Burns* (1934) 'The First Mrs Tanqueray'

14 I am not at all the sort of person you and I took me for.
- **Jane Carlyle** 1801-66 wife of Thomas Carlyle: letter to Thomas Carlyle, 7 May 1822

15 If you are afraid of loneliness, don't get married.
- **Anton Chekhov** 1860-1904 Russian dramatist and short-story writer: attributed

16 *of her future son-in-law John Betjeman:*
We invite people like that to our houses, but we don't marry them.
- **Lady Chetwode** d. 1946: Maurice Bowra *Memories 1898-1939* (1966)

17 He has a future and I have a past so we should be all right.
on her marriage to Montagu Porch in 1918

(he was forty-one, three years younger than her son Winston)
- **Lady Jennie Churchill** 1851-1921 American-born society hostess: Anita Leslie *Jennie: the life of Lady Randolph Churchill* (1969)

18 If you're married for more than ten minutes, you're going to have to forgive somebody for something.
- **Hillary Rodham Clinton** 1947- American lawyer and politician: on ABC *Primetime Live* 30 January 1992

19 The most happy marriage I can picture or imagine to myself would be the union of a deaf man to a blind woman.
- **Samuel Taylor Coleridge** 1772-1834 English poet, critic, and philosopher: Thomas Allsop *Letters, Conversations, and Recollections of S. T. Coleridge* (1836)

20 *asked about the age difference on returning from her honeymoon with her husband, 32 years her junior:*
If he dies, he dies.
- **Joan Collins** 1933- British actress: in *Daily Mail* 5 March 2002

21 Marriage is a feast where the grace is sometimes better than the dinner.
- **Charles Caleb Colton** 1780-1832 English clergyman and writer: *Lacon* (1822)

22 Tho' marriage makes man and wife one flesh, it leaves 'em still two fools.
- **William Congreve** 1670-1729 English dramatist: *The Double Dealer* (1694)

23 SHARPER: Thus grief still treads upon the heels of pleasure:
Married in haste, we may repent at leisure.
SETTER: Some by experience find those words mis-placed:
At leisure married, they repent in haste.
- **William Congreve** 1670-1729 English dramatist: *The Old Bachelor* (1693)

24 Marriage is a wonderful invention; but, then again, so is a bicycle repair kit.
- **Billy Connolly** 1942- Scottish comedian: Duncan Campbell *Billy Connolly* (1976)

25 One of those looks which only a quarter-century of wedlock can adequately marinate.
- **Alan Coren** 1938-2007 English humorist: *Seems Like Old Times* (1989)

26 So basically you're saying marriage is just a way of getting out of an embarrassing pause in conversation.
- **Richard Curtis** 1956- New Zealand-born writer: *Four Weddings and a Funeral* (1994 film)

27 We sleep in separate rooms, we have dinner apart, we take separate vacations—we're doing everything we can to keep our marriage together.
- **Rodney Dangerfield** 1921-2004 American comedian: attributed

28 Nothing was happening in my marriage. I nicknamed our waterbed Lake Placid.
- **Phyllis Diller** 1917-2012 American actress: attributed

29 I have always thought that every woman should marry, and no man.
- **Benjamin Disraeli** 1804-81 British Tory statesman and novelist: *Lothair* (1870)

30 No man is regular in his attendance at the House of Commons until he is married.
- **Benjamin Disraeli** 1804-81 British Tory statesman and novelist: Hesketh Pearson *Dizzy* (1951)

31 I don't think matrimony consistent with the liberty of the subject.
- **George Farquhar** 1678-1707 Irish dramatist: *The Twin Rivals* (1703)

32 His designs were strictly honourable, as the phrase is; that is, to rob a lady of her fortune by way of marriage.
- **Henry Fielding** 1707-54 English novelist and dramatist: *Tom Jones* (1749)

33 Keep your eyes wide open before marriage, half shut afterwards.
- **Benjamin Franklin** 1706-90 American politician, inventor, and scientist: *Poor Richard's Almanack* (1738)

34 I support gay marriage because I believe they have a right to be just as miserable as the rest of us.
- **Kinky Friedman** 1944- American singer and politician: quoted on CBS News, 21 August 2005

35 A man in love is incomplete until he has married. Then he's finished.
- **Zsa Zsa Gabor** 1917- Hungarian-born film actress: in *Newsweek* 28 March 1960

36 POLLY: Then all my sorrows are at an end.
MRS PEACHUM: A mighty likely speech, in troth, for a wench who is just married!
- **John Gay** 1685-1732 English poet and dramatist: *The Beggar's Opera* (1728)

37 By god, D. H. Lawrence was right when he had said there must be a dumb, dark, dull, bitter belly-tension between a man and a woman, and how else could this be achieved save in the long monotony of marriage?
- **Stella Gibbons** 1902-89 English novelist: *Cold Comfort Farm* (1932)

38 My mother said it was simple to keep a man, you must be a maid in the living room, a cook in the kitchen and a whore in the bedroom. I said I'd hire the other two and take care of the bedroom bit.
- **Jerry Hall** 1956- American model: in *Observer* 6 October 1985 'Sayings of the Week'

39 The critical period in matrimony is breakfast-time.
- **A. P. Herbert** 1890-1971 English writer and humorist: *Uncommon Law* (1935) 'Is Marriage Lawful?'

40 Holy deadlock.
- **A. P. Herbert** 1890-1971 English writer and humorist: title of novel (1934)

41 The concept of two people living together for 25 years without having a cross word suggests a lack of spirit only to be admired in sheep.
- **A. P. Herbert** 1890-1971 English writer and humorist: in *News Chronicle*, 1940

42 Marriage is a good deal like a circus: there is not as much in it as is represented in the advertising.
- **E. W. Howe** 1853-1937 American novelist and editor: *Country Town Sayings* (1911)

43 Do you think I'd marry anyone who would marry *me*?
- **Henry James** 1843-1916 American novelist: *The Princess Casamassima* (1886)

44 Hogamus, higamous
Man is polygamous

Higamus, hogamous
Woman monogamous.
- **William James** 1842-1910 American philosopher: in *Oxford Book of Marriage* (1990)

45 *of a man who remarried immediately after the death of a wife with whom he had been unhappy:*
The triumph of hope over experience.
- **Samuel Johnson** 1709-84 English poet, critic, and lexicographer: James Boswell *Life of Samuel Johnson* (1791) 1770

46 The most difficult year of marriage is the one you're in.
- **Franklin P. Jones** 1887-1929 American businessman: attributed

47 I'm sick of these conventional marriages. One woman and one man was good enough for your grandmother. But who wants to marry your grandmother?
- **George S. Kaufman** 1889-1961 and **Morrie Ryskind** 1895-1985 screenwriters: *Animal Crackers* (1930 film), spoken by Groucho Marx as Captain Spaulding

48 The honeymoon is over when he phones that he'll be late for supper— and she has already left a note that it's in the refrigerator.
- **Bill Lawrence** 1968- American screenwriter: in *Reader's Digest* 1955

49 Many a man in love with a dimple makes the mistake of marrying the whole girl.
- **Stephen Leacock** 1869-1944 Canadian humorist: attributed

50 Don't worry if you never marry. It will save you a lot of vexation.
last words of advice to Petronella Wyatt
- **Princess Margaret** 1930-2002: in *Sunday Times* 17 February 2002

51 *to her husband, who had asked the age of a flirtatious starlet with noticeably thick legs:*
For God's sake, Walter, why don't you chop off her legs and read the rings?
- **Carol Matthau** 1925-2003 American actress: Truman Capote *Answered Prayers* (1986)

52 No matter how happily a woman may be married, it always pleases her to

discover that there is a nice man who wishes she were not.

- **H. L. Mencken** 1880-1956 American journalist and literary critic: *Chrestomathy* (1949)

53 One doesn't have to get anywhere in a marriage. It's not a public conveyance.
- **Iris Murdoch** 1919-99 English novelist: *A Severed Head* (1961)

54 Marriage is the alliance of two people one of whom never remembers birthdays and the other never forgetsam.
- **Ogden Nash** 1902-71 American humorist: 'I do, I will, I have' (1949)

55 Marriage may often be a stormy lake, but celibacy is almost always a muddy horsepond.
- **Thomas Love Peacock** 1785-1866 English novelist and poet: *Melincourt* (1817)

56 Strange to say what delight we married people have to see these poor fools decoyed into our condition.
- **Samuel Pepys** 1633-1703 English diarist: diary, 25 December 1665

57 Tolerance is the one essential ingredient…You can take it from me that the Queen has the quality of tolerance in abundance.
his recipe for a successful marriage, 19 November 1997, marking their golden wedding anniversary
- **Prince Philip, Duke of Edinburgh** 1921– husband of Elizabeth II: in *Times* 20 November 1997

58 They dream in courtship, but in wedlock wake.
- **Alexander Pope** 1688-1744 English poet: *Translations from Chaucer* (1714)

59 Advice to persons about to marry.—'Don't.'
- **Punch** 1841-1992 English humorous weekly periodical: vol. 8 (1845)

60 BISHOP: Who is it that sees and hears all we do, and before whom even I am but as a crushed worm?
PAGE: The Missus, my Lord.
- **Punch** 1841-1992 English humorous weekly periodical: vol. 79 (1880)

61 *the Lord Chief Justice was once asked by a lady what was the maximum punishment for bigamy:*
Two mothers-in-law.
- **Lord Russell of Killowen** 1832-1900 Irish lawyer and politician: Edward Abinger *Forty Years at the Bar* (1930)

62 A young man married is a man that's marred.
- **William Shakespeare** 1564-1616 English dramatist: *All's Well that Ends Well* (1603-4)

63 Many a good hanging prevents a bad marriage.
- **William Shakespeare** 1564-1616 English dramatist: *Twelfth Night* (1601)

64 It is a woman's business to get married as soon as possible, and a man's to keep unmarried as long as he can.
- **George Bernard Shaw** 1856-1950 Irish dramatist: *Man and Superman* (1903)

65 Marriage is popular because it combines the maximum of temptation with the maximum of opportunity.
- **George Bernard Shaw** 1856-1950 Irish dramatist: *Man and Superman* (1903) 'Maxims: Marriage'

66 'Tis safest in matrimony to begin with a little aversion.
- **Richard Brinsley Sheridan** 1751-1816 Irish dramatist and Whig politician: *The Rivals* (1775)

67 Take care of him. And make him feel important. And if you can do that, you'll have a happy and wonderful marriage. Like two out of every ten couples.
- **Neil Simon** 1927– American dramatist: *Barefoot in the Park* (1964)

68 My definition of marriage…it resembles a pair of shears, so joined that they cannot be separated; often moving in opposite directions, yet always punishing anyone who comes between them.
- **Sydney Smith** 1771-1845 English clergyman and essayist: Lady Holland *Memoir* (1855)

69 The concerts you enjoy together
Neighbours you annoy together
Children you destroy together,

That keep marriage intact.
- **Stephen Sondheim** 1930- American songwriter: 'The Little Things You Do Together' (1970 song)

70 My brother Toby, quoth she, is going to be married to Mrs Wadman. Then he will never, quoth my father, lie *diagonally* in his bed again as long as he lives.
- **Laurence Sterne** 1713-68 English novelist: *Tristram Shandy* (1759-67)

71 Even if we take matrimony at its lowest, even if we regard it as no more than a sort of friendship recognised by the police.
- **Robert Louis Stevenson** 1850-94 Scottish novelist: *Virginibus Puerisque* (1881)

72 *asked who wore the trousers at home:*
I do. I wear the trousers. And I wash and iron them, too.
- **Denis Thatcher** 1915-2003 English businessman: attributed; in *Times* 27 June 2003

73 It should be a very happy marriage—they are both so much in love with *him*.
- **Irene Thomas** 1919-2001 British broadcaster: *The Bandsman's Daughter* (1979)

74 Marriage isn't a word...it's a *sentence*!
- **King Vidor** 1895-1982 American film director: in *The Crowd* (1928 film)

75 He is dreadfully married. He's the most married man I ever saw in my life.
- **Artemus Ward** 1834-67 American humorist: *Artemus Ward's Lecture* (1869) 'Brigham Young's Palace'

76 Marriage is a great institution, but I'm not ready for an institution yet.
- **Mae West** 1892-1980 American film actress: Laurence J. Peter (ed.) *Quotations for our Time* (1977); attributed

77 A good marriage is like Dr Who's Tardis, only small and banal from the outside, but spacious and interesting from within.
- **Katharine Whitehorn** 1928- English journalist: *View from a Column* (1981)

78 'Tis my maxim, he's a fool that marries, but he's a greater that does not marry a fool.
- **William Wycherley** c.1640-1716 English dramatist: *The Country Wife* (1675)

Medicine

see also **SICKNESS**

A hospital is no place to be sick. **Sam Goldwyn**

1 I am dying with the help of too many physicians.
- **Alexander the Great** 356-323 BC Greek king: attributed

2 *doctor's advice to Bond star Roger Moore after he had been fitted with a heart pacemaker:*
Keep paying the electricity bill.
- **Anonymous**: in *Mail on Sunday* 4 January 2004 'Quotes of the Year'

3 Medicinal discovery,
It moves in mighty leaps,
It leapt straight past the common cold
And gave it us for keeps.
- **Pam Ayres** 1947- English writer of humorous verse: 'Oh no, I got a cold' (1976)

4 Psychiatrist: a man who asks you a lot of expensive questions your wife asks you for nothing.
- **Sam Bardell**: attributed

5 Hark! the herald angels sing!
Beecham's Pills are just the thing,
Two for a woman, one for a child...
Peace on earth and mercy mild!
- **Thomas Beecham** 1879-1961 English conductor: advertising jingle devised for his father, but not used; Neville Cardus *Sir Thomas Beecham* (1961)

6 Physicians of the Utmost Fame
Were called at once; but when they came
They answered, as they took their Fees,

'There is no Cure for this Disease.'
- **Hilaire Belloc** 1870-1953 British writer and Liberal politician: 'Henry King' (1907)

7 I was in for ten hours and had 40 pints, beating my previous record by 20 minutes.
comparing transfusions after his liver transplant with drinking, during the BBC's Sports Personality of the Year Awards
- **George Best** 1946-2005 Northern Irish footballer: in *Mail on Sunday* 15 December 2002

8 *definition of a physician:*
One on whom we set our hopes when ill, and our dogs when well.
- **Ambrose Bierce** 1842-c.1914 American writer: *The Devil's Dictionary* (1911)

9 I used to believe that chiropractors were charlatans, but then I went to one and now I stand corrected.
- **Shmuel Breban** American comedian: attributed

10 A fashionable surgeon, like a pelican, can be recognized by the size of his bill.
- **John Chalmers DaCosta** 1863-1933 American surgeon: *The Trials and Triumphs of the Surgeon* (1944)

11 *epigram on Dr John Lettsom, who would sign his prescriptions 'I. Lettsom':*
Whenever patients come to I,
I physics, bleeds, and sweats 'em;
If after that they choose to die,
What's that to me!—*I letts 'em.*
- **Thomas Erskine** 1750-1823 British lawyer: *Poetical Works* (1823)

12 A Harvard medical school study has determined that rectal thermometers are still the best way to tell a baby's temperature. Plus it really teaches the baby who's boss.
- **Tina Fey** 1970- American comedian and actress: attributed

13 A cousin of mine who was a casualty surgeon in Manhattan tells me that he and his colleagues had a one-word nickname for bikers: Donors.
- **Stephen Fry** 1957- English comedian, actor, and writer: *Paperweight* (1992)

14 I came in here in all good faith to help my country. I don't mind giving a reasonable amount [of blood], but a pint…why that's very nearly an armful. I'm sorry. I'm not walking around with an empty arm for anybody.
- **Ray Galton** 1930- and **Alan Simpson** 1929- English writers: *The Blood Donor* (1961 television programme, words spoken by Tony Hancock)

15 A hospital is no place to be sick.
- **Sam Goldwyn** 1882-1974 American film producer: Arthur Marx *Goldwyn* (1976)

16 What's the bleeding time?
- **Richard Gordon** 1921- English writer: *Doctor in the House* (1954 film), spoken by James Robertson Justice

17 If you have a stomach ache, in France you get a suppository, in Germany a health spa, in the United States they cut your stomach open and in Britain they put you on a waiting list.
- **Phil Hammond** 1955- and **Michael Mosley**: *Trust Me (I'm a Doctor)* (1999)

18 When our organs have been transplanted
And the new ones made happy to lodge in us,
Let us pray one wish be granted—
We retain our zones erogenous.
- **E. Y. Harburg** 1898-1981 American songwriter: 'Seated One Day at the Organ' (1965)

19 Hungry Joe collected lists of fatal diseases and arranged them in alphabetical order so that he could put his finger without delay on any one he wanted to worry about.
- **Joseph Heller** 1923-99 American novelist: *Catch-22* (1961)

20 As to diseases, make a habit of two things—to help, or at least to do no harm.
- **Hippocrates** c.460-357 BC Greek physician: *Epidemics*

21 The kind of doctor I want is one who, when he's not examining me, is home studying medicine.
- **George S. Kaufman** 1889-1961 American dramatist: Howard Teichmann *George S. Kaufman* (1973)

22 In disease Medical Men guess: if they
cannot ascertain a disease, they call it
nervous.
- **John Keats** 1795-1821 English poet: J. A. Gere
and John Sparrow (eds.) *Geoffrey Madan's
Notebooks* (1981); attributed

23 One of the most difficult things to
contend with in a hospital is the
assumption on the part of the staff that
because you have lost your gall bladder
you have also lost your mind.
- **Jean Kerr** 1923-2003 American writer:
How I Got to be Perfect (1979)

24 A specialist is a man who knows more
and more about less and less.
- **William Mayo** 1861-1939 American
physician: attributed

25 I fear that being a patient in any hospital
in Ireland calls for two things—holy
resignation and an iron constitution.
- **Flann O'Brien** 1911-66 Irish novelist and
journalist: *Myles Away from Dublin* (1990)

26 The desire to take medicine is perhaps
the greatest feature which distinguishes
man from animals.
- **William Osler** 1849-1919 Canadian-born
physician: H. Cushing *Life of Sir William
Osler* (1925)

27 He said my bronchial tubes were
entrancing,
My epiglottis filled him with glee,
He simply loved my larynx
And went wild about my pharynx,
But he never said he loved me.
- **Cole Porter** 1891-1964 American
songwriter: 'The Physician' (1933)

28 Cured yesterday of my disease,
I died last night of my physician.
- **Matthew Prior** 1664-1721 English poet: 'The
Remedy Worse than the Disease' (1727)

29 A friend of mine confused her Valium
with her birth control pills—she had
14 kids but didn't give a shit.
- **Joan Rivers** 1933- American comedienne:
attributed

30 There would never be any public
agreement among doctors if they did
not agree to agree on the main point
of the doctor being always in the right.
- **George Bernard Shaw** 1856-1950 Irish
dramatist: preface to *The Doctor's Dilemma*
(1911)

31 There is at bottom only one genuinely
scientific treatment for all diseases, and
that is to stimulate the phagocytes.
- **George Bernard Shaw** 1856-1950 Irish
dramatist: *The Doctor's Dilemma* (1911)

32 I can't stand whispering. Every time a
doctor whispers in the hospital, next
day there's a funeral.
- **Neil Simon** 1927- American dramatist:
The Gingerbread Lady (1970)

33 Randolph Churchill went into
hospital...to have a lung removed. It
was announced that the trouble was not
'malignant'...it was a typical triumph of
modern science to find the only part of
Randolph that was not malignant and
remove it.
- **Evelyn Waugh** 1903-66 English novelist:
'Irregular Notes 1960-65'; diary March
1964

34 Sir Roderick Glossop...is always
called a nerve specialist, because it
sounds better, but everybody knows
that he's really a sort of janitor to the
looney-bin.
- **P. G. Wodehouse** 1881-1975 English-born
writer: *The Inimitable Jeeves* (1923)

Members of Parliament

see also **POLITICS**

....

Being an MP feeds your vanity and starves your self-respect.   **Matthew Parris**

1 Being an MP is the sort of job all
working-class parents want for their
children—clean, indoors and no heavy
lifting.
   - **Diane Abbott** 1953-   British Labour
   politician: in *Observer* 30 January 1994
   'Sayings of the Week'

2 Happiness is the constituency in the
rear view mirror.
   - **Anonymous**: in 1991; Gyles Brandreth
   Something Sensational to Read in the Train
   (2010)

3 As an MP, you only meet two types
of people: people with problems and
people who are right.
   - **Gyles Brandreth** 1948-   English writer and
   broadcaster: diary, 18 May 1997, *Something
   Sensational to Read in the Train* (2010)

4 CHURCHILL: I am the humble servant of
the Lord Jesus Christ and of the House
of Commons.
CRIPPS: I hope you treat Jesus better
than you treat the H of C.
   - **Stafford Cripps** 1889-1952 British Labour
   politician: diary, April 1950

5 The only safe pleasure for a
parliamentarian is a bag of boiled
sweets.
   - **Julian Critchley** 1930-2000 British
   Conservative politician and journalist: in
   Listener 10 June 1982

6 The occupational hazards are the three
As: arrogance, alcoholism and adultery.
If you suffer from only one, it's thought

you're doing quite well.
advice for women MPs
   - **Edwina Currie** 1946-   British Conservative
   politician: in *Daily Telegraph* 8 June 2010

7 The prospect of a lot
Of dull MPs in close proximity,
All thinking for themselves is what
No man can face with equanimity.
   - **W. S. Gilbert** 1836-1911 English writer:
   Iolanthe (1882)

8 When in that House MPs divide,
If they've a brain and cerebellum too,
They have to leave that brain outside,
And vote just as their leaders tell 'em to.
   - **W. S. Gilbert** 1836-1911 English writer:
   Iolanthe (1882)

9 Being an MP feeds your vanity and
starves your self-respect.
   - **Matthew Parris** 1949-   British journalist
   and former politician: in *Times* 9 February
   1994

10 Under the present circumstances,
I would rather be a lap dancer than a
woman MP—the hours are better and
unruly male members are shown the
door.
   - **Allison Pearson** 1960-   Welsh journalist: in
   Evening Standard 9 May 2001

11 I never saw so many shocking bad hats
in my life.
*on seeing the first Parliament after the 1832
Reform Bill*
   - **Duke of Wellington** 1769-1852 British
   soldier and statesman: W. Fraser *Words on
   Wellington* (1889)

Memory

The older I get, the better I used to be. **John McEnroe**

1 Our memories are card-indexes consulted, and then put back in disorder by authorities whom we do not control.
  - **Cyril Connolly** 1903-74 English writer: *The Unquiet Grave* (1944)

2 H: We met at nine
  G: We met at eight
  H: I was on time
  G: No, you were late
  H: Ah yes! I remember it well.
  - **Alan Jay Lerner** 1918-86 American songwriter: 'I Remember It Well' (1957)

3 The older I get, the better I used to be.
  quoting basketball star Connie Hawkins
  - **John McEnroe** 1959- American tennis player: on *Charlie Rose* WNET 4 February 1999

4 The fondest memory I have is not really of the Goons. It is a girl called Julia with enormous breasts.
  - **Spike Milligan** 1918-2002 Irish comedian: attributed

5 The selective memory isn't selective enough.
  - **Blake Morrison** 1950- English poet: in *Independent on Sunday* 16 June 1991

6 My memory is so very untrustworthy. It's as fickle as a fox. Ask me to name the third lateral bloodvessel from the extremity of my index finger that runs east to west when I lie on my face at sundown, or the percentage of chalk to be found in the knuckles of an average spinster in her fifty-seventh year, ha, ha, ha!—or even ask me, my dear boy, to give details of the pulse rate of frogs two minutes before they die of scabies—these things are no tax upon my memory, ha, ha, ha! but ask me to remember exactly what you said your problems were, a minute ago and you will find that my memory has forsaken me utterly.
  - **Mervyn Peake** 1911-68 English artist and writer: *Titus Groan* (1946)

Men

see also **MEN AND WOMEN**

Men are animals and as such are entitled to humane treatment.
Germaine Greer

1 My mother's two categories: nice men did things for you, bad men did things to you.
  - **Margaret Atwood** 1939- Canadian novelist: *Lady Oracle* (1976)

2 It is a truth universally acknowledged, that a single man in possession of a good fortune, must be in want of a wife.
  - **Jane Austen** 1775-1817 English novelist: *Pride and Prejudice* (1813)

3 A man is two people, himself and his cock. A man always takes his friend to the party. Of the two, the friend is the nicer, being more able to show his feelings.
  - **Beryl Bainbridge** 1934-2010 English novelist: Judy Allen *Picking on Men* (1985)

4 A man who correctly guesses a woman's age may be smart, but he's not very bright.
  - **Lucille Ball** 1911-89 American actress: attributed

5 Women were brought up to believe that men were the answer. They weren't. They weren't even one of the questions.
  ▪ **Julian Barnes** 1946- English novelist: *Staring at the Sun* (1986)

6 Men in their forties are like the New York Times Sunday crossword puzzle: tricky, complicated, and you're never really sure you got the right answer.
  ▪ **Candace Bushnell** 1958- , **Darren Star** 1961- , and **Patrick King** 1954- American writers: *Sex and the City* (HBO TV, 1998) Sarah Jessica Parker as Carrie

7 All men are children anyway and if you understand that, a woman understands everything.
  ▪ **Coco Chanel** 1883-1971 French couturière: John Fairchild *The Fashionable Savages* (1965)

8 My mother wanted me to be a nice boy. I didn't let her down. I don't smoke, drink or mess around with women.
  ▪ **Julian Clary** 1959- Englsih comedian: in *Independent* 2 March 1996 'Quote Unquote'

9 Beware of men who cry. It's true that men who cry are sensitive to and in touch with feelings, but the only feelings they tend to be sensitive to and in touch with are their own.
  ▪ **Nora Ephron** 1941-2012 American screenwriter and director: *Heartburn* (1983)

10 Summer bachelors, like summer breezes, are never as cool as they pretend to be.
  ▪ **Nora Ephron** 1941-2012 American screenwriter and director: in *New York Post* 22 August 1965

11 It struck me as pretty ridiculous to be called Mr Darcy and to stand on your own looking snooty at a party. It's like being called Heathcliff and insisting on spending the entire evening in the garden, shouting 'Cathy' and banging your head against a tree.
  ▪ **Helen Fielding** 1958- British writer: *Bridget Jones's Diary* (1996)

12 I want a man who's kind and understanding. Is that too much to ask of a millionaire?
  ▪ **Zsa Zsa Gabor** 1917- Hungarian-born actress: attributed

13 Francesca di Rimini, miminy, piminy, *Je-ne-sais-quoi* young man!
  ▪ **W. S. Gilbert** 1836-1911 English writer: *Patience* (1881)

14 Men are animals and as such are entitled to humane treatment.
  ▪ **Germaine Greer** 1939- Australian feminist: in *Mail on Sunday* 7 March 1999 'Quotes of the Week'

15 Behind every successful man stands a surprised mother-in-law.
  ▪ **Hubert Humphrey** 1911-78 American Democratic politician: attributed, 1960s

16 To men, porno movies are beautiful love stories with all the boring stuff taken out.
  ▪ **Richard Jeni** 1957-2007 American comedian: attributed

17 When a man brings his wife flowers for no reason—there's a reason!
  ▪ **Marian Jordan** 1898-1961 American actress: attributed, as Molly McGee in *Fibber McGee and Molly* (NBC radio, 1935-59)

18 Years ago, manhood was an opportunity for achievement, and now it is a problem to be overcome.
  ▪ **Garrison Keillor** 1942- American humorous writer and broadcaster: *The Book of Guys* (1994)

19 There are no available men in their thirties in New York. Giuliani had them removed along with the homeless.
  ▪ **Michael Patrick King**: *Sex and the City* 'Valley of the Twenty-Something Guys' (1998); spoken by Miranda

20 Most men think monogamy is something you make dining-room tables out of.
  ▪ **Kathy Lette** 1958- Australian writer: *Men: A User's Guide* (2010)

21 A man's home may seem to be his castle on the outside; inside it is more often his nursery.
  ▪ **Clare Booth Luce** 1903-87 American diplomat, politician, and writer: attributed

22 Men are those creatures with two legs and eight hands
  ▪ **Jayne Mansfield** 1933-67 American actress: attributed

23 Bachelors have consciences, married men have wives.
- **H. L. Mencken** 1880-1956 American journalist and literary critic: *A Little Book in C major* (1916)

24 In men this blunder still you find,
All think their little set—mankind.
- **Hannah More** 1745-1833 English writer: *Florio* (1786)

25 If you want to scare your boyfriend next Halloween, come dressed as what he fears most. Commitment.
- **Peter Nelson**: *Real Man Tells All* (1988)

26 The follies which a man regrets most, in his life, are those which he didn't commit when he had the opportunity.
- **Helen Rowland** 1875-1950 American writer: *A Guide to Men* (1922)

27 The typical public schoolboy is acceptable at a dance and invaluable in a shipwreck.
- **J. F. Roxburgh** 1885-1951 English headmaster: *Eleutheros* (1930)

28 Men's bums never grow up. Like school satchels, they evoke in an instant memories of childhood.
- **Arundhati Roy** 1961- Indian novelist: *The God of Small Things* (1997)

29 I like men to behave like men—strong and childish.
- **Françoise Sagan** 1935-2004 French novelist: attributed; Jonathon Green *A Dictionary of Contemporary Quotations* (1982)

30 God made him, and therefore let him pass for a man.
- **William Shakespeare** 1564-1616 English dramatist: *The Merchant of Venice* (1596-8)

31 A hard man is good to find.
- **Mae West** 1892-1980 American film actress: attributed

32 A man in the house is worth two in the street.
- **Mae West** 1892-1980 American film actress: *Belle of the Nineties* (1934 film)

33 There is, of course, no reason for the existence of the male sex except that sometimes one needs help with moving the piano.
- **Rebecca West** 1892-1983 English novelist and journalist: in *Sunday Telegraph* 28 June 1970

34 A fox is a wolf who sends flowers.
- **Ruth Weston** 1906-55 American actress: attributed; in R. L. Woods *A Modern Handbook of Humour* (1967)

35 Many a fellow who looks like the dominant male and has himself photographed smoking a pipe curls up like carbon paper when confronted by an aunt.
- **P. G. Wodehouse** 1881-1975 English-born writer: *The Mating Season* (1949)

Men and Women

see also **DATING, MEN, WOMEN**

....

When women go wrong, men go right after them.　**Mae West**

1 The average girl would rather have beauty than brains because she knows that the average man can see much better than he can think.
- **Anonymous**: saying, from 1940s on

2 If you catch a man, throw him back.
- **Anonymous**: women's liberation slogan, Australia, 1975

3 Why is it hard for women to find men who are sensitive, caring, and good-looking? Because those men already have boyfriends.
- **Anonymous**: modern saying

4 A gentleman is one who never swears at his wife when ladies are present.
- **Anonymous**: saying, Evan Esar *20,000 Quips and Quotes* (1968)

5 In passing, also, I would like to say that the first time Adam had a chance he laid the blame on woman...
  - **Nancy Astor** 1879-1964 American-born British Conservative politician: *My Two Countries* (1923)

6 Zuleika, on a desert island, would have spent most of her time in looking for a man's footprint.
  - **Max Beerbohm** 1872-1956 English critic, essayist, and caricaturist: *Zuleika Dobson* (1911)

7 All women dress like their mothers, that is their tragedy. No man ever does. That is his.
  - **Alan Bennett** 1934- English dramatist and actor: *Forty Years On* (1969)

8 You never see a man walking down the street with a woman who has a little pot belly and a bald spot.
  - **Elayne Boosler** 1952- American comedian: attributed

9 Guys are like dogs. They keep coming back. Ladies are like cats. Yell at a cat one time, they're gone.
  - **Lenny Bruce** 1925-66 American comedian: attributed

10 A woman can become a man's friend only in the following stages—first an acquaintance, next a mistress, and only then a friend.
  - **Anton Chekhov** 1860-1904 Russian dramatist and short-story writer: *Uncle Vanya* (1897)

11 Certain women should be struck regularly, like gongs.
  - **Noël Coward** 1899-1973 English dramatist, actor, and composer: *Private Lives* (1930)

12 *on his regret at not being born female:*
  I'd have opened a knitting shop in Carlisle and been a part of life.
  - **Quentin Crisp** 1908-99 English writer: in *Spectator* 20 November 1999

13 I wouldn't be seen dead with a woman old enough to be my wife.
  - **Tony Curtis** 1925-2010 American actor: attributed

14 Last year my wife ran off with the fellow next door and I must admit, I still miss him.
  - **Les Dawson** 1934-93 Englsih comedian: attributed

15 A coachman's a privileged indiwidual... 'cos a coachman may be on the wery amicablest terms with eighty mile o' females, and yet nobody think that he ever means to marry any vun among them.
  - **Charles Dickens** 1812-70 English novelist: *Pickwick Papers* (1837)

16 The feminist movement seems to have beaten the manners out of men, but I didn't see them put up a lot of resistance.
  - **Clarissa Dickson Wright** 1947- English chef and broadcaster: in *Mail on Sunday* 24 September 2000 'Quotes of the Week'

17 Plain women he regarded as he did the other severe facts of life, to be faced with philosophy and investigated by science.
  - **George Eliot** 1819-80 English novelist: *Middlemarch* (1871-2)

18 *a fellow Congressman attacked a piece of women's rights legislation with the words, 'I've always thought of women as kissable, cuddly, and smelling good':*
  That's what I feel about men. I only hope you haven't been disappointed as often as I have.
  - **Millicent Fenwick** 1910-92 American Republican politician: in *Ned Sherrin in his Anecdotage* (1993)

19 *estranged husband of Liza Minnelli:*
  I'd give up all my Shirley Temple dolls to get Liza back.
  - **David Gest** 1953- : in *Sunday Times* 14 December 2003

20 If they ever invent a vibrator that can open pickle jars, we've had it.
  on the bleak future facing men
  - **Jeff Green** 1964- English comedian: in *Mail on Sunday* 21 March 1999

21 Couldn't sleep
  And wouldn't sleep
  Until I could sleep where I shouldn't sleep—

Bewitched, bothered and bewildered
am I.
- **Lorenz Hart** 1895-1943 American
songwriter: 'Bewitched, Bothered and
Bewildered' (1940)

22 Take him, I won't put a price on him
Take him, he's yours
Take him, pyjamas look nice on him
But how he snores!
- **Lorenz Hart** 1895-1943 American
songwriter: 'Take Him' (1940)

23 Women and cats do as they please, and
men and dogs might as well relax to it.
- **Robert Heinlein** 1907-88 American science
fiction writer: *Glory Road* (1963)

24 A woman's mind is cleaner than a
man's; she changes it more often.
- **Oliver Herford** 1863-1935 English-born
American humorist: attributed; Evan Esar
and Nicolas Bentley (eds.) *Treasury of
Humorous Quotations* (1951)

25 Can you imagine a world without men?
No crime and lots of happy fat women.
- **Nicole Hollander** 1939- American
cartoonist: attributed

26 Brought up in an epoch when ladies
apparently rolled along on wheels,
Mr Quarles was peculiarly susceptible
to calves.
- **Aldous Huxley** 1894-1963 English novelist:
Point Counter Point (1928)

27 Women speak because they wish to
speak, whereas a man speaks only when
driven to speech by something outside
himself—like, for instance, he can't find
any clean socks.
- **Jean Kerr** 1923-2003 American writer:
The Snake Has All the Lines (1962)

28 No one will ever win the battle of the
sexes; there's too much fraternizing
with the enemy.
- **Henry Kissinger** 1923- American
politician: attributed

29 Behind every great man is a woman
rolling her eyes.
- **Steve Koren**, **Mark O'Keefe**, and **Steve
Oedekerk** screenwriters: *Bruce Almighty*
(2003 film), spoken by Jim Carrey as
Bruce Nolan

30 The female sex has no greater fan than
I, and I have the bills to prove it.
- **Alan Jay Lerner** 1918-86 American
songwriter: *The Street Where I Live* (1978)

31 Yes, why can't a woman be more like a
man?
Men are so honest, so thoroughly
square;
Eternally noble, historically fair;
Who when you win will always give
your back a pat—
Why can't a woman be like that?
- **Alan Jay Lerner** 1918-86 American
songwriter: 'A Hymn to Him' (1956 song)

32 Why do men like smart women?
Because opposites attract.
- **Kathy Lette** 1958- Australian writer: *Dead
Sexy* (2003)

33 *comment made by the estranged wife of
Selwyn Lloyd:*
How could any woman love a man who
wears a cardigan over his pyjamas?
- **Elizabeth Lloyd** 1928- : attributed; Alan
Watkins in *Spectator* 14 June 2003

34 Brother, do you know a nicer
occupation,
Matter of fact, neither do I,
Than standing on the corner
Watching all the girls go by?
- **Frank Loesser** 1910-69 American
songwriter: 'Standing on the Corner' (1956)

35 Oh! to be loved by a man I respect,
To bask in the glow of his perfectly
understandable neglect.
- **Frank Loesser** 1910-69 American
songwriter: 'Happy to Keep his Dinner
Warm' (1961)

36 Women are brighter than men. That's
true, but it should be kept very quiet or
it ruins the whole racket.
- **Anita Loos** 1893-1981 American writer:
attributed

37 Men talk to women so they can sleep
with them and women sleep with men
so they can talk to them.
- **Jay McInerney** 1955- American writer:
Brightness Falls (1992)

38 I suppose true sexual equality will come
when a general called Anthea is found
having an unwise lunch with a young,

unreliable male model from Spain.
remark after a series of sex scandals involving military men
- **John Mortimer** 1923-2009 English novelist, barrister, and dramatist: in *The Spectator* 26 March 1994

39 A little incompatibility is the spice of life, particularly if he has income and she is pattable.
- **Ogden Nash** 1902-71 American humorist: *Versus* (1949)

40 Twenty years ago when we had no respect for women they just used to say, 'You're chucked.' And now we do respect them we have to lie to them sensitively.
- **Simon Nye** 1958- English screenwriter: *Men Behaving Badly* (ITV, series 1, 1992) 'Intruders'

41 Men seldom make passes
At girls who wear glasses.
- **Dorothy Parker** 1893-1967 American critic and humorist: 'News Item' (1937)

42 Woman lives but in her lord;
Count to ten, and man is bored.
With this the gist and sum of it,
What earthly good can come of it?
- **Dorothy Parker** 1893-1967 American critic and humorist: 'General Review of the Sex Situation' (1937)

43 Of course, I'm awfly glad that Mother
had to marry Father,
But I hate men.
- **Cole Porter** 1891-1964 American songwriter: 'I Hate Men' (1948)

44 All my life I've loved a womanly woman and admired a manly man, but I never could stand a boily boy.
- **Lord Rosebery** 1847-1929 British Liberal statesman: George Cornwallis-West *Edwardian Heydays* (1930)

45 The material for this book was collected directly from nature at great personal risk by the author.
in capitals, on the flyleaf of her book
- **Helen Rowland** 1875-1950 American writer: *A Guide to Men* (1922)

46 Men hate to lose. I once beat my husband at tennis. I asked him 'Are we going to have sex again?' He said 'Yes, but not with each other'.
- **Rita Rudner** 1953- American comedienne and writer: attributed

47 It was always women who did the choosing, and men's place was to be grateful if they were lucky enough to be the chosen ones.
- **Salman Rushdie** 1947- Indian-born British novelist: *Joseph Anton* (2012)

48 LYDIA: Every great man has had a woman behind him.
JANET: And every great woman has had some man or other in front of her, tripping her up.
- **Dorothy L. Sayers** 1893-1957 English writer: *Love All* (1940)

49 Only the male intellect, clouded by sexual impulse, could call the undersized, narrow-shouldered, broad-hipped, and short-legged sex the fair sex.
- **Arthur Schopenhauer** 1788-1860 German philosopher: 'On Women' (1851), tr. E. Belfort Bax

50 Men want the same thing from their underwear that they want from women: a little bit of support and a little bit of freedom.
- **Jerry Seinfeld** 1954- American comedian: attributed

51 *an unknown woman wrote to Shaw suggesting that as he had the greatest brain in the world, and she the most beautiful body, they ought to produce the most perfect child. He replied:*
What if the child inherits my body and your brains?
- **George Bernard Shaw** 1856-1950 Irish dramatist: Hesketh Pearson *Bernard Shaw* (1942)

52 You've got to understand, in a way a thirty-three-year-old guy is a lot younger than a twenty-four-year-old girl. That is, he may not be ready for marriage yet.
- **Neil Simon** 1927- American dramatist: *Come Blow Your Horn* (1961)

53 Werther had a love for Charlotte
Such as words could never utter;
Would you know how first he met her?

She was cutting bread and butter.
- **William Makepeace Thackeray** 1811-63 English novelist: 'Sorrows of Werther' (1855)

54 If you want anything said, ask a man. If you want anything done, ask a woman.
- **Margaret Thatcher** 1925-2013 British Conservative stateswoman: in *People* (New York) 15 September 1975

55 Sure he was great, but don't forget that Ginger Rogers did everything he did backwards…and in high heels!
caption to 'Frank and Ernest' cartoon showing a Fred Astaire film festival
- **Bob Thaves** 1924-2006 American cartoonist: Ginger Rogers *Ginger: My Story* (1991)

56 A man has one hundred dollars and you leave him with two dollars, that's subtraction.
- **Mae West** 1892-1980 American film actress: Joseph Weintraub *Peel Me a Grape* (1975)

57 Is that a gun in your pocket, or are you just glad to see me?
- **Mae West** 1892-1980 American film actress: Joseph Weintraub *Peel Me a Grape* (1975), usually quoted as 'Is that a pistol in your pocket…'

58 When women go wrong, men go right after them.
- **Mae West** 1892-1980 American film actress: in *She Done Him Wrong* (1933 film)

59 *asked by the gossip columnist Hedda Hopper*

how she knew so much about men:
Baby, I went to night school.
- **Mae West** 1892-1980 American film actress: Max Wilk *The Wit and Wisdom of Hollywood* (1972)

60 Whatever women do they must do twice as well as men to be thought half as good. Luckily, this is not difficult.
- **Charlotte Whitton** 1896-1975 Canadian writer and politician: in *Canada Month* June 1963

61 Girls are just friends who give you erections.
reporting his teenage son's words
- **Nigel Williams** 1948- English writer: *Fortysomething* (1999)

62 The only time a woman really succeeds in changing a man is when he's a baby.
- **Natalie Wood** 1938-81 American actress: attributed

63 A man is designed to walk three miles in the rain to phone for help when the car breaks down—and a woman is designed to say, 'You took your time' when he comes back dripping wet.
- **Victoria Wood** 1953- British writer and comedienne: attributed

64 A mistress should be like a little country retreat near the town, not to dwell in constantly, but only for a night and away.
- **William Wycherley** c.1640-1716 English dramatist: *The Country Wife* (1675)

Mental Health

see also **MIND**

....

O Lord, Sir—when a heroine goes mad she always goes into white satin.
Richard Brinsley Sheridan

1 A neurotic is a person who builds a castle in the air. A psychotic is the person who lives in it. A psychiatrist is the one who collects the rent.
- **Anonymous**: popular saying, from 1950s

2 The statistics on sanity are that one out of every four Americans is suffering from some form of mental illness.

Think of your three best friends. If they're okay, then it's you.
- **Rita Mae Brown** 1944- American novelist and poet: attributed

3 I told my wife the truth. I told her I was seeing a psychiatrist. Then she told *me* the truth; that she was seeing a psychiatrist, two plumbers

and a bartender.
- **Rodney Dangerfield** 1921-2004 American comedian: attributed

4 Any man who goes to a psychiatrist should have his head examined.
- **Sam Goldwyn** 1882-1974 American film producer: Norman Zierold *Moguls* (1969)

5 There was only one catch and that was Catch-22, which specified that a concern for one's own safety in the face of dangers that were real and immediate was the process of a rational mind...Orr would be crazy to fly more missions and sane if he didn't, but if he was sane he had to fly them. If he flew them he was crazy and didn't have to; but if he didn't want to he was sane and had to.
- **Joseph Heller** 1923-99 American novelist: *Catch-22* (1961)

6 Show me a sane man and I will cure him for you.
- **Carl Gustav Jung** 1875-1961 Swiss psychologist: Vincent Brome *Jung* (1978)

7 Insanity runs in my family, it practically *gallops!*
- **Joseph Kesselring** 1902-67 American writer: *Arsenic and Old Lace* (1941), spoken by Cary Grant as Mortimer Brewster in the 1944 film version

8 Psychiatry is a waste of good couches. Why should I make a psychiatrist laugh, and then pay him?
- **Kathy Lette** 1958- Australian writer: in *Times* 27 October 2001

9 If the nineteenth century was the age of the editorial chair, ours is the century of the psychiatrist's couch.
- **Marshall McLuhan** 1911-80 Canadian communications scholar: *Understanding Media* (1964)

10 O Lord, Sir—when a heroine goes mad she always goes into white satin.
- **Richard Brinsley Sheridan** 1751-1816 Irish dramatist and Whig politician: *The Critic* (1779)

11 A psychiatrist is a man who goes to the Folies-Bergère and looks at the audience.
- **Mervyn Stockwood** 1913-95 English clergyman: in *Observer* 15 October 1961

12 You're only given a little spark of madness. You mustn't lose it.
- **Robin Williams** 1952- American actor: D. Houseman and J. Frank-Keyes *Funny Business* (1992)

Middle Age

see also **OLD AGE**, **YOUTH**

....

Whenever the talk turns to age, I say I am 49 plus VAT. **Lionel Blair**

1 Years ago we discovered the exact point, the dead centre of middle age. It occurs when you are too young to take up golf and too old to rush up to the net.
- **Franklin P. Adams** 1881-1960 American journalist and humorist: *Nods and Becks* (1944)

2 I recently turned 60. Practically a third of my life is over.
- **Woody Allen** 1935- American film director, writer, and actor: in *Observer* 'Sayings of the Week' 10 March 1996

3 You are thirty-two. You are rapidly approaching the age when your body, whether it embarrasses you or not, begins to embarrass other people.
- **Alan Bennett** 1934- English dramatist and actor: *Getting On* (1972)

4 Whenever the talk turns to age, I say I am 49 plus VAT.
- **Lionel Blair** 1936- British actor and dancer: in *Mail on Sunday* 6 June 1999

5 Middle age is when your broad mind and

narrow waist begin to change places.
- **E. Joseph Cossman**: attributed

6 Nobody loves a fairy when she's forty.
- **Arthur W. D. Henley** British songwriter: title of song (1934)

7 *of Zsa Zsa Gabor:*
She's discovered the secret of perpetual middle age.
- **Oscar Levant** 1906-72 American pianist: attributed

8 I have a bone to pick with Fate.
Come here and tell me, girlie,
Do you think my mind is maturing late,
Or simply rotted early?
- **Ogden Nash** 1902-71 American humorist: 'Lines on Facing Forty' (1942)

9 As invariably happens after one passes 40, the paper sagged open to the obituary page.
- **S. J. Perelman** 1904-79 American humorist: 'Swindle Sheet with Blueblood Engrailed Arrant Fibs Rampant'

10 Maturity is a high price to pay for growing up.
- **Tom Stoppard** 1937- British dramatist: *Where Are They Now?* (1973)

11 From birth to 18 a girl needs good parents. From 18 to 35, she needs good looks. From 35 to 55, good personality. From 55 on, she needs good cash.
- **Sophie Tucker** 1884-1966 Russian-born American vaudeville artiste: Michael Freedland *Sophie* (1978)

12 Youth is when you are allowed to stay up late on New Year's Eve. Middle age is when you are forced to.
- **Bill Vaughan** 1915-77 American columnist: attributed

13 Thirty-five is a very attractive age. London society is full of women of the very highest birth who have, of their own free choice, remained thirty-five for years.
- **Oscar Wilde** 1854-1900 Irish dramatist and poet: *The Importance of Being Earnest* (1895)

The Mind

see also **INTELLIGENCE, MENTAL HEALTH**

Insanity is hereditary. You can get it from your children.   **Sam Levenson**

1 If a cluttered desk is a sign of a cluttered mind, then what are we to think of an empty desk?
- **Anonymous**: modern saying, often wrongly attributed to Albert Einstein

2 if you judge a fish by its ability to climb a tree, it will live its whole life believing it's stupid.
- **Anonymous**: modern saying, often wrongly attributed to Albert Einstein

3 If I am out of my mind, it's all right with me.
- **Saul Bellow** 1915-2005 American novelist: *Herzog* (1961) opening sentence

4 An apparatus with which we think that we think.
definition of the brain
- **Ambrose Bierce** 1842-c.1914 American writer: *Cynic's Word Book* (1906)

5 *Charles Condomine declining psychoanalysis:*
I refuse to endure months of expensive humiliation only to be told at the end of it that at the age of four I was in love with my rocking-horse.
- **Noël Coward** 1899-1973 English dramatist, actor, and composer: *Blithe Spirit* (1941)

6 Minds are like parachutes. They only function when they are open.
- **Lord Dewar** 1864-1930 British industrialist: attributed

7 Insanity is hereditary. You can get it from your children.
- **Sam Levenson** 1911-80 American humorist: *You Can Say That Again, Sam!* (1975)

8 If I knew what I was so anxious about I wouldn't be anxious.
- **Mignon McLaughlin** 1913-83 American writer: *Complete Neurotic's Notebook* (1981)

9 The trouble with having an open mind, of course, is that people will insist on coming along and trying to put things in it.
  ▪ **Terry Pratchett** 1948– English fantasy writer: *Diggers* (1990)

10 'Do you know if there was any insanity in her family?' 'Insanity? No, I never heard of any. Her father lives in West Kensington, but I believe he's sane on all other subjects.'
  ▪ **Saki** 1870–1916 Scottish writer: *Beasts and Super-Beasts* (1914)

11 Not body enough to cover his mind decently with; his intellect is improperly exposed.
  ▪ **Sydney Smith** 1771–1845 English clergyman and essayist: Lady Holland *Memoir* (1855)

12 I must have a prodigious quantity of mind; it takes me as much as a week, sometimes, to make it up.
  ▪ **Mark Twain** 1835–1910 American writer: *The Innocents Abroad* (1869)

13 A neurosis is a secret you don't know you're keeping.
  ▪ **Kenneth Tynan** 1927–80 English theatre critic: Kathleen Tynan *Life of Kenneth Tynan* (1987)

14 Right now I'm having amnesia and déja vu at the same time. I think I've forgotten this before.
  ▪ **Steven Wright** 1955– American comedian: attributed

Mistakes and Misfortunes

Calamities are of two kinds: misfortune to ourselves, and good fortune to others.   **Ambrose Bierce**

1 STRIKER: Surely you can't be serious.
  DR RUMACK: I am serious. And don't call me Shirley.
  ▪ **Jim Abrahams** and **others** screenwriters: *Airplane!* (1980 film)

2 Instead of being arrested, as we stated, for kicking his wife down a flight of stairs and hurling a lighted kerosene lamp after her, the Revd James P. Wellman died unmarried four years ago.
  ▪ **Anonymous**: from an American newspaper, quoted by Burne-Jones in a letter to Lady Horner; J. A. Gere and John Sparrow (eds.) *Geoffrey Madan's Notebooks* (1981)

3 *waiter delivering champagne to George Best's hotel room:*
  Tell me, Mr Best, where did it all go wrong?
  £20,000 in cash was scattered on the bed, which also contained Miss World
  ▪ **Anonymous**: attributed

4 My only solution for the problem of habitual accidents…is to stay in bed all day. Even then, there is always the chance that you will fall out.
  ▪ **Robert Benchley** 1889–1945 American humorist: *Chips off the old Benchley* (1949) 'Safety Second'

5 *on being told by her son that lesbians are women who sleep together:*
  MRS HOPKINS: Well, that's nothing. I slept with your Auntie Phyllis all during the air raids.
  ▪ **Alan Bennett** 1934– English dramatist and actor: *Me! I'm Afraid of Virginia Woolf* (1978)

6 George the Third
  Ought never to have occurred.
  One can only wonder
  At so grotesque a blunder.
  ▪ **Edmund Clerihew Bentley** 1875–1956 English writer: 'George the Third' (1929)

7 My misdeeds are accidental happenings and merely the result of having been in the wrong bar or bed at the wrong time, say most days between midday and midnight.
  ▪ **Jeffrey Bernard** 1932–97 English journalist: in *The Spectator* 18 July 1992

8 Calamities are of two kinds: misfortune to ourselves, and good fortune to others.
- **Ambrose Bierce** 1842–c.1914 American writer: *The Cynic's Word Book* (1906)

9 *on premature calls of a win in Florida in the presidential election of 2000:*
We don't just have egg on our face. We have omelette all over our suits.
- **Tom Brokaw** 1940– American journalist: in *Atlanta Constitution-Journal* 9 November 2000 (online edition)

10 Of all the horrid, hideous notes of woe, Sadder than owl-songs or the midnight blast,
Is that portentous phrase, 'I told you so.'
- **Lord Byron** 1788–1824 English poet: *Don Juan* (1819–24)

11 I've learned from my mistakes, and I'm sure I can repeat them.
as Sir Arthur Streeb-Greebling
- **Peter Cook** 1937–95 English comedian and actor: attributed

12 *Edith Evans repeatedly inserted the word 'very' into a line of* Hay Fever:
No, no, Edith. The line is, 'You can see as far as Marlow on a clear day.' On a *very* clear day you can see Marlow *and* Beaumont and Fletcher.
- **Noël Coward** 1899–1973 English dramatist, actor, and composer: Cole Lesley *The Life of Noël Coward* (1976)

13 If Gladstone fell into the Thames, that would be misfortune; and if anybody pulled him out, that, I suppose, would be a calamity.
- **Benjamin Disraeli** 1804–81 British Tory statesman and novelist: Leon Harris *The Fine Art of Political Wit* (1965)

14 Something nasty in the woodshed.
- **Stella Gibbons** 1902–89 English novelist: *Cold Comfort Farm* (1932)

15 The babe with a cry brief and dismal, Fell into the water baptismal;
Ere they gathered its plight,
It had sunk out of sight,
For the depth of the font was abysmal.
- **Edward Gorey** 1925–2000 American illustrator: *The Listing Attic* (1954)

16 'There's been an accident,' they said, 'Your servant's cut in half; he's dead!'

'Indeed!' said Mr Jones, 'and please, Send me the half that's got my keys.'
- **Harry Graham** 1874–1936 British writer and journalist: 'Mr Jones' (1899)

17 I left the room with silent dignity, but caught my foot in the mat.
- **George Grossmith** 1847–1912 and **Weedon Grossmith** 1854–1919: *The Diary of a Nobody* (1894)

18 If, of all words of tongue and pen, The saddest are, 'It might have been,' More sad are these we daily see: 'It is, but hadn't ought to be!'
- **Bret Harte** 1836–1902 American poet: 'Mrs Judge Jenkins' (1867)

19 Well, I'm still here.
after erroneous reports of his death, marked by tributes paid to him in Congress
- **Bob Hope** 1903–2003 American comedian: in *Mail on Sunday* 7 June 1998 'Quotes of the Week'

20 My father told me all about the birds and the bees, the liar—I went steady with a woodpecker until I was 21.
- **Bob Hope** 1903–2003 American comedian: attributed; in *Times* 29 July 2003

21 You were only supposed to blow the bloody doors off!
- **Troy Kennedy-Martin** 1932–2009 British screenwriter: *The Italian Job* (1969 film); spoken by Michael Caine as Charlie Croker

22 When I make a mistake, it's a beaut.
- **Fiorello H. La Guardia** 1882–1947 American Republican politician: on his appointment of Herbert O'Brien as a judge; William Manners *Patience and Fortitude* (1976)

23 No snowflake in an avalanche ever feels responsible.
- **Stanislaw Lec** 1909–66 Polish writer: *More Unkempt Thoughts* (1968)

24 now and then
there is a person born
who is so unlucky
that he runs into accidents
which started to happen
to somebody else.
- **Don Marquis** 1878–1937 American poet and journalist: *archys life of mehitabel* (1933) 'archy says'

25 Erratum. In my article on the price of milk, 'horses' should have read 'cows' throughout.
- **J. B. Morton** 1893-1975 British journalist: *Sideways Through Borneo* (1937)

26 I had never had a piece of toast
Particularly long and wide,
But fell upon the sanded floor,
And always on the buttered side.
- **James Payn** 1830-98 English writer: in *Chambers's Journal* 2 February 1884

27 I actually slipped on a hamburger in Hamburg once, and almost fell off stage.
- **Keith Richards** 1943- English rock musician: *Keith Richards: in His Own Words* (1994)

28 *a postcard of the Venus de Milo sent to his niece:*
See what'll happen to you if you don't stop biting your finger-nails.
- **Will Rogers** 1879-1935 American actor and humorist: Bennett Cerf *Shake Well Before Using* (1948)

29 *For Pheasant read Peasant, throughout.*
- **W. C. Sellar** 1898-1951 and **R. J. Yeatman** 1898-1968: *1066 and All That* (1930); errata

30 Well, if I called the wrong number, why did you answer the phone?
- **James Thurber** 1894-1961 American humorist: cartoon caption in *New Yorker* 5 June 1937

31 Wardrobe malfunction.
explanation for the exposure of Janet Jackson's right breast on prime time American television during the Super Bowl
- **Justin Timberlake** 1981- American singer: in *Daily Telegraph* 3 February 2004 (online edition)

32 MR BINKS: One of my ancestors fell at Waterloo.
LADY CLARE: Ah? Which platform?
- **F. H. Townsend** 1868-1920 British illustrator: in *Punch* 1 November 1905

33 If we had had more time for discussion we should probably have made a great many more mistakes.
- **Leon Trotsky** 1879-1940 Russian revolutionary: *My Life* (1930)

34 *to his troop sergeant after sustaining serious wounds trying to unblock a jammed machine gun:*
Kiss me, Chudleigh.
- **Auberon Waugh** 1939-2001 English writer: anecdote; in *Daily Telegraph* 18 January 2001

35 Unseen, in the background, Fate was quietly slipping the lead into the boxing gloves.
- **P. G. Wodehouse** 1881-1975 English writer: *Very Good, Jeeves* (1930)

36 He felt like a man who, chasing rainbows, has had one of them suddenly turn and bite him in the leg.
- **P. G. Wodehouse** 1881-1975 English writer: *Eggs, Beans, and Crumpets* (1940)

Modern Life

The trouble with the rat race is that even if you win, you're still a rat! **Lily Tomlin**

1 What happens when the human body is completely submerged in water? The telephone rings.
- **Anonymous**: modern saying

2 Facebook is for people who can't face books.
- **Madeline Beard** English writer: said to the Editor

3 I don't like little chip and pin machines. I don't like that they tell you what to do. 'Hand me back to the merchant!' like a bossy toddler.
- **Russell Brand** 1975- British comedian: attributed

4 The other line moves faster…And don't try to change lines. The other line—the

one you were in originally—will then move faster.

usually quoted as 'The other line always moves faster'

- **Barbara Ettore**: in *Harper's* August 1974

5 Change is inevitable—except from a vending machine.

- **Robert C. Gallagher**: attributed

6 I was standing behind a man in Starbucks the other day, he was ordering 'a tall skinny black Americano'. I said, 'What are you ordering, coffee or a President?'

- **Michael McIntyre** 1976- English comedian: attributed

7 Men who blow themselves up are promised 72 virgins in paradise. That's a high price to pay for a shag.

- **Shazia Mirza** 1976- English comedian: at the Edinburgh Festival, 2006, in *Independent* 26 August 2006

8 Starbucks says they are going to start putting religious quotes on cups. The very first one will say, 'Jesus! This cup is expensive!'

- **Conan O'Brien** 1963- American comedian and broadcaster: attributed

9 Why would I tweet when I've not yet read *The Brothers Karamazov*?

- **Michael Palin** 1953- British comedian and broadcaster: in *Time Out* 5 July 2012

10 Somebody just gave me a shower radio. Thanks a lot. Do you really want music in the shower? I guess there's no better place to dance than a slick surface next to a glass door.

- **Jerry Seinfeld** 1954- American comedian: *Seinlanguage* (1993)

11 Now they show you how detergents take out bloodstains, a pretty violent image there. I think if you've got a T-shirt with a bloodstain all over it, maybe laundry isn't your biggest problem. Maybe you should get rid of the body before you do the wash.

- **Jerry Seinfeld** 1954- American comedian: attributed

12 The trouble with the rat race is that even if you win you're still a rat.

- **Lily Tomlin** 1939- American comedienne and actress: in *People* 26 December 1977

13 I'm the modern, intelligent, independent-type woman—in other words, a girl who can't get a man.

- **Shelley Winters** 1922-2006 American actress: in *Saturday Evening Post* 1952

Money

see also **DEBT, POVERTY, WEALTH**

....

We don't wake up for less than $10,000 a day.   **Linda Evangelista**

1 Money is better than poverty, if only for financial reasons.

- **Woody Allen** 1935- American film director, writer, and actor: *Without Feathers* (1976) 'Early Essays'

2 That money talks
I'll not deny,
I heard it once,
It said goodbye.

- **Richard Armour** 1906-89 American poet: attributed; L. Dunkling and A. Room *Guinness Book of Money* (1990)

3 Money, it turned out, was exactly like sex, you thought of nothing else if you didn't have it and thought of other things if you did.

- **James Baldwin** 1924-87 American novelist and essayist: in *Esquire* May 1961 'Black Boy looks at the White Boy'

4 We live by the Golden Rule. Those who have the gold make the rules.

- **Buzzie Bavasi** 1914-2008 American baseball manager: attributed; A. J. Maikovich and M. D. Brown (eds.) *Sports Quotations* (2000)

5 I'm tired of Love: I'm still more tired of Rhyme.

But Money gives me pleasure all the time.
- **Hilaire Belloc** 1870-1953 British writer and Liberal politician: 'Fatigued' (1923)

6 HOLDUP MAN: Quit stalling—I said your money or your life.
JACK BENNY: I'm thinking it over!
- **Jack Benny** 1894-1974 American comedian and actor: one of Jack Benny's most successful gags; Irving Fein *Jack Benny* (1976)

7 I live in a two-income household, but who knows how long my mom can keep that up.
- **Shmuel Breban** American comedian: attributed

8 I never loved a dear gazelle—
Nor anything that cost me much:
High prices profit those who sell,
But why should I be fond of such?
- **Lewis Carroll** 1832-98 English writer and logician: 'Tema con Variazioni'

9 Saving is a very fine thing. Especially when your parents have done it for you.
- **Winston Churchill** 1874-1965 British Conservative statesman: J. A. Sutcliffe (ed.) *The Sayings of Winston Churchill* (1992)

10 My rule is, if it flies, floats, or fornicates, rent it. It's cheaper in the long run.
- **Felix Dennis** 1947- English publisher: *How To Get Rich* (2006)

11 When you don't have any money, the problem is food. When you have money, it's sex. When you have both it's health.
- **J. P. Donleavy** 1926- Irish-American novelist: *The Ginger Man* (1955)

12 We don't wake up for less than $10,000 a day.
of herself and supermodel Christy Turlington; often quoted as, 'I don't get out of bed for less than $10,000 a day'
- **Linda Evangelista** 1965- Canadian supermodel: in *Vogue* October 1990

13 I want an old-fashioned house
With an old-fashioned fence
And an old-fashioned millionaire.
- **Marve Fisher** American songwriter: 'An Old-Fashioned Girl' (1954 song)

14 A fool and his money are soon parted. What I want to know is how they got together in the first place.
- **Cyril Fletcher** 1913-2005 English comedian: attributed to Fletcher from the late 1960s, but the saying is found earlier

15 My main problem is reconciling my gross habits with my net income.
- **Errol Flynn** 1909-59 Australian-born American actor: in *New York Times* 6 March 1955

16 A bank is a place where they lend you an umbrella in fair weather and ask for it back when it begins to rain.
- **Robert Frost** 1874-1963 American poet: in *Muscatine Journal* 22 August 1961

17 Economy was always 'elegant', and money-spending always 'vulgar' and ostentatious— a sort of sour-grapeism, which made us very peaceful and satisfied.
- **Elizabeth Gaskell** 1810-65 English novelist: *Cranford* (1853)

18 Money, wife, is the true fuller's earth for reputations, there is not a spot or a stain but what it can take out.
- **John Gay** 1685-1732 English poet and dramatist: *The Beggar's Opera* (1728)

19 The shares are a penny, and ever so many are taken by Rothschild and Baring,
And just as a few are allotted to you, you awake with a shudder despairing.
- **W. S. Gilbert** 1836-1911 English writer: *Iolanthe* (1882)

20 *on being told that money doesn't buy happiness:*
But it upgrades despair so beautifully.
- **Richard Greenberg** 1958- American dramatist: *Hurrah at Last* (1999)

21 Money is what you'd get on beautifully without if only other people weren't so crazy about it.
- **Margaret Case Harriman** American writer: Laurence J. Peter (ed.) *Quotations for our Time* (1977)

22 Insurance is like a pyramid...huge, incomprehensible, hideously expensive, completely unnecessary and designed

only to be of benefit to you once you're dead
- **Tom Holt** 1961- English novelist: *Djinn Rummy* (1995)

23 A bank is a place that will lend you money if you can prove that you don't need it.
- **Bob Hope** 1903-2003 American comedian: Alan Harrington *Life in the Crystal Palace* (1959)

24 When a feller says, 'It hain't the money, but th' principle o' th' thing', it's the money.
- **Frank McKinney Hubbard** 1868-1930 American humorist: *Hoss Sense and Nonsense* (1926)

25 Nobody works as hard for his money as the man who marries it.
- **Frank McKinney Hubbard** 1868-1930 American humorist: attributed

26 Never say you know a man until you have divided an inheritance with him.
- **Johann Kaspar Lavater** 1741-1801 Swiss theologian: attributed

27 All I ask is the chance to prove that money can't make me happy.
- **Spike Milligan** 1918-2002 Irish comedian: attributed

28 Money is like manure. If you spread it around it does a lot of good, but if you pile it up in one place it stinks like hell.
- **Clint Murchison** 1923-87 American businessman: attributed

29 I finally know what distinguishes man from the other beasts: financial worries.
- **Jules Renard** 1864-1910 French novelist and dramatist: attributed

30 'My boy,' he says, 'always try to rub up against money, for if you rub up against money long enough, some of it may rub off on you.'
- **Damon Runyon** 1884-1946 American writer: in *Cosmopolitan* August 1929, 'A Very Honourable Guy'

31 I'm living so far beyond my income that we may also be said to be living apart.
- **Saki** 1870-1916 Scottish writer: *The Unbearable Bassington* (1912)

32 I do want to get rich but I never want to do what there is to do to get rich.
- **Gertrude Stein** 1874-1946 American writer: *Everybody's Autobiography* (1937)

33 *on being asked what* Rosencrantz and Guildenstern are Dead *was about:*
It's about to make me very rich.
- **Tom Stoppard** 1937- British dramatist: attributed; in *Daily Telegraph* 27 February 1999

34 Money talks, but credit has an echo.
- **Bob Thaves** 1924-2006 American cartoonist: attributed

35 Pennies don't fall from heaven. They have to be earned on earth.
- **Margaret Thatcher** 1925-2013 British Conservative stateswoman: in *Observer* 18 November 1979 'Sayings of the Week'

36 Money won't buy happiness, but it will pay the salaries of a large research staff to study the problem.
- **Bill Vaughan**: Laurence J. Peter (ed.) *Quotations for Our Time* (1977)

Morality

see also **VIRTUE**

Throwing acid is wrong—in some people's eyes.   **Jimmy Carr**

1 Guilt: the gift that keeps on giving.
  - **Erma Bombeck** 1927-96 American humorist: attributed

2 Throwing acid is wrong—in some people's eyes.
  - **Jimmy Carr** 1972- Irish comedian: in *Guardian* 19 August 2002

3 A woman can look both moral and exciting—if she also looks as if it was quite a struggle.
  - **Edna Ferber** 1887-1968 American writer: in *Reader's Digest* December 1954

4 To be absolutely honest, what I feel really bad about is that I don't feel worse. That's the ineffectual liberal's problem in a nutshell.
  - **Michael Frayn** 1933- English writer: in *Observer* 8 August 1965

5 When it comes to the morality of our ancestors, none of us can boast much; the records do not show that Adam and Eve were married.
  - **E. W. Howe** 1853-1937 American novelist and editor: *Country Town Sayings* (1911)

6 We know no spectacle so ridiculous as the British public in one of its periodical fits of morality.
  - **Lord Macaulay** 1800-59 English politician and historian: *Essays Contributed to the Edinburgh Review* (1843)

7 If people want a sense of purpose, they should get it from their archbishops. They should not hope to receive it from their politicians.
  - **Harold Macmillan** 1894-1986 British Conservative statesman: in conversation 1963; Henry Fairlie *The Life of Politics* (1968)

8 Those are my principles, and if you don't like them...well, I have others.
  - **Groucho Marx** 1890-1977 American film comedian: widely attributed, but probably apocryphal

9 Being moral isn't what you *do*...it's what you *mean* to do.
  - **Bette Midler** 1945- American actress: *A View from a Broad* (1980)

10 I think fidelity is a very good idea—now that I can't walk.
  - **John Mortimer** 1923-2009 English novelist, barrister, and dramatist: in *Mail on Sunday* 4 January 2004 'Quotes of the Year'

11 That woman speaks eighteen languages, and can't say No in any of them.
  - **Dorothy Parker** 1893-1967 American critic and humorist: Alexander Woollcott *While Rome Burns* (1934)

12 And there was that wholesale libel on a Yale prom. If all the girls attending it were laid end to end, Mrs Parker said, she wouldn't be at all surprised.
  - **Dorothy Parker** 1893-1967 American critic and humorist: Alexander Woollcott *While Rome Burns* (1934)

13 I'm very mild, I'm very meek, My will is strong, but my won't is weak.
  - **Cole Porter** 1891-1964 American songwriter: 'Don't Look at Me That Way' (*Paris*, 1928 musical)

14 Dost thou think, because thou art virtuous, there shall be no more cakes and ale?
  - **William Shakespeare** 1564-1616 English dramatist: *Twelfth Night* (1601)

15 When a stupid man is doing something he is ashamed of, he always declares that it is his duty.
  - **George Bernard Shaw** 1856-1950 Irish dramatist: *Caesar and Cleopatra* (1901)

16 PICKERING: Have you no morals, man? DOOLITTLE: Can't afford them, Governor.
  - **George Bernard Shaw** 1856-1950 Irish dramatist: *Pygmalion* (1916)

17 If your morals make you dreary, depend upon it they are wrong.
   - **Robert Louis Stevenson** 1850-94 Scottish novelist: *Across the Plains* (1892)

18 BELINDA: Ay, but you know we must return good for evil.
   LADY BRUTE: That may be a mistake in the translation.
   - **John Vanbrugh** 1664-1726 English architect and dramatist: *The Provoked Wife* (1697)

19 Moral indignation is jealousy with a halo.
   - **H. G. Wells** 1866-1946 English novelist: *The Wife of Sir Isaac Harman* (1914)

20 On an occasion of this kind it becomes more than a moral duty to speak one's mind. It becomes a pleasure.
   - **Oscar Wilde** 1854-1900 Irish dramatist and poet: *The Importance of Being Earnest* (1895)

21 A Tory minister can sleep in ten different women's beds in a week. A Labour minister gets it in the neck if he looks at his neighbour's wife over the garden fence.
   - **Harold Wilson** 1916-95 British Labour statesman: *Memoirs* (1986)

Mothers

My mother had a good deal of trouble with me, but I think she enjoyed it.
Mark Twain

1 When your mother asks, 'Do you want a piece of advice?' it's a mere formality. It doesn't matter if you answer yes or no. You're going to get it anyway.
   - **Erma Bombeck** 1927-96 American humorist: attributed

2 Any suburban mother can state her role sardonically enough in a sentence: it is to deliver children obstetrically once and by car forever after.
   - **Peter De Vries** 1910-93 American novelist and humorist: in *Life* 24 December 1956

3 Few misfortunes can befall a boy which bring worse consequences than to have a really affectionate mother.
   - **W. Somerset Maugham** 1874-1965 English novelist: *A Writer's Notebook* (1949), written in 1896

4 I really am a mother's boy. I adore her and she adores me. She's not just proud of me—she faints when she sees me. She gets hysterical. If she were here now she'd want me to sit on her knee.
   - **Omar Sharif** 1932- Egyptian-born actor: in *Times* 11 July 1983

5 My mother had a good deal of trouble with me, but I think she enjoyed it.
   - **Mark Twain** 1835-1910 American writer: *Autobiography* (1924)

Movies *see* CINEMA

Murder

English law *does not permit good persons, as such, to strangle bad persons, as such.*   **T. H. Huxley**

1 Lizzie Borden took an axe
And gave her mother forty whacks;
When she saw what she had done
She gave her father forty-one!
  • **Anonymous**: popular rhyme in circulation
  after the acquittal of Lizzie Borden, in
  June 1893, from the charge of murdering
  her father and stepmother at Fall River,
  Massachusetts on 4 August 1892

2 You can't chop your poppa up in
  Massachusetts,
Not even if it's planned as a surprise
No you can't chop your poppa up in
  Massachusetts
You know how neighbours love to
  criticize.
  • **Michael Brown**: 'Lizzie Borden' (1952)

3 Every murderer is probably somebody's
old friend.
  • **Agatha Christie** 1890-1976 English writer:
  The Mysterious Affair at Styles (1920)

4 I married many men,
A ton of them,
And yet I was untrue to none of them
Because I bumped off ev'ry one of
  them
To keep my love alive.
  • **Lorenz Hart** 1895-1943 American
  songwriter: 'To Keep My Love Alive' (1943)

5 Television has brought back murder
into the home—where it belongs.
  • **Alfred Hitchcock** 1899-1980 British-born
  film director: in *Observer* 19 December 1965

6 English law does not permit good
persons, as such, to strangle bad
persons, as such.
  • **T. H. Huxley** 1825-95 English biologist: letter
  in *Pall Mall Gazette*, 31 October 1866

7 The National Rifle Association says
guns don't kill people, people do. But
I think the gun helps. Just standing
there, going 'Bang!'—that's not going
to kill too many people.
  • **Eddie Izzard** 1962-   British comedian:
  Dress to Kill (stageshow, San Francisco,
  1998)

8 You can always count on a murderer for
a fancy prose style.
  • **Vladimir Nabokov** 1899-1977 Russian
  novelist: *Lolita* (1955)

9 *Julius Caesar of his assassins:*
Infamy, infamy, they've all got it in for
me!
  • **Talbot Rothwell** 1916-74 English
  screenwriter: *Carry on, Cleo* (1964), spoken
  by Kenneth Williams; according to Frank
  Muir's letter to the *Guardian*, 22 July 1995,
  the line had actually been written by him
  and Denis Norden for a radio sketch for
  'Take It From Here', and was later used by
  Rothwell with their permission

10 *justification for poisoning his sister-in-law:*
She had very thick ankles.
  • **Thomas Griffiths Wainewright** 1794-1852
  English artist: in *Dictionary of National
  Biography* (1917-)

Music

see also **MUSICIANS, OPERA, SONGS**

....

Wagner has lovely moments but awful quarters of an hour.   **Gioacchino Rossini**

1 Whenever I don't know what to write about, I just close my eyes and think of Essex.
  - **Damon Albarn** 1968- English musician: attributed

2 I can't listen to too much Wagner, ya know? I start to get the urge to conquer Poland.
  - **Woody Allen** 1935- American film director, writer, and actor: *Manhattan Murder Mystery* (1998 film)

3 Writing about music is like dancing about architecture.
  also found in the form 'Talking about music…'
  - **Anonymous**: attributed to Elvis Costello, David Bowie, Frank Zappa, and many others, but of unknown origin

4 All music is folk music, I ain't never heard no horse sing a song.
  - **Louis Armstrong** 1901-71 American singer and jazz musician: in *New York Times* 7 July 1971

5 *when asked what jazz is:*
  If you still have to ask…shame on you.
  - **Louis Armstrong** 1901-71 American singer and jazz musician: Max Jones et al. *Salute to Satchmo* (1970) (sometimes quoted 'Man, if you gotta ask you'll never know')

6 There is nothing to it. You only have to hit the right notes at the right time and the instrument plays itself.
  when complimented on his organ playing
  - **Johann Sebastian Bach** 1685-1750 German composer: K. Geiringer *The Bach Family* (1954)

7 I love Wagner, but the music I prefer is that of a cat hung up by its tail outside a window and trying to stick to the panes of glass with its claws.
  - **Charles Baudelaire** 1821-67 French poet and critic: Nat Shapiro (ed.) *An Encyclopedia of Quotations about Music* (1978)

8 What can you do with it? It's like a lot of yaks jumping about.
  on the third movement of Beethoven's Seventh Symphony
  - **Thomas Beecham** 1879-1961 English conductor: Harold Atkins and Archie Newman *Beecham Stories* (1978)

9 The musical equivalent of the Towers of St Pancras Station.
  - **Thomas Beecham** 1879-1961 English conductor: describing Elgar's 1st Symphony; Neville Cardus *Sir Thomas Beecham* (1961)

10 There are two golden rules for an orchestra: start together and finish together. The public doesn't give a damn what goes on in between.
  - **Thomas Beecham** 1879-1961 English conductor: Harold Atkins and Archie Newman *Beecham Stories* (1978)

11 [The piano is] a parlour utensil for subduing the impenitent visitor. It is operated by depressing the keys of the machine and the spirits of the audience.
  - **Ambrose Bierce** 1842-c.1914 American writer: *The Enlarged Devil's Dictionary* (1967)

12 ANDRÉ PREVIN: You're playing all the wrong notes.
  ERIC MORECAMBE: I'm playing all the *right* notes. But not *necessarily* in the right order.
  playing the Grieg Piano Concerto
  - **Eddie Braben** 1930-2013 English comedy writer: *The Morecambe and Wise Show* BBC TV 25 December 1971

13 Extraordinary how potent cheap music is.
  - **Noël Coward** 1899-1973 English dramatist, actor, and composer: *Private Lives* (1930)

14 The tuba is certainly the most intestinal of instruments—the very lower bowel of music.
  - **Peter De Vries** 1910-93 American novelist: *The Glory of the Hummingbird* (1974)

15 I don't like composers who think. It gets in the way of their plagiarism.
- **Howard Dietz** 1896-1983 American songwriter: *Dancing in the Dark* (1974)

16 I hate music, especially when it's played.
- **Jimmy Durante** 1893-1980 American comedian and singer: Nat Shapiro (ed.) *An Encyclopedia of Quotations about Music* (1978)

17 Playing 'Bop' is like scrabble with all the vowels missing.
- **Duke Ellington** 1899-1974 American jazz pianist, composer, and band-leader: in *Look* 10 August 1954

18 *message sent after the Grenadier Guards had played an arrangement of Richard Strauss'* Elektra:
His Majesty does not know what the Band has just played, but it is *never* to be played again.
- **George V** 1865-1936 British king: Osbert Sitwell *Left Hand, Right Hand* (1945)

19 I only know two tunes. One of them is 'Yankee Doodle' and the other isn't.
- **Ulysses S. Grant** 1822-85 American Unionist general and statesman: Nat Shapiro (ed.) *An Encyclopedia of Quotations about Music* (1978)

20 Music helps not the toothache.
- **George Herbert** 1593-1633 English poet and clergyman: *Outlandish Proverbs* (1640)

21 Classic music is th'kind that we keep thinkin'll turn into a tune.
- **Frank McKinney Hubbard** 1868-1930 American humorist: *Comments of Abe Martin and His Neighbors* (1923)

22 *on the performance of a celebrated violinist:*
Difficult do you call it, Sir? I wish it were impossible.
- **Samuel Johnson** 1709-84 English poet, critic, and lexicographer: William Seward *Supplement to the Anecdotes of Distinguished Persons* (1797)

23 HAMMERSTEIN: Here is a story laid in China about an Italian told by an Irishman. What kind of music are you going to write?
KERN: It'll be good Jewish music.
in the 1930s, discussing with Oscar Hammerstein II a musical to be based on

Donn Byrne's novel Messer Marco Polo
- **Jerome Kern** 1885-1945 American composer: Gerald Bordman *Jerome Kern* (1980)

24 I don't like jazz. When I hear jazz, it's as if I had gas on the stomach. I used to think it was static when I heard it on the radio.
- **Nikita Khrushchev** 1894-1971 Soviet statesman: in *Encounter* April 1963

25 A carpenter's hammer, in a warm summer noon, will fret me into more than midsummer madness. But those unconnected, unset sounds are nothing to the measured malice of music.
- **Charles Lamb** 1775-1834 English writer: *Elia* (1823)

26 *to another musician:*
Very well, my dear. You continue to play Bach your way and I'll continue to play him *his* way.
- **Wanda Landowska** 1877-1959 Polish-born American pianist and harpsichordist: Harold C. Schonberg *The Great Pianists* (1963)

27 A squeak's heard in the orchestra
The leader draws across
The intestines of the agile cat
The tail of the noble hoss.
- **G. T. Lanigan** 1845-86: *The Amateur Orlando* (1875)

28 If I play Tchaikovsky I play his melodies and skip his spiritual struggles...If there's any time left over I fill in with a lot of runs up and down the keyboard.
- **Liberace** 1919-87 American showman: Stuart Hall and Paddy Whannel (eds.) *The Popular Arts* (1964)

29 I don't like my music, but what is my opinion against that of millions of others.
- **Frederick Loewe** 1904-88 American composer: Nat Shapiro (ed.) *An Encyclopedia of Quotations about Music* (1978)

30 *on seeing Niagara Falls:*
Fortissimo at last!
- **Gustav Mahler** 1860-1911 Austrian composer: K. Blaukopf *Gustav Mahler* (1973)

31 If you're in jazz and more than ten

people like you, you're labelled commercial.
- **Herbie Mann** 1930– American jazz musician: Henry Pleasants *Serious Music and all that Jazz!* (1969)

32 *lead singer of Coldplay:*
I know you think we just sit and count money, but sometimes we do other things, like teach the drummer to play piano.
- **Chris Martin** 1977– English musician: in *Sunday Times* 12 June 2005

33 I don't like country music, but I don't mean to denigrate those who do. And for the people who like country music, denigrate means 'put down'.
- **Bob Newhart** 1929– American comedian: attributed

34 If I had the power, I would insist on all oratorios being sung in the costume of the period—with a possible exception in the case of *The Creation*.
- **Ernest Newman** 1868–1959 English music critic: in *New York Post* 1924; Nat Shapiro (ed.) *An Encyclopedia of Quotations about Music* (1978)

35 I have been told that Wagner's music is better than it sounds.
- **Bill Nye** 1850–96 American humorist: Mark Twain *Autobiography* (1924)

36 *the hypocritical Quaker, Ephraim Smooth, hears violin music:*
I must shut my ears. The man of sin rubbeth the hair of the horse to the bowels of the cat.
- **John O'Keeffe** 1747–1833 Irish dramatist: *Wild Oats* (1791)

37 I am afraid that all musical instruments are incredibly expensive to repair, with the possible exception of the triangle.
- **Terry Pratchett** 1948– English fantasy writer: *Maskerade* (1995)

38 If anyone has conducted a Beethoven performance, and then doesn't have to go to an osteopath, then there's something wrong.
- **Simon Rattle** 1955– English conductor: in *Guardian* 31 May 1990

39 Of course we've all *dreamed* of reviving the *castrati*; but it's needed Hilda to take

the first practical steps towards making them a reality...She's drawn up a list of well-known singers who she thinks would benefit...It's only a question of getting them to agree.
- **Henry Reed** 1914–86 English poet and dramatist: *Private Life of Hilda Tablet* (1954)

40 To the social-minded, a definition for Concert is: that which surrounds an intermission.
- **Ned Rorem** 1923– American composer: *The Final Diary* (1974)

41 Wagner has lovely moments but awful quarters of an hour.
- **Gioacchino Rossini** 1792–1868 Italian composer: to Emile Naumann, April 1867

42 Applause is a receipt, not a note of demand.
- **Artur Schnabel** 1882–1951 Austrian-born pianist: in *Saturday Review of Literature* 29 September 1951

43 You are there and I am here; but where is Beethoven?
to his conductor during a Beethoven rehearsal
- **Artur Schnabel** 1882–1951 Austrian-born pianist: Nat Shapiro (ed.) *An Encyclopedia of Quotations about Music* (1978)

44 I am delighted to add another unplayable work to the repertoire. I want the Concerto to be difficult and I want the little finger to become longer. I can wait.
of his Violin Concerto
- **Arnold Schoenberg** 1874–1951 Austrian-born American composer: Joseph Machlis *Introduction to Contemporary Music* (1963)

45 *of the piano:*
A large, rectangular monster that screams when you touch its teeth.
- **Andrés Segovia** 1893–1987 Spanish guitarist: in *Washington Post* 2 March 1980

46 I have a reasonable good ear in music: let us have the tongs and the bones.
- **William Shakespeare** 1564–1616 English dramatist: *A Midsummer Night's Dream* (1595-6)

47 Hell is full of musical amateurs: music is the brandy of the damned.
- **George Bernard Shaw** 1856–1950 Irish dramatist: *Man and Superman* (1903)

48 If one will only take the precaution to go in long enough after it commences and to come out long before it is over you will not find it wearisome.
of Gounod's La Rédemption
- **George Bernard Shaw** 1856-1950 Irish dramatist: in *The World* 22 February 1893

49 I play all my country and western music backwards. Your lover returns, your dog comes back to life and you cease to be an alcoholic.
- **Linda Smith** 1958-2006 British comedian: in *Daily Telegraph* (obituary), 1 March 2006

50 I would like to thank Beethoven, Brahms, Wagner, Strauss, Rimsky-Korsakov.
- **Dmitri Tiomkin** 1899-1979 Russian-born composer: Oscar acceptance speech for the score of *The High and the Mighty* in 1955; Nat Shapiro (ed.) *An Encyclopedia of Quotations about Music* (1978)

51 I assure you that the typewriting machine, when played with expression, is not more annoying than the piano when played by a sister or near relation.
- **Oscar Wilde** 1854-1900 Irish dramatist and poet: letter to Robert Ross from Reading Prison, 1 April 1897

52 Musical people are so absurdly unreasonable. They always want one to be perfectly dumb at the very moment when one is longing to be absolutely deaf.
- **Oscar Wilde** 1854-1900 Irish dramatist and poet: *An Ideal Husband* (1895)

53 You have Van Gogh's ear for music.
- **Billy Wilder** 1906-2002 American screenwriter and director: to actor Cliff Ormand, Tom Wood *The Bright Side of Billy Wilder, Primarily* (1970)

54 He reminds us how cheap potent music can be.
of the popular pianist Richard Clayderman
- **Richard Williams**: Ned Sherrin *Cutting Edge* (1984); see **music** 13

Musicians

see also **MUSIC**

Please do not shoot the pianist. He is doing his best.   **Anonymous**

1 The music teacher came twice each week to bridge the awful gap between Dorothy and Chopin.
- **George Ade** 1866-1944 American humorist and dramatist: Nat Shapiro (ed.) *An Encyclopedia of Quotations about Music* (1978)

2 I prefer to face the wrath of the police than the wrath of Sir John Barbirolli.
a member of the Hallé orchestra on a speeding charge
- **Anonymous**: Ned Sherrin *Cutting Edge* (1984)

3 *printed notice in an American dancing saloon:*
Please do not shoot the pianist. He is doing his best.
- **Anonymous**: Oscar Wilde *Impressions of America* 'Leadville' (c.1882-3)

4 A musicologist is a man who can read music but can't hear it.
- **Thomas Beecham** 1879-1961 English conductor: H. Proctor-Gregg *Beecham Remembered* (1976)

5 Why do we have to have all these third-rate foreign conductors around—when we have so many second-rate ones of our own?
- **Thomas Beecham** 1879-1961 English conductor: L. Ayre *Wit of Music* (1966)

6 No wonder Bob Geldof is such an expert on famine. He's been feeding off 'I Don't Like Mondays' for 30 years.
- **Russell Brand** 1975- British comedian: at the Edinburgh Festival, 2006, in *Independent* 26 August 2006

7 JOURNALIST: Why do you continue
to practise the cello for several hours
each day?
CASALS (AGED OVER 90): Because I think
I'm improving.
- **Pablo Casals** 1876-1973 Spanish cellist:
attributed

8 Tchaikovsky thought of committing
suicide for fear of being discovered as
a homosexual, but today, if you are a
composer and *not* homosexual, you
might as well put a bullet through your
head.
- **Sergei Diaghilev** 1872-1929 Russian ballet
impresario: Vernon Duke *Listen Here!*
(1963)

9 Everybody told me you can't get far
On thirty-seven dollars and a Jap guitar.
- **Steve Earle** 1954- American singer and
songwriter: 'Guitar Town' (1986 song)

10 QUESTION: Mr. Sullivan's music…
reminds me so much of dear Baytch
[Bach]. Do tell me: what is Baytch
doing just now? Is he still composing?
ANSWER: Just now, as a matter of fact,
dear Baytch is by way of decomposing.
- **W. S. Gilbert** 1836-1911 English writer:
Hesketh Pearson *Gilbert and Sullivan*
(1947)

11 QUESTION: Do you play the guitar with
your teeth?
HENDRIX: No, with my ears.
- **Jimi Hendrix** 1942-70 American rock
musician: in *International Times*
2-15 February 1968

12 There is no doubt that the first
requirement for a composer is to be
dead.
- **Arthur Honegger** 1892-1955 Swiss
composer: *Je suis compositeur* (1951)

13 ANONYMOUS: Is Ringo the best
drummer in the world?
JOHN LENNON: He's not even the best
drummer in the band.
- **John Lennon** 1940-80 English pop singer
and songwriter: attributed

14 In the 1960s, the record companies
seemed to sign anything with long hair;
if it was a sheepdog, so what.
- **Nick Mason** 1944- English drummer:
N. Shaffner *A Saucerful of Secrets: the Pink
Floyd Odyssey* (1991)

15 *on Stravinsky's Symphony of Wind
Instruments in memory of Debussy:*
I had no idea Stravinsky disliked
Debussy so much as this.
- **Ernest Newman** 1868-1959 English music
critic: in *Musical Times* 1921

16 I'm told that Saint-Saëns has informed
a delighted public that since the war
began he has composed music for the
stage, melodies, an elegy and a piece
for the trombone. If he'd been making
shell-cases instead it might have been all
the better for music.
- **Maurice Ravel** 1875-1937 French composer:
letter to Jean Marnold, 7 October 1916

17 *asked how he could play so well when he was
loaded:*
I practise when I'm loaded.
- **Zoot Sims** 1925-85 American jazz musician:
Bill Crow *Jazz Anecdotes* (1990)

18 'What do you think of Beethoven?'
'I love him, especially his poems.'
- **Ringo Starr** 1940- English rock musician:
at a press conference during the Beatles'
first American tour in 1964; Hunter Davies
The Beatles (1985)

19 On matters of intonation and
technicalities I am more than a
martinet—I am a martinetissimo!
- **Leopold Stokowski** 1882-1977 English-born
American conductor: Nat Shapiro (ed.) *An
Encyclopedia of Quotations about Music*
(1978)

20 After I die, I shall return to earth as the
doorkeeper of a bordello and I won't let
one of you in.
to his orchestra during a difficult rehearsal
- **Arturo Toscanini** 1867-1957 Italian conductor:
Nat Shapiro (ed.) *An Encyclopedia of
Quotations about Music* (1978)

Names

Every Tom, Dick and Harry is called Arthur. **Sam Goldwyn**

1 I never really needed a nickname at school. Although it was bad for me it was much worse for my sister Ophelia.
   ▪ **Ed Balls** 1967– British Labour politician: in *Independent* 24 September 2007

2 *of Arianna Stassinopoulos:*
   So boring you fall asleep halfway through her name.
   ▪ **Alan Bennett** 1934– English dramatist and actor: attributed; in *Observer* 18 September 1983

3 *fashionable children's names of which Camden disapproved:*
   The new names, Free-gift, Reformation, Earth, Dust, Ashes…which have lately been given by some to their children.
   ▪ **William Camden** 1551–1623 English antiquary: *Remains* (1605)

4 *of Alfred Bossom:*
   Who is this man whose name is neither one thing nor the other?
   ▪ **Winston Churchill** 1874–1965 British Conservative statesman: attributed

5 If you don't give your child a middle name, how are they ever to know when you are cross with them?
   ▪ **Vivienne Clore** British showbusiness agent: in *Mail on Sunday* 24 February 2013

6 *nickname for Cecil Beaton:*
   Malice in Wonderland.
   ▪ **Jean Cocteau** 1889–1963 French dramatist and film director: attributed; Hugo Young in *Guardian* 24 January 2004

7 Rip-Van-With-It.
   nickname for Cecil Beaton
   ▪ **Cyril Connolly** 1903–74 English writer: Hugo Vickers (ed.) *The Unexpurgated Beaton* (2002)

8 One theory is that I was named after the opera and the other that my mum was sitting in her boudoir wondering what to call me and glanced at her Carmen rollers. I prefer the Bizet theory.
   ▪ **Carmen Ejogo** 1974– British actress: in *Observer* 26 March 2000 'They said what…?'

9 *on J. P. Horrocks-Taylor's slipping Mick English's rugby tackle to score:*
   Horrocks went one way, Taylor went the other, and I was left holding his bloody hyphen.
   ▪ **Mick English** d. 2010 Irish rugby player: in *Sunday Times* 2 September 1990

10 Colin is the sort of name you give your goldfish for a joke.
   ▪ **Colin Firth** 1960– British actor: in *Observer* 1 September 2002

11 *to Arthur Hornblow, who was planning to name his son Arthur:*
   Every Tom, Dick and Harry is called Arthur.
   ▪ **Sam Goldwyn** 1882–1974 American film producer: Michael Freedland *The Goldwyn Touch* (1986)

12 *comment at a Test Match as Michael Holding faced Peter Willey:*
   The batsman's Holding, the bowler's Willey.
   ▪ **Brian Johnston** 1912–94 British cricket commentator: attributed

13 In the last Parliament, the House of Commons had more MPs called John than all the women MPs put together.
   ▪ **Tessa Jowell** 1947– British Labour politician: in *Independent on Sunday* 14 March 1999 'Quotes'

14 One day I'll be famous! I'll be proper and prim;
   Go to St James so often I will call it St Jim!
   ▪ **Alan Jay Lerner** 1918–86 American songwriter: 'Just You Wait' (*My Fair Lady*, 1956 musical)

15 *when asked if Groucho were his real name:*
   No, I'm breaking it in for a friend.
   ▪ **Groucho Marx** 1890–1977 American film comedian: attributed

16 *on why she had named her canary 'Onan':*
Because he spills his seed on the ground.
- **Dorothy Parker** 1893-1967 American critic and humorist: John Keats *You Might as Well Live*

17 But I must not go on singling out names. One must not be a name-dropper, as Her Majesty remarked to me yesterday.
- **Lord St John of Fawsley** 1929-2012 British Conservative politician: speech, 20 June 1979

18 *wondering why, since he was Irish, he was not O'Sheridan:*
For in truth we owe everybody.
- **Richard Brinsley Sheridan** 1751-1816 Irish dramatist and Whig politician: Walter Jerrold *Bon-Mots* (1893)

19 I remember your name perfectly; but I just can't think of your face.
- **William Archibald Spooner** 1844-1930 English clergyman and academic: attributed; in *Penguin Dictionary of Quotations* (1960)

20 *on being asked by William Carlos Williams how he had chosen the name 'West':*
Horace Greeley said, 'Go West, young man.' So I did.
West was born Nathan von Wallenstein Weinstein
- **Nathanael West** 1903-40 American writer: Jay Martin *Nathanael West* (1970)

21 A good name will wear out; a bad one may be turned; a nickname lasts forever.
- **Johann Georg Zimmerman** 1728-95 Swiss physician and writer: attributed

Nature and the Country

....

Anybody can be good in the country. **Oscar Wilde**

1 I am at two with nature.
- **Woody Allen** 1935- American film director, writer, and actor: attributed; Bill Adler and Jerry Feinman *Woody Allen: Clown Prince of American Humour* (1976)

2 Pollution: cirrhosis of the river.
- **Anonymous**: saying

3 Hedgehogs—why can't they just share the hedge?
- **Dan Antopolski** 1972- English comedian: voted the funniest joke at the 2009 Edinburgh Festival; in *Sunday Times* 30 August 2009

4 The tree which moves some to tears of joy is in the eyes of others only a green thing that stands in the way.
- **William Blake** 1757-1827 English poet: letter to Rev. Dr Trusler, 23 August 1799

5 I'm proud of George. He's learned a lot about ranching since that first year when he tried to milk the horse. What's worse, it was a male horse.
- **Laura Bush** 1946- American First Lady: White House Correspondents' Association dinner, 30 April 2005

6 He likes the country, but in truth must own,
Most likes it, when he studies it in town.
- **William Cowper** 1731-1800 English poet: 'Retirement' (1782)

7 God made the country, and man made the town.
- **William Cowper** 1731-1800 English poet: *The Task* (1785)

8 Worms have played a more important part in the history of the world than most persons would at first suppose.
- **Charles Darwin** 1809-82 English natural historian: *The Formation of Vegetable Mould through the Action of Worms* (1881)

9 A weekend in the country—
Trees in the orchard call.
When you've examined one tree,
Then you've examined them all.
- **Ira Gershwin** 1896-1983 American songwriter: 'A Weekend in the Country' (*The Barkleys of Broadway*, 1949 film)

10 June is bustin' out all over
The sheep aren't sleepin' any more!
All the rams that chase the ewe sheep

Are determined there'll be new sheep
And the ewe sheep aren't even keepin'
   score!
- **Oscar Hammerstein II** 1895-1960
  American songwriter: 'June is Bustin' Out
  All Over' (1945)

11 There is nothing good to be had in the
country, or if there is, they will not let
you have it.
- **William Hazlitt** 1778-1830 English essayist:
  The Round Table (1817)

12 The Pacific Ocean was a body of water
surrounded on all sides by elephantiasis
and other dread diseases.
- **Joseph Heller** 1923-99 American novelist:
  Catch-22 (1961)

13 The Farmer will never be happy again;
He carries his heart in his boots;
For either the rain is destroying his
   grain
Or the drought is destroying his roots.
- **A. P. Herbert** 1890-1971 English writer and
  humorist: 'The Farmer' (1922)

14 *a London clubman's view of the country:*
A damp sort of place where all sorts of
birds fly about uncooked.
- **Joseph Wood Krutch** 1893-1970 American
  critic and naturalist: *The Twelve Seasons* (1949)

15 There is nothing so desperately
monotonous as the sea, and I no longer
wonder at the cruelty of pirates.
- **James Russell Lowell** 1819-91 American
  poet: *Fireside Travels* (1884) 'At Sea'

16 So *that's* what hay looks like.
*said at Badminton House, where she was
evacuated during the Second World War*
- **Queen Mary** 1867-1953 British Queen
  Consort: James Pope-Hennessy *Life of
  Queen Mary* (1959)

17 It is no good putting up notices saying
'Beware of the bull' because very rude
things are sometimes written on them.
I have found that one of the most effective
notices is 'Beware of the Agapanthus'.
- **Lord Massereene and Ferrard** 1914-93:
  speech on the Wildlife and Countryside
  Bill, House of Lords 16 December 1980

18 A farm is an irregular patch of
nettles bounded by short-term notes,
containing a fool and his wife who
didn't know enough to stay in the city.
- **S. J. Perelman** 1904-79 American humorist:
  The Most of S. J. Perelman (1959) 'Acres and
  Pains'

19 I have no relish for the country; it is a
kind of healthy grave.
- **Sydney Smith** 1771-1845 English clergyman
  and essayist: letter to Miss G. Harcourt,
  1838

20 A weekend in the country
With the panting
And the yawns
With the crickets and the pheasants
And the orchards and the hay,
With the servants and the peasants,
We'll be laying our plans
While we're playing croquet
For a weekend in the country
So inactive one has to lie down.
A weekend in the country
Where we're twice as upset
As in town.
- **Stephen Sondheim** 1930- American
  songwriter: 'A Weekend in the Country'
  (1972)

21 Anybody can be good in the country.
- **Oscar Wilde** 1854-1900 Irish dramatist and
  poet: *The Picture of Dorian Gray* (1891)

22 What do we see at once but a little
robin! There is no need to burst
into tears fotherington-tomas swete
tho he be. Nor to buzz a brick at it,
molesworth 2.
a nature walk at St Custards
- **Geoffrey Willans** 1911-58 and **Ronald
  Searle** 1920-2012: *Down with Skool!* (1953)

23 BRICK: Well, they say nature hates a
vacuum, Big Daddy.
BIG DADDY: That's what they say, but
sometimes I think that a vacuum is a
hell of a lot better than some of the
stuff that nature replaces it with.
- **Tennessee Williams** 1911-83 American
  dramatist: *Cat on a Hot Tin Roof* (1955)

Newspapers and Journalism

Journalism could be described as turning one's enemies into money.
Craig Brown

1 *to Nicholas Phipps, who had announced that he was an efficient hack rather than a creative writer:*
Creative writers are two a penny. Efficient hacks are very rare.
- **Lord Beaverbrook** 1879-1964 Canadian-born British newspaper proprietor and Conservative politician: in *Daily Telegraph* 17 July 2004 (obituary of Nicholas Phipps)

2 I read the newspapers avidly. It is my one form of continuous fiction.
- **Aneurin Bevan** 1897-1960 British Labour politician: in *Times* 29 March 1960

3 When a dog bites a man, that is not news, because it happens so often. But if a man bites a dog, that is news.
- **John B. Bogart** 1848-1921 American journalist: F. M. O'Brien *The Story of the [New York] Sun* (1918); often attributed to Charles A. Dana

4 *on being asked whether George Mair had been a fastidious journalist:*
He once telephoned a semicolon from Moscow.
- **James Bone** 1872-1962 British journalist: James Agate diary, 31 October 1935

5 Journalism could be described as turning one's enemies into money.
- **Craig Brown** 1957- British satirist: in *Daily Telegraph* 28 September 1990

6 I've been watching the TV News for forty years. It hasn't got any better.
- **Michele Brown** 1947- British writer and publisher: attributed

7 A would-be satirist, a hired buffoon,
A monthly scribbler of some low lampoon,
Condemned to drudge, the meanest of the mean,
And furbish falsehoods for a magazine.
of journalists
- **Lord Byron** 1788-1824 English poet: 'English Bards and Scotch Reviewers' (1809)

8 More than one newspaper has been ruined by the brilliant writer in the editor's chair.
- **Lord Camrose** 1879-1954 British newspaper proprietor: Leonard Russell et al. *The Pearl of Days: An Intimate Memoir of the Sunday Times* (1972)

9 Let's face it, sports writers, we're not hanging around with brain surgeons.
- **Jimmy Cannon** 1910-73 American journalist: attributed

10 When seagulls follow a trawler, it is because they think sardines will be thrown into the sea.
- **Eric Cantona** 1966- French footballer: at the end of a press conference, 31 March 1995

11 Journalism largely consists in saying 'Lord Jones Dead' to people who never knew that Lord Jones was alive.
- **G. K. Chesterton** 1874-1936 English essayist, novelist, and poet: *Wisdom of Father Brown* (1914)

12 You are misunderstood, maligned, viewed by the press as a Pulitzer Prize ready to be won.
on the problems of investigative journalism for politicians
- **Lawton Chiles** 1930-98 American Democratic politician: in *St Petersburg (Florida) Times* 6 March 1991

13 The first law of journalism—to confirm existing prejudice rather than contradict it.
- **Alexander Cockburn** 1941-2012 Irish-born American journalist: in 1974; Jonathon Green *Says Who?* (1988)

14 We have a saying in Fleet Street: the editor who writes for his own newspaper has a fool for a contributor.
- **Bill Deedes** 1913-2007 British journalist and Coonservative politician: in *Hansard* (1957)

15 Everything is copy.
- **Phoebe Ephron** 1914-71 American writer: Nora Ephron *I Feel Bad About My Neck* (2008)

16 If you can't get a job as a pianist in a brothel you become a royal reporter.
- **Max Hastings** 1945- British journalist and historian: in *Daily Express* 9 June 1992

17 Editor: a person employed by a newspaper, whose business it is to separate the wheat from the chaff, and to see that the chaff is printed.
- **Elbert Hubbard** 1859-1915 American writer: *The Roycroft Dictionary* (1914)

18 Like a Goth swaggering around Rome wearing an onyx toilet seat for a collar, he exudes self-confidence.
of Rupert Murdoch
- **Clive James** 1939- Australian critic and writer: in *Observer* 16 October 1989

19 To rinse the gutters of public life you need a gutter press.
- **Boris Johnson** 1964- British Conservative politician: in *Spectator* 3 November 2012

20 Power without responsibility: the prerogative of the harlot throughout the ages.
summing up the view of Lord Beaverbrook, who had said to Kipling: 'What I want is power. Kiss 'em one day and kick 'em the next'; Stanley Baldwin, Kipling's cousin, subsequently obtained permission to use the phrase in a speech in London on 18 March 1931
- **Rudyard Kipling** 1865-1936 English writer and poet: in *Kipling Journal* December 1971

21 A newspaper which weighs as much as the *Oxford Dictionary of Quotations* and a very large haddock.
of the Sunday edition of the New York Times
- **Bernard Levin** 1928-2004 British journalist: *In These Times* (1986)

22 I think it well to remember that, when writing for the newspapers, we are writing for an elderly lady in Hastings who has two cats of which she is passionately fond. Unless our stuff can successfully compete for her interest with those cats, it is no good.
- **Willmott Lewis** 1877-1950 British journalist: Claud Cockburn *In Time of Trouble* (1957)

23 The British Press is always looking for stuff to fill the space between their cartoons.
- **Bernadette Devlin McAliskey** 1947- Northern Irish politician: comment, 1970

24 You should always believe all you read in the newspapers, as this makes them more interesting.
- **Rose Macaulay** 1881-1958 English novelist: *A Casual Commentary* (1926)

25 People don't actually read newspapers. They get into them every morning, like a hot bath.
- **Marshall McLuhan** 1911-80 Canadian communications scholar: in 1965; Jonathon Green (ed.) *A Dictionary of Contemporary Quotations* (1982)

26 The art of newspaper paragraphing is to stroke a platitude until it purrs like an epigram.
- **Don Marquis** 1878-1937 American poet and journalist: E. Anthony *O Rare Don Marquis* (1962)

27 Exclusives aren't what they used to be. We tend to put 'exclusive' on everything just to annoy other papers. I once put 'exclusive' on the weather by mistake.
- **Piers Morgan** 1965- English journalist: in *Independent on Sunday* 14 March 1999 'Quotes'

28 If as Graham Greene said every novelist needs an icicle in his heart, a successful editor needs a small iceberg.
of Daily Mail editor David English
- **Ferdinand Mount** 1939- British writer and politician: *Cold Cream* (2008)

29 *asked why he had allowed the unclothed models feature on Page 3 to develop:*
I don't know. The editor did it when I was away.
- **Rupert Murdoch** 1931- Australian-born American media entrepreneur: in *Guardian* 25 February 1994

30 Four hostile newspapers are more to be feared than a thousand bayonets.
- **Napoleon I** 1769-1821 French emperor: attributed from the late 19th century

31 I like to do my principal research in bars, where people are more likely to tell the truth or, at least, lie less

convincingly than they do in briefings and books.
- **P. J. O'Rourke** 1947- American humorous writer: *Holidays in Hell* (1988)

32 My belief is that 'recluse' is a codeword generated by journalists...meaning 'doesn't like to talk to reporters'.
- **Thomas Pynchon** 1937- American novelist: in a telephone conversation with CNN, 1997; in *Guardian* 5 May 2003

33 No self-respecting fish would be wrapped in a Murdoch newspaper.
- **Mike Royko** 1932-97 American journalist: before resigning from the Chicago *Sun-Times* when the paper was sold to Rupert Murdoch in 1984; Karl E. Meyer (ed.) *Pundits, Poets, and Wits* (1990)

34 *of the* Daily Mail*:*
By office boys for office boys.
- **Lord Salisbury** 1830-1903 British Conservative statesman: H. Hamilton Fyfe *Northcliffe, an Intimate Biography* (1930)

35 Ever noticed that no matter what happens in one day, it exactly fits in the newspaper?
- **Jerry Seinfeld** 1954- American comedian: in *Mail on Sunday* 11 February 2007

36 People who read tabloids deserve to be lied to.
- **Jerry Seinfeld** 1954- American comedian: interview, 60 *Minutes* March 1997

37 If our newspapers...could discriminate between the news value of a bicycle accident in Clapham and that of a capsize of civilization...
usually quoted as 'Newspapers are unable, seemingly, to discriminate between a bicycle accident and the collapse of civilization'
- **George Bernard Shaw** 1856-1950 Irish dramatist: *Too True to Be Good* (1931) preface

38 Accuracy to a newspaper is what virtue is to a lady; but a newspaper can always print a retraction.
- **Adlai Stevenson** 1900-65 American Democratic politician: *The Wit and Wisdom of Adlai Stevenson* (1965)

39 Comment is free but facts are on expenses.
- **Tom Stoppard** 1937- British dramatist: *Night and Day* (1978)

40 Freedom of the press in Britain means freedom to print such of the proprietor's prejudices as the advertisers don't object to.
- **Hannen Swaffer** 1879-1962 British journalist: Tom Driberg *Swaff* (1974)

41 There are laws to protect the freedom of the press's speech, but none that are worth anything to protect the people from the press.
- **Mark Twain** 1835-1910 American writer: 'License of the Press' (1873)

42 They had loitered together of old on many a doorstep and forced an entry into many a stricken home.
- **Evelyn Waugh** 1903-66 English novelist: *Scoop* (1938)

43 Of course, I believe in the Devil. How otherwise would I account for the existence of Lord Beaverbrook?
of the proprietor of the Express newspapers
- **Evelyn Waugh** 1903-66 English novelist: L. Gourlay *The Beaverbrook I Knew* (1984)

44 *the difference between journalism and literature:*
Journalism is unreadable, and literature is not read.
- **Oscar Wilde** 1854-1900 Irish dramatist and poet: 'The Critic as Artist' (1891)

45 Newspapers, even, have degenerated. They may now be absolutely relied upon.
- **Oscar Wilde** 1854-1900 Irish dramatist and poet: *The Decay of Lying* (1891)

46 You cannot hope
to bribe or twist,
thank God! the
British journalist.
But, seeing what
the man will do
unbribed, there's
no occasion to.
- **Humbert Wolfe** 1886-1940 British poet: 'Over the Fire' (1930)

47 Rock journalism is people who can't write interviewing people who can't talk for people who can't read.
- **Frank Zappa** 1940-93 American rock musician: Linda Botts *Loose Talk* (1980)

Office Life

What I don't like about office Christmas parties is looking for a job the next day.
Phyllis Diller

1 *on accountancy:*
A profession whose idea of excitement is sharpening a bundle of no. 2 pencils.
- **Anonymous**: in *Time* magazine 1993

2 *of the cramped office he shared with Dorothy Parker:*
One square foot less and it would be adulterous.
- **Robert Benchley** 1889-1945 American humorist: in *New Yorker* 5 January 1946

3 BROWN: I've never worked *anywhere*... without being sexually involved with *somebody* in the office.
QUESTIONER: What about the *boss*?
BROWN: Why discriminate against *him*?
- **Helen Gurley Brown** 1922-2012 American journalist: in *New York Magazine* 27 September 1982

4 Meetings...are rather like cocktail parties. You don't want to go, but you're cross not to be asked.
- **Jilly Cooper** 1937- English writer: *How to Survive from Nine to Five* (1970)

5 What I don't like about office Christmas parties is looking for a job the next day.
- **Phyllis Diller** 1917-2012 American actress: attributed

6 'Noel,' he pipes, 'Noel, Noel.'
Some wag beats tempo with a ruler.
And the plump blonde from Personnel
Is sick behind the water cooler.
- **Phyllis McGinley** 1905-78 American poet: 'Office Party' (1960)

7 An office party is not, as is sometimes supposed, the Managing Director's chance to kiss the tea-girl. It is the tea-girl's chance to kiss the Managing Director.
- **Katharine Whitehorn** 1928- English journalist: *Roundabout* (1962) 'The Office Party'

8 I yield to no one in my admiration for the office as a social centre, but it's no place actually to get any work done.
- **Katharine Whitehorn** 1928- English journalist: *Sunday Best* (1976)

9 A team effort is a lot of people doing what I say.
- **Michael Winner** 1935-2013 British film director and producer: in *Sunday Times* 5 April 1970

10 Sexual harassment at work—is it a problem for the self-employed?
- **Victoria Wood** 1953- British writer and comedienne: *Lucky Bag: an Evening with Victoria Wood* (1984)

Old Age

see also **AGE, MIDDLE AGE, YOUTH**

To what do I attribute my longevity? Bad luck. **Quentin Crisp**

1 Mr Salteena was an elderly man of 42.
- **Daisy Ashford** 1881-1972 English child author: *The Young Visiters* (1919)

2 The only thing for old age is a brave face, a good tailor and comfortable shoes.
- **Alan Ayckbourn** 1939- English dramatist: *Table Manners* (1975)

3 To me old age is always fifteen years older than I am.
- **Bernard Baruch** 1870-1965 American financier and presidential adviser: in *Newsweek* 29 August 1955

4 If you live to be ninety in England and can still eat a boiled egg they think you

deserve the Nobel Prize.
- **Alan Bennett** 1934- English dramatist and actor: *An Englishman Abroad* (1989)

5 Here I sit, alone and sixty,
Bald, and fat, and full of sin,
Cold the seat and loud the cistern,
As I read the Harpic tin.
- **Alan Bennett** 1934- English dramatist and actor: 'Place Names of China' (parody of John Betjeman)

6 *on reaching the age of 100:*
If I'd known I was gonna live this long,
I'd have taken better care of myself.
- **Eubie Blake** 1883-1983 American ragtime pianist: in *Observer* 13 February 1983 'Sayings of the Week'; also claimed by Adolph Zukor on reaching 100

7 Old age is the outpatients' department of Purgatory.
- **Lord Hugh Cecil** 1869-1956 British Conservative politician and educationist: John Betjeman, letter to Tom Driberg, 21 July 1976

8 *in his old age Churchill overheard one of two new MPs whisper to the other, 'They say the old man's getting a bit past it':*
And they say the old man's getting deaf as well.
- **Winston Churchill** 1874-1965 British Conservative statesman: K. Halle *The Irrepressible Churchill* (1985)

9 *it was pointed out to the aged Winston Churchill that his fly-button was undone:*
No matter. The dead bird does not leave the nest.
- **Winston Churchill** 1874-1965 British Conservative statesman: Rupert Hart-Davis letter to George Lyttelton, 5 January 1957

10 How foolish to think that one can ever slam the door in the face of age. Much wiser to be polite and gracious and ask him to lunch in advance.
- **Noël Coward** 1899-1973 English dramatist, actor, and composer: diary, 3 June 1956

11 To what do I attribute my longevity? Bad luck.
- **Quentin Crisp** 1908-99 English writer: in *Spectator* 20 November 1999

12 *approaching his 80th birthday:*
While there's snow on the roof, it

doesn't mean the fire has gone out in the furnace.
- **John G. Diefenbaker** 1895-1979 Canadian Progressive Conservative statesman: attributed, 1991

13 Before I go to meet my Maker,
I want to use the salt left in my shaker.
- **Howard Dietz** 1896-1983 American songwriter: 'Before I Kiss the World Goodbye' (1963)

14 As Groucho Marx once said, 'Anyone can get old—all you have to do is to live long enough.'
- **Elizabeth II** 1926- British queen: speech at her official 80th birthday lunch, 15 June 2006, in *Independent on Sunday* 18 June 2006

15 Being an old maid is like death by drowning, a really delightful sensation after you cease to struggle.
- **Edna Ferber** 1887-1968 American writer: R. E. Drennan *Wit's End* (1973)

16 After the age of 80, you seem to be having breakfast every five minutes.
- **Christopher Fry** 1907-2005 English dramatist: attributed; in *Spectator* 7 December 2002

17 Methus'lah live nine hundred years
But who calls dat livin'
When no gal'll give in
To no man what's nine hundred years?
- **Ira Gershwin** 1896-1983 American songwriter: 'It Ain't Necessarily So' (1935)

18 At forty I lost my illusions,
At fifty I lost my hair,
At sixty my hope and teeth were gone,
And my feet were beyond repair.
At eighty life has clipped my claws,
I'm bent and bowed and cracked;
But I can't give up the ghost because
My follies are intact.
- **E. Y. Harburg** 1898-1981 American songwriter: 'Gerontology or Springtime for Senility' (1965)

19 It's amazing how much 'mature wisdom' resembles being too tired.
- **Robert Heinlein** 1907-88 American science fiction writer: *Time Enough for Love* (1973)

20 To my deafness I'm accustomed,
To my dentures I'm resigned,

I can manage my bifocals,
But Oh, how I miss my mind.
- **Lord Home** 1903-95 British Conservative
  statesman: John G. Murray *A Gentleman
  Publisher's Commonplace Book* (1996)

21 Nobody in Beverly Hills grows old. It's
a violation of a city ordinance.
- **Bob Hope** 1903-2003 American comedian:
  attributed; in *Times* 24 September 2003

22 I still go up my 44 stairs two at a time,
but that is in hopes of dropping dead at
the top.
- **A. E. Housman** 1859-1936 English poet:
  letter to Laurence Housman, 9 June 1935

23 In one old people's home they changed
the words of the song to 'When I'm
84' as they considered 64 to be young.
I might do that.
- **Paul McCartney** 1942- English pop singer
  and songwriter: in *Times* 14 October 2006

24 Senescence begins
And middle age ends
The day your descendants
Outnumber your friends.
- **Ogden Nash** 1902-71 American humorist:
  'Crossing the Border' (1964)

25 Growing old is like being increasingly
penalized for a crime you haven't
committed.
- **Anthony Powell** 1905-2000 English
  novelist: *Temporary Kings* (1973)

26 *when his age was contrasted with that of his
opponent Walter Mondale (born 1928):*
I am not going to make age an issue in
this campaign. I am not going to exploit
for political purposes my opponent's
youth and inexperience.
- **Ronald Reagan** 1911-2004 American
  Republican statesman: television debate,
  21 October 1984

27 As I grow older and older,
And totter towards the tomb,
I find that I care less and less
Who goes to bed with whom.
- **Dorothy L. Sayers** 1893-1957 English writer:
  'That's Why I Never Read Modern Novels';
  Janet Hitchman *Such a Strange Lady* (1975)

28 *a final letter to a young correspondent, a year
before his death:*
Dear Elise,
Seek younger friends; I am extinct.
- **George Bernard Shaw** 1856-1950 Irish
  dramatist: letter, 1949

29 *on how he knows he's getting old:*
My children are doing me in history now.
- **David Trimble** 1944- Northern Irish
  politician: in *Mail on Sunday* 27 May 2007

30 One should never make one's début
with a scandal. One should reserve that
to give an interest to one's old age.
- **Oscar Wilde** 1854-1900 Irish dramatist and
  poet: *The Picture of Dorian Gray* (1891)

Opera

Italian chefs screaming risotto recipes at each other.   **Aristotle Onassis**

1 I do not mind what language an opera
is sung in so long as it is a language
I don't understand.
- **Edward Appleton** 1892-1965 English
  physicist: in *Observer* 28 August 1955

2 The opera ain't over 'til the fat lady
sings.
- **Dan Cook** 1926-2008 American journalist:
  in *Washington Post* 3 June 1978

3 People are wrong when they say that the

opera isn't what it used to be. It is what it
used to be—that's what's wrong with it.
- **Noël Coward** 1899-1973 English dramatist,
  actor, and composer: *Design for Living*
  (1933)

4 Opera is when a guy gets stabbed in the
back and, instead of bleeding, he sings.
- **Ed Gardner** 1901-63 American radio
  comedian: *Duffy's Tavern* (US radio
  programme, 1940s)

5 Opera in English is, in the main, just
about as sensible as baseball in Italian.
  - **H. L. Mencken** 1880-1956 American
    journalist and literary critic: Laurence J.
    Peter (ed.) *Quotations for our Time* (1977)

6 *view of opera before he met Maria Callas:*
Italian chefs screaming risotto recipes at
each other.
  - **Aristotle Onassis** 1906-75 Greek shipping
    magnate and international businessman:
    Peter Evans *Nemesis: the True Story of
    Aristotle* (2004)

7 *Parsifal* is the kind of opera that starts
at six o'clock. After it has been going
three hours, you look at your watch

and it says 6.20.
  - **David Randolph** 1914-2010 American
    conductor: Nat Shapiro (ed.) *An
    Encyclopedia of Quotations about Music*
    (1978)

8 It is a music one must hear several
times. I am not going again.
of Tannhäuser
  - **Gioacchino Rossini** 1792-1868 Italian
    composer: L. de Hegermann-Lindencrone
    In the Courts of Memory (1912)

9 The first act of the three occupied
two hours. I enjoyed that in spite of the
singing.
  - **Mark Twain** 1835-1910 American writer:
    What is Man? (1906)

Optimism and Pessimism

see also **HOPE**

....

An optimist is a girl who mistakes a bulge for a curve.   **Ring Lardner**

1 I don't consider myself a pessimist.
I think of a pessimist as someone who is
waiting for it to rain. And I feel soaked
to the skin.
  - **Leonard Cohen** 1934- Canadian singer
    and writer: in *Observer* 2 May 1993

2 A pessimist is a man who thinks all
women are bad. An optimist is a man
who hopes that they are.
  - **Chauncey Depew** 1834-1928 American
    businessman and politician: attributed,
    c. 1898

3 I guess I just prefer to see the dark
side of things. The glass is always half
empty. And cracked. And I just cut my
lip on it. And chipped a tooth.
  - **Janeane Garofalo** 1964- American
    comedian: attributed

4 The people who live in a Golden Age
usually go around complaining how
yellow everything looks.
  - **Randall Jarrell** 1914-65 American poet:
    A Sad Heart at the Supermarket (1965)

5 My friends, as I have discovered
myself, there are no disasters,

only opportunities. And, indeed,
opportunities for fresh disasters.
  - **Boris Johnson** 1964- British Conservative
    politician: in *Daily Telegraph* 2 December
    2004

6 An optimist is a girl who mistakes a
bulge for a curve.
  - **Ring Lardner** 1885-1933 American writer:
    Evan Esar *The Treasury of Humorous
    Quotations* (1952)

7 *on hearing the doorbell or a ringing telephone:*
What fresh hell is this?
  - **Dorothy Parker** 1893-1967 American critic
    and humorist: Marion Meade *What Fresh
    Hell Is This?* (1988)

8 'Do you know what a pessimist is?'
'A man who thinks everybody is as nasty
as himself, and hates them for it.'
  - **George Bernard Shaw** 1856-1950 Irish
    dramatist: *An Unsocial Socialist* (1887)

9 The nice part about being a pessimist
is that you are constantly being either
proven right or pleasantly surprised.
  - **George F. Will** 1941- American columnist:
    The Levelling Wind (1994)

The Paranormal

Apart from the known and the unknown, what else is there? **Harold Pinter**

1 Those who believe in telekinesis, raise my hand.
- **Anonymous**: modern saying, sometimes associated with the writer Kurt Vonnegut

2 *on spiritualism:*
I always knew the living talked rot, but it's nothing to the rot the dead talk.
- **Margot Asquith** 1864-1945 British political hostess: Chips Channon diary, 20 December 1937

3 I don't believe in astrology; I'm a Sagittarius and we're sceptical.
- **Arthur C. Clarke** 1917-2008 English science fiction writer: attributed; Nigel Rees *Cassell Dictionary of Humorous Quotations* (1999)

4 But where is everybody?
on the existence of extra-terrestrials, given the lack of contact
- **Enrico Fermi** 1901-54 Italian-born American atomic physicist: attributed, c.1950

5 *supposed opening words of a letter of dismissal to the Sun's astrologer:*
As you will no doubt have foreseen…
- **Kelvin Mackenzie** 1946- British journalist: attributed, probably apocryphal

6 The only contact I ever made with the dead was when I spoke to a journalist from the *Sun*.
- **Morrissey** 1959- English singer and songwriter: David Bret *Morrissey: Landscapes of the Mind* (1994)

7 Apart from the known and the unknown, what else is there?
- **Harold Pinter** 1930-2008 English dramatist: *The Homecoming* (1965)

8 Mr Geller may have psychic powers by means of which he can bend spoons; if so, he appears to be doing it the hard way.
- **James Randi** 1928- Canadian-born American conjuror: *The Supernatural A-Z: the truth and the lies* (1995)

Parents

see also **CHILDREN, FAMILY, MOTHERS**

A Jewish man with parents alive is a fifteen-year-old boy. **Philip Roth**

1 Maternity is a matter of fact. Paternity is a matter of opinion.
- **Walter Bagehot** 1826-77 English economist: *Physics and Politics* (1872)

2 I'm still working. I need the money. Money, I've discovered, is the one thing keeping me in touch with my children.
- **Gyles Brandreth** 1948- English writer and broadcaster: *The One to One Show* (2010)

3 If you have never been hated by your child, you have never been a parent.
- **Bette Davis** 1908-89 American actress: *The Lonely Life* (1962)

4 Most children threaten at times to run away from home. This is the only thing that keeps some parents going.
- **Phyllis Diller** 1917-2012 American actress: attributed

5 [A successful parent is one] who raises a child who grows up and is able to pay for his or her own psychoanalysis.
- **Nora Ephron** 1941-2012 American screenwriter and director: in *People* 10 November 1986

6 Mom and Pop were just a couple of kids when they got married. He was

eighteen, she was sixteen, and I was
three.

- **Billie Holiday** 1915-59 American singer:
  Lady Sings the Blues (1958) opening words

7 *on hearing a report that his son Charles James
Fox was to be married:*
He will be obliged to go to bed at least
one night of his life.
- **Lord Holland** 1705-74 English Whig
  politician: Christopher Hobhouse *Fox* (1934)

8 In case it is one of mine.
*patting children in Chelsea on the head as he
passed by*
- **Augustus John** 1878-1961 British painter:
  Michael Holroyd *Augustus John* (1975)

9 They fuck you up, your mum and dad.
They may not mean to, but they do.
They fill you with the faults they had
And add some extra, just for you.
- **Philip Larkin** 1922-85 English poet: 'This Be
  The Verse' (1974)

10 Having children makes you no more a
parent than having a piano makes you
a pianist.
- **Michael Levine**: *Lessons at the Halfway
  Point* (1995)

11 Parents should conduct their arguments
in quiet, respectful tones, but in a
foreign language. You'd be surprised
what an inducement that is to the
education of children.
- **Judith Martin** 1938- American journalist:
  'Advice from Miss Manners', column in
  Washington Post 1979-82

12 Your folks are like God because you
want to know they're out there and you
want them to approve of your life, still
you only call them when you're in crisis

and need something.
- **Chuck Palahniuk** 1962- American writer:
  Invisible Monsters (1999)

13 A Jewish man with parents alive is a
fifteen-year-old boy, and will remain a
fifteen-year-old boy until *they die*!
- **Philip Roth** 1933- American novelist:
  Portnoy's Complaint (1967)

14 I did not throw myself into the struggle
for life: I threw my mother into it.
- **George Bernard Shaw** 1856-1950 Irish
  dramatist: preface to *The Irrational Knot*
  (1905)

15 If you must hold yourself up to your
children as an object lesson (which is
not at all necessary), hold yourself up
as a warning and not as an example.
- **George Bernard Shaw** 1856-1950 Irish
  dramatist: *Parents and Children* (1914)

16 I wish either my father or my mother,
or indeed both of them, as they were
in duty both equally bound to it, had
minded what they were about when
they begot me.
- **Laurence Sterne** 1713-68 English novelist:
  Tristram Shandy (1759-67)

17 I have four sons and three stepsons.
I have learnt what it is like to step on
Lego with bare feet.
- **Fay Weldon** 1931- British novelist and
  scriptwriter: in *Independent* 6 July 2002

18 All women become like their mothers.
That is their tragedy. No man does.
That's his.
- **Oscar Wilde** 1854-1900 Irish dramatist
  and poet: *The Importance of Being Earnest*
  (1895); the same words occur in dialogue
  form in *A Woman of No Importance* (1893)

Parties and Hospitality

see also **SOCIETY**

....

Some people can stay longer in an hour than others can in a week.
William Dean Howells

1 If the soup had been as warm as the wine, the wine as old as the fish, and the fish as young as the maid, and the maid as willing as the hostess, it would have been a very good meal.
- **Anonymous**: saying of unknown origin

2 *opening a lecture at Strathclyde University, immediately after her husband's trial for perjury; the audience included many journalists:*
Good morning, and a special welcome to those of you who are new to the field of quantum solar energy conversion.
- **Mary Archer** 1944- British scientist: in *Sunday Times* 29 July 2001

3 It is amazing how nice people are to you when they know you are going away.
- **Michael Arlen** 1895-1963 British novelist: attributed

4 Mankind is divisible into two great classes: hosts and guests.
- **Max Beerbohm** 1872-1956 English critic, essayist, and caricaturist: *And Even Now* (1920)

5 *on the arrival of the champagne after a series of poor dishes at a dinner:*
Thank God for something warm!
- **Benjamin Disraeli** 1804-81 British Tory statesman and novelist: Christopher Hibbert *Disraeli and his World* (1978)

6 Hospitality consists in a little fire, a little food, and an immense quiet.
- **Ralph Waldo Emerson** 1803-82 American philosopher and poet: journal, 1865

7 Here you are again, older faces and younger clothes.
habitual greeting to guests
- **Mamie Stuyvesant Fish** 1853-1915 American socialite: attributed

8 My idea of hell is a very large party in a cold room, where everybody has to play hockey properly.
- **Stella Gibbons** 1902-89 English novelist: *Cold Comfort Farm* (1932)

9 The best number for a dinner party is two—myself and a dam' good head waiter.
- **Nubar Gulbenkian** 1896-1972 British industrialist and philanthropist: in *Daily Telegraph* 14 January 1965

10 A host is like a general: misfortunes often reveal his genius.
- **Horace** 65-8 BC Roman poet: *Satires*

11 Some people can stay longer in an hour than others can in a week.
- **William Dean Howells** 1837-1920 American novelist and critic: attributed

12 At every party there are two kinds of people—those who want to go home and those who don't. The trouble is, they are usually married to each other.
- **Ann Landers** 1918-2002 American advice columnist: in *International Herald Tribune* 19 June 1991

13 I really felt for you in the scene in which you tried to make the party go.
to Judith Anderson after her Lady Macbeth *in 1937*
- **Queen Mary** 1867-1953 British Queen Consort: Adrian Woolhouse *Angus Macbean Face-maker* (2006)

14 At a dinner party one should eat wisely but not too well, and talk well but not too wisely.
- **W. Somerset Maugham** 1874-1965 English novelist: *Writer's Notebook* (1949); written in 1896

15 Home is heaven and orgies are vile, But you *need* an orgy, once in a while.
- **Ogden Nash** 1902-71 American humorist: 'Home, 99⁴⁴/₁₀₀% Sweet Home' (1935)

16 Gee, what a terrific party. Later on we'll get some fluid and embalm each other.
- **Neil Simon** 1927– American dramatist: *The Gingerbread Lady* (1970)

17 I must ask anyone entering the house never to contradict me or differ from me in any way, as it interferes with the functioning of the gastric juices and prevents my sleeping at night.
his habitual greeting to guests arriving at Renishaw
- **George Sitwell** 1860–1943 English antiquary: attributed, *Oxford Dictionary of National Biography*

18 I made a terrible social gaffe. I went to a Ken and Barbie party dressed as Klaus Barbie.
- **Arthur Smith** 1954– and **Chris England**: *An Evening with Gary Lineker* (1990)

19 I once went to one of those parties where everyone throws their car keys into the middle of the room. I don't know who got my moped but I drove that Peugeot for years.
- **Victoria Wood** 1953– British writer and comedienne: attributed

Past, Present, and Future

Cheer up! the worst is yet to come! **Philander Chase Johnson**

1 'The first ten million years were the worst,' said Marvin, 'and the second ten million years, they were the worst too. The third ten million I didn't enjoy at all. After that I went into a bit of a decline.'
- **Douglas Adams** 1952–2001 English science fiction writer: *Restaurant at the End of the Universe* (1980)

2 Nothing is more responsible for the good old days than a bad memory.
- **Franklin P. Adams** 1881–1960 American journalist and humorist: Howard Teichmann *Smart Aleck* (1976)

3 Nostalgia isn't what it used to be.
- **Anonymous**: graffito (taken as title of book by Simone Signoret, 1978)

4 The world has turned upside down. The best golfer in the world is black; the best rapper in the world is white; and now there is a war and, guess what, Germany doesn't want to be in it.
- **Alan Bennett** 1934– English dramatist and actor: diary 2003, in *London Review of Books* 8 January 2004

5 *definition of the future:*
That period of time in which our affairs prosper, our friends are true, and our happiness is assured.
- **Ambrose Bierce** 1842–c.1914 American writer: *The Cynic's Word Book* (1906)

6 Predictions can be very difficult— especially about the future.
- **Niels Bohr** 1885–1962 Danish physicist: attributed

7 Posterity is as likely to be wrong as anybody else.
- **Heywood Broun** 1888–1939 American journalist: *Sitting on the World* (1924)

8 The rule is, jam to-morrow and jam yesterday—but never jam today.
- **Lewis Carroll** 1832–98 English writer and logician: *Through the Looking-Glass* (1872)

9 For my part, I consider that it will be found much better by all Parties to leave the past to history, especially as I propose to write that history myself.
- **Winston Churchill** 1874–1965 British Conservative statesman: speech in the House of Commons, 23 January 1948

10 I never think of the future. It comes soon enough.
- **Albert Einstein** 1879–1955 German-born theoretical physicist: interview given on the *Belgenland*, December 1930

11 Why should I write for posterity?
What, if I may be free
To ask a ridiculous question,
Has posterity done for me?
- **E. Y. Harburg** 1898-1981 American songwriter: 'Posterity is Right Around the Corner' (1976)

12 In times like these, it helps to recall that there have always been times like these.
- **Paul Harvey** 1918-2009 American radio broadcaster: attributed

13 You can only predict things after they have happened.
- **Eugène Ionesco** 1912-94 French dramatist: *Le Rhinocéros* (1959)

14 Cheer up! the worst is yet to come!
- **Philander Chase Johnson** 1866-1939 American journalist: in *Everybody's Magazine* May 1920

15 I do not know which makes a man more conservative—to know nothing but the present, or nothing but the past.
- **John Maynard Keynes** 1883-1946 English economist: *The End of Laissez-Faire* (1926)

16 Industrial archaeology...believes that a thing that doesn't work any more is far more interesting than a thing that still works.
- **Miles Kington** 1941-2008 English humorist: *Nature Made Ridiculously Simple* (1983)

17 Soon we'll be sliding down the razor-blade of life.
- **Tom Lehrer** 1928- American humorist: 'Bright College Days' (c.1960)

18 They spend their time mostly looking forward to the past.
- **John Osborne** 1929-94 English dramatist: *Look Back in Anger* (1956)

19 We mustn't prejudge the past.
- **William Whitelaw** 1918-99 British Conservative politician: in *Times* 2 July 1999; attributed

20 Hindsight is always twenty-twenty.
- **Billy Wilder** 1906-2002 American screenwriter and director: J. R. Columbo *Wit and Wisdom of the Moviemakers* (1979)

People and Personalities

....

I had to pull him out, otherwise nobody would have believed I didn't push him in.
Peter Cook

1 Jimmy [Connors] was such an out-and-out 'personality' that he managed to get into a legal dispute with the president of his own fan club.
- **Martin Amis** 1949- English novelist: in *New Yorker* 5 September 1994

2 On no account is this man to be put in charge of others.
Army selection board on the young Peter Ustinov, c.1942
- **Anonymous**: quoted in *Daily Telegraph* 30 March 2004

3 He was my knight on a shining bicycle.
of Boris Johnson after he rescued her from a gang of girls
- **Franny Armstrong** 1972- British film director: in *Times* 4 November 2009

4 Agatha Christie has given more pleasure in bed than any other woman.
- **Nancy Banks-Smith** 1929- British journalist: attributed

5 I will take questions from the guys, but from the girls I want telephone numbers.
- **Silvio Berlusconi** 1936- Italian statesman: at a youth rally in Rome, 9 September 2009

6 She has perfected the art of answering questions at length and saying absolutely nothing. She would never, even under torture, admit that pink was her favourite colour for fear of offending orange and mauve.
of Margot Fonteyn
- **Richard Buckle** 1916-2001 English ballet critic: in *Sunday Times* 30 March 1969

7 *of Viscount Montgomery:*
In defeat unbeatable: in victory
unbearable.
- **Winston Churchill** 1874-1965 British
  Conservative statesman: Edward Marsh
  Ambrosia and Small Beer (1964)

8 *after meeting Irving Berlin and supposing him
to be Isaiah Berlin:*
Berlin's just like most bureaucrats.
Wonderful on paper but disappointing
when you meet them face to face.
- **Winston Churchill** 1874-1965 British
  Conservative statesman: Laurence
  Bergreen *As Thousands Cheer* (1990)

9 He has all the virtues I dislike and none
of the vices I admire.
on Sir Stafford Cripps
- **Winston Churchill** 1874-1965 British
  Conservative statesman: attributed

10 I had to pull him out, otherwise nobody
would have believed I didn't push
him in.
on rescuing David Frost from drowning
- **Peter Cook** 1937-95 English satirist and
  actor: Nigel Rees (ed.) *A Year of Stings and
  Squelches* (1985)

11 *on a visit to Washington:*
If there were anything I could take
back to France with me, it would be
Mrs Kennedy.
- **Charles de Gaulle** 1890-1970 French
  statesman: attributed

12 *of David Steel, Leader of the Liberal Party:*
He's passed from rising hope to elder
statesman without any intervening
period whatsoever.
- **Michael Foot** 1913-2010 British Labour
  politician: in the House of Commons,
  28 March 1979

13 *on Richard Chartres, Bishop of London:*
The sort of bishop you would get if you
went to Harrods.
- **Giles Fraser** 1964- English Anglican
  clergyman: quoting one of his congregation,
  17 April 2013

14 *Lady Carina Fitzalan-Howard was asked if
her future husband David Frost were religious:*
Yes, he thinks he's God Almighty.
- **Carina Frost** 1952- : in *Sunday Times* 28 July
  1985

15 He's the angriest man you'll ever meet.
He's like a man with a fork in a world
of soup.
on his brother Liam
- **Noel Gallagher** 1967- English pop singer:
  in *Sun* 21 April 2009

16 I like a drink as much as the next man,
unless the next man is Mel Gibson.
*introducing the convicted drink-driver on stage
to present an award*
- **Ricky Gervais** 1961- English comedian: at
  the Golden Globes, 17 January 2010

17 Vladimir, Vladimir, Vladimir Kuts
Nature's attempt at an engine in boots.
on the Russian runner Vladimir Kuts
- **A. P. Herbert** 1890-1971 English writer and
  humorist: in 1956; Ned Sherrin *Cutting Edge*
  (1984)

18 Twin miracles of mascara, her eyes
looked like the corpses of two small
crows that had crashed into a chalk
cliff.
on Barbara Cartland
- **Clive James** 1939- Australian critic and
  writer: in *Observer* 2 August 1981

19 *on her son Karl writing a book about capital:*
If only Karl had made capital instead.
- **Henrietta Marx** German mother of Karl
  Marx: remark reported by Marx in 1868;
  S. K. Padover *Letters of Karl Marx* (1979)

20 The thinking man's crumpet.
of Joan Bakewell
- **Frank Muir** 1920-98 English writer and
  broadcaster: attributed

21 *of Errol Flynn:*
You always knew precisely where you
stood with him because he *always* let
you down.
- **David Niven** 1910-83 English actor: *Bring
  On the Empty Horses* (1975)

22 I was the toast of two continents:
Greenland and Australia.
- **Dorothy Parker** 1893-1967 American critic
  and humorist: attributed

23 *on Michael Jackson:*
He's the guy that makes Liberace look
like Clint Eastwood.
- **Joan Rivers** 1933- American comedienne:
  Graham Jones *I Don't Hate Men, But–*;
  I Don't Hate Women, But– (1986)

24 *on Mick Jagger:*
The lips, the lips! He could French kiss a
moose or blow a tuba from both ends at
the same time.
- **Joan Rivers** 1933- American comedienne:
Graham Jones *I Don't Hate Men, But–;
I Don't Hate Women, But–* (1986)

25 He seemed to have been cut out of very
thin cardboard.
of Lytton Strachey
- **Edith Sitwell** 1887-1964 English poet and
critic: *Taken Care Of* (1965)

26 *on Marilyn Monroe:*
Her body has gone to her head.
- **Barbara Stanwyck** 1907-90 American
actress: attributed, perhaps apocryphal

27 A genius with the IQ of a moron.
of Andy Warhol
- **Gore Vidal** 1925-2012 American novelist
and critic: in *Observer* 18 June 1989

28 *to a gentleman who had accosted him in the
street saying, 'Mr Jones, I believe?':*
If you believe that, you'll believe anything.
George Jones RA (1786–1869), painter of

*military subjects, bore a striking resemblance
to Wellington*
- **Duke of Wellington** 1769-1852 British
soldier and statesman: Elizabeth Longford
Pillar of State (1972)

29 I think his fate is rather like Humpty
Dumpty's, quite as tragic and quite as
impossible to put right.
on her husband, Oscar Wilde
- **Constance Wilde** 1859-98: letter to her
brother, 26 March 1897

30 *on Burt Reynolds:*
He's the kind of guy who would
stop on his way down the aisle to get
married to say hello to a pretty girl.
- **Tammy Wynette** 1942-98 American singer:
in *Winnipeg Free Press* 22 September 1978

31 Q: Who does George Michael sleep
with?
A: Nobody. You can't get two on a
sunbed.
- **Paula Yates** 1959-2000 British television
presenter: Graham Jones *I Don't Hate Men,
But–; I Don't Hate Women, But–* (1986)

Peoples *see* COUNTRIES AND PEOPLES

Personalities *see* PEOPLE AND PERSONALITIES

Pessimism *see* OPTIMISM AND PESSIMISM

Philosophy

Sometimes I sits and thinks, and then again I just sits.   **Punch**

1 What if everything is an illusion and
nothing exists? In that case I definitely
overpaid for my carpet.
- **Woody Allen** 1935- American film
director, writer, and actor: *Without Feathers*
(1975)

2 *intervening at a New York party between
Mike Tyson and Naomi Campbell:*
TYSON: Do you know who the f— I am?

I'm the heavyweight champion of the
world.
AYER: And I am the former Wykeham
Professor of Logic. We are both pre-
eminent in our field. I suggest we talk
about this like rational men.
- **A. J. Ayer** 1910-89 English philosopher:
Ben Rogers *A. J. Ayer: a Life* (1999)

3 Some people see things that are and

ask, Why? Some people dream of things that never were and ask, Why not? Some people have to go to work and don't have time for all that.

- **George Carlin** 1937-2008 American comedian: *Brain Droppings* (1997)

4 I have tried too in my time to be a philosopher; but, I don't know how, cheerfulness was always breaking in.

- **Oliver Edwards** 1711-91 English lawyer: James Boswell *Life of Samuel Johnson* (1934 ed.) 17 April 1778

5 Philosophy consists very largely of one philosopher arguing that all others are jackasses. He usually proves it, and I should add that he usually proves that he is one himself.

- **H. L. Mencken** 1880-1956 American journalist and literary critic: *Minority Report* (1956)

6 I like your playing very much.
to Jean-Paul Sartre

- **Charlie Parker** 1920-55 American jazz saxophonist: John Szwed *So What: the life of Miles Davis* (2002)

7 The universe is full of magical things patiently waiting for our wits to grow sharper.

- **Eden Phillpotts** 1862-1960 English writer: *A Shadow Passes* (1918)

8 It's a strange thing about determined seekers-after-wisdom that, no matter where they happen to be, they'll always seek that wisdom which is a long way off. Wisdom is one of the few things that looks bigger the further away it is.

- **Terry Pratchett** 1948- English fantasy writer: *Witches Abroad* (1991)

9 Sometimes I sits and thinks, and then again I just sits.

- **Punch** 1841-1992 English humorous weekly periodical: vol. 131 (1906)

10 It is better to be vaguely right than exactly wrong.

- **Carveth Read** 1848-1931 English philosopher: *Logic, Deductive and Inductive* (1898)

11 My German engineer, I think is a fool. He thinks nothing empirical is Knowable—I asked him to admit that there was not a rhinoceros in the room, but he wouldn't.
of Wittgenstein

- **Bertrand Russell** 1872-1970 British philosopher and mathematician: letter to Lady Ottoline Morrell, November 1911

12 I have a new philosophy; I'm only going to dread one day at a time.

- **Charles Monroe Schulz** 1922-2000 American cartoonist: attributed

13 *on the speaker's choice of subject at university:*
Almost everyone who didn't know what to do, did philosophy. Well, that's logical.

- **Tom Stoppard** 1937- British dramatist: *Albert's Bridge* (1969)

14 The safest general characterization of the European philosophical tradition is that it consists of a series of footnotes to Plato.

- **Alfred North Whitehead** 1861-1947 English philosopher and mathematician: *Process and Reality* (1929)

15 What is your aim in philosophy?— To show the fly the way out of the fly-bottle.

- **Ludwig Wittgenstein** 1889-1951 Austrian-born philosopher: *Philosophische Untersuchungen* (1953)

16 You would not like Nietzsche, sir. He is fundamentally unsound.
Jeeves to Bertie Wooster

- **P. G. Wodehouse** 1881-1975 English-born writer: *My Man Jeeves* (1919)

Poetry

see also **LITERATURE, POETS, WRITING**

....

I'd as soon write free verse as play tennis with the net down.　**Robert Frost**

1　There was a young man called
　　MacNabbiter
　　Who had an organ of prodigious
　　diameter.
　　But it was not the size
　　That gave girls the surprise,
　　'Twas his rhythm—Iambic Pentameter.
　　▪ **Anonymous**: in *Ned Sherrin in his
　　Anecdotage* (1993)

2　There was a young man from Peru
　　Whose limericks stopped at line two.
　　▪ **Anonymous**: Harry Mathews and Alastair
　　Brotchie (eds) *Oulipo Compendium* (1998)

3　Haikus are easy. But sometimes they
　　don't make sense. Refrigerator.
　　▪ **Anonymous**: saying

4　'*I* can repeat poetry as well as other folk
　　if it comes to that—' 'Oh, it needn't
　　come to that!' Alice hastily said.
　　▪ **Lewis Carroll** 1832-98 English writer and
　　logician: *Through the Looking-Glass* (1872)

5　'By God,' quod he, 'for pleynly, at a
　　word,
　　Thy drasty rymyng is nat worth a
　　toord!'
　　▪ **Geoffrey Chaucer** c.1343-1400 English poet:
　　The Canterbury Tales 'Sir Thopas'

6　Poets have been mysteriously silent on
　　the subject of cheese.
　　▪ **G. K. Chesterton** 1874-1936 English
　　essayist, novelist, and poet: *Alarms and
　　Discursions* (1910)

7　*on the haiku:*
　　To convey one's mood in seventeen
　　syllables is very diffic.
　　▪ **John Cooper Clarke** 1949-　English poet:
　　attributed

8　*Laman Blanchard, a young poet, had
　　submitted some verses entitled 'Orient Pearls
　　at Random Strung' to* Household Words*:
　　Dear Blanchard, too much string—

Yours. C.D.
　　▪ **Charles Dickens** 1812-70 English novelist:
　　Frederick Locker-Lampson *My Confidences*
　　(1896)

9　Immature poets imitate; mature poets
　　steal.
　　▪ **T. S. Eliot** 1888-1965 American-born British
　　poet, critic, and dramatist: *The Sacred Wood*
　　(1920) 'Philip Massinger'

10　I'd as soon write free verse as play
　　tennis with the net down.
　　▪ **Robert Frost** 1874-1963 American poet:
　　Edward Lathem *Interviews with Robert Frost*
　　(1966)

11　There are the women whose husbands
　　I meet on aeroplanes
　　Who close their briefcases and ask,
　　'What are *you* in?'
　　I look in their eyes, I tell them I am in
　　poetry....
　　▪ **Donald Hall** 1928-　American poet: 'To a
　　Waterfowl' (1971)

12　The notion of expressing sentiments
　　in short lines having similar sounds at
　　their ends seems as remote as mangoes
　　on the moon.
　　▪ **Philip Larkin** 1922-85 English poet: letter to
　　Barbara Pym, 22 January 1975

13　Writing a book of poetry is like
　　dropping a rose petal down the Grand
　　Canyon and waiting for the echo.
　　▪ **Don Marquis** 1878-1937 American poet and
　　journalist: E. Anthony *O Rare Don Marquis*
　　(1962)

14　My favourite poem is the one that starts
　　'Thirty days hath September' because it
　　actually tells you something.
　　▪ **Groucho Marx** 1890-1977 American film
　　comedian: Ned Sherrin *Cutting Edge* (1984);
　　attributed

15 All that is not prose is verse; and all that
is not verse is prose.
- **Molière** 1622-73 French comic dramatist:
Le Bourgeois Gentilhomme (1671)

16 Of all the literary scenes
Saddest this sight to me:
The graves of little magazines
Who died to make verse free.
- **Keith Preston** 1884-1927 American poet:
'The Liberators'

17 *response on being told by Philip Larkin that
there was no known rhyme for Stoke Poges:*
An incontinent man from Stoke Poges
At the theatre would often soak loges.
To take care of that
He'd pee in his hat

Or a chamber pot made in Limoges.
- **Ken Thomson** Australian writer and editor:
in 1946; told to the Editor

18 *to Rousseau, of his 'Ode to Posterity':*
It will never reach its address.
- **Voltaire** 1694-1778 French writer and
philosopher: attributed

19 All bad poetry springs from genuine
feeling.
- **Oscar Wilde** 1854-1900 Irish dramatist and
poet: 'The Critic as Artist' (1891)

20 Peotry is sissy stuff that rhymes. Weedy
people sa la and fie and swoon when
they see a bunch of daffodils.
- **Geoffrey Willans** 1911-58 and **Ronald
Searle** 1920-2012: *Down with Skool!* (1953)

Poets

see also **POETRY**

··

Dr Donne's verses are like the peace of God; they pass all understanding.   **James I**

1 We learn from Horace, Homer
sometimes sleeps;
We feel without him: Wordsworth
sometimes wakes.
- **Lord Byron** 1788-1824 English poet: *Don Juan*
(1819-24)

2 Even the greatest poets need something
to cling to. Keats had Beauty; Milton had
God. T. S. Eliot's standby was Worry.
- **John Carey** 1934- British literary scholar:
in *Sunday Times* 25 September 1988

3 I used to think all poets were Byronic.
They're mostly wicked as a ginless tonic
And wild as pension plans.
- **Wendy Cope** 1945- English poet: 'Triolet'
(1986)

4 *the young Stephen Spender had told Eliot of
his wish to become a poet:*
I can understand your wanting to write
poems, but I don't quite know what you
mean by 'being a poet'…
- **T. S. Eliot** 1888-1965 American-born
British poet, critic, and dramatist: Stephen
Spender *World within World* (1951)

5 Osbert was wonderful, as you would

expect, and Edith, of course, but then
we had this rather lugubrious man in a
suit, and he read a poem…I think it was
called The Desert. And first the girls got
the giggles and then I did and then even
the King.
*of an evening at Windsor during the war,
arranged by Osbert Sitwell, at which T. S.
Eliot read from 'The Waste Land' to the King
and Queen and the Princesses*
- **Queen Elizabeth, the Queen Mother**
1900-2002: private conversation, reported
in *Spectator* 30 June 1990

6 A poet who reads his work in public
may have other nasty habits.
- **Robert Heinlein** 1907-88 American science
fiction writer: *Time Enough for Love* (1973)

7 What is a modern poet's fate?
To write his thoughts upon a slate;
The critic spits on what is done,
Gives it a wipe—and all is gone.
- **Thomas Hood** 1799-1845 English poet and
humorist: 'A Joke', in Hallam Tennyson
Alfred Lord Tennyson (1897); not found in
Hood's *Complete Works*

8 I wish Shelley had been at Harrow.
- **James John Hornby** 1826-1909 English headmaster of Eton: Henry S. Salt *Percy Bysshe Shelley* (1896)

9 My poetry, so far as I could make out, sprang chiefly from physical conditions, such as a relaxed sore throat during my most prolific period.
- **A. E. Housman** 1859-1936 English poet: letter, 5 February 1933

10 Dr Donne's verses are like the peace of God; they pass all understanding.
- **James I** 1566-1625 British king: remark recorded by Archdeacon Plume (1630-1704)

11 *on the relative merits of two minor poets:*
Sir, there is no settling the point of precedency between a louse and a flea.
- **Samuel Johnson** 1709-84 English poet, critic, and lexicographer: James Boswell *Life of Samuel Johnson* (1791) 1783

12 We had the old crow over at Hull recently, looking like a Christmas present from Easter Island.
of Ted Hughes
- **Philip Larkin** 1922-85 English poet: letter, 1975

13 *on being asked by Stephen Spender in the 1930s how best a poet could serve the Communist cause:*
Go to Spain and get killed.

The movement needs a Byron.
- **Harry Pollitt** 1890-1960 British Communist politician: Frank Johnson *Out of Order* (1982); attributed, perhaps apocryphal

14 While pensive poets painful vigils keep, Sleepless themselves, to give their readers sleep.
- **Alexander Pope** 1688-1744 English poet: *The Dunciad* (1742)

15 Sir, I admit your gen'ral rule
That every poet is a fool:
But you yourself may serve to show it,
That every fool is not a poet.
- **Alexander Pope** 1688-1744 English poet: 'Epigram from the French' (1732)

16 For years a secret shame destroyed my peace—
I'd not read Eliot, Auden or MacNeice.
But then I had a thought that brought me hope—
Neither had Chaucer, Shakespeare, Milton, Pope.
- **Justin Richardson** 1900-75 British poet: 'Take Heart, Illiterates' (1966)

17 Meredith's a prose Browning, and so is Browning.
- **Oscar Wilde** 1854-1900 Irish dramatist and poet: *Intentions* (1891) 'The Critic as Artist'

18 ACQUAINTANCE: How are you?
YEATS: Not very well. I can only write prose today.
- **W. B. Yeats** 1865-1939 Irish poet: attributed

Political Parties

The Labour Party is going around stirring up apathy.   **William Whitelaw**

1 CHILD: Mamma, are Tories born wicked, or do they grow wicked afterwards?
MOTHER: They are born wicked, and grow worse.
- **Anonymous**: G. W. E. Russell *Collections and Recollections* (1898)

2 A liberal is a man who leaves the room before the fight begins.
- **Heywood Broun** 1888-1939 American journalist: R. E. Drennan *Wit's End* (1973)

3 There's nothing so improves the mood of the Party as the imminent execution of a senior colleague.
- **Alan Clark** 1928-99 British Conservative politician: diary, 13 July 1990

4 Vote Labour and you build castles in the air. Vote Conservative and you can live in them.
- **David Frost** 1939- English broadcaster: *That Was The Week That Was* (BBC TV, 1962)

5 I never dared be radical when young
For fear it would make me conservative
when old.
- **Robert Frost** 1874-1963 American poet:
'Precaution' (1936)

6 I often think it's comical
How Nature always does contrive
That every boy and every gal,
That's born into the world alive,
Is either a little Liberal,
Or else a little Conservative!
- **W. S. Gilbert** 1836-1911 English writer:
Iolanthe (1882)

7 Conservatives do not believe that the
political struggle is the most important
thing in life…The simplest of them
prefer fox-hunting—the wisest religion.
- **Lord Hailsham** 1907-2001 British
Conservative politician: *The Case for
Conservatism* (1947)

8 *at a photocall when Lady Thatcher said to
him 'You should be on my right':*
That would be difficult.
- **Edward Heath** 1916-2005 British
Conservative statesman: in *Times* 24 April
1999 'Quotes of the Week'

9 Voting Tory will cause your wife to
have bigger breasts and increase your
chances of owning a BMW M3.
- **Boris Johnson** 1964- British Conservative
politician: attributed, in *Sunday Times* 1 May
2005

10 The Tory Party only panics in a crisis.
- **Iain Macleod** 1913-70 British Conservative
politician: attributed

11 As usual the Liberals offer a mixture
of sound and original ideas.
Unfortunately none of the sound
ideas is original and none of the
original ideas is sound.
- **Harold Macmillan** 1894-1986 British
Conservative statesman: speech to London
Conservatives, 7 March 1961

12 I have only one firm belief about the
American political system, and that
is this: God is a Republican and Santa
Claus is a Democrat.
- **P. J. O'Rourke** 1947- American humorous
writer: *Parliament of Whores* (1991)

13 I will make a bargain with the
Republicans. If they will stop telling
lies about Democrats, we will stop
telling the truth about them.
- **Adlai Stevenson** 1900-65 American
Democratic politician: speech during 1952
Presidential campaign; Leon Harris *The Fine
Art of Political Wit* (1965)

14 The Labour Party is going around
stirring up apathy.
- **William Whitelaw** 1918-99 British
Conservative politician: recalled by Alan
Watkins as a characteristic 'Willieism', in
Observer 1 May 1983

Politicians

see also **PEOPLE, POLITICS, PRESIDENTS, PRIME MINISTERS**

a politician is an arse upon which everyone has sat except a man.   **e. e. cummings**

1 When the political columnists say 'Every
thinking man' they mean themselves,
and when candidates appeal to 'Every
intelligent voter' they mean everybody
who is going to vote for them.
- **Franklin P. Adams** 1881-1960 American
journalist and humorist: *Nods and Becks*
(1944)

2 My name is George Nathaniel Curzon,
I am a most superior person.
My face is pink, my hair is sleek,
I dine at Blenheim once a week.
of Lord Curzon
- **Anonymous**: *The Masque of Balliol* (c.1880),
in W. G. Hiscock *The Balliol Rhymes* (1939,
the last two lines are a later addition)

3 Dalton McGuinty: He's an evil reptilian kitten-eater from another planet.
Canadian Conservative press release attacking the Liberal leader during September 2003 Ontario election campaign
- **Anonymous**: in *London Free Press News* 13 September 2003

4 Beaverbrook is so pleased to be in the Government that he is like the town tart who has finally married the Mayor!
- **Beverley Baxter** 1891-1964 Canadian-born British journalist and Conservative politician: Chips Channon diary 12 June 1940

5 I am the very master of the
    multipurpose metaphor,
I put them into speeches which I always
    feel the better for.
The speed of my delivery is totally
    vehicular,
I'm burning with a passion about
    nothing in particular.
I'm well acquainted too with matters
    technological,
I'm able to explain myself in phrases
    tautological.
My language is poetical and full of
    hidden promises…
It's like the raging torrent of a thousand
    Dylan Thomases.
- **Alistair Beaton** 1947- Scottish satirist: 'I am the very Model…', sung by Pooh-Bach (*Minister for everything else. Formerly Neil Kinnock*) in Ned Sherrin and Alistair Beaton *The Metropolitan Mikado* (1985)

6 The right kind of leader for the Labour Party…a desiccated calculating machine.
generally taken as referring to Hugh Gaitskell, although Bevan specifically denied it in an interview with Robin Day on 28 April 1959
- **Aneurin Bevan** 1897-1960 British Labour politician: Michael Foot *Aneurin Bevan* (1973) vol. 2

7 *Attlee is said to have remarked that Herbert Morrison was his own worst enemy:*
Not while I'm alive he ain't.
- **Ernest Bevin** 1881-1951 British Labour politician and trade unionist: Paul Johnson (ed.) *The Oxford Book of Political Anecdotes* (1986), introduction; also attributed to Bevin of Aneurin Bevan

8 JONES: What's your favourite political joke?
CAMERON: Nick Clegg.
- **David Cameron** 1966- British Conservative statesman: *Cameron on Cameron: conversations with Dylan Jones* (2008)

9 QUESTION: What are the desirable qualifications for any young man who wishes to become a politician?
MR CHURCHILL: It is the ability to foretell what is going to happen tomorrow, next week, next month, and next year. And to have the ability afterwards to explain why it didn't happen.
- **Winston Churchill** 1874-1965 British Conservative statesman: B. Adler *Churchill Wit* (1965)

10 There but for the grace of God, goes God.
of Stafford Cripps
- **Winston Churchill** 1874-1965 British Conservative statesman: P. Brendon *Churchill* (1984)

11 In the end we are all sacked and it's always awful.
- **Alan Clark** 1928-99 British Conservative politician: diary 21 June 1983

12 a politician is an arse upon which everyone has sat except a man.
- **e. e. cummings** 1894-1962 American poet: *1 x 1* (1944)

13 I view this able and energetic man with some detachment. He is loyal to his own career but only incidentally to anything or anyone else.
of Richard Crossman
- **Hugh Dalton** 1887-1962 British Labour politician: diary 17 September 1941

14 It is not necessary that every time he rises he should give his famous imitation of a semi-house-trained polecat.
of Norman Tebbit
- **Michael Foot** 1913-2010 British Labour politician: speech in the House of Commons 2 March 1978

15 *on being asked immediately after the Munich crisis if he were not worn out by the late nights:*
No, not exactly. But it spoils one's eye

for the high birds.

- **Lord Halifax** 1881-1959 British Conservative politician: Paul Johnson (ed.) *The Oxford Book of Political Anecdotes* (1986)

16 Peter Mandelson is someone who can skulk in broad daylight.

- **Simon Hoggart** 1946- English journalist: in *Guardian* 10 July 1998

17 Hello. I'm your MP. Actually I'm your candidate. Gosh!

- **Boris Johnson** 1964- British Conservative politician: canvassing in Henley, 2005

18 All politicians in the end are like crazed wasps in a jam jar, each individually convinced that they are going to make it.

- **Boris Johnson** 1964- British Conservative politician: on *Desert Island Discs* BBC Radio 4, 30 October 2005

19 Like some cut-price edition of David Cameron hastily knocked off by a Shanghai sweatshop to satisfy unexpected market demand.
of Nick Clegg

- **Boris Johnson** 1964- British Conservative politician: in *Daily Telegraph* 8 February 2010

20 *of her fellow members of the Afghan parliament:*
A stable or a zoo is better, at least there you have a donkey that carries a load and a cow that provides milk.

- **Malalai Joya** 1978- Afghan politician: in *Independent* 22 May 2007

21 I once said cynically of a politician, 'He'll double-cross that bridge when he comes to it.'

- **Oscar Levant** 1906-72 American pianist: *Memoirs of an Amnesiac* (1965)

22 Many people see Eva Peron as either a saint or the incarnation of Satan. That means I can definitely identify with her.

- **Madonna** 1958- American pop singer and actress: in *Newsweek* 5 February 1996

23 did you ever
notice that when
a politician
does get an idea

he usually
gets it all wrong.

- **Don Marquis** 1878-1937 American poet and journalist: *archys life of mehitabel* (1933) 'archygrams'

24 You can put lipstick on a pig, but it's still a pig.

- **Barack Obama** 1961- American Democratic statesman: speech in Lebanon, Virginia, 9 September 2008; see **politicians** 27

25 If I saw Mr Haughey buried at midnight at a crossroads, with a stake driven through his heart—politically speaking—I should continue to wear a clove of garlic round my neck, just in case.

- **Conor Cruise O'Brien** 1917-2008 Irish politician, writer, and journalist: in *Observer* 10 October 1982

26 The majority of the members of the Irish parliament are professional politicians, in the sense that otherwise they would not be given jobs minding mice at a crossroads.

- **Flann O'Brien** 1911-66 Irish novelist and journalist: *The Hair of the Dogma* (1977)

27 What's the difference between a hockey mom and a pitbull? Lipstick.

- **Sarah Palin** 1964- American Republican politician: speech to Republican Party convention, 3 September 2008; see **politicians** 24

28 DEMOSTHENES: The Athenians will kill thee, Phocion, should they go crazy.
PHOCION: But they will kill thee, should they come to their senses.

- **Phocion** c.402-317 BC Athenian soldier: Plutarch *Life of Phocion and Cato the Younger* (Loeb ed., 1919)

29 Gordon Brown is from Mars, David Cameron is from Venus.

- **Andrew Rawnsley** 1962- English journalist: in *Observer* 19 November 2006

30 He may be a son of a bitch, but he's our son of a bitch.
on President Somoza of Nicaragua, 1938

- **Franklin D. Roosevelt** 1882-1945 American Democratic statesman: Jonathon Green *The Book of Political Quotes* (1982)

31 *on deciding to run for Governor of California:*
The most difficult decision I've ever made in my entire life, except for the one in 1978 when I decided to get a bikini wax.
- **Arnold Schwarzenegger** 1947- Austrian-born American actor and Republican politician: on the NBC TV *Tonight Show* 6 August 2003

32 *explaining why he avoided meeting MPs:*
If I knew them, it might spoil the purity of my hatred.
- **Norman Shrapnel** 1912-2004 English journalist: in *Guardian* 3 February 2004

33 A politician is a man who understands government, and it takes a politician to run a government. A statesman is a politician who's been dead 10 or 15 years.
- **Harry S. Truman** 1884-1972 American Democratic statesman: in *New York World Telegram and Sun* 12 April 1958

34 If you want a friend in Washington, get a dog.
- **Harry S. Truman** 1884-1972 American Democratic statesman: attributed

35 I cannot bring myself to vote for a woman who has been voice-trained to speak to me as though my dog has just died.
of Margaret Thatcher
- **Keith Waterhouse** 1929-2009 British journalist and writer: in 1979, attributed

36 It's a pity, as my husband says, that more politicians are not bastards by birth instead of vocation.
- **Katharine Whitehorn** 1928- English journalist: in *Observer* 12 January 1964

Politics

see also **DEMOCRACY, DIPLOMACY, GOVERNMENT, HOUSE OF LORDS, MEMBERS, POLITICAL PARTIES, PRESIDENTS, PRIME MINISTERS**

....

If voting changed anything they'd abolish it.   **Ken Livingstone**

1 Practical politics consists in ignoring facts.
- **Henry Brooks Adams** 1838-1918 American historian: *The Education of Henry Adams* (1907)

2 Politics is the gentle art of getting votes from the poor and campaign funds from the rich by promising to protect each from the other.
- **Oscar Ameringer** 1870-1943 American humorist: Ferdinand Lundberg *Scoundrels All* (1968)

3 *Je suis Marxiste—tendance Groucho.*
I am a Marxist—of the Groucho tendency.
- **Anonymous**: slogan found at Nanterre in Paris, 1968

4 Vote for the man who promises least; he'll be the least disappointing.
- **Bernard Baruch** 1870-1965 American financier and presidential adviser: Meyer Berger *New York* (1960)

5 There are two ways of getting into the Cabinet—you can crawl in or kick your way in.
- **Aneurin Bevan** 1897-1960 British Labour politician: attributed

6 *definition of politics:*
A strife of interests masquerading as a contest of principles. The conduct of public affairs for private advantage.
- **Ambrose Bierce** 1842-c.1914 American writer: *The Enlarged Devil's Dictionary* (1967)

7 The liberals can understand everything but people who don't understand them.
- **Lenny Bruce** 1925-66 American comedian: John Cohen (ed.) *The Essential Lenny Bruce* (1967)

8 Politics is like a chicken-coop, and those inside get to behave as if their little run

were all the world.

- **John Buchan** 1875-1940 Scottish novelist: *Greenmantle* (1916)

9   Have you ever seen a candidate talking to a rich person on television?

- **Art Buchwald** 1925-2007 American humorist: Laurence J. Peter (ed.) *Quotations for our Time* (1977)

10 Dear Chief Secretary, I'm afraid there is no money.

- **Liam Byrne** 1970- British Labour politician: letter left for his successor as Chief Secretary to the Treasury, David Laws, revealed by Laws, 17 May 2010

11 *to Franklin Roosevelt on the likely duration of the Yalta conference with Stalin:*
I do not see any other way of realizing our hopes about World Organization in five or six days. Even the Almighty took seven.

- **Winston Churchill** 1874-1965 British Conservative statesman: *The Second World War* (1954) vol. 6

12 Politics are almost as exciting as war and quite as dangerous. In war you can only be killed once, but in politics— many times.

- **Winston Churchill** 1874-1965 British Conservative statesman: attributed

13 There are no true friends in politics. We are all sharks circling, and waiting, for traces of blood to appear in the water.

- **Alan Clark** 1928-99 British Conservative politician: diary, 30 November 1990

14 *on being attacked by Egyptian protesters:*
I felt bad that good tomatoes were wasted.

- **Hillary Rodham Clinton** 1947- American lawyer and politician: press conference, Washington, 16 July 2012

15 M is for Marx
And Movement of Masses
And Massing of Arses.
And Clashing of Classes.

- **Cyril Connolly** 1903-74 English writer: 'Where Engels Fears to Tread'

16 The duty of an Opposition [is] very simple...to oppose everything, and

propose nothing.

- **Lord Derby** 1799-1869 British Conservative statesman: quoting 'Mr Tierney, a great Whig authority'; House of Lords 4 June 1841

17 'It's always best on these occasions to do what the mob do.' 'But suppose there are two mobs?' suggested Mr Snodgrass. 'Shout with the largest,' replied Mr Pickwick.

- **Charles Dickens** 1812-70 English novelist: *Pickwick Papers* (1837)

18 Men destined to the highest places should beware of badinage...An insular country subject to fogs, and with a powerful middle class, requires grave statesmen.

- **Benjamin Disraeli** 1804-81 British Tory statesman and novelist: *Endymion* (1880)

19 *of Labour's 'prawn cocktail offensive' prior to the 1992 election campaign:*
Never before have so many crustaceans died in vain.

- **Michael Heseltine** 1933- British Conservative politician: speech, 1992

20 *on Mussolini's allowing himself to be photographed in a bathing suit:*
A really great statesman doesn't do that.

- **Adolf Hitler** 1889-1945 German dictator: Joachim C. Fest *The Face of the Third Reich* (1970)

21 My policy on cake is still pro having it and pro eating it!

- **Boris Johnson** 1964- British Conservative politician: interview in *Observer* 19 October 2008

22 BOSWELL: So, Sir, you laugh at schemes of political improvement.
JOHNSON: Why, Sir, most schemes of political improvement are very laughable things.

- **Samuel Johnson** 1709-84 English poet, critic, and lexicographer: James Boswell *Life of Samuel Johnson* (1791) 26 October 1769

23 Gratitude is not a normal feature of political life.

- **Lord Kilmuir** 1900-67 British Conservative politician and lawyer: *Political Adventure* (1964)

24 *on her husband's election as leader of the Labour Party in 1983:*
I don't see how I can get Neil to help with the shopping ever again.
- **Glenys Kinnock** 1944- British politician: attributed, in *Guardian* 4 October 1994

25 Politics is just show business for ugly people.
- **Jay Leno** 1950- American comedian: attributed, 1995

26 If voting changed anything they'd abolish it.
- **Ken Livingstone** 1945- British Labour politician: in *Independent* 12 April 1996

27 If you want to succeed in politics, you must keep your conscience well under control.
- **David Lloyd George** 1863-1945 British Liberal statesman: Lord Riddell diary 23 April 1919

28 Being in politics is like being a football coach. You have to be smart enough to understand the game, and dumb enough to think it's important.
while campaigning for the presidency
- **Eugene McCarthy** 1916-2005 American Democratic politician: in an interview, 1968

29 There are three bodies no sensible man directly challenges: the Roman Catholic Church, the Brigade of Guards and the National Union of Mineworkers.
- **Harold Macmillan** 1894-1986 British Conservative statesman: in *Observer* 22 February 1981

30 I have never found in a long experience of politics that criticism is ever inhibited by ignorance.
- **Harold Macmillan** 1894-1986 British Conservative statesman: Leon Harris *The Fine Art of Politcal Wit* (1965)

31 *when Rab Butler produced a pile of papers:*
MACMILLAN: What are those?
BUTLER: Policies.
MACMILLAN: Oh, I beg you, not policies. They come back to haunt you. Give them broad sunlit uplands, dear boy.
- **Harold Macmillan** 1894-1986 British Conservative statesman: at a meeting in the family home, Birch grove in Sussex, recalled by Macmillan's grandson, the Earl of Stockton; attributed, in *Times* 16 July 2006

32 *on privatization:*
First of all the Georgian silver goes, and then all that nice furniture that used to be in the saloon. Then the Canalettos go.
- **Harold Macmillan** 1894-1986 British Conservative statesman: speech to the Tory Reform Group, 8 November 1985

33 A political culture that has no time for lunch is no culture at all.
- **Andrew Marr** 1959- British journalist: in *Independent* 11 January 2003

34 WOMAN HECKLER: I wouldn't vote for you if you were the Archangel Gabriel.
MENZIES: If I were the Archangel Gabriel, madam, I'm afraid you would not be in my constituency.
- **Robert Gordon Menzies** 1894-1978 Australian Liberal statesman: R. Robinson *The Wit of Sir Robert Menzies* (1966)

35 Politics is the diversion of trivial men who, when they succeed at it, become important in the eyes of more trivial men.
- **George Jean Nathan** 1882-1958 American critic: attributed

36 When I want a peerage, I shall buy it like an honest man.
- **Lord Northcliffe** 1865-1922 British newspaper proprietor: Tom Driberg *Swaff* (1974)

37 It's important to realize that I was actually black before the election.
on racism
- **Barack Obama** 1961- American Democratic statesman: interview, *The Late Show with David Letterman* 21 September 2009

38 Politics are, like God's infinite mercy, a last resort.
- **P. J. O'Rourke** 1947- American humorous writer: *Parliament of Whores* (1991)

39 Men enter local politics solely as a result of being unhappily married.
- **C. Northcote Parkinson** 1909-93 English writer: *Parkinson's Law* (1958)

40 Have I inadvertently said something foolish?
upon his opinion being cheered by the populace
- **Phocion** c.402-317 BC Athenian soldier: Plutarch *Parallel Lives* 'Phocion'

41 Politics is supposed to be the second
oldest profession. I have come to realize
that it bears a very close resemblance to
the first.
- **Ronald Reagan** 1911-2004 American
Republican statesman: at a conference in
Los Angeles, 2 March 1977

42 Status quo, you know, that is Latin for
'the mess we're in'.
- **Ronald Reagan** 1911-2004 American
Republican statesman: speech,
Washington, 16 March 1981

43 Politics is not a bad profession. If you
succeed there are many rewards, if you
disgrace yourself you can always write
a book.
- **Ronald Reagan** 1911-2004 American
Republican statesman: attributed

44 Communism is like prohibition, it's a
good idea but it won't work.
- **Will Rogers** 1879-1935 American actor
and humorist: in 1927; *Weekly Articles* (1981)
vol. 3

45 It's not cricket to picket.
- **Harold Rome** 1908-93 American
songwriter: song-title (1937)

46 He knows nothing; and he thinks he
knows everything. That points clearly
to a political career.
- **George Bernard Shaw** 1856-1950 Irish
dramatist: *Major Barbara* (1907)

47 Nature has no cure for this sort of
madness [Marxism], though I have
known a legacy from a rich relative
work wonders.
- **F. E. Smith** 1872-1930 British Conservative
politician and lawyer: *Law, Life and Letters*
(1927)

48 Minorities…are almost always in the
right.
- **Sydney Smith** 1771-1845 English clergyman
and essayist: H. Pearson *The Smith of Smiths*
(1934)

49 An independent is a guy who wants to
take the politics out of politics.
- **Adlai Stevenson** 1900-65 American
Democratic politician: Bill Adler
The Stevenson Wit (1966)

50 WOMAN AT A RALLY: Governor, every
thinking person will be voting for you.
STEVENSON: Madam, that's not enough.
I need a majority.
campaigning against Eisenhower
- **Adlai Stevenson** 1900-65 American
Democratic politician: attributed

51 I always cheer up immensely if
an attack is particularly wounding
because I think, well, if they attack me
personally, it means they have not a
single political argument left.
- **Margaret Thatcher** 1925-2013 British
Conservative stateswoman: in 1975; Iain
Dale *As I Said to Denis* (1997)

52 The country is going down the drain,
and they are squabbling about the size
of the plughole.
- **Jeremy Thorpe** 1929- British Liberal
politician: in *Time*, 1975

53 The people have spoke—the bastards.
*after being defeated in the California Senate
primary c.1962; usually quoted as 'The people
have spoken—the bastards'*
- **Dick Tuck** 1924- American Democratic
politician: in *Time* 13 August 1973

54 *on Marxism, from an expert on ants:*
Wonderful theory, wrong species.
- **Edward O. Wilson** 1929- American
sociobiologist: in *Los Angeles Times*
21 October 1994

Poverty

see also **DEBT, MONEY**

It's no disgrace t'be poor, but it might as well be.   **Frank McKinney Hubbard**

1 It's the same the whole world over,
  It's the poor wot gets the blame,
  It's the rich wot gets the gravy.
  Ain't it all a bleedin' shame?
  ▪ **Anonymous**: 'She was Poor but she was
  Honest'; sung by British soldiers in the First
  World War

2 Anyone who has ever struggled
  with poverty knows how extremely
  expensive it is to be poor.
  ▪ **James Baldwin** 1924-87 American novelist
  and essayist: *Nobody Knows My Name*
  (1961) 'Fifth Avenue, Uptown: a letter from
  Harlem'

3 What throws a monkey wrench in
  A fella's good intention?
  That nasty old invention—
  Necessity!
  ▪ **E. Y. Harburg** 1898-1981 American
  songwriter: 'Necessity' (1947)

4 It's no disgrace t'be poor, but it might
  as well be.
  ▪ **Frank McKinney Hubbard** 1868-1930
  American humorist: *Short Furrows* (1911)

5 We were so poor that if we woke up on
  Christmas day without an erection, we
  had nothing to play with.
  ▪ **Frank McCourt** 1930-2009 Irish writer:
  attributed, in *Observer* 16 November 1997

6 If only Bapu [Gandhi] knew the cost of
  setting him up in poverty!
  ▪ **Sarojini Naidu** 1879-1949 Indian politician:
  A. Campbell-Johnson *Mission with
  Mountbatten* (1951)

7 Look at me. Worked myself up from
  nothing to a state of extreme poverty.
  ▪ **S. J. Perelman** 1904-79 and **others**
  screenwriters: *Monkey Business* (1931 film)

8 Poverty is no disgrace to a man, but it is
  confoundedly inconvenient.
  ▪ **Sydney Smith** 1771-1845 English clergyman
  and essayist: J. Potter Briscoe *Sydney Smith:
  His Wit and Wisdom* (1900)

9 He was a gentleman who was generally
  spoken of as having nothing a-year, paid
  quarterly.
  ▪ **R. S. Surtees** 1805-64 English novelist:
  Mr Sponge's Sporting Tour (1853)

10 As for the virtuous poor, one can
  pity them, of course, but one cannot
  possibly admire them.
  ▪ **Oscar Wilde** 1854-1900 Irish dramatist and
  poet: *Sebastian Melmoth* (1891)

11 Like dear St Francis of Assisi I am
  wedded to Poverty: but in my case the
  marriage is not a success.
  ▪ **Oscar Wilde** 1854-1900 Irish dramatist and
  poet: letter June 1899

Power

The Pope! How many divisions has *he* got?   **Joseph Stalin**

1 She cannot see an institution without
  hitting it with her handbag.
  of Margaret Thatcher
  ▪ **Julian Critchley** 1930-2000 British
  Conservative politician and journalist: in
  Times 21 June 1982

2 So long as men worship the Caesars
  and Napoleons, Caesars and Napoleons
  will duly arise and make them
  miserable.
  ▪ **Aldous Huxley** 1894-1963 English novelist:
  Ends and Means (1937)

3 I don't want loyalty. I want *loyalty*. I want him to kiss my ass in Macy's window at high noon and tell me it smells like roses. I want his pecker in my pocket.
- **Lyndon Baines Johnson** 1908–73 American Democratic statesman: David Halberstam *The Best and the Brightest* (1972)

4 Better to have him inside the tent pissing out, than outside pissing in.
of J. Edgar Hoover
- **Lyndon Baines Johnson** 1908–73 American Democratic statesman: David Halberstam *The Best and the Brightest* (1972)

5 Knowledge is power, if you know it about the right person.
- **Ethel Watts Mumford** 1878–1940 American writer and humorist: attributed

6 Castro couldn't even go to the bathroom unless the Soviet Union put the nickel in the toilet.
- **Richard Milhous Nixon** 1913–94 American Republican statesman: interview, September 1980

7 Powerful men often succeed through the help of their wives. Powerful women only succeed in spite of their husbands.
- **Lynda Lee-Potter** 1935–2004 British journalist: in *Daily Mail* 16 May 1984

8 I'll make him an offer he can't refuse.
- **Mario Puzo** 1920–99 American novelist: *The Godfather* (1969)

9 Seven months ago I could give a single command and 541,000 people would immediately obey it. Today I can't get a plumber to come to my house.
- **H. Norman Schwarzkopf III** 1934–2012 American general: in *Newsweek* 11 November 1991

10 The Pope! How many divisions has *he* got?
on being asked to encourage Catholicism in Russia by way of conciliating the Pope
- **Joseph Stalin** 1879–1953 Soviet dictator: on 13 May 1935

Praise and Flattery

What really flatters a man is that you think him worth flattering.
George Bernard Shaw

1 I once had a rose named after me and I was very flattered. But then I read the description in the catalogue: no good in a bed, but fine up against a wall.
- **Anonymous**: saying, very recently associated with Eleanor Roosevelt

2 The advantage of doing one's praising for oneself is that one can lay it on so thick and exactly in the right places.
- **Samuel Butler** 1835–1902 English novelist: *The Way of All Flesh* (1903) ch. 34

3 If a man is vain, flatter. If timid, flatter. If boastful, flatter. In all history, too much flattery never lost a gentleman.
- **Kathryn Cravens** 1898–1991 American broadcaster: *Pursuit of Gentlemen* (1951)

4 We authors, Ma'am.
to Queen Victoria after the publication of Leaves from the Journal of our Life in the Highlands in 1868
- **Benjamin Disraeli** 1804–81 British Tory statesman and novelist: Elizabeth Longford *Victoria R.I.* (1964); attributed

5 The others were only my wives. But you, my dear, will be my widow.
allaying his fifth wife's jealousy of his previous wives
- **Sacha Guitry** 1885–1957 French actor and dramatist: attributed

6 I live for your agglomerated lucubrations.
to H. G. Wells
- **Henry James** 1843–1916 American novelist: letter, 18 November 1902

7 [Women] hate flattery, so they tell you; and when you say, 'Ah, darling, it isn't flattery in your case, it's plain, sober truth; you really are, without

exaggeration, the most beautiful...the most perfect human creature...' they will smile a quiet approving smile.
- **Jerome K. Jerome** 1859-1927 English writer: *Idle Thoughts of an Idle Fellow* (1886)

8 To refuse to accept praise is to want to be praised twice over.
- **Duc de la Rochefoucauld** 1613-80 French moralist: *Maxims* (1678)

9 Nine out of ten males will believe anything, especially if it confirms their virility.
- **Andrea Martin** 1947- American actress: attributed; Mary Unterbrink *Funny Women* (1987)

10 What really flatters a man is that you think him worth flattering.
- **George Bernard Shaw** 1856-1950 Irish dramatist: *John Bull's Other Island* (1907)

11 Among the smaller duties of life, I hardly know one more important than that of not praising where praise is not due.
- **Sydney Smith** 1771-1845 English clergyman and essayist: Saba Holland *Memoir* (1855)

12 I suppose flattery hurts no one, that is, if he doesn't inhale.
- **Adlai Stevenson** 1900-65 American Democratic politician: television broadcast, 30 March 1952

Pregnancy *see* BIRTH AND PREGNANCY

Prejudice and Tolerance

Tolerance is only another name for indifference.   **W. Somerset Maugham**

1 You take the girl, and I'll keep the car, okay?
to a policeman, on being stopped in Philadelphia while driving his Ferrari with a white woman passenger
- **Miles Davis** 1926-91 American jazz musician: John Szwed *So What: the life of Miles Davis* (2002)

2 Being a star has made it possible for me to get insulted in places where the average Negro could never *hope* to go and get insulted.
- **Sammy Davis Jnr.** 1925-90 American entertainer: *Yes I Can* (1965)

3 I am free of all prejudice. I hate everyone equally.
- **W. C. Fields** 1880-1946 American humorist: attributed, in *Saturday Review* 28 January 1967

4 CONGRESSMAN STARNES: You are quoting from this Marlowe. Is he a Communist?
HALLIE FLANAGAN: I am very sorry. I was quoting from Christopher Marlowe.
- **Hallie Flanagan** 1890-1969 American theatre director: in hearing on the Federal Theatre Project by the House Un-American Activities Committee, 6 December 1938

5 Wouldn't it be a hell of a thing if all this was burnt cork and you people were being tolerant for nothing?
- **Dick Gregory** 1932- American comedian and civil rights activist: *Nigger* (1965)

6 You gotta say this for the white race—its self-confidence knows no bounds. Who else could go to a small island in the South Pacific where there's no poverty, no crime, no unemployment, no war and no worry—and call it a 'primitive society'?
- **Dick Gregory** 1932- American comedian and civil rights activist: *From the Back of the Bus* (1962)

7 Without the aid of prejudice and custom, I should not be able to find my way across the room.
- **William Hazlitt** 1778-1830 English essayist: 'On Prejudice' (1830)

8 If there were any of Australia's original inhabitants living in Melbourne they were kept well out of the way of nice people; unless, of course, they could sing.
- **Barry Humphries** 1934- Australian actor and writer: *More Please* (1992)

9 When they call you articulate, that's another way of saying 'He talks good for a black guy'.
- **Ice-T** 1958- American rap musician: in *Independent* 30 December 1995 'Interviews of the Year'

10 Though I've belted you and flayed you,
By the livin' Gawd that made you,
You're a better man than I am, Gunga Din!
- **Rudyard Kipling** 1865-1936 English writer and poet: 'Gunga Din' (1892)

11 *refused admittance to a smart Californian beach club:*
Since my daughter is only half-Jewish, could she go in the water up to her knees?
- **Groucho Marx** 1890-1977 American film comedian: in *Observer* 21 August 1977

12 Tolerance is only another name for indifference.
- **W. Somerset Maugham** 1874-1965 English novelist: *A Writer's Notebook* (1949) written in 1896

13 The South African police would leave no stone unturned to see that nothing disturbed the even terror of their lives.
- **Tom Sharpe** 1928- British novelist: *Indecent Exposure* (1973)

14 You must always look for the *Ulsterior motive.*
of C. S. Lewis as an Ulsterman
- **J. R. R. Tolkien** 1892-1973 British philologist and writer: A. N. Wilson *Life of C. S. Lewis* (1986)

Present *see* PAST, PRESENT, AND FUTURE

Presidents

see also **POLITICIANS, POLITICS**

The vice-presidency isn't worth a pitcher of warm piss.   **John Nance Garner**

1 Richard Nixon impeached himself. He gave us Gerald Ford as his revenge.
- **Bella Abzug** 1920-98 American Democratic politician: in *Rolling Stone*; Linda Botts *Loose Talk* (1980)

2 Anybody that wants the presidency so much that he'll spend two years organizing and campaigning for it is not to be trusted with the office.
- **David Broder** 1929- American columnist: in *Washington Post* 18 July 1973

3 *of President Nixon:*
I worship the quicksand he walks on.
- **Art Buchwald** 1925-2007 American humorist: attributed, 1974

4 The US presidency is a Tudor monarchy plus telephones.
- **Anthony Burgess** 1917-93 English novelist and critic: George Plimpton (ed.) *Writers at Work* 4th Series (1977)

5 I said to him the other day, 'George, if you really want to end tyranny in this world, you're going to have to stay up later'...Nine o'clock and Mr Excitement here is in bed, and I am watching *Desperate Housewives.*
on George W. Bush's habit of being in bed by 9 p.m.
- **Laura Bush** 1946- American First Lady: White House Correspondents' Association dinner, 30 April 2005

6 God Almighty was satisfied with
Ten Commandments. Mr Wilson
requires Fourteen Points.
- **Georges Clemenceau** 1841-1929 French
statesman: during the Peace Conference
negotiations in 1919; Leon Harris *The Fine
Art of Political Wit* (1965)

7 Being president is like running a
cemetery; you've got a lot of people
under you and nobody's listening.
- **Bill Clinton** 1946- American Democratic
statesman: speech in Galesburg, Illinois,
10 January 1995

8 A hard dog to keep on the porch.
on her husband, Bill Clinton
- **Hillary Rodham Clinton** 1947- American
lawyer and Democratic politician: in
Guardian 2 August 1999

9 It is a great advantage to a President, and
a major source of safety to the country,
for him to know he is not a great man.
- **Calvin Coolidge** 1872-1933 American
Republican statesman: *Autobiography* (1929)

10 Mr Speaker, the Honourable
Gentleman has conceived three times
and brought forth nothing.
*when Lincoln, making his first speech in the
Illinois legislature, had three times begun
'Mr Speaker, I conceive'*
- **Stephen A. Douglas** 1813-61 American
politician: Leon Harris *The Fine Art of
Political Wit* (1965)

11 *on his office:*
The vice-presidency isn't worth a
pitcher of warm piss.
- **John Nance Garner** 1868-1967 American
Democratic politician: O. C. Fisher *Cactus
Jack* (1978) ch. 11

12 I was happy when I first heard Ronald
Reagan was running for the presidency.
I've always thought, once you're in
show business you should stay in it.
- **Bob Hope** 1903-2003 American comedian:
attributed

13 So dumb he can't fart and chew gum at
the same time.
of Gerald Ford
- **Lyndon Baines Johnson** 1908-73 American
Democratic statesman: Richard Reeves
A Ford, not a Lincoln (1975)

14 Ronald Reagan, the President who
never told bad news to the American
people.
- **Garrison Keillor** 1942- American
humorous writer and broadcaster: *We Are
Still Married* (1989), introduction

15 The pay is good and I can walk to work.
on becoming President of the U.S.A.
- **John F. Kennedy** 1917-63 American
Democratic statesman: attributed; James B.
Simpson (ed.) *Simpson's Contemporary
Quotations* (1988)

16 BARBARA WALTERS: What would be your
first act on becoming President?
JOHN F. KENNEDY JNR: Call Uncle Teddy
and gloat.
- **John F. Kennedy Jnr.** 1960-99 American
lawyer: in *Sunday Telegraph* 25 July 1999;
recalled by Ted Kennedy at his nephew's
memorial service on 23 July 1999

17 He looked at me as if I was a side dish
he hadn't ordered.
referring to President Taft
- **Ring Lardner** 1885-1933 American writer:
attributed, in A. K. Adams *The Home Book
of Humorous Quotations* (1969)

18 He [Calvin Coolidge] slept more than
any other President, whether by day or
by night. Nero fiddled, but Coolidge
only snored.
- **H. L. Mencken** 1880-1956 American
journalist and literary critic: in *American
Mercury* April 1933

19 The battle for the mind of Ronald
Reagan was like the trench warfare
of World War I. Never have so many
fought so hard for such barren terrain.
- **Peggy Noonan** 1950- American writer:
What I Saw at the Revolution (1990)

20 I trust Bush with my daughter, but
I trust Clinton with my job.
- **Craig Paterson**: in *Independent* 1 February
2003

21 Poor George, he can't help it—he was
born with a silver foot in his mouth.
of George Bush Snr
- **Ann Richards** 1933-2006 American
Democratic politician: keynote speech at
the Democratic convention, in *Independent*
20 July 1988

22 McKinley has no more backbone than a chocolate éclair!
- **Theodore Roosevelt** 1858-1919 American Republican statesman: Harry Thurston Peck *Twenty Years of the Republic* (1906)

23 *on his outspoken daughter Alice Roosevelt Longworth*
I can do one of two things. I can be president of the United States or I can control Alice. I cannot possibly do both.
- **Theodore Roosevelt** 1858-1919 American Republican statesman: John Lewis-Stempel *Fatherhood: An Anthology* (2001)

24 He didn't inhale, he didn't insert. He won't invade.
on Bill Clinton and Kosovo
- **Neil Shand**: *Loose Ends* monologue, 1999

25 *of Eisenhower's presidential campaign in 1956:*
The General has dedicated himself so many times he must feel like the cornerstone of a public building.
- **Adlai Stevenson** 1900-65 American Democratic politician: Leon Harris *The Fine Art of Political Wit* (1965)

26 He'll sit right here and he'll say do this, do that! And nothing will happen. Poor Ike—it won't be a bit like the Army.
- **Harry S. Truman** 1884-1972 American Democratic statesman: *Harry S. Truman* (1973); see

27 A triumph of the embalmer's art.
of Ronald Reagan
- **Gore Vidal** 1925-2012 American writer: in *Observer* 26 April 1981

Prime Ministers

see also **POLITICIANS, POLITICS**

....

Every Prime Minister needs a Willie.   **Margaret Thatcher**

1 *of Gordon Brown:*
A man who can lighten a room by leaving it.
- **Anonymous**: Tom Bower *Gordon Brown* (2004)

2 It is fitting that we should have buried the Unknown Prime Minister [Bonar Law] by the side of the Unknown Soldier.
- **Herbert Asquith** 1852-1928 British Liberal statesman: Robert Blake *The Unknown Prime Minister* (1955)

3 He [Lloyd George] can't see a belt without hitting below it.
- **Margot Asquith** 1864-1945 British political hostess: in *Listener* 11 June 1953 'Margot Oxford' by Lady Violet Bonham Carter

4 Few thought he was even a starter
There were many who thought themselves smarter
But he ended PM
CH and OM

An earl and a knight of the garter.
- **Clement Attlee** 1883-1967 British Labour statesman: describing himself; letter to Tom Attlee, 8 April 1956

5 There are three classes which need sanctuary more than others—birds, wild flowers, and Prime Ministers.
- **Stanley Baldwin** 1867-1947 British Conservative statesman: in *Observer* 24 May 1925

6 [Lloyd George] did not seem to care which way he travelled providing he was in the driver's seat.
- **Lord Beaverbrook** 1879-1964 Canadian-born British newspaper proprietor and Conservative politician: *The Decline and Fall of Lloyd George* (1963)

7 Sir! you have disappointed us!
We had intended you to be
The next Prime Minister but three:
The stocks were sold; the Press was squared;

The Middle Class was quite prepared.
But as it is!…My language fails!
Go out and govern New South Wales!
- **Hilaire Belloc** 1870-1953 British writer and Liberal politician: 'Lord Lundy' (1907)

8 Listening to a speech by Chamberlain is like paying a visit to Woolworth's: everything in its place and nothing above sixpence.
- **Aneurin Bevan** 1897-1960 British Labour politician: Michael Foot *Aneurin Bevan* (1962) vol.1

9 HOW DARE YOU BECOME PRIME MINISTER WHEN I'M AWAY GREAT LOVE CONSTANT THOUGHT VIOLET.
to her father, H. H. Asquith, 7 April 1908
- **Violet Bonham Carter** 1887-1969 British Liberal politician: Mark Bonham Carter and Mark Pottle (eds.) *Lantern Slides* (1996)

10 If he ever went to school without any boots it was because he was too big for them.
referring to Harold Wilson
- **Ivor Bulmer-Thomas** 1905-93 British Conservative politician: speech at the Conservative Party Conference, in *Manchester Guardian* 13 October 1949

11 That's the trouble with Anthony—half mad baronet, half beautiful woman.
of Anthony Eden
- **R. A. Butler** 1902-82 British Conservative politician: attributed

12 Ah yes, the foreign affairs debate. Dear Anthony will make the speech which dear Anthony always makes so well.
on Anthony Eden
- **R. A. Butler** 1902-82 British Conservative politician: attributed; in *Spectator* 14 June 2003

13 Pitt is to Addington
As London is to Paddington.
- **George Canning** 1770-1827 British Tory statesman: 'The Oracle' (c.1803)

14 For the purposes of recreation he [Gladstone] has selected the felling of trees, and we may usefully remark that his amusements, like his politics, are essentially destructive…The forest

laments in order that Mr Gladstone may perspire.
- **Lord Randolph Churchill** 1849-94 British Conservative politician: speech on Financial Reform, delivered in Blackpool, 24 January 1884

15 *comparing Herbert Asquith with Arthur Balfour:*
The difference between him and Arthur is that Arthur is wicked and moral, Asquith is good and immoral.
- **Winston Churchill** 1874-1965 British Conservative statesman: E. T. Raymond *Mr Balfour* (1920)

16 He occasionally stumbled over the truth, but hastily picked himself up and hurried on as if nothing had happened.
of Stanley Baldwin
- **Winston Churchill** 1874-1965 British Conservative statesman: J. L. Lane (ed.) *The Sayings of Winston Churchill* (1992)

17 COMMENT: One never hears of Baldwin nowadays — he might as well be dead.
CHURCHILL: No, not dead. But the candle in that great turnip has gone out.
- **Winston Churchill** 1874-1965 British Conservative statesman: Harold Nicolson's diary, August 1950

18 An empty taxi arrived at 10 Downing Street, and when the door was opened Attlee got out.
- **Winston Churchill** 1874-1965 British Conservative statesman: attributed to Churchill, but strongly repudiated by him; Kenneth Harris *Attlee* (1982)

19 [Clement Attlee is] a modest man who has a good deal to be modest about.
- **Winston Churchill** 1874-1965 British Conservative statesman: in *Chicago Sunday Tribune Magazine of Books* 27 June 1954

20 A sheep in sheep's clothing.
of Clement Attlee
- **Winston Churchill** 1874-1965 British Conservative statesman: Lord Home *The Way the Wind Blows* (1976)

21 *on stepping from his bath in the presence of a startled President Roosevelt:*
The Prime Minister has nothing to

hide from the President of the United States.

- **Winston Churchill** 1874-1965 British Conservative statesman: as recalled by Roosevelt's son in *Churchill* (BBC television series presented by Martin Gilbert, 1992)

22 *Disraeli was asked on what, offering himself for Marylebone, he intended to stand:*
On my head.

- **Benjamin Disraeli** 1804-81 British Tory statesman and novelist: *Lord Beaconsfield's Correspondence with his Sister 1832-1852* (1886)

23 Margaret Thatcher has added the diplomacy of Alf Garnett to the economics of Arthur Daley.

- **Denis Healey** 1917- British Labour politician: in *Observer* 31 December 1989

24 INTERVIEWER: What three skills should every great Prime Minister have? Did you have them?
HEATH: Patience, stamina and good luck. Two out of three isn't bad!

- **Edward Heath** 1916-2005 British Conservative statesman: in *Independent* 25 November 1998

25 It was not totally inconceivable that she could have joined me as my wife at No. 10.
on the TV starlet Jayne Mansfield

- **Edward Heath** 1916-2005 British Conservative statesman: in *Sunday Times* 6 February 2000

26 He is a mixture of Harry Houdini and a greased piglet…Nailing Blair is like trying to pin jelly to a wall.
on the Hutton Report on the Iraq War

- **Boris Johnson** 1964- British Conservative politician: in *Daily Telegraph* 29 January 2004

27 *on being asked what place Arthur Balfour would have in history:*
He will be just like the scent on a pocket handkerchief.

- **David Lloyd George** 1863-1945 British Liberal statesman: Thomas Jones diary, 9 June 1922

28 [Churchill] would make a drum out of the skin of his mother in order to sound his own praises.

- **David Lloyd George** 1863-1945 British Liberal statesman: Paul Johnson (ed.) *The Oxford Book of Political Anecdotes* (1986)

29 He might make an adequate Lord Mayor of Birmingham in a lean year.
of Neville Chamberlain, whose family came from Birmingham

- **David Lloyd George** 1863-1945 British Liberal statesman: Leon Harris *The Fine Art of Political Wit* (1965)

30 Well, it was the best I could do, seated as I was between Jesus Christ and Napoleon Bonaparte.
on the outcome of the Peace Conference negotiations in 1919 between himself, Woodrow Wilson, and Georges Clemenceau

- **David Lloyd George** 1863-1945 British Liberal statesman: Leon Harris *The Fine Art of Political Wit* (1965)

31 *after forming the National Government, 25 August 1931:*
Tomorrow every Duchess in London will be wanting to kiss me!

- **Ramsay MacDonald** 1866-1937 British Labour statesman: Viscount Snowden *An Autobiography* (1934)

32 A C-3PO made of ham. His resemblance to a slightly camp gammon robot is extraordinary.
on David Cameron

- **Caitlin Moran** 1975- English journalist: in *Times* 13 March 2010

33 He was not only a bore; he bored for England.
of Anthony Eden

- **Malcolm Muggeridge** 1903-90 British journalist: *Tread Softly* (1966)

34 A big cat detained briefly in a poodle parlour, sharpening her claws on the velvet.
of Lady Thatcher in the House of Lords

- **Matthew Parris** 1949- British journalist and former politician: *Look Behind You!* (1993)

35 Every Prime Minister needs a Willie.
at the farewell dinner for William Whitelaw

- **Margaret Thatcher** 1925-2013 British Conservative stateswoman: in *Guardian* 7 August 1991

36 The House has done me a great honour by commissioning this fine and imposing statue. I might have preferred iron, but bronze will do.
unveiling a statue of herself in the Members Lobby in the House of Commons
- **Margaret Thatcher** 1925-2013 British Conservative stateswoman: on 21 February 2007

37 If my critics saw me walking over the Thames, they would say it was because I couldn't swim.
- **Margaret Thatcher** 1925-2013 British Conservative stateswoman: attributed, but probably apocryphal

38 In the 1964 Government...I had to occupy almost every position on the field, goalkeeper, defence, attack—I had to take the corner-kicks and penalties, administer to the wounded and bring on the lemons at half-time.
- **Harold Wilson** 1916-95 British Labour statesman: *Final Term: The Labour Government 1974-76* (1979)

Progress

see also **SCIENCE, TECHNOLOGY**

A swell house with…all the modern inconveniences.　**Mark Twain**

1 All progress is based upon a universal innate desire on the part of every organism to live beyond its income.
- **Samuel Butler** 1835-1902 English novelist: *Notebooks* (1912)

2 Now, *here*, you see, it takes all the running *you* can do, to keep in the same place. If you want to get somewhere else, you must run at least twice as fast as that!
- **Lewis Carroll** 1832-98 English writer and logician: *Through the Looking-Glass* (1872)

3 To you, Baldrick, the Renaissance was just something that happened to other people, wasn't it?
- **Richard Curtis** 1956-　and **Ben Elton** 1959-screenwriters: *Blackadder II* (1987) television series

4 The civilized man has built a coach, but has lost the use of his feet.
- **Ralph Waldo Emerson** 1803-82 American philosopher and poet: 'Self-Reliance' (1841)

5 *on being asked what he thought of modern civilization:*
That would be a good idea.
- **Mahatma Gandhi** 1869-1948 Indian statesman: while visiting England in 1930, E. F. Schumacher *Good Work* (1979)

6 In my youth there were words you couldn't say in front of a girl; now you can't say 'girl'.
- **Tom Lehrer** 1928-　American humorist: in *Sunday Telegraph* 10 March 1996 'Spirits of the Age'

7 Progress might have been all right once, but it has gone on too long.
- **Ogden Nash** 1902-71 American humorist: attributed

8 You can't say civilization don't advance, however, for in every war they kill you in a new way.
- **Will Rogers** 1879-1935 American actor and humorist: in *New York Times* 23 December 1929

9 A swell house with…all the modern inconveniences.
- **Mark Twain** 1835-1910 American writer: *Life on the Mississippi* (1883)

Publishing

I suppose publishers are untrustworthy. They certainly always look it.
Oscar Wilde

1 *telegram from an impatient author who had sent her play to a theatrical management:*
AUTHOR: Please give immediate decision; have other irons in the fire.
MANAGEMENT: Suggest removing irons and inserting manuscript.
- **Anonymous**: Christine Campbell Thomson *I am a Literary Agent* (1951)

2 *of an author who was executed for murdering his publisher:*
When the author was on the scaffold he said goodbye to the minister and to the reporters, and then he saw some publishers sitting in the front row below, and to them he did not say goodbye. He said instead, 'I'll see you later.'
- **J. M. Barrie** 1860-1937 Scottish writer and dramatist: speech at Aldine Club, New York, 5 November 1896

3 In a profession where simple accountancy is preferable to a degree in English, illiteracy is not considered to be a great drawback.
- **Dominic Behan** 1928- Irish writer: *The Public World of Parable Jones* (1989)

4 The world needs your book, just not many copies of it.
- **Derek Brewer** 1923-2008 British academic and publisher: to an author, in *Times* 18 November 2008

5 The poem will please if it is lively—if it is stupid it will fail—but I will have none of your damned cutting and slashing.
- **Lord Byron** 1788-1824 English poet: letter to his publisher John Murray, 6 April 1819

6 *at a literary dinner during the Napoleonic Wars, Thomas Campbell proposed a toast to Napoleon:*
Gentlemen, you must not mistake me. I admit that the French Emperor is a tyrant. I admit he is a monster. I admit that he is the sworn foe of our nation, and, if you will, of the whole human race. But, gentlemen, we must be just to our great enemy. We must not forget that he once shot a bookseller.
- **Thomas Campbell** 1777-1844 Scottish poet: G. O. Trevelyan *The Life of Lord Macaulay* (1876)

7 Aren't we due a royalty statement?
to his literary agent
- **Charles, Prince of Wales** 1948- heir apparent to the British throne: Giles Gordon *Aren't We Due a Royalty Statement?* (1993)

8 *on being sent the manuscript of* Travels with my Aunt, *Greene's American publishers had cabled, 'Terrific book, but we'll need to change the title':*
No need to change title. Easier to change publishers.
- **Graham Greene** 1904-91 English novelist: telegram to his American publishers in 1968; Giles Gordon *Aren't We Due a Royalty Statement?* (1993)

9 Manuscript: something submitted in haste and returned at leisure.
- **Oliver Herford** 1863-1935 English-born American humorist: attributed

10 The relationship of an agent to a publisher is that of a knife to a throat.
- **Marvin Josephson** American agent: Ned Sherrin *Cutting Edge* (1984)

11 A publisher who writes is like a cow in a milk bar.
- **Arthur Koestler** 1905-83 Hungarian-born writer: Jonathon Green (ed.) *A Dictionary of Contemporary Quotations* (1982)

12 And he dreamed the dream of all those who publish books, which was to have so much gold in your pockets that you would have to employ two people just to hold your trousers up.
- **Terry Pratchett** 1948- English fantasy writer: *Maskerade* (1995)

13 I suppose publishers are untrustworthy. They certainly always look it.
- **Oscar Wilde** 1854-1900 Irish dramatist and poet: letter February 1898

14 All a publisher has to do is write cheques at intervals, while a lot of deserving and industrious chappies rally round and do the real work.
- **P. G. Wodehouse** 1881-1975 English-born writer: *My Man Jeeves* (1919)

15 Being published by the Oxford University Press is rather like being married to a duchess: the honour is almost greater than the pleasure.
- **G. M. Young** 1882-1959 English historian: Rupert Hart-Davis letter to George Lyttelton, 29 April 1956

Punishment *see* CRIME AND PUNISHMENT

Puns

see also WIT

....

You can lead a horticulture, but you can't make her think.   **Dorothy Parker**

1 Hanging is too good for a man who makes puns; he should be drawn and quoted.
- **Fred Allen** 1894-1956 American humorist: attributed; Laurence Peter *Quotations for Our Time* (1996)

2 An ill-favoured thing, but Minoan.
supposedly a comment by the archaeologist Sir Arthur Evans on finding a fragment of Cretan pottery
- **Anonymous**: in 'Quote...Unquote' Newsletter, April 1995

3 *to incoming Foreign Secretary Anthony Eden, following Samuel Hoare's resignation, 1935:*
I said to your predecessor: 'You know what they're all saying, no more coals to Newcastle, no more Hoares to Paris.' The fellow didn't even laugh.
- **George V** 1865-1936 British king: Earl of Avon *Facing the Dictators* (1962)

4 *explaining her mother's insistence on taking her own bidet with her when she travelled:*
My poor, dear mother suffers from a bidet-fixe.
- **Karen Lancaster** d. 1964: Osbert Lancaster *With an Eye to the Future* (1967)

5 Many of us can still remember the social nuisance of the inveterate punster. This man followed conversation as a shark follows a ship.
- **Stephen Leacock** 1869-1944 Canadian humorist: *The Boy I Left Behind Me* (1947)

6 Broadbosomed, bold, becalm'd, benign
Lies Balham foursquare on the
    Northern Line.
Matched by no marvel save in Eastern
    scene,
A rose-red city half as gold as green.
- **Frank Muir** 1920-98 and **Denis Norden** 1922- : 'Balham—Gateway to the South' *Third Division* (BBC Third Programme, 1948); Nigel Rees (ed.) *Cassell Dictionary of Humorous Quotations* (1999)

7 She was as happy as the dey was long.
of the relationship between Caroline of Brunswick, estranged wife of George IV, and the dey (or governor) of Algiers
- **Lord Norbury** 1745-1831: attributed; Nigel Rees *Cassell Dictionary of Humorous Quotations* (1998)

8 A jester unemployed is nobody's fool.
- **Norman Panama** 1914-2003 and **Melvin Frank** 1913-88 American screenwriters: *The Court Jester* (1955 film), spoken by Danny Kaye as Hubert Hawkins

9 *on her abortion:*
It serves me right for putting all my
eggs in one bastard.
- **Dorothy Parker** 1893-1967 American critic
  and humorist: John Keats *You Might as well
  Live* (1970)

10 You can lead a horticulture, but you
can't make her think.
- **Dorothy Parker** 1893-1967 American critic
  and humorist: John Keats *You Might as well
  Live* (1970)

11 'I want to be a lawn.' Greta Garbo.
- **W. C. Sellar** 1898-1951 and **R. J. Yeatman**
  1898-1968: *Garden Rubbish* (1930); chapter
  heading

12 *of Sir Charles Napier's conquest of Sindh:*
Peccavi—I have Sindh.
reworking Latin peccavi *I have sinned*
- **Catherine Winkworth** 1827-78 English
  hymnwriter: in *Punch* 18 May 1844,
  supposedly sent by Napier to Lord
  Ellenborough

Quotations

I always have a quotation for everything—it saves original thinking.
Dorothy L. Sayers

1 It isn't difficult, you know, to be witty
or amusing when one has something to
say that is destructive, but damned hard
to be clever and quotable when you are
singing someone's praises.
- **Noël Coward** 1899-1973 English dramatist,
  actor, and composer: William Marchant
  The Pleasure of His Company (1981)

2 I know heaps of quotations, so I can
always make quite a fair show of
knowledge.
- **O. Douglas** 1877-1948 Scottish writer:
  The Setons (1917)

3 Next to the originator of a good
sentence is the first quoter of it.
- **Ralph Waldo Emerson** 1803-82 American
  philosopher and poet: *Letters and Social
  Aims* (1876)

4 *advice for House of Commons quotations:*
No Greek; as much Latin as you like:
never French in any circumstance: no
English poet unless he has completed
his century.
- **Charles James Fox** 1749-1806 English Whig
  politician: J. A. Gere and John Sparrow
  (eds.) *Geoffrey Madan's Notebooks* (1981)

5 You can get a happy quotation
anywhere if you have the eye.
- **Oliver Wendell Holmes Jr.** 1841-1935
  American lawyer: letter to Harold Laski,
  31 May 1923

6 You must not treat my immortal works
as quarries to be used at will by the
various hacks whom you may employ
to compile anthologies.
- **A. E. Housman** 1859-1936 English poet:
  letter to his publisher Grant Richards,
  29 June 1907

7 He liked those literary cooks
Who skim the cream of others' books;
And ruin half an author's graces
By plucking bon-mots from their
places.
- **Hannah More** 1745-1833 English writer:
  Florio (1786)

8 His works contain nothing worth
quoting; and a book that furnishes no
quotations is, *me judice*, no book—it's a
plaything.
- **Thomas Love Peacock** 1785-1866 English
  novelist and poet: *Crotchet Castle* (1831)

9 A widely-read man never quotes
accurately, for the rather obvious reason
that he has read too widely.
- **Hesketh Pearson** 1887-1964 English actor
  and biographer: *Common Misquotations*
  (1934) introduction

10 An anthology is like all the plums and
orange peel picked out of a cake.
- **Walter Raleigh** 1861-1922 English lecturer
  and critic: letter to Mrs Robert Bridges,
  15 January 1915

11 I always have a quotation for everything—it saves original thinking.
  - **Dorothy L. Sayers** 1893-1957 English writer: *Have His Carcase* (1932)

12 It's better to be quotable than honest.
  - **Tom Stoppard** 1937- British dramatist: in *Guardian* 21 March 1973

13 What a good thing Adam had. When he said a good thing he knew nobody had said it before.
  - **Mark Twain** 1835-1910 American writer: *Notebooks* (1935)

Reading

I read part of it all the way through. **Sam Goldwyn**

1 The world may be full of fourth-rate writers but it's also full of fourth-rate readers.
  - **Stan Barstow** 1928- English novelist: in *Daily Mail* 15 August 1989

2 You couldn't even read the Gettysburg Address.
  So who cares anyway where Gettysburg lived?
  - **Betty Comden** 1917-2006 and **Adolph Green** 1915-2002: *Singin' in the Rain* (1952)

3 *on the difficulties of reading the novels of Sir Walter Scott:*
  He shouldn't have written in such small print.
  - **O. Douglas** 1877-1948 Scottish writer: *The Setons* (1917)

4 I read part of it all the way through.
  - **Sam Goldwyn** 1882-1974 American film producer: N. Zierold *Hollywood Tycoons* (1969)

5 ELPHINSTON: What, have you not read it through?
  JOHNSON: No, Sir, do *you* read books *through*?
  - **Samuel Johnson** 1709-84 English poet, critic, and lexicographer: James Boswell *Life of Samuel Johnson* (1791) 19 April 1773

6 [*The Compleat Angler*] is acknowledged to be one of the world's books. Only the trouble is that the world doesn't read its books, it borrows a detective story instead.
  - **Stephen Leacock** 1869-1944 Canadian humorist: *The Boy I Left Behind Me* (1947)

7 Reading isn't an occupation we encourage among police officers.
  We try to keep the paper work down to a minimum.
  - **Joe Orton** 1933-67 English dramatist: *Loot* (1967)

8 People say that life is the thing, but I prefer reading.
  - **Logan Pearsall Smith** 1865-1946 American-born man of letters: *Afterthoughts* (1931) 'Myself'

9 'Classic.' A book which people praise and don't read.
  - **Mark Twain** 1835-1910 American writer: *Following the Equator* (1897)

Relationships

see also **DATING**

··

We had a lot in common. I loved him and he loved him. **Shelley Winters**

1 A relationship, I think, is like a shark, you know? It has to constantly move forward or it dies. And I think what we got on our hands is a dead shark.
   - **Woody Allen** 1935- American film director, writer, and actor: *Annie Hall* (1977 film), spoken as Alvy

2 The feeling of friendship is like that of being comfortably filled with roast beef; love, like being enlivened with champagne.
   - **James Boswell** 1740-95 Scottish lawyer and biographer: *Life of Samuel Johnson* (1791) 16 April 1775

3 Once the trust goes out of a relationship it's really no fun lying to them anymore.
   - **Glen Charles** 1943- and **Les Charles** American screenwriters: *Cheers* (NBC TV, 1984) spoken by George Wendt as Norm

4 Once a woman has forgiven her man, she must not reheat his sins for breakfast.
   - **Marlene Dietrich** 1901-92 German-born American actress and singer: *Marlene Dietrich's ABC* (1962)

5 Never go to bed mad. Stay up and fight.
   - **Phyllis Diller** 1917-2012 American actress: *Phyllis Diller's Housekeeping Hints* (1966)

6 I know a lot of people didn't expect our relationship to last—but we've just celebrated our two months anniversary.
   - **Britt Ekland** 1942- Swedish actress: attributed

7 Men love women, women love children; children love hamsters—it's quite hopeless.
   - **Alice Thomas Ellis** 1932-2005 English novelist: attributed, 1987

8 Can officially confirm that the way to a man's heart these days is not through beauty, food, sex, or alluringness of character, but merely the ability to seem not very interested in him.
   - **Helen Fielding** 1958- British writer: *Bridget Jones's Diary* (1996)

9 A woman who can't forgive should never have more than a nodding acquaintance with a man.
   - **E. W. Howe** 1853-1937 American novelist and editor: attributed, but probably apocryphal

10 The trouble with Ian [Fleming] is that he gets off with women because he can't get on with them.
   - **Rosamund Lehmann** 1901-90 English novelist: John Pearson *The Life of Ian Fleming* (1966)

11 Take me or leave me; or, as is the usual order of things, both.
   - **Dorothy Parker** 1893-1967 American critic and humorist: in *New Yorker* 4 February 1928

12 My love life is like a piece of Swiss cheese. Most of it's missing and what's there stinks.
   - **Joan Rivers** 1933- American comedienne: attributed

13 Whenever I date a guy, I think: Is this the man I want my children to spend their weekends with?
   - **Rita Rudner** 1953- American comedienne and writer: attributed

14 We had a lot in common. I loved him and he loved him.
   on divorcing Vittorio Gassman
   - **Shelley Winters** 1922-2006 American actress: attributed; Susan Strasberg *Bittersweet* (1980)

Religion

see also **CLERGY**, **GOD**

....

An atheist is a man who has no invisible means of support.   **John Buchan**

1 Anyone who thinks sitting in church can make you a Christian must also think that sitting in a garage can make you a car.
   ▪ **Anonymous**: modern saying

2 To be Catholic or Jewish isn't chic. Chic is Episcopalian.
   ▪ **Elizabeth Arden** c.1880-1966 Canadian-born American businesswoman: A. A. Lewis and C. Woodworth *Miss Elizabeth Arden* (1972)

3 Bernard always had a few prayers in the hall and some whiskey afterwards as he was rarther pious.
   ▪ **Daisy Ashford** 1881-1972 English child author: *The Young Visiters* (1919)

4 I've a definite sense of spirituality. I want Brooklyn to be christened, but don't know into what religion yet.
   ▪ **David Beckham** 1975- English footballer: in *Daily Mail* 5 September 2002

5 Gentlemen, I am a Catholic…If you reject me on account of my religion, I shall thank God that He has spared me the indignity of being your representative.
   ▪ **Hilaire Belloc** 1870-1953 British writer and Liberal politician: speech to voters of South Salford, 1906

6 FOSTER: I'm still a bit hazy about the Trinity, sir.
   SCHOOLMASTER: Three in one, one in three, perfectly straightforward. Any doubts about that see your maths master.
   ▪ **Alan Bennett** 1934- English dramatist and actor: *Forty Years On* (1969)

7 Broad of Church and 'broad of Mind',
   Broad before and broad behind,
   A keen ecclesiologist,
   A rather dirty Wykehamist.
   ▪ **John Betjeman** 1906-84 English poet: 'The Wykehamist' (1931)

8 So, Lord, reserve for me a crown,
   And do not let my shares go down.
   ▪ **John Betjeman** 1906-84 English poet: 'In Westminster Abbey' (1940)

9 *of Bede Griffiths's visiting India with the intention of reconciling the Roman Catholic and Hindu faiths:*
   I suppose he's trying to combine Mumbo with Jumbo in roughly equal proportions.
   ▪ **John Betjeman** 1906-84 English poet: Bevis Hillier *Betjeman: the Bonus of Laughter* (2004)

10 The Vatican is against surrogate mothers. Good thing they didn't have that rule when Jesus was born.
   ▪ **Elayne Boosler** 1952- American comedian: attributed

11 We Romans are rich. We've got a lot of gods. We've got a god for everything. The only thing we don't have a god for is premature ejaculation…but I hear that's coming quickly.
   ▪ **Mel Brooks** 1926- American film director and comic actor: *History of the World Part I* (1981 film), as Comicus

12 If Jesus had been killed 20 years ago, Catholic school children would be wearing little electric chairs around their necks instead of crosses.
   ▪ **Lenny Bruce** 1925-66 American comedian: attributed

13 An atheist is a man who has no invisible means of support.
   ▪ **John Buchan** 1875-1940 Scottish novelist: H. E. Fosdick *On Being a Real Person* (1943)

14 Thanks to God, I am still an atheist.
   ▪ **Luis Buñuel** 1900-83 Spanish film director: *Le Monde* 16 December 1959

15 BERNIE: Can you help me? I have lost my sense of direction.

KERMIT: Have you tried Hare Krishna?
- **Jack Burns** 1933- and **Jerry Juhl** 1938-2005 American screenwriters: *The Muppet Movie* (1979 film)

16 Christians have burnt each other, quite persuaded
That all the Apostles would have done as they did.
- **Lord Byron** 1788-1824 English poet: *Don Juan* (1819-24)

17 The one excuse for being pagan is to enjoy it thoroughly.
- **Roy Campbell** 1901-57 South African poet: Cressida Connolly *The Rare and the Beautiful* (2004)

18 Atheism is a non-prophet organization.
- **George Carlin** 1937-2008 American comedian: attributed, re-working an old saying

19 Blessed are the cheesemakers.
a misheard beatitude
- **Graham Chapman** 1941-89, **John Cleese** 1939- , and **others** British comedians: *Monty Python's Life of Brian* (1979 film)

20 It is the test of a good religion whether you can joke about it.
- **G. K. Chesterton** 1874-1936 English writer: *All Things Considered* (1908)

21 I read about an Eskimo hunter who asked the local missionary priest, "If I did not know about God and sin, would I go to hell?" "No," said the priest, "not if you did not know." "Then why," asked the Eskimo earnestly, "did you tell me?"
- **Annie Dillard** 1945- American writer: *Pilgrim at Tinker Creek* (1974)

22 A Protestant, if he wants aid or advice on any matter, can only go to his solicitor.
- **Benjamin Disraeli** 1804-81 British Tory statesman and novelist: *Lothair* (1870)

23 Said Waldershare, 'Sensible men are all of the same religion.' 'And pray what is that?'...'Sensible men never tell.'
- **Benjamin Disraeli** 1804-81 British Tory statesman and novelist: *Endymion* (1880)

24 A lady, if undressed at Church, looks silly,

One cannot be devout in dishabilly.
- **George Farquhar** 1678-1707 Irish dramatist: *The Stage Coach* (1704)

25   What after all
Is a halo? It's only one more thing to keep clean.
- **Christopher Fry** 1907-2005 English dramatist: *The Lady's not for Burning* (1949)

26 I find it hard to understand why one should look for sermons in stones when the inability to preach is so attractive a feature of stones.
- **Northrop Frye** 1912-91 Canadian literary critic: *The Bush Garden* (1971)

27 The three kinds of services you generally find in the Episcopal churches. I call them either low-and-lazy, broad-and-hazy, or high-and-crazy.
- **Willa Gibbs** Canadian writer: *All the Golden Doors* (1957)

28 A Consumer's Guide to Religion—The Best Buy—Church of England. It's a jolly friendly faith. If you are one, there's no onus to make everyone else join. In fact no one need ever know.
- **Robert Gillespie** and **Charles Lewson**: *That Was The Week That Was* BBC television 1962

29 *at Oxford, to an angry crowd who thought she was Charles II's French Catholic mistress the Duchess of Portsmouth:*
Pray, good people, be civil. I am the Protestant whore.
- **Nell Gwyn** 1650-87 English actress and courtesan: B. Bevan *Nell Gwyn* (1969)

30 No matter how I probe and prod
I cannot quite believe in God.
But oh! I hope to God that he
Unswervingly believes in me.
- **E. Y. Harburg** 1898-1981 American songwriter: 'The Agnostic' (1965)

31 For a halo up in heaven
I have never been too keen.
Who needs another gadget
That a fellow has to clean?
- **E. Y. Harburg** 1898-1981 American songwriter: 'The Man who has Everything' (1965)

32 *imagining how a Church of England Inquisition might have worked*
'Cake or death?' 'Cake, please.'
- **Eddie Izzard** 1962- British comedian: *Dress to Kill* (stage show, San Francisco, 1998)

33 All moanday, tearsday, wailsday, thumpsday, frightday, shatterday till the fear of the Law.
- **James Joyce** 1882-1941 Irish novelist: *Finnegans Wake* (1939)

34 *the closing moment of Baroness Thatcher's funeral service, 17 April 2013:*
The Archbishop of Canterbury, whose crisp sign of the Cross has something of a window cleaner reaching into every last crevice, gave his blessing.
- **Quentin Letts** 1963- English journalist: in *Daily Mail* 18 April 2013

35 It's nice to have a nun around. Gives the place a bit of glamour.
- **Graham Linehan** 1968- and **Arthur Mathews** 1959- screenwriters: 'Grant Unto Him Eternal Rest' (1995), episode from *Father Ted* (Channel 4 TV, 1995-8)

36 You can't run the Church on Hail Marys.
view of a Vatican banker
- **Paul Marcinkus** 1922-2006 American Roman Catholic archbishop: in *Independent* 23 February 2006

37 *on hearing an evangelical sermon:*
Things have come to a pretty pass when religion is allowed to invade the sphere of private life.
- **Lord Melbourne** 1779-1848 British Whig statesman: G. W. E. Russell *Collections and Recollections* (1898)

38 Puritanism. The haunting fear that someone, somewhere, may be happy.
- **H. L. Mencken** 1880-1956 American journalist and literary critic: *Chrestomathy* (1949)

39 It is now quite lawful for a Catholic woman to avoid pregnancy by a resort to mathematics, though she is still forbidden to resort to physics and chemistry.
- **H. L. Mencken** 1880-1956 American journalist and literary critic: *Notebooks* (1956) 'Minority Report'

40 I celebrate everyone's religious holidays. If it's good enough for the righteous, it's good enough for the self-righteous I always say.
- **Bette Midler** 1945- American actress: tweet, September 2010

41 The orgasm has replaced the Cross as the focus of longing and the image of fulfilment.
- **Malcolm Muggeridge** 1903-90 British journalist: *Tread Softly* (1966)

42 God is a man, so it must be all rot.
just before her marriage to Robert Graves in 1917
- **Nancy Nicholson** 1899-1977 British artist: R. Graves *Goodbye to All That* (1929)

43 You are not an agnostic...You are just a fat slob who is too lazy to go to Mass.
- **Conor Cruise O'Brien** 1917-2008 Irish politician, writer, and journalist: attributed

44 There's no reason to bring religion into it. I think we ought to have as great a regard for religion as we can, so as to keep it out of as many things as possible.
- **Sean O'Casey** 1880-1964 Irish dramatist: *The Plough and the Stars* (1926)

45 Good manners can replace religious beliefs. In the Anglican Church they already have. Etiquette (and quiet, well-cut clothes) are devoutly worshipped by Anglicans.
- **P. J. O'Rourke** 1947- American humorous writer: *Modern Manners* (1984)

46 He was an embittered atheist (the sort of atheist who does not so much disbelieve in God as personally dislike Him), and took a sort of pleasure in thinking that human affairs would never improve.
- **George Orwell** 1903-50 English novelist: *Down and Out In Paris and London* (1933)

47 No praying, it spoils business.
- **Thomas Otway** 1652-85 English dramatist: *Venice Preserved* (1682)

48 God and the doctor we alike adore
But only when in danger, not before;
The danger o'er, both are alike requited,
God is forgotten, and the Doctor slighted.
- **John Owen** c.1563-1622 Welsh epigrammatist: *Epigrams*

49 *on long sermons:*
The mind cannot absorb what the
backside cannot endure.
- **Prince Philip, Duke of Edinburgh** 1921–
British prince: attributed, Robert Hardman
Our Queen (2011)

50 I have wondered at times about what
the Ten Commandments would have
looked like if Moses had run them
through the US Congress.
- **Ronald Reagan** 1911–2004 American
Republican statesman: attributed

51 Prove to me that you're no fool
Walk across my swimming pool.
- **Tim Rice** 1944– English songwriter:
'Herod's Song' (1970)

52 I always claim the mission workers
came out too early to catch any sinners
on this part of Broadway. At such an
hour the sinners are still in bed resting
up from their sinning of the night
before, so they will be in good shape for
more sinning a little later on.
- **Damon Runyon** 1884–1946 American
writer: in *Collier's* 28 January 1933, 'The Idyll
of Miss Sarah Brown'

53 The Chinese said they would...build
a shrine to my memory. I have some
slight regret that this did not happen
as I might have become a god, which
would have been very *chic* for an atheist.
- **Bertrand Russell** 1872–1970 British
philosopher and mathematician:
Autobiography (1968)

54 People may say what they like about
the decay of Christianity; the religious
system that produced green Chartreuse
can never really die.
- **Saki** 1870–1916 Scottish writer: *Reginald*
(1904)

55 You can't expect the fatted calf to share
the enthusiasm of the angels over the
prodigal's return.
- **Saki** 1870–1916 Scottish writer: *Reginald*
(1904)

56 Didn't some cynical critic say the
Church of England is the only barrier
between England and Christianity?
- **Saki** 1870–1916 Scottish writer: *Mrs Elmsley*
(1911, published as by Hector Munro)

57 How can what an Englishman believes
be heresy? It is a contradiction in terms.
- **George Bernard Shaw** 1856–1950 Irish
dramatist: *Saint Joan* (1924)

58 I made my then famous declaration
(among 100 people) 'I am a Socialist, an
Atheist and a Vegetarian' (ergo, a true
Shelleyan), whereupon two ladies who
had been palpitating with enthusiasm
for Shelley under the impression that
he was a devout Anglican, resigned on
the spot.
- **George Bernard Shaw** 1856–1950 Irish
dramatist: letter 1 March 1908

59 Baptists are only funny underwater.
- **Neil Simon** 1927– American dramatist:
Laughter on the 23rd Floor (1994)

60 I'm a dyslexic Satanist; I worship the
drivel.
- **Linda Smith** 1958–2006 British comedian:
in *Daily Telegraph* (obituary), 1 March 2006

61 Deserves to be preached to death by
wild curates.
- **Sydney Smith** 1771–1845 English clergyman
and essayist: Lady Holland *Memoir* (1855)

62 Protestant women may take the pill.
Roman Catholic women must keep
taking The Tablet.
- **Irene Thomas** 1919–2001 British writer and
broadcaster: in *Guardian* 28 December
1990

63 When the missionaries came to Africa,
they had the Bible and we had the land.
They said: 'Let us pray'. We closed our
eyes. When we opened them we had
the Bible and they had the land.
- **Desmond Tutu** 1931– South African
Anglican clergyman: attributed; in *Mail on
Sunday* 14 March 2004

64 Why do born-again people so often
make you wish they'd never been born
the first time?
- **Katharine Whitehorn** 1928– English
journalist: attributed

65 I don't go to church. Kneeling bags my
nylons.
- **Billy Wilder** 1906–2002 and **others**
screenwriters: *Ace in the Hole* (1951 film),
spoken by Jan Sterling as Lorraine

Restaurants

I went to a restaurant that serves 'breakfast any time'. So I ordered French toast during the Renaissance. **Steven Wright**

1 WAITER WITH FISH ORDER: Are you smelt, sir?
JOHN BETJEMAN: Only by the discerning.
- **John Betjeman** 1906-84 English poet: Bevis Hillier *Betjeman: the Bonus of Laughter* (2004)

2 Any restaurant featuring French cuisine and Ice-cold Grape Slush in the same window can't be trusted.
- **Peg Bracken** 1918-2007 American writer: *But I Wouldn't Have Missed It for the World* (1973)

3 I love restaurants and that's the thing now, they always boast about now, restaurants, home-made cooking…I don't want home-made cooking, that's why I'm here!
- **Lee Evans** 1964- English comedian: attributed

4 *to diners, while being carried on a stretcher from his suite at the Savoy when dying of cancer:*
It was the food. It was the food.
- **Richard Harris** 1930-2002 Irish actor: in *Limerick Leader* (online edition) 7 December 2002

5 'Can I have a table near the floor?'
'Certainly, I'll have the waiter saw the legs off.'
- **Groucho Marx** 1890-1977 American film comedian: attributed

6 Avoid any restaurant where the waiter arrives with a handful of knives and forks just as you reach the punchline of your best story and says 'Which of you is having fish?'
- **John Mortimer** 1923-2009 English writer and barrister: attributed

7 Someone at the table, whose order had not yet arrived, said, 'I think "waiter" is such a funny word. It is we who wait.'
- **Muriel Spark** 1918-2006 British novelist: *The Finishing School* (2004)

8 MARGARET THATCHER: This food is absolutely delicious.
DENIS THATCHER: So it should be. They're charging like the Light Brigade.
eating in Harry's Bar
- **Denis Thatcher** 1915-2003 English businessman: attributed; in *Spectator* 20 March 2004

9 Restaurant critics—even great critics are like very bad lovers. They only come once a year, they don't care if you're not ready, they leave without saying a word and then they tell everyone what you did was wrong.
- **Trevor White** 1972- Irish food critic: *Kitchen Con* (2006)

10 I went to a restaurant that serves 'breakfast any time'. So I ordered French toast during the Renaissance.
- **Steven Wright** 1955- American comedian: attributed

Retirement

The transition from Who's Who to Who's He.   **Eddie George**

1 Retirement means twice as much husband on half as much money.
   ▪ **Anonymous**: modern saying

2 If anything could have pulled me out of retirement, it would have been an Indiana Jones film. But in the end, retirement is just too damned much fun.
   ▪ **Sean Connery** 1930–   Scottish actor: in *Observer* 10 June 2007

3 The transition from Who's Who to Who's He.
   view of the former Governor of the Bank of England on retirement
   ▪ **Eddie George** 1938–2009 English banker: in *Independent* 29 December 2003

4 I remember one of my staff asking me when I was going to retire. I said when I could no longer hear the sound of laughter. He said, 'That never stopped you before.'
   ▪ **Bob Hope** 1903–2003 American comedian: attributed

Romance

see also **DATING, LOVE**

I still love you, see last year's card for details.   **Michael McIntyre**

1 Where's the romance gone? Destroyed by cynics and liberationists…Forget the flowers, the chocolates, the soft words—rather, woo her with a self-defence manual in one hand and a family planning leaflet in the other.
   ▪ **Alan Ayckbourn** 1939–   English dramatist: *Round and Round the Garden* (1975)

2 I've always felt reading romantic novels was a bit like eating a whole box of chocolates or going to bed with a rotter. You can't stop because it's so nice but afterwards you wish you hadn't.
   ▪ **Jilly Cooper** 1937–   English writer: in *Observer* 17 February 1980

3 I'm afraid I was very much the traditionalist. I went down on one knee and dictated a proposal which my secretary faxed over straight away.
   ▪ **Stephen Fry** 1957–   and **Hugh Laurie** 1959– : *A Bit More Fry and Laurie* (1991)

4 Christian said he'd call the next day, but in boy time that meant Thursday.
   ▪ **Amy Heckkerling** 1954–   American film director: *Clueless* (1995 film), spoken by Alicia Silverstone as Cher

5 *on Valentine's Day:*
   Just last week I wrote 'I still love you, see last year's card for full details.'
   ▪ **Michael McIntyre** 1976–   English comedian: attributed

6 Some people claim that marriage interferes with romance. There is no doubt about it. Anytime you have a romance, your wife is bound to interfere.
   ▪ **Groucho Marx** 1890–1977 American film comedian: *The Groucho Phile* (1976)

7 A man on a date wonders if he'll get lucky. The woman already knows.
   ▪ **Monica Piper**: attributed

Royalty

I left England when I was four because I found out I could never be King.
Bob Hope

1 *on her passion for horses:*
When I appear in public people expect me to neigh, grind my teeth, paw the ground and swish my tail—none of which is easy.
▪ **Anne, Princess Royal** 1950– British princess: in *Observer* 22 May 1977

2 King's Moll Reno'd in Wolsey's Home Town.
▪ **Anonymous**: US newspaper headline on Wallis Simpson's divorce proceedings in Ipswich

3 Most Gracious Queen, we thee implore
To go away and sin no more,
But if that effort be too great,
To go away at any rate.
▪ **Anonymous**: epigram on Queen Caroline, quoted in a letter from Francis Burton to Lord Colchester, 15 November 1820

4 Lousy but loyal.
▪ **Anonymous**: London East End slogan at George V's Jubilee, 1935

5 How different, how very different from the home life of our own dear Queen!
▪ **Anonymous**: comment overheard at a performance of Cleopatra by Sarah Bernhardt (probably apocryphal)

6 Green with lust and sick with shyness
Let me lick your lacquered toes,
Gosh, oh gosh, your Royal Highness,
Put your finger up my nose.
parodic poem on John Betjeman's being presented with the Duff Cooper Memorial Prize by Princess Margaret
▪ **Maurice Bowra** 1898–1971 English scholar and literary critic: attributed; in *Daily Telegraph* 10 February 2002 (online edition)

7 I shall be an autocrat: that's my trade. And the good Lord will forgive me: that's his.
▪ **Catherine the Great** 1729–96 Russian empress: attributed

8 We saw Queen Mary looking like the Jungfrau, white and sparkling in the sun.
▪ **Chips Channon** 1897–1958 American-born British Conservative politician: diary, 22 June 1937

9 I've tried him drunk and I've tried him sober but there's nothing in him.
of his niece Anne's husband George of Denmark
▪ **Charles II** 1630–85 British king: Gila Curtis *The Life and Times of Queen Anne* (1972)

10 This is very true: for my words are my own, and my actions are my ministers'.
▪ **Charles II** 1630–85 British king: reply to 'The King's Epitaph', see **Royalty** 33; *Thomas Hearne: Remarks and Collections* (1885–1921) 17 November 1706

11 *on having to watch scantily-dressed dancers' displays:*
It's become an occupational hazard. You take a deep breath and do it for England.
▪ **Charles, Prince of Wales** 1948– heir apparent to the British throne: in *Mirror* 22 March 2002

12 *on being asked the identity of the small man sharing an open carriage with the large Queen Salote of Tonga in the British Coronation procession:*
Her lunch.
▪ **Noël Coward** 1899–1973 English dramatist, actor, and composer: attributed, but denied by Coward as offensive to Queen Salote; Dick Richards *The Wit and Wisdom of Noël Coward* (1968)

13 Everyone likes flattery; and when you come to Royalty you should lay it on with a trowel.
▪ **Benjamin Disraeli** 1804–81 British Tory statesman and novelist: G. W. E. Russell *Collections and Recollections* (1898)

14 I never deny; I never contradict;
I sometimes forget.
*of his dealings as Prime Minister with
Queen Victoria*
- **Benjamin Disraeli** 1804-81 British Tory
statesman and novelist: Elizabeth Longford
Victoria R. I. (1964)

15 *to the Archbishop of Canterbury after
the service of celebration at St Paul's for
Queen Victoria's Diamond Jubilee in 1897:*
I have no objection whatsoever to the
notion of the Eternal Father, but every
objection to the concept of an eternal
mother.
- **Edward VII** 1841-1910 British king:
attributed, perhaps apocryphal

16 *on being asked if Queen Victoria would be
happy in heaven:*
She will have to walk behind the
angels—and she won't like that.
- **Edward VII** 1841-1910 British king:
attributed, perhaps apocryphal

17 I think everybody really will concede
that on this, of all days, I should begin
my speech with the words 'My husband
and I'.
- **Elizabeth II** 1926- British queen: speech
at Guildhall, London, on her 25th wedding
anniversary

18 *of Prince Andrew:*
He's the only one who knows how to
work the video.
- **Elizabeth II** 1926- British queen: in
Observer 29 December 1985

19 The whole world is in revolt. Soon
there will be only five Kings left—the
King of England, the King of Spades,
the King of Clubs, the King of Hearts
and the King of Diamonds.
- **Farouk** 1920-65 Egyptian king: said to Lord
Boyd-Orr at a conference in Cairo, 1948;
As I Recall (1966) ch. 21

20 *on H. G. Wells's comment on 'an alien and
uninspiring court':*
I may be uninspiring, but I'll be damned
if I'm an alien!
- **George V** 1865-1936 British monarch: Sarah
Bradford *George VI* (1989); attributed

21 Ah'm sorry your Queen has to pay taxes.

She's not a wealthy woman.
- **John Paul Getty** 1892-1976 American
industrialist: in *Ned Sherrin in his Anecdotage*
(1993); attributed

22 I left England when I was four because
I found out I could never be King.
- **Bob Hope** 1903-2003 American comedian:
William Robert Faith *Bob Hope* (1983)

23 *on the British royal family's increasing
tendency to marry commoners:*
The monarchy, an institution that has
cleverly embraced what might be called
'downward nobility' for decades now.
- **Rachel Johnson** 1965- English writer: in
Mail on Sunday 9 December 2012

24 *notice on a playbill sent to her former lover,
the Duke of Clarence, refusing repayment of
her allowance:*
Positively no money refunded after the
curtain has risen.
- **Mrs Jordan** 1761-1816 Irish-born actress:
Duke of Windsor 'My Hanoverian
Ancestors' (unpublished reminiscences);
Elizabeth Longford (ed.) *The Oxford Book of
Royal Anecdotes* (1989)

25 My children are not royal, they just
happen to have the Queen as their aunt.
- **Princess Margaret** 1930-2002 British
princess: Elizabeth Longford (ed.) *The
Oxford Book of Royal Anecdotes* (1989)

26 *on the abdication of her son, Edward VIII,
1936:*
Really, this might be Rumania.
- **Queen Mary** 1867-1953 British Queen
Consort: Michael Hill (ed.) *Right Royal
Remarks* (2003)

27 Such an active lass. So outdoorsy. She
loves nature in spite of what it did
to her.
on Princess Anne
- **Bette Midler** 1945- American actress:
A View from a Broad (1980)

28 For 50 years and more, Elizabeth
Windsor has maintained her dignity,
her sense of duty, and her hairstyle.
*accepting an Oscar for Best actress for her part
in* The Queen
- **Helen Mirren** 1945- English actress: in
Independent on Sunday 4 March 2007

29 How vulgar of those American women to call him David. Either one calls him Sir or one calls him Darling.
talking of her friend the Prince of Wales, later King Edward VIII
- **Lady Victor Paget** 1892–1975: Kenneth Rose *Who's Who in the Royal House of Windsor* (1985)

30 I declare this thing open—whatever it is.
- **Prince Philip, Duke of Edinburgh** 1921– husband of Elizabeth II: opening an annexe at Vancouver City Hall, 1969; Basil Boothroyd *Philip: an informal biography* (1971)

31 The Right Divine of Kings to govern wrong.
- **Alexander Pope** 1688–1744 English poet: *The Dunciad* (1742)

32 *on Charles, Prince of Wales:*
He's so gay. He can't wait for his mother to die so he can be Queen.
- **Joan Rivers** 1933– American comedienne: from stand up routine, early 1980s

33 Here lies a great and mighty king Whose promise none relies on; He never said a foolish thing, Nor ever did a wise one.
- **Lord Rochester** 1647–80 English poet: 'The King's Epitaph' (an alternative first line reads: 'Here lies our sovereign lord the King'); see **Royalty** 10

34 The *éminence cerise*, the bolster behind the throne.
of Queen Elizabeth the Queen Mother
- **Will Self** 1961– British writer: in *Independent on Sunday* 8 August 1999

35 He speaks to Me as if I was a public meeting.
of Gladstone
- **Victoria** 1819–1901 British queen: G. W. E. Russell *Collections and Recollections* (1898)

36 *when forced by a mob to cheer George IV's estranged wife Caroline of Brunswick:*
God Save the Queen, and may all your wives be like her!
- **Duke of Wellington** 1769–1852 British soldier and statesman: Elizabeth Longford *Wellington: Pillar of State* (1972); also attributed to Lord Anglesey and others

37 *having been wakened with the news of his accession, William IV returned to bed:*
To enjoy the novelty of sleeping with a queen.
- **William IV** 1765–1837 British king: Duke of Windsor 'My Hanoverian Ancestors' (unpublished reminiscences); Elizabeth Longford (ed.) *The Oxford Book of Royal Anecdotes* (1989)

38 *to Edward IV whom she later married:*
My liege, I know I am not good enough to be your queen, but I am far too good to become your mistress.
- **Elizabeth Woodville** c.1437–92 English queen of Edward IV: Agnes and Elizabeth Strickland *Lives of the Queens of England* (1840)

39 I'm doing pretty well considering. In the past, when anyone left the Royal family they had you beheaded.
- **Sarah, Duchess of York** 1959– : in *Independent* 8 July 2000 'Quotes of the Week'

Satisfaction and Discontent

see also **HAPPINESS, HOPE**

....

If not actually disgruntled, he was far from being gruntled.   **P. G. Wodehouse**

1 *when asked what was the best day of her life:*
It was a night.
- **Brigitte Bardot** 1934– French actress: in *Independent on Sunday* 3 October 2004

2 The world has treated me very well, but then I haven't treated it so badly either.
- **Noël Coward** 1899–1973 English dramatist, actor, and composer: Sheridan Morley *The Quotable Noël Coward* (1999)

3 Frankly, my dear, I don't give a damn.
- **Sidney Howard** 1891–1939 American dramatist and screenwriter: *Gone with the Wind* (1939 film, based on the novel by Margaret Mitchell); spoken by Clark Gable as Rhett Butler

4 When fortune empties her chamberpot on your head, smile—and say 'we are going to have a summer shower'.
- **John A. Macdonald** 1851–91 Scottish-born Canadian statesman: spoken *c.* 1875

5 I test my bath before I sit,
And I'm always moved to wonderment

That what chills the finger not a bit
Is so frigid upon the fundament.
- **Ogden Nash** 1902–71 American humorist: 'Samson Agonistes' (1942)

6 His strongest tastes were negative. He abhorred plastics, Picasso, sunbathing and jazz—everything in fact that had happened in his own lifetime.
- **Evelyn Waugh** 1903–66 English novelist: *The Ordeal of Gilbert Pinfold* (1957)

7 It's better to be looked over than overlooked.
- **Mae West** 1892–1980 American film actress: *Belle of the Nineties* (1934 film)

8 Too much of a good thing can be wonderful.
- **Mae West** 1892–1980 American film actress: *Goodness had Nothing to Do with It* (1959)

9 If not actually disgruntled, he was far from being gruntled.
- **P. G. Wodehouse** 1881–1975 English-born writer: *The Code of the Woosters* (1938)

Science

see also **PROGRESS, TECHNOLOGY**

....

Such wholesale returns of conjecture out of such a trifling investment of fact.
Mark Twain

1 Basic research is like shooting an arrow into the air and, where it lands, painting a target.
- **Homer Burton Adkins** 1892–1949 American organic chemist: A. Mackay (ed.), *A Dictionary of Scientific Quotations* (1991)

2 Multiplication is vexation,
Division is as bad;

The Rule of Three doth puzzle me,
And Practice drives me mad.
- **Anonymous**: in *Lean's Collectanea* (1904), possibly 16th-century

3 The Higgs boson walks into a Catholic Church and the priest says: 'What are you doing here?' The Higgs says, 'Well, you can't have mass without me.'
- **Anonymous**: popular saying

4 When I find myself in the company of scientists, I feel like a shabby curate who has strayed by mistake into a drawing room full of dukes.
- **W. H. Auden** 1907-73 English poet: *The Dyer's Hand* (1963)

5 The Microbe is so very small
You cannot make him out at all.
But many sanguine people hope
To see him through a microscope.
- **Hilaire Belloc** 1870-1953 British writer and Liberal politician: 'The Microbe' (1897)

6 Sir Humphrey Davy
Abominated gravy.
He lived in the odium
Of having discovered Sodium.
- **Edmund Clerihew Bentley** 1875-1956 English writer: 'Sir Humphrey Davy' (1905)

7 Basic research is what I am doing when I don't know what I am doing.
- **Wernher von Braun** 1912-77 German-born American rocket engineer: R. L. Weber *A Random Walk in Science* (1973)

8 There was a young lady named Bright,
Whose speed was far faster than light;
She set out one day
In a relative way
And returned on the previous night.
- **Arthur Buller** 1874-1944 British botanist and mycologist: 'Relativity' (1923)

9 If an elderly but distinguished scientist says that something is possible he is almost certainly right, but if he says that it is impossible he is very probably wrong.
- **Arthur C. Clarke** 1917-2008 English science fiction writer: in *New Yorker* 9 August 1969

10 I have no more faith in men of science being infallible than I have in men of God being infallible, principally on account of them being men.
- **Noël Coward** 1899-1973 English dramatist, actor, and composer: diary, 1 July 1946

11 Someone told me that each equation I included in the book would halve the sales.
- **Stephen Hawking** 1942- English theoretical physicist: *A Brief History of Time* (1988)

12 Cosmologists are often in error, but never in doubt.
- **Lev Landau** 1908-68 Russian physicist: attributed in Simon Singh *Big Bang* (2004)

13 It was Einstein who made the real trouble. He announced in 1905 that there was no such thing as absolute rest. After that there never was.
- **Stephen Leacock** 1869-1944 Canadian humorist: *The Boy I Left Behind Me* (1947)

14 It is a good morning exercise for a research scientist to discard a pet hypothesis every day before breakfast.
- **Konrad Lorenz** 1903-89 Austro-German zoologist: *On Aggression* (1966)

15 Aristotle maintained that women have fewer teeth than men; although he was twice married, it never occurred to him to verify this statement by examining his wives' mouths.
- **Bertrand Russell** 1872-1970 British philosopher and mathematician: *Impact of Science on Society* (1952)

16 He had been eight years upon a project for extracting sun-beams out of cucumbers, which were to be put into vials hermetically sealed, and let out to warm the air in raw inclement summers.
- **Jonathan Swift** 1667-1745 Irish poet and satirist: *Gulliver's Travels* (1726)

17 Her own mother lived the latter years of her life in the horrible suspicion that electricity was dripping invisibly all over the house.
- **James Thurber** 1894-1961 American humorist: *My Life and Hard Times* (1933)

18 There is something fascinating about science. One gets such wholesale returns of conjecture out of such a trifling investment of fact.
- **Mark Twain** 1835-1910 American writer: *Life on the Mississippi* (1883)

19 It was absolutely marvellous working for Pauli. You could ask him anything. There was no worry that he would think a particular question was stupid, since he thought *all* questions were stupid.
- **Victor Weisskopf** 1908-2002 American physicist: in *American Journal of Physics* 1977

Scotland

That state of mind which cartographers seek to define as Scotland.
Claud Cockburn

1 There are few more impressive sights in the world than a Scotsman on the make.
- **J. M. Barrie** 1860-1937 Scottish writer and dramatist: *What Every Woman Knows* (performed 1908)

2 That state of mind which cartographers seek to define as Scotland.
- **Claud Cockburn** 1904-81 British writer and journalist: *Crossing the Line* (1958)

3 There are two seasons in Scotland: June and winter.
- **Billy Connolly** 1942- Scottish comedian: attributed

4 *to a Boer who had told her that he could never quite forgive the British for having conquered his country:*
I understand that perfectly. We feel very much the same in Scotland.
- **Queen Elizabeth, the Queen Mother** 1900-2002: Elizabeth Longford (ed.) *The Oxford Book of Royal Anecdotes* (1989)

5 They christened their game golf because they were Scottish and revelled in meaningless Celtic noises in the back of the throat.
- **Stephen Fry** 1957- English comedian, actor, and writer: *Paperweight* (1992)

6 Sir, let me tell you, the noblest prospect which a Scotchman ever sees, is the high road that leads him to England!
- **Samuel Johnson** 1709-84 English poet, critic, and lexicographer: James Boswell *Life of Samuel Johnson* (1791) 6 July 1763

7 *Oats.* A grain, which in England is generally given to horses, but in Scotland supports the people.
- **Samuel Johnson** 1709-84 English poet, critic, and lexicographer: *A Dictionary of the English Language* (1755)

8 No McTavish
Was ever lavish.
- **Ogden Nash** 1902-71 American humorist: 'Genealogical Reflection' (1931)

9 That knuckle-end of England—that land of Calvin, oat-cakes, and sulphur.
- **Sydney Smith** 1771-1845 English clergyman and essayist: Lady Holland *Memoir* (1855)

10 It is never difficult to distinguish between a Scotsman with a grievance and a ray of sunshine.
- **P. G. Wodehouse** 1881-1975 English writer: *Blandings Castle and Elsewhere* (1935)

Secrecy

The best leaks always take place in the urinal.   **John Cole**

1 A Company for carrying on an undertaking of Great Advantage, but no one to know what it is.
- **Anonymous**: Company Prospectus at the time of the South Sea Bubble (1711)

2 See all your best work go unnoticed.
- **Anonymous**: advertisement for staff for MI5, 2005

3 The best leaks always take place in the urinal.
- **John Cole** 1927- Northern Irish journalist and broadcaster: in *Independent* 3 June 1996

4 Secrets with girls, like loaded guns with boys,

Are never valued till they make a noise.
- **George Crabbe** 1754-1832 English poet:
  Tales of the Hall (1819) 'The Maid's Story'

5 Once the toothpaste is out of the tube,
it is awfully hard to get it back in.
- **H. R. Haldeman** 1929-93 American
  Presidential assistant to Richard Nixon:
  to John Dean; *Hearings Before the Select
  Committee on Presidential Campaign
  Activities of US Senate: Watergate and
  Related Activities* (1973)

6 Truth is suppressed, not to protect
the country from enemy agents but
to protect the Government of the day
against the people.
- **Roy Hattersley** 1932- British Labour
  politician: in *Independent* 18 February 1995

7 That's another of those irregular verbs,
isn't it? I give confidential briefings; you
leak; he has been charged under Section
2a of the Official Secrets Act.
- **Jonathan Lynn** 1943- and **Antony Jay**
  1930- English writers: *Yes Prime Minister*
  (1987) vol. 2 'Man Overboard'

8 The most difficult secret for a man to
keep is his own opinion of himself.
- **Marcel Pagnol** 1895-1974 French dramatist
  and film-maker: attributed

9 It's been a huge advantage during my
professional career that I've always
looked like a cheerful, fat missionary.
It wouldn't be any use if you went
around looking sinister, would it?
- **Daphne Park** 1921- British diplomat and
  senior controller of MI6: in *Daily Telegraph*
  24 April 2003

Self-Knowledge and Self-Deception

see also **CHARACTER**

....

I wouldn't say I was the best manager, but I was in the top one.　**Brian Clough**

1 A person of low taste, more interested
in himself than in me.
definition of an egotist
- **Ambrose Bierce** 1842-c.1914 American
  writer: *Cynic's Word Book* (1906)

2 Our polite recognition of another's
resemblance to ourselves.
definition of admiration
- **Ambrose Bierce** 1842-c.1914 American
  writer: *Cynic's Word Book* (1906)

3 I think that most people who have dealt
with me think that I am a pretty straight
sort of guy.
*on the handling of the decision to exempt
Formula One motor racing from a proposed
ban on tobacco advertising*
- **Tony Blair** 1953- British Labour statesman:
  'On the Record' interview with John
  Humphrys, 16 November 1997

4 The reward for conformity is that
everyone likes you except yourself.
- **Rita Mae Brown** 1944- American novelist
  and poet: *Bingo* (1988)

5 They misunderestimated me.
- **George W. Bush** 1946- American
  Republican statesman: speech in
  Bentonville, Arkansas, November 2000

6 The Crown Prince Umberto is charm
itself, but has no great intelligence. He
reminds me of myself.
- **Chips Channon** 1897-1958 American-
  born British Conservative politician: diary
  (undated entry); introduction to *Chips: the
  Diaries of Sir Henry Channon* (1993)

7 I wouldn't say I was the best manager,
but I was in the top one.
- **Brian Clough** 1935-2004 English football
  manager: attributed; in *Scotsman*
  21 September 2004 (online edition)

8 All my shows are great. Some of them
are bad. But they are all great.
- **Lew Grade** 1906-98 British television
  producer and executive: in *Observer*
  14 September 1975

9 It's been my experience that people
who make proclamations about

themselves are usually the opposite of what they claim to be.
- **Chelsea Handler** 1975- American comedienne and writer: *Are You There, Vodka? It's Me, Chelsea* (2008)

10 The photograph is not quite true to my own notion of my gentleness and sweetness of nature, but neither perhaps is my external appearance.
- **A. E. Housman** 1859-1936 English poet: letter, 12 June 1922

11 For self-revelation, whether it be a Tudor villa on the by-pass or a bomb-proof chalet at Berchtesgaden, there's no place like home.
- **Osbert Lancaster** 1908-86 English writer and cartoonist: *Homes Sweet Homes* (1939)

12 I am not the type who wants to go back to the land; I am the type who wants to go back to the hotel.
- **Fran Lebowitz** 1946- American writer: *Social Studies* (1981)

13 A journey of self-discovery starts with a single step...But so does falling down a flight of stairs.
- **Kathy Lette** 1958- Australian writer: *The Boy Who Fell to Earth* (2012)

14 Underneath this flabby exterior is an enormous lack of character.
- **Oscar Levant** 1906-72 American pianist: *Memoirs of an Amnesiac* (1965)

15 It was not till quite late in life that I discovered how easy it is to say 'I don't know'.
- **W. Somerset Maugham** 1874-1965 English novelist: *The Partial View* (1954)

16 Every person is the star of their life story. No one goes through the world thinking: 'Well, I'm just a cameo'.
- **John C. Reilly** 1965- American actor: in *Observer* 10 February 2013

17 [I am] a doormat in a world of boots.
- **Jean Rhys** c.1890-1979 British novelist and short-story writer: in *Guardian* 6 December 1990

18 You're so vain
You probably think this song is about you.
- **Carly Simon** 1945- American singer and songwriter: 'You're So Vain' (1972 song)

19 I have often wished I had time to cultivate modesty...But I am too busy thinking about myself.
- **Edith Sitwell** 1887-1964 English poet and critic: in *Observer* 30 April 1950

20 How awful to reflect that what people say of us is true!
- **Logan Pearsall Smith** 1865-1946 American-born man of letters: *Afterthoughts* (1931)

21 The kind of person who embarks on an endless leap-frog down to the great moral issues. I put a position, rebut it, refute it, refute the rebuttal and rebut the refutation. Endlessly.
on himself
- **Tom Stoppard** 1937- British dramatist: Mel Gussow *Conversations with Stoppard* (1995)

22 Satire is a sort of glass, wherein beholders do generally discover everybody's face but their own.
- **Jonathan Swift** 1667-1745 Irish poet and satirist: *The Battle of the Books* (1704) preface

23 I am extraordinarily patient, provided I get my own way in the end.
- **Margaret Thatcher** 1925-2013 British Conservative stateswoman: in *Observer* 4 April 1989

24 Pavarotti is not vain, but conscious of being unique.
- **Peter Ustinov** 1921-2004 British actor, director, and writer: in *Independent on Sunday* 12 September 1993

25 I'm the girl who lost her reputation and never missed it.
- **Mae West** 1892-1980 American film actress: P. F. Boller and R. L. Davis *Hollywood Anecdotes* (1988)

26 I don't at all like knowing what people say of me behind my back. It makes me far too conceited.
- **Oscar Wilde** 1854-1900 Irish dramatist and poet: *An Ideal Husband* (1895)

27 Early in life I had to choose between honest arrogance and hypocritical humility. I chose honest arrogance and have seen no occasion to change.
- **Frank Lloyd Wright** 1867-1959 American architect: Herbert Jacobs *Frank Lloyd Wright* (1965)

Sex

see also **LOVE, MARRIAGE**

....

I've been around so long, I knew Doris Day before she was a virgin.   **Groucho Marx**

1 STEVE ROSSI: What is the difference between erotic sex and kinky sex?
ALLEN: Erotic sex, you use a feather.
ROSSI: And, what about kinky sex?
ALLEN: You use the whole chicken.
- **Marty Allen** 1922– American comedian: CNN News, 16 March 1993

2 Don't knock masturbation. It's sex with someone I love.
- **Woody Allen** 1935– American film director, writer, and actor: *Annie Hall* (1977 film, with Marshall Brickman)

3 That [sex] was the most fun I ever had without laughing.
- **Woody Allen** 1935– American film director, writer, and actor: *Annie Hall* (1977 film, with Marshall Brickman)

4 My love life is terrible. The last time I was inside a woman was when I visited the Statue of Liberty.
- **Woody Allen** 1935– American film director, writer, and actor: *Crimes and Misdemeanors* (1989 film)

5 Is sex dirty? Only if it's done right.
- **Woody Allen** 1935– American film director, writer, and actor: *Everything You Always Wanted to Know about Sex* (1972 film)

6 My brain? It's my second favourite organ.
- **Woody Allen** 1935– American film director, writer, and actor: *Sleeper* (1973 film, with Marshall Brickman)

7 A fast word about oral contraception. I asked a girl to go to bed with me and she said 'no'.
- **Woody Allen** 1935– American film director, writer, and actor: at a night-club in Washington, April 1965

8 On bisexuality: It immediately doubles your chances for a date on Saturday night.
- **Woody Allen** 1935– American film director, writer, and actor: in *New York Times* 1 December 1975

9 Have you seen that movie? Maris and I rented the video. I don't mind telling you we pushed our beds together that night! And that was no mean feat; her room, as you know, is across the hall!
- **David Angell** 1946-2001, **Peter Casey**, and **David Lee** American television producers: *Frasier* (NBC TV, 1993) 'Selling Out', written by Lloyd Garver; spoken by David Hyde Pierce as Niles

10 You should make a point of trying every experience once, excepting incest and folk-dancing.
- **Anonymous**: Arnold Bax *Farewell My Youth* (1943), quoting 'a sympathetic Scot'

11 Would you like to sin
With Elinor Glyn
On a tigerskin?
Or would you prefer
To err
With her
On some other fur?
- **Anonymous**: verse alluding to Elinor Glyn's romantic novel *Three Weeks* (1907); A. Glyn *Elinor Glyn* (1955)

12 'My mother made me a homosexual.'
'If I send her the wool will she make me one?'
- **Anonymous**: New York graffito of the 1970s

13 Let us honour if we can
The vertical man
Though we value none
But the horizontal one.
- **W. H. Auden** 1907-73 English poet: 'To Christopher Isherwood' (1930)

14 Give me chastity and continency—but not yet!
- **St Augustine of Hippo** AD 354-430 Roman Christian theologian: *Confessions* (AD 397-8)

15 My mother used to say, Delia, if S-E-X ever rears its ugly head, close your eyes

before you see the rest of it.
- **Alan Ayckbourn** 1939- English dramatist: *Bedroom Farce* (1978)

16 I'll come and make love to you at five o'clock. If I'm late start without me.
- **Tallulah Bankhead** 1903-68 American actress: Ted Morgan *Somerset Maugham* (1980)

17 *at the age of ninety-seven, Blake was asked at what age the sex drive goes:*
You'll have to ask somebody older than me.
- **Eubie Blake** 1883-1983 American ragtime pianist: in *Ned Sherrin in his Anecdotage* (1993)

18 On life's long road I have found the penis to be a most unreliable compass.
- **David L. Bloomer** 1912-96 Scottish badminton player: told to Jeremy Nicholas in 1972

19 Sex has never been an obsession with me. It's just like eating a bag of crisps. Quite nice, but nothing marvellous.
- **Boy George** 1961- English pop singer and songwriter: in *Sun* 21 October 1982

20 Genitals are a great distraction to scholarship.
- **Malcolm Bradbury** 1932-2000 English novelist and critic: *Cuts* (1987)

21 I could never understand what Sir Godfrey Tearle saw in Jill Bennett, until I saw her at the Caprice eating corn-on-the-cob.
a romance between a young actress and a Grand Old Man of the theatre
- **Coral Browne** 1913-91 Australian actress: attributed

22 If homosexuality were the normal way, God would have made Adam and Bruce.
- **Anita Bryant** 1940- American singer: in *New York Times* 5 June 1977

23 Sexual intercouse is kicking death in the ass while singing.
- **Charles Bukowski** 1920-94 German-born American writer: *Notes of a Dirty Old Man* (1969)

24 It was the afternoon of my eighty-first birthday, and I was in bed with my catamite when Ali announced that the archbishop had come to see me.
- **Anthony Burgess** 1917-93 English novelist and critic: *Earthly Powers* (1980); opening sentence

25 He said it was artificial respiration, but now I find I am to have his child.
- **Anthony Burgess** 1917-93 English novelist and critic: *Inside Mr Enderby* (1963)

26 MIRANDA: What's the big mystery? It's my clitoris, not the sphinx.
CARRIE: I think you just found the title of your autobiography.
- **Candace Bushnell** 1958- , **Darren Star** 1961- , and **Patrick King** 1954- American writers: *Sex and the City* (HBO TV, 1999), Cynthia Nixon as Miranda and Sarah Jessica Parker as Carrie

27 What men call gallantry, and gods adultery,
Is much more common where the climate's sultry.
- **Lord Byron** 1788-1824 English poet: *Don Juan* (1819-24)

28 *on homosexuality:*
It doesn't matter what you do in the bedroom as long as you don't do it in the street and frighten the horses.
- **Mrs Patrick Campbell** 1865-1940 English actress: Daphne Fielding *The Duchess of Jermyn Street* (1964)

29 I don't have a sex 'drive'. I have a sex 'just sit in the car and hope someone gets in.'
- **Louis C.K.** 1967- American comedian: attributed

30 Do not adultery commit;
Advantage rarely comes of it.
- **Arthur Hugh Clough** 1819-61 English poet: 'The Latest Decalogue' (1862)

31 I am that twentieth-century failure, a happy undersexed celibate.
- **Denise Coffey** 1936- English actress: Ned Sherrin *Cutting Edge* (1984)

32 *asked if he was superstitious:*
Only about thirteen in a bed.
- **Noël Coward** 1899-1973 English dramatist, actor, and composer: Anna Massey *Telling Some Tales* (2007)

33 *to one of Laurence Olivier's small children
who asked what two dogs were doing:*
The doggie in front has suddenly gone
blind and the other one has very kindly
offered to push him all the way to
St Dunstan's.
- **Noël Coward** 1899-1973 English dramatist,
actor, and composer: Kenneth Tynan *The
Sound of Two Hands Clapping* (1975)

34 I became one of the stately homos of
England.
- **Quentin Crisp** 1908-99 English writer:
The Naked Civil Servant (1968)

35 For flavour, Instant Sex will never
supersede the stuff you had to peel
and cook.
- **Quentin Crisp** 1908-99 English writer: in
Sunday Telegraph 28 September 1999

36 *in 1951 the homosexual Tom Driberg married
a widow; he later complained:*
She broke her marriage vows; she tried
to sleep with me.
- **Tom Driberg** 1905-76 British Labour
politician: in *Ned Sherrin in his Anecdotage*
(1993)

37 Seduction is often difficult to distinguish
from rape. In seduction, the rapist
bothers to buy a bottle of wine.
- **Andrea Dworkin** 1946-2005 American
feminist and writer: *Letters from a War Zone*
(1988)

38 When choosing sexual partners
remember: Talent is not sexually
transmittable.
- **Tina Fey** 1970- American comedian and
actress: *Bossypants* (2011)

39 He in a few minutes ravished this
fair creature, or at least would have
ravished her, if she had not, by a timely
compliance, prevented him.
- **Henry Fielding** 1707-54 English novelist and
dramatist: *Jonathan Wild* (1743)

40 *on oral fixation:*
Sometimes a cigar is just a cigar.
- **Sigmund Freud** 1856-1939 Austrian
psychiatrist: often attributed, but almost
certainly apocryphal

41 *on her boyfriend Porfirio Rubirosa:*
He may be the best lover in the world,
but what do you do the other twenty-
two hours of the day?
- **Zsa Zsa Gabor** 1917- Hungarian-born film
actress: attributed

42 Women need a reason to have sex, men
just need a place.
- **Lowell Ganz** 1948- and **Babaloo Mandel**
1949- American screenwriters: *City
Slickers* (1991 film), spoken by Billy Crystal
as Mitch Robbins

43 Masturbation is the thinking man's
television.
- **Christopher Hampton** 1946- English
dramatist: *The Philanthropist* (1970)

44 Men don't realize that if we're sleeping
with them on the first date, we're
probably not interested in seeing them
again either.
- **Chelsea Handler** 1975- American
comedienne and writer: attributed

45 I regret to say that we of the FBI are
powerless to act in cases of oral-genital
intimacy, unless it has in some way
obstructed interstate commerce.
- **J. Edgar Hoover** 1895-1972 American
director of the FBI: Irving Wallace et al.
Intimate Sex Lives of Famous People (1981)

46 There is no unhappier creature on earth
than a fetishist who yearns to embrace
a woman's shoe and has to embrace the
whole woman.
- **Karl Kraus** 1874-1936 Austrian satirist:
Aphorisms and More Aphorisms (1909)

47 Sexual intercourse began
In nineteen sixty-three
(Which was rather late for me)—
Between the end of the *Chatterley* ban
And the Beatles' first L.P.
- **Philip Larkin** 1922-85 English poet: 'Annus
Mirabilis' (1974)

48 He was into animal husbandry—until
they caught him at it.
- **Tom Lehrer** 1928- American humorist:
in *An Evening Wasted with Tom Lehrer*
(record album, 1953); Nigel Rees (ed.)
Cassell Dictionary of Humorous Quotations
(1999)

49 All this male angst over size. It's *attitude*
women are interested in. Women like a
penis which says 'G'day! God am I glad

to see *you*.'
- **Kathy Lette** 1958– Australian writer: *Mad Cows* (1996)

50 What's the worst thing about oral sex? The view.
- **Maureen Lipman** 1946– English actress: *How Was It For You?* (1985)

51 *on lesbianism:*
I can understand two men. There is something to get hold of. But how do two insides make love?
- **Lydia Lopokova** 1892–1981 Russian ballerina: A. J. P. Taylor letter 5 November 1973

52 What's a promiscuous person? It's usually someone who is getting more sex than you are.
- **Victor Lownes** 1928– American businessman: attributed, N. Mackwood *In and Out* (1980)

53 Many years ago I chased a woman for almost two years, only to discover that her tastes were exactly like mine: we both were crazy about girls.
- **Groucho Marx** 1890–1977 American film comedian: letter 28 March 1955

54 I've been around so long, I knew Doris Day before she was a virgin.
- **Groucho Marx** 1890–1977 American film comedian: Max Wilk *The Wit and Wisdom of Hollywood* (1972)

55 I always thought music was more important than sex—then I thought if I don't hear a concert for a year-and-a-half it doesn't bother me.
- **Jackie Mason** 1931– American comedian: in *Guardian* 17 February 1989

56 A man marries to have a home, but also because he doesn't want to be bothered with sex and all that sort of thing.
- **W. Somerset Maugham** 1874–1965 English novelist: *The Circle* (1921)

57 Continental people have sex life; the English have hot-water bottles.
- **George Mikes** 1912–87 Hungarian-born writer: *How to be an Alien* (1946)

58 Contraceptives should be used on every conceivable occasion.
- **Spike Milligan** 1918–2002 Irish comedian: *The Last Goon Show of All* (1972)

59 *on tantric sex:*
I prefer the plumber position. You stay in all day and nobody comes.
- **John Mortimer** 1923–2009 English novelist, barrister, and dramatist: in *Times* 24 February 2003

60 Not tonight, Josephine.
- **Napoleon I** 1769–1821 French emperor: attributed, but probably apocryphal; R. H. Horne *The History of Napoleon* (1841) describes the circumstances in which the affront might have occurred

61 Your idea of fidelity is not having more than one man in bed at the same time.
- **Frederic Raphael** 1931– British novelist and screenwriter: *Darling* (1965 film)

62 It's so long since I've had sex I've forgotten who ties up whom.
- **Joan Rivers** 1933– American comedienne: attributed

63 Is it not strange that desire should so many years outlive performance?
- **William Shakespeare** 1564–1616 English dramatist: *Henry IV, Part 2* (1597)

64 How long do you want to wait until you start enjoying life? When you're sixty-five you get social security, not girls.
- **Neil Simon** 1927– American dramatist: *Come Blow Your Horn* (1961)

65 There are times when a woman reading *Playboy* feels a little like a Jew reading a Nazi manual.
- **Gloria Steinem** 1934– American journalist: interviewing Hugh Heffner in 1970; Steven Watts *Mr Playboy: Hugh Heffner and the American Dream* (2009)

66 A lady, if surprised by melancholy, might go to bed with a chap, once; or a thousand times if consumed by passion. But twice...*twice*...A lady might think she'd been taken for a tart.
- **Tom Stoppard** 1937– British dramatist: *Night and Day* (1978)

67 CHAIRMAN OF MILITARY TRIBUNAL: What would you do if you saw a German soldier trying to violate your sister?

STRACHEY: I would try to get between them.

- **Lytton Strachey** 1880-1932 English biographer: in Robert Graves *Good-bye to All That* (1929); otherwise rendered as, 'I should interpose my body'

68 Masturbation: the primary sexual activity of mankind. In the nineteenth century, it was a disease; in the twentieth, it's a cure.

- **Thomas Szasz** 1920-2012 Hungarian-born psychiatrist: *The Second Sin* (1973)

69 Dip me in chocolate and throw me to the lesbians.

- **Richard Thomas** and **Stewart Lee**: *Jerry Springer—the Opera* (2003)

70 Enjoy your supper, Mr Percy, the port is on the chim-a-ney piece, and don't forget it's *still* adultery!
on finding her husband Herbert Beerbohm Tree dining à deux with the young and handsome actor Esmé Percy

- **Lady Tree** 1863-1937 English actress: attributed, perhaps apocryphal

71 I'm all for bringing back the birch, but only between consenting adults.

- **Gore Vidal** 1925-2012 American novelist and critic: in *Sunday Times Magazine* 16 September 1973

72 All this fuss about sleeping together. For physical pleasure I'd sooner go to my dentist any day.

- **Evelyn Waugh** 1903-66 English novelist: *Vile Bodies* (1930)

73 Why don't you come up sometime, and see me?
usually quoted as, 'Why don't you come up and see me sometime?'

- **Mae West** 1892-1980 American film actress: in *She Done Him Wrong* (1933 film)

74 It's not the men in my life that counts— it's the life in my men.

- **Mae West** 1892-1980 American film actress: in *I'm No Angel* (1933 film)

75 It is no longer enough to be lusty. One must be a sexual gourmet.

- **George F. Will** 1941- American columnist: *The Pursuit of Happiness, and Other Sobering Thoughts* (1978)

Sickness and Health

see also **EXERCISE, MEDICINE**

A man is as old as his arteries.   **Thomas Sydenham**

1 You know my father died of cancer when I was a teenager. He had it before it became popular.

- **Goodman Ace** 1899-1982 American humorist: in *New Yorker* 1977

2 I've got this terrible pain in all the diodes down my left side.

- **Douglas Adams** 1952-2001 English science fiction writer: *The Hitchhiker's Guide to the Galaxy* (BBC radio, 1978), Marvin the Paranoid Android

3 I feel as young as I ever did, apart from the occasional heart attack.

- **Robert Benchley** 1889-1945 American humorist: attributed

4 I don't deserve this award, but I have arthritis, and I don't deserve that either.

- **Jack Benny** 1894-1974 American comedian: attributed

5 In 1969 I gave up women and alcohol. It was the worst 20 minutes of my life.

- **George Best** 1946-2005 Northern Irish footballer: attributed

6 In the face of such overwhelming statistical possibilities, hypochondria has always seemed to me to be the only rational position to take on life.

- **John Diamond** 1953-2001 British journalist: *C: Because Cowards Get Cancer Too* (1998)

7 Health...what my friends are always drinking to before they fall down.
  ▪ **Phyllis Diller** 1917-2012 American actress: *The Joys of Aging—And How to Avoid Them* (1981)

8 I wish I had the voice of Homer
  To sing of rectal carcinoma,
  Which kills a lot more chaps, in fact,
  Than were bumped off when Troy was
      sacked.
  ▪ **J. B. S. Haldane** 1892-1964 Scottish mathematical biologist: 'Cancer's a Funny Thing'; Ronald Clark *J. B. S.* (1968)

9 The average, healthy, well-adjusted adult gets up at seven-thirty in the morning feeling just plain terrible.
  ▪ **Jean Kerr** 1923-2003 American writer: *How I Got To Be Perfect* (1979)

10 Besides death, constipation is the big fear in hospitals.
  ▪ **Robert McCrum** 1953- British writer: *My Year Off* (1998)

11 *on hearing of the illness of Traill, who in 1904 had beaten him for the Provostship of Trinity Dublin:*
  Nothing trivial, I hope.
  ▪ **John Pentland Mahaffy** 1839-1919 Irish writer: Ulick O'Connor *Oliver St John Gogarty* (1964)

12 I think the worst time to have a heart attack is during a game of charades.
  ▪ **Demetri Martin** 1973- American comedian: attributed

13 It's no longer a question of staying healthy. It's a question of finding a sickness you like.
  ▪ **Jackie Mason** 1931- American comedian: attributed

14 *on her replacement hips and knee:*
  I'm Dorothy's daughter up top and the Tin Man down below.
  ▪ **Liza Minelli** 1946- American actress and singer: in *Daily Telegraph* 30 June 2011

15 There is no danger of my getting scurvy [while in England], as I have to consume at least two gin-and-limes every evening to keep the cold out.
  ▪ **S. J. Perelman** 1904-79 American humorist: letter, 13 December 1953

16 Hypochondria is the one disease I haven't got.
  ▪ **David Renwick** 1951- and **Andrew Marshall**: *The Burkiss Way* (BBC Radio, 1978); Nigel Rees *Cassell Dictionary of Humorous Quotations* (1999)

17 A man is as old as his arteries.
  ▪ **Thomas Sydenham** 1624-89 English physician: attributed, but probably apocryphal

18 When people discussed tonics, pick-me-ups after a severe illness, she kept to herself the prescription of a quick dip in bed with someone you liked but were not in love with. A shock of sexual astonishment which could make you feel astonishingly well and high spirited.
  ▪ **Mary Wesley** 1912-2002 English novelist: *Not That Sort of Girl* (1987)

19 *on hearing that Peter Sellers had suffered a heart attack:*
  What do you mean, heart attack? You've got to have a heart before you can have an attack.
  ▪ **Billy Wilder** 1906-2002 American screenwriter and director: Roger Lewis *The Life and Death of Peter Sellers* (1994)

Singing *see* SONGS AND SINGING

Sleep and Dreams

There ain't no way to find out why a snorer can't hear himself snore. **Mark Twain**

1 The amount of sleep required by the average person is about five minutes more.
   - **Anonymous**: saying, sometimes attibuted to Max Kauffman or Wilson Mizner

2 Sleep is when all the unsorted stuff comes flying out as from a dustbin upset in a high wind.
   - **William Golding** 1911-93 English novelist: *Pincher Martin* (1956)

3 I love sleep because it is both pleasant and safe to use.
   - **Fran Lebowitz** 1946- American writer: *Metropolitan Life* (1978)

4 And so to bed.
   - **Samuel Pepys** 1633-1703 English diarist: diary 20 April 1660

5 Sometimes I lie awake at night and I ask, 'Where have I gone wrong?' Then a voice says to me, 'This is going to take more than one night.'
   - **Charles Monroe Schulz** 1922-2000 American cartoonist: attributed

6 Many's the long night I've dreamed of cheese—toasted, mostly.
   - **Robert Louis Stevenson** 1850-94 Scottish novelist: *Treasure Island* (1883)

7 There ain't no way to find out why a snorer can't hear himself snore.
   - **Mark Twain** 1835-1910 American writer: *Tom Sawyer Abroad* (1894)

8 I haven't been to sleep for over a year. That's why I go to bed early. One needs more rest if one doesn't sleep.
   - **Evelyn Waugh** 1903-66 English novelist: *Decline and Fall* (1928)

Snobbery

see also **CLASS**

The trouble with Michael [Heseltine] is that he had to buy all his furniture.
Michael Jopling

1 NILES: She's been afraid to fly since her harrowing incident.
   DAPHNE: Oh, dear…Did a plane almost crash?
   NILES: No, she was bumped from first class. She still wakes up screaming.
   - **David Angell** 1946-2001, **Peter Casey**, and **David Lee** American television producers: *Frasier* (NBC TV, 1994) 'Can't Buy Me Love', written by Chuck Ranberg and Anne Flett-Giordano; spoken by David Hyde Pierce and Jane Leeves

2 Sir Walter Elliot, of Kellynch-hall, in Somersetshire, was a man who, for his own amusement, never took up any book but the Baronetage; there he found occupation for an idle hour, and consolation in a distressed one.
   - **Jane Austen** 1775-1817 English novelist: *Persuasion* (1818)

3 Vulgarity has its uses. Vulgarity often cuts ice which refinement scrapes at vainly.
   - **Max Beerbohm** 1872-1956 English critic, essayist, and caricaturist: letter, 21 May 1921

4 Sapper, Buchan, Dornford Yates, practitioners in that school of Snobbery with Violence that runs like a thread of good-class tweed through twentieth-century literature.
   - **Alan Bennett** 1934- English dramatist and actor: *Forty Years On* (1969)

5 Gaily into Ruislip Gardens
Runs the red electric train,
With a thousand Ta's and Pardon's
Daintily alights Elaine.
- **John Betjeman** 1906-84 English poet:
'Middlesex' (1954)

6 And this is good old Boston,
The home of the bean and the cod,
Where the Lowells talk to the Cabots
And the Cabots talk only to God.
- **John Collins Bossidy** 1860-1928 American
oculist: verse spoken at Holy Cross College
alumni dinner in Boston, Massachusetts,
1910

7 From Poland to polo in one generation.
of Darryl Zanuck
- **Arthur Caesar** 1892-1953 American
screenwriter: Max Wilk *The Wit and
Wisdom of Hollywood* (1972)

8 The trouble with Michael is that he had
to buy all his furniture.
of Michael Heseltine
- **Michael Jopling** 1930- British Conservative
politician: Alan Clark diary 17 June 1987

9 *to undergraduate Lord Curzon who requested
permission from his Head of College to attend
a ball in London in honour of the Empress
Augusta of Germany:*
I don't think much of Empresses. Good
morning.
- **Benjamin Jowett** 1817-93 English classicist:
Kenneth Rose *Superior Person* (1969)

10 *alleged response to being addressed as
'Mr Kingsley' rather than 'Sir Ben' on the
set of his new film:*
It's a small word. It's not long. And it's
not difficult to remember.
- **Ben Kingsley** 1943- English actor:
attributed; in *Times* 17 June 2003

11 We always feel kindly disposed towards
noble authors.
- **Lord Macaulay** 1800-59 English politician and
historian: in *Edinburgh Review* January 1833

12 *when the Duchess of Devonshire apologized
to Queen Mary for her son's marrying the
American dancer Adele Astaire:*
Don't worry. I have a niece called Smith.
- **Queen Mary** 1867-1953 British Queen
Consort: in *Times* 1 June 1994; obituary of
Lady May Abel Smith

13 Thank goodness for Tesco. It keeps the
riff-raff out of Waitrose.
- **Royce Mills** 1942- English actor: as Widow
Twankay in *Aladddin* at the Yvonne Arnaud
Theatre, Guildford, 2012

14 *Ogden Nash had had his car broken into in
Boston:*
I'd expect to be robbed in Chicago
But not in the land of the cod,
So I hope that the Cabots and Lowells
Will mention the matter to God.
- **Ogden Nash** 1902-71 American humorist:
David Frost and Michael Shea *The Mid-
Atlantic Companion* (1986)

15 *on being told that Clare Boothe Luce was
always kind to her inferiors:*
And where does she find them?
- **Dorothy Parker** 1893-1967 American critic
and humorist: Marion Meade *What Fresh
Hell is This?* (1988)

16 There is no stronger craving in the
world than that of the rich for titles,
except perhaps that of the titled for
riches.
- **Hesketh Pearson** 1887-1964 English actor
and biographer: *The Pilgrim Daughters*
(1961)

17 I am his Highness' dog at Kew;
Pray, tell me sir, whose dog are you?
- **Alexander Pope** 1688-1744 English poet:
'Epigram Engraved on the Collar of a Dog
which I gave to his Royal Highness' (1738)

18 You can be in the Horseguards and still
be common, dear.
- **Terence Rattigan** 1911-77 English dramatist:
Separate Tables (1954) 'Table Number
Seven'

19 Good God! I've never drunk a vintage
that starts with the number two
before.
- **Nicholas Soames** 1948- British Conservative
politician: in *Daily Mail* 5 June 2003

20 Whenever he met a great man he
grovelled before him, and my-lorded
him as only a free-born Briton can do.
- **William Makepeace Thackeray** 1811-63
English novelist: *Vanity Fair* (1847-8)

Society and Social Life

see also **PARTIES**

....

I don't want to belong to any club that will accept me as a member.
Groucho Marx

1 It was a delightful visit;—perfect, in being much too short.
   - **Jane Austen** 1775-1817 English novelist: *Emma* (1816)

2 Though you would often in the fifteenth century have heard the snobbish Roman say, in a would-be off-hand tone, 'I am dining with the Borgias tonight,' no Roman ever was able to say, 'I dined last night with the Borgias.'
   - **Max Beerbohm** 1872-1956 English critic, essayist, and caricaturist: *And Even Now* (1920)

3 Phone for the fish-knives, Norman
   As Cook is a little unnerved;
   You kiddies have crumpled the serviettes
   And I must have things daintily served.
   - **John Betjeman** 1906-84 English poet: 'How to get on in Society' (1954)

4 I'm a man more dined against than dining.
   - **Maurice Bowra** 1898-1971 English scholar and literary critic: John Betjeman *Summoned by Bells* (1960)

5 In London, at the Café de Paris, I sang to café society; in Las Vegas, at the Desert Inn, I sang to Nescafé society.
   - **Noël Coward** 1899-1973 English dramatist, actor, and composer: Sheridan Morley *The Quotable Noël Coward* (1999)

6 I'm Burlington Bertie
   I rise at ten thirty and saunter along like a toff,
   I walk down the Strand with my gloves on my hand,
   Then I walk down again with them off.
   - **W. F. Hargreaves** 1846-1919 British songwriter: 'Burlington Bertie from Bow' (1915)

7 Dear Miss Manners: If you had a single piece of advice to offer a couple who want to break into society, what would it be?
   Gentle Reader, Don't bother.
   - **Judith Martin** 1938- American journalist: *Miss Manners Guide to Excruciatingly Correct Behaviour* (1979)

8 PLEASE ACCEPT MY RESIGNATION. I DON'T WANT TO BELONG TO ANY CLUB THAT WILL ACCEPT ME AS A MEMBER.
   - **Groucho Marx** 1890-1977 American film comedian: telegram; *Groucho and Me* (1959)

9 The truly free man is the one who will turn down an invitation to dinner without giving an excuse.
   - **Jules Renard** 1864-1910 French novelist and dramatist: *Journal* October 1895

10 All decent people live beyond their incomes nowadays, and those who aren't respectable live beyond other peoples'.
   - **Saki** 1870-1916 Scottish writer: *Chronicles of Clovis* (1911)

11 MENDOZA: I am a brigand: I live by robbing the rich.
   TANNER: I am a gentleman: I live by robbing the poor.
   - **George Bernard Shaw** 1856-1950 Irish dramatist: *Man and Superman* (1903)

12 GERALD: I suppose society is wonderfully delightful!
   LORD ILLINGWORTH: To be in it is merely a bore. But to be out of it simply a tragedy.
   - **Oscar Wilde** 1854-1900 Irish dramatist and poet: *A Woman of No Importance* (1893)

Songs and Singing

see also OPERA

....

I was just wondering, is this the place where I'm supposed to be drowned by the waves or by the orchestra? **John Coates**

1 Today if something is not worth saying, people sing it.
  - **Pierre-Augustin Caron de Beaumarchais** 1732-99 French dramatist: *Le Barbier de Séville* (1775)

2 *to the tenor Heddle Nash, lying on the bed in Mimi's deathbed scene:*
  'I can't hear you. Sing up!'
  'How do you expect me to sing my best in this position, Sir Thomas?'
  'In that position, my dear fellow, I have performed some of my greatest achievements.'
  - **Thomas Beecham** 1879-1961 English conductor: Neville Cardus *Sir Thomas Beecham* (1961)

3 I love to sing. And I love to drink scotch. Most people would rather hear me drink scotch.
  - **George Burns** 1896-1996 American comedian: in *New York Magazine* 13 May 1974

4 I was just wondering, is this the place where I'm supposed to be drowned by the waves or by the orchestra?
  the tenor in The Wreckers *explaining to Sir Thomas Beecham why he had stopped*
  - **John Coates** 1865-1941 English tenor: C. Reid *Sir Thomas Beecham* (1961)

5 Swans sing before they die: 'twere no bad thing
  Should certain persons die before they sing.
  - **Samuel Taylor Coleridge** 1772-1834 English poet, critic, and philosopher: 'On a Volunteer Singer' (1834)

6 DYLAN: I *do* know what my songs are about.

PLAYBOY: And what's that?
DYLAN: Oh, some are about four minutes; some are about five, and some, believe it or not, are about eleven.
  - **Bob Dylan** 1941- American singer and songwriter: interview in *Playboy* March 1966

7 People never talked about my music. They just counted how many knickers were on the stage.
  - **Tom Jones** 1940- Welsh pop singer: in *Sunday Times* 18 June 2000

8 *refusing to accept further changes to lyrics:*
  Call me Miss Birdseye. This show is frozen!
  - **Ethel Merman** 1909-84 American singer and actress: in *Times* 13 July 1985

9 'Who wrote that song?'
  'Rodgers and Hammerstein. If you can imagine it taking *two* men to write one song.'
  of 'Some Enchanted Evening' (1949)
  - **Cole Porter** 1891-1964 American songwriter: G. Eells *The Life that Late He Led* (1967)

10 Tenors are usually short, stout men (except when they are Wagnerian tenors, in which case they are large, stout men).
  - **Harold Schonberg** 1915-2003 American music critic: in *Show* December 1961

11 *the president of CBS Records to Leonard Cohen:*
  Leonard, we know you're great, but we don't know if you're any good.
  - **Walter Yetnikoff** 1933- American businessman: in 1984; Ira B. Nadel *Various Positions: a life of Leonard Cohen* (1996)

Speeches

The most popular speaker is the one who sits down before he stands up.
John Pentland Mahaffy

1 An after dinner speech should be like a lady's dress: long enough to cover the subject but short enough to be interesting.
 • **Anonymous**: traditional saying

2 There are three golden rules for Parliamentary speakers: 'Stand up. Speak up. Shut up.'
 • **Anonymous**: traditional saying, sometimes associated with James W. Lowther (1855–1949), Speaker of the House of Commons

3 I do not object to people looking at their watches when I am speaking. But I strongly object when they start shaking them to make certain they are still going.
 • **Lord Birkett** 1883-1962 English judge: in *Observer* 30 October 1960

4 Castroenteritis.
describing Fidel Castro's speaking style
 • **Guillermo Cabrera Infante** 1929-2005 Cuban writer: *Mea Cuba* (1994)

5 *encountering A. P. Herbert after his maiden speech in the House of Commons:*
That wasn't a maiden speech—it was a brazen hussy of a speech—a painted tart of a speech.
 • **Winston Churchill** 1874-1965 British Conservative statesman: Collin Brooks, diary 9 December 1935

6 ALEXANDER SMYTH: You, sir, speak for the present generation, but I speak for posterity.
HENRY CLAY: Yes, and you seem resolved to speak until the arrival of *your* audience.
 • **Henry Clay** 1777-1852 American politician: in the US Senate; Robert V. Remini *Henry Clay* (1991)

7 If you don't say anything, you won't be called on to repeat it.
 • **Calvin Coolidge** 1872-1933 American Republican statesman: attributed

8 I dreamt I was making a speech in the House. I woke up, and by Jove I was!
 • **Duke of Devonshire** 1833-1908 British Conservative politician: Winston Churchill *Thoughts and Adventures* (1932)

9 A sophistical rhetorician, inebriated with the exuberance of his own verbosity.
of Gladstone
 • **Benjamin Disraeli** 1804-81 British Tory statesman and novelist: in *Times* 29 July 1878

10 Hubert Humphrey talks so fast that listening to him is like trying to read *Playboy* magazine with your wife turning the pages.
 • **Barry Goldwater** 1909-98 American Republican politician: attributed; Ned Sherrin *Cutting Edge* (1984)

11 Please can we have no more complaints about the pauses in Tony Blair's speeches. They are the best parts.
 • **David Guest**: letter to *Daily Telegraph* 17 February 2005

12 *a 'close second' to Robert Benchley's choice of the most disagreeable combination of words in English:*
Would you care to say a few words?
 • **Richard Ingrams** 1937- English satirical journalist: in *Observer* 29 August 2004 (see also **words** 5)

13 The human brain starts working the moment you are born and never stops until you stand up to speak in public.
 • **George Jessel** 1898-1981 American comedian: in *Observer* 7 August 1949

14 I may not know much, but I know chicken shit from a chicken salad.
on a speech by Richard Nixon
 • **Lyndon Baines Johnson** 1908-73 American Democratic statesman: Merle Miller *Lyndon* (1980)

15 Did you ever think that making a
speech on economics is a lot like pissing
down your leg? It seems hot to you, but
it never does to anyone else.
to J. K. Galbraith
- **Lyndon Baines Johnson** 1908-73 American
Democratic statesman: J. K. Galbraith *A Life
in Our Times* (1981)

16 I appreciate your welcome. As the cow
said to the Maine farmer 'Thank you for
a warm hand on a cold morning'.
- **John F. Kennedy** 1917-63 American
Democratic statesman: speech,
2 November 1960

17 How can one best summon up the
exquisite, earnest tedium of the speech
of Sir Geoffrey Howe in yesterday's
South African debate? It was rather like
watching a much-loved family tortoise
creeping over the lawn in search of a
distant tomato.
on the then British Foreign Secretary
- **David McKie** 1935- British journalist: in
Guardian 17 July 1986

18 The most popular speaker is the one
who sits down before he stands up.
- **John Pentland Mahaffy** 1839-1919 Irish
writer: W. B. Stanford and R. B. McDowell
Mahaffy (1971)

19 A speech is like a love affair: any fool
can start one but to end one requires
considerable skill.
- **Lord Mancroft** 1914-87 British Conservative
politician: attributed

20 According to most studies, people's
number one fear is public speaking.
Number two is death. Death is number
two. Does that sound right? This means
to the average person, if you go to a
funeral, you're better off in the casket
than doing the eulogy.
- **Jerry Seinfeld** 1954- American comedian:
attributed

21 He has devoted the best years of his life
to preparing his impromptu speeches.
on Winston Churchill
- **F. E. Smith** 1872-1930 British Conservative
politician and lawyer: S. E. Ayling *Twelve
Portraits of Power* (1962)

22 I fear I cannot make an amusing speech.
I have just been reading a book which
says that 'all geniuses are devoid of
humour'.
- **Stephen Spender** 1909-95 English poet:
speech in a debate at the Cambridge
Union, January 1938

23 Nixon's farm policy is vague, but he is
going a long way toward solving the
corn surplus by his speeches.
- **Adlai Stevenson** 1900-65 American
Democratic politician: Bill Adler *The
Stevenson Wit* (1966)

24 The last time I was in this hall was
when my late beloved boss, Frank
Knox, the secretary of the Navy, spoke
here, and it was a better speech than the
one I'll be giving here tonight. I should
know, I wrote them both.
- **Adlai Stevenson** 1900-65 American
Democratic politician: attributed

25 Whales only get killed when they
spout.
declining a request to be interviewed
- **Denis Thatcher** 1915-2003 British
businessman: in *Times* 8 July 2003

26 To remain silent is the most useful
service that a mediocre speaker can
render to the public good.
- **Alexis de Tocqueville** 1805-59 French
historian and politician: *Democracy in
America* (1840)

27 I am here to propose a toast to the
sports writers. It's up to you whether
you stand or not.
- **Freddie Trueman** 1931-2006 English
cricketer: Michael Parkinson *Sporting Lives*
(1993)

28 Better to keep your mouth shut and
appear stupid than to open it and
remove all doubt.
- **Mark Twain** 1835-1910 American writer:
James Munson (ed.) *The Sayings of
Mark Twain* (1992); attributed, perhaps
apocryphal

Sports and Games

see also **BASEBALL, BOXING, CRICKET, FOOTBALL, GOLF, TENNIS**

··

We break bones and we lose teeth. We play rugby. **Martin Johnson**

1 HE: Excuse me won't you—I'm a little stiff from badminton.
SHE: It doesn't matter where you're from.
- **Anonymous**: traditional, now often associated with Morecambe and Wise

2 Bridge, because of its tendency to encourage prolonged smoking and its deadly immobility, is probably the most dangerous game played in England now.
a doctor's view
- **Anonymous**: in *Medical World* May 1960

3 *on being asked why he did not hunt:*
I do not see why I should break my neck because a dog chooses to run after a nasty smell.
- **Arthur James Balfour** 1848-1930 British Conservative statesman: Ian Malcolm *Lord Balfour: A Memory* (1930)

4 Playing snooker gives you firm hands and helps to build up character. It is the ideal recreation for dedicated nuns.
view of the Pope's emissary, attending a sponsored snooker championship at Tyburn convent
- **Luigi Barbarito** 1922- Italian Roman Catholic clergyman: in *Daily Telegraph* 15 November 1989

5 Rugby is a beastly game played by gentlemen.
Soccer is a gentleman's game played by beasts.
[American] Football is a beastly game played by beasts.
- **Henry Blaha** American football player: attributed

6 I do not participate in any sport with ambulances at the bottom of the hill.
- **Erma Bombeck** 1927-96 American humorist: attributed; A. J. Maikovich and M. Brown (eds.) *Sports Quotations* (2000)

7 If a man watches three games of football in a row, he should be declared legally dead.
- **Erma Bombeck** 1927-96 American humorist: attributed; A. J. Maikovich and M. Brown (eds.) *Sports Quotations* (2000)

8 A couple of weeks ago I knew nothing about the Olympics. Now I can't wait for next year's.
- **Frankie Boyle** 1972- British comedian: in *Sun* 10 August 2012

9 *on running the London Marathon:*
I've set myself a target. I'm going for less than eleven-and-a-half days.
- **Jo Brand** 1957- English comedian: in *Observer* 27 February 2005

10 Life's too short for chess.
- **H. J. Byron** 1835-84 English dramatist: *Our Boys* (1875)

11 *on fox-hunting*
The only little red pests I pursue these days are in this House.
- **David Cameron** 1966- British Conservative statesman: in the House of Commons, 9 January 2013

12 The trouble with referees is that they just don't care which side wins.
- **Tom Canterbury** American basketball player: in *Guardian* 24 December 1980

13 As elaborate a waste of human intelligence as you could find anywhere outside an advertising agency.
on chess
- **Raymond Chandler** 1888-1959 American writer: *The Long Goodbye* (1953)

14 If you lived in Sheffield and were called Sebastian, you had to learn to run fast at a very early stage.
- **Sebastian Coe** 1956- English athlete: in *Times* 26 May 1998

15 I went to a fight the other night and an ice hockey game broke out.
- **Rodney Dangerfield** 1921-2004 American comedian: attributed

16 Deer-stalking would be a very fine sport if only the deer had guns.
- **W. S. Gilbert** 1836-1911 English writer: Hesketh Pearson *Gilbert and Sullivan* (1951)

17 The thing about sport, any sport, is that swearing is very much part of it.
- **Jimmy Greaves** 1940- English footballer: in *Observer* 1 January 1989 'Sayings of the Year'

18 I was watching sumo wrestling on the TV for two hours before I realized it was darts.
- **Hattie Hayridge** 1959- English comedienne: attributed

19 What you've got to remember about Michael is that under that cold professional Germanic exterior beats a heart of stone.
of Michael Schumacher
- **Damon Hill** 1960- English motor-racing driver: in May 2000

20 Get your retaliation in first.
- **Carwyn James** 1929-83 Welsh Rugby Football coach: to the British Lions team in 1971; quoted in David Pickering (ed.) *Cassell's Sports Quotations* (2002)

21 The only athletic sport I ever mastered was backgammon.
- **Douglas Jerrold** 1803-57 English dramatist and journalist: Walter Jerrold *Douglas Jerrold* (1914)

22 We break bones and we lose teeth. We play rugby.
- **Martin Johnson** 1970- English rugby player: Martin Johnson *Autobiography* (2003)

23 It is very strange, and very melancholy, that the paucity of human pleasures should persuade us ever to call hunting one of them.
- **Samuel Johnson** 1709-84 English poet, critic, and lexicographer: Hester Lynch Piozzi *Anecdotes of ... Johnson* (1786)

24 I remain of the opinion that there is no game from bridge to cricket that is not improved by a little light conversation;

a view which...is shared only by a small and unjustly despised minority.
- **Osbert Lancaster** 1908-86 English writer and cartoonist: *All Done From Memory* (1953)

25 If you play bridge badly you make your partner suffer, but if you play poker badly you make everybody happy.
- **Joe Laurie Jr.** 1892-1954 American comedian: attributed

26 If you don't have confidence, you'll always find a way not to win.
- **Carl Lewis** 1961- American athlete: attributed

27 Rodeoing is about the only sport you can't fix. You'd have to talk to the bulls and the horses, and they wouldn't understand you.
- **Bill Linderman** 1920-65 American rodeo cowboy: in 1961; Jonathon Green and Don Atyeo (eds.) *The Book of Sports Quotes* (1979)

28 Swimming is a confusing sport, because sometimes you do it for fun, and other times you do it to not die. And when I'm swimming, sometimes I'm not sure which one it is.
- **Demetri Martin** 1973- American comedian: attributed

29 I hate all sports as rabidly as a person who likes sports hates common sense.
- **H. L. Mencken** 1880-1956 American journalist and literary critic: Laurence J. Peter (ed.) *Quotations for our Time* (1977)

30 Athletic sports, save in the case of young boys, are designed for idiots.
- **George Jean Nathan** 1882-1958 American critic and writer: *Testament of a Critic* (1931)

31 The sport of ski-ing consists of wearing three thousand dollars' worth of clothes and equipment and driving two hundred miles in the snow in order to stand around at a bar and get drunk.
- **P. J. O'Rourke** 1947- American humorous writer: *Modern Manners* (1984)

32 *Goering's excuse for being late was a shooting party:*
Animals, I hope.
- **Eric Phipps** 1875-1945 British diplomat: Ned Sherrin *Cutting Edge* (1984); attributed

33 The atmosphere here is a cross between
the Munich Beer Festival and the
Coliseum at Rome when the Christians
were on the menu.
at a darts match
- **Sid Waddell** 1940-2012 English sports
commentator: in 1980, attributed

34 I have observed in women of her type
a tendency to regard all athletics as
inferior forms of foxhunting.
- **Evelyn Waugh** 1903-66 English novelist:
Decline and Fall (1928)

35 The English country gentleman
galloping after a fox—the unspeakable
in full pursuit of the uneatable.
- **Oscar Wilde** 1854-1900 Irish dramatist and
poet: *A Woman of No Importance* (1893); see
law 30

36 *on American football:*
Football combines the two worst
features of modern American life: it's
violence punctuated by committee
meetings.
- **George F. Will** 1941- American columnist:
Baseball (PBS TV, 1994)

37 The fascination of shooting as a sport
depends almost wholly on whether
you are at the right or wrong end of
a gun.
- **P. G. Wodehouse** 1881-1975 English writer:
attributed

38 Jogging is for people who aren't
intelligent enough to watch television.
- **Victoria Wood** 1953- British writer and
comedienne: *Mens Sana in Thingummy
Doodah* (1990)

Statistics

Statistics are like a bikini. What they reveal is suggestive, but what they
conceal is vital.   **Aaron Levenstein**

1 [The War Office kept three sets of
figures:] one to mislead the public,
another to mislead the Cabinet, and the
third to mislead itself.
- **Herbert Asquith** 1852-1928 British Liberal
statesman: Alistair Horne *Price of Glory*
(1962)

2 There are three kinds of lies: lies,
damned lies and statistics.
- **Benjamin Disraeli** 1804-81 British Tory
statesman and novelist: attributed to
Disraeli in Mark Twain *Autobiography*
(1924)

3 He uses statistics as a drunken man uses
lamp posts—for support rather than
illumination.
- **Andrew Lang** 1844-1912 Scottish man of
letters: attributed

4 Statistics are like a bikini. What they
reveal is suggestive, but what they
conceal is vital.
- **Aaron Levenstein** 1911-86 American
academic: attributed, Laurence J. Peter
Quotations for Our Time (1977)

5 I treat opinion polls with a pinch of
sugar.
- **Ed Miliband** 1969- British Labour
politician: in *Sunday Times* 22 January 2012

Success

see also **FAILURE**

....

Be nice to people on your way up because you'll meet 'em on your way down.
Wilson Mizner

1 Eighty per cent of success is showing up.
- **Woody Allen** 1935- American film director, writer, and actor: attributed

2 The road to success is always under construction.
- **Anonymous**: traditional saying, today associated with Lily Tomlin

3 Success is the one unpardonable sin against our fellows.
- **Ambrose Bierce** 1842-c.1914 American writer: *The Enlarged Devil's Dictionary* (1967)

4 Where did we go right?
of an unexpected success
- **Mel Brooks** 1926- American film director and actor: *The Producers* (1967 film), spoken by Zero Mostel

5 Behind every successful man you'll find a woman who has nothing to wear.
- **Harold Coffin** d. 1981 American columnist: attributed in *Reader's Digest* (1960)

6 Whom the gods wish to destroy they first call promising.
- **Cyril Connolly** 1903-74 English writer: *Enemies of Promise* (1938)

7 Nothing succeeds, they say, like success. And certainly nothing fails like failure.
- **Margaret Drabble** 1939- English novelist: *The Millstone* (1965)

8 Success is a lousy teacher. It seduces smart people into thinking they can't lose.
- **Bill Gates** 1955- American computer entrepreneur: *The Road Ahead* (1996)

9 *formula for success:*
Rise early. Work late. Strike oil.
- **John Paul Getty** 1892-1976 American industrialist: attributed

10 Behind every man's achievement is a proud wife and a surprised mother-in-law.
- **Brooks Hays** 1898-1981 American Democratic politician: introducing his ninety-five-year-old mother-in-law to President Kennedy, 1 December 1961

11 Well, we knocked the bastard off!
on conquering Mount Everest, 1953
- **Edmund Hillary** 1919-2008 New Zealand mountaineer: *Nothing Venture, Nothing Win* (1975)

12 Luck, like a Russian car, generally only works if you push it.
- **Tom Holt** 1961- English novelist: *My Hero* (1996)

13 This very remarkable man
Commends a most practical plan:
You can do what you want
If you don't think you can't,
So don't think you can't think you can.
- **Charles Inge** 1868-1957: 'On Monsieur Coué' (1928)

14 Success didn't spoil me. I've always been insufferable.
- **Fran Lebowitz** 1946- American writer: attributed

15 It is sobering to consider that when Mozart was my age he had already been dead for a year.
- **Tom Lehrer** 1928- American humorist: N. Shapiro (ed.) *An Encyclopedia of Quotations about Music* (1978)

16 How to succeed in business without really trying.
- **Shepherd Mead** 1914-94 American advertising executive: title of book (1952)

17 The theory seems to be that as long as a man is a failure he is one of God's children, but that as soon as he succeeds he is taken over by the Devil.
- **H. L. Mencken** 1880-1956 American journalist and literary critic: *Minority Report* (1956)

18 Be nice to people on your way up because you'll meet 'em on your way down.
- **Wilson Mizner** 1876-1933 American dramatist: Alva Johnston *The Legendary Mizners* (1953)

19 On the highest throne in the world, we still sit only on our bottom.
- **Montaigne** 1533-92 French moralist and essayist: *Essays* (1580)

20 The world is divided into people who do things and people who get the credit. Try, if you can, to belong to the first class. There's far less competition.
- **Dwight Morrow** 1873-1931 American lawyer, banker, and diplomat: letter to his son; Harold Nicolson *Dwight Morrow* (1935)

21 David Frost has risen without trace.
- **Kitty Muggeridge** 1903-94 English writer: said c.1965 to Malcolm Muggeridge

22 It is difficult to soar like an eagle when you are surrounded by turkeys.
words embroidered on a cushion for her husband John Osborne
- **Helen Osborne** 1939-2004: in *Daily Telegraph* 14 January 2004

23 The man of talent is like a marksman who hits a mark others cannot hit; the man of genius is like a marksman who hits a mark they cannot even see to.
- **Arthur Schopenhauer** 1788-1860 German philosopher: *The World as Will and Representation* (1886)

24 I never climbed any ladder: I have achieved eminence by sheer gravitation.
- **George Bernard Shaw** 1856-1950 Irish dramatist: preface to *The Irrational Knot* (1905)

25 Our business in this world is not to succeed, but to continue to fail, in good spirits.
- **Robert Louis Stevenson** 1850-94 Scottish novelist: *Ethical Studies* (1924)

26 President George W. Bush overcame an incredible lack of obstacles to achieve his success.
- **Jon Stewart** 1962- American satirist: in concert at the Prince Edward Theatre, 11 December 2005

27 There's no deodorant like success.
- **Elizabeth Taylor** 1932-2011 English-born American actress: in *Life* 18 December 1964

28 Success is the necessary misfortune of life, but it is only to the very unfortunate that it comes early.
- **Anthony Trollope** 1815-82 English novelist: *Orley Farm* (1862)

29 Whenever a friend succeeds, a little something in me dies.
- **Gore Vidal** 1925-2012 American novelist and critic: in *Sunday Times Magazine* 16 September 1973

30 It matters not whether you win or lose: what matters is whether I win or lose.
- **Darin Weinberg**: attributed

31 Moderation is a fatal thing, Lady Hunstanton. Nothing succeeds like excess.
- **Oscar Wilde** 1854-1900 Irish dramatist and poet: *A Woman of No Importance* (1893)

32 Success is a science; if you have the conditions, you get the result.
- **Oscar Wilde** 1854-1900 Irish dramatist and poet: letter ?March-April 1883

33 *to fellow Welshman, the actor Victor Spinetti:*
Ah, Victor, still struggling to keep your head below water.
- **Emlyn Williams** 1905-87 Welsh dramatist: attributed; Ned Sherrin *Cutting Edge* (1984)

Taxes

....

Income Tax has made more Liars out of the American people than Golf.
Will Rogers

1 I believe we should all pay our tax bill with a smile. I tried—but they wanted cash.
   - **Anonymous**: modern saying

2 Why does a slight tax increase cost you two hundred dollars and a substantial tax cut save you thirty cents?
   - **Peg Bracken** 1918-2007 American writer: *I Didn't Come Here To Argue* (1969)

3 Mansions can't run away to Switzerland.
   on taxing the homes of the wealthy
   - **Vince Cable** 1943- British Liberal Democrat politician: in *Independent on Sunday* 31 July 2011

4 It was as true…as taxes is. And nothing's truer than them.
   - **Charles Dickens** 1812-70 English novelist: *David Copperfield* (1850)

5 In the first year the Income Tax paper arrived and I filled it up to show that I was not liable. They returned the paper with 'Most unsatisfactory' scrawled across it. I wrote 'I entirely agree' under the words, and returned it once more.
   - **Arthur Conan Doyle** 1859-1930 Scottish-born writer: *Memories and Adventures* (1924)

6 Why sir, there is every possibility that you will soon be able to tax it!
   to Gladstone, when asked about the usefulness of electricity
   - **Michael Faraday** 1791-1867 English physicist and chemist: W. E. H. Lecky *Democracy and Liberty* (1899 ed.)

7 *Excise*. A hateful tax levied upon commodities.
   - **Samuel Johnson** 1709-84 English poet, critic, and lexicographer: *A Dictionary of the English Language* (1755)

8 Logic and taxation are not always the best of friends.
   - **James C. McReynolds** 1862-1946 American lawyer: concurring in *Sonneborn Bros. v. Cureton* 1923

9 A fat policeman chasing a speeding Ferrari.
   on revenue attempts to keep up with the banks' tax avoidance
   - **Lord Oakeshott** 1947- British Liberal Democrat politician: in *Guardian* 17 March 2009

10 Taxation, gentlemen, is very much like dairy farming. The task is to extract the maximum amount of milk with the minimum of moo.
   - **Terry Pratchett** 1948- English fantasy writer: *Jingo* (1997)

11 I'm up to my neck in the real world, every day. Just you try doing your VAT return with a head full of goblins.
   - **Terry Pratchett** 1948- English fantasy writer: in *Sunday Times* 27 February 2000 'Talking Heads'

12 Next to being shot at and missed, nothing is quite as satisfying as an income tax refund.
   - **F. J. Raymond**: attributed

13 Income Tax has made more Liars out of the American people than Golf.
   - **Will Rogers** 1879-1935 American actor and humorist: *The Illiterate Digest* (1924) 'Helping the Girls with their Income Taxes'

14 What is the difference between a taxidermist and a tax collector? The taxidermist takes only your skin.
   - **Mark Twain** 1835-1910 American writer: *Notebook* 30 December 1902

Technology

see also **PROGRESS, SCIENCE**

. . . .

The thing with high-tech is that you always end up using scissors.
David Hockney

1 When all else fails, read the instructions.
  • **Anonymous**: twentieth-century saying

2 When man wanted to make a machine that would walk he created the wheel, which does not resemble a leg.
  • **Guillaume Apollinaire** 1880–1918 French poet: *Les Mamelles de Tirésias* (1918)

3 Inanimate objects are classified scientifically into three major categories—those that don't work, those that break down, and those that get lost.
  • **Russell Baker** 1925– American journalist and columnist: in *New York Times* 18 June 1968

4 Let's be frank, the Italians' technological contribution to humankind stopped with the pizza oven.
  • **Bill Bryson** 1951– American travel writer: *Neither Here Nor There* (1991)

5 The first rule of intelligent tinkering is to save all the parts.
  • **Paul Ralph Ehrlich** 1932– American biologist: in *Saturday Review* 5 June 1971

6 Technology…the knack of so arranging the world that we need not experience it.
  • **Max Frisch** 1911–91 Swiss novelist and dramatist: *Homo Faber* (1957)

7 Oh, it's a marvellous invention, this is. I don't know what I'd do without this… Friends all over the world. None in this country, but all over the world.
  • **Ray Galton** 1930– and **Alan Simpson** 1929– English scriptwriters: *Hancock's Half Hour* (BBC radio, 1961) 'The Radio Ham'

8 Desks are really bacteria cafeterias.
  on research which showed that keyboards, computer mice and telephone dials are more infested with microbes than toilet seats
  • **Charles Gerba** American microbiologist: attributed, in *Times* 16 March 2004

9 If it weren't for electricity, we'd all be watching television by candlelight.
  • **George Gobel** 1919–91 America comedian: attributed, in *Cue* 6 November 1954

10 The itemised phone bill ranks up there with suspender belts, Sky Sports Channels and Loaded magazine as inventions women could do without.
  • **Maeve Haran** 1932– British writer: in *Mail on Sunday* 25 April 1999

11 The thing with high-tech is that you always end up using scissors.
  • **David Hockney** 1937– British artist: in *Observer* 10 July 1994 'Sayings of the Week'

12 Our toaster works on either AC or DC but not on bread. It has two settings—too soon or too late.
  • **Sam Levenson** 1911–80 American humorist: *In One Era and Out the Other* (1973)

13 Xerox: a trademark for a photocopying device that can make rapid reproductions of human error, perfectly.
  • **Merle L. Meacham**: Laurence J. Peter *Quotations for Our Time* (1977)

14 No man can hear his telephone ring without wishing heartily that Alexander Graham Bell had been run over by an ice wagon at the age of four.
  • **H. L. Mencken** 1880–1956 American journalist and literary critic: Marion Elizabeth Rodgers *Mencken: The American Iconoclast* (2005)

15 When the inventor of the drawing board messed things up, what did he go back to?
  • **Bob Monkhouse** 1928–2003 English entertainer: attributed; in *Guardian* 29 December 2003 (online edition)

16 praise without end the go-ahead zeal
   of whoever it was invented the wheel;
   but never a word for the poor soul's
      sake
   that thought ahead, and invented

the brake.
■ **Howard Nemerov** 1920-91 American
poet and novelist: 'To the Congress of the
United States, Entering Its Third Century'
26 February 1989

Telegrams

. . . .

PUT CORPSE ON ICE TILL CLOSE OF PLAY. **E. M. Grace**

1 Along the electric wire the message
      came:
   He is not better—he is much the same.
   *parodic poem on the illness of the Prince of
   Wales, later King Edward VII*
   ■ **Anonymous**: F. H. Gribble *Romance of
   the Cambridge Colleges* (1913); sometimes
   attributed to Alfred Austin (1835-1913), Poet
   Laureate

2 *as a young* Times *correspondent in America,
   Claud Cockburn received a telegram
   authorizing him to report a murder in
   Al Capone's Chicago:*
   BY ALL MEANS COCKBURN
   CHICAGOWARDS. WELCOME STORIES
   EX-CHICAGO NOT UNDULY EMPHASISING
   CRIME.
   ■ **Anonymous**: Claud Cockburn *In Time of
   Trouble* (1956)

3 *telegraph message on arriving in Venice:*
   STREETS FLOODED. PLEASE ADVISE.
   ■ **Robert Benchley** 1889-1945 American
   humorist: R. E. Drennan *Wit's End* (1973)

4 *appeal to his wife:*
   AM IN MARKET HARBOROUGH. WHERE
   OUGHT I TO BE?
   ■ **G. K. Chesterton** 1874-1936 English
   essayist, novelist, and poet: *Autobiography*
   (1936)

5 Dear Mrs A.,
   Hooray, hooray,
   At last you are deflowered.
   On this as every other day
   I love you—Noel Coward.
   ■ **Noël Coward** 1899-1973 English dramatist,
   actor, and composer: telegram to Gertrude
   Lawrence, 5 July 1940 (the day after her
   wedding)

6 HAVE MOVED HOTEL EXCELSIOR
   COUGHING MYSELF INTO A FIRENZE.
   telegram from Florence
   ■ **Noël Coward** 1899-1973 English dramatist,
   actor, and composer: Angus McGill and
   Kenneth Thomson *Live Wires* (1982)

7 LEGITIMATE AT LAST WONT MOTHER BE
   PLEASED.
   on Gertrude Lawrence's first straight role
   ■ **Noël Coward** 1899-1973 English dramatist,
   actor, and composer: Sheridan Morley
   A Talent to Amuse (1969)

8 *despite the threat of World War II,
   arrangements for the revue* Set to Music
   went ahead:
   SUGGEST YOU ENGAGE EIGHT REALLY
   BEAUTIFUL SHOWGIRLS MORE OR
   LESS SAME HEIGHT NO REAL TALENT
   REQUIRED.
   ■ **Noël Coward** 1899-1973 English dramatist,
   actor, and composer: telegram to Jack
   Wilson; Sheridan Morley *A Talent to Amuse*
   (1969)

9 *sent by W. G. Grace's elder brother, a cricket-
   playing coroner, to postpone an inquest:*
   PUT CORPSE ON ICE TILL CLOSE OF PLAY.
   ■ **E. M. Grace** 1841-1911 English cricketer:
   A. A. Thomson *The Great Cricketer* (1957);
   perhaps apocryphal

10 *response to a telegraphic enquiry,* HOW OLD
   CARY GRANT?:
   OLD CARY GRANT FINE. HOW YOU?
   ■ **Cary Grant** 1904-86 British-born American
   actor: R. Schickel *Cary Grant* (1983)

11 LAST SUPPER AND ORIGINAL CAST
   COULDN'T DRAW IN THIS HOUSE.
   telegram to his father during a bad week

with a stock acting company
- **George S. Kaufman** 1889-1961 American dramatist: Angus McGill and Kenneth Thomson *Live Wires* (1982)

12 *Carl Laemmle Jr. had sent a telegram to his father,* PLEASE WIRE MORE MONEY AM TALKING TO FRENCH COUNT RE MOVIE: NO MONEY TILL YOU LEARN TO SPELL.
- **Carl Laemmle** 1867-1939 American film producer: Angus McGill and Kenneth Thomson *Live Wires* (1982)

13 *an estate agent in Bermuda told her that the house she was considering came with a maid, a secretary, and a chauffeur:* AIRMAIL PHOTOGRAPH OF CHAUFFEUR.
- **Beatrice Lillie** 1894-1989 Canadian-born comedienne: Angus McGill and Kenneth Thomson *Live Wires* (1982)

14 *telegram to Mrs Sherwood on the arrival of her baby:* GOOD WORK, MARY. WE ALL KNEW YOU HAD IT IN YOU.
- **Dorothy Parker** 1893-1967 American critic and humorist: Alexander Woollcott *While Rome Burns* (1934)

15 *to a couple who had married after living together:* WHAT'S NEW?
- **Dorothy Parker** 1893-1967 American critic and humorist: S. T. Brownlow (ed.) *The Sayings of Dorothy Parker* (1992)

16 Satisfied great success.
reply to telegram from Billy Rose, suggesting that reorchestration by Robert Russell Bennett might make a ballet which was 'a great success' even more successful
- **Igor Stravinsky** 1882-1971 Russian composer: in *Ned Sherrin in his Anecdotage* (1993)

17 *cables were soon arriving…'Require earliest name life story photograph American nurse upblown Adowa.' We replied:* NURSE UNUPBLOWN.
- **Evelyn Waugh** 1903-66 English novelist: *Waugh in Abyssinia* (1936)

18 FEAR I MAY NOT BE ABLE TO REACH YOU IN TIME FOR THE CEREMONY. DON'T WAIT.
telegram of apology for missing Oscar Wilde's wedding
- **James McNeill Whistler** 1834-1903 American-born painter: E. J. and R. Pennell *The Life of James McNeill Whistler* (1908)

19 *his wife had requested him, when in Paris, to buy and send her a bidet:* UNABLE OBTAIN BIDET. SUGGEST HANDSTAND IN SHOWER.
- **Billy Wilder** 1906-2002 American screenwriter and director: Leslie Halliwell *Filmgoer's Book of Quotes* (1973)

Television

....

Never miss a chance to have sex or appear on television.   **Gore Vidal**

1 TV—a clever contraction derived from the words Terrible Vaudeville…we call it a medium because nothing's well done.
- **Goodman Ace** 1899-1982 American humorist: letter to Groucho Marx, *c.*1953

2 Television is a triumph of equipment over people, and the minds that control it are so small that you could put them in a gnat's navel with room left over for two caraway seeds and an agent's heart.
- **Fred Allen** 1894-1956 American humorist: attributed

3 The best that can be said for Norwegian television is that it gives you the sensation of a coma without the worry and inconvenience.
- **Bill Bryson** 1951- American travel writer: *Neither Here Nor There* (1991)

4 Theatre actors look down on film actors, who look down on TV actors. Thank God for reality shows or we wouldn't have anybody to look down on.
- **George Clooney** 1961- American actor and director: in *Observer* 10 February 2008

5 Television is more interesting than people. If it were not, we should have people standing in the corners of our rooms.
- **Alan Coren** 1938-2007 English humorist: attributed; in *The Penguin Dictionary of Twentieth-Century Quotations* (1993)

6 We hope to amuse the customers with music and with rhyme
But ninety minutes is a long, long time.
- **Noël Coward** 1899-1973 English dramatist, actor, and composer: '90 Minutes is a Long, Long Time' (1955); opening song for a CBS television live special starring Noël Coward and Mary Martin

7 Television is for appearing on, not looking at.
- **Noël Coward** 1899-1973 English dramatist, actor, and composer: Dick Richards *The Wit of Noël Coward* (1968)

8 Television is an invention that permits you to be entertained in your living room by people you wouldn't have in your home.
- **David Frost** 1939- English broadcaster and writer: attributed

9 IAN ST JOHN: Is he speaking to you yet?
JIMMY GREAVES: Not yet, but I hope to be incommunicado with him in a very short space of time.
- **Jimmy Greaves** 1940- English footballer: Barry Fantoni (ed.) *Private Eye's Colemanballs 2* (1984)

10 To goad the BBC is a rewarding sport in itself. It makes a tabloid feel like a heavyweight.
- **Clive James** 1939- Australian critic and writer: *The Dreaming Swimmer* (1992)

11 Television is simultaneously blamed, often by the same people, for worsening the world and for being powerless to change it.
- **Clive James** 1939- Australian critic and writer: *Glued to the Box* (1981); introduction

12 Television has proved that people will look at anything rather than each other.
- **Ann Landers** 1918-2002 American advice columnist: attributed

13 I find television very educational. Every time someone switches it on I go into another room and read a good book.
- **Groucho Marx** 1890-1977 American film comedian: attributed, Stefan Kanfer *The Essential Groucho* (2000) 'King Leer'

14 Something half way between a girls' school and a lunatic asylum.
on the atmosphere at the BBC
- **George Orwell** 1903-50 English novelist: wartime diary, 14 March 1942

15 The BBC is rather like a cross between the Church of England and the Post Office.
- **Jeremy Paxman** 1950- British journalist: *Friends in High Places* (1990)

16 No matter what the critics say, it's hard to believe that a television programme that keeps four children quiet for an hour can be all bad.
- **Beryl Pfizer** American writer: attributed

17 *Television?* The word is half Greek, half Latin. No good can come of it.
- **C. P. Scott** 1846-1932 British journalist: view of the editor of the *Manchester Guardian*; Asa Briggs *The BBC: the First Fifty Years* (1985)

18 The media. It sounds like a convention of spiritualists.
- **Tom Stoppard** 1937- British dramatist: *Night and Day* (1978)

19 Never miss a chance to have sex or appear on television.
- **Gore Vidal** 1925-2012 American novelist and critic: attributed; Bob Chieger *Was It Good For You Too?* (1983)

20 *of television:*
It used to be that we in films were the lowest form of art. Now we have something to look down on.
- **Billy Wilder** 1906-2002 American screenwriter and director: A. Madsen *Billy Wilder* (1968)

Tennis

You cannot be serious! **John McEnroe**

1 Miss J. Hunter Dunn, Miss J. Hunter
Dunn,
Furnish'd and burnish'd by Aldershot sun,
What strenuous singles we played after
tea,
We in the tournament—you against me.
Love-thirty, love-forty, oh! weakness of
joy,
The speed of a swallow, the grace of a
boy,
With carefullest carelessness, gaily you
won,
I am weak from your loveliness, Joan
Hunter Dunn.
  ▪ **John Betjeman** 1906-84 English poet:
  'A Subaltern's Love-Song' (1945)

2 I call tennis the McDonald's of sport—
you go in, they make a quick buck out
of you, and you're out.
  ▪ **Pat Cash** 1965- Australian tennis player: in
  Independent on Sunday 4 July 1999

3 New Yorkers love it when you spill
your guts out there. Spill your guts at
Wimbledon and they make you stop

and clean it up.
  ▪ **Jimmy Connors** 1952- American tennis
  player: at Flushing Meadow; in *Guardian*
  24 December 1984 'Sports Quotes of the
  Year'

4 The depressing thing about tennis is
that no matter how good I get, I'll never
be as good as a wall.
  ▪ **Mitch Hedberg** 1968-2005 American
  comedian: attributed

5 Like a Volvo, Borg is rugged, has good
after-sales service, and is very dull.
  ▪ **Clive James** 1939- Australian critic and
  writer: in *Observer* 29 June 1980

6 You cannot be serious!
  ▪ **John McEnroe** 1959- American tennis
  player: challenging a tennis umpire at
  Wimbledon, early 1980s

7 I threw the kitchen sink at him, but he
went to the bathroom and got his tub.
*defeated by Roger Federer in the Wimbledon
Final, 2004*
  ▪ **Andy Roddick** 1982- American tennis
  player: interview (BBC1), 4 July 2004

The Theatre

see also **ACTING, AUDIENCES**

Don't clap too hard—it's a very old building. **John Osborne**

1 Welcome to the Theatre,
To the magic, to the fun!
Where painted trees and flowers grow,
And laughter rings fortissimo,
And treachery's sweetly done.
  ▪ **Lee Adams** 1924- American songwriter:
  'Welcome to the Theatre' (1970)

2 Shaw's plays are the price we pay for
Shaw's prefaces.
  ▪ **James Agate** 1877-1947 British drama critic
  and novelist: diary 10 March 1933

3 Why don't actors look out of the window
in the morning? Because then they'd have
nothing to do in the afternoon.
old theatre joke
  ▪ **Anonymous**: Michael Simkins *What's My
  Motivation?* (2004)

4 YOUNG ACTOR: Did Hamlet actually
sleep with Ophelia?
OLD ACTOR: I don't know about the West
End, laddie, but we always did on tour.
  ▪ **Anonymous**: traditional theatre saying

5 This [*Oh, Calcutta!*] is the kind of show
to give pornography a dirty name.
- **Clive Barnes** 1927-2008 British journalist
and critic: in *New York Times* 18 June 1969

6 God, send me some good actors.
Cheap.
- **Lilian Baylis** 1874-1937 English theatre
manager: Sybil Thorndike *Lilian Baylis*
(1938)

7 *on being asked 'What was the message of your
play' after a performance of* The Hostage:
Message? Message? What the hell do
you think I am, a bloody postman?
- **Brendan Behan** 1923-64 Irish dramatist:
Dominic Behan *My Brother Brendan* (1965)

8 I go to the theatre to be entertained,
I want to be taken out of myself, I don't
want to see lust and rape and incest and
sodomy and so on, I can get all that at
home.
- **Alan Bennett** 1934- English dramatist and
actor and **others**: *Beyond the Fringe* (1963)
'Man of Principles'

9 Heralded by a sprinkling of glitter dust
and much laying on of microphones,
Godspell is back in London at The Young
Vic. For those who missed it the first
time, this is your golden opportunity:
you can miss it again.
- **Michael Billington** 1939- English critic:
review in *Guardian* 1981; Diana Rigg *No Turn
Unstoned* (1983)

10 ANONYMOUS: Why did you go on stage?
MICHAEL BLAKEMORE: To get out of the
audience.
- **Michael Blakemore** 1928- Australian
actor and director: attributed; in *Times*
29 December 2003

11 Anyone can do theatre. Even actors.
And theatre can be done everywhere.
Even in a theatre.
- **Augusto Boal** 1931-2009 Brazilian theatre
director: in *New York Times* 9 May 2009

12 Tonight's late show is a burlesque
cabaret, but, please, don't let that
put you off. These aren't your
ordinary burlesque dancers—slightly
podgy middle-class girls with body
dysmorphia and father issues. No, these
burlesque dancers are very good—why,

they could have made it as real strippers
if they had wanted to.
- **Benet Brandreth** 1975- English lawyer:
The Brandreth Papers (2011)

13 *on being told there was no part suitable for
her first husband in a production of* King
Lear, *she refused to take no for an answer and
after searching painstakingly through the text
triumphantly came up with the stage direction:*
A camp near Dover.
- **Coral Browne** 1913-91 Australian actress:
Ned Sherrin *Cutting Edge* (1984)

14 *on hearing the London playwright Henry
Arthur Jones reading his play* Michael and
his Lost Angel *(1896) in a very strong
Cockney accent:*
But it's so *long*, Mr. Jones—even *without*
the *h*'s.
- **Mrs Patrick Campbell** 1865-1940 English
actress: Margot Peters *Mrs Pat* (1984)

15 Shut up, Arnold, or I'll direct this play
the way you wrote it!
- **John Dexter** 1925-90 English director: to
the playwright Arnold Wesker; in *Ned
Sherrin in his Anecdotage* (1993)

16 *after a play about Napoleon had failed:*
Never, never, will I do another play
where a guy writes with a feather.
- **Max Gordon** 1892-1978 American Broadway
producer: attributed by Arthur Miller; in *Ned
Sherrin's Theatrical Anecdotes* (1991)

17 The difficulty about a theatre job is that
it interferes with party-going.
- **Barry Humphries** 1934- Australian actor
and writer: *More Please* (1992)

18 I'll come no more behind your scenes,
David; for the silk stockings and white
bosoms of your actresses excite my
amorous propensities.
*John Wilkes recalls the remark [to Garrick]
in the form: 'the silk stockings and white
bosoms of your actresses do make my genitals
to quiver'*
- **Samuel Johnson** 1709-84 English poet,
critic, and lexicographer: James Boswell
Life of Samuel Johnson (1791) 1750

19 Satire is what closes Saturday night.
- **George S. Kaufman** 1889-1961 American
dramatist: Scott Meredith *George S.
Kaufman and his Friends* (1974)

20 Beware of flu. Avoid crowds. See
Someone in the House.
advertisement for his unsuccessful revision
of the Broadway play, staged during the
influenza epidemic of 1918
- **George S. Kaufman** 1889-1961 American
dramatist: Howard Teichmann *George S.*
Kaufman: an intimate portrait (1972)

21 Stand upstage of me and do your worst.
stage direction to any new cast he worked with
- **Edmund Kean** c.1787-1833 English actor:
attributed

22 A play in which nothing happens, twice.
reviewing Waiting for Godot *in* Irish
Times, *1954*
- **Vivian Mercier** 1919-89 Irish literary
historian: *Beckett/Beckett* (1977)

23 Don't clap too hard—it's a very old
building.
- **John Osborne** 1929-94 English dramatist:
The Entertainer (1957)

24 Another pain where the ulcers grow,
Another op'nin' of another show.
- **Cole Porter** 1891-1964 American
songwriter: 'Another Op'nin', Another
Show' (1948)

25 Brush up your Shakespeare,
Start quoting him now.
Brush up your Shakespeare
And the women you will wow.
- **Cole Porter** 1891-1964 American songwriter:
'Brush Up your Shakespeare' (1948)

26 It is better to have written a damned
play, than no play at all—it snatches a
man from obscurity.
- **Frederic Reynolds** 1764-1841 English
dramatist: *The Dramatist* (1789)

27 You've got to perform in a role
hundreds of times. In keeping it
fresh one can become a large, madly
humming, demented refrigerator.
- **Ralph Richardson** 1902-83 English actor: in
Time 21 August 1978

28 Something appealing,
Something appalling,
Something for everyone:
A comedy tonight!
- **Stephen Sondheim** 1930- American
songwriter: 'Comedy Tonight' (1962)

29 Do you imagine I am going to
pronounce the name of my beautiful
theatre in a hired cab?
refusing to give directions to His Majesty's
theatre to a cab-driver
- **Herbert Beerbohm Tree** 1852-1917 English
actor-manager: Neville Cardus *Sir Thomas*
Beecham (1961)

30 *Moby Dick* nearly became the tragedy
of a man who could not make up his
nose.
on Welles's production of Moby Dick *in*
1955, when his false nose fell off on the first
night, alluding to the publicity for Olivier's
Hamlet *as 'the tragedy of a man who could*
not make up his mind'
- **Kenneth Tynan** 1927-80 English theatre
critic: *A View of the English Stage* (1975)

31 In the old days, you went from ingénue
to old bag with a long stretch of
unemployment in between.
- **Julie Walters** 1950- British actress: in
Sunday Times 26 May 2002

32 *on Irving's revival of* Macbeth *at the Lyceum,*
with Ellen Terry as Lady Macbeth:
Judging from the banquet, Lady
Macbeth seems an economical
housekeeper and evidently patronises
local industries for her husband's
clothes and the servants' liveries, but
she takes care to do all her shopping in
Byzantium.
- **Oscar Wilde** 1854-1900 Irish dramatist and
poet: Rupert Hart-Davis (ed.) *The Letters of*
Oscar Wilde (1962)

33 I think it (nudity on stage) is disgusting
and shameful and damaging to all
things American. But if I were 22 with a
great body, it would be artistic, tasteful,
patriotic and a progressive, religious
experience.
- **Shelley Winters** 1922-2006 American
actress: in *Jet* 10 July 1969

34 Musical comedy is the Irish stew of
drama. Anything may be put into it,
with the certainty that it will improve
the general effect.
- **P. G. Wodehouse** 1881-1975 English-born
writer: *The Man with Two Left Feet* (1917)

Time

Life is too short to stuff a mushroom. **Shirley Conran**

1 This must be Thursday. I never could get the hang of Thursdays.
  - **Douglas Adams** 1952-2001 English science fiction writer: *The Hitchhiker's Guide to the Galaxy* (BBC radio, 1978)

2 Time is an illusion. Lunchtime doubly so.
  - **Douglas Adams** 1952-2001 English science fiction writer: *The Hitch Hiker's Guide to the Galaxy* (1979)

3 I do love deadlines. I love the whooshing sound they make as they go past.
  - **Douglas Adams** 1952-2001 English science fiction writer: in *Guardian* 14 May 2001

4 And meanwhile time goes about its immemorial work of making everyone look and feel like shit.
  - **Martin Amis** 1949- English novelist: *London Fields* (1989)

5 The trouble with being punctual is that there is no-one there to appreciate it.
  - **Anonymous**: mid 20th-century saying, now associated with American businessman Franklin P. Jones (1887-1929)

6 *on receiving an invitation for 9 a.m.:*
  Oh, are there two nine o'clocks in the day?
  - **Tallulah Bankhead** 1903-68 American actress: attributed, perhaps apocryphal

7 *to an effusive greeting 'I haven't seen you for 41 years':*
  I thought I told you to wait in the car.
  - **Tallulah Bankhead** 1903-68 American actress: attributed; Nigel Rees *Cassell Dictionary of Humorous Quotations* (1999)

8 VLADIMIR: That passed the time.
  ESTRAGON: It would have passed in any case.
  VLADIMIR: Yes, but not so rapidly.
  - **Samuel Beckett** 1906-89 Irish dramatist, novelist, and poet: *Waiting for Godot* (1955)

9 I am a sundial, and I make a botch
  Of what is done much better by a watch.
  - **Hilaire Belloc** 1870-1953 British writer and Liberal politician: 'On a Sundial' (1938)

10 *arriving at Dublin Castle for the handover by British forces on 16 January 1922, and being told that he was seven minutes late:*
  We've been waiting 700 years, you can have the seven minutes.
  - **Michael Collins** 1880-1922 Irish revolutionary: Tim Pat Coogan *Michael Collins* (1990); attributed, perhaps apocryphal

11 Life is too short to stuff a mushroom.
  - **Shirley Conran** 1932- English writer: *Superwoman* (1975)

12 I'll be with you in the squeezing of a lemon.
  - **Oliver Goldsmith** 1730-74 Irish writer: *She Stoops to Conquer* (1773)

13 We have passed a lot of water since then.
  - **Sam Goldwyn** 1882-1974 American film producer: E. Goodman *The Fifty-Year Decline of Hollywood* (1961); attributed, possibly apocryphal

14 Morning comes whether you set the alarm or not.
  - **Ursula K. Le Guin** 1929- American writer: *Dancing at the Edge of the World* (1985)

15 Time spent on any item of the agenda will be in inverse proportion to the sum involved.
  - **C. Northcote Parkinson** 1909-93 English writer: *Parkinson's Law* (1958)

16 Wherever I travel I'm too late. The orgy has moved elsewhere.
  - **Mordecai Richler** 1931-2001 Canadian writer: *Shovelling Trouble* (1972) 'A Sense of the Ridiculous'

17 Three o'clock is always too late or too early for anything you want to do.
  - **Jean-Paul Sartre** 1905-80 French philosopher: *La Nausée* (1938)

18 Eternity's a terrible thought. I mean, where's it all going to end?
- **Tom Stoppard** 1937- British dramatist: *Rosencrantz and Guildenstern are Dead* (1967)

19 *to a man in the street, carrying a grandfather clock:*
My poor fellow, why not carry a watch?
- **Herbert Beerbohm Tree** 1852-1917 English actor-manager: Hesketh Pearson *Beerbohm Tree* (1956)

Tolerance *see* **PREJUDICE AND TOLERANCE**

Towns and Cities

Toronto is a kind of New York operated by the Swiss.   **Peter Ustinov**

1 God made the harbour, and that's all right, but Satan made Sydney.
- **Anonymous**: unnamed Sydney citizen; Mark Twain *More Tramps Abroad* (1897)

2 New York is big but this is Biggar.
- **Anonymous**: slogan for the town of Biggar in Saskatchewan

3 I passed through Glasgow on my way here and couldn't help noticing how different it was from Venice.
- **Raymond Asquith** 1878-1916 English lawyer: letter to Mrs Horner, 28 September 1904

4 One has no great hopes from Birmingham. I always say there is something direful in the sound.
- **Jane Austen** 1775-1817 English novelist: *Emma* (1816)

5 Come, friendly bombs, and fall on Slough!
It isn't fit for humans now.
- **John Betjeman** 1906-84 English poet: 'Slough' (1937)

6 For Cambridge people rarely smile, Being urban, squat, and packed with guile.
- **Rupert Brooke** 1887-1915 English poet: 'The Old Vicarage, Grantchester' (1915)

7 Venice is like eating an entire box of chocolate liqueurs in one go.
- **Truman Capote** 1924-84 American writer: in *Observer* 26 November 1961

8 A big hard-boiled city with no more personality than a paper cup.
of Los Angeles
- **Raymond Chandler** 1888-1959 American writer: *The Little Sister* (1949)

9 People don't talk in Paris; they just look lovely...and eat.
- **Chips Channon** 1897-1958 American-born British Conservative politician: diary 22 May 1951

10 New York, New York,—a helluva town, The Bronx is up but the Battery's down, And people ride in a hole in the ground.
- **Betty Comden** 1917-2006 and **Adolph Green** 1915-2002: 'New York, New York' (1945 song)

11 In Manhattan, every flat surface is a potential stage and every inattentive waiter an unemployed, possibly unemployable, actor.
- **Quentin Crisp** 1908-99 English writer: 'Love Lies Bleeding' (Channel 4 TV), 6 August 1991; Nigel Rees (ed.) *Cassell Dictionary of Humorous Quotations* (1999)

12 This is Soho, where anything goes, just make sure it's not your wallet.
- **Len Deighton** 1929- English writer: 'Soho', in Len Deighton and Adrian Bailey *Len Deighton's London Dossier* (1967)

13 Last week, I went to Philadelphia, but it was closed.
- **W. C. Fields** 1880-1946 American humorist: Richard J. Anobile *Godfrey Daniels* (1975); attributed

14 They used to say that Cambridge was the first stopping place for the wind that swept down from the Urals: in the thirties that was as true of the politics as the weather.
- **Stephen Fry** 1957– English comedian, actor, and writer: *The Liar* (1991)

15 The people of Berlin are doing very exciting things with their city at the moment. Basically they had this idea of just knocking it through.
- **Stephen Fry** 1957– and **Hugh Laurie** 1959– : *A Bit More Fry and Laurie* (1991)

16 Liverpool, though not very delightful as a place of residence, is a most convenient and admirable point to get away from.
- **Nathaniel Hawthorne** 1804-64 American novelist: *Our Old Home* (1863)

17 Taunton is no longer a one-horse town; these days, they have a bicycle as well.
- **Tom Holt** 1961– English novelist: *Expecting Someone Taller* (1987)

18 When a man is tired of London, he is tired of life; for there is in London all that life can afford.
- **Samuel Johnson** 1709-84 English lexicographer: James Boswell *Life of Samuel Johnson* (1791) 20 September 1777

19 New York, New York, so good they named it twice.
- **Gerard Kenny** 1947– American singer-songwriter: 'New York, New York' (1978 song)

20 According to legend, Telford is so dull that the bypass was built before the town.
on the Midlands new-town
- **Victor Lewis-Smith** British television producer: in *Evening Standard* 9 December 1994

21 A car is useless in New York, essential everywhere else. The same with good manners.
- **Mignon McLaughlin** 1913-83 American writer: *Complete Neurotic's Notebook* (1981)

22 *sitting in a New York bar in the 1940s:*
Oh, to be back in Hollywood, wishing I was back in New York.
- **Herman J. Mankiewicz** 1897-1953 American screenwriter: James Sanders *Celluloid Skyline: New York and the Movies* (2001)

23 When it's three o'clock in New York, it's still 1938 in London.
- **Bette Midler** 1945– American actress: attributed

24 Saigon is like all the other great modern cities of the world. It's the mess left over from people getting rich.
- **P. J. O'Rourke** 1947– American humorous writer: *Give War a Chance* (1992)

25 There was a certain something about the air in the city. You got the feeling that it was air that had seen life. You couldn't help noting with every breath that thousands of other people were very close to you and nearly all of them had armpits.
- **Terry Pratchett** 1948– English fantasy writer: *Mort* (1987)

26 City of perspiring dreams.
of Cambridge
- **Frederic Raphael** 1931– British novelist: *The Glittering Prizes* (1976)

27 New York's like a disco, but without the music.
- **Elaine Stritch** 1925– American actress: in *Observer* 17 February 1980

28 He took offence at my description of Edinburgh as the Reykjavik of the South.
- **Tom Stoppard** 1937– British dramatist: *Jumpers* (1972)

29 The difference between Los Angeles and a yogurt is that yogurt has real culture.
- **Tom Taussik**: attributed

30 Toronto is a kind of New York operated by the Swiss.
- **Peter Ustinov** 1921-2004 British actor: in *Globe & Mail* 1 August 1987; attributed

31 Brighton looks like a town that is constantly helping the police with their enquiries.
- **Keith Waterhouse** 1929-2009 English writer: quoted by the author in conversation with Ned Sherrin

Transport

Walk! Not bloody likely. I am going in a taxi.   **George Bernard Shaw**

1 Railways and the Church have their critics, but both are the best ways of getting a man to his ultimate destination.
 ▪ **Revd W. Awdry** 1911–97 English writer of children's books: in *Daily Telegraph* 22 March 1997; obituary

2 He [Benchley] came out of a night club one evening and, tapping a uniformed figure on the shoulder, said, 'Get me a cab.' The uniformed figure turned around furiously and informed him that he was not a doorman but a rear admiral. 'O.K.,' said Benchley, 'Get me a battleship.'
 ▪ **Robert Benchley** 1889–1945 American humorist: in *New Yorker* 5 January 1946

3 I encountered Mr. Hackman, an Englishman, who has been walking the length and breadth of Europe for several years. I enquired of him what were his chief observations. He replied gruffly, 'I never look up', and went on his way.
 ▪ **N. Brooke**: in 1796; Duncan Minshull *The Vintage Book of Walking* (2000)

4 Q: If Mrs Thatcher were run over by a bus…?
 LORD CARRINGTON: It wouldn't dare.
 ▪ **Lord Carrington** 1919– British Conservative politician: during the Falklands War; Russell Lewis *Margaret Thatcher* (1984)

5 The only way of catching a train I ever discovered is to miss the train before.
 ▪ **G. K. Chesterton** 1874–1936 English essayist, novelist, and poet: attributed; Evan Esar and Nicolas Bentley (eds.) *Treasury of Humorous Quotations* (1951)

6 I prefer to travel on French ships because there is none of that 'women and children first' nonsense.
 ▪ **Noël Coward** 1899–1973 English dramatist, actor, and composer: attributed; the saying is attributed to various authors and first occurs anonymously

7 That monarch of the road,
 Observer of the Highway Code,
 That big six-wheeler
 Scarlet-painted
 London Transport
 Diesel-engined
 Ninety-seven horse power
 Omnibus!
 ▪ **Michael Flanders** 1922–75 and **Donald Swann** 1923–94: 'A Transport of Delight' (c.1956)

8 Sir, Saturday morning, although recurring at regular and well-foreseen intervals, always seems to take this railway by surprise.
 ▪ **W. S. Gilbert** 1836–1911 English writer of comic and satirical verse: letter to the station-master at Baker Street, on the Metropolitan line; John Julius Norwich *Christmas Crackers* (1980)

9 What is this that roareth thus?
 Can it be a Motor Bus?
 Yes, the smell and hideous hum
 Indicat Motorem Bum!…
 How shall wretches live like us
 Cincti Bis Motoribus?
 Domine, defende nos
 Contra hos Motores Bos!
 ▪ **A. D. Godley** 1856–1925 English classicist: letter to C. R. L. Fletcher, 10 January 1914

10 Aunt Jane observed, the second time
 She tumbled off a bus,
 'The step is short from the Sublime
 To the Ridiculous.'
 ▪ **Harry Graham** 1874–1936 British writer and journalist: 'Equanimity' (1899)

11 *of Bishop Patrick's fatal error in crossing the street:*
 The light of God was with him,
 But the traffic light was not.
 ▪ **E. Y. Harburg** 1898–1981 American songwriter: 'Lead Kindly Light' (1965)

12 There once was a man who said,
  'Damn!

It is borne in upon me I am
An engine that moves
In predestinate grooves,
I'm not even a bus, I'm a tram.'
- **Maurice Evan Hare** 1886-1967 English
limerick writer: 'Limerick' (1905)

13 Home James, and don't spare the horses.
- **Fred Hillebrand** 1893- American
songwriter: title of song (1934)

14 The automobile changed our dress,
manners, social customs, vacation
habits, the shape of our cities, consumer
purchasing patterns, common tastes and
positions in intercourse.
- **John Keats** 1920- American journalist:
The Insolent Chariots (1958)

15 *seeing the Morris Minor prototype in 1945:*
It looks like a poached egg—we can't
make that.
- **Lord Nuffield** 1877-1963 British motor
manufacturer and philanthropist: attributed

16 Why is it no one ever sent me yet
One perfect limousine, do you suppose?
Ah no, it's always just my luck to get
One perfect rose.
- **Dorothy Parker** 1893-1967 American critic
and humorist: 'One Perfect Rose' (1937)

17 What is better than presence of mind in
a railway accident? Absence of body.
- **Punch** 1841-1992 English humorous weekly
periodical: vol. 16 (1849)

18 I don't even like *old* cars. I mean they
don't even interest me. I'd rather have
a goddam horse. A horse is at least
human, for God's sake.
- **J. D. Salinger** 1919-2010 American novelist
and short-story writer: *The Catcher in the
Rye* (1951)

19 Walk! Not bloody likely. I am going in
a taxi.
- **George Bernard Shaw** 1856-1950 Irish
dramatist: *Pygmalion* (1916), spoken by
Eliza Doolittle

20 BOATMAN: I 'ad that Christopher
Marlowe in the back of my boat.
- **Tom Stoppard** 1937- British dramatist:
Shakespeare in Love (1999 film, screenplay
by Tom Stoppard and Mark Norman)

21 Commuter—one who spends his life
In riding to and from his wife;
A man who shaves and takes a train,
And then rides back to shave again.
- **E. B. White** 1899-1985 American humorist:
'The Commuter' (1982)

Travel and Exploration

Worth seeing, yes; but not worth going to see. **Samuel Johnson**

1 A trip is what you take when you can't
take any more of what you've been
taking.
- **Adeline Ainsworth**: attributed

2 In America there are two classes of
travel—first class, and with children.
- **Robert Benchley** 1889-1945 American
humorist: *Pluck and Luck* (1925)

3 It is easier to find a travelling companion
than to get rid of one.
- **Peg Bracken** 1918-2007 American writer:
But I Wouldn't Have Missed It for the World
(1973)

4 The longer the cruise, the older the
passengers.
- **Peg Bracken** 1918-2007 American writer: *But
I Wouldn't Have Missed It for the World* (1973)

5 (Newton's Law of the Ever-level
Suitcase) At the same time an object is
lost, used up, given away, thrown out,
or otherwise disposed of, another object
of equal size and weight rushes in to fill
the vacuum.
- **Peg Bracken** 1918-2007 American writer:
But I Wouldn't Have Missed It for the World
(1973)

6 The perpetual lamentations after
beef and beer, the stupid bigoted
contempt for every thing foreign, and
insurmountable incapacity of acquiring

even a few words of any language, rendered him like all other English servants, an encumbrance.
- **Lord Byron** 1788-1824 English poet: letter, 14 January 1811

7 I like my 'abroad' to be Catholic and sensual.
- **Chips Channon** 1897-1958 American-born British Conservative politician: diary 18 January 1924

8 Polar exploration is at once the cleanest and most isolated way of having a bad time which has been devised.
- **Apsley Cherry-Garrard** 1882-1959 English polar explorer: *The Worst Journey in the World* (1922)

9 They say travel broadens the mind; but you must have the mind.
- **G. K. Chesterton** 1874-1936 English writer: 'The Shadow of the Shark' (1921)

10 Why do the wrong people travel, travel, travel,
When the right people stay back home?
- **Noël Coward** 1899-1973 English dramatist, actor, and composer: 'Why do the Wrong People Travel?' (1961)

11 *on his arrival in Turkey:*
I am of course known here as English Delight.
- **Noël Coward** 1899-1973 English dramatist, actor, and composer: Sheridan Morley *The Quotable Noël Coward* (1999)

12 Like all great travellers, I have seen more than I remember, and remember more than I have seen.
- **Benjamin Disraeli** 1804-81 British Tory statesman and novelist: attributed

13 At my age travel broadens the behind.
- **Stephen Fry** 1957- English comedian, actor, and writer: *The Liar* (1991)

14 Abroad is bloody.
- **George VI** 1895-1952 British king: W. H. Auden *A Certain World* (1970)

15 *on the Giant's Causeway:*
Worth seeing, yes; but not worth going to see.
- **Samuel Johnson** 1709-84 English lexicographer: James Boswell *Life of Samuel Johnson* (1791) 12 October 1779

16 If you look like your passport photo, you're too ill to travel.
- **Will Kommen**: attributed; Laurence J. Peter *Peter's People* (1979)

17 What good is speed if the brain has oozed out on the way?
- **Karl Kraus** 1874-1936 Austrian satirist: 'The Discovery of the North Pole'

18 Thanks to the interstate highway system, it is now possible to travel from coast to coast without seeing anything.
- **Charles Kuralt** 1934-97 American journalist and broadcaster: *On the Road* (1980)

19 I wouldn't mind seeing China if I could come back the same day.
- **Philip Larkin** 1922-85 English poet: *Required Writing* (1983), interview with *Observer*, 1979

20 At first, you fear you will die; then, after it has a good hold on you, you fear you won't die.
on seasickness
- **Jack London** 1876-1916 American novelist: *The Cruise of the Snark* (1911)

21 The highest compliment that can be paid to a foreigner is to be stopped in the street and asked the way by a native.
- **E. V. Lucas** 1868-1938 English journalist, essayist, and critic: *Giving and Receiving* (1922)

22 A sure cure for seasickness is to sit under a tree.
- **Spike Milligan** 1918-2002 Irish comedian: attributed; in *Daily Telegraph* 28 February 2002

23 She said that all the sights in Rome were called after London cinemas.
- **Nancy Mitford** 1904-73 English writer: *Pigeon Pie* (1940)

24 As every student of exploration knows, the prize goes not to the explorer who first sets foot upon the virgin soil but to the one who gets that foot home first. If it is still attached to his leg, this is a bonus.
- **Terry Pratchett** 1948- English fantasy writer: *Jingo* (1997)

25 Granny Weatherwax didn't like maps. She felt instinctively that they sold the landscape short.
- **Terry Pratchett** 1948- English fantasy writer: *Witches Abroad* (1991)

26 All my wife has ever taken from the Mediterranean—from that whole vast intuitive culture—are four bottles of Chianti to make into lamps.
- **Peter Shaffer** 1926- English dramatist: *Equus* (1973)

27 If it's Tuesday, this must be Belgium.
- **David Shaw**: film title (1969)

28 *asked why he had come to America:*
In pursuit of my life-long quest for naked women in wet mackintoshes.
- **Dylan Thomas** 1914-53 Welsh poet: Constantine Fitzgibbon *Dylan Thomas* (1965); attributed

29 J. M. BARRIE: What was your most dangerous journey?
THOMSON: Crossing Piccadilly Circus.
- **Joseph Thomson** 1858-94 Scottish explorer: Janet Dunbar *J. M. Barrie: The Man Behind the Image* (1970)

30 It is not worthwhile to go around the world to count the cats in Zanzibar.
- **Henry David Thoreau** 1817-62 American writer: *Walden* (1854) 'Conclusion'

31 It used to be a good hotel, but that proves nothing—I used to be a good boy.
- **Mark Twain** 1835-1910 American writer: *The Innocents Abroad* (1869)

Trust and Treachery

Defectors are like grapes. The first pressings from them are the best.
Maurice Oldfield

1 Outside Shakespeare the word treason to me means nothing. Only, you pissed in our soup and we drank it.
Coral Browne to the traitor Guy Burgess
- **Alan Bennett** 1934- English dramatist and actor: *An Englishman Abroad* (1989)

2 The only recorded instance in history of a rat swimming *towards* a sinking ship.
of a former Conservative who proposed to stand as a Liberal
- **Winston Churchill** 1874-1965 British Conservative statesman: Leon Harris *The Fine Art of Political Wit* (1965)

3 When I was at Cambridge it was…my ambition to be approached in some way by an elderly homosexual don and asked to spy for or against my country.
- **Stephen Fry** 1957- English comedian, actor, and writer: *Paperweight* (1992)

4 *Pension.* Pay given to a state hireling for treason to his country.
- **Samuel Johnson** 1709-84 English poet, critic, and lexicographer: *A Dictionary of the English Language* (1755)

5 Never trust a man who combs his hair straight from his left armpit.
of the careful distribution of hair on General MacArthur's balding head
- **Alice Roosevelt Longworth** 1884-1980 American socialite: Michael Teague *Mrs L* (1981)

6 Defectors are like grapes. The first pressings from them are the best. The third and fourth lack body.
- **Maurice Oldfield** 1915-81 English intelligence officer: Chapman Pincher in *Mail on Sunday* 19 September 1982; attributed

7 Never take a reference from a clergyman. They always want to give someone a second chance.
- **Lady Selborne** 1858-1950 English suffragist: K. Rose *The Later Cecils* (1975)

8 [Treason], Sire, is a question of dates.
- **Charles-Maurice de Talleyrand** 1754-1838 French statesman: Duff Cooper *Talleyrand* (1932)

Truth

see also LIES

....

The truth is rarely pure, and never simple.   **Oscar Wilde**

1   Too much truth
    Is uncouth.
    ▪ **Franklin P. Adams** 1881–1960 American
      journalist and humorist: *Nods and Becks*
      (1944)

2   'Tis strange—but true; for truth is
       always strange;
    Stranger than fiction.
    ▪ **Lord Byron** 1788–1824 English poet: *Don Juan*
      (1819–24)

3   Our old friend...economical with the
    actualité.
    ▪ **Alan Clark** 1928–99 British Conservative
      politician: under cross-examination at the
      Old Bailey during the Matrix Churchill case;
      in *Independent* 10 November 1992

4   Something unpleasant is coming when
    men are anxious to tell the truth.
    ▪ **Benjamin Disraeli** 1804–81 British Tory
      statesman and novelist: *The Young Duke*
      (1831)

5   It is always the best policy to speak the
    truth—unless, of course, you are an

exceptionally good liar.
▪ **Jerome K. Jerome** 1859–1927 English writer:
  in *The Idler* February 1892

6   Never tell a story because it is true: tell
    it because it is a good story.
    ▪ **John Pentland Mahaffy** 1839–1919 Irish
      writer: W. B. Stanford and R. B. McDowell
      Mahaffy (1971)

7   I never give them [the public] hell.
    I just tell the truth, and they think it
    is hell.
    ▪ **Harry S. Truman** 1884–1972 American
      Democratic statesman: in *Look* 3 April
      1956

8   Get your facts first, and then you can
    distort 'em as much as you please.
    ▪ **Mark Twain** 1835–1910 American writer:
      Rudyard Kipling *From Sea to Sea* (1899)

9   The truth is rarely pure, and never
    simple.
    ▪ **Oscar Wilde** 1854–1900 Irish dramatist
      and poet: *The Importance of Being Earnest*
      (1895)

Unintended Humour

....

I know the human being and fish can coexist peacefully.   **George W. Bush**

1   *comment made to Cecil Beaton by a lady-*
    in-waiting to the exiled Queen Geraldine of
    Albania:
    Of course, we'll go back there one day.
    Meanwhile, we have to make a new life
    for ourselves at the Ritz.
    ▪ **Anonymous:** Cecil Beaton diary 1940

2   I make no apology for returning to
    the subject of premature ejaculation,
    because my postbag is full of it.
    beginning of an agony column in the
    Hampstead and Highgate Express, as

recounted by Michael Grade to Marjorie
Proops
▪ **Anonymous:** in *Independent* 10 February 1993

3   I am the Jesus Christ of politics...I
    sacrifice myself for everyone.
    ▪ **Silvio Berlusconi** 1936– Italian statesman:
      speech, 12 February 2006

4   When I have my photo taken, I don't
    say 'cheese'. I say 'sex'.
    ▪ **Carla Bruni** 1967– Italian-French singer
      and model: in *Observer* 30 March 2008

5 *talking about Ronald Reagan:*
I'm proud to be his partner. We've had triumphs, we've made mistakes, we've had sex.
quickly corrected to 'setbacks, we've had setbacks'
- **George Bush** 1924– American Republican statesman: speech, College of Southern Idaho, 6 May 1988

6 I know the human being and fish can coexist peacefully.
- **George W. Bush** 1946– American Republican statesman: speech, 29 September 2000

7 Our enemies are innovative and resourceful, and so are we. They never stop thinking about new ways to harm our country and our people, and neither do we.
- **George W. Bush** 1946– American Republican statesman: speech, 5 August 2004

8 That's the fastest time ever run—but it's not as fast as the world record.
- **David Coleman** 1926– British sports commentator: Barry Fantoni (ed.) *Private Eye's Colemanballs* 3 (1986)

9 There is a wealth of poverty in Northern Ireland which must be overcome.
- **Lord Enniskillen** 1918–89: speech in the House of Lords, 3 December 1968

10 There's been a colour clash: both teams are wearing white.
- **John Motson** 1945– English football commentator: in 'Colemanballs' column in *Private Eye*; Ned Sherrin *Cutting Edge* (1984)

11 Haven't you run before? This isn't your first time?
to double Olympic gold medallist Mo Farah as winner of the New Orleans half-marathon
- **LaTonya Norton** American television presenter: interview, WDSU TV, 24 February 2013

12 All my concerts had no sounds in them: they were completely silent…People had to make their own music in their minds.
- **Yoko Ono** 1933– Japanese poet and songwriter: interview in *Rolling Stone* 1968

13 Having committed political suicide, the Conservative Party is now living to regret it.
- **Chris Patten** 1944– British Conservative politician: attributed, 2003; the remark was subsequently considered for a Plain English Foot in Mouth Award

14 I think that gay marriage is something that should be between a man and a woman.
- **Arnold Schwarzenegger** 1947– Austrian-born American actor and Republican politician: in *CCN.com* (online edition) 28 August 2003

15 I can't see who's in the lead but it's either Oxford or Cambridge.
- **John Snagge** 1904–96 English sports commentator: C. Dodd *Oxford and Cambridge Boat Race* (1983)

16 I don't have time to sit down and write. When I think of a melody, I call my answering machine and sing it.
- **Britney Spears** 1981– American pop singer: in *Observer* 9 January 2005

17 We have become a grandmother.
- **Margaret Thatcher** 1925–2013 British Conservative stateswoman: in *Times* 4 March 1989

18 Comrade Zhdanov is no professional musician. But oh, how well he knows folk song! When he recently visited our Piatnitzky Choir, we asked him: 'Is it true, Comrade Zhdanov, that you know 600 folk songs?' 'No,' he said, 'not 600, but I suppose I do know about 300.' How much better our composers would write if they knew folk songs as Andrei Alexandrovich does!
on the musical expertise of A. A. Zhdanov, Stalin's 'cultural commissar'
- **Vladimir Zakharov** 1901–56 Russian composer: Alexander Werth *Musical Uproar in Moscow* (1949)

The Universe

Space is almost infinite. As a matter of fact, we think it is infinite.   **Dan Quayle**

1 Had I been present at the Creation,
I would have given some useful hints
for the better ordering of the universe.
  ▪ **Alfonso, King of Castile** 1221-84: on
  studying the Ptolemaic system (attributed)

2 'I quite realized,' said Columbus,
'That the Earth was not a rhombus,
But I *am* a little annoyed
To find it an oblate spheroid.'
  ▪ **Edmund Clerihew Bentley** 1875-1956
  English writer: 'Columbus' (1929)

3 After one look at this planet any visitor
from outer space would say 'I WANT TO
SEE THE MANAGER'.
  ▪ **William S. Burroughs** 1914-97 American
  novelist: *The Adding Machine* (1985)

4   Listen: there's a hell
Of a good universe next door; let's go.
  ▪ **e. e. cummings** 1894-1962 American poet:
  1 x 1 (1944)

5 Now, my own suspicion is that the
universe is not only queerer than we
suppose, but queerer than we *can*
suppose.
  ▪ **J. B. S. Haldane** 1892-1964 Scottish
  mathematical biologist: *Possible Worlds*
  (1927)

6 Space isn't remote at all. It's only an
hour's drive away if your car could go
straight upwards.
  ▪ **Fred Hoyle** 1915-2001 English astrophysicist:
  in *Observer* 9 September 1979 'Sayings of
  the Week'

7 I am sorry to say that there is too
much point to the wisecrack that life is
extinct on other planets because their
scientists were more advanced than
ours.
  ▪ **John F. Kennedy** 1917-63 American
  Democratic statesman: speech,
  11 December 1959

8 I don't think there's intelligent life on
other planets. Why should other planets
be any different from this one?
  ▪ **Bob Monkhouse** 1928-2003 English
  entertainer: attributed; in *BBC News*
  29 December 2003 (online edition)

9 Space is almost infinite. As a matter of
fact, we think it is infinite.
  ▪ **Dan Quayle** 1947- American Republican
  politician: in *Daily Telegraph* 8 March 1989

10 Sometimes I think the surest sign that
intelligent life exists elsewhere in the
universe is that none of it has tried to
contact us.
  ▪ **Bill Watterson** 1958- American cartoonist:
  Calvin and Hobbes (comic strip) 8 November
  1989

Virtue and Vice

see also **MORALITY**

....

I think I could be a good woman if I had five thousand a year.
William Makepeace Thackeray

1 Most plain girls are virtuous because of the scarcity of opportunity to be otherwise.
- **Maya Angelou** 1928- American writer: *I Know Why the Caged Bird Sings* (1969)

2 I'm as pure as the driven slush.
- **Tallulah Bankhead** 1903-68 American actress: in *Saturday Evening Post* 12 April 1947

3 *definition of a saint:*
A dead sinner revised and edited.
- **Ambrose Bierce** 1842-c.1914 American writer: *The Devil's Dictionary* (1911)

4 The rain, it raineth on the just
And also on the unjust fella:
But chiefly on the just, because
The unjust steals the just's umbrella.
- **Lord Bowen** 1835-94 English judge: Walter Sichel *Sands of Time* (1923)

5 Lead me not into temptation; I can find the way myself.
- **Rita Mae Brown** 1944- American novelist and poet: attributed

6 A little still she strove, and much repented,
And whispering 'I will ne'er consent'—consented.
- **Lord Byron** 1788-1824 English poet: *Don Juan* (1819-24)

7 I fear I have nothing original in me—
Excepting Original Sin.
- **Thomas Campbell** 1777-1844 Scottish poet: 'To a Young Lady, Who Asked Me to Write Something Original for Her Album' (1843)

8 What terrible sins I have working for me. I suppose it's the wages.
- **Peter Cook** 1937-95 English satirist and actor: *Bedazzled* (1967 film), spoken by Cook as the Devil

9 Lydia was tired of being good...It made her feel a little dowdy, as though she had taken up residence in the suburbs of morality.
- **Alice Thomas Ellis** 1932-2005 English novelist: *Unexplained Laughter* (1985)

10 The louder he talked of his honour, the faster we counted our spoons.
- **Ralph Waldo Emerson** 1803-82 American philosopher and poet: *The Conduct of Life* (1860)

11 If you resolve to give up smoking, drinking and loving, you don't actually live longer, it just seems longer.
- **Clement Freud** 1924-2009 English politician, broadcaster, and writer: in *Observer* 27 December 1964

12 But if he does really think that there is no distinction between virtue and vice, why, Sir, when he leaves our houses, let us count our spoons.
- **Samuel Johnson** 1709-84 English poet, critic, and lexicographer: James Boswell *Life of Samuel Johnson* (1791) 14 July 1763

13 He that but looketh on a plate of ham and eggs to lust after it, hath already committed breakfast with it in his heart.
- **C. S. Lewis** 1898-1963 English literary scholar: letter, 10 March 1954

14 honesty is a good
thing but
it is not profitable to
its possessor
unless it is
kept under control.
- **Don Marquis** 1878-1937 American poet and journalist: *archys life of mehitabel* (1933) 'archygrams'

15 Decency is Indecency's conspiracy of silence.
- **George Bernard Shaw** 1856-1950 Irish dramatist: *Man and Superman* (1903) 'Maxims: Decency'

16 Self-denial is not a virtue: it is only the effect of prudence on rascality.
- **George Bernard Shaw** 1856–1950 Irish dramatist: *Man and Superman* (1903)

17 I think I could be a good woman if I had five thousand a year.
- **William Makepeace Thackeray** 1811–63 English novelist: *Vanity Fair* (1847–8), spoken by Becky Sharpe

18 When I'm good, I'm very, very good, but when I'm bad, I'm better.
- **Mae West** 1892–1980 American film actress: in *I'm No Angel* (1933 film)

19 I used to be Snow White…but I drifted.
- **Mae West** 1892–1980 American film actress: Joseph Weintraub *Peel Me a Grape* (1975)

20 Between two evils, I always pick the one I never tried before.
- **Mae West** 1892–1980 American film actress: in *Klondike Annie* (1936 film)

21 To err is human—but it feels divine.
- **Mae West** 1892–1980 American film actress: attributed; Fred Metcalf (ed.) *Penguin Dictionary of Modern Humorous Quotations* (1987)

22 Charity, dear Miss Prism, charity! None of us are perfect. I myself am peculiarly susceptible to draughts.
- **Oscar Wilde** 1854–1900 Irish dramatist and poet: *The Importance of Being Earnest* (1895)

23 I can resist everything except temptation.
- **Oscar Wilde** 1854–1900 Irish dramatist and poet: *Lady Windermere's Fan* (1892)

24 A little sincerity is a dangerous thing, and a great deal of it is absolutely fatal.
- **Oscar Wilde** 1854–1900 Irish dramatist and poet: 'The Critic as Artist' (1891)

Wales

The land of my fathers. My fathers can have it. **Dylan Thomas**

1 It profits a man nothing to give his soul for the whole world…But for Wales—!
- **Robert Bolt** 1924–95 English dramatist: *A Man for All Seasons* (1960)

2 I am Anglo Welsh. My grandparents were Anglo Welsh. My parents were Anglo Welsh; indeed my parents burned down their own cottage.
- **Gyles Brandreth** 1948– English writer and broadcaster: *The One to One Show* Edinburgh Festival Fringe, 2010

3 The land of my fathers. My fathers can have it.
- **Dylan Thomas** 1914–53 Welsh poet: *Adam* December 1953

4 There are still parts of Wales where the only concession to gaiety is a striped shroud.
- **Gwyn Thomas** 1913–81 Welsh novelist and dramatist: in *Punch* 18 June 1958

5 'I often think,' he continued, 'that we can trace almost all the disasters of English history to the influence of Wales!'
- **Evelyn Waugh** 1903–66 English novelist: *Decline and Fall* (1928)

War

see also **ARMED FORCES**

The quickest way of ending a war is to lose it.   **George Orwell**

1 *of the retreat from Dunkirk, May 1940:*
The noise, my dear! And the people!
- **Anonymous**: Anthony Rhodes *Sword of Bone* (1942)

2 War does not determine who is right—only who is left.
- **Anonymous**: early twentieth century saying, often later attributed to Bertrand Russell

3 War is God's way of teaching Americans geography.
- **Anonymous**: widely attributed to Ambrose Bierce, but not found before the early 1990s

4 War is never a picnic. Although obviously soldiers do end up eating outdoors a lot.
- **Jesse Armstrong** and **Sam Bain** 1971– British screenwriters: *Peep Show* (Channel 4 TV, 2008), spoken by David Mitchell as Mark

5 After each war there is a little less democracy to save.
- **Brooks Atkinson** 1894–1984 American journalist and critic: *Once Around the Sun* (1951) 7 January

6 Well, if you knows of a better 'ole, go to it.
- **Bruce Bairnsfather** 1888–1959 British cartoonist: *Fragments from France* (1915) cartoon caption

7 We need a futile gesture at this stage. It will raise the whole tone of the war.
- **Peter Cook** 1937–95 English comedian and actor: *Beyond the Fringe* (1961)

8 They found more dangerous chemicals in Coca-Cola's Dasani mineral water than they did in the whole of Iraq.
- **Robin Cook** 1946–2005 British Labour politician: in *Observer* 29 August 2004

9 Men love war because it allows them to look serious. Because they imagine it is the one thing that stops women laughing at them.
- **John Fowles** 1926–2005 English novelist: *The Magus* (1966)

10 There never was a good war, or a bad peace.
- **Benjamin Franklin** 1706–90 American politician, inventor, and scientist: letter to Josiah Quincy, 11 September 1783

11 The Gulf War was like teenage sex. We got in too soon and out too soon.
- **Tom Harkin** 1939– American Democratic politician: in *Independent on Sunday* 29 September 1991

12 I'd like to see the government get out of war altogether and leave the whole field to private industry.
- **Joseph Heller** 1923–99 American novelist: *Catch-22* (1961)

13 *to George VI, summer 1940:*
All the same, sir, I would put some of the colonies in your wife's name.
- **Joseph Herman Hertz** 1872–1946 Slovakian-born British chief rabbi: Chips Channon diary, 3 June 1943

14 *of war in Iraq:*
Vietnam without the mosquitoes.
- **Carl Hiaasen** 1953– American writer: attributed; in *Guardian* 23 October 2004

15 TRENTINO (LOUIS CALHERN): I am willing to do anything to prevent this war.
FIREFLY (GROUCHO MARX): It's too late. I've already paid a month's rent on the battlefield.
- **Bert Kalmar** 1884–1947 and **others** screenwriters: *Duck Soup* (1933 film)

16 I think from now on they're shooting without a script.
comment on the German invasion of Russia
- **George S. Kaufman** 1889–1961 American dramatist: Howard Teichmann *George S. Kaufman* (1973)

17 All castles had one major weakness.

The enemy used to get in through the gift shop.

- **Peter Kay** 1973- British comedian: attributed; in *Nuts* May 2005

18 A nation is only at peace when it's at war.

- **Hugh Kingsmill** 1889-1949 English man of letters: Richard Ingrams *God's Apology* (1977)

19 If we'd had as many soldiers as that, we'd have won the war!
on seeing the number of Confederate troops in Gone with the Wind *at the 1939 premiere*

- **Margaret Mitchell** 1900-49 American novelist: W. G. Harris *Gable and Lombard* (1976)

20 Like many men of my generation, I had an opportunity to give war a chance, and I promptly chickened out.

- **P. J. O'Rourke** 1947- American humorous writer: *Give War a Chance* (1992)

21 The quickest way of ending a war is to lose it.

- **George Orwell** 1903-50 English novelist: in *Polemic* May 1946 'Second Thoughts on James Burnham'

22 Little girl…Sometime they'll give a war and nobody will come.

- **Carl Sandburg** 1878-1967 American poet: *The People, Yes* (1936); 'Suppose They Gave a War and Nobody Came?' was the title of a 1970 film

23 Retreat, hell! We're only attacking in another direction.

- **Oliver P. Smith** 1893-1977 American general: vicinity of Chosin Reservoir, Korea, 4 December, 1950

24 *Evelyn Waugh, returning from Crete in 1941, was asked his impression of his first battle:*
Like German opera, too long and too loud.

- **Evelyn Waugh** 1903-66 English novelist: Christopher Sykes *Evelyn Waugh* (1975)

25 As Lord Chesterfield said of the generals of his day, 'I only hope that when the enemy reads the list of their names, he trembles as I do.'
usually quoted 'I don't know what effect these men will have upon the enemy, but, by God, they frighten me'

- **Duke of Wellington** 1769-1852 British soldier and statesman: letter, 29 August 1810

26 *of an early attempt to write about Waterloo:*
Write the history of a battle? As well write the history of a ball!

- **Duke of Wellington** 1769-1852 British soldier and statesman: Richard Holmes *Firing Line* (1986)

Wealth

see also **MONEY, POVERTY**

The meek shall inherit the earth, but not the mineral rights.   **John Paul Getty**

1 If you would know what the Lord God thinks of money, you have only to look at those to whom he gives it.

- **Maurice Baring** 1874-1945 British writer: Malcolm Cowley (ed.) *Writers at Work* (1958) 1st series

2 I can walk. It's just that I'm so rich I don't need to.

- **Alan Bennett** 1934- English dramatist and actor: *Forty Years On* (1969)

3 People say I wasted my money. I say 90 per cent went on women, fast cars and booze. The rest I wasted.

- **George Best** 1946-2005 Northern Irish footballer: in *Daily Telegraph* 29 December 1990

4 A very rich person should leave his kids enough to do anything but not enough to do nothing.

- **Warren Buffett** 1930- American businessman: quoted in *Fortune Magazine* (online edition) 25 June 2006

5 Mrs Budge Bulkeley, worth £32,000,000, has arrived here [Isfahan] accompanied by some lesser millionairesses. They are in great misery because the caviar is running out.
on fellow travellers in Persia
- **Robert Byron** 1905-41 English traveller, art critic, and historian: *The Road to Oxiana* (1937)

6 When I hear a rich man described as a colourful character I figure he's a bum with money.
- **Jimmy Cannon** 1910-73 American journalist: in *New York Post* c.1955 'Nobody Asked Me, But...'

7 I really love having money, because it lets me be lazy. Work's really overrated.
- **Charlotte Church** 1986- Welsh soprano: in *Times* 9 September 2007

8 The Rich aren't like us—they pay less taxes.
- **Peter De Vries** 1910-93 American novelist: in *Washington Post* 30 July 1989

9 £40,000 a year [is] a moderate income—such a one as a man might jog on with.
- **Lord Durham** 1792-1840 English Whig politician: Herbert Maxwell *The Creevey Papers* (1903); letter from Mr Creevey to Miss Elizabeth Ord, 13 September 1821

10 A rich man is nothing but a poor man with money.
- **W. C. Fields** 1880-1946 American humorist: attributed

11 The meek shall inherit the earth, but not the mineral rights.
- **John Paul Getty** 1892-1976 American industrialist: Robert Lenzner *The Great Getty*; attributed

12 *aged seven, when his brother asked why he was not interested in learning to read:*
Because when I grow up I'm going to be a millionaire and hire someone to read for me.
- **James Goldsmith** 1933-97 British financier and politician: Juan Fallon *Billionaire: the life and times of Sir James Goldsmith* (1991)

13 Poor Harold, he can live on his income all right, but he no longer can live on the income from his income.
of Harold Vanderbilt
- **George S. Kaufman** 1889-1961 American dramatist: Howard Teichmann *George S. Kaufman* (1973)

14 Wealth and power are much more likely to be the result of breeding than they are of reading.
on self-help books
- **Fran Lebowitz** 1946- American writer: *Social Studies* (1981)

15 Wealth—any income that is at least $100 more a year than the income of one's wife's sister's husband.
- **H. L. Mencken** 1880-1956 American journalist and literary critic: *A Book of Burlesques* (1920)

16 I don't mind their having a lot of
   money, and I don't care how they
   employ it,
But I do think that they damn well
   ought to admit they enjoy it.
- **Ogden Nash** 1902-71 American humorist: 'The Terrible People' (1933)

17 The average millionaire is only the average dishwasher dressed in a new suit.
- **George Orwell** 1903-50 English novelist: *Down and Out in Paris and London* (1933)

18 I am a Millionaire. That is my religion.
- **George Bernard Shaw** 1856-1950 Irish dramatist: *Major Barbara* (1907)

19 It is the wretchedness of being rich that you have to live with rich people.
- **Logan Pearsall Smith** 1865-1946 American-born man of letters: *Afterthoughts* (1931)

20 To suppose, as we all suppose, that we could be rich and not behave as the rich behave, is like supposing that we could drink all day and keep absolutely sober.
- **Logan Pearsall Smith** 1865-1946 American-born man of letters: *Afterthoughts* (1931)

21 It was very prettily said, that we may learn the little value of fortune by the persons on whom heaven is pleased to bestow it.
- **Richard Steele** 1672-1729 Irish-born essayist and dramatist: *The Tatler* 27 July 1710

22 I've been poor and I've been rich—rich is better.
- **Sophie Tucker** 1884-1966 Russian-born American vaudeville artiste: attributed

23 Real diamonds! They must be worth their weight in gold.
- **Billy Wilder** 1906-2002 and **I. A. L. Diamond** 1915-88 screenwriters: *Some Like it Hot* (1959 film); spoken by Marilyn Monroe as Sugar Kane

24 I am grateful for the blessings of wealth, but it hasn't changed who I am. My feet are still on the ground. I'm just wearing better shoes.
- **Oprah Winfrey** 1954- American talk-show host: in *Independent on Sunday* 18 July 2004

The Weather

It was such a lovely day I thought it was a pity to get up.   **W. Somerset Maugham**

1 The English winter—ending in July, To recommence in August.
- **Lord Byron** 1788-1824 English poet: *Don Juan* (1819-24)

2 Summer has set in with its usual severity.
- **Samuel Taylor Coleridge** 1772-1834 English poet, critic, and philosopher: letter to Vincent Novello, 9 May 1826

3 *to his cat, who disliked rain:*
I know what's wrong, my dear, but I really do not know how to turn it off.
- **Albert Einstein** 1879-1955 German-born theoretical physicist: Banesch Hoffmann *Albert Einstein: Creator and Rebel* (1972)

4 There is no such thing as bad weather, only inappropriate clothing.
- **Ranulph Fiennes** 1944- English explorer: attributed, re-working an old saying

5 A woman rang to say she heard there was a hurricane on the way. Well don't worry, there isn't.
weather forecast on the night before catastrophic gales in southern England
- **Michael Fish** 1944- British weather forecaster: BBC TV, 15 October 1987

6 The weather is like the Government, always in the wrong.
- **Jerome K. Jerome** 1859-1927 English writer: *Idle Thoughts of an Idle Fellow* (1889)

7 When two Englishmen meet, their first talk is of the weather.
- **Samuel Johnson** 1709-84 English poet, critic, and lexicographer: *The Idler* 24 June 1758

8 The most serious charge which can be brought against New England is not Puritanism but February.
- **Joseph Wood Krutch** 1893-1970 American critic and naturalist: *The Twelve Seasons* (1949) 'February'

9 *commenting on the stifling heat of summer in Miami:*
The sensation of breathing, then living, was not unlike being obliged to make love to a 300-pound woman who has decided to get on top.
- **Norman Mailer** 1923-2007 American novelist and essayist: *Miami and the Siege of Chicago* (1968)

10 It was such a lovely day I thought it was a pity to get up.
- **W. Somerset Maugham** 1874-1965 English novelist: *Our Betters* (1923)

11 Winter is icummen in, Lhude sing Goddamm, Raineth drop and staineth slop, And how the wind doth ramm! Sing: Goddamm.
- **Ezra Pound** 1885-1972 American poet: 'Ancient Music' (1917)

12 Come December, people always say, 'Isn't it cold?' Well, of course it's cold.

It's the middle of winter. You don't wander around at midnight saying, 'Isn't it dark?'
- **Arthur Smith** 1954- English comedian: *Arthur Smith's Hamlet*

13 Thank heavens, the sun has gone in, and I don't have to go out and enjoy it.
- **Logan Pearsall Smith** 1865-1946 American-born man of letters: *Afterthoughts* (1931)

14 Let no man boast himself that he has got through the perils of winter till at least the seventh of May.
- **Anthony Trollope** 1815-82 English novelist: *Doctor Thorne* (1858)

15 The way to ensure summer in England is to have it framed and glazed in a comfortable room.
- **Horace Walpole** 1717-97 English writer and connoisseur: letter to Revd William Cole, 28 May 1774

16 It was the wrong kind of snow.
explaining disruption on British Rail
- **Terry Worrall** British spokesman for British Rail: as quoted in *Evening Standard* 12 February 1991

Weddings

see also **MARRIAGE**

....

A bride's attitude towards her betrothed can be summed up in three words: Aisle. Altar. Hymn.   **Frank Muir**

1 If it were not for the presents, an elopement would be preferable.
- **George Ade** 1866-1944 American humorist and dramatist: *Forty Modern Fables* (1901)

2 *a rhyming marriage licence, said to have been composed for an al fresco ceremony outside Lichfield:*
Under an oak in stormy weather
I joined this rogue and whore together;
And none but he who rules the thunder
Can put this rogue and whore asunder.
- **Anonymous**: has been attributed to Swift, but of doubtful authenticity; C. H. Wilson *Swiftiana* (1804)

3 'What are you giving the bride and groom?'
'Oh, about three months.'
- **Anonymous**: said to have been overheard at a Hollywood wedding

4 Egghead weds hourglass.
on the marriage of Arthur Miller and Marilyn Monroe
- **Anonymous**: headline in *Variety* 1956; attributed

5 *to guests as they arrived at the reception given for a smart society wedding:*
Don't go upstairs. The bride's hideous.
- **Margot Asquith** 1864-1945 British political hostess: John Gielgud *Distinguished Company* (1972)

6 We had a civil ceremony—his mother couldn't come.
on her wedding
- **Phyllis Diller** 1917-2012 American actress: attributed

7 A bride's attitude towards her betrothed can be summed up in three words: Aisle. Altar. Hymn.
- **Frank Muir** 1920-98 English writer and broadcaster: Frank Muir and Denis Norden *The Complete and Utter 'My Word' Collection* (1983)

8   The trouble
with being best man is, you don't get a chance to prove it.
- **Les A. Murray** 1938- Australian poet: *The Boys Who Stole the Funeral* (1989)

9 *agreeing with the comment, at her remarriage to Alan Campbell in 1950, that some of those*

present had not spoken to each other for years:
Including the bride and groom.
- **Dorothy Parker** 1893-1967 American critic and humorist: Marion Meade *What Fresh Hell Is This?* (1988)

10 In olden times sacrifices were made at the altar—a custom which is still continued.
- **Helen Rowland** 1875-1950 American writer: *Reflections of a Bachelor Girl* (1909)

11 You can always surprise your husband on your anniversary just by mentioning it.
- **Al Schock** 1920-2009 American businessman: *Jokes for All Occasions* (1979)

12 We're supposed to have just a small family affair.
on his wedding
- **Prince William** 1982– British prince: to his father-in-law Michael Middleton at Westminster Abbey, 29 April 2011

13 Nothing so surely introduces a sour note into a wedding ceremony as the abrupt disappearance of the groom in a cloud of dust.
- **P. G. Wodehouse** 1881-1975 English writer: *A Pelican at Blandings* (1969)

Wine

see also **CHAMPAGNE, DRINK**

....

A good general rule is to state that the bouquet is better than the taste, and vice versa.   **Stephen Potter**

1 *of claret:*
It would be port if it could.
- **Richard Bentley** 1662-1742 English classical scholar: R. C. Jebb *Bentley* (1902)

2 And Noah he often said to his wife
   when he sat down to dine,
'I don't care where the water goes if it
   doesn't get into the wine.'
- **G. K. Chesterton** 1874-1936 English essayist, novelist, and poet: 'Wine and Water' (1914)

3 *when the Queen accepted a second glass of wine at lunch:*
Do you think it's wise, darling? You know you've got to rule this afternoon.
- **Queen Elizabeth, the Queen Mother** 1900-2002: Compton Miller *Who's Really Who* (1983)

4 I cook with wine, sometimes I even add it to food.
- **W. C. Fields** 1880-1946 American humorist: attributed, probably apocryphal

5 Behold the rain which descends from heaven upon our vineyards, and which incorporates itself with the grapes to be changed into wine; a constant proof that God loves us, and loves to see us happy!
- **Benjamin Franklin** 1706-90 American politician, inventor, and scientist: letter to the Abbé Morellet, *c.* July, 1779

6 A good general rule is to state that the bouquet is better than the taste, and vice versa.
on wine-tasting
- **Stephen Potter** 1900-69 British writer: *One-Upmanship* (1952)

7 It's the old wine ramp, vicar! Cheapish, reddish and Spanish.
- **Tom Stoppard** 1937– British dramatist: *Where Are They Now?* (1973)

8 It's a naïve domestic Burgundy without any breeding, but I think you'll be amused by its presumption.
- **James Thurber** 1894-1961 American humorist: cartoon caption in *New Yorker* 27 March 1937

9 Poor wine at the table of a rich host is an insult without an apology.
- **Johann Georg Zimmerman** 1728-95 Swiss physician and writer: *Aphorisms and Reflections on Men, Morals, and Things* (1800)

Wit and Wordplay

see also **HUMOUR, PUNS**

....

I'm on the horns of a Dalai Lama. **Dick Vosburgh**

1 HONEY: I wonder if you could show me where the...I want to...put some powder on my nose.
GEORGE: Martha, won't you show her where we keep the...euphemism?
- **Edward Albee** 1928- American dramatist: *Who's Afraid of Virginia Woolf* (1964)

2 *after reports that cafeterias in Washington had changed the name of 'french fries' to 'freedom fries' in response to French criticism of American policy in Iraq:*
I don't want to have to refer to my French fry potatoes as freedom fries, and I don't want to have to freedom kiss my wife.
- **Woody Allen** 1935- American film director, writer, and actor: in *Independent* 7 June 2003

3 *notice affixed to the gates of St James's Palace during one of George II's absences in Hanover:*
Lost or strayed out of this house a man who has left a wife and six children on the parish...[A reward of four shillings and sixpence is offered] Nobody judging him to deserve a crown.
- **Anonymous**: Duke of Windsor 'My Hanoverian Ancestors' (unpublished reminiscences); Elizabeth Longford (ed.) *The Oxford Book of Royal Anecdotes* (1989)

4 *it was said that aboard ship Caroline of Brunswick, the estranged wife of George IV, would sleep in a tent on deck with her majordomo, and take a bath in her cabin with him:*
The Grand Master of St Caroline has
    found promotion's path;
He is made both Knight Companion
    and Commander of the Bath.
- **Anonymous**: Roger Fulford *The Trial of Queen Caroline* (1967)

5 *version of an old joke:*
VICTOR LEWIS SMITH: You clearly don't know the difference between a Joist and a Girder.
IRISH BUILDER: Yes I do. Joist wrote Ulysses and Girder wrote Faust.
- **Anonymous**: in *Evening Standard* 12 September 2003

6 *Christopher Isherwood apologized for his bad cold, saying he should have cancelled his dinner invitation to Axelrod and Frederic Raphael:*
My dear Christopher, any cold of yours is a cold of mine.
- **George Axelrod** 1922-2003 American writer: quoted by Frederic Raphael in *Times Literary Supplement* 4 February 2000

7 My problem was that I was always missing. Miss World, Miss England, Miss UK...
- **George Best** 1946-2005 Northern Irish footballer: Joe Lovejoy *Bestie* (1998)

8 I'm a trisexual. I'll try anything once.
- **Jenny Bicks**: *Sex and the City* 'Boy, Girl, Boy, Girl...' (2000), spoken by Samantha (Kim Cattrall)

9 *on being told he should not marry anyone as plain as his fiancée:*
My dear fellow, buggers can't be choosers.
- **Maurice Bowra** 1898-1971 English scholar and literary critic: Hugh Lloyd-Jones *Maurice Bowra: a Celebration* (1974)

10 They *will* call me Mrs Pat. I can't stand it. The 'Pat' is the last straw that breaks the Campbell's back.
- **Mrs Patrick Campbell** 1865-1940 English actress: attributed

11 Wit ought to be a glorious treat, like caviar. It should be served in small elegant portions; never spread it about like marmalade.
- **Noël Coward** 1899-1973 English dramatist, actor, and composer: attributed; Margaret Hainson *Never Spread Like Marmalade* (1975)

12 His wit invites you by his looks to
    come,
   But when you knock it never is at
    home.
   ▪ **William Cowper** 1731-1800 English poet:
   'Conversation' (1782)

13 *L'esprit de l'escalier.*
   Staircase wit.
   *the witty riposte one thinks of only when one
   has left the drawing-room and is already on
   the way downstairs*
   ▪ **Denis Diderot** 1713-84 French philosopher:
   in *Paradoxe sur le Comédien* (written 1773-8,
   published 1830)

14 *to an author who had presented him with an
   unwelcome book:*
   Many thanks. I shall lose no time in
   reading it.
   ▪ **Benjamin Disraeli** 1804-81 British Tory
   statesman and novelist: Wilfrid Meynell
   The Man Disraeli (1903)

15 *to a footman who had accidentally spilt cream
   over him:*
   My good man, I'm not a strawberry!
   ▪ **Edward VII** 1841-1910 British king: William
   Lanceley *From Hall-Boy to House-Steward*
   (1925)

16 I can answer you in two words,
   im-possible.
   ▪ **Sam Goldwyn** 1882-1974 American film
   producer: Alva Johnston *The Great Goldwyn*
   (1937); apocryphal

17 My son, the world is your lobster.
   ▪ **Leon Griffiths** 1928-92 English writer:
   Minder (TV series); Nigel Rees (ed.) *Cassell
   Dictionary of Humorous Quotations* (1999)

18 *cannibal Hannibal Lecter:*
   I do wish we could chat longer, but I'm
   having an old friend for dinner.
   ▪ **Thomas Harris** 1940- and **Ted Tally** 1952-
   screenwriters: *The Silence of the Lambs*
   (1991 film)

19 *after Edward Heath had told Norman St
   John Stevas not to appear on a television
   programme:*
   ST JOHN STEVAS: I hope that
   disagreement about the television
   programme is water under the bridge?
   HEATH: No, not water under the bridge,

promotion down the drain.
   ▪ **Edward Heath** 1916-2005 British
   Conservative statesman: attributed

20 Dentist fills wrong cavity.
   *report of a dentist convicted of interfering
   with a patient*
   ▪ **Ben Hecht** 1894-1964 American
   screenwriter: attributed

21 Lisp: to call a spade a thpade.
   ▪ **Oliver Herford** 1863-1935 American
   humorist: attributed; Evan Esar and Nicolas
   Bentley (eds.) *The Treasury of Humorous
   Quotations* (1951)

22 I am trisexual. The Army, the Navy, and
   the Household Cavalry.
   ▪ **Brian Desmond Hurst** 1895-1986 Irish film
   director: Christopher Robbins *The Empress
   of Ireland* (2004)

23 The Tuscan Palazzo of Count Girolamo
   Strozzi where he [Tony Blair] forged
   one of New Labour's few hard-edged
   ideological positions: he was pro-sciutto
   and anti-pasto.
   ▪ **Boris Johnson** 1964- British Conservative
   politician: in *Daily Telegraph* 22 July 2008

24 *Ira Gershwin had noticed two aged men
   entering the theatre:*
   GERSHWIN: That must be Gilbert and
   Sullivan coming to fix the show.
   KAUFMAN: Why don't you put jokes like
   that into your lyrics?
   ▪ **George S. Kaufman** 1889-1961 American
   dramatist: Howard Teichmann *George S.
   Kaufman* (1973)

25 'Succès d'estime' translates as 'a success
   that ran out of steam'.
   ▪ **George S. Kaufman** 1889-1961 American
   dramatist: Philip Furia *Ira Gershwin* (1996)

26 MRS WHITEHEAD: That's bigamy.
   CAPTAIN SPAULDING: Yes, and it's big of
   me, too.
   ▪ **George S. Kaufman** 1889-1961 and **Morrie
   Ryskind** 1895-1985 screenwriters: *Animal
   Crackers* (1930 film), spoken by Margaret
   Irving and Groucho Marx

27 The greatest thing since they reinvented
   unsliced bread.
   ▪ **William Keegan** 1938- British journalist: in
   Observer 13 December 1987

28 The first thing I do in the morning is
brush my teeth and sharpen my tongue.
- **Oscar Levant** 1906-72 American pianist:
attributed; Evan Esar *Treasury of Humorous
Quotations* (1951)

29 *for a poem on being Poet Laureate:*
It's hard to get your words' worth from
a poet.
- **Roger McGough** 1937- English poet:
attributed

30 Said Hamlet to Ophelia,
I'll draw a sketch of thee.
What kind of pencil shall I use?
2B or not 2B?
- **Spike Milligan** 1918-2002 Irish comedian:
'Hamlet'

31 I must go down to the sea again
To the lonely sea and the sky;
I left my shoes and socks there—
I wonder if they're dry?
parodying John Masefield's 'Sea Fever'
- **Spike Milligan** 1918-2002 Irish comedian:
'Return to Sorrento (3rd Class)'

32 If lawyers are disbarred and clergymen
defrocked, doesn't it follow that
electricians can be delighted, musicians
denoted, cowboys deranged, models
deposed, tree surgeons debarked and
dry cleaners depressed?
- **Virginia Ostman**: attributed; Laurence J.
Peter *Quotations for our Time* (1977)

33 *to the British actor Herbert Marshall who
annoyed her by repeated references to his busy
'shedule':*
I think you're full of skit.
- **Dorothy Parker** 1893-1967 American critic
and humorist: Marion Meade *What Fresh
Hell Is This?* (1988)

34 The pellet with the poison's in the
vessel with the pestle. The chalice from
the palace has the brew that is true.
- **Norman Panama** 1914-2003 and **Melvin
Frank** 1913-88 American screenwriters: *The
Court Jester* (1955 film); spoken by Danny Kaye

35 You beat your pate, and fancy wit will
come:
Knock as you please, there's nobody at
home.
- **Alexander Pope** 1688-1744 English poet:
'Epigram: You beat your pate' (1732)

36 ADVERTISEMENT: Rice is nice, but ricicles
are twicicles as nicicles.
CEDRIC PRICE: But testicles is besticles.
*in a Cambridge cinema watching the
advertisments*
- **Cedric Price** 1934-2003 English architect:
Alan Bennett diary 2003, in *London Review
of Books* 8 January 2004

37 No, no; for my virginity,
When I lose that, says Rose, I'll die:
Behind the elms last night, cried Dick,
Rose, were you not extremely sick?
- **Matthew Prior** 1664-1721 English poet:
'A True Maid' (1718)

38 The cruel Queen died and a post-
mortem examination revealed the word
'CALLOUS' engraved on her heart.
*of Mary Tudor, who had said CALAIS would
be engraved on her heart*
- **W. C. Sellar** 1898-1951 and **R. J. Yeatman**
1898-1968: *1066 and All That* (1930)

39 Comparisons are odorous.
- **William Shakespeare** 1564-1616 English
dramatist: *Much Ado About Nothing*
(1598-9)

40 *of Jeffrey Archer's title:*
Lord Archer of Weston-Super-Mare—
the only seaside pier on which Danny
La Rue has not performed.
- **Neil Shand**: *Loose Ends* monologue, 1999

41 An aspersion upon my parts of speech!
- **Richard Brinsley Sheridan** 1751-1816 Irish
dramatist and Whig politician: *The Rivals*
(1775)

42 He is the very pineapple of politeness!
- **Richard Brinsley Sheridan** 1751-1816 Irish
dramatist and Whig politician: *The Rivals*
(1775)

43 MRS MALAPROP: No caparisons, Miss, if
you please!—Caparisons don't become
a young woman.
- **Richard Brinsley Sheridan** 1751-1816 Irish
dramatist and Whig politician: *The Rivals*
(1775)

44 MRS MALAPROP: She's as headstrong as
an allegory on the banks of the Nile.
- **Richard Brinsley Sheridan** 1751-1816 Irish
dramatist and Whig politician: *The Rivals*
(1775)

45 LADY SNEERWELL: There's no possibility
of being witty without a little ill-nature;
the malice of a good thing is the barb
that makes it stick.
- **Richard Brinsley Sheridan** 1751-1816 Irish
dramatist and Whig politician: *The School
for Scandal* (1777)

46 *on seeing Mrs Grote in a huge rose-coloured
turban:*
Now I know the meaning of the word
'grotesque'.
- **Sydney Smith** 1771-1845 English clergyman
and essayist: Peter Virgin *Sydney Smith*
(1994)

47 *the Earl of Snowdon, asking Sir Anthony
Wagner, Garter King of Arms, for greater
flexibility when making arrangements for
the Investiture of the Prince of Wales at
Carmarthen Castle in 1969:*
Garter, darling, can't you be a little
more elastic?
- **Lord Snowdon** 1930- English
photographer: as told to the editor

48 *a toast:*
To our queer old dean.
- **William Archibald Spooner** 1844-1930
English academic: *Oxford University What's
What* (1948); attributed, perhaps apocryphal

49 *to an undergraduate:*
You have tasted your worm, you have
hissed my mystery lectures, and you
must leave by the first town drain.
- **William Archibald Spooner** 1844-1930
English academic: *Oxford University
What's What* (1948); attributed, perhaps
apocryphal

50 My parents bought a lavatory from a
travelling circus, under the fond delusion
that a Chipperfield commode was a
desirable thing to have about the house.
*at a British Antique Dealers' Association
dinner in the 1970s*
- **Tom Stoppard** 1937- British dramatist:
attributed; in *Spectator* 19 December 1998

51 To those waiting with bated breath
for that favourite media catchphrase,
the U-turn, I have only this to say. 'You
turn if you want to; the lady's not for
turning.'
- **Margaret Thatcher** 1925-2013 British
Conservative stateswoman: speech at
Conservative Party Conference in Brighton,
10 October 1980

52 When you see the sign 'African Primates
Meeting' you expect someone to
produce bananas.
*address at his retirement service, Cape Town,
23 June 1996*
- **Desmond Tutu** 1931- South African
Anglican clergyman: in *Daily Telegraph*
24 June 1996

53 Enter the strumpet voluntary.
- **Kenneth Tynan** 1927-80 English theatre
critic: of a guest at an Oxford party;
attributed

54 I'm on the horns of a Dalai Lama.
- **Dick Vosburgh** 1929-2007 American writer:
A Saint She Ain't (1999)

55 *the American lexicographer Noah Webster
was said to have been found by his wife
embracing a chambermaid:*
MRS WEBSTER: Noah, I'm surprised.
NOAH WEBSTER: No, my dear. You are
amazed. It is we who are surprised.
- **Noah Webster** 1758-1843 American
lexicographer: apocryphal; William Safire
in *New York Times* 15 October 1973

56 OSCAR WILDE: How I wish I had said
that.
WHISTLER: You will, Oscar, you will.
- **James McNeill Whistler** 1834-1903
American-born painter: in R. Ellman *Oscar
Wilde* (1987)

57 I thought coq au vin was love in a
lorry.
- **Victoria Wood** 1953- British writer and
comedienne: *Talent* (1978)

Wives

see also **MARRIAGE**

....

When you marry your mistress you create a job vacancy.   **James Goldsmith**

1 Many a man owes his success to his
first wife and his second wife to his
success.
- **Jim Backus** 1913-89 American actor:
attributed

2 *to his butler, who had resigned because of
Lady Braxfield's constant scolding:*
Lord! ye've little to complain o': ye may
be thankfu' ye're no married to her.
- **Lord Braxfield** 1722-99: Henry Cockburn
Memorials of his Time (1856)

3 Think you, if Laura had been Petrarch's
wife,
He would have written sonnets all his
life?
- **Lord Byron** 1788-1824 English poet: *Don Juan*
(1819-24)

4 Translations (like wives) are seldom
strictly faithful if they are in the least
attractive.
- **Roy Campbell** 1901-57 South African poet:
in *Poetry Review* June-July 1949

5 It's my old girl that advises. She has the
head. But I never own to it before her.
Discipline must be maintained.
- **Charles Dickens** 1812-70 English novelist:
Bleak House (1853)

6 Here lies my wife; here let her lie!
Now she's at peace and so am I.
- **John Dryden** 1631-1700 English poet, critic,
and dramatist: epitaph; attributed but not
traced in his works

7 The comfortable estate of widowhood,
is the only hope that keeps up a wife's
spirits.
- **John Gay** 1685-1732 English poet and
dramatist: *The Beggar's Opera* (1728)

8 When you marry your mistress you
create a job vacancy.
marrying Lady Annabel Birley in 1978
- **James Goldsmith** 1933-97 British financier
and politician: G. Wansell *Tycoon* (1987)

9 I...chose my wife, as she did her
wedding gown, not for a fine glossy
surface, but such qualities as would
wear well.
- **Oliver Goldsmith** 1730-74 Irish writer:
The Vicar of Wakefield (1766)

10 Only two things are necessary to keep
one's wife happy. One is to let her think
she is having her own way, and the
other, to let her have it.
- **Lyndon Baines Johnson** 1908-73 American
Democratic statesman: attributed

11 There's nothing like a good dose
of another woman to make a man
appreciate his wife.
- **Clare Booth Luce** 1903-87 American
diplomat, politician, and writer: *The Women*
(1937)

12 There once was an old man of Lyme
Who married three wives at a time,
When asked 'Why a third?'
He replied, 'One's absurd!
And bigamy, Sir, is a crime!'
- **William Cosmo Monkhouse** 1840-1901
English art critic: *Nonsense Rhymes* (1902)

13 Who was that lady I saw you with last
night?
She ain't no lady; she's my wife.
- **Joe Weber** 1867-1942 and **Lew Fields**
1867-1941 American comedians: vaudeville
lines, 1887

14 Twenty years of romance make a
woman look like a ruin; but twenty
years of marriage make her something
like a public building.
- **Oscar Wilde** 1854-1900 Irish dramatist and
poet: *A Woman of No Importance* (1893)

15 Marriage is a bribe to make a
housekeeper think she's a householder.
- **Thornton Wilder** 1897-1975 American
novelist and dramatist: *The Merchant of
Yonkers* (1939)

16 There are men who fear repartee in a
wife more keenly than a sword.
- **P. G. Wodehouse** 1881-1975 English writer:
Jill the Reckless (1922)

Women and Woman's Role

see also **FEMINISM, MEN AND WOMEN**

....

A woman needs a man like a fish needs a bicycle. **Irina Dunn**

1 The nightingale will run out of
songs before a woman runs out of
conversation.
- **Anonymous**: Spanish proverb

2 We women do talk too much, but even
then we don't tell half we know.
- **Nancy Astor** 1879-1964 American-
born British Conservative politician:
attributed,1934

3 I believe a woman's place is in the home—
or anyway in some cosy nightclub.
- **Lucille Ball** 1911-89 American actress:
attributed; Michèle Brown and Ann
O'Connor *Hammer and Tongues* (1986)

4 Women complain about premenstrual
syndrome, but I think of it as the only
time of the month I can be myself.
- **Roseanne Barr** 1953- American
comedienne and actress: attributed

5 The trouble with women in an
orchestra is that if they are attractive it
will upset my players and if they're not
it will upset me.
- **Thomas Beecham** 1879-1961 English
conductor: Harold Atkins and Archie
Newman *Beecham Stories* (1978)

6 A woman who looks like a girl and
thinks like a man is the best sort, the
most enjoyable to be and the most
pleasurable to have and to hold.
- **Julie Burchill** 1960- English journalist and
writer: *Damaged Goods* (1986)

7 I heard a man say that brigands demand
your money *or* your life, whereas
women require both.
- **Samuel Butler** 1835-1902 English novelist:
Further Extracts from Notebooks (1934)

8 The trouble with some women is that
they get all excited about nothing—and
then marry him.
- **Cher** 1946- American singer and actress:
attributed

9 A good uniform must work its way with
the women, sooner or later.
- **Charles Dickens** 1812-70 English novelist:
Pickwick Papers (1837)

10 A woman needs a man like a fish needs
a bicycle.
- **Irina Dunn** 1948- Australian writer and
politician: graffito written 1970; attributed to
Dunn by Gloria Steinem in *Time* 9 October
2000

11 Women are like elephants to me; I like
to look at them, but I wouldn't want to
own one.
- **W. C. Fields** 1880-1946 American humorist:
attributed

12 'O! help me, heaven,' she prayed, 'to be
decorative and to do right!'
- **Ronald Firbank** 1886-1926 English novelist:
The Flower Beneath the Foot (1923)

13 The more underdeveloped the country,
the more overdeveloped the women.
- **J. K. Galbraith** 1908-2006 Canadian-born
American economist: in *Time* 17 October
1969

14 She had the loaded handbag of
someone who camps out and seldom
goes home.
- **Mavis Gallant** 1922- Canadian writer:
A Fairly Good Time (1970)

15 Nothing is ever so wrong in this world
that a sensible woman can't set it right

in the course of an afternoon.
- **Jean Giraudoux** 1882-1944 French dramatist: *The Madwoman of Chaillot* (1945)

16 The Conservative Establishment has always treated women as nannies, grannies and fannies.
- **Teresa Gorman** 1931- British Conservative politician: in *Times* 7 November 1998

17 She who must be obeyed.
- **H. Rider Haggard** 1856-1925 English writer: *She* (1887)

18 When Grandma was a lassie
That tyrant known as man
Thought a woman's place
Was just the space
Around a fryin' pan.
It was good enough for Grandma
But it ain't good enough for us!
- **E. Y. Harburg** 1898-1981 American songwriter: 'It was Good Enough for Grandma' (1944)

19 Other people's babies—
That's my life!
Mother to dozens,
And nobody's wife.
of a nanny
- **A. P. Herbert** 1890-1971 English writer and humorist: 'Other People's Babies' (1930)

20 Every woman should have four pets in her life: a mink in her closet, a Jaguar in her garage, a tiger in her bed and a jackass who pays for everything.
- **Paris Hilton** 1981- American heiress: in *The Gazette* [Montreal] 5 February 2005

21 A woman's preaching is like a dog's walking on his hinder legs. It is not done well; but you are surprised to find it done at all.
- **Samuel Johnson** 1709-84 English poet, critic, and lexicographer: James Boswell *Life of Samuel Johnson* (1791) 31 July 1763

22 Remember, you're fighting for this woman's honour…which is probably more than she ever did.
- **Bert Kalmar** 1884-1947 and **others** screenwriters: *Duck Soup* (1933 film); spoken by Groucho Marx

23 When you get to a man in the case,
They're like as a row of pins—
For the Colonel's Lady an' Judy O'Grady
Are sisters under their skins!
- **Rudyard Kipling** 1865-1936 English writer and poet: 'The Ladies' (1896)

24 Being a woman is of special interest only to aspiring male transsexuals. To actual women, it is merely a good excuse not to play football.
- **Fran Lebowitz** 1946- American writer: *Metropolitan Life* (1978)

25 I can stretch a greenback dollar from here to Kingdom Come.
I can play the numbers, pay my bills, an' still end up with some
I got a twenty dollar piece says
There ain't nothin' I can't do.
I can make a dress out of a feed bag an' I can make a man out of you.
'Cause I'm a woman
W-O-M-A-N
I'll say it again.
- **Jerry Leiber** 1933-2011 American songwriter: 'I'm a Woman' (1962 song)

26 The standards women set for themselves these days are incredibly high and we can't live up to them. Whatever we do, we can never make the perfect soufflé – and be up in the bedroom in the black lacy underwear at the right time, or, if we are, the plumber's bound to be in there.
- **Maureen Lipman** 1946- English actress: attributed

27 Women do not find it difficult nowadays to behave like men, but they often find it extremely difficult to behave like gentlemen.
- **Compton Mackenzie** 1883-1972 English novelist: *Literature in My Time* (1933)

28 You know that look women get when they want to have sex? Me neither.
- **Steve Martin** 1945- American comedian: attributed

29 Women's hearts are like old china… none the worse for a break or two.
- **W. Somerset Maugham** 1874-1965 English novelist: *Lady Frederick* (1947)

30 'Always be civil to the girls, you never know who they may marry' is an aphorism which has saved many an English spinster from being treated like an Indian widow.
- **Nancy Mitford** 1904-73 English writer: *Love in a Cold Climate* (1949)

31 Be plain in dress and sober in your diet; In short my deary, kiss me, and be quiet.
- **Lady Mary Wortley Montagu** 1689-1762 English writer: 'A Summary of Lord Lyttelton's Advice'

32 Though she be but little, she is fierce.
- **William Shakespeare** 1564-1616 English dramatist: *A Midsummer Night's Dream* (1595-6)

33 The lady doth protest too much, methinks.
- **William Shakespeare** 1564-1616 English dramatist: *Hamlet* (1601)

34 The fickleness of the women I love is only equalled by the infernal constancy of the women who love me.
- **George Bernard Shaw** 1856-1950 Irish dramatist: *The Philanderer* (1898)

35 A woman seldom writes her mind but in her postscript.
- **Richard Steele** 1672-1729 Irish-born essayist and dramatist: *The Spectator* 31 May 1711

36 We are becoming the men we wanted to marry.
- **Gloria Steinem** 1934- American journalist: in *Ms* July/August 1982

37 There are worse occupations in this world than feeling a woman's pulse.
- **Laurence Sterne** 1713-68 English novelist: *A Sentimental Journey* (1768)

38 She was a blonde—with a brunette past.
- **Gwyn Thomas** 1913-81 Welsh novelist and dramatist: attributed, 1969; Nigel Rees *Chambers Dictionary of Modern Quotations* (1993)

39 When once a woman has given you her heart, you can never get rid of the rest of her body.
- **John Vanbrugh** 1664-1726 English architect and dramatist: *The Relapse* (1696)

40 The world is full of care, much like unto a bubble; Woman and care, and care and women, and women and care and trouble.
- **Nathaniel Ward** 1578-1652 English clergyman: epigram, attributed by Ward to a lady at the Court of the Queen of Bohemia; *The Simple Cobbler of Aggawam in America* (1647)

41 I will not stand for being called a woman in my own house.
- **Evelyn Waugh** 1903-66 English novelist: *Scoop* (1938)

42 You may admire a girl's curves on first introduction, but the second meeting shows up new angles.
- **Mae West** 1892-1980 American film actress: Joseph Weintraub *The Wit and Wisdom of Mae West* (1967)

43 Many a woman has a past, but I am told that she has at least a dozen, and that they all fit.
- **Oscar Wilde** 1854-1900 Irish dramatist and poet: *Lady Windermere's Fan* (1892)

Wordplay *see* WIT AND WORDPLAY

Words

see also **LANGUAGE**

....

Some word that teems with hidden meaning—like Basingstoke.   **W. S. Gilbert**

1 The most beautiful words in the English language are not 'I love you' but 'It's benign'.
  - **Woody Allen** 1935- American film director, writer, and actor: *Deconstructing Harry* (1997 film)

2 *as a young serviceman Dennis Potter was summoned for help with spelling by an elderly Major:*
  How you do spell 'accelerator'? I've been all through the blasted 'Ex's' in this bloody dictionary.
  - **Anonymous**: related by Dennis Potter during the launch of his television show *Lipstick on Your Collar*; in *Ned Sherrin in his Anecdotage* (1993)

3 Serendipity means searching for a needle in a haystack and instead finding a farmer's daughter.
  - **Anonymous**: in 'Quote...Unquote' Newsletter, July 1995, as quoted by Sir Herman Bondi

4 Bendor says that Beauchamp is a bugler.
  when Bendor, Duke of Westminster, tried to explain his brother-in-law's homosexuality to his sister
  - **Lady Beauchamp** 1876-1936: in *Daily Telegraph* 16 November 2005

5 The English language may hold a more disagreeable combination of words than 'The doctor will see you now.'
  I am willing to concede something to the phrase 'Have you anything to say before the current is turned on'.
  - **Robert Benchley** 1889-1945 American humorist: *Love Conquers All* (1923)

6 It depends on what the meaning of 'is' is.
  videotaped evidence to the grand jury, when questioned in relation to Monica Lewinsky
  - **Bill Clinton** 1946- American Democratic statesman: tapes broadcast 21 September 1998; in *Guardian* 22 September 1998

7 Euphemisms are unpleasant truths wearing diplomatic cologne.
  - **Quentin Crisp** 1908-99 English writer: *Manners from Heaven* (1984)

8 Some word that teems with hidden meaning—like Basingstoke.
  - **W. S. Gilbert** 1836-1911 English writer: *Ruddigore* (1887)

9 I had always assumed that Cliché was a suburb of Paris, until I discovered it to be a street in Oxford.
  - **Philip Guedalla** 1889-1944 British historian and biographer: *Supers and Supermen* (1920)

10 Words are chameleons, which reflect the colour of their environment.
  - **Learned Hand** 1872-1961 American judge: in *Commissioner v. National Carbide Corp.* (1948)

11 The greatest romance in the life of a lyricist is when the right word meets the right note; often however, a Park Avenue phrase elopes with a Bleeker Street chord resulting in a shotgun wedding and a quickie divorce.
  - **E. Y. Harburg** 1898-1981 American songwriter: lecture given at the New York YMCA in 1970

12 I understand your new play is full of single entendre.
  - **George S. Kaufman** 1889-1961 American dramatist: to Howard Dietz on *Between the Devil*; Howard Teichmann *George S. Kaufman* (1973)

13 Avant-garde? That's the French for bullshit.
  - **John Lennon** 1940-80 English pop singer and songwriter: attributed

14 Hypochondria is Greek for 'men'.
  - **Kathy Lette** 1958- Australian writer: in *Mail on Sunday* 4 April 2004

15 They say the definition of ambivalence is watching your mother-in-law drive over a cliff in your new Cadillac.
- **David Mamet** 1947- American dramatist and director: in *Guardian* 19 February 2000

16 Words are like leaves; and where they most abound,
Much fruit of sense beneath is rarely found.
- **Alexander Pope** 1688-1744 English poet: *An Essay on Criticism* (1711)

17 The trouble with words is that you never know whose mouth they've been in.
- **Dennis Potter** 1935-94 English television dramatist: attributed

18 *suggested remedy when J. H. Thomas complained of 'an 'ell of an 'eadache':*
A couple of aspirates.
- **F. E. Smith** 1872-1930 British Conservative politician and lawyer: in *Ned Sherrin in his Anecdotage* (1993)

19 Man does not live by words alone, despite the fact that he sometimes has to eat them.
- **Adlai Stevenson** 1900-65 American Democratic politician: *The Wit and Wisdom of Adlai Stevenson* (1965)

20 By hard, honest labour I've dug all the large words out of my vocabulary...I never write metropolis for seven cents because I can get the same money for city. I never write policeman, because I can get the same money for *Cop*.
- **Mark Twain** 1835-1910 American writer: *Mark Twain's Speeches* (1923)

21 A chair is a piece of furniture. I am not a chair because no one has ever sat on me.
on Jack Straw's announcement that Parliamentary language will now be gender-neutral
- **Ann Widdecombe** 1947- British Conservative politician: in *Observer* 11 March 2007

Work

see also **HOLIDAYS** and Leisure

....

Work is always so much more fun than fun.   **Noël Coward**

1 I will undoubtedly have to seek what is happily known as gainful employment, which I am glad to say does not describe holding public office.
- **Dean Acheson** 1893-1971 American politician: in *Time* 22 December 1952

2 A professional is a man who can do his job when he doesn't feel like it. An amateur is a man who can't do his job when he does feel like it.
- **James Agate** 1877-1947 British drama critic and novelist: diary, 19 July 1945

3 We often miss opportunity because it's dressed in overalls and looks like work.
- **Anonymous**: saying found from the 1920s, later often associated with Thomas Edison

4 Nothing is really work unless you would rather be doing something else.
- **J. M. Barrie** 1860-1937 Scottish writer and dramatist: attributed

5 Lord Finchley tried to mend the Electric Light
Himself. It struck him dead: And serve him right!
It is the business of the wealthy man
To give employment to the artisan.
- **Hilaire Belloc** 1870-1953 British writer and Liberal politician: 'Lord Finchley' (1911)

6 Oh you hate your job? Why didn't you say so? There's a support group for that. It's called EVERYBODY and they meet at the bar.
- **Drew Carey** 1958- American comedian and actor: attributed

7 *when criticized for continually arriving late for work:*
But think how early I go.
- **Lord Castlerosse** 1891-1943: while working in the City in 1919 for his uncle Lord Revelstoke; Leonard Mosley *Castlerosse* (1956); remark also claimed by Howard Dietz at MGM

8 Work is always so much more fun than fun.
- **Noël Coward** 1899-1973 English dramatist, actor, and composer: Sheridan Morley *The Quotable Noël Coward* (1999)

9 I never work. Work does age you so.
- **Quentin Crisp** 1908-99 English writer: in *Observer* 10 January 1999 'Sayings of the Week'

10 By working faithfully eight hours a day, you may eventually get to be a boss and work twelve hours a day.
- **Robert Frost** 1874-1963 American poet: attributed

11 I have long been of the opinion that if work were such a splendid thing the rich would have kept more of it for themselves.
- **Bruce Grocott** 1940- British Labour politician: in *Observer* 22 May 1988 'Sayings of the Week'

12 HOMER: The three little sentences that will get you through life. Number 1: Cover for me. Number 2: Oh, good idea, Boss! Number 3: It was like that when I got here.
- **Matt Groening** 1954- American humorist and satirist: *The Simpsons* 'One Fish, Two Fish, Blowfish, Blue Fish' (1991) written by Nell Scovell

13 I like work: it fascinates me. I can sit and look at it for hours.
- **Jerome K. Jerome** 1859-1927 English writer: *Three Men in a Boat* (1889)

14 There are so many things that we wish we had done yesterday, so few that we feel like doing today.
- **Mignon McLaughlin** 1913-83 American writer: *Complete Neurotic's Notebook* (1981)

15 Work expands so as to fill the time available for its completion.
- **C. Northcote Parkinson** 1909-93 English writer: *Parkinson's Law* (1958)

16 It's true hard work never killed anybody, but I figure why take the chance?
- **Ronald Reagan** 1911-2004 American Republican statesman: interview; in *Guardian* 31 March 1987

17 It is not more vacation we need—it is more vocation.
- **Eleanor Roosevelt** 1884-1962 American humanitarian and diplomat: *Tomorrow is Now* (1963)

18 I have yet to hear a man ask for advice on how to combine marriage and a career.
- **Gloria Steinem** 1934- American journalist: attributed

19 Work is the curse of the drinking classes.
- **Oscar Wilde** 1854-1900 Irish dramatist and poet: Hesketh Pearson *Life of Oscar Wilde* (1946)

Writers

see also **BOOKS, LITERATURE, POETRY, POETS, READING, WRITING**

I know no person so perfectly disagreeable and even dangerous as an author.
William IV

1 By appointment: teddy bear to the
nation.
heading to profile of John Betjeman
- **Anonymous:** Alan Bell 'Times Profile: Sir John
Betjeman' in *Times* 20 September 1982

2 *of the Bloomsbury Group:*
They lived in squares and loved in
triangles.
- **Anonymous:** unattributed saying

3 Wanting to know an author because
you like his work is like wanting to
know a duck because you like pâté.
- **Margaret Atwood** 1939- Canadian
novelist: in *Globe and Mail* 7 September
1996

4 We were put to Dickens as children but
it never quite took. That unremitting
humanity soon had me cheesed off.
- **Alan Bennett** 1934- English dramatist and
actor: *The Old Country* (1978)

5 *on being telephoned by the* Evening News
*to ask if he had any comment to offer on the
occasion of Harold Pinter's fiftieth birthday:*
I don't; it's only later I realize I could
have suggested two minutes' silence.
- **Alan Bennett** 1934- English dramatist and
actor: *Writing Home* (1994)

6 He's always backing into the limelight.
of T. E. Lawrence
- **Lord Berners** 1883-1950 English composer,
artist, and writer: oral tradition

7 *of Dr Johnson and her husband James Boswell:*
I have seen many a bear led by a man:
but I never before saw a man led by a
bear.
- **Margaret Boswell** c.1738-89: James Boswell
Life of Samuel Johnson (1791) 27 November
1773

8 Mark Twain was a mop-headed male
Whose narratives sparkled like ale
And this Prince of the Grin
Who fathered Huck Finn
Can still hold the world by the tale!
- **Mrs W. S. Burgess:** winner of a competition
in *The Mark Twain Quarterly* 1942

9 In general I do not draw well with
literary men—not that I dislike them
but—I never know what to say to
them after I have praised their last
publication.
- **Lord Byron** 1788-1824 English poet:
'Detached Thoughts' 15 October 1821

10 *of the vegetarian George Bernard Shaw:*
If you give him meat no woman in
London will be safe.
- **Mrs Patrick Campbell** 1865-1940 English
actress: Frank Harris *Contemporary Portraits*
(1919)

11 Oh, Jack Kerouac—that isn't writing,
it's typing.
- **Truman Capote** 1924-84 American
writer: M. Thomas Inge *Truman Capote:
Conversations* (1987)

12 In America only the successful writer
is important, in France all writers are
important, in England no writer is
important, and in Australia you have to
explain what a writer is.
- **Geoffrey Cotterell** 1919-2010 English writer:
in *New York Journal-American* 22 September
1961

13 Most people are vain, so I try to ensure
that any author who comes to stay will
find at least one of their books in their
room.
- **Duke of Devonshire** 1920-2004: in *The
Spectator* 22 January 1994

14 I love being a writer. What I can't stand
is the paperwork.
- **Peter De Vries** 1910-93 American novelist:
Laurence J. Peter (ed.) *Quotations for our
Time* (1977)

15 An author who speaks about his own
books is almost as bad as a mother who
talks about her own children.
- **Benjamin Disraeli** 1804-81 British Tory
statesman and novelist: at a banquet given
in Glasgow on his installation as Lord
Rector, 19 November 1873

16 *on Henry James:*
He had a mind so fine no idea could
violate it.
- **T. S. Eliot** 1888-1965 American-born British
poet, critic, and dramatist: in *The Little
Review* January 1918

17 The mama of dada.
of Gertrude Stein
- **Clifton Fadiman** 1904-99 American critic:
Party of One (1955)

18 The nicest old lady I ever met.
of Henry James
- **William Faulkner** 1897-1962 American
novelist: Edward Stone *The Battle and the
Books* (1964)

19 It is splendid to be a great writer,
to put men into the frying pan of
your words and make them pop like
chestnuts.
- **Gustave Flaubert** 1821-80 French novelist:
letter to Louise Colet, 3 November 1851

20 The work of Henry James has always
seemed divisible by a simple dynastic
arrangement into three reigns: James I,
James II, and the Old Pretender.
- **Philip Guedalla** 1889-1944 British historian
and biographer: *Supers and Supermen* (1920)
'Some Critics'

21 The cheerful clatter of Sir James
Barrie's cans as he went round with the
milk of human kindness.
- **Philip Guedalla** 1889-1944 British historian
and biographer: *Supers and Supermen* (1920)
'Some Critics'

22 The defendant, Mr. Haddock, is,
among other things, an author, which
fact should alone dispose you in the
plaintiff's favour.
- **A. P. Herbert** 1890-1971 English writer and
humorist: *Misleading Cases* (1935)

23 The book of my enemy has been
remaindered

And I rejoice.
- **Clive James** 1939- Australian critic and
writer: 'The Book of My Enemy has been
Remaindered' (1986)

24 Whatever Wells writes is not only alive,
but kicking.
on H. G. Wells
- **Henry James** 1843-1916 American novelist:
G. K. Chesterton *Autobiography* (1936)

25 *a young admirer had asked if he might kiss
the hand that wrote Ulysses:*
No, it did lots of other things too.
- **James Joyce** 1882-1941 Irish novelist:
Richard Ellmann *James Joyce* (1959)

26 Mr Ruskin, whose distinction it was
to express in prose of incomparable
grandeur thought of an unparalleled
confusion.
- **Osbert Lancaster** 1908-86 English writer
and cartoonist: *Pillar to Post* (1938)

27 E. M. Forster never gets any further
than warming the teapot. He's a rare
fine hand at that. Feel this teapot. Is it
not beautifully warm? Yes, but there
ain't going to be no tea.
- **Katherine Mansfield** 1888-1923 New
Zealand-born short-story writer: diary,
May 1917

28 Dear Willie, you may well be right in
thinking you write like Shakespeare.
Certainly I have noticed during these
last few months an adulation of your
name in the more vulgar portions of
the popular press. And one word of
brotherly advice. *Do Not Attempt the
Sonnets.*
- **Viscount Maugham** 1866-1958 British
lawyer: letter to his brother Somerset
Maugham, in *Ned Sherrin in his Anecdotage*
(1993)

29 I am the kind of writer that people
think other people are reading.
- **V. S. Naipaul** 1932- Trinidadian writer of
Indian descent: in *Radio Times* 14 March
1979

30 The triumph of sugar over diabetes.
of J. M. Barrie, author of Peter Pan
- **George Jean Nathan** 1882-1958 American
critic: Robin May *The Wit of the Theatre*
(1969)

31 Oh, that Bernadette Shaw! What a chatterbox! Nags away from arsehole to breakfast-time but never sees what's staring her in the face.
- **Peter Nichols** 1927– English dramatist: *Privates on Parade* (1977)

32 Those of us who had a perfectly happy childhood should be able to sue for deprivation of literary royalties.
- **Chris Patten** 1944– British Conservative politician: in *Times* 2 February 2006

33 *on being asked to appear in a charity programme in support of imprisoned writers:*
No, on the whole I think all writers should be in prison.
- **Ralph Richardson** 1902–83 English actor: in *Ned Sherrin in his Anecdotage* (1993)

34 Virginia Woolf, I enjoyed talking to her, but thought *nothing* of her writing. I considered her 'a beautiful little knitter'.
- **Edith Sitwell** 1887–1964 English poet and critic: letter to Geoffrey Singleton, 11 July 1955

35 He [Macaulay] is like a book in breeches.
- **Sydney Smith** 1771–1845 English clergyman and essayist: Lady Holland *Memoir* (1855)

36 The shelf life of the modern hardback writer is somewhere between the milk and the yoghurt.
- **Calvin Trillin** 1935– American journalist and writer: in *Sunday Times* 9 June 1991; attributed

37 Truman made lying an art form—a minor art form.
on Truman Capote
- **Gore Vidal** 1925–2012 American novelist and critic: in *People* 25 June 1979

38 What other culture could have produced someone like Hemingway and *not* seen the joke?
- **Gore Vidal** 1925–2012 American novelist and critic: *Pink Triangle and Yellow Star* (1982)

39 To see him [Stephen Spender] fumbling with our rich and delicate language is to experience all the horror of seeing a Sèvres vase in the hands of a chimpanzee.
- **Evelyn Waugh** 1903–66 English novelist: in *The Tablet* 5 May 1951

40 A magnificent but painful hippopotamus resolved at any cost, even at the cost of its dignity, upon picking up a pea which has got into a corner of its den.
of Henry James
- **H. G. Wells** 1866–1946 English novelist: *Boon* (1915) ch. 4

41 Mr. [Henry] James writes fiction as if it were a painful duty.
- **Oscar Wilde** 1854–1900 Irish dramatist and poet: 'The Decay of Lying' (1891)

42 Meredith! Who can define him? His style is chaos illuminated by flashes of lightning. As a writer he has mastered everything except language: as a novelist he can do everything except tell a story. As an artist he is everything, except articulate.
- **Oscar Wilde** 1854–1900 Irish dramatist and poet: 'The Decay of Lying' (1891)

43 I know no person so perfectly disagreeable and even dangerous as an author.
- **William IV** 1765–1837 British king: Philip Ziegler *King William IV* (1971)

44 She is so odd a blend of Little Nell and Lady Macbeth.
of Dorothy Parker
- **Alexander Woollcott** 1887–1943 American writer: *While Rome Burns* (1934)

Writing

see also **BOOKS, LITERATURE, POETRY, POETS, READING, WRITERS**

....

As to the Adjective: when in doubt, strike it out.   **Mark Twain**

1 After being turned down by numerous publishers, he had decided to write for posterity.
   - **George Ade** 1866-1944 American humorist and dramatist: *Fables in Slang* (1900)

2 He writes so well, he makes me feel like putting my quill back in my goose.
   - **Fred Allen** 1894-1956 American humorist: attributed, Fred Metcalf *Penguin Dictionary of Modern Humorous Quotations* (2001)

3 If you can't annoy somebody with what you write, I think there's little point in writing.
   - **Kingsley Amis** 1922-95 English novelist and poet: in *Radio Times* 1 May 1971

4 The biggest obstacle to professional writing is the necessity for changing a typewriter ribbon.
   - **Robert Benchley** 1889-1945 American humorist: *Chips off the old Benchley* (1949)

5 Authors with a mortgage never get writer's block.
   - **Mavis Cheek** 1948- English novelist: in *Bookseller* 19 September 2003

6 A good novel tells us the truth about its hero; but a bad novel tells us the truth about its author.
   - **G. K. Chesterton** 1874-1936 English essayist, novelist, and poet: *Heretics* (1905)

7 He who writes badly thinks badly.
   - **William Cobbett** 1762-1835 English political reformer: *A Grammar of the English Language* (1818)

8 Writing a novel is like driving a car at night. You can see only as far as your headlights, but you can make the whole trip that way.
   - **E. L. Doctorow** 1931- American novelist: in *Vanity Fair* 1989

9 I suppose most editors are failed writers—but so are most writers.
   - **T. S. Eliot** 1888-1965 Anglo-American poet, critic, and dramatist: to Robert Giroux in conversation in 1948; Robert Giroux *The Education of an Editor* (1982)

10 You just have to work with what God sends, and if God doesn't seem to understand the concept of commercial success, then that's your bad luck.
   - **Michael Frayn** 1933- English writer: in *Sunday Times* 3 February 2002

11 *to Edward Gibbon, author of* The Decline and Fall of the Roman Empire:
   Another damned, thick, square book! Always scribble, scribble, scribble! Eh! Mr Gibbon?
   - **Duke of Gloucester** 1743-1805: Henry Best *Personal and Literary Memorials* (1829); also attributed to the Duke of Cumberland and King George III

12 *explaining why he wrote opinions while standing:*
   Nothing conduces to brevity like a caving in of the knees.
   - **Oliver Wendell Holmes Jr.** 1841-1935 American lawyer: Catherine Drinker Bowen *Yankee from Olympus* (1944); attributed

13 Read over your compositions, and where ever you meet with a passage which you think is particularly fine, strike it out.
   - **Samuel Johnson** 1709-84 English poet, critic, and lexicographer: quoting a college tutor; James Boswell *Life of Samuel Johnson* (1791) 30 April 1773

14 No man but a blockhead ever wrote, except for money.
   - **Samuel Johnson** 1709-84 English poet, critic, and lexicographer: James Boswell *Life of Samuel Johnson* (1791) 5 April 1776

15 'The cat sat on the mat' is not a story. 'The cat sat on the dog's mat' is a story.
  - **John le Carré** 1931- English thriller writer: in *New York Times* 25 September 1977

16 If you want to get rich from writing, write the sort of thing that's read by persons who move their lips when reading.
  - **Don Marquis** 1878-1937 American poet and journalist: attributed; Peter Kemp (ed.) *Oxford Dictionary of Literary Quotations* (1997)

17 The art of writing, like the art of love, runs all the way from a kind of routine hard to distinguish from piling bricks to a kind of frenzy closely related to delirium tremens.
  - **H. L. Mencken** 1880-1956 American journalist and literary critic: *Minority Report* (1956)

18 If you steal from one author, it's plagiarism; if you steal from many, it's research.
  - **Wilson Mizner** 1876-1933 American dramatist: Alva Johnston *The Legendary Mizners* (1953)

19 Anybody who can write home for money can write for the magazines.
  - **Wilson Mizner** 1876-1933 American dramatist: Alva Johnston *The Legendary Mizners* (1953)

20 　　　　I'm glad you'll write,
You'll furnish paper when I shite.
  - **Lady Mary Wortley Montagu** 1689-1762 English writer: 'Reasons that Induced Dr S— to write a Poem called the Lady's Dressing Room'

21 It is our national joy to mistake for the first-rate, the fecund rate.
  - **Dorothy Parker** 1893-1967 American critic and humorist: review of Sinclair Lewis *Dodsworth*; in *New Yorker* 16 March 1929

22 As to the Adjective: when in doubt, strike it out.
  - **Mark Twain** 1835-1910 American writer: *Pudd'nhead Wilson* (1894)

23 Anyone could write a novel given six weeks, pen, paper, and no telephone or wife.
  - **Evelyn Waugh** 1903-66 English novelist: Chips Channon diary 16 December 1934

Youth

see also **CHILDREN, MIDDLE AGE, OLD AGE**

The only way to stay young is to avoid old people. **James D. Watson**

1 It is better to waste one's youth than to do nothing with it at all.
  - **Georges Courteline** 1858-1929 French writer and dramatist: *La Philosophie de Georges Courteline* (1948)

2 Everybody my age should be issued with a 2lb fresh salmon. If you see someone young, beautiful and happy, you should slap them as hard as you can with it.
  - **Richard Griffiths** 1947-2013 English actor: in *Independent* 11 October 2006

3 Remember that as a teenager you are at the last stage in your life when you will be happy to hear that the phone is for you.
  - **Fran Lebowitz** 1946- American writer: *Social Studies* (1981)

4 The invention of the teenager was a mistake. Once you identify a period of life in which people get to stay out late but don't have to pay taxes—naturally no one wants to live any other way.
  - **Judith Martin** 1938- American journalist: attributed

5 Youth is wasted on the young. I'm 52 now and I just can't stay up all night like I did.
  - **Camille Paglia** 1947- American writer and critic: interview in *Sunday Times* 6 June 1999

6 It's all that the young can do for the old,
to shock them and keep them up to date.
- **George Bernard Shaw** 1856–1950 Irish
  dramatist: *Fanny's First Play* (1914) 'Induction'

7 What music is more enchanting than
the voices of young people, when you
can't hear what they say?
- **Logan Pearsall Smith** 1865–1946 American-
  born man of letters: *Afterthoughts* (1931)

8 The only way to stay young is to avoid
old people.
- **James D. Watson** 1928– American
  biologist: in *Times* 9 March 2002

9 Being young is not having any money;
being young is not minding not having
any money.
- **Katharine Whitehorn** 1928– English
  journalist: *Observations* (1970)

10 I have been in a youth hostel. I know
what they're like. You are put in a
kitchen with seventeen venture scouts
with behavioural difficulties and made
to wash swedes.
- **Victoria Wood** 1953– British writer and
  comedienne: *Mens Sana in Thingummy
  Doodah* (1990)

Author Index

Breban, Shmuel
Medicine 9,
Money 7
Brebner, John Bartlet 1895–1957
Canada 3
Brecht, Bertolt 1898–1956
Crime 7
Bremner, Rory 1961–
Advice 4
Brenan, Gerald 1894–1987
Bores 2
Brenner, Sydney 1927–
Computers 4
Brewer, Derek 1923–2008
Publishing 4
Bridges, Edward 1892–1969
Civil Servants 1
Brien, Alan 1925–2008
Actors 4,
Anger 4
Brillat-Savarin, Anthelme
1755–1826
Cookery 6
Brilliant, Ashleigh 1933–
Anger 5
Britt, Stewart Henderson 1907–79
Advertising 3
Broder, David 1929–
Presidents 2
Brokaw, Tom 1940–
Fishing 1,
Mistakes 9
Brooke, N.
Transport 3
Brooke, Rupert 1887–1915
History 5,
Towns 6
Brookner, Anita 1928–
Literature 3
Brooks, Louise 1906–85
Acting 3
Brooks, Mel 1926–
Comedy Routines 18,
Manners 5,
Religion 11,
Success 4
Brophy, Brigid 1929–95
Books 5
Broun, Heywood 1888–1939
Censorship 3,
Past 7,
Political Parties 2
Brown, A. Whitney 1952–
America 3
Brown, Craig 1957–
Hypocrisy 1,
Newspapers 5
Brown, Helen Gurley 1922–2012
Office Life 3
Brown, John Mason 1900–69
Actors 5
Brown, Michael
Murder 2

Brown, Michele 1947–
Newspapers 6
Brown, Rita Mae 1944–
Mental Health 2,
Self-Knowledge 4,
Virtue 5
Brown, Thomas 1663–1704
Enemies 3
Browne, Cecil 1932–
God 12
Browne, Coral 1913–91
Acting 4,
Critics 10,
Sex 21,
Theatre 13
Bruce, Lenny 1925–66
Education 4,
Family 4,
Men and Women 9,
Politics 7,
Religion 12
Brummell, Beau 1778–1840
Food 17
Bruni, Carla 1967–
Unintended 4
Bryant, Anita 1940–
Sex 22
Bryson, Bill 1951–
Academic 3,
America 4,
Animals 8,
British 2,
Business 5,
Faces 6,
Humour 3,
Life 9,
Lifestyle 5,
Technology 4,
Television 3
Buchan, John 1875–1940
Humour 4,
Politics 8,
Religion 13
Buchwald, Art 1925–2007
Politics 9,
Presidents 3
Buckle, Richard 1916–2001
People 6
Buffett, Warren 1930–
Business 6, 7, 8,
Wealth 4
Bukowski, Charles 1920–94
Character 3,
Life 10,
Sex 23
Buller, Arthur 1874–1944
Science 8
Bulmer-Thomas, Ivor 1905–93
Prime Ministers 10
Buñuel, Luis 1900–83
Religion 14
Burchill, Julie 1960–
Beauty 1,

Books 6,
Feminism 3,
Insults 9,
Women 6
Burgess, Anthony 1917–93
Presidents 4,
Sex 24, 25
Burgess, Mrs W. S.
Writers 8
Burke, Johnny 1908–64
Dictionaries 2
Burnier, Jeanine
Comedy 1
Burns, George 1896–1996
Age 3,
Comedy Routines 12,
Happiness 4,
Songs 3
Burns, Jack 1933– and **Juhl, Jerry**
1938–2005
Religion 15
Burroughs, William S. 1914–97
Universe 3
Burrows, Abe 1910–85
Gifts 3
Burt, Benjamin Hapgood
1880–1950
Drunkenness 3
Burton, Tim 1958–
Actors 6
Busby, Matt 1909–94
Football 2
Bush, George 1924–
Bores 3,
Food 18,
Unintended 5
Bush, George W. 1946–
Languages 5,
Self-Knowledge 5,
Unintended 6, 7
Bush, Laura 1946–
Nature 5,
Presidents 5
Bushnell, Candace 1958– , **Star,
Darren** 1961– , and **King, Patrick**
1954–
Betting 2,
Comebacks 4,
Men 6,
Sex 26
Butler, R. A. 1902–82
Prime Ministers 11, 12
Butler, Samuel 1835–1902
Animals 9,
Bible 1,
Bores 4,
Eating 5,
Marriage 10,
Praise 2,
Progress 1,
Women 7
Bygraves, Max see Sykes, Eric and
Bygraves, Max

Fleming, Ian 1908–64
 Animals 13
Flers, Robert, Marquis de
 1872–1927 and Caillavet, Armand
 de 1869–1915
 Democracy 5
Fletcher, Cyril 1913–2005
 Money 14
Fletcher, John 1579–1625
 Drink 19
Flynn, Errol 1909–59
 Money 15
Fonda, Jane 1937–
 Acting 10,
 Age 8,
 Hollywood 7
Foot, Alistair see Marriott, Anthony
 and Foot, Alistair
Foot, Michael 1913–2010
 People 12,
 Politicians 14
Foote, Samuel 1720–77
 Bores 6
Ford, Betty 1918–2011
 Drink 20
Ford, Gerald 1909–2006
 Hair 5
Ford, Henry 1863–1947
 Bores 7,
 Colours 4,
 History 9
Ford, John 1895–1973
 Books 8
Foreman, George 1948–
 Boxing 5
Forster, E. M. 1879–1970
 Life 15,
 Literature 9
Fowler, Gene 1890–1960
 Censorship 5
Fowles, John 1926–2005
 War 9
Fox, Charles James 1749–1806
 Quotations 4
Fox, Robin Lane 1946–
 Gardens 3
Frank, Melvin see Panama, Norman
 and Frank, Melvin
Franklin, Benjamin 1706–90
 Death 24,
 Epitaphs 12,
 Marriage 33,
 War 10,
 Wine 5
Franks, Oliver 1905–92
 Bureaucracy 5,
 Gossip 3
Fraser, Antonia 1932–
 God 24
Fraser, Giles 1964–
 People 13
Fraser-Sampson, Guy
 France 5

Frayn, Michael 1933–
 Morality 4,
 Writing 10
Frazer, James George 1854–1941
 Family Life 4
Frederick the Great 1712–86
 Crime 17,
 Literature 10
Frei, Matt 1963–
 Countries 13
French, Dawn 1957–
 Art 11,
 Christmas 4
Freud, Clement 1924–2009
 Countries 14,
 Virtue 11
Freud, Sigmund 1856–1939
 Sex 40
Friedan, Betty 1921–2006
 Feminism 5
Friedman, Kinky 1944–
 Marriage 34
Friedman, Shelby
 Cookery 13
Frisch, Max 1911–91
 Technology 6
Frisco, Joe 1889–1958
 Hollywood 8
Frost, Carina 1952–
 People 14
Frost, David 1939–
 Depression 2,
 Political Parties 4,
 Television 8
Frost, Robert 1874–1963
 God 25,
 Home 10,
 Law 6,
 Money 16,
 Poetry 10,
 Political Parties 5,
 Work 10
Fry, Christopher 1907–2005
 Language 6,
 Old Age 16,
 Religion 25
Fry, Stephen 1957–
 Academic 5,
 Body 14,
 Computers 8,
 Family 12,
 Ideas 3,
 Medicine 13,
 Scotland 5,
 Towns 14,
 Travel 13,
 Trust 3
Fry, Stephen 1957– and
 Laurie, Hugh 1959–
 Romance 3,
 Towns 15
Frye, Northrop 1912–91
 Religion 26

Fuller, Thomas 1654–1734
 Class 8,
 Food 24,
 Manners 11
Gabor, Zsa Zsa 1917–
 Advice 7,
 Age 9,
 Divorce 4,
 Husbands 18, 19,
 Jewellery 4,
 Marriage 35,
 Men 12,
 Sex 41
Gaiman, Neil see Pratchett, Terry
 and Gaiman, Neil
Gainsborough, Thomas 1727–88
 Art 12, 13
Galbraith, J. K. 1908–2006
 Economics 7,
 Fame 14,
 Food 25,
 Management 3,
 Women 13
Gallagher, Noel 1967–
 People 15
Gallagher, Robert C.
 Modern Life 5
Gallant, Mavis 1922–
 Women 14
Galton, Ray 1930– and
 Simpson, Alan 1929–
 Censorship 6,
 Comedy Routines 38, 46,
 History 10,
 Medicine 14,
 Technology 7
Gandhi, Indira 1917–84
 Ambition 4
Gandhi, Mahatma 1869–1948
 Progress 5
Ganz, Lowell 1948– and
 Mandel, Babaloo 1949–
 Sex 42
Gardner, Ed 1901–63
 Opera 4
Garland, Judy 1922–69
 Hollywood 9
Garner, John Nance 1868–1967
 Presidents 11
Garofalo, Janeane 1964–
 Optimism 3
Garrick, David 1717–79
 Cookery 14
Garrick, David 1717–79 see
 Colman, George, the Elder and
 Garrick, David
Gaskell, Elizabeth 1810–65
 Anger 9,
 Family Life 5,
 Insults 19,
 Money 17
Gates, Bill 1955–
 Success 8

Keyword Index

....

I say bugger B.   HOLIDAYS 6
boiled bag of b. sweets   MEMBERS 5
   cold b. veal   ENEMIES 5
boiler 10 years in a b. suit   FASHION 20
boils unwatched pot b. *immediately*   COOKERY 12
boily stand a b. boy   MEN AND WOMEN 44
bomb b. the country next   AMERICA 15
   time to put a b. under it   FASHION 11
bombs Come, friendly b.   TOWNS 5
   Our b. are incredibly smart   AMERICA 3
bones tongs and the b.   MUSIC 46
   we break b.   SPORTS 22
bonhomie natural *b.*   ECONOMICS 3
bon-mots plucking b. from   QUOTATIONS 7
bonnet b. in Germany   COUNTRIES 24
bonus that's a b.   BODY 33
book b. cannot take the place   CRITICS 50
   b. in breeches   WRITERS 35
   b. is depicted being cut   DRESS 14
   b. of my enemy   WRITERS 23
   B. of Life begins   BIBLE 6
   covers of this b. are too far   BOOKS 4
   damned, thick, square b.   WRITING 11
   get a lawyer—not a b.   LAW 16
   had written a b.   BOOKS 3
   He's *got* a b.   BOOKS 8
   knows this out of the b.   EDUCATION 5
   moment I picked up your b.   LITERATURE 17
   no b.—it's a plaything   QUOTATIONS 8
   only ever read one b. in my life   LITERATURE 20
   read the b.   CRITICS 27
   sent a new b.   BOOKS 6
   to finish her b.   INSULTS 17
   What is the use of a b.   LITERATURE 5
   with a good b.   HOLIDAYS 11
   without mentioning a single b.   LITERATURE 24
   world needs your b.   PUBLISHING 4
   written a b.   BOOKS 10
bookcase TV is bigger than your b.   CLASS 3
books B. are well written   BOOKS 28
   b. were read   DEATH 11
   do *you* read b. *through*   READING 5
   If my b. had been any worse   LITERATURE 6
   I hate b.   BOOKS 17
   one of their b. in their room   WRITERS 13
   provided with no b.   BOOKS 9
   regular supply of b.   LIFESTYLE 11
   respected b.   LIBRARIES 7
   showed me his b.   LIBRARIES 6
   so charming as b.   BOOKS 21
bookseller he once shot a b.   PUBLISHING 6
boot pour piss out of a b.   INSULTS 26
bootboy b. at Claridges   BOOKS 30
boots engine in b.   PEOPLE 17
   school without any b.   PRIME MINISTERS 10
   too small for its b.   ENGLAND 10
   top of his b.   ARMED FORCES 19
   when I take my b. off   BODY 9
   world of b.   SELF-KNOWLEDGE 17
booze fool with b.   DRINK 15
bop 'B.' is like scrabble   MUSIC 17
bordello doorkeeper of a b.   MUSICIANS 20
Borden Lizzie B. took an axe   MURDER 1

bore avoid is being a b. to oneself   BORES 2
   b. is a man   BORES 14
   b. people at dinner parties   FAME 17
   God is a b.   GOD 33
   is an old b.   BORES 16
   merely a b.   SOCIETY 12
   not only a b.   PRIME MINISTERS 33
   Thou shalt not b.   FILM PRODUCERS 20
bored man is b.   MEN AND WOMEN 42
boredom b. occasioned   BORES 10
bores destiny of b.   BORES 8
Borg Like a Volvo, B. is rugged   TENNIS 5
Borgias I dined last night with the B.   SOCIETY 2
boring b. kind of guy   BORES 3
   b. old Swede   FILM STARS 4
   b. you fall asleep   NAMES 2
   not b. you   BORES 5
   Somebody's b. me   BORES 15
born b. an Englishman   ENGLAND 8
   b. in a manger   BIRTH 1
   he was b. in Australia   AUSTRALIA 6
   man is b. in a stable   IRELAND 9
   never been b. the first time   RELIGION 64
   some men are b. great   HEROES 6
   That's b. into the world alive   POLITICAL PARTIES 6
born-again b. people so often   RELIGION 64
borrow b. his body   BODY 20
   b. the money   HAPPINESS 15
   well enough to b. from   DEFINITIONS 1
borrowers to catch out b.   BOOKS 13
borrows b. a detective story   READING 6
bosom no b. and no behind   ENGLAND 36
boson Higgs b. walks into a Catholic   SCIENCE 3
boss eventually get to be a b.   WORK 10
   funny man or a great b.   MANAGEMENT 4
   Oh, good idea, B.   WORK 12
   What about the *b.*   OFFICE LIFE 3
Boston B., the home of the bean   SNOBBERY 6
botch I make a b.   TIME 9
both b. so much in love with him   MARRIAGE 73
   friends in b. places   HEAVEN 6
bother B. it   LANGUAGE 9
   Gentle Reader, Don't b.   SOCIETY 7
   I didn't b. with it   LITERATURE 10
   no time to b.   LETTERS 2
bothered Bewitched, b.   MEN AND WOMEN 21
Botticelli B.'s a *cheese*   FOOD 54
   If B. were alive   FASHION 21
bottle b. just going to sit   DRINK 48
   catsup b.   FOOD 4
bottles English have hot-water b.   SEX 57
bottom reach the b. first   CHILDREN 13
   sit only on our b.   SUCCESS 19
   your b. will follow   DIETS 12
bounded b. on the north   HOLLYWOOD 5
bouquet b. is better   WINE 6
Bourbon Wheaties with B.   DRINK 12
bourgeois afraid to look b.   CLASS 22
Bovril does her hair with B.   ACTORS 8
bovvered Am I b.   COMEDY ROUTINES 2
bow b., ye tradesmen   CLASS 10
bowel lower b. of music   MUSIC 14
Bowery Late of the B.   EPITAPHS 14

Cambridge (cont.)
it's either Oxford or C.   UNINTENDED 15
When I was at C.   TRUST 3
camel c. is a horse designed   BUREAUCRACY 9
camels distrust c., and anyone   DRINK 30
none but she-c.   ANIMALS 15
cameo I'm just a c.   SELF-KNOWLEDGE 16
Cameron David C. is from Venus   POLITICIANS 29
camp c. near Dover   THEATRE 13
campaigning organizing and c.   PRESIDENTS 2
Campbell breaks the C.'s back   WIT 10
camps someone who c. out   WOMEN 14
can C. I do you now   COMEDY ROUTINES 4
He who c., does   EDUCATION 17
I c. do that   AMERICA 12
think you c.   SUCCESS 13
Canada all over C.   CANADA 9
Drink C. Dry   DRINK 6
what street C. is on   CANADA 4
Canalettos Then the C. go   POLITICS 32
can-can you can c. too   DANCE 10
cancer my father died of c.   SICKNESS 1
candidate Actually I'm your c.   POLITICIANS 17
c. talking to a rich person   POLITICS 9
candle c. in that great turnip   PRIME MINISTERS 17
candles c. cost more than the cake   AGE 11
candy C. is dandy   DRINK 36
cannibal Said the c.   FOOD 27
cannibalism if ever I had to practice c.   EATING 2
cannon c.-ball took off his legs   ARMED FORCES 13
canoe make love in a c.   CANADA 2
cant c. of criticism   CRITICS 37
canting this c. world   CRITICS 37
cap small feather in my c.   DICTIONARIES 6
caparisons No c., Miss   WIT 43
cape Risorgimento c.   APPEARANCE 10
capital made c. instead   PEOPLE 19
car c. is useless in New York   TOWNS 21
get in the back of the c.   GOVERNMENT 22
if your c. could go straight upwards   UNIVERSE 6
I'll keep the c.   PREJUDICE 1
just sit in the c. and hope   SEX 29
like driving a c. at night   WRITING 8
like the passengers in his c.   DEATH 6
Take up c. maintenance   EDUCATION 7
wait in the c.   TIME 7
caraway left over for two c. seeds   TELEVISION 2
carbuncle monstrous c.   ARCHITECTURE 6
carcinoma sing of rectal c.   SICKNESS 8
card insulting Christmas c.   CHRISTMAS 5
last year's c. for full details   ROMANCE 5
cardboard cut out of very thin c.   PEOPLE 25
cardigan c. over his pyjamas   MEN AND WOMEN 33
card-indexes memories are c. consulted   MEMORY 1
cards c. that just say, 'Yes, I am'   FAME 10
c. with a man called Doc   ADVICE 1
care I c. less and less   OLD AGE 27
Take c. of him   MARRIAGE 67
taken better c. of myself   OLD AGE 6
women and c. and trouble   WOMEN 40
career c. must be slipping   AWARDS 2
combine marriage and a c.   WORK 18
Good c. move   DEATH 59

loyal to his own c.   POLITICIANS 13
stomach went in for a c.   BODY 16
careful cannot be too c.   ENEMIES 10
make them more c.   FLYING 3
carelessness looks like c.   FAMILY 36
cares they have no c.   LAWYERS 6
think nobody c. if you're alive   HOPE 11
Carlyle good of God to let C.   MARRIAGE 10
Carmen glanced at her C. rollers   NAMES 8
carpenter being the c.   ACTING 25
carpet definitely overpaid for my c.   PHILOSOPHY 1
carrier c. who carried his can   EPITAPHS 6
carrots naked, raw c.   FOOD 34
carry He could c. no more   EPITAPHS 6
cartographers c. seek to define   SCOTLAND 2
cartoons space between their c.   NEWSPAPERS 23
Cary OLD C. GRANT FINE   TELEGRAMS 10
case civil servant a good c.   CIVIL SERVANTS 2
In c. it is one of mine   PARENTS 8
cash she needs good c.   MIDDLE AGE 11
casinos go to c. for the same reason   BETTING 2
cassowary If I were a c.   ANIMALS 30
castle builds a c. in the air   MENTAL HEALTH 1
castles All c. had one major weakness   WAR 17
castrati dreamed of reviving the c.   MUSIC 39
Castro C. couldn't even go   POWER 6
Castroenteritis C.   SPEECHES 4
cat bowels of the c.   MUSIC 36
c. detained briefly   PRIME MINISTERS 34
c. has fallen asleep on your lap   CATS 1
c. hung up by its tail   MUSIC 7
'c. sat on the mat' is not   WRITING 15
intestines of the agile c.   MUSIC 27
man could be crossed with a c.   CATS 11
swing a c.   HOME 7
to throw at a noisy c.   BOOKS 24
catalogue entire c.   BOOKS 1
in the c. descriptions   ART 6
catamite in bed with my c.   SEX 24
catastrophe education and c.   HISTORY 21
catch If you c. a man   MEN AND WOMEN 2
To c. a husband is an art   HUSBANDS 16
catch-22 as good as C.   CRITICS 21
one catch and that was C.   MENTAL HEALTH 5
catching c. a train   TRANSPORT 5
catholic C. and sensual   TRAVEL 7
C. school children   RELIGION 21
C. woman to avoid pregnancy   RELIGION 39
C. women must keep taking   RELIGION 62
I am a C.   RELIGION 5
Roman C. Church   POLITICS 29
Catholics pigeons, or C.   MARRIAGE 1
cats C. look down on us   ANIMALS 10
count the c. in Zanzibar   TRAVEL 30
has two c.   NEWSPAPERS 22
If c. looked like frogs   CATS 8
Ladies are like c.   MEN AND WOMEN 9
why women love c.   CATS 5
Women and c. do as they please   MEN AND WOMEN 23
catsup c. bottle   FOOD 4
cauliflower C. is nothing   FOOD 62
cause c. of dullness   BORES 6
cavalry Navy, and the Household C.   WIT 22

c. is ever inhibited by ignorance · POLITICS 30
criticize Never c. Americans · AMERICA 11
critics C. search for ages · CRITICS 44
know who the c. are · CRITICS 17
murderers or c. · ART 18
of Music Among C. · CRITICS 34
Restaurant c.—even great critics · RESTAURANTS 9
crocodile it's c. land · APPEARANCE 17
crooning c. like a bilious pigeon · LANGUAGES 19
cross attempt to c. it · FACES 7
crisp sign of the C. · RELIGION 34
double c. that bridge · POLITICIANS 21
having a c. word · MARRIAGE 41
orgasm has replaced the C. · RELIGION 41
un-nailed from the c. · ACTORS 10
cross-counter In boxing the right c. · BOXING 7
cross-dressing about c. · DRESS 16
crossed Was the cow c. · LAW 11
crosses instead of c. · RELIGION 12
crossroads faces a c. · CHOICE 1
crossword New York Times Sunday c. puzzle · MEN 6
crow had the old c. over · POETS 12
crowds Avoid c. · THEATRE 20
crown deserve a c. · WIT 3
Lord, reserve for me a c. · RELIGION 8
crows corpses of two small c. · PEOPLE 18
crucifixion after the C. · FILM 11
cruel rather c. and incompetent · BUSINESS 10
cruise longer the c., the older · TRAVEL 4
crumpet thinking man's c. · PEOPLE 20
crustaceans c. died in vain · POLITICS 19
crutch kick in the c. · ANGER 3
Reality is a c. · DRUGS 7
cry babe with a c. · MISTAKES 15
Beware of men who c. · MEN 9
c. into your beer · DRINK 33
especially when they c. · CHILDREN 24
cryptogram charm of a c. · AUTOBIOGRAPHY 8
crystals Rose Geranium bath c. · BUSINESS 3
cuckoo c. clock · COUNTRIES 30
cucumber c. should be well sliced · COOKERY 16
when c. is added · FOOD 37
cucumbers sun-beams out of c. · SCIENCE 16
cuddled c. by a complete stranger · CHILDREN 1
cuddling C. up to a piece of gristle · BODY 23
cuddly c. as a cornered ferret · DESCRIPTION 3
kissable, c., and smelling · MEN AND WOMEN 18
cuisine French c. and Ice-cold Grape Slush · RESTAURANTS 2
people who have such bad c. · COOKERY 9
culture c. could have produced · WRITERS 38
hear the word c. · INTELLIGENCE 10
political c. · POLITICS 33
pursue C. in bands · ART 42
cultured real or c. · FAME 19
cultures other people's c. and the Dutch · COUNTRIES 22
cunning I have a c. plan · COMEDY ROUTINES 20
curable Love's a disease. But c. · LOVE 24
curate albino c. · FRIENDS 17
bland country c. · FACES 5
I feel like a shabby c. · SCIENCE 4
like a Protestant c. · DANCE 8

remember the average c. · CLERGY 7
very name of a C. · CLERGY 13
curates preached to death by wild c. · RELIGION 61
curb sit on the c. and clap · HEROES 5
cure c. for sea sickness · TRAVEL 22
in the twentieth, it's a c. · SEX 68
I will c. him for you · MENTAL HEALTH 6
no C. for this Disease · MEDICINE 6
once-bitten there is no c. · FISHING 3
that reincarnation won't c. · INSULTS 29
cured C. yesterday of my disease · MEDICINE 28
curiosity lost all c. · AUTOBIOGRAPHY 11
Love, c., freckles, and doubt · LOVE 27
curls c. up like carbon paper · MEN 35
current c. is turned on · WORDS 5
curse c. of the drinking classes · WORK 19
curtain after the c. has risen · ROYALTY 24
Bring down the c. · LAST WORDS 13
c. was up · CRITICS 28
her c. calls · ACTORS 10
remove the c. rings · DRESS 5
shower c. on the inside · LAST WORDS 7
curtains sew rings on the new c. · INSULTS 10
curtsey C. while you're thinking · MANNERS 7
curve mistakes a bulge for a c. · OPTIMISM 6
curves admire a girl's c. · WOMEN 42
custard bathed us like warm c. · DESCRIPTION 4
never invented c. · EATING 10
custom aid of prejudice and c. · PREJUDICE 7
cut c. you down to my size · COMEBACKS 7
right of final c. · FILM PRODUCERS 20
cutting damned c. and slashing · PUBLISHING 5
cuttings press c. to prove it · ACTING 18
cymbal like an ill-tuned c. · JUDGES 13
cynic What is a c. · CHARACTER 20
d I never use a big, big D · LANGUAGE 9
dad d.'s name all over his underwear · FASHION 10
fuck you up, your mum and d. · PARENTS 9
Wherever my d. is now · FAMILY 35
dada art belongs to D. · ART 28
mama of d. · WRITERS 17
daddy D. sat up very late · DRINK 8
keep D. off her · FAMILY 21
Dalai horns of a D. Lama · WIT 54
Dali D. is the only painter of LSD · ART 23
dammed saved by being d. · COUNTRIES 18
damn don't give a d. · SATISFACTION 3
no general idea is worth a d. · IDEAS 5
old man who said 'D.' · TRANSPORT 12
one d. thing over and over · LIFE 27
damned lies, d. lies and statistics · STATISTICS 2
Life is just one d. thing · LIFE 17
music is the brandy of the d. · MUSIC 47
public be d. · BUSINESS 24
those d. dots · ECONOMICS 5
written a d. play · THEATRE 26
dance acceptable at a d. · MEN 27
rather d. with the cows · DANCE 5
towers of Notre Dame to d. · CERTAINTY 18
danced hadn't d. on TV · EATING 4
dancer object to the fan d. · HUMAN RACE 9
dances Also d. · FILM STARS 1
dancing like d. about architecture · MUSIC 3

danger be in less d.   FAMILY LIFE 9
   But only when in d.   RELIGION 48
dangerous d. as an author   WRITERS 43
   d. when active   CENSORSHIP 4
   found more d. chemicals   WAR 8
   horse is d. at both ends   ANIMALS 13
   most d. game played   SPORTS 2
Daniel lionized was D.   HUMAN RACE 11
Darcy to be called Mr D.   MEN 11
dare It wouldn't d.   TRANSPORT 4
dark Hellish d., and smells   DRUNKENNESS 11
   Isn't it d.   WEATHER 12
   thrives in the d.. Like celery   FAME 16
   too d. to read   CATS 6
   winking at a girl in the d.   ADVERTISING 3
darken Never d. my Dior   DRESS 9
darling or one calls him D.   ROYALTY 29
darts realized it was d.   SPORTS 18
date keep them up to d.   YOUTH 6
   man on a d. wonders if he'll get   ROMANCE 7
   sleeping with them on the first d.   SEX 44
dates broken d.   LOVE 20
   question of d.   TRUST 8
daughter Don't put your d.   ACTING 6
   Elderly ugly d.   LOVE 16
   I trust Bush with my d.   PRESIDENTS 20
daughter-in-law her own d.   FAMILY 16
Davy D. Abominated gravy   SCIENCE 6
day about to ruin your d.   LIFE 10
   d. away from Tallulah   DESCRIPTION 9
   dread one d. at a time   PHILOSOPHY 12
   I knew Doris D.   SEX 54
   Start every d. with a smile   ADVICE 6
   what happens in one d.   NEWSPAPERS 35
   when people write every other d.   LETTERS 7
daylight d. coming the other way   FOOLISHNESS 10
   doesn't suit d.   APPEARANCE 1
   skulk in broad d.   POLITICIANS 16
days d. should be rigorously planned   LIFE 22
   good old d. than a bad memory   PAST 2
   lost three d. already   DIETS 3
   takes less than three d.   BASEBALL 9
dead all our best men are d.   LITERATURE 23
   blooming well d.   DEATH 51
   character d.   GOSSIP 11
   composer is to be d.   MUSICIANS 12
   contact I ever made with the d.   PARANORMAL 6
   d. bird   OLD AGE 9
   d. for a year   SUCCESS 15
   d. for the next two months   LETTERS 11
   d. on holiday   LIFE 23
   d., or my watch has stopped   DEATH 36
   d. sinner revised   VIRTUE 3
   declared legally d.   SPORTS 7
   For being d.   DEATH 12
   got on our hands is a d. shark   RELATIONSHIPS 1
   if I am d.   DEATH 28
   in hopes of dropping d. at the top   OLD AGE 22
   Lord Jones D.   NEWSPAPERS 11
   must be d.   DEATH 8
   Not many d.   HEADLINES 9
   Once you're d.   DEATH 27
   quick, and the d.   DRIVING 7

   rot the d. talk   PARANORMAL 2
   seen d. with   DEATH 60
   was alive and is d.   EPITAPHS 4
   wealthy and d.   DEATH 54
deadlier email of the species is d.   COMPUTERS 8
deadline met his own d.   EPITAPHS 1
deadlines I love d.   TIME 3
deadlock Holy d.   MARRIAGE 40
deadly d. in the long run   EDUCATION 19
deaf be dead, extremely d., or   FRIENDS 8
   d. man to a blind woman   MARRIAGE 19
   longing to be absolutely d.   MUSIC 52
   old man's getting d. as well   OLD AGE 8
deafness To my d. I'm accustomed   OLD AGE 20
dean To our queer old d.   WIT 48
dear D. 338171   LETTERS 4
   D. Desk   LETTERS 5
death between wife and d.   DEATH 40
   Cake or d.   RELIGION 32
   d. and taxes   DEATH 24
   D. and taxes and childbirth   DEATH 37
   D. has got something   DEATH 3
   D. is always a great pity   DEATH 53
   D. is the most convenient   DEATH 35
   d. is unreliable   DEATH 9
   d., sex and jewels   ART 39
   d. of a political economist   ECONOMICS 1
   D. to anyone who drops   CRIME 23
   improved by d.   DEATH 50
   kicking d. in the ass   SEX 23
   makes d. a long-felt want   INSULTS 53
   my d. duties   DEATH 55
   no drinking after d.   DRINK 19
   old maid is like d. by drowning   OLD AGE 15
   preached to d.   RELIGION 61
   Reports of my d.   DEATH 56
   terror to d.   BIOGRAPHY 8
debauchery Drink and d.   GOLF 1
debt midst of life we are in d.   DEBT 6
   National D.   DEBT 9
debts If I hadn't my d.   DEBT 10
Debussy idea Stravinsky disliked D.   MUSICIANS 15
début d. with a scandal   OLD AGE 30
deceiving nearly d. your friends   LIES 4
decency D. is Indecency's conspiracy   VIRTUE 15
decent d. people live beyond   SOCIETY 10
   too d., too old   HUSBANDS 3
decided course already d. on   ADVICE 3
decipherable was d.   HANDWRITING 5
deciphering only hope of d.   HANDWRITING 2
decision difficult d. I've ever made   POLITICIANS 31
decisions d. he is allowed to take   MANAGEMENT 6
declare d. except my genius   INTELLIGENCE 17
decline d. two drinks   LANGUAGES 22
   I went into a bit of a d.   PAST 1
decompose d. in a barrel   DEATH 22
decomposing Baytch is d.   MUSICIANS 10
decorations uninhibitedly on the d.   LIFE 20
decorative be d. and to do right   WOMEN 12
decoyed see these poor fools d.   MARRIAGE 56
dedicated d. himself so many times   PRESIDENTS 25
deer if only the d. had guns   SPORTS 16
defeat In d. unbeatable   PEOPLE 7

draw COULDN'T D. IN THIS HOUSE   TELEGRAMS 11
   d. right to the finish   FUNERALS 4
   right arm to d.   ART 4
drawback great d.   PUBLISHING 3
drawbacks everything has its d.   DEATH 30
drawing inventor of the d. board   TECHNOLOGY 15
dread d. one day at a time   PHILOSOPHY 12
dream They d. in courtship   MARRIAGE 58
dreamed d. of cheese   SLEEP 6
dreams City of perspiring d.   TOWNS 26
dreamt d. I was making a speech   SPEECHES 8
dreary morals make you d.   MORALITY 17
dress automobile changed our d.   TRANSPORT 14
   d. has no meaning unless   DRESS 19
   d. like their mothers   MEN AND WOMEN 7
   like a lady's d.: long enough   SPEECHES 1
   like to d. egos   FASHION 22
   plain in d.   WOMEN 31
   they d. to be annoying   FASHION 19
   woman's d. should be   DRESS 10
dressed d. as richly upholstered   APPEARANCE 5
   d. with pepper   COOKERY 16
dresser They leave it on the d.   ACTORS 22
drier Or come up d.   IGNORANCE 3
drifted Snow White…but I d.   VIRTUE 19
drink buy a d. from both   EXERCISE 12
   don't d. liquor   DRINK 29
   D. and debauchery   GOLF 1
   d. and women   ACADEMIC 15
   d. as much as the next man   PEOPLE 16
   D. Canada Dry   DRINK 6
   d. it himself   FOOD 67
   d. it when I am happy   CHAMPAGNE 2
   d. one another's healths   DRINK 25
   D., sir, is a great provoker   DRINK 41
   has taken to d.   DRINK 49
   in favour iv d.   DRINK 14
   One more d.   DRUNKENNESS 9
   Then the d. takes a drink   DRINK 47
   vanity and sometimes d.   APPEARANCE 2
   we could d. all day   WEALTH 20
   woman drove me to d.   DRINK 18
   your husband I would d. it   COMEBACKS 1
drinking curse of the d. classes   WORK 19
   d. so you're more fun   DRINK 24
   d. to before they fall   SICKNESS 7
   no d. after death   DRINK 19
   stop d. to get a hangover   DRUNKENNESS 6
drinks d. as much as you do   DRUNKENNESS 12
dripping electricity was d. invisibly   SCIENCE 17
drive can't d. the car   CRITICS 42
   if I tell him how to d.   ADVICE 14
drivel I worship the d.   RELIGION 60
driven pure as the d. slush   VIRTUE 2
driver in the d.'s seat   PRIME MINISTERS 6
   woman d. is one who drives like   DRIVING 8
drove woman d. me to drink   DRINK 18
drown d. it in the bathtub   GOVERNMENT 20
drowned d. by the waves   SONGS 4
drowning d. other people's kittens   CRITICS 12
   death by d.   OLD AGE 15
drudge harmless d.   DICTIONARIES 5
drugs both on d.   GENERATION GAP 1

   can't cope with d.   DRUGS 7
   doing d. so you can still play   DRUGS 4
drum d. out of the skin   PRIME MINISTERS 28
drummer best d. in the band   MUSICIANS 13
   teach the d. to play piano   MUSIC 32
drunk d. as a lord   COMEBACKS 13
   d. as a lord   DRINK 23
   d. or running for office   ADVICE 10
   dad was the town d.   DRUNKENNESS 15
   Guinness makes you d.   DRUNKENNESS 2
   I've tried him d.   ROYALTY 9
   not so think as you d.   DRUNKENNESS 10
   stand around at a bar and get d.   SPORTS 31
   well educated, and a little d.   AUDIENCES 1
   Winston, you're d.   COMEBACKS 5
   You're not d.   DRUNKENNESS 7
dry Drink Canada D.   DRINK 6
   d. she ain't   FILM STARS 14
   I am on d. land   HOPE 10
   into a d. Martini   DRINK 1
   wonder if they're d.   WIT 31
Dubliners real D. lead   IRELAND 6
duchess d. in a bath towel   ARISTOCRACY 7
   every D. in London   PRIME MINISTERS 31
   married to a d.   PUBLISHING 15
duchesses four bereaved D.   ARISTOCRACY 1
duck After that everything's a d.   ANIMALS 26
   know a d. because you like pâté   WRITERS 3
ducks if you look at his d.   ART 9
duke enough who knows a d.   CLERGY 5
dukes drawing room full of d.   SCIENCE 4
dull after-sales service, and is very d.   TENNIS 5
   always d.   ENGLAND 39
   Anger makes d. men witty   ANGER 2
   d. in a new way   BORES 9
   d. in himself   BORES 6
   it should be so d.   HISTORY 1
   land of the d.   AMERICA 21
   more d. than a discreet diary   DIARIES 2
   Only d. people   BORES 17
   paper appears d.   BORES 12
   Telford is so d.   TOWNS 20
   that he be d.   GOVERNMENT 1
dullness cardinal sin is d.   CINEMA 2
   cause of d.   BORES 6
   D. is so much stronger   BORES 4
dumb d. at the very moment when   MUSIC 52
   d. enough to think   POLITICS 28
   not a d. blonde   INSULTS 40
   Our D. Friends   DRUNKENNESS 8
   so d. he can't fart   PRESIDENTS 13
dumping eternal d. ground   FAME 7
dumps Whenever I'm down in the d.   FASHION 2
dunce d. with wits   INSULTS 42
   How much a d.   FOOLISHNESS 3
dust d. on a Venetian blind   CRITICS 10
   Excuse My D.   EPITAPHS 20
dustbin d. upset in a high wind   SLEEP 2
Dutch other people's cultures and the D.   COUNTRIES 22
duties my death d.   DEATH 55
   smaller d. of life   PRAISE 11
duty as if it were a painful d.   WRITERS 41

eighty (cont.)

At e. life has clipped my claws	OLD AGE	18
twenty goes into e.	AGE	15

eighty-four When I'm e.   OLD AGE 23
Einstein E. who made the real   SCIENCE 13
either How happy I could be with e.   LOVE 14
ejaculation god for is premature e.   RELIGION 11
   subject of premature e.   UNINTENDED 2
elastic be a little more e.   WIT 47
elbow e. has a fascination   BEAUTY 3
elder to e. statesman   PEOPLE 12
elderly e. man of 42   OLD AGE 1
   writing for an e. lady   NEWSPAPERS 22
eldest not the e. son   FAMILY 12
election black before the e.   POLITICS 37
electric biggest e. train set   HOLLYWOOD 22
   little e. chairs   RELIGION 12
   mend the E. Light   WORK 5
electricity e. was dripping invisibly   SCIENCE 17
   If it weren't for e.   TECHNOLOGY 9
   paying the e. bill   MEDICINE 2
   usefulness of e.   TAXES 6
elegant Economy was always 'e.'   MONEY 17
elementary E., my dear Watson   CRIME 15
elephant They couldn't hit an e.   LAST WORDS 15
elephantiasis e. and other dread   NATURE 12
elephants Women are like e.   WOMEN 11
eleven e. at night   DRINK 43
   just fought World War E.   INTELLIGENCE 14
   less than e.-and-a-half days   SPORTS 9
elf Cheese it is a peevish e.   FOOD 56
   Love is a perky e. dancing   LOVE 17
   Oh fuck, not another e.!   LITERATURE 8
Elginbrodde Martin E.   EPITAPHS 16
Eliot E.'s standby was Worry   POETS 2
   I'd not read E.   POETS 16
Elizabeth E. Windsor has maintained   ROYALTY 28
elms Behind the e. last night   WIT 37
elopement e. would be preferable   WEDDINGS 1
else happening to Somebody E.   HUMOUR 18
elsewhere something that happens e.   LIFE 8
email e. of the species is deadlier   COMPUTERS 8
emasculated has not been e.   AUTOBIOGRAPHY 7
embalm e. each other   PARTIES 16
embalmer triumph of the e.'s art   PRESIDENTS 27
embarrass e. other people   MIDDLE AGE 3
embarrassing e. pause   MARRIAGE 26
embarrassment life in a state of e.   ENGLAND 15
emblem e. of mortality   DEATH 21
emeralds I wish they were e.   GIFTS 5
emergency If an e., notify   BUREAUCRACY 2
eminence e. by sheer gravitation   SUCCESS 24
éminence é. cerise   ROYALTY 34
emotional e., we're not Spanish   FAMILY 14
emotions gamut of the e.   ACTORS 27
   Paleolithic e., medieval institutions   HUMAN RACE 15
employment known as gainful e.   WORK 1
empresses I don't think much of E.   SNOBBERY 9
empty Bring on the e. horses   CINEMA 3
   glass is always half e.   OPTIMISM 3
   so adventurous as an e. pocket   AMBITION 6
end ignorance that it can ever e.   LOVE 12
   noise at one e.   CHILDREN 18

   where's it all going to e.   TIME 18
endangered even as an e. species   LAW 13
   they were an e. species   LOVE 8
ending quickest way of e. a war   WAR 21
ends e. I think criminal   GOVERNMENT 14
   see how it e.   EXAMINATIONS 9
   similar sounds at their e.   POETRY 12
enemies also to love our e.   ENEMIES 4
   choice of his e.   ENEMIES 10
   conciliates e.   FRIENDS 2
   e. are innovative and resourceful   UNINTENDED 7
   forgiving one's e.   ENEMIES 9
   hundred e.   HUMOUR 20
   no time for making new e.   LAST WORDS 18
   pain it brings to your e.   AWARDS 1
   turning one's e. into money   NEWSPAPERS 5
   wish their e. dead   ENEMIES 6
enemy acute e.   BIOGRAPHY 1
   better class of e.   FRIENDS 11
   book of my e.   WRITERS 23
   e. of good art   ART 8
   hasn't an e.   FRIENDS 19
   men will have upon the e.   WAR 25
   sleeps with the e.   MARRIAGE 3
   your e. and your friend   FRIENDS 16
engagement e. should come   DATING 14
   Every e. ring should have   JEWELLERY 1
engine e. in boots   PEOPLE 17
   e. of pollution   CATS 9
England amusements in E.   ENGLAND 37
   between E. and Christianity   RELIGION 56
   do it for E.   ROYALTY 11
   dowdiness in E.   ENGLAND 32
   E. and America   COUNTRIES 25
   E. did for cricket   CRICKET 7
   expect to convert E.   FASHION 12
   he bored for E.   PRIME MINISTERS 33
   I left E. when I was four   ROYALTY 22
   road that leads him to E.   SCOTLAND 6
   stately homos of E.   SEX 34
   summer in E.   WEATHER 15
English E. and as such crave   ENGLAND 5
   E. approach to ideas   IDEAS 8
   E. are bipolar   ENGLAND 30
   E. are busy   ENGLAND 28
   E. can be explained   ENGLAND 13
   E. cooking: put things   COOKERY 1
   E. Delight   TRAVEL 11
   E. have hot-water bottles   SEX 57
   E. how to talk   CONVERSATION 30
   E. manners   MANNERS 13
   E., not being a spiritual   CRICKET 9
   E. servants   TRAVEL 6
   E. up with which I will not put   LANGUAGE 5
   Jesus can't have been E.   DRESS 20
   King's E. was good enough   LANGUAGES 7
   Not to be E.   ENGLAND 22
   old E. belief   ENGLAND 23
   Opera in E.   OPERA 5
   so little E.   LANGUAGE 10
   strong E. accent   FASHION 18
   think of the E. for a thing   LANGUAGES 6
   understand E.   LANGUAGES 2

fiction (cont.)

one form of continuous f.	NEWSPAPERS 2
Stranger than f.	TRUTH 2
what f. means	BOOKS 29
work of f.	AUTOBIOGRAPHY 8

fidelity f. is a very good idea — MORALITY 10
  f. is not having more than one — SEX 61
field loaf with a f. in it — FOOD 66
fields lies W. C. F. — EPITAPHS 11
fifteen always f. years older — OLD AGE 3
fifth came f. and lost the job — FAILURE 7
fifty f. million Frenchmen — FRANCE 13
  F. Things To Do Before — DEATH 14
  until he's f. — DRINK 15
fight before the f. begins — POLITICAL PARTIES 2
  Citizen Army will f. — ARMED FORCES 5
  f. for freedom — DRESS 6
  If I don't f. — BOXING 5
  size of the dog in the f. — ANGER 8
  Stay up and f. — RELATIONSHIPS 5
  strength of character to f. — AWARDS 4
  went to a f. the other night — SPORTS 15
fighting f. for this woman's honour — WOMEN 22
  stop f. for it — FOOTBALL 1
figment like it to say 'f.' — EPITAPHS 23
figure losing her f. or her face — APPEARANCE 7
file f. your waste-paper basket — LIBRARIES 2
fill better than trying to f. them — IDLENESS 2
  knowing how to f. a sweater — ACTORS 13
  stuff to f. the space — NEWSPAPERS 23
fills f. wrong cavity — WIT 20
film and that is f. — HOLLYWOOD 21
  deal with the f. lab — FILM STARS 13
  length of a f. should be directly — CINEMA 10
filmmaking no rules in f. — CINEMA 2
films f. were the lowest form — TELEVISION 20
financial other beasts: f. worries — MONEY 29
  seek f. succour — BETTING 1
Finchley Lord F. tried — WORK 5
find f. out what everyone is doing — LAW 10
  f. out who we were playing — CRICKET 5
  f. out why a snorer — SLEEP 7
  f. the way myself — VIRTUE 5
  where does she f. them — SNOBBERY 15
fine f., strike it out — WRITING 13
  OLD CARY GRANT F. — TELEGRAMS 10
finest f. bloody fast bowler — CRICKET 15
finger little f. to become longer — MUSIC 44
  what chills the f. not a bit — SATISFACTION 5
fingernails biting your f. — MISTAKES 28
  finished the f. — FILM 8
finish draw right to the f. — FUNERALS 4
  start together and f. together — MUSIC 10
  until I f. talking — MANAGEMENT 10
finished now she's f. with you — LOVE 1
  Then he's f. — MARRIAGE 35
Finland worst food after F. — COOKERY 9
fire f., a little food — PARTIES 6
  f. has gone out — OLD AGE 12
  I have a f. inside me — COMEBACKS 4
  other irons in the f. — PUBLISHING 1
Firenze COUGHING MYSELF INTO A F. — TELEGRAMS 6
fires Husbands are like f. — HUSBANDS 18

fireside by his own f. — HOME 20
first f. class, and with children — TRAVEL 2
  f. ten million years — PAST 1
  never been born the f. time — RELIGION 64
  to mistake for the f.-rate — WRITING 21
fish as old as the f. — PARTIES 1
  came up with the f. — FOOD 38
  f. are having their revenge — ANIMALS 12
  f. needs a bicycle — WOMEN 10
  He eats a lot of f. — INTELLIGENCE 18
  his intelligence against a f. — FISHING 6
  human being and f. can coexist — UNINTENDED 6
  judge a f. by its ability — MIND 2
  like f. into a letterbox — FILM PRODUCERS 11
  no self-respecting f. — NEWSPAPERS 33
  surrounded by f. — BUREAUCRACY 3
  throw her a f. — ACTORS 31
  watching f. dart about a pool — CRICKET 16
  Which of you is having f. — RESTAURANTS 6
fishes Luca Brasi sleeps with the f. — DEATH 47
fishing f. is a religion — FISHING 1
  name given to f. — FISHING 5
fish-knives Phone for the f., Norman — SOCIETY 3
fishy f. about the French — FRANCE 2
fit It isn't f. for humans now — TOWNS 5
five count to f. — ANGER 13
  I have wedded f. — HUSBANDS 12
  only f. Kings left — ROYALTY 19
  sound like a f.-year-old — CHILDREN 17
fix coming to f. the show — WIT 24
  only sport you can't f. — SPORTS 27
fjord Betty F. Clinic — DRINK 50
flabby f. redundant figure — APPEARANCE 21
flag High as a f. — AMERICA 8
flair only f. is in her nostrils — INSULTS 27
flamingo very large f. — DEBT 8
flashes f. of silence — CONVERSATION 24
flat Fell half so f. — CRITICS 2
  how f. he really did want it — CRITICS 3
  just how f. and empty — AMERICA 4
  Very f., Norfolk — ENGLAND 12
flats can't walk in f. — FASHION 8
flatter If a man is vain, f. — PRAISE 3
  they'd be rather f. — COUNTRIES 27
flattered f. by the censorship — CENSORSHIP 13
flattering you think him worth f. — PRAISE 10
flattery Everyone likes f. — ROYALTY 13
  f. hurts no one — PRAISE 12
  give them f. — ART 36
  isn't f. in your case — PRAISE 7
flaunt f. it — COMEDY ROUTINES 18
flavour chewing-gum lose its f. — FOOD 57
  gives success its f. — FAILURE 2
flaw no fault or f. — LAW 8
flea between a louse and a f. — POETS 11
fleas smaller f. to bite 'em — ANIMALS 29
fleet F.'s lit up — DRUNKENNESS 14
flesh delicate white human f. — LOVE 13
  have more f. — BODY 26
  makes man and wife one f. — MARRIAGE 22
flies f., floats, or fornicates — MONEY 10
flooded STREETS F. PLEASE ADVISE — TELEGRAMS 3
floor lie on the f. — DRUNKENNESS 7

fortune (cont.)

in possession of a good f.	MEN 2
little value of f.	WEALTH 21
rob a lady of her f.	MARRIAGE 32

forty f.-nine plus VAT — MIDDLE AGE 4

Life begins at f.	AGE 7
loves a fairy when she's f.	MIDDLE AGE 6
one passes f.	MIDDLE AGE 9

forward looking f. to the past — PAST 18
foul really f. things up — COMPUTERS 2
founding f. a bank — CRIME 7
fountain f.-pen filler — GOSSIP 7
four at the age of f. — ARMED FORCES 25

F. legs good	ANIMALS 24

fourteen Wilson requires F. Points — PRESIDENTS 6
fourteenth f. Mr Wilson — ARISTOCRACY 5
fourth full of f.-rate writers — READING 1
fowl liver-wing of a f. — AWARDS 8
fowls f. for dissenters — FOOD 59
fox gentlemen galloping after a f. — SPORTS 35

metaphysical f.	CONVERSATION 26

fox-hunting inferior forms of f. — SPORTS 34

prefer f.	POLITICAL PARTIES 7

frailty therefore more f. — BODY 26
framed f. and glazed — WEATHER 15
France Everything is easier in F. — FRANCE 15

F. is a country	FRANCE 16
F. is the only place	FRANCE 1
F. we are fighting for	CHAMPAGNE 3
take back to F.	PEOPLE 11

Francesca di Rimini F., miminy, piminy — MEN 13
Francis Like dear St F. — POVERTY 11
frank many f. words — DIPLOMACY 2
Frankenstein F. get married — EDUCATION 24
frankly F., my dear — SATISFACTION 3
frappé now completely f. — CHILDREN 14
fraternizing f. with the enemy

— MEN AND WOMEN 28

Frazier F. is so ugly — FACES 1
freak ticket to the f. show — AMERICA 5
freckles Love, curiosity, f., and doubt — LOVE 27
Fred Here lies F. — EPITAPHS 4
free bring it to you, f. — DEATH 3

favours f. speech	CENSORSHIP 3
f. in America	AMERICA 16
F. your mind	DIETS 12
I'm f.	COMEDY ROUTINES 21
in favour of f. expression	CENSORSHIP 2
This is a f. country	MANNERS 25

freedom as f. fries — WIT 2

fight for f.	DRESS 6
F. of the press	CENSORSHIP 8
F. of the press in Britain	NEWSPAPERS 40

French answering you in F. — FRANCE 9

Englishman is about to talk F.	LANGUAGES 24
fishy about the F.	FRANCE 2
F., they say, live to eat	EATING 1
F. are always too wordy	FRANCE 8
F. are masters	DIPLOMACY 10
F. / British relationship	DIPLOMACY 9
F. for bullshit	WORDS 13
F. fry potatoes	WIT 2
F. Revolution	FAMILY 37

F. widow in every bedroom	HOLIDAYS 5
how it's improved her F.	LANGUAGES 9
not too F. French bean	ART 14
prefer to travel on F. ships	TRANSPORT 6
serve the F.	FOOD 13
Speak in F.	LANGUAGES 6
trouble with the F.	LANGUAGES 5

Frenchman Englishman to a F. — FRANCE 7
Frenchmen fifty million F. — FRANCE 13

What asses these F. are	LANGUAGES 25

frenzy f. closely related to delirium — WRITING 17
fresh What f. hell is this — OPTIMISM 7
Freud trouble with F. — HUMOUR 7
friend become a man's f. — MEN AND WOMEN 10

breaking it in for a f.	NAMES 15
Diamonds are a girl's best f.	JEWELLERY 5
find a f.	FRIENDS 7
f. is not standing	DEMOCRACY 16
goodnatured f.	FRIENDS 13
having an old f. for dinner	WIT 18
man's best f.	CATS 6
my f. Evelyn Waugh	FRIENDS 5
probably somebody's old f.	MURDER 3
Reagan for his best f.	FILM STARS 15
takes his f. to the party	MEN 3
want a f. in Washington	POLITICIANS 34
Whenever a f. succeeds	SUCCESS 29
your enemey and your f.	FRIENDS 16

friends at all her f. — GOSSIP 7

Champagne for my real f.	FRIENDS 3
couldn't buy f.	FRIENDS 11
descendants Outnumber your f.	OLD AGE 24
deserting one's f.	FRIENDS 2
Family F. are a bit too numerous	FAMILY 19
f. all over the world	TECHNOLOGY 7
f. are true	PAST 5
F. come and go	ENEMIES 2
f. except two	CHRISTMAS 3
f. in both places	HEAVEN 6
f. who took exercise	EXERCISE 8
F. who give you erections	MEN AND WOMEN 61
keep your eye on your f.	ADVICE 9
lay down his f.	FRIENDS 15
nearly deceiving your f.	LIES 4
none of his f.	FRIENDS 19
not always the best of f.	TAXES 8
no true f. in politics	POLITICS 13
only two f.	FRIENDS 14
Seek younger f.	OLD AGE 28
two real f.	LIFESTYLE 11
your three best f.	MENTAL HEALTH 2

friendship degree of f. called slight — FRIENDS 4

sort of f.	MARRIAGE 71
swear eternal f.	FOOD 60

fries as freedom f. — WIT 2
frighten f. the horses — SEX 28

by God, they f. me	WAR 25

frightening feminist is about f. men — FEMINISM 3
Frigidaire popped him in the F. — CHILDREN 14
frilly Hope is a f., pink dress — HOPE 9
frivolity how precious is f. — LITERATURE 9
frivolous Memoirs of the f. — AUTOBIOGRAPHY 1
frock history of that f. — DRESS 5

geniuses g. are devoid of humour   SPEECHES 22

gentleman being a g.   CLASS 21

    Every other inch a g.   INSULTS 56

    g. is someone who can play   CHARACTER 1

    g. never eats   CLASS 1

    g....Someone who can   CLASS 16

    He was a g.   POVERTY 9

    I am a g.   SOCIETY 11

    teach you to be a g.   ACADEMIC 14

gentlemanly werry g. ideas   CHAMPAGNE 7

gentlemen beastly game played by g.   SPORTS 5

    behave like g.   WOMEN 27

    G. do not take soup   CLASS 6

    G. never wear   COLOURS 3

    most of the g. does   ACADEMIC 16

genuine springs from g. feeling   POETRY 19

geography feel like the g. teacher   ECONOMICS 12

    G. is about Maps   BIOGRAPHY 2

    teaching Americans g.   WAR 3

George G.—don't do that   COMEDY ROUTINES 11

    G. the Third   MISTAKES 6

    give the ball to G.   FOOTBALL 2

Georgian G. silver goes   POLITICS 32

geriatric five years in the g. ward   HAPPINESS 9

    g. set   FUNERALS 9

    What's a g.   FOOTBALL 15

German G. footballer   FOOTBALL 15

    G. soldier trying to violate   SEX 67

    G. spoken underwater   LANGUAGES 1

    performed for G. literature   LITERATURE 10

    Speak G.   LANGUAGES 17

    than one G. adjective   LANGUAGES 22

    Waiting for the G. verb   LANGUAGES 15

Germans at the end, the G. win   FOOTBALL 13

    beastly to the G.   COUNTRIES 8

    G. are extremely diligent   COUNTRIES 11

    Not all G. believe in God   ECONOMICS 6

    They're G.   COUNTRIES 5

Germany G. doesn't want   PAST 4

germs get enough g. to catch   KISSING 1

gerund Save the g.   LANGUAGE 18

gesture futile g. at this stage   WAR 7

get g. where I am today   COMEDY ROUTINES 16

Gettysburg where G. lived   READING 2

ghastly G. good taste   ARCHITECTURE 3

ghost never mind Banquo's g.   ACTORS 4

gibberish printed g. all over it   EDUCATION 1

gibbon Eh! Mr G.   WRITING 11

Gibson Mel G. could play a Scot   ACTORS 3

    next man is Mel G.   PEOPLE 16

gift get in through the g. shop   WAR 17

    Guilt: the g. that keeps on   MORALITY 1

gifts most minor of g.   ACTING 15

    their guilt g.   GIFTS 1

giggles girls got the g.   POETS 5

Gilbert That must be G.   WIT 24

gin flavour of g.   DRINK 10

    get out the g.   DRINK 40

    g. will make them run   DRESS 4

    G. was mother's milk   DRINK 44

    such as g.   DRINK 51

    two g.-and-limes   SICKNESS 15

girder Joist and a G.   WIT 5

girdle helps you with your g.   HUSBANDS 23

girl Diamonds are a g.'s best friend   JEWELLERY 5

    nice g.'s ambition   AMBITION 1

    Now you can't say 'g.'   PROGRESS 6

    When I'm not near the g. I love   LOVE 19

    You take the g.   PREJUDICE 1

girls At g. who wear glasses   MEN AND WOMEN 41

    both were crazy about g.   SEX 53

    g. I liked   FASHION 5

    g. I want telephone numbers   PEOPLE 5

    G. are just friends   MEN AND WOMEN 61

    In Little G.   CHILDREN 4

    knowingness of little g.   CHILDREN 22

    social security, not g.   SEX 64

    Watching all the g. go by   MEN AND WOMEN 34

give g. a war and nobody will come   WAR 22

    g. them ours   GOVERNMENT 16

    g. the public something   FUNERALS 10

GKC poor G.   EPITAPHS 15

glad are you just g. to see me   MEN AND WOMEN 57

Gladstone G. may perspire   PRIME MINISTERS 14

    G....spent his declining years   IRELAND 7

    If G. fell into the Thames   MISTAKES 13

    sitting next to Mr G.   CONVERSATION 1

glamour G. is on a life-support   APPEARANCE 9

    Gives the place a bit of g.   RELIGION 35

Glasgow passed through G.   TOWNS 3

    play the old G. Empire   HUMOUR 7

glass g.-bottomed boat   HOLLYWOOD 14

    g. is always half empty   OPTIMISM 3

    in a dirty g.   DRINK 37

    panes of g. with its claws   MUSIC 7

    Satire is a sort of g.   SELF-KNOWLEDGE 22

    take a g. of wine   HOME 20

glasses At girls who wear g.   MEN AND WOMEN 41

    wears dark g.   FAME 1

gloat Call Uncle Teddy and g.   PRESIDENTS 16

Glyn sin with Elinor G.   SEX 11

gnu look his g. in the face   ENGLAND 43

go all g. together   COUNTRIES 19

    as cooks g.   COOKERY 21

    delighted to see them g.   CHILDREN 33

    g. away at any rate   ROYALTY 3

    g. in long enough after   MUSIC 48

    I g.   COMEDY ROUTINES 19

    Let my people g.   CRITICS 33

    One of us must g.   DEATH 62

    when you have to g. there   HOME 10

goad g. the BBC   TELEVISION 10

goal g. they finally got   FOOTBALL 9

    Woman's place was in the g.   FEMINISM 2

goalkeeper g., defence, attack   PRIME MINISTERS 38

goals scoring three g.   FOOTBALL 15

goblins head full of g.   TAXES 11

God All G.'s children are not beautiful

    HUMAN RACE 5

    believe in G.   GOD 19

    By G. what a site   AUSTRALIA 7

    choose A Jewish G.   GOD 12

    decides he is not G.   GOD 28

    don't believe in G.   GOD 20

    don't do G.   GOD 14

    don't think G. comes well   BIBLE 7

governor *Stewart* for g. FILM STARS 15
  g. is bound to ask you CLASS 13
goyim g. Annoy 'im GOD 7
grabs Benn g. child HEADLINES 8
grace g. is sometimes better MARRIAGE 21
  There but for the g. of God POLITICIANS 10
Gracie goodnight, G. COMEDY ROUTINES 12
grades into four g. EDUCATION 20
graffiti No g. COUNTRIES 15
grammar don't want to talk g. CLASS 20
  talking bad g. LAST WORDS 3
Grammarians Conan the G. ACADEMIC 11
grammatical seven g. errors EPITAPHS 8
grand Ain't it g. DEATH 51
Grand Canyon rose petal down the G. POETRY 13
grandchild fourteenth g. BIRTH 8
grandchildren G. don't make a man AGE 4
  grandparents and g. get along FAMILY LIFE 8
granddaughter seventh g. BIRTH 8
grandiose taste for the g. ARCHITECTURE 9
grandma It was good enough for G. WOMEN 18
grandmother g. took a bath MANNERS 2
  married to a g. AGE 4
  wants to marry your g. MARRIAGE 47
  We have become a g. UNINTENDED 17
grandparents g. and grandchildren get along FAMILY LIFE 8
grannies nannies, g. and fannies WOMEN 16
grape how to jump on a g. COUNTRIES 6
  peel me a g. FOOD 63
grapefruit g. deserves all the credit COMEBACKS 12
  g. throughout the day DIETS 4
grapes Defectors are like g. TRUST 6
grass Keep off the g. EPITAPHS 22
  shit on g. FOOTBALL 23
gratitude G. is not a normal feature POLITICS 23
gratuitous is the most g. AUTOBIOGRAPHY 10
grave g. yawns for him BORES 16
  kind of healthy g. NATURE 19
gravel fished out of a g. pit FOOD 16
graves dig our g. with our teeth EATING 11
  g. of little magazines POETRY 16
gravitation eminence by sheer g. SUCCESS 24
gravy person who disliked g. FOOD 60
great All my shows are g. SELF-KNOWLEDGE 8
  Behind every g. man MEN AND WOMEN 29
  every g. woman has had MEN AND WOMEN 48
  feeling that he is g. JUDGES 4
  g. being a priest CLERGY 10
  know he is not a g. man PRESIDENTS 9
  Leonard, we know you're g. SONGS 11
  some men are born g. HEROES 6
  think him g. BORES 9
  Whenever he met a g. man SNOBBERY 20
greater G. love FRIENDS 15
greatly g. to his credit ENGLAND 16
greatness g. thrust upon them HEROES 6
  some achieve g. BUSINESS 4
greed swallow with g. COUNTRIES 7
Greek half G., half Latin TELEVISION 17
  is G. for 'men'. WORDS 14
  No G.; as much Latin QUOTATIONS 4
  original G. CRITICS 43

green big g. one out there FOOTBALL 25
  g. about the gills DRUGS 5
  g. belt was a labour idea ARCHITECTURE 11
  g. thing that stands in NATURE 4
  G. with lust ROYALTY 6
  just as g. GARDENS 2
grew when I g. up GENERATION GAP 10
grey g. around the underwear region BRITISH 3
grievance Scotsman with a g. SCOTLAND 10
grill not to look like a mixed g. APPEARANCE 11
grindstone nose to the g. IDLENESS 6
gristle Cuddling up to a piece of g. BODY 23
grocer photograph of the G. DIPLOMACY 13
groom disappearance of the g. WEDDINGS 13
  Including the bride and g. WEDDINGS 9
grooves In predestinate g. TRANSPORT 12
gross g. habits with my net income MONEY 15
grosser your g. reminiscences LETTERS 14
Grosvenor violence in G. Square EDUCATION 23
grotesque meaning of the word g. WIT 46
Groucho Marxist—of the G. tendency POLITICS 3
ground worship the g. DATING 15
grouse make a g. do for six CLASS 16
grovelled g. before him SNOBBERY 20
grow never g. out of it ARMED FORCES 25
growing price to pay for g. up MIDDLE AGE 10
grown-ups G. never GENERATION GAP 4
gruntled far from being g. SATISFACTION 9
guaranteed g. only to those CENSORSHIP 8
guardian reading *The G.* FOOTBALL 17
guess g. what a man is going to do DANCE 7
  In disease Medical Men g. MEDICINE 22
guesses correctly g. a woman's age MEN 4
guests g. are so pleased to feel HOME 17
  hosts and g. PARTIES 4
guile squat, and packed with g. TOWNS 6
guilt G.: the gift that keeps on MORALITY 1
  their g. gifts GIFTS 1
guilty g. never escape unscathed LAWYERS 1
guineas two hundred g. ART 45
Guinness G., sarcasm and late nights IRELAND 6
  G. makes you drunk DRUNKENNESS 2
guitar play the g. with your teeth MUSICIANS 11
  thirty-seven dollars and a Jap g. MUSICIANS 9
gulf G. War was like teenage sex WAR 11
gum chew g. at the same time PRESIDENTS 13
gun g. across the Savoy Grill BUSINESS 19
  Is that a g. in your pocket MEN AND WOMEN 57
  with a miniature machine g. LOVE 17
  wrong end of a g. SPORTS 37
Gunga G. Din PREJUDICE 10
guns G. aren't lawful DEATH 44
  g. don't kill people MURDER 7
  if only the deer had g. SPORTS 16
  loaded g. with boys SECRECY 4
guts Spill your g. at Wimbledon TENNIS 3
gutter you need a g. press NEWSPAPERS 19
guy straight sort of g. SELF-KNOWLEDGE 3
gym love to go to the g. EXERCISE 1
h even *without* the h's THEATRE 14
ha funny h.-ha HUMOUR 10
habit court is just an expensive h. LAW 21
habit-forming Cocaine h. DRUGS 3

life (cont.)

loved I l. him and he loved him RELATIONSHIPS 14
  l. in triangles WRITERS 2
  wish I l. HUMAN RACE 8
loveliness miracle of l. BEAUTY 3
lovely I looked l. APPEARANCE 6
  It was such a l. day WEATHER 10
  Shoulders back, l. boy COMEDY ROUTINES 36
lover best l. in the world SEX 41
  Scratch a l. FRIENDS 12
  what is left of a l. HUSBANDS 27
  which husband was the best l. COMEBACKS 6
lovers like very bad l. RESTAURANTS 9
  women should tell our l. ADVICE 14
loving help l. the land FRANCE 12
  lovely l. LOVE 20
lower cheaper to l. the Atlantic FILM 7
  lies much l. BODY 18
  l. orders don't set CLASS 23
  L. Seymour Street CLASS 19
loyal Lousy but l. ROYALTY 4
  l. to his own career POLITICIANS 13
loyalty I want l. POWER 3
LSD L.? Nothing much happened DRUGS 2
  painter of L. without LSD ART 23
luck Bad l. OLD AGE 11
  bring him l. CERTAINTY 6
  l. to get One perfect rose TRANSPORT 16
  L., like a Russian car SUCCESS 12
  stamina and good l. PRIME MINISTERS 24
lucky l. if he gets out of it alive LIFE 11
  wonders if he'll get l. ROMANCE 7
lucrative l. to cheat CRIME 9
lucubrations your agglomerated l. PRAISE 6
lugubrious l. man in a suit POETS 5
lunatic girls' school and a l. asylum TELEVISION 14
lunatics l. have taken charge CINEMA 12
lunch cork out of my l. DRINK 16
  Her l. ROYALTY 12
  hour off for l. GOVERNMENT 12
  L. Hollywood-style HOLLYWOOD 11
  L. is for wimps MANAGEMENT 8
  no time for l. POLITICS 33
luncheon soup at l. CLASS 6
lunches l. of fifty-seven years BODY 32
lunchtime L. doubly so TIME 2
  legend in his own l. FAME 9
lust Green with l. ROYALTY 6
  ham and eggs to l. after it VIRTUE 13
lusty no longer enough to be l. SEX 75
luxury l. was lavished CHILDREN 26
lying l. in state DIPLOMACY 5
  made l. an art form WRITERS 37
  no fun l. to them anymore RELATIONSHIPS 3
  One of you is l. LIES 7
Lyme old man of L. WIVES 12
Macaulay M. is like a book in breeches WRITERS 35
Macbeth don't care for Lady M. ACTING 27
  Little Nell and Lady M. WRITERS 44
  Perhaps M. ACTORS 24
machine desiccated calculating m. POLITICIANS 6
  ingenious m. BODY 10
  make a m. that would walk TECHNOLOGY 2
mackintoshes wet m. TRAVEL 28

mad Don't get m. DIVORCE 9
  m. rocking-horse FILM STARS 5
  M., is he? ARMED FORCES 8
  M. dogs ENGLAND 11
  when a heroine goes m. MENTAL HEALTH 10
made m. for life DEATH 27
madness Fishing is a form of m. FISHING 3
  little spark of m. MENTAL HEALTH 12
  sort of m. [Marxism] POLITICS 47
Madonna only thing M. will ever do INSULTS 35
Mafia it's the M. CRIME 26
magazine falsehoods for a m. NEWSPAPERS 7
magazines graves of little m. POETRY 16
Magna Carta M. mean nothing to you HISTORY 10
magnificent more than m. FILM 5
maid old m. is like death by drowning OLD AGE 15
  second wife always has a m. HOME 6
maiden That wasn't a m. speech SPEECHES 5
mail deadlier than the m. COMPUTERS 8
Mailer M. is, as usual CRITICS 45
maintenance Take up car m. EDUCATION 7
majesty as Her M. remarked to me NAMES 17
Major M. Major it had been all three INSULTS 24
major John M.'s self-control in cabinet ANGER 18
Major-General modern M. ARMED FORCES 10
majority admit to be the m. DEMOCRACY 12
  big enough m. FOOLISHNESS 14
  m. is always the best DEMOCRACY 3
majors college m. ACADEMIC 13
make movie I want to m. FILM PRODUCERS 13
  People who m. history HISTORY 6
  Scotsman on the m. SCOTLAND 1
  to m. it up MIND 12
maker prepared to meet my M. GOD 16
male as my m. organ AUTOBIOGRAPHY 3
  existence of the m. sex MEN 33
  it was a m. horse NATURE 5
malfunction Wardrobe m. MISTAKES 31
malice M. in Wonderland NAMES 6
  m. of a good thing WIT 45
  measured m. of music MUSIC 25
malignant part of Randolph that was not m.
  MEDICINE 33
Malvern Perrier or M. water CHOICE 2
mama but it's M. AGE 9
  m. of dada WRITERS 17
Mammon God and M. GOD 38
man Clothes by a m. FASHION 6
  get M. to shut up GOD 4
  God is a m. RELIGION 42
  hard m. is good to find MEN 31
  let him pass for a m. MEN 30
  m. bites a dog NEWSPAPERS 3
  m. could be crossed with a cat CATS 11
  M. does not live by words WORDS 19
  M. he eat the barracuda CLASS 12
  M. is one of the toughest HUMAN RACE 7
  m. is *so* in the way FAMILY LIFE 5
  m. led by a bear WRITERS 7
  m. more dined against than dining SOCIETY 4
  m. to a worm EATING 3
managed world is disgracefully m. GOD 23
manager m. gets the blame FOOTBALL 12

mistake (cont.)

publication praised their last p. WRITERS 9
publicity fifty per cent of the p. HOLLYWOOD 2
now called p. FAME 21
winds up with the bitch P. FAME 12
publicly not insult his wife p. HUSBANDS 30
public relations hire p. officers BUSINESS 4
published before this book is p. BIOGRAPHY 5
publisher agent to a p. PUBLISHING 10
murdering his p. PUBLISHING 2
p. has to do is write cheques PUBLISHING 14
p. who writes is like a cow PUBLISHING 11
publishers Easier to change p. PUBLISHING 8
p. and printers CENSORSHIP 7
p. are untrustworthy PUBLISHING 13
turned down by numerous p. WRITING 1
pubs all the p. in Dublin DEATH 22
Pulitzer as a P. Prize NEWSPAPERS 12
pull had to p. him out PEOPLE 10
pulls p. a lady through HOPE 5
pulse feeling a woman's p. WOMEN 37
punch start a p.-up CRITICS 24
punch-line meditation with a p. FISHING 2
punctual trouble with being p. TIME 5
would always be p. FILM STARS 17
punctuation p. where he pleases APOLOGY 5
punishing p. anyone who comes MARRIAGE 68
punishment My fees are sufficient p. LAWYERS 1
Teenagers are God's p. FAMILY LIFE 1
punster inveterate p. PUNS 5
pupped come down and p. ARCHITECTURE 13
pure has not a p. heart COOKERY 2
p. as the driven slush VIRTUE 1
truth is rarely p. TRUTH 9
purgatory department of P. OLD AGE 7
purge p., and leave sack ARISTOCRACY 9
puritanism not P. but February WEATHER 8
P. The haunting fear RELIGION 38
purity spoil the p. of my hatred POLITICIANS 32
purple walk by the colour p. COLOURS 8
purpose If people want a sense of p. MORALITY 7
purrs stroke a platitude until it p. NEWSPAPERS 26
pursuit man in p. of happiness HUSBANDS 11
push didn't p. him in PEOPLE 10
pushed bloody well p. BIRTH 5
Did he fall or was he p. DEATH 29
pushing P. forty? She's clinging AGE 1
put up with which I will not p. LANGUAGE 5
putts missed short p. GOLF 10
when he p. GOLF 3
pyjamas cardigan over his p. MEN AND WOMEN 33
p. look nice on him MEN AND WOMEN 22
pyramid Insurance is like a p. MONEY 22
quad no one about in the Q. GOD 30
qualities such q. as would wear WIVES 9
quantum q. solar energy PARTIES 2
quarrels Books and harlots have their q. BOOKS 2
in q. interpose ANGER 10
quarries q. to be used at will QUOTATIONS 6
quarterly nothing a-year, paid q. POVERTY 9
queen being a drag q. FASHION 8
die so he can be Q. ROYALTY 32
God save the Q. ROYALTY 36
have the Q. as their aunt ROYALTY 25

home life of our own dear Q. ROYALTY 5
Q. is most anxious FEMINISM 14
Q. Mary looking like ROYALTY 8
Q. Mother of football FOOTBALL 22
Q. to skip Chuck nups HEADLINES 3
sleeping with a q. ROYALTY 37
trying for the Q. CINEMA 9
your Q. has to pay taxes ROYALTY 21
queer To our q. old dean WIT 48
very q. things in it BIBLE 3
What a q. thing Life is LIFE 37
queerer q. than we *can* suppose UNIVERSE 5
queers hate for q. EPITAPHS 9
query always q. them DEBT 5
question any clear q. MANNERS 6
any q. from the bench JUDGES 10
Irish secretly changed the Q. IRELAND 7
number of the q. EXAMINATIONS 3
put the q. in wrong COMPUTERS 3
rephrase the q. LOVE 29
Schleswig-Holstein q. DIPLOMACY 11
questions all q. were stupid SCIENCE 19
ask q. of those EXAMINATIONS 6
even one of the q. MEN 3
lot of expensive q. MEDICINE 4
queue q. of one ENGLAND 27
quick q., and the dead DRIVING 7
quicker liquor Is q. DRINK 36
quicksand worship the q. he walks PRESIDENTS 3
quiet four children q. for an hour TELEVISION 16
immense q. PARTIES 1
They just want q. FAMILY LIFE 3
very well and q. CHILDREN 6
quill q. back in my goose WRITING 2
quit try again. Then q. FAILURE 5
quotable hard to be clever and q. QUOTATIONS 1
q. than honest QUOTATIONS 12
quotation happy q. anywhere QUOTATIONS 5
q. for everything QUOTATIONS 11
quotations furnishes no q. QUOTATIONS 8
I know heaps of q. QUOTATIONS 2
quote Q. Learned JUDGES 9
quoted should be drawn and q. PUNS 1
quoter first q. of it QUOTATIONS 3
quotes never q. accurately QUOTATIONS 9
putting religious q. on cups MODERN LIFE 8
rabbits r. in Windsor Park BIRTH 8
race r. between education HISTORY 21
r. is not always BETTING 1
trouble with the rat r. MODERN LIFE 12
racing obstacle r. HOME 23
racist Alcoholic and a r. ACTORS 3
racket ruins the whole r. MEN AND WOMEN 36
radical dared be r. when young POLITICAL PARTIES 5
radio I had the r. on FILM STARS 12
just gave me a shower r. MODERN LIFE 10
r. lark's a wonderful hobby TECHNOLOGY 7
rage I fall in a r. ANGER 17
raids during the air r. MISTAKES 5
railings Iron r. HANDWRITING 4
railway takes this r. by surprise TRANSPORT 8
railways R. and the Church TRANSPORT 1
rain back when it begins to r. MONEY 16

wretchedness of being r.   WEALTH 19
riches that of the titled for r.   SNOBBERY 16
ricicles r. are twicicles   WIT 36
rickshaw except a motorised r.   LAW 14
rid before getting r. of it   BUREAUCRACY 6
rides Don't accept r. from strange men   ADVICE 11
ridiculous no spectacle so r.   MORALITY 6
   see people looking r.   LOVE 5
   Sublime To the R.   TRANSPORT 10
riff-raff keeps the r. out of Waitrose   SNOBBERY 13
Riga young lady of R.   ANIMALS 3
right almost always in the r.   POLITICS 48
   be decorative and to do r.   WOMEN 12
   decide I was r.   FOOTBALL 3
   doctor being always in the r.   MEDICINE 30
   give my r. arm   ART 4
   half of the people are r.   DEMOCRACY 14
   In boxing the r. cross-counter   BOXING 7
   it's all r. with me   MIND 3
   know it about the r. person   POWER 5
   men go r. after them   MEN AND WOMEN 58
   not determine who is r.   WAR 2
   nothing against your r. leg   ACTING 5
   people who are r.   MEMBERS 3
   proven r. or pleasantly surprised   OPTIMISM 9
   R. but Repulsive   HISTORY 14
   r. notes at the right time   MUSIC 6
   should be on my r.   POLITICAL PARTIES 8
   Whenever you're r., shut up   HUSBANDS 24
   Where did we go r.   SUCCESS 4
righteous good enough for the r.   RELIGION 40
rights folly of 'Woman's r.'   FEMINISM 14
Rimbauds always chasing R.   LITERATURE 21
ring Every engagement r. should have   JEWELLERY 1
rings read the r.   MARRIAGE 51
rioting r. and learning   ACADEMIC 3
rip R.-Van-With-It   NAMES 7
ripen but nice to r.   AGE 2
risen Frost has r. without trace   SUCCESS 21
rising from r. hope   PEOPLE 12
risk at great personal r.   MEN AND WOMEN 45
risks one of the r.   AMERICA 18
risotto screaming r. recipes   OPERA 6
Ritz life for ourselves at the R.   UNINTENDED 1
   like the R. Hotel   LAW 17
road and not the r.   EPITAPHS 19
   r. that leads him to England   SCOTLAND 6
   r. to success is always under   SUCCESS 2
roads cosy little A-r. in England   FRANCE 5
roam sent to r.   FOOLISHNESS 3
roar I storm and I r.   ANGER 17
   r. their ribs out   HUMOUR 9
roareth What is this that r. thus   TRANSPORT 9
roast r. beef and rain   ENGLAND 13
   R. Beef, Medium   FOOD 23
rob r. a lady of her fortune   MARRIAGE 32
robbed I'd expect to be r. in Chicago   SNOBBERY 14
robbing r. a bank   CRIME 7
robin little r.   NATURE 22
Robin Hood modern-day R.   FILM PRODUCERS 18
robot camp gammon r.   PRIME MINISTERS 32
robs r. Peter   GOVERNMENT 26
rock dealing in r.'n'roll   HUMAN RACE 10

R. Journalism   NEWSPAPERS 47
rocking-horse in love with my r.   MIND 5
   mad r.   FILM STARS 5
rock 'n' roll start out playing r.   DRUGS 4
rodeoing R. is about the only sport   SPORTS 27
rogue this r. and whore together   WEDDINGS 2
rogues couple of r.   ART 13
roll Assistant heads must r.   MANAGEMENT 1
rollers glanced at her Carmen r.   NAMES 8
Roman concept of R. numerals   INTELLIGENCE 14
   no R. ever was able to say   SOCIETY 2
   R. Conquest   BRITISH 7
Roman Catholic is a R.   FRIENDS 5
romance lifelong r.   LOVE 31
   r. with no kisses   DATING 7
   r. with no kisses   KISSING 2
   Twenty years of r.   WIVES 14
romantic For something r.   LITERATURE 26
Rome all the sights in R. were called   TRAVEL 23
room All I need is r.   HOME 15
   always r. at the top   AMBITION 11
   find my way across the r.   PREJUDICE 7
   lighten a r.   PRIME MINISTERS 1
   not a rhinoceros in the r.   PHILOSOPHY 11
   Twenty-four hour r. service generally   HOLIDAYS 7
rooms sleep in separate r.   MARRIAGE 27
Roosevelt Once we had a R.   AMERICA 9
Roosian might have been a R.   COUNTRIES 16
rope spare a r.   AMERICA 9
rose r. named after me   PRAISE 1
   r.-red city   PUNS 6
   r.-red sissy   DESCRIPTION 16
   One perfect r.   TRANSPORT 16
roses my r. to see you   DATING 12
   Wars of the R.   FILM PRODUCERS 1
rot it must be all r.   RELIGION 42
   living talked r.   PARANORMAL 2
Rothschild taken by R. and Baring   MONEY 19
rotted Or simply r. early   MIDDLE AGE 8
rotter going to bed with a r.   ROMANCE 2
rouge too much r.   DRESS 22
rough R. diamonds are a girl's best   FRIENDS 6
round R. up the usual suspects   CRIME 16
routine r. hard to distinguish   WRITING 17
royal become a r. reporter   NEWSPAPERS 16
   when anyone left the R. family   ROYALTY 39
royalties deprivation of literary r.   WRITERS 32
royalty due a r. statement   PUBLISHING 7
   when you come to R.   ROYALTY 13
rub if you r. up against money   MONEY 30
rubbish R.   COMEDY ROUTINES 43
   someone who puts out the r.   HUSBANDS 20
Rubens If I were alive in R.'s time   ART 11
rugby we play r.   SPORTS 22
rugger nuns in a r. scrum   ARCHITECTURE 10
ruin about to r. your day   LIFE 10
   increasingly to resemble a r.   HUSBANDS 14
   make a woman look like a r.   WIVES 14
ruined r. by literature   LITERATURE 3
   r. by our parents   FAMILY 6
Ruislip Gaily into R. Gardens   SNOBBERY 5
rule r. all afternoon   WINE 3
   infallible r.   CLASS 21

Sindh I have S.   PUNS 12
sing answering machine and s.   UNINTENDED 16
  blues for people who can't s.   COMEDY 6
  die before they s.   SONGS 5
  heard no horse s. a song   MUSIC 4
  people s. it   SONGS 1
  s. my best in this position   SONGS 2
  they could s.   PREJUDICE 8
singing don't want you s.   FUNERALS 6
  in spite of the s.   OPERA 9
single desire to be s. again   HUSBANDS 17
  s. man in possession   MEN 2
singles What strenuous s. we played   TENNIS 1
sings instead of bleeding, he s.   OPERA 4
sinister went around looking s.   SECRECY 9
sink stare sullenly at the s.   FOOD 15
  threw the kitchen s.   TENNIS 7
sinking desert a s. ship   CERTAINTY 4
  like a s. ship   ACTORS 35
  swimming *towards* a s. ship   TRUST 2
sinner Or I of her a s.   LOVE 7
  s. revised and edited   VIRTUE 3
sinning in good shape for more s.   RELIGION 52
sins s. were scarlet   DEATH 11
  terrible s. I have working   VIRTUE 8
sir Either one calls him S.   ROYALTY 29
sissy rose-red s.   DESCRIPTION 16
  s. stuff that rhymes   POETRY 20
sister bury my s.   FUNERALS 7
  trying to violate your s.   SEX 67
sisterly s. animosity   FAMILY 28
sisters s. under their skins   WOMEN 23
sit allowed to s. down   DIPLOMACY 16
  come and s. by me   GOSSIP 6
  s. down and shut up   CHILDREN 2
site By God what a s.   AUSTRALIA 7
  s. for sore eyes   COMPUTERS 15
sits down before he stands up   SPEECHES 18
  Sometimes I s. and thinks   PHILOSOPHY 4
sitting He struts s. down   INSULTS 16
  stay s. down   APPEARANCE 7
  unsportsmanlike to hit a s. ball   GOLF 6
  you're s. on it   FILM STARS 8
six forget the s. feet   BODY 29
sixpence shot at for s.   ARMED FORCES 7
sixty alone and s.   OLD AGE 5
  recently turned s.   MIDDLE AGE 2
sixty-five s. you get social security   SEX 64
size cut you down to my s.   COMEBACKS 7
  s. of the onion, the dish   COOKERY 18
  this male angst over s.   SEX 49
sizzle sell the steak, sell the s.   ADVERTISING 11
skate I could s. on them   JEWELLERY 3
skating s. on thin ice   ACTORS 7
skay s. is only seen   ACTING 31
Skegness I say stuff S.   HOLIDAYS 6
ski they s. and eat chocolate   COUNTRIES 9
ski-ing s. consists of wearing   SPORTS 31
skill Imagination without s.   ART 37
  S. is fine and genius is   BUSINESS 16
skin taxidermist takes only your s.   TAXES 14
skinny tall s. black Americano   MODERN LIFE 6
skins sisters under their s.   WOMEN 23

skit I think you're full of s.   WIT 33
Skugg S. Lies snug   EPITAPHS 12
skulk s. in broad daylight   POLITICIANS 16
sky s. falls on my head   FILM PRODUCERS 13
slab Beneath this s.   EPITAPHS 19
slam Don't s. the lid   DRUNKENNESS 13
  s. the door in the face of age   OLD AGE 10
slamming s. Doors   CHILDREN 4
slap s. them as hard as you can   YOUTH 2
slapped s. my mother   APPEARANCE 28
slashed s.-wrist shot   FILM PRODUCERS 17
slashing damned cutting and s.   PUBLISHING 5
slate thoughts upon a s.   POETS 7
slaves never will be s.   ENGLAND 34
slax Little snax, Bigger s.   DIETS 11
sleep been to s. for over a year   SLEEP 8
  die in my s. like my grandfather   DEATH 6
  I love s.   SLEEP 3
  like men who s. badly   HAPPINESS 10
  she tried to s. with me   SEX 36
  s. is so deep   LIBRARIES 3
  s. my way to the middle   AMBITION 3
  when you can't get to s.   LIFE 21
  women s. with men so   MEN AND WOMEN 37
  won't get much s.   ANIMALS 1
sleeping s. with a queen   ROYALTY 37
  s. with them on the first date   SEX 44
  wake which knows no s.   IRELAND 4
sleepless S. themselves   POETS 14
sleeps Luca Brasi s. with the fishes   DEATH 47
  s. alone at last   EPITAPHS 5
  s. with the enemy   MARRIAGE 3
slept hearing that a judge had s.   JUDGES 11
  s. more than any other   PRESIDENTS 18
  s. with your Auntie Phyllis   MISTAKES 5
slice S. him where you like   CHARACTER 23
sliding s. down a barrister   INSULTS 38
slightly he was S. in *Peter Pan*   ACTORS 32
slime doin' 'The S.'   DANCE 6
slipped s. on a hamburger   MISTAKES 27
slipping career must be s.   AWARDS 2
slob You are just a fat s.   RELIGION 43
Slough fall on S.   TOWNS 5
slow Talk s.   ACTING 34
  telling you to s. down   DEATH 5
  was s. poison   DRINK 7
slower anybody driving s. than you   DRIVING 3
slums intimacy of the s.   EDUCATION 21
slush French cuisine and Ice-cold Grape S.   RESTAURANTS 2
  pure as the driven s.   VIRTUE 2
small as a s. whisky   DRINK 21
  It's a s. word   SNOBBERY 10
  Microbe is so very s.   SCIENCE 5
  pictures that got s.   FILM STARS 9
  so s., he's the only man   BODY 7
  too s. for its boots   ENGLAND 10
smaller s. fleas to bite 'em   ANIMALS 29
smallest s. room of my house   COMEBACKS 11
smart men like s. women   MEN AND WOMEN 32
  s. enough to understand   POLITICS 28
smarter thought themselves s.   PRIME MINISTERS 4
smell investigate a s.   LIFE 26

spaghetti (cont.)

lonely eating s.   FOOD 43

Spain Go to S. and get killed   POETS 13

Spanish emotional, we're not S.   FAMILY 14

expects the S. Inquisition   COMEDY ROUTINES 27

reddish and S.   WINE 7

spare s. a rope   AMERICA 9

spark little s. of madness   MENTAL HEALTH 12

sparrows know s. from starlings   ANIMALS 26

to the road for the s.   ECONOMICS 7

speak let it s. to you first   ART 32

s. ill of everybody   AUTOBIOGRAPHY 9

s. it fluently   LANGUAGES 13

Stand up. S. up   SPEECHES 2

stand up to s. in public   SPEECHES 13

speaker most popular s.   SPEECHES 18

speaking fear is public s.   SPEECHES 20

Is he s. to you   TELEVISION 9

when I am s.   SPEECHES 3

speaks man s. only when driven   MEN AND WOMEN 27

s. to Me as if I was   ROYALTY 35

specialist s. is a man who knows   MEDICINE 24

species they were an endangered s.   LOVE 8

Wonderful theory, wrong s.   POLITICS 54

specific should have been more s.   AMBITION 10

spectacle intimate s.   FILM PRODUCERS 4

no s. so ridiculous   MORALITY 6

speculate when he should not s.   BETTING 11

speech Anthony will make the s.   PRIME MINISTERS 12

aspersion upon my parts of s.   WIT 41

better s. than the one   SPEECHES 24

dreamt I was making a s.   SPEECHES 8

make a s. on conservation   INSULTS 49

s. by Chamberlain   PRIME MINISTERS 8

s. on economics   SPEECHES 15

speeches corn surplus by his s.   SPEECHES 23

preparing his impromptu s.   SPEECHES 21

speed begin to pick up s.   AGE 20

No-one obeys the s. limit   LAW 14

S. has never killed anyone   DRIVING 4

what good is s.   TRAVEL 17

spell couldn't s. *Indescribable*   INSULTS 2

foreigners always s. better   LANGUAGES 21

How do you s. 'accelerator'   WORDS 2

inability to s.   HANDWRITING 3

NO MONEY TILL YOU LEARN TO S.   TELEGRAMS 1

s. football, never mind   FOOTBALL 11

spelling My s. is Wobbly   LANGUAGE 15

s. mistakes have been left in   BOOKS 16

spend s. more time with me   FAMILY 22

spent realize what you s.   CHRISTMAS 9

spheroid oblate s.   UNIVERSE 2

sphinx my clitoris, not the s.   SEX 26

spill S. your guts at Wimbledon   TENNIS 3

spills s. his seed   NAMES 16

spinach I say it's s.   FOOD 64

spine shiver looking for a s.   INSULTS 28

s. for a safety-pin   CHARACTER 16

spinster saved many an English s.   WOMEN 30

spirits fail, in good s.   SUCCESS 25

spiritual detestable s. qualities   CHARACTER 3

not being a s. people   CRICKET 9

skip his s. struggles   MUSIC 28

spiritualists convention of s.   TELEVISION 18

spirituality sense of s.   RELIGION 4

split I s. it so it will stay split.   LANGUAGE 4

split-level s. and open-plan   ARCHITECTURE 5

spoil some skill to s. a breakfast   FOOD 25

s. our own   DRINK 25

Success didn't s. me   SUCCESS 14

spoiled good walk s.   GOLF 8

spoke people have s.   POLITICS 53

spoken s. word is repeated   DEBT 7

spoons faster we counted our s.   VIRTUE 10

he can bend s.   PARANORMAL 8

let us count our s.   VIRTUE 12

locks up its s.   ARMED FORCES 24

sport only s. can be   BIOGRAPHY 3

s., any sport   SPORTS 17

s. with ambulances at the bottom   SPORTS 6

sports person who likes s.   SPORTS 29

sports writers Let's face it, s.   NEWSPAPERS 9

propose a toast to the s.   SPEECHES 27

spotless houses were so s.   HOME 5

spout killed when they s.   SPEECHES 25

spring In the s. a young man's fancy   LOVE 18

springs like Jell-O on s.   BODY 30

spy s. for or against my country   TRUST 3

square country so s.   CANADA 1

so thoroughly s.   MEN AND WOMEN 31

squares lived in s.   WRITERS 2

squeezing with you in the s. of a lemon   TIME 12

stabbed get s. in the back   HOLLYWOOD 6

guy gets s. in the back   OPERA 4

stable Because a man is born in a s.   IRELAND 9

s. or a zoo is better   POLITICIANS 20

stage daughter on the s.   ACTING 6

go on s.   THEATRE 10

nudity on s.   THEATRE 33

On the s. he was natural   ACTORS 18

She comes on s. as if   INSULTS 10

staircase S. wit   WIT 13

stairs falling down a flight of s.   SELF-KNOWLEDGE 13

fool a flight of s.   AGE 16

still go up my 44 s. two at a time   OLD AGE 22

wife down a flight of s.   MISTAKES 2

stake s. driven through his heart   POLITICIANS 25

stamina Patience, s. and   PRIME MINISTERS 24

stand he intended to s.   PRIME MINISTERS 22

now I s. corrected   MEDICINE 1

s. for nothing fall for anything   CHARACTER 8

s. up to anything   ARMED FORCES 23

S. up. Speak up   SPEECHES 2

up to you whether you s.   SPEECHES 27

standards s. women set for themselves   WOMEN 26

standing even the men were s.   MANNERS 17

s. on the corner   MEN AND WOMEN 34

stands sits down before he s. up   SPEECHES 18

star Being a s. has made it possible   PREJUDICE 2

discovery of a new s.   COOKERY 6

s. of their life story   SELF-KNOWLEDGE 16

Wet, she was a s.   FILM STARS 14

stardom S. isn't a profession   FAME 4

stare s. sullenly at the sink   FOOD 15

stupid (cont.)

interesting…but s.   COMEDY ROUTINES 42
It's the economy, s.   ECONOMICS 4
You s. boy   COMEDY ROUTINES 49

stupidity inherited s. of the race   ENGLAND 41
Seriousness is s.   EDUCATION 10
universe and human s.   FOOLISHNESS 4

style failure may be your s.   FAILURE 3
one's s. is one's signature   LETTERS 12
taste, and s.   MANNERS 20
whatever happens to be in s.   INSULTS 52

subjunctive s. mood is in its death   LANGUAGE 14
sublime step is short from the S.   TRANSPORT 10
submerged completely s. in water   MODERN LIFE 1
substitution s. of 'kwik' for 'quick'   ADVERTISING 2
subtraction dollars, that's s.   MEN AND WOMEN 56
subtracts woman s. from her age   AGE 5
suburbs s. of morality   VIRTUE 9
succeed How to s. in business   SUCCESS 16
If at first you don't s.   FAILURE 3
If at first you don't s.   FAILURE 5
if at first you don't s.   FAMILY 12
want to s. in politics   POLITICS 27

succeeds Nothing s. like excess   SUCCESS 31
Whenever a friend s.   SUCCESS 29

succès S. d'estime   WIT 25
success gives s. its flavour   FAILURE 2
If A is a s. in life   LIFESTYLE 7
no deodorant like s.   SUCCESS 27
obstacles to achieve his s.   SUCCESS 26
Satisfied great s.   TELEGRAMS 16
second wife to his s.   WIVES 1
s. is showing up   SUCCESS 1
s. that ran out of   WIT 25
S. is a lousy teacher   SUCCESS 8
S. is the one unpardonable sin   SUCCESS 3

successful Behind every s. man   MEN 15
s. in your profession   CRIME 12
s. writer is important   WRITERS 12

succession s. of opposing certainties   CERTAINTY 17
sucker Never give a s.   BETTING 4
sucking all that s. and blowing   MARRIAGE 6
suffragettes s. were triumphant   FEMINISM 2
sugar shower you with s. lumps   ANIMALS 17
triumph of s. over diabetes   WRITERS 30
with a pinch of s.   STATISTICS 5

suggestions In Rome, they are s.   DRIVING 9
suicide call a 's. blonde'   HAIR 2
committed political s.   UNINTENDED 13
Santa has committed s.   CHRISTMAS 2
where they commit s.   COUNTRIES 2

suit lugubrious man in a s.   POETS 5
point his s.   FILM STARS 7
wears a white s. all the time   DRESS 11

suitcase Law of the Ever-level S.   TRAVEL 5
rawhide s.   FILM STARS 5

suits omelette all over our s.   MISTAKES 9
sulk I will not…s.   DATING 6
sultry where the climate's s.   SEX 27
summer S. bachelors, like summer breezes   MEN 10
S. has set in   WEATHER 2
s. in England   WEATHER 15

sumo watching s. wrestling   SPORTS 18

sums like s. with letters   EDUCATION 13
sun journalist from the S.   PARANORMAL 6
s. go down on his wrath   ANGER 22
s. never sets   COUNTRIES 29
S. Wot Won It   HEADLINES 5
Thank heavens, the s. has gone   WEATHER 13

sunbeams s. out of cucumbers   SCIENCE 16
sunbed can't get two on a s.   PEOPLE 31
sunburn S. is very becoming   APPEARANCE 11
Sunday English S.   CRITICS 18
S.-school superintendent   CRIME 22

sundial I am a s.   TIME 9
sunlit Give them broad s. uplands   POLITICS 31
sunny s. place for shady people   FRANCE 11
sunsets colourful s.   ANGER 22
sunshine are the s.   BOOKS 22
grievance and a ray of s.   SCOTLAND 10

superior I am a most s. person   POLITICIANS 2
which is the s. sex   FEMINISM 10

superseded knowledge, been s.   HYPOCRISY 7
support invisible means of s.   RELIGION 13
little bit of s.   MEN AND WOMEN 50
s. of Paul   GOVERNMENT 26
s. rather than illumination   STATISTICS 1
There's a s. group for that.   WORK 6

suppose queerer than we can s.   UNIVERSE 5
suppository give you a s.   MEDICINE 17
suppressed Truth is s.   SECRECY 6
sure nobody is s. about   CERTAINTY 5
surely Shome mishtake, s.   COMEDY ROUTINES 35
surgeon fashionable s., like a pelican   MEDICINE 10
surgeons with brain s.   NEWSPAPERS 2
surprise girl as a s.   DATING 14
takes this railway by s.   TRANSPORT 8

surprised devilish s.   ART 31
It is we who are s.   WIT 55
proven right or pleasantly s.   OPTIMISM 9
she was so s.   DATING 3
she wouldn't be at all s.   MORALITY 12

surrender cheese-eating s. monkeys   FRANCE 6
surrogate Vatican is against s. mothers

     RELIGION 10

survive paranoid s.   MANAGEMENT 5
susceptible peculiarly s. to draughts   VIRTUE 22
suspect S. all   MANNERS 11
suspects Round up the usual s.   CRIME 16
suspender up there with s. belts   TECHNOLOGY 10
suspicion recurrent s.   DEMOCRACY 2
suttee committing s.   ARISTOCRACY 1
swamps across primeval s.   FAMILY 39
swans S. sing   SONGS 5
sward delectable s.   GARDENS 2
swear Don't s., boy   LANGUAGE 2
swearing s. is very much part of it   SPORTS 17
swears never s. at his wife   MEN AND WOMEN 4
sweater knowing how to fill a s.   ACTORS 13
sweatshop Shanghai s. to satisfy   POLITICIANS 19
Swede boring old S.   FILM STARS 4
travelling S.   COUNTRIES 7

swedes made to wash s.   YOUTH 10
sweeter mountain sheep are s.   FOOD 49
sweetheart cutting your s.'s toe-nails   LOVE 3
sweetie run a s.-shop   HUMOUR 4